THE BOOK ®

Vauxhall/Opel Calibra
Service and Repair Manual

Michael Gascoigne BSc, MS, CEng, MIChemE, MISTC

Models covered

(3502-288-5AC1)

Vauxhall/Opel Calibra front-wheel-drive models with four-cylinder petrol engines, including special/limited editions; 1998 cc SOHC and DOHC

Does not cover V6 engine, four-wheel-drive models or air conditioning systems

© Haynes Publishing 1999

A book in the **Haynes Service and Repair Manual Series**

ISBN 1 85960 502 8

British Library Cataloguing in Publication Data
A catalogue record for this book is available from the British Library.

ABCDE
FGHIJ
KLMNO
PQ

Printed in the USA

Haynes Publishing
Sparkford, Nr Yeovil, Somerset BA22 7JJ, England

Haynes North America, Inc
861 Lawrence Drive, Newbury Park, California 91320, USA

Editions Haynes S.A.
Tour Aurore - IBC, 18 Place des Reflets,
92975 Paris La Défense 2, Cedex, France

Haynes Publishing Nordiska AB
Box 1504, 751 45 Uppsala, Sverige

Contents

Contents

The Calibra covered by this manual was first introduced to the UK market in June 1990. The engine and other mechanical components are based on the Cavalier, but the bodywork has been redesigned for improved aerodynamics with a drag coefficient of only 0.26, lower than any other production four-seater in the world when it was introduced. This manual covers models with non-turbo petrol engines and front-wheel-drive. Turbo and four-wheel drive is available on certain other models.

The engines covered in this manual are:
a) The 2.0 litre C20NE single overhead camshaft (SOHC) engine with Motronic M1.5 injection/ignition.
b) The 2.0 litre C20XE double overhead camshaft (DOHC) engine with Motronic 2.5 or 2.8 injection/ignition. This was produced until 1995 and then discontinued.
c) The 2.0 litre X20XEV (DOHC) engine, introduced in 1994 as a replacement for the C20XE. This engine is the 'ECOTEC' type, designed to meet strict EEC exhaust gas limits for 1996 and has Simtec injection/ignition.

All the engines are of well-proven design and, provided regular maintenance is carried out, are unlikely to give trouble.

The body styles are all Coupe, and the DTM model introduced in 1995 is fitted with a rear spoiler and a lowered sports suspension.

Five-speed manual transmission is available on all models, and four-speed automatic transmission is available as an option on C20NE and X20XEV models.

A wide range of standard and optional equipment is available within the Calibra range to suit most tastes.

Safety features include a full-size driver's airbag from 1993, and a passenger airbag from 1994. Anti-lock braking is fitted as standard to all models.

For the home mechanic, the Calibra is a straightforward vehicle to maintain, and most of the items requiring frequent attention are easily accessible.

Calibra 2.0 litre Coupe

The Vauxhall Calibra Team

Haynes manuals are produced by dedicated and enthusiastic people working in close co-operation. The team responsible for the creation of this book included:

Author	Michael Gascoigne
Sub-editor	Sophie Yar
Editor & Page Make-up	Steve Churchill
Workshop manager	Paul Buckland
Photo Scans	Steve Tanswell John Martin
Cover illustration & Line Art	Roger Healing

We hope the book will help you to get the maximum enjoyment from your car. By carrying out routine maintenance as described you will ensure your car's reliability and preserve its resale value.

Your Vauxhall Calibra Manual

The aim of this manual is to help you get the best value from your vehicle. It can do so in several ways. It can help you decide what work must be done (even should you choose to get it done by a garage). It will also provide information on routine maintenance and servicing, and give a logical course of action and diagnosis when random faults occur. However, it is hoped that you will use the manual by tackling the work yourself. On simpler jobs it may even be quicker than booking the car into a garage and going there twice, to leave and collect it. Perhaps most important, a lot of money can be saved by avoiding the costs a garage must charge to cover its labour and overheads.

The manual has drawings and descriptions to show the function of the various components so that their layout can be understood. Tasks are described and photographed in a clear step-by-step sequence.

References to the 'left' or 'right' of the vehicle are in the sense of a person in the driver' seat facing forwards.

Acknowledgements

Thanks are due to Champion Spark Plug who supplied the illustrations showing spark plug conditions and to Duckhams Oils who provided lubrication data. Thanks are also due to Draper Tools Limited, who provided some of the workshop tools, to Vauxhall dealer J. Davy, of West Ham, Basingstoke for assistance with vehicles, and to all those people at Sparkford who helped in the production of this manual. Certain illustrations are the copyright of Vauxhall Motors Ltd and are used with their permission.

We take great pride in the accuracy of information given in this manual, but vehicle manufacturers make alterations and design changes during the production run of a particular vehicle of which they do not inform us. No liability can be accepted by the authors or publishers for loss, damage or injury caused by errors in, or omissions from, the information given.

Working on your car can be dangerous. This page shows just some of the potential risks and hazards, with the aim of creating a safety-conscious attitude.

General hazards

Scalding

• Don't remove the radiator or expansion tank cap while the engine is hot.
• Engine oil, automatic transmission fluid or power steering fluid may also be dangerously hot if the engine has recently been running.

Burning

• Beware of burns from the exhaust system and from any part of the engine. Brake discs and drums can also be extremely hot immediately after use.

Crushing

• When working under or near a raised vehicle, always supplement the jack with axle stands, or use drive-on ramps. *Never venture under a car which is only supported by a jack.*
• Take care if loosening or tightening high-torque nuts when the vehicle is on stands. Initial loosening and final tightening should be done with the wheels on the ground.

Fire

• Fuel is highly flammable; fuel vapour is explosive.
• Don't let fuel spill onto a hot engine.
• Do not smoke or allow naked lights (including pilot lights) anywhere near a vehicle being worked on. Also beware of creating sparks (electrically or by use of tools).
• Fuel vapour is heavier than air, so don't work on the fuel system with the vehicle over an inspection pit.
• Another cause of fire is an electrical overload or short-circuit. Take care when repairing or modifying the vehicle wiring.
• Keep a fire extinguisher handy, of a type suitable for use on fuel and electrical fires.

Electric shock

• Ignition HT voltage can be dangerous, especially to people with heart problems or a pacemaker. Don't work on or near the ignition system with the engine running or the ignition switched on.

• Mains voltage is also dangerous. Make sure that any mains-operated equipment is correctly earthed. Mains power points should be protected by a residual current device (RCD) circuit breaker.

Fume or gas intoxication

• Exhaust fumes are poisonous; they often contain carbon monoxide, which is rapidly fatal if inhaled. Never run the engine in a confined space such as a garage with the doors shut.
• Fuel vapour is also poisonous, as are the vapours from some cleaning solvents and paint thinners.

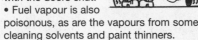

Poisonous or irritant substances

• Avoid skin contact with battery acid and with any fuel, fluid or lubricant, especially antifreeze, brake hydraulic fluid and Diesel fuel. Don't syphon them by mouth. If such a substance is swallowed or gets into the eyes, seek medical advice.
• Prolonged contact with used engine oil can cause skin cancer. Wear gloves or use a barrier cream if necessary. Change out of oil-soaked clothes and do not keep oily rags in your pocket.
• Air conditioning refrigerant forms a poisonous gas if exposed to a naked flame (including a cigarette). It can also cause skin burns on contact.

Asbestos

• Asbestos dust can cause cancer if inhaled or swallowed. Asbestos may be found in gaskets and in brake and clutch linings. When dealing with such components it is safest to assume that they contain asbestos.

Special hazards

Hydrofluoric acid

• This extremely corrosive acid is formed when certain types of synthetic rubber, found in some O-rings, oil seals, fuel hoses etc, are exposed to temperatures above 400ºC. The rubber changes into a charred or sticky substance containing the acid. *Once formed, the acid remains dangerous for years. If it gets onto the skin, it may be necessary to amputate the limb concerned.*
• When dealing with a vehicle which has suffered a fire, or with components salvaged from such a vehicle, wear protective gloves and discard them after use.

The battery

• Batteries contain sulphuric acid, which attacks clothing, eyes and skin. Take care when topping-up or carrying the battery.
• The hydrogen gas given off by the battery is highly explosive. Never cause a spark or allow a naked light nearby. Be careful when connecting and disconnecting battery chargers or jump leads.

Air bags

• Air bags can cause injury if they go off accidentally. Take care when removing the steering wheel and/or facia. Special storage instructions may apply.

Diesel injection equipment

• Diesel injection pumps supply fuel at very high pressure. Take care when working on the fuel injectors and fuel pipes.

⚠ *Warning: Never expose the hands, face or any other part of the body to injector spray; the fuel can penetrate the skin with potentially fatal results.*

Remember...

DO

• Do use eye protection when using power tools, and when working under the vehicle.

• Do wear gloves or use barrier cream to protect your hands when necessary.

• Do get someone to check periodically that all is well when working alone on the vehicle.

• Do keep loose clothing and long hair well out of the way of moving mechanical parts.

• Do remove rings, wristwatch etc, before working on the vehicle – especially the electrical system.

• Do ensure that any lifting or jacking equipment has a safe working load rating adequate for the job.

DON'T

• Don't attempt to lift a heavy component which may be beyond your capability – get assistance.

• Don't rush to finish a job, or take unverified short cuts.

• Don't use ill-fitting tools which may slip and cause injury.

• Don't leave tools or parts lying around where someone can trip over them. Mop up oil and fuel spills at once.

• Don't allow children or pets to play in or near a vehicle being worked on.

The following pages are intended to help in dealing with common roadside emergencies and breakdowns. You will find more detailed fault finding information at the back of the manual, and repair information in the main chapters.

If your car won't start and the starter motor doesn't turn

☐ If it's a model with automatic transmission, make sure the selector is in 'P' or 'N'.
☐ Open the bonnet and make sure that the battery terminals are clean and tight.
☐ Switch on the headlights and try to start the engine. If the headlights go very dim when you're trying to start, the battery is probably flat. Get out of trouble by jump starting (see next page) using a friend's car.

If your car won't start even though the starter motor turns as normal

☐ Is there fuel in the tank?
☐ Is there moisture on electrical components under the bonnet? Switch off the ignition, then wipe off any obvious dampness with a dry cloth. Spray a water-repellent aerosol product (WD-40 or equivalent) on ignition and fuel system electrical connectors like those shown in the photos. Pay special attention to the ignition coil wiring connector and HT leads.

A Check that the spark plug HT leads are securely connected by pushing them home.

B The fuel injection system wiring plug may cause problems if not connected securely.

C Check the ECU multi-plug for security (where fitted), with the ignition switched off.

Check that electrical connections are secure (with the ignition switched off) and spray them with a water dispersant spray like WD40 if you suspect a problem due to damp

D Check the security and condition of the battery connections.

E Check that the ignition coil wiring plug is secure, and spray with water-dispersant if necessary.

HAYNES HiNT

Jump starting will get you out of trouble, but you must correct whatever made the battery go flat in the first place. There are three possibilities:

1 *The battery has been drained by repeated attempts to start, or by leaving the lights on.*

2 *The charging system is not working properly (alternator drivebelt slack or broken, alternator wiring fault or alternator itself faulty).*

3 *The battery itself is at fault (electrolyte low, or battery worn out).*

When jump-starting a car using a booster battery, observe the following precautions:

✔ Before connecting the booster battery, make sure that the ignition is switched off.

✔ Ensure that all electrical equipment (lights, heater, wipers, etc) is switched off.

✔ Take note of any special precautions printed on the battery case.

Jump starting

✔ Make sure that the booster battery is the same voltage as the discharged one in the vehicle.

✔ If the battery is being jump-started from the battery in another vehicle, the two vehicles MUST NOT TOUCH each other.

✔ Make sure that the transmission is in neutral (or PARK, in the case of automatic transmission).

1 Connect one end of the red jump lead to the positive (+) terminal of the flat battery

2 Connect the other end of the red lead to the positive (+) terminal of the booster battery.

3 Connect one end of the black jump lead to the negative (-) terminal of the booster battery

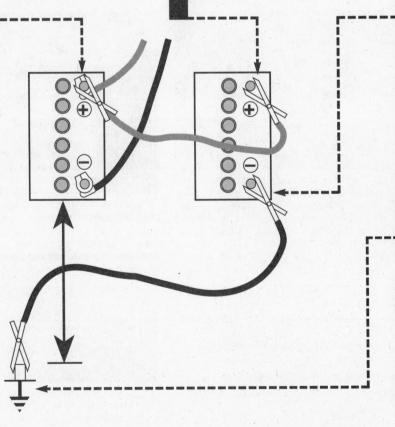

4 Connect the other end of the black jump lead to a bolt or bracket on the engine block, well away from the battery, on the vehicle to be started.

5 Make sure that the jump leads will not come into contact with the fan, drive-belts or other moving parts of the engine.

6 Start the engine using the booster battery and run it at idle speed. Switch on the lights, rear window demister and heater blower motor, then disconnect the jump leads in the reverse order of connection. Turn off the lights etc.

Wheel changing

Some of the details shown here will vary according to model. For instance, the location of the spare wheel and jack is not the same on all cars. However, the basic principles apply to all vehicles.

Warning: Do not change a wheel in a situation where you risk being hit by another vehicle. On busy roads, try to stop in a lay-by or a gateway. Be wary of passing traffic while changing the wheel - it is easy to become distracted by the job in hand.

Preparation

☐ When a puncture occurs, stop as soon as it is safe to do so.
☐ Park on firm level ground, if possible, and well out of the way of other traffic.
☐ Use hazard warning lights if necessary.

☐ If you have one, use a warning triangle to alert other drivers of your presence.
☐ Apply the handbrake and engage first or reverse gear (or Park on models with automatic transmission.

☐ Chock the wheel diagonally opposite the one being removed – a couple of large stones will do for this.
☐ If the ground is soft, use a flat piece of wood to spread the load under the jack.

Changing the wheel

1 Clear the luggage compartment and lift up the carpet, then unscrew the clamp and remove the spare wheel. No tools are required.

2 Remove the jack and tools from the spare wheel compartment.

3 Remove the jacking point cover from the sill. For safety, place the spare wheel under the car near the jacking point.

4 With the wheel still on the ground, remove the wheel trim, if fitted, then remove the plastic caps from the wheel bolts. One of them is a locking cap, recessed into the wheel, which has to be removed with a special tool supplied with the jack. Then slacken each wheel bolt by half a turn.

5 Raise the jack whilst locating below the jacking point. Ensure that the jack is on firm ground and located correctly. Turn the handle clockwise until the wheel is raised clear of the ground. Remove the bolts and lift the wheel clear.

6 Position the spare wheel and fit the bolts. Hand tighten with the wheel brace and lower the car to the ground. Then tighten the wheel bolts in a diagonal sequence. Note that the spare wheel on the Calibra is thinner than a normal wheel and is only for emergency use. Do not exceed 80 km/h with the spare wheel fitted.

Finally...

☐ Remove the wheel chocks.

☐ Stow the jack and tools in the correct locations in the car.

☐ Check the tyre pressure on the wheel just fitted. If it is low, or if you don't have a pressure gauge with you, drive slowly to the nearest garage and inflate the tyre to the right pressure.

☐ Have the damaged tyre or wheel repaired as soon as possible.

Identifying leaks

Puddles on the garage floor or drive, or obvious wetness under the bonnet or underneath the car, suggest a leak that needs investigating. It can sometimes be difficult to decide where the leak is coming from, especially if the engine bay is very dirty already. Leaking oil or fluid can also be blown rearwards by the passage of air under the car, giving a false impression of where the problem lies.

 Warning: Most automotive oils and fluids are poisonous. Wash them off skin, and change out of contaminated clothing, without delay.

 The smell of a fluid leaking from the car may provide a clue to what's leaking. Some fluids are distinctively coloured. It may help to clean the car carefully and to park it over some clean paper overnight as an aid to locating the source of the leak.

Remember that some leaks may only occur while the engine is running.

Sump oil

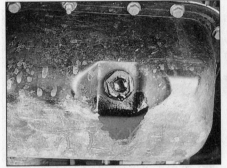

Engine oil may leak from the drain plug...

Oil from filter

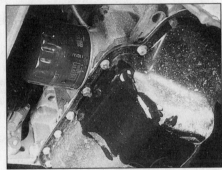

...or from the base of the oil filter.

Gearbox oil

Gearbox oil can leak from the seals at the inboard ends of the driveshafts.

Antifreeze

Leaking antifreeze often leaves a crystalline deposit like this.

Brake fluid

A leak occurring at a wheel is almost certainly brake fluid.

Power steering fluid

Power steering fluid may leak from the pipe connectors on the steering rack.

Towing

When all else fails, you may find yourself having to get a tow home – or of course you may be helping somebody else. Long-distance recovery should only be done by a garage or breakdown service. For shorter distances, DIY towing using another car is easy enough, but observe the following points:

☐ Use a proper tow-rope – they are not expensive. The vehicle being towed must display an 'ON TOW' sign in its rear window.

☐ Always turn the ignition key to the 'on' position when the vehicle is being towed, so that the steering lock is released, and that the direction indicator and brake lights will work.

☐ Only attach the tow-rope to the towing eyes provided.

☐ Before being towed, release the handbrake and select neutral on the transmission.

☐ Note that greater-than-usual pedal pressure will be required to operate the brakes, since the vacuum servo unit is only operational with the engine running.

☐ On models with power steering, greater-than-usual steering effort will also be required.

☐ The driver of the car being towed must keep the tow-rope taut at all times to avoid snatching.

☐ Make sure that both drivers know the route before setting off.

☐ Only drive at moderate speeds and keep the distance towed to a minimum. Drive smoothly and allow plenty of time for slowing down at junctions.

☐ On models with automatic transmission, special precautions apply. If in doubt, do not tow, or transmission damage may result.

Introduction

There are some very simple checks which need only take a few minutes to carry out, but which could save you a lot of inconvenience and expense.

These "Weekly checks" require no great skill or special tools, and the small amount of time they take to perform could prove to be very well spent, for example;

☐ Keeping an eye on tyre condition and pressures, will not only help to stop them wearing out prematurely, but could also save your life.

☐ Many breakdowns are caused by electrical problems. Battery-related faults are particularly common, and a quick check on a regular basis will often prevent the majority of these.

☐ If your car develops a brake fluid leak, the first time you might know about it is when your brakes don't work properly. Checking the level regularly will give advance warning of this kind of problem.

☐ If the oil or coolant levels run low, the cost of repairing any engine damage will be far greater than fixing the leak, for example.

Underbonnet check points

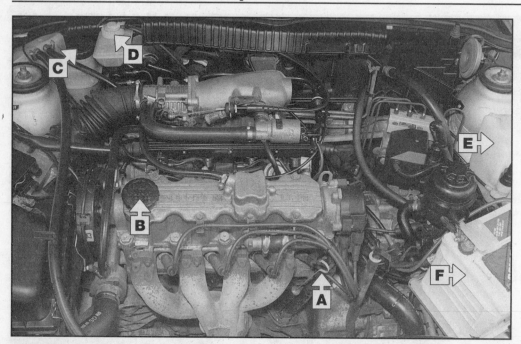

◀ **C 20 NE model**

A Engine oil level dipstick

B Engine oil filler cap

C Coolant expansion tank cap

D Brake fluid reservoir

E Screen washer fluid reservoir

F Battery

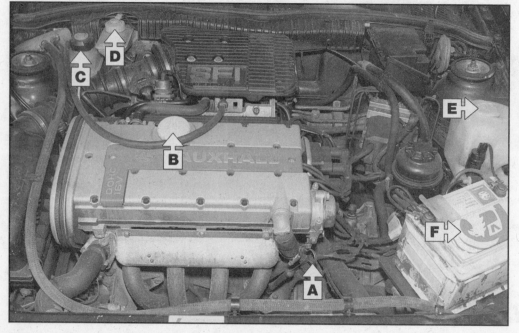

◀ **C 20 XE model**

A Engine oil level dipstick

B Engine oil filler cap

C Coolant expansion tank cap

D Brake fluid reservoir

E Screen washer fluid reservoir

F Battery

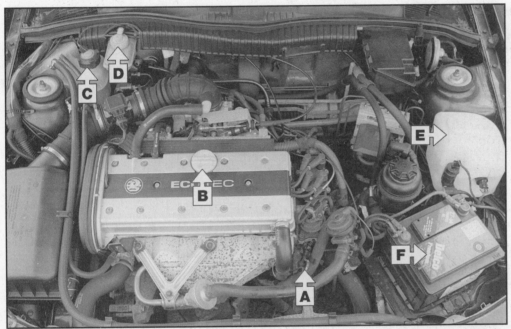

◀ **X 20 XEV model
(up to 1997)**

A *Engine oil level dipstick*

B *Engine oil filler cap*

C *Coolant expansion tank cap*

D *Brake fluid reservoir*

E *Screen washer fluid reservoir*

F *Battery*

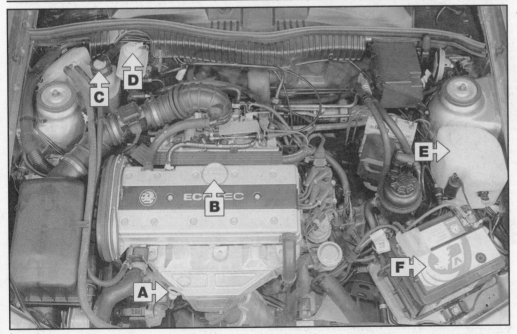

◀ **X 20 XEV model
(1997 onwards)**

A *Engine oil level dipstick*

B *Engine oil filler cap*

C *Coolant expansion tank cap*

D *Brake fluid reservoir*

E *Screen washer fluid reservoir*

F *Battery*

Engine oil level

Before you start

✔ Make sure that your car is on level ground.
✔ Check the oil level before the car is driven, or at least 5 minutes after the engine has been switched off.

HAYNES HiNT *If the oil is checked immediately after driving the vehicle, some of the oil will remain in the upper engine components, resulting in an inaccurate reading on the dipstick!*

The correct oil

Modern engines place great demands on their oil. It is very important that the correct oil for your car is used (See "Lubricants, fluids and tyre pressures").

Car Care

● If you have to add oil frequently, you should check whether you have any oil leaks. Place some clean paper under the car overnight, and check for stains in the morning. If there are no leaks, the engine may be burning oil *(see "Fault Finding").*

● Always maintain the level between the upper and lower dipstick marks (see photo 3). If the level is too low severe engine damage may occur. Oil seal failure may result if the engine is overfilled by adding too much oil.

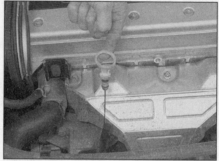

1 The dipstick top is often brightly coloured for easy identification (see *"Underbonnet check points"* on pages 0•10 and 0•11 for exact location). Withdraw the dipstick.

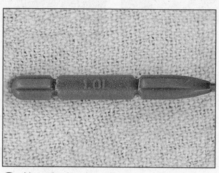

3 Note the level on the end of the dipstick, which should be between the upper and lower mark. One litre of oil is required to raise the level between the marks.

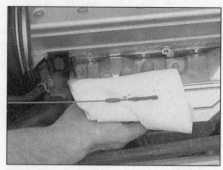

2 Using a clean rag or paper towel remove all oil from the dipstick. Insert the clean dipstick into the tube as far as it will go, then withdraw it again.

4 Oil is added through the filler cap. Unscrew the cap and top-up the level; a funnel may help to reduce spillage. Add the oil slowly, checking the level on the dipstick often. Don't overfill (see *"Car Care"* left).

Coolant level

Warning: DO NOT attempt to remove the expansion tank pressure cap when the engine is hot, as there is a very great risk of scalding. Do not leave open containers of coolant about, as it is poisonous.

Car Care

● With a sealed-type cooling system, adding coolant should not be necessary on a regular basis. If frequent topping-up is required, it is likely there is a leak. Check the radiator, all hoses and joint faces for signs of staining or wetness, and rectify as necessary.

● It is important that antifreeze is used in the cooling system all year round, not just during the winter months. Don't top-up with water alone, as the antifreeze will become too diluted.

1 The coolant level varies with the temperature of the engine. When the engine is cold, the coolant level should be near the "COLD" (or "KALT") mark.

2 If topping-up is necessary, **wait until the engine is cold**. Slowly turn the expansion tank cap anti-clockwise to relieve the system pressure. Once any pressure is released, turn the cap anti-clockwise until it can be lifted off.

3 Add a mixture of water and antifreeze through the expansion tank filler neck until the coolant reaches the "COLD" level mark. Refit the cap, turning it clockwise as far as it will go until it is secure.

Screen washer fluid level

Screenwash additives not only keep the winscreen clean during foul weather, they also prevent the washer system freezing in cold weather - which is when you are likely to need it most. Don't top up using plain water as the screenwash will become too diluted, and will freeze during cold weather. *On no account use coolant antifreeze in the washer system - this could discolour or damage paintwork.*

1 The windscreen washer fluid reservoir is located in the rear left-hand corner of the engine compartment. The washer level can be seen through the reservoir body. If topping-up is necessary, open the cap.

2 When topping-up the reservoir, add a screenwash additive in the quantities recommended on the bottle.

Brake fluid level

Warning:
● *Brake fluid can harm your eyes and damage painted surfaces, so use extreme caution when handling and pouring it.*
● *Do not use fluid that has been standing open for some time, as it absorbs moisture from the air, which can cause a dangerous loss of braking effectiveness.*

 HAYNES HINT
• *Make sure that your car is on level ground.*
• *The fluid level in the reservoir will drop slightly as the brake pads wear down, but the fluid level must never be allowed to drop below the "MIN" mark.*

Safety First!

● If the reservoir requires repeated topping-up this is an indication of a fluid leak somewhere in the system, which should be investigated immediately.

● If a leak is suspected, the car should not be driven until the braking system has been checked. Never take any risks where brakes are concerned.

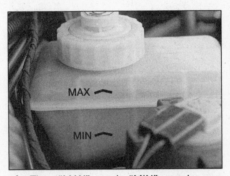

1 The "MAX" and "MIN" marks are indicated on the side of the reservoir. The fluid level must be kept between the marks.

2 If topping-up is necessary, first wipe the area around the filler cap with a clean rag before removing the cap.

3 When adding fluid, it's a good idea to inspect the reservoir. The system should be drained and refilled if dirt is seen in the fluid (see Chapter 9 for details).

4 Carefully add fluid avoiding spilling it on surrounding paintwork. Use only the specified hydraulic fluid; mixing different types of fluid can cause damage to the system. After filling to the correct level, refit the cap securely, to prevent leaks and the entry of foreign matter. Wipe off any spilt fluid.

Power steering fluid level

Before you start:
✔ Park the vehicle on level ground.
✔ Set the steering wheel straight-ahead.
✔ The engine should be turned off.

 For the check to be accurate, the steering must not be turned once the engine has been stopped.

Safety First!
● The need for frequent topping-up indicates a leak, which should be investigated immediately.

1 The fluid level is checked with a dipstick attached to the reservoir filler cap. The reservoir is located on the left-hand side of the engine compartment (viewed from the driver's seat) behind the battery.

2 Clean the area around the reservoir cap, then unscrew the cap and wipe the dipstick with a clean rag. When the engine is cold, the fluid should come up to the lower "ADD" mark; when hot, it should come up to the "FULL" mark.

3 If topping up is required, use the specified type of fluid, and do not overfill the reservoir. When the level is correct, refit the cap.

Electrical system

✔ Check all external lights and the horn. Refer to the appropriate Sections of Chapter 12 for details if any of the circuits are found to be inoperative.

✔ Visually check all accessible wiring connectors, harnesses and retaining clips for security, and for signs of chafing or damage.

 If you need to check your brake lights and indicators unaided, back up to a wall or garage door and operate the lights. The reflected light should show if they are working properly.

1 If a single indicator light, brake light or headlight has failed, it is likely that a bulb has blown and will need to be replaced. Refer to Chapter 12 for details. If both brake lights have failed, it is possible that the brake light switch above the brake pedal needs adjusting. This simple operation is described in Chapter 9.

2 If more than one indicator light or headlight has failed it is likely that either a fuse has blown or that there is a fault in the circuit (refer to *"Electrical fault-finding"* in Chapter 12). The fuses are mounted in a panel located at the lower right-hand corner of the facia under a removable cover.

3 To replace a blown fuse, simply pull it out. Fit a new fuse of the same rating, available from car accessory shops. It is important that you find the reason that the fuse blew - a checking procedure is given in Chapter 12.

Battery

Caution: *Before carrying out any work on the vehicle battery, read the precautions given in "Safety first" at the start of this manual.*

✔ Make sure that the battery tray is in good condition, and that the clamp is tight. Corrosion on the tray, retaining clamp and the battery itself can be removed with a solution of water and baking soda. Thoroughly rinse all cleaned areas with water. Any metal parts damaged by corrosion should be covered with a zinc-based primer, then painted.

✔ Periodically (approximately every three months), check the charge condition of the battery as described in Chapter 5.

✔ If the battery is flat, and you need to jump start your vehicle, see **Roadside Repairs**.

HAYNES HINT

Battery corrosion can be kept to a minimum by applying a layer of petroleum jelly to the clamps and terminals after they are reconnected.

1 The battery is located on the left-hand side of the engine compartment. The exterior of the battery should be inspected periodically for damage such as a cracked case or cover.

3 If corrosion (white, fluffy deposits) is evident, remove the cables from the battery terminals, clean them with a small wire brush, then refit them. Automotive stores sell a tool for cleaning the battery post . . .

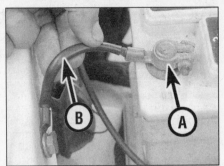

2 Check the tightness of battery clamps (A) to ensure good electrical connections. You should not be able to move them. Also check each cable (B) for cracks and frayed conductors.

4 . . . as well as the battery cable clamps

Wiper blades

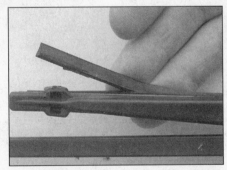

1 Check the condition of the wiper blades; if they are cracked or show any signs of deterioration, or if the glass swept area is smeared, renew them. For maximum clarity of vision, wiper blades should be renewed annually, as a matter of course.

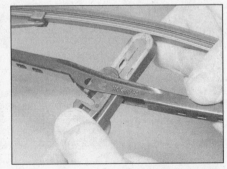

2 To remove a wiper blade, pull the arm fully away from the glass until it locks. Swivel the blade through 90°, press the locking tab(s) with your fingers, and slide the blade out of the arm's hooked end. On refitting, ensure that the blade locks securely into the arm.

Tyre condition and pressure

It is very important that tyres are in good condition, and at the correct pressure - having a tyre failure at any speed is highly dangerous. Tyre wear is influenced by driving style - harsh braking and acceleration, or fast cornering, will all produce more rapid tyre wear. As a general rule, the front tyres wear out faster than the rears. Interchanging the tyres from front to rear ("rotating" the tyres) may result in more even wear. However, if this is completely effective, you may have the expense of replacing all four tyres at once! Remove any nails or stones embedded in the tread before they penetrate the tyre to cause deflation. If removal of a nail does reveal that the tyre has been punctured, refit the nail so that its point of penetration is marked. Then immediately change the wheel, and have the tyre repaired by a tyre dealer.

Regularly check the tyres for damage in the form of cuts or bulges, especially in the sidewalls. Periodically remove the wheels, and clean any dirt or mud from the inside and outside surfaces. Examine the wheel rims for signs of rusting, corrosion or other damage. Light alloy wheels are easily damaged by "kerbing" whilst parking; steel wheels may also become dented or buckled. A new wheel is very often the only way to overcome severe damage.

New tyres should be balanced when they are fitted, but it may become necessary to re-balance them as they wear, or if the balance weights fitted to the wheel rim should fall off. Unbalanced tyres will wear more quickly, as will the steering and suspension components. Wheel imbalance is normally signified by vibration, particularly at a certain speed (typically around 50 mph). If this vibration is felt only through the steering, then it is likely that just the front wheels need balancing. If, however, the vibration is felt through the whole car, the rear wheels could be out of balance. Wheel balancing should be carried out by a tyre dealer or garage.

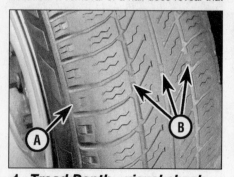

1 Tread Depth - visual check
The original tyres have tread wear safety bands (B), which will appear when the tread depth reaches approximately 1.6 mm. The band positions are indicated by a triangular mark on the tyre sidewall (A).

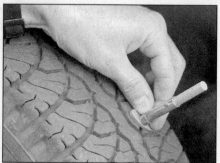

2 Tread Depth - manual check
Alternatively, tread wear can be monitored with a simple, inexpensive device known as a tread depth indicator gauge.

3 Tyre Pressure Check
Check the tyre pressures regularly with the tyres cold. Do not adjust the tyre pressures immediately after the vehicle has been used, or an inaccurate setting will result.

Tyre tread wear patterns

Shoulder Wear

Underinflation (wear on both sides)
Under-inflation will cause overheating of the tyre, because the tyre will flex too much, and the tread will not sit correctly on the road surface. This will cause a loss of grip and excessive wear, not to mention the danger of sudden tyre failure due to heat build-up.
Check and adjust pressures
Incorrect wheel camber (wear on one side)
Repair or renew suspension parts
Hard cornering
Reduce speed!

Centre Wear

Overinflation
Over-inflation will cause rapid wear of the centre part of the tyre tread, coupled with reduced grip, harsher ride, and the danger of shock damage occurring in the tyre casing.
Check and adjust pressures

If you sometimes have to inflate your car's tyres to the higher pressures specified for maximum load or sustained high speed, don't forget to reduce the pressures to normal afterwards.

Uneven Wear

Front tyres may wear unevenly as a result of wheel misalignment. Most tyre dealers and garages can check and adjust the wheel alignment (or "tracking") for a modest charge.
Incorrect camber or castor
Repair or renew suspension parts
Malfunctioning suspension
Repair or renew suspension parts
Unbalanced wheel
Balance tyres
Incorrect toe setting
Adjust front wheel alignment
Note: *The feathered edge of the tread which typifies toe wear is best checked by feel.*

Lubricants and fluids

Component or system	Lubricant type/specification
Engine	Multigrade engine oil, viscosity SAE 10W/40 to 20W/50, to API SG/CD *(Duckhams QXR Premium Petrol Engine Oil, or Duckhams Hypergrade Petrol Engine Oil)*
Cooling system	Ethylene glycol-based antifreeze *(Duckhams Antifreeze & Summer Coolant)*
Manual transmission	Gear oil, viscosity SAE 80 EP *(Duckhams Hypoid Gear Oil 80W GL-4)*
Automatic transmission	Dexron II type ATF *(Duckhams ATF Autotrans III)*
Braking system	Hydraulic fluid to SAE J1703F or DOT 4 *(Duckhams Universal Brake and Clutch Fluid)*
Power steering	Dexron II type ATF *(Duckhams ATF Autotrans III)*

Choosing your engine oil

Engines need oil, not only to lubricate moving parts and minimise wear, but also to maximise power output and to improve fuel economy. By introducing a simplified and improved range of engine oils, Duckhams has taken away the confusion and made it easier for you to choose the right oil for your engine.

HOW ENGINE OIL WORKS

• *Beating friction*

Without oil, the moving surfaces inside your engine will rub together, heat up and melt, quickly causing the engine to seize. Engine oil creates a film which separates these moving parts, preventing wear and heat build-up.

• *Cooling hot-spots*

Temperatures inside the engine can exceed 1000° C. The engine oil circulates and acts as a coolant, transferring heat from the hot-spots to the sump.

• *Cleaning the engine internally*

Good quality engine oils clean the inside of your engine, collecting and dispersing combustion deposits and controlling them until they are trapped by the oil filter or flushed out at oil change.

OIL CARE - FOLLOW THE CODE

To handle and dispose of used engine oil safely, always:

OIL CARE FOLLOW THE CODE
OIL BANK LINE
0800 66 33 66

- *Avoid skin contact with used engine oil. Repeated or prolonged contact can be harmful.*
- *Dispose of used oil and empty packs in a responsible manner in an authorised disposal site. Call 0800 663366 to find the one nearest to you. Never tip oil down drains or onto the ground.*

Tyre pressures (cold)

	Front	Rear
Up to 3 passengers:		
Up to 1993 model year	33 psi (2.3 bar)	30 psi (2.1 bar)
1993 model year onwards	34 psi (2.4 bar)	31.5 psi (2.2 bar)
Full load	36 psi (2.5 bar)	46 psi (3.2 bar)
Temporary spare wheel	61 psi (4.2 bar)	61 psi (4.2 bar)

Notes

Chapter 1
Routine maintenance and servicing

Contents

Degrees of difficulty

Easy, suitable for novice with little experience

Fairly easy, suitable for beginner with some experience

Fairly difficult, suitable for competent DIY mechanic

Difficult, suitable for experienced DIY mechanic

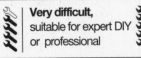
Very difficult, suitable for expert DIY or professional

Lubricants and fluids .... Refer to *"Weekly Checks"*

Capacities

Engine oil

Including filter:

All engines except DOHC (non-Ecotec) .... 4.0 litres

DOHC (non-Ecotec) .... 4.5 litres

Quantity of oil required to raise level from "MIN" to "MAX" .... 1.0 litre

Cooling system (approx.) .... 7.2 litres

Transmission

Manual transmission .... 1.9 litres

Automatic transmission:

At fluid change .... 3.0 to 3.5 litres

Difference between dipstick MAX and MIN marks - approximate:

+ 20°C side .... 0.25 litre

+ 80°C side .... 0.40 litre

Power steering fluid (approx.) .... 1.0 litre (approx.)

Fuel tank (approx.) .... 63.0 litres

Washer fluid

Without headlamp washers .... 2.6 litres

With headlamp washers .... 4.5 litres

Engine

Oil filter .... Champion G102

Cooling system

Antifreeze mixture:

28% antifreeze .... Protection down to -15°C

50% antifreeze .... Protection down to -30°C

Note: *Refer to antifreeze manufacturer for latest recommendations.*

Fuel system

Note: *Idle speed adjustment is not possible on some models, shown for information only. For further details refer to Chapter 4A.*

Idle speed:

SOHC engine .... 800 ± 80 rpm

DOHC engine:

Non-Ecotec .... 940 ± 80 rpm

Ecotec .... 850 ± 160 rpm

Idle mixture CO content .... 0.3 % (at 2800 to 3200 rpm)

Air filter element .... Champion U554

Fuel filter .... Champion L201

Ignition system

Ignition timing .... Refer to Chapter 5

Spark plugs:

	Type	Electrode gap*
SOHC engine		
Up to 1995	Champion RN9YCC	0.8 mm
1996-on	Champion RC10DMC	Not adjustable
DOHC engine:		
Non-Ecotec engine	Champion RC9MCC	0.8 mm
Ecotec engine	Champion RC10DMC	Not adjustable

* *Information on spark plug types and electrode gaps is as recommended by Champion Spark Plug. Where alternative types are used, refer to the manufacturer's recommendations*

Brakes

Minimum pad friction material thickness (including backing plate) .... 7.0 mm

Minimum shoe friction material thickness .... 0.5 mm above rivet heads

Tyres

Pressures .... See *"Weekly checks"*

Torque wrench settings

	Nm	lbf ft
Automatic transmission drain plug	45	33
Engine oil (sump) drain plug	55	41
Roadwheels	110	81
Spark plugs	25	18

The maintenance intervals in this manual are provided with the assumption that you, not the dealer, will be carrying out the work. These are the minimum maintenance intervals recommended by the manufacturer for vehicles driven daily. If you wish to keep your vehicle in peak condition at all times, you may wish to perform some of these procedures more often. We encourage frequent maintenance, because it enhances the efficiency, performance and resale value of your vehicle.

If the vehicle is driven in dusty areas, used to tow a trailer, or driven frequently at slow speeds (idling in traffic) or on short journeys, more frequent maintenance intervals are recommended. Vauxhall recommend that the service intervals are halved for vehicles that are used under these conditions.

When the vehicle is new, it should be serviced by a factory-authorised dealer service department, to preserve the factory warranty.

Maintenance is essential for ensuring safety and for getting the best in terms of performance and economy from your vehicle. Over the years, the need for periodic lubrication - oiling, greasing, and so on - has been drastically reduced, if not eliminated. This has unfortunately tended to lead some owners to think that because no action is required, components either no longer exist, or will last for ever. This is certainly not the case; it is essential to carry out regular visual examination comprehensively to spot any possible defects at an early stage before they develop into major expensive repairs.

The following service schedules are a list of the maintenance requirements, and the intervals at which they should be carried out, as recommended by the manufacturers. Where applicable, these procedures are covered in greater detail near the beginning of each relevant Chapter.

Every 250 miles (400 km) or weekly
☐ Refer to "Weekly checks"

Basic service, every 9000 miles (15 000 km) or 12 months - whichever comes sooner

Along with the items in "Weekly checks", carry out the following:
☐ Renew the engine oil and oil filter (Section 3).
☐ Renew the pollen filter (Section 4).
☐ Check all hoses and other components for fluid leaks (Section 5).
☐ Check the steering and suspension components (Section 6).
☐ Check the condition of the driveshaft rubber gaiters (Section 7).
☐ Check the automatic transmission fluid level (if applicable) (Section 8).
☐ Check the radiator for blockage (e.g. dead insects) and clean as necessary (Section 9).
☐ Check the idle speed and mixture (Section 10).
☐ Check the throttle linkage and lubricate if necessary (Section 11).
☐ Check the exhaust system for corrosion, leaks and security (Section 12).
☐ Check all wiring for condition and security (Section 13).
☐ Check and adjust the ignition timing (if applicable) (Section 14).
☐ Renew the brake fluid (Section 15).
☐ Check the brake pad friction material for wear (Section 16).
☐ Check the handbrake linkage (Section 17).
☐ Check the power steering fluid level (Section 18).
☐ Check the power steering pump drivebelt (if applicable) (Section 19).
☐ Check the bodywork (Section 20).
☐ Lubricate all locks and hinges (Section 21).
☐ Check the alternator V-belt (Section 22).
☐ Check the headlamp alignment (Section 23).
☐ Replace battery in the door lock key (if applicable) (Section 24).
☐ Carry out a road test (Section 25).
Note: Vauxhall specify that an Exhaust Emissions Test should be carried out at least annually. However, this requires special equipment, and is performed as part of the MOT test (refer to the end of the manual).

Full service, every 18 000 miles (30 000 km) or 24 months - whichever comes sooner

Along with the "basic service", carry out the following:
☐ Renew the coolant (Section 26).
☐ Renew the air cleaner element (Section 27).
☐ Renew the fuel filter (Section 28).
☐ Renew the spark plugs (SOHC only) (Section 29).
☐ Inspect and clean the distributor cap and HT leads (Section 30).
☐ Check the clutch cable adjustment (Section 31).
☐ Check the manual transmission fluid level (Section 32).
☐ Check the automatic transmission (Section 33).
☐ Check the brake shoes for wear (Section 34).

Major service, every 36 000 miles (60 000 km) or 48 months - whichever comes sooner

Along with the "full service", carry out the following:
☐ Renew the timing belt (Section 35).
☐ Renew the spark plugs (DOHC models only) (Section 36).
☐ Renew the automatic transmission fluid (Section 37)*.
* **Note:** If a vehicle is used for heavy-duty work (e.g. taxi work, caravan/trailer towing, mostly short-distance, stop-start city driving) the fluid must be changed every 36 months or 27 000 miles (45 000 km), whichever occurs first.

1

Underbonnet view of a SOHC engine with Motronic M1.5

1 Anti-theft alarm horn
2 Air cleaner casing
3 Airflow meter
4 Suspension strut top
5 Coolant expansion tank
6 Brake fluid reservoir
7 Throttle body
8 Relay box
9 ABS control unit
10 Washer fluid reservoir
11 Battery
12 Power steering fluid
   reservoir
13 Power steering fluid hoses
14 Distributor cap
15 Engine oil level dipstick
16 Idle speed adjuster
17 Fuel pressure regulator
18 Oil filler cap
19 Thermostat housing

Underbonnet view of an early DOHC (non-Ecotec) engine with Motronic M2.5

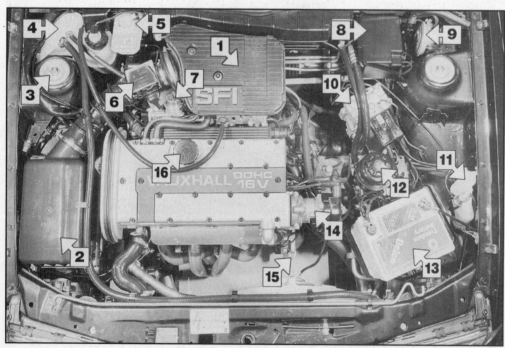

1 Pre-volume chamber to
   throttle
2 Air cleaner casing
3 Suspension strut top
4 Coolant expansion tank
5 Brake fluid reservoir
6 Air mass meter (hot wire)
7 Fuel pressure regulator
8 Relay box
9 Anti-theft alarm horn
10 ABS hydraulic modulator
11 Washer fluid reservoir
12 Power steering fluid
   reservoir
13 Battery
14 Hall-effect distributor
15 Engine oil level dipstick
16 Oil filler cap

Underbonnet view of a late DOHC (non-Ecotec) engine with Motronic M2.8

1 Pre-volume chamber to throttle
2 Air cleaner casing
3 Suspension strut top
4 Coolant expansion tank
5 Brake fluid reservoir
6 Air mass meter (hot film)
7 Fuel pressure regulator
8 Relay box
9 Anti-theft alarm horn
10 ABS hydraulic modulator
11 Washer fluid reservoir
12 Power steering fluid reservoir
13 Battery
14 Camshaft phase sensor
15 DIS module
16 Engine oil level dipstick
17 Oil filler cap

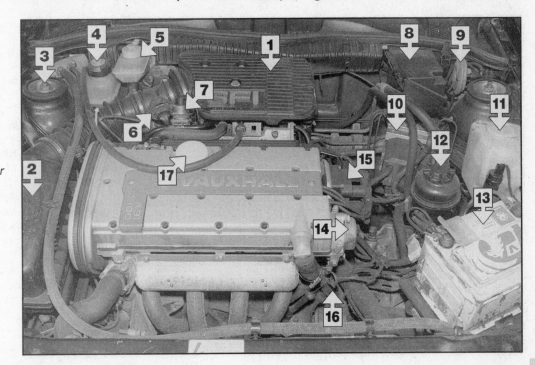

Underbonnet view of an early DOHC (Ecotec) engine with Simtec 56.1

1 Air cleaner casing
2 Suspension strut top
3 Coolant expansion tank
4 Brake fluid reservoir
5 Air mass meter (hot film)
6 Relay box
7 Anti-theft alarm horn
8 ABS hydraulic modulator
9 Washer fluid reservoir
10 Power steering fluid reservoir
11 Battery
12 Cable to camshaft phase sensor
13 DIS module
14 Exhaust gas recirculation valve
15 Secondary air cut-off valve
16 Secondary air non-return valve
17 Engine oil level dipstick
18 Oil filler cap

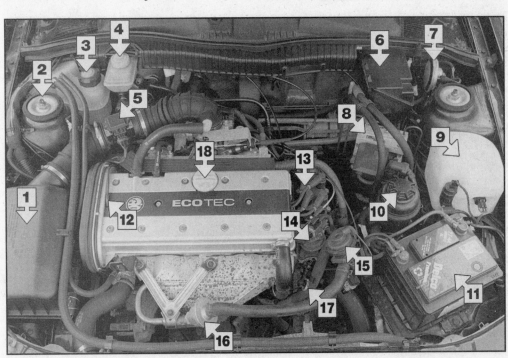

Underbonnet view of a late DOHC (Ecotec) engine with Simtec 56.5

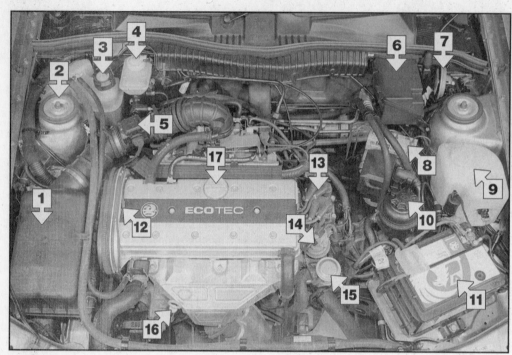

1　Air cleaner casing
2　Suspension strut top
3　Coolant expansion tank
4　Brake fluid reservoir
5　Air mass meter (hot film)
6　Relay box
7　Anti-theft alarm horn
8　ABS hydraulic modulator
9　Washer fluid reservoir
10　Power steering fluid
　　reservoir
11　Battery
12　Cable to camshaft phase
　　sensor
13　DIS module
14　Exhaust gas recirculation
　　valve
15　Secondary air cut-off valve
16　Engine oil level dipstick
17　Oil filler cap

Front underbody view of a DOHC (Ecotec) engine

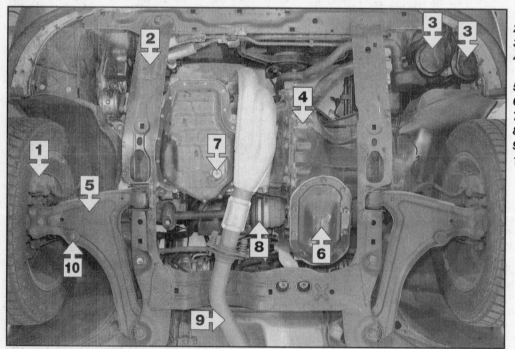

1　Brake caliper
2　Subframe
3　Twin horns
4　Clutch and transmission
　　bellhousing
5　Suspension lower arm
6　Differential cover plate
7　Engine oil drain plug
8　Driveshaft gaiter
9　Exhaust pipe
10　Anti-roll bar securing nut

Rear underbody view of a DOHC (Ecotec) engine model

1 Fuel tank securing strap
2 Shock absorber
3 ABS wheel sensor
4 Semi-trailing arm
5 Suspension crossmember
  mounting bracing bracket
6 Handbrake cable
7 Suspension crossmember
8 Exhaust expansion box
9 Fuel filter

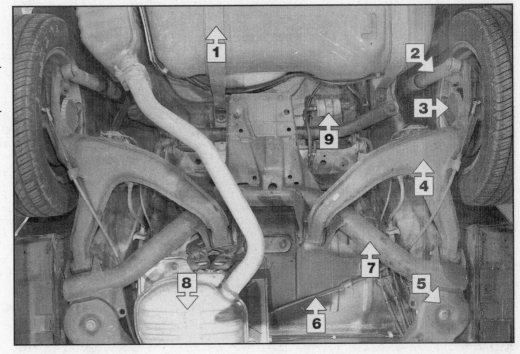

Maintenance procedures

1 Introduction

This Chapter is designed to help the home mechanic maintain his/her vehicle for safety, economy, long life and peak performance.

The Chapter contains a master maintenance schedule, followed by Sections dealing specifically with each task in the schedule. Visual checks, adjustments, component renewal and other helpful items are included. Refer to the accompanying illustrations of the engine compartment and the underside of the vehicle for the locations of the various components.

Servicing your vehicle according to the mileage/time maintenance schedule and the following Sections will provide a planned maintenance programme, which should result in a long and reliable service life. This is a comprehensive plan, so maintaining some items but not others at the specified service intervals, will not produce the same results.

As you service your vehicle, you will discover that many of the procedures can - and should - be grouped together, because of the particular procedure being performed, or because of the proximity of two otherwise-unrelated components to one another. For example, if the vehicle is raised for any reason, the exhaust can be inspected at the same time as the suspension and steering components.

The first step in this maintenance programme is to prepare yourself before the actual work begins. Read through all the Sections relevant to the work to be carried out, then make a list and gather all the parts and tools required. If a problem is found, seek advice from a parts specialist, or a dealer service department.

2 Intensive maintenance

If, from the time the vehicle is new, routine maintenance schedule is followed closely, frequent checks made of fluid levels and high-wear items, as recommended, the engine will be kept in relatively good running condition The need for additional work will be minimised

It is possible that there will be times when the engine is running poorly due to the lack of regular maintenance. This is even more likely if a used vehicle, which has not received regular and frequent maintenance checks, is purchased. In such cases, additional work may need to be carried out, outside of the regular maintenance intervals.

If engine wear is suspected, a compression test (refer to Chapter 2A) will provide valuable information regarding the overall performance of the main internal components. Such a test can be used as a basis to decide on the extent of the work to be carried out. If, for example, a compression test indicates serious internal engine wear, conventional maintenance as described in this Chapter will not greatly improve the performance of the engine. It may also prove a waste of time and money, unless extensive overhaul work is carried out first.

The following series of operations are those most often required to improve the performance of a generally poor-running engine:

Primary operations

a) *Clean, inspect and test the battery (See "Weekly Checks")*
b) *Check all the engine related fluids (See "Weekly Checks")*
c) *Check the condition and tension of the auxiliary drivebelt (Sections 19 and 22, as appropriate).*
d) *Renew the spark plugs (Sections 29 and 36, as appropriate).*
e) *Inspect the distributor cap, rotor arm and HT leads, as applicable (Section 30).*
f) *Check the condition of the air filter, and renew if necessary (Section 27).*
g) *Check the fuel filter (Section 28).*
h) *Check the condition of all hoses, and check for fluid leaks (Section 5).*
i) *Check the idle speed and mixture settings (Section 10).*

If the above operations do not prove fully effective, carry out the following secondary operations:

Secondary operations

All items listed under "Primary operations", plus the following:

a) *Check the charging system (Chapter 5).*
b) *Check the ignition system (Chapter 5).*
c) *Check the fuel system (Chapters 4A and 4B).*
d) *Renew the distributor cap and rotor arm (Section 30).*
e) *Renew the ignition HT leads (Section 30).*

Basic service, every 9000 miles (15 000 km) or 12 months

3 Engine oil and filter - renewal

1 Ideally, the oil should be drained with the engine hot, just after the vehicle has been driven.
2 On DOHC models, remove the engine undershield, if there is one, to expose the sump drain plug and the oil filter.
3 Place a container beneath the oil drain plug at the rear of the sump.
4 Remove the oil filler cap from the camshaft cover, then using a socket or spanner, unscrew the oil drain plug, and allow the oil to drain **(see illustration)**. Take care to avoid scalding if the oil is hot.

HAYNES HiNT *As the drain plug releases from the threads, move it away quickly so the stream of oil, running out of the sump, goes into the container not up your sleeve.*

5 Allow ten to fifteen minutes for the oil to drain completely, then move the container and position it under the oil filter.
6 Improved access to the oil filter can be gained by jacking up the front of the vehicle and removing the right-hand roadwheel **(see illustration)**. Ensure that the handbrake is applied, and that the vehicle is securely supported on axle stands (see "*Jacking and Vehicle Support*"). Note that further oil may drain from the sump as the vehicle is raised.
7 Using a strap wrench or a filter removal tool if necessary, slacken the filter and unscrew it from the mounting. Alternatively, if the filter is very tight, a screwdriver can be driven through the filter casing and used as a lever. Discard the filter.
8 Wipe the mating face on the filter mounting with a lint-free rag, then smear the sealing ring of the new filter with clean engine oil of the specified grade.
9 Screw the new filter into position and tighten it by hand only, do not use any tools.
10 Where applicable, refit the roadwheel and lower the vehicle to the ground. Fully tighten the roadwheel bolts with the vehicle resting on its wheels.
11 Examine the condition of the oil drain plug sealing ring and renew if necessary, then refit the drain plug and tighten it to the specified torque.
12 Refill the engine through the filler on the camshaft cover, using the specified grade and quantity of oil. Fill until the level reaches the "MAX" mark on the dipstick, allowing time for the oil to drain through the engine to the sump.
13 Refit the oil filler cap, then start the engine and check for leaks. Note that the oil pressure warning lamp may stay illuminated for a few seconds when the engine is started as the oil filter fills with oil.

14 Stop the engine and recheck the oil level, topping-up if necessary.
15 On DOHC models, refit the engine undershield, if there is one.
16 Dispose of the old engine oil safely; do not pour it down a drain.
Note: It is antisocial and illegal to dump oil down the drain. To find the location of your local oil recycling bank, call this number free - 0800 66 33 66.

4 Pollen filter - renewal

1 Open the bonnet and detach the windscreen cowl panel to access the components underneath, as described in Chapter 11. It is not necessary to completely remove the panel.
2 Release the clips from the front of the pollen filter, then remove the filter and replace it with a new one **(see illustration)**.
3 Refit the cowl panel.

5 Hose and fluid leak check

1 Visually inspect the engine joint faces, gaskets and seals for any signs of water or oil leaks. Pay particular attention to the areas

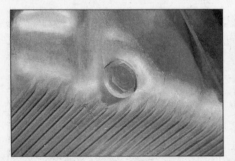
3.4 Sump drain plug location - DOHC (non-Ecotec) model (engine undershield removed)

3.6 Oil filter viewed through right-hand wheel arch - SOHC model

4.2 Removing the pollen filter

around the camshaft cover, cylinder head, oil filter and sump joint faces. Remember that, over a period of time, some very slight seepage from these areas is to be expected - what you are really looking for is any indication of a serious leak. Should a leak be found, renew the offending gasket or oil seal by referring to the appropriate Chapters in this manual.

2 Also check the security and condition of all the engine related pipes and hoses. Ensure that all cable-ties or securing clips are in place, and in good condition. Clips that are broken or missing can lead to chafing of the hoses, pipes or wiring, which could cause more serious problems in the future.

3 Carefully check the radiator hoses and heater hoses along their entire length. Renew any hose that is cracked, swollen or deteriorated. Cracks will show up better if the hose is squeezed. Pay close attention to the hose clips that secure the hoses to the cooling system components. Hose clips can pinch and puncture hoses, resulting in cooling system leaks. It is always beneficial to renew hose clips whenever possible.

4 Inspect all the cooling system components (hoses, joint faces, etc.) for leaks.

HAYNES HINT

A leak in the cooling system will usually show up as white or rust coloured deposits on the area adjoining the leak

5 Where any problems are found on system components, renew the component or gasket with reference to Chapter 3.

6 Where applicable, inspect the automatic transmission fluid cooler hoses for leaks or deterioration.

7 With the vehicle raised, inspect the petrol tank and filler neck for punctures, cracks and other damage. The connection between the filler neck and tank is especially critical. Sometimes a rubber filler neck or connecting hose will leak due to loose retaining clamps or deteriorated rubber.

8 Carefully check all rubber hoses and metal fuel lines leading away from the petrol tank. Check for loose connections, deteriorated hoses, crimped lines, and other damage. Pay particular attention to the vent pipes and hoses, which often loop up around the filler neck and can become blocked or crimped. Follow the lines to the front of the vehicle, carefully inspecting them all the way. Renew damaged sections as necessary.

9 From within the engine compartment, check the security of all fuel hose attachments and pipe unions, and inspect the fuel hoses and vacuum hoses for kinks, chafing and deterioration.

10 Check the condition of the power steering fluid hoses and pipes.

6 Steering and suspension check

Front suspension and steering check

1 Raise the front of the car, and support on axle stands (see *"Jacking and Vehicle Support"*).

2 Visually inspect the balljoint dust covers and the steering rack-and-pinion gaiters for splits, chafing or deterioration. Any wear of these components will cause loss of lubricant, together with dirt and water entry, resulting in rapid wear of the balljoints or steering gear.

3 Check the power steering fluid hoses for chafing or deterioration, and the pipe and hose unions for fluid leaks. Also check for signs of fluid leakage under pressure from the steering gear rubber gaiters, which would indicate failed fluid seals within the steering gear.

4 Grasp the roadwheel at the 12 o'clock and 6 o'clock positions, and try to rock it **(see illustration)**. Very slight free play may be felt, but if the movement is appreciable, further investigation is necessary to determine the source. Continue rocking the wheel while an assistant depresses the footbrake. If the movement is now eliminated or significantly reduced, it is likely that the hub bearings are at fault. If the free play is still evident with the footbrake depressed, then there is wear in the suspension joints or mountings.

5 Now grasp the wheel at the 9 o'clock and 3 o'clock positions, and try to rock it as before. Any movement felt now may again be caused by wear in the hub bearings or the steering track-rod balljoints. If the inner or outer balljoint is worn, the visual movement will be obvious.

6 Using a large screwdriver or flat bar, check for wear in the suspension mounting bushes by levering between the relevant suspension component and its attachment point. Some movement is to be expected as the mountings are made of rubber, but excessive wear should be obvious. Also check the condition of any visible rubber bushes, looking for splits, cracks or contamination of the rubber.

7 Inspect the front suspension lower arms for distortion or damage (Chapter 10, Section 5).

8 With the car standing on its wheels, have an assistant turn the steering wheel back and forth about an eighth of a turn each way. There should be very little, if any, lost movement between the steering wheel and roadwheels. If this is not the case, closely observe the joints and mountings previously described, but in addition, check the steering column universal joints for wear, and the rack-and-pinion steering gear itself.

6.4 Check for wear in the hub bearings by grasping the wheel and trying to rock it

Suspension strut/shock absorber check

Note: *Suspension struts/shock absorbers should always be renewed in pairs on the same axle.*

9 Check for any signs of fluid leakage around the suspension strut/shock absorber body, or from the rubber gaiter around the piston rod. Should any fluid be noticed, the suspension strut/shock absorber is defective internally, and should be renewed.

10 The efficiency of the suspension strut/shock absorber may be checked by bouncing the vehicle at each corner. The body will return to its normal position and stop after being depressed. If it rises and returns on a rebound, the suspension strut/shock absorber is probably suspect. Examine also the suspension strut/shock absorber upper and lower mountings for any signs of wear.

7 Driveshaft gaiter check

1 With the vehicle raised and securely supported on stands, turn the steering onto full lock, then slowly rotate the roadwheel. Inspect the condition of the outer constant velocity (CV) joint rubber gaiters, squeezing the gaiters to open out the folds **(see illustration)**. Check for signs of cracking, splits or deterioration of the rubber, which may allow the grease to escape, and lead to water and grit entry into the joint. Also check

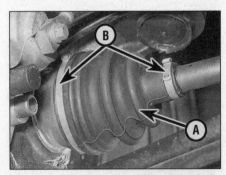

7.1 Check the condition of the driveshaft gaiters (A) and clips (B)

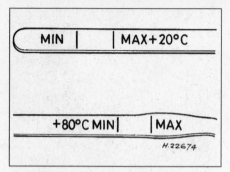

8.4 When checking the fluid level, ensure side of dipstick used corresponds with fluid temperature

the security and condition of the retaining clips. Repeat these checks on the inner CV joints. If any damage or deterioration is found, the gaiters should be renewed as described in Chapter 8.

2 At the same time, check the general condition of the CV joints themselves by first holding the driveshaft and attempting to rotate the wheel. Repeat this check by holding the inner joint and attempting to rotate the driveshaft. Any appreciable movement indicates wear in the joints, wear in the driveshaft splines, or a loose driveshaft retaining nut.

8 Automatic transmission fluid level check

Note: *The transmission fluid level can be checked either when it is cold (only below 35°C (100°F) outside temperature) or when it is fully warmed up to normal operating temperature (after driving for a distance of approximately 12 miles/20 km). Since the fluid level must be checked with the engine running, ensure that the vehicle is parked on level ground with the handbrake firmly applied before leaving the driver's seat. Be careful to keep loose clothing, long hair, etc., well clear of hot or moving components when working under the bonnet.*

Transmission cold

1 Park the vehicle on level ground and apply the handbrake firmly. With the engine running at no more than idle speed and your foot firmly on the brake pedal, move the selector lever through all positions, ending in position "P". Allow the engine to idle for one minute, then check the level within two minutes.

2 With the engine still idling and position "P" still selected, open the bonnet and withdraw the transmission dipstick from the filler tube located in the front of the transmission casing, at the left-hand end of the engine.

3 Note the fluid's condition (see below), then wipe clean the dipstick using a clean, non-fluffy rag, insert it fully back into the tube and withdraw it again.

4 The level should be up to the "MAX" mark on the "+20°C" side of the dipstick **(see illustration).**

5 If topping-up is required, switch off the ignition and add only good quality fluid of the specified type through the filler tube. If significant amounts of fluid are being lost (carefully note the amounts being added, and how often), check the transmission for leaks and either repair the fault or take the vehicle to a Vauxhall dealer for attention.

6 When the level is correct, ensure that the dipstick is pressed firmly into the filler tube.

Transmission fully warmed up

7 Work exactly as described above, but take the level reading from the "+80°C" side of the dipstick. In this case, the level must be between the dipstick "MAX" and "MIN" marks.

Checking the fluid's condition

8 Whenever the fluid level is checked, examine the condition of the fluid and compare its colour, smell and texture with that of new fluid.

9 If the fluid is dark, almost black, and smells burnt, it is possible that the transmission friction material is worn or disintegrating. The vehicle should be taken to a Vauxhall dealer or automatic transmission specialist for immediate attention.

10 If the fluid is milky, this is due to the presence of emulsified droplets of water. This may be caused either by condensation after a prolonged period of short journeys or by the entry of water through the dipstick/filler tube or breather. If the fluid does not revert to its normal appearance after a long journey it must be renewed or advice should be sought from a Vauxhall dealer or automatic transmission specialist.

11 If the fluid is varnish-like (i.e. light to dark brown and tacky) it has oxidised due to overheating or to over or under filling. If renewal of the fluid does not cure the problem, the vehicle should be taken to a Vauxhall dealer or automatic transmission specialist for immediate attention.

12 If at any time on checking the fluid level or on draining the fluid, particles of dirt, metal chips or other foreign matter are found in the fluid, the vehicle must be taken to a Vauxhall dealer or automatic transmission specialist for immediate attention. It may be necessary to strip, clean and reassemble at least the valve body, if not the complete transmission, to rectify any fault.

9 Radiator inspection and cleaning

1 Inspect the radiator for leaks or corrosion, especially around the outlet or inlet connectors.
2 Clean the radiator with a soft brush or compressed air. Remove any debris, like dead insects or leaves.

3 If leaks are visible, replace the radiator. Refer to Chapter 3, if necessary.

10 Idle speed and mixture check

The idle speed and mixture are automatically adjusted by the control unit, and cannot be altered. If either of these is outside the specified limits, there is a system fault and the problem should be referred to a dealer. See Chapter 4A for details of how to check the idle mixture.

11 Throttle linkage maintenance

On models built before 1992, lubricate the throttle linkage.

12 Exhaust system check

1 With the engine off, check the security of the exhaust system. Pay particular attention to the rubber mountings that suspend the exhaust.
2 Start the engine and check underneath for leaks, which can be heard. This job is made easier if you have access to a ramp.
3 Listen for exhaust leaks from around the front pipe to exhaust manifold joint.
4 For further information, refer to Chapter 4B.

13 Wiring check

1 Check all wiring in both the engine compartment and under the car.
2 Ensure that all wiring clips/clamps are secure.
3 Pay particular attention to wiring near components that get hot, i.e. exhaust systems.
4 Make sure that all electrical connections are secure and undamaged.

14 Ignition timing

⚠ *Warning: Voltages produced by an electronic ignition system are considerably higher than those produced by conventional ignition systems. Extreme care must be taken when working on the system with the ignition switched on. Persons with surgically implanted cardiac pacemaker devices should keep away from the ignition circuits, components and test equipment.*

Refer to Chapter 5 for details.

15 Brake fluid renewal

Warning: *Brake hydraulic fluid can harm your eyes and damage painted surfaces, so use extreme caution when handling and pouring it. Do not use fluid that has been standing open for some time, as it absorbs moisture from the air. Excess moisture can cause a dangerous loss of braking effectiveness.*

HAYNES HINT *Old hydraulic fluid is usually darker in colour than new fluid.*

Renew the brake and bleed the system. Refer to Chapter 9 for full details.

16 Brake pad check

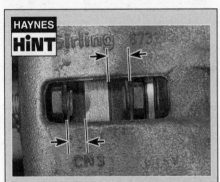

For a quick check, the thickness of the friction material on each brake pad can be measured through the aperture in the caliper body.

With the front or rear (as applicable) of the vehicle raised, remove the wheels and check the brake pads for wear. Renew the pads if the lining is below that specified. See Chapter 9 for full details.

17 Handbrake linkage check

With the vehicle raised, check the operation of the handbrake and lubricate the linkages. Refer to Chapter 9, for further details.

18 Power steering fluid check

1 With the engine off, remove the cap from the power steering reservoir. It is fitted with a dipstick.

2 The fluid should be visible up to the 'MAX' mark. If not, top it up using specified fluid, **(see illustration)**.

3 Start the engine and immediately top-up the fluid to the 'MIN' mark.

4 Do not allow the reservoir to run dry.

5 For details on how to bleed the system, refer to Chapter 10.

19 Power steering pump drivebelt check

Note: *Later models, from 1993 onwards, are fitted with a single serpentine belt which drives the alternator, power steering pump and air conditioning pump (if fitted). This type of belt has an automatic tensioner and cannot be adjusted.*

Checking

1 A special gauge is available for measuring the belt tension, and the values for use with this gauge are given in the Specifications in Chapter 10. If the gauge is not available, a good approximation is achieved with a belt deflection of approximately 10.0 mm (0.4 in) under moderate thumb pressure at the midpoint of the belt run between the pulleys. If in doubt, err on the slack side, as an excessively tight belt may cause pump damage.

2 Check the condition of the belt and renew it if there are any signs of damage or excessive wear.

Adjustment

3 Slacken the pump mounting and adjuster bolts.

4 Slacken the adjuster nuts and adjust the length of the threaded rod to remove or tension the belt as required **(see illustration)**.

5 Tighten the adjuster nuts and tighten the adjuster and mounting bolts to the specified torque (see Chapter 10), on completion.

6 If a new drivebelt has been fitted, recheck the tension after a few hundred miles.

20 Bodywork check

1 Clean the outside of the vehicle. If possible, clean underneath as well. If using a pressure cleaner take care not to damage any electrical components, especially in the engine compartment.

2 Check all around for signs of damage or corrosion and treat accordingly. Repair stone chips when you can to prevent rusting.

3 Read Chapter 11 for more details.

18.2 Topping-up the power steering fluid level

21 Lock and hinge check

1 Lubricate locks and hinges on all doors, tailgates and bonnet.

2 Check for wear or damage and ensure correct operation of safety catches.

3 Check the security of the bonnet stay and its securing clip.

4 Read Chapter 11 for further details.

22 Alternator V-belt check

Note: *Later models, from 1993 onwards, are fitted with a single serpentine belt which drives the alternator, power steering pump and air conditioning pump (if fitted). This type of belt has an automatic tensioner and cannot be adjusted.*

Checking

1 Correct tensioning of the drivebelt will ensure that it has a long life. Although special tools are available for measuring the belt tension, a good approximation can be achieved with approximately 13.0 mm (0.5 in) of free movement under firm thumb pressure at the mid-point of the longest run between pulleys. Make sure the belt is not too tight as this can cause excessive wear in the alternator.

19.4 Adjusting the length of the power steering pump threaded rod - models with V-belts

1

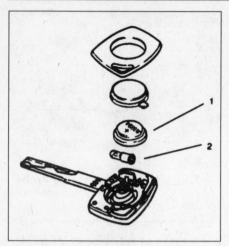

24.3 Replacing the battery in the door lock key

1 Battery (note, positive '+' side up)
2 Bulb

Adjustment

2 With the mounting bolts just holding the unit, lever the alternator away from the engine using a wooden lever at the mounting bracket end until the correct tension is achieved. Then tighten the mounting nuts and bolts. On no account lever at the free end of the alternator, as serious internal damage could be caused.
3 For details of replacement, see Chapter 5. When a new belt has been fitted, it will probably stretch slightly when it is first run, and the tension should be rechecked and if necessary adjusted after approximately 250 miles (400 km).

23 Headlamp alignment

Refer to Chapter 12 for details.

24 Door lock key battery - replacement

1 Carefully prise open the outer cover from the key. Take care not to lose any of the internal components, as they are loose.
2 Remove the battery and discard it safely.
3 Place the new battery, "+" side up **(see illustration)**. Check the operation of the key. If the bulb does not light obtain a replacement.
4 Replace the outer cover.

25 Road test

Instruments and electrical equipment

1 Check the operation of all instruments and electrical equipment.
2 Make sure that all instruments read correctly, and switch on all electrical equipment in turn to check that it functions properly.

Steering and suspension

3 Check for any abnormalities in the steering, suspension, handling or road "feel".
4 Drive the vehicle, and check that there are no unusual vibrations or noises.
5 Check that the steering feels positive, with no excessive "sloppiness", or roughness, and check for any suspension noises when cornering, or when driving over bumps.

Drivetrain

6 Check the performance of the engine, clutch, transmission and driveshafts.
7 Turn the radio/cassette off and listen for any unusual noises from the engine, clutch and transmission.
8 Make sure that the engine runs smoothly when idling, and that there is no hesitation when accelerating.
9 Check that the clutch action is smooth and progressive, that the drive is taken up smoothly, and that the pedal travel is not excessive. Also listen for any noises when the clutch pedal is depressed.
10 Check that all gears can be engaged smoothly, without noise, and that the gear lever action is not abnormally vague or "notchy".
11 Listen for a metallic clicking sound from the front of the vehicle, as the vehicle is driven slowly in a circle with the steering on full lock. Carry out this check in both directions. If a clicking noise is heard, this indicates wear in a driveshaft joint, in which case, the complete driveshaft must be renewed (see Chapter 8).

Full service, every 18 000 miles (30 000 km) or 24 months

26 Coolant renewal

⚠ *Warning: Wait until the engine is cold before starting the procedure. Do not allow antifreeze to come in contact with your skin or with painted*

27.2 Lift the cover and remove the air cleaner element

surfaces of the vehicle. Rinse off spills with plenty of water. Never leave antifreeze lying around in an open container. Always clean spilt fluids, as it can be harmful if swallowed.

Refer to Chapter 3 for details.

27 Air cleaner element - renewal

1 Unclip the coolant expansion tank hose from the air cleaner cover.
2 Release the two clips from the left-hand side of the cover, and undo the two screws from the right-hand side, then lift the cover and remove the air cleaner element **(see illustration)**.
3 Wipe clean the inside surfaces of the cover and main body.
4 Refitting is the reverse of removal, noting that the element fits with the rubber locating flange uppermost.

28 Fuel filter renewal

⚠ *Warning: Before carrying out the following operation, refer to the precautions given in "Safety first!" at the beginning of this manual, and follow them implicitly. Petrol is a highly dangerous and volatile liquid, and the precautions necessary when handling it cannot be overstressed.*

Refer to Chapter 4A.

29 Spark plug renewal (SOHC)

1 The correct functioning of the spark plugs is vital for the correct running and efficiency of the engine. It is essential that the plugs fitted are appropriate for the engine. Refer to the specifications at the beginning of this Chapter.

29.3 Removing a spark plug - SOHC models

If this type is used and the engine is in good condition, the spark plugs should not need attention between scheduled service replacement intervals. Spark plug cleaning is rarely necessary and should not be attempted unless specialised equipment is available, as damage can easily be caused to the firing ends.

2 Identify each HT lead for position so that the leads can be refitted to their correct cylinders. Then disconnect the leads from the plugs by pulling on the connectors, not the leads.

3 Clean the area around each spark plug using a small paintbrush, then using a plug spanner (preferably with a rubber insert), unscrew and remove the plugs **(see illustration)**. Cover the spark plug holes with a clean rag to prevent the ingress of any foreign matter.

4 The condition of the spark plugs will tell much about the overall condition of the engine.

5 If the insulator nose of the spark plug is clean and white, with no deposits, this is a sign of a weak mixture, or too hot a plug (a hot plug transfers heat away from the electrode slowly - a cold plug transfers heat away quickly).

6 If the tip and insulator nose is covered with hard black-looking deposits, this indicates that the mixture is too rich. Should the plug be black and oily, then it is likely that the engine is fairly worn, as well as the mixture being too rich.

7 If the insulator nose is covered with light tan to greyish brown deposits, then the mixture is correct, and it is likely that the engine is in good condition.

8 The spark plug gap is of considerable importance, because if it is either too large or too small, the size of the spark and its efficiency will be seriously impaired. The spark plug gap should be set to the figure given in the Specifications.

9 To set it, measure the gap with a feeler blade and then bend open, or close, the outer plug electrode until the correct gap is achieved. The centre electrode should never be bent, as this may crack the insulation and cause plug failure, if nothing worse **(see illustrations)**.

10 Before fitting new spark plugs check that their threaded connector sleeves are tight.

11 Screw in the plugs by hand, then tighten them to the specified torque. Do not exceed the torque figure.

12 Push the HT leads firmly onto the spark plugs, ensuring that they are connected to their correct cylinders.

It is very often difficult to insert spark plugs into their holes without cross-threading them. To avoid this, fit a short length of 8 mm (internal diameter), rubber hose over the end of the spark plug. The flexible hose acts as a universal joint to help align the plug correctly. Should the plug begin to cross-thread, the hose will slip on the spark plug, preventing damage to the thread in the cylinder head.

30 Distributor and HT lead check

1 Remove the distributor cap, HT leads and rotor arm, as described in Chapter 5, and wipe them clean. Also wipe clean the coil connections.

2 Visually check the distributor cap, rotor arm and HT leads for hairline cracks, and signs of arcing.

> **HAYNES HiNT** *Number the HT leads before removal to ensure correct refitting.*

3 When refitting the distributor cap, check that the ends of the HT leads are fitted securely to the cap, plugs and coil. Also make sure that the spring-tensioned carbon brush in the centre of the distributor cap moves freely, and that the HT segments are not worn excessively.

4 Inspect the electrical and vacuum connections of the ignition/engine management systems, and make sure that they are clean and secure.

31 Clutch cable check

1 Check the clutch cable adjustment, as described in Chapter 6.

2 Check also the condition of the cable. Inspect the cable strands for fraying, and ensure that the cable is correctly routed, to avoid chafing against surrounding components. Renew the cable, as described in Chapter 6, if excessive wear or damage is evident.

32 Manual transmission fluid check

Note: *On models built after 1994 it is no longer necessary to check levels.*

1 Ensure that the vehicle is on level ground.

1

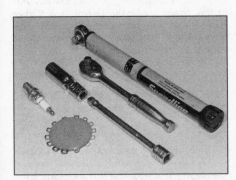

29.9a Tools required for spark plug removal, gap adjustment and refitting

29.9b Measuring the spark plug gap with a wire gauge

29.9c Measuring the spark plug gap with a feeler blade

32.2 Transmission oil level plug (arrowed) - F16 type transmission, viewed from below with driveshaft removed

32.3 Transmission breather/filler plug (arrowed) - F16 type transmission

2 Unscrew the transmission oil level plug, which is located in the rear right-hand side of the differential housing **(see illustration)**. The oil level should be up to the bottom of the level plug orifice.

3 If necessary, top-up the oil level through the breather/filler orifice in the gear selector cover. Unscrew the breather/filler plug **(see illustration)**, and top-up with the specified grade of oil, until it just begins to run from the level plug orifice. Refit the level plug and the breather/filler plug on completion.

4 Renewal of the transmission oil is not specified by the manufacturers, and no drain plug is provided. If you wish to renew the oil as a precaution, drained it by removing the differential cover plate. Use a new gasket when refitting the cover plate. Fill the transmission through the breather/filler orifice, as described in paragraphs 1 to 3.

5 Periodically inspect the transmission for oil leaks, and check the gear selector linkage components for wear and smooth operation.

33 Automatic transmission check

1 Carry out a thorough road test, ensuring that all gearchanges occur smoothly, without snatching and with no increase in engine speed between changes.

2 Check the operation of the kickdown. Check that all gear positions can be engaged at the appropriate movement of the selector lever and with the vehicle at rest, check that the operation of the parking pawl in position "P" prevents it from being moved. Ensure that the starter motor will work only with the selector lever in positions "P" or "N", and that the reversing lamps light only when position "R" is selected.

3 The manufacturer's schedule calls for a regular check of the electrical control system using the special Vauxhall test equipment;

owners will have to have this check carried out by a Vauxhall dealer.

4 Periodically inspect the transmission casing, checking all joint surfaces and seals for signs of fluid leaks. If any are found, the fault must be rectified immediately.

5 Check also that the transmission breather hose (under the battery mounting bracket) is clear and not blocked, kinked or twisted.

34 Brake shoe check

Note: *All models have front and rear disc brakes. The handbrake operates rear drum brakes that are combined with the rear disc brakes.*

Refer to Chapter 9 for details.

Major service, every 36 000 miles (60 000 km) or 48 months

35 Timing belt renewal

1 To minimise the risk of major damage to the engine, the timing belt (or cambelt, as it is sometimes called) needs replacing at least on every major service.

2 It is good practise however, not only to renew the belt whenever major engine work is carried out, but also if you buy a used car with unclear service history.

3 Some models are fitted with an inspection cover to view the condition of the belt, but others involve a lot more work.

4 Full details of checking and replacement are shown in Chapters 2A or 2B, as appropriate.

36 Spark plug renewal (DOHC)

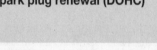

1 This procedure is basically the same shown in Section 29. However on these models, a spark plug cover needs to be removed from the camshaft cover before the plugs can be removed.

2 Take great care when removing and refitting spark plugs on these engines **(see illustration)**. Hairline cracks in the ceramic of the plug can cause occasional or complete ignition failure. Damage to the catalytic converter may also occur.

3 A special tool (Vauxhall No. KM-194-B), with a 3 part conical sliding element, is

available to reduce the risk of plug damage **(see illustration)**.

36.2 Removing a spark plug - DOHC model

4 After refitting the spark plugs, remember to replace the plug cover.

37 Automatic transmission fluid renewal

Renew the transmission fluid as detailed in Chapter 7B.

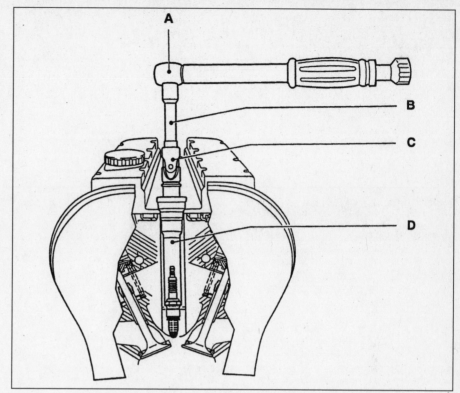

36.3 Removing spark plugs using special adapter - DOHC models

A Torque wrench   B Extension   C Joint   D Special adapter (P/N KM-194-B)

1

Chapter 2 Part A:
SOHC engine procedures

Contents

Camshaft front oil seal - removal and refitting 13
Camshaft housing and camshaft - general 15
Camshaft housing and camshaft - dismantling, inspection and
   reassembly 16
Camshaft rear oil seal - removal and refitting 14
Camshafts, "undersize" - general 17
Compression test - description 3
Crankcase ventilation system - description and maintenance 2
Crankshaft and bearings - examination 33
Crankshaft and bearings - removal and refitting 32
Crankshaft front oil seal - renewal 25
Crankshaft rear oil seal - renewal 26
Cylinder block and bores - examination and renovation 34
Cylinder head - dismantling and reassembly 20
Cylinder head - inspection and renovation 21
Cylinder head - removal and refitting (engine in vehicle) 18
Cylinder head - removal and refitting (engine removed) 19
Engine - removal and refitting (leaving transmission in car) 7
Engine and transmission mountings - renewal 9
Engine and transmission - removal, separation, reconnection and
   refitting 8

Engine oil and filter - renewal . . . . See Chapter 1
Engine dismantling and reassembly - general 10
Examination and renovation - general 35
Flexplate (automatic transmission) - removal and refitting 24
Flywheel - removal, inspection and refitting 23
General description 1
Hydraulic valve lifters - inspection 22
Initial start-up after major overhaul or repair 36
Major operations possible with the engine in the vehicle 4
Major operations requiring engine removal 5
Method of engine removal 6
Oil pump - dismantling, inspection and reassembly 29
Oil pump - removal and refitting 28
Pistons and connecting rods - examination and renovation 31
Pistons and connecting rods - removal and refitting 30
Sump - removal and refitting 27
Timing belt and sprockets (without automatic tensioner) - removal,
   refitting and adjustment 11
Timing belt, sprockets and tensioner - removal, refitting and
   adjustment 12

2A

Degrees of difficulty

Easy, suitable for novice with little experience	Fairly easy, suitable for beginner with some experience	Fairly difficult, suitable for competent DIY mechanic	Difficult, suitable for experienced DIY mechanic	Very difficult, suitable for expert DIY or professional

Specifications

General

Type (all models) . . . . Four-cylinder, in-line, water-cooled, transversely mounted at front of vehicle. Single belt-driven overhead camshaft, acting on hydraulic valve lifters

Manufacturer's engine code:
  C20 NE . . . . 2.0 litre (1998 cc) + catalyst
Pistons:
  Bore . . . . 86.0 mm
  Stroke . . . . 86.0 mm
Compression ratio . . . . 9.2 : 1
Maximum power . . . . 85 kW (115 bhp) at 5200 rpm
Maximum torque . . . . 170 Nm at 2600 rpm
Firing order . . . . 1-3-4-2 (No 1 cylinder at timing belt end)

Cylinder block

Material . . . . Cast iron
Maximum permissible bore out-of round . . . . 0.013 mm
Maximum permissible bore taper . . . . 0.013 mm
Maximum permissible rebore oversize . . . . 0.5 mm

Crankshaft and bearings

Number of main bearings 5
Main bearing journal diameter (mm):
  Standard .... 57.974 to 57.995
  0.25 mm undersize .... 57.732 to 57.745
  0.50 mm undersize .... 57.482 to 57.495
Main bearing shell colour codes:
  Standard .... Brown/green/white
  0.25 mm undersize .... Brown/blue and Green/blue
  0.50 mm undersize .... Brown/white and Green/white
Centre (thrust) main bearing journal width (mm):
  Standard .... 25.950 to 26.002
  0.25 mm undersize .... 26.150 to 26.202
  0.50 mm undersize .... 26.350 to 26.402
Big-end bearing journal diameter (mm):
  Standard .... 48.970 to 48.988
  0.25 mm undersize .... 48.720 to 48.738
  0.50 mm undersize .... 48.470 to 48.488
Big-end bearing shell colour codes (all models):
  Standard .... None
  0.25 mm undersize .... Blue
  0.50 mm undersize .... White
Main and big-end bearing journal out-of-round (all models) .... 0.04 mm maximum
Main bearing permissible movement (mm) .... 0.015 to 0.040
Big-end bearing permissible movement (mm) .... 0.006 to 0.031
Crankshaft endfloat (mm) .... 0.050 to 0.152
Connecting rod endfloat (mm) .... 0.07 to 0.24

Piston and cylinder bores (Ø in mm)

	Bore diameter	Piston diameter	ID mark
Production size 1	85.98 mm	85.96 mm	8
Production size 2	85.99 mm	85.97 mm	99
	86.00 mm	85.98 mm	00
	86.01 mm	85.99 mm	01
	86.02 mm	86.00 mm	02
0.5 mm oversize	86.47 mm	86.45 mm	7 + 0.5

Piston clearance in bore (mm) .... 0.02 to 0.04

Piston rings

Number (per piston) .... 2 compression, 1 oil control
Ring end gap (mm):
  Compression .... 0.3 to 0.5
  Oil control (top and bottom sections) .... 0.4 to 1.4
  Ring gap offset (to gap of adjacent ring)* .... 180°
See Section 31 for oil control ring sections

Cylinder head

Material .... Light alloy
Maximum permissible distortion of sealing face .... 0.025 mm
Height of cylinder head (sealing surface to sealing surface) .... 96.00 ± 0.25 mm
Valve seat width (mm):
  Inlet .... 1.0 to 1.5
  Exhaust .... 1.7 to 2.2

Camshaft

Camshaft bearing journal diameter:	Normal (mm)	0.1 mm undersize
No 1	42.455 to 42.470	42.355 to 42.370
No 2	42.705 to 42.720	42.605 to 42.620
No 3	42.955 to 42.970	42.855 to 42.870
No 4	43.205 to 43.220	43.105 to 43.120
No 5	43.455 to 43.470	43.355 to 43.370
Camshaft bearing diameter in housing:		
No 1	42.500 to 42.525	42.400 to 42.425
No 2	42.750 to 42.775	42.650 to 42.675
No 3	43.000 to 43.025	42.900 to 42.925
No 4	43.250 to 43.275	43.150 to 43.175
No 5	43.500 to 43.525	43.400 to 43.425

Cam lift (mm) (inlet and exhaust) 6.67
Maximum permissible radial run-out (mm) 0.04
Endfloat (mm) .... 0.09 to 0.21

Timing belt (engines without automatic tension roller)

Tension, using Vauxhall gauge KM-51 0-A (see Section 11):

New belt, cold	4.5
New belt, warm	7.5
Used belt, cold	2.5
Used belt, warm	7.0

Valves and guides

	Inlet	Exhaust
Overall length - production (mm)	104.2	104.0
Overall length - service (mm)	103.8	103.6
Head diameter (mm)	41.8	36.5
Stem diameter (mm):		
Standard	6.998 to 7.012	6.978 to 6.992
0.075 mm oversize	7.073 to 7.087	7.053 to 7.067
0.150 mm oversize	7.148 to 7.162	7.128 to 7.142
0.250 mm oversize	7.248 to 7.262	7.228 to 7.242
Valve guide bore (mm):		
Standard	7.030 to 7.050	
0.075 mm oversize	7.105 to 7.125	
0.150 mm oversize	7.180 to 7.200	
0.250 mm oversize	7.280 to 7.300	
Valve clearance in guide (mm):		
Inlet	0.018 to 0.052	
Exhaust	0.038 to 0.072	
Valve seat angle	44°	
Valve clearances	Automatic adjustment by hydraulic lifters	

Flywheel

Maximum permissible lateral run-out of starter ring gear	0.5 mm
Refinishing limit - maximum depth of material that may be removed from clutch friction surface	0.3 mm

Lubrication system

Lubricant type/specification	See "Lubricants and fluids"
Lubricant capacity	See Chapter 1 Specifications
Oil pump clearances:	
Inner-to-outer gear teeth clearance (backlash)	0.0 to 0.2 mm
Gear-to-housing clearance (endfloat)	0.03 to 0.10 mm
Oil pressure at idle (engine warm)	1.5 bar (21.8 lbf/in^2)

Torque wrench settings

Note: Use new bolts where asterisked (*). The torque settings stated for the cylinder head are only applicable to latest specification bolts, available from Vauxhall. Earlier type or alternative make, head bolts may require different torques. Consult your supplier.

	Nm	lbf ft
Air inlet pre-heat to exhaust manifold	8	6
Alternator and inlet manifold to brackets	18	13
Alternator to bracket:		
M8	30	22
M10	40	30
Alternator to shackle	25	18
Big-end bearing cap: *		
Stage 1	35	26
Stage 2	Angle tighten by 45°	
Stage 3	Angle tighten by 15°	
Camshaft housing cover to housing	8	6
Camshaft sprocket to camshaft	45	33
Camshaft thrust plate	8	6
Coolant outlet to thermostat housing	8	6
Coolant pump to cylinder block (M8)	25	18
Crankshaft sensor wheel	13	10
Cylinder head to cylinder block: *		
Stage 1	25	18
Stage 2	Angle tighten by 90°	
Stage 3	Angle tighten by 90°	
Stage 4	Angle tighten by 90°	
Drivebelt pulley to timing belt drive sprocket	20	15
Drivebelt (ribbed) tensioner to cylinder block	20	15
Drivebelt (ribbed) tensioner to support	18	13

2A

Torque wrench settings

	Nm	lbf ft
Engine mounting, left:		
Bracket to transmission	60	44
Mounting bush to bracket	60	44
Mounting bush to bodywork * (use locking compound)	65	48
Engine mounting, right:		
Bracket to engine block	60	44
Damping bush to bracket	35	26
Damping bush to bodywork * (use locking compound)	65	48
Engine mounting, rear:		
Bracket to transmission (use new locking plates)	60	44
Damping bush to bracket	45	33
Damping bush to front subframe	40	30
Exhaust manifold to cylinder head	22	16
Exhaust pipe to manifold	25	18
Flexplate to crankshaft	60	44
Flywheel to crankshaft: *		
Stage 1	65	48
Stage 2	Angle tighten by 30°	
Stage 3	Angle tighten by 15°	
Front timing belt cover to rear cover	4	3
Fuel pump to camshaft housing	18	13
Guide sleeve, release bearing to transmission	22	16
Heat shield sleeves to cylinder head	30	22
Inlet manifold to cylinder head	22	16
Main bearing cap: *		
Stage 1	50	37
Stage 2	Angle tighten by 45°	
Stage 3	Angle tighten by 15°	
Oil filter to oil pump/cylinder block	6	4
Oil pick-up pipe bracket to cylinder block	6	4
Oil pick-up pipe to oil pump	8	6
Oil pipes to radiator	22	16
Oil pressure switch to oil pump	40	30
Oil pressure relief valve to oil pump	30	22
Oil pump cover to oil pump	6	4
Oil pump to cylinder block	6	4
Oxygen sensor to exhaust manifold	30	22
Power steering pump bracket to support	18	13
Power steering pump to support	25	18
Shackle to alternator	25	18
Spark plugs	25	18
Starter to cylinder block:		
M10	45	33
M12	60	44
Sump	15	11
Sump drain plug	55	41
Temperature sender to cylinder head	20	15
Thermostat housing	15	11
Timing belt cover to oil pump/camshaft housing	6	4
Timing belt drive sprocket to crankshaft:		
Stage 1	130	96
Stage 2	Angle tighten by between 40° to 50°	
Transmission to engine:		
M10	45	33
M12	60	44

1 General description

General

The engine is the four-cylinder, in-line single or double overhead camshaft type (depending on model), mounted transversely at the front of the vehicle.

The crankshaft runs in five shell-type bearings, and the centre bearing incorporates a thrust bearing shell to control crankshaft endfloat.

The connecting rods are attached to the crankshaft by horizontally split shell-type big-end bearings. On single overhead camshaft (SOHC) models, the pistons are attached to the connecting rods by gudgeon pins, which are an interference fit in the connecting rod small-end bore. The aluminium alloy pistons are fitted with three piston rings: two compression rings and an oil control ring.

The camshaft on SOHC engines is driven from the crankshaft by a toothed composite rubber belt. Each cylinder has two valves (one inlet and one exhaust), operated through rocker arms that are supported at their pivot ends by hydraulic self-adjusting valve lifters (tappets).

The inlet and exhaust valves are each closed by a single valve spring, and operate in guides pressed into the cylinder head.

A gear-type oil pump is located in a housing attached to the front of the cylinder block, and is driven directly from the crankshaft. A full-flow type oil filter is fitted.

The distributor is driven directly from the end of the camshaft. The coolant pump is located at the front of the cylinder block, and is driven by the timing belt.

This Chapter describes the SOHC engine repair procedures. Many repairs and specifications to the DOHC engine are similar to the SOHC. However where they differ, details can be found in Chapter 2B.

Engine identification codes - general

Before ordering spare parts, or carrying out any repair or overhaul operations on the engine, it is essential to identify the exact engine type being worked on.

Check the engine identification code first, which is located on a horizontal surface on the exhaust manifold side of the cylinder block, at the distributor end. On later engines, the code is on the cylinder block-to-transmission flange, next to the engine oil dipstick.

2 Crankcase ventilation system - description and maintenance

Description

1 A crankcase ventilation system is fitted.
2 Oil fumes and blow-by gases (combustion gases that have passed by the piston rings) are drawn from the crankcase into the area of the cylinder head above the camshaft through a hose. From here the gases are drawn into the inlet manifold/throttle body, where they are re-burnt with fresh air/fuel mixture, hence reducing harmful exhaust emissions.

Maintenance

3 Certain models have a mesh filter inside the camshaft cover, which should be cleaned in paraffin if clogging is evident.
4 On high mileage vehicles, particularly when regularly used for short journeys, a jelly-like deposit may be evident inside the crankcase ventilation system hoses. If excessive deposits are present, the relevant hose(s) should be removed and cleaned.
5 Periodically inspect the system hoses for security and damage, and renew as necessary. Note that damaged or loose hoses can cause various engine running problems that can be difficult to trace.
6 The crankcase breather/dipstick tube can be unbolted from the cylinder block after disconnecting the hose. Use a new gasket when refitting.

3 Compression test - description

1 If engine performance is poor, or if misfiring occurs which cannot be attributed to the ignition or fuel system, a compression test can provide diagnostic clues. If the test is performed regularly, it can give warning of trouble on a high mileage engine before any other symptoms become apparent.
2 The engine must be at operating temperature, the battery must be fully charged, and the spark plugs must be removed. The help of an assistant will also be required.
3 Disable the ignition system by disconnecting the coil LT ("+15") wire. Fit the compression tester to No 1 cylinder spark plug hole.
4 Have the assistant hold the throttle wide open and crank the engine on the starter. Record the highest reading obtained on the compression tester.
5 Repeat the test on the remaining cylinders, recording the pressure developed in each.
6 The difference in pressure between any two cylinders should be no more than 1.0 bar (14.5 lbf/in²). If the pressure in any cylinder is low, pour a teaspoonful of clean engine oil into the spark plug hole, and repeat the test.
7 If the addition of oil temporarily improves the compression pressure, this indicates that cylinder bore or piston ring wear was responsible for the pressure loss. No improvement suggests that leaking or burnt valves, or a blown head gasket may be to blame.
8 A low reading from two adjacent cylinders is almost certainly due to the head gasket leaking between them.
9 On completion of the test, refit the spark plugs and reconnect the coil LT wire.

4 Major operations possible with the engine in the vehicle

The following operations may be carried out without removing the engine from the vehicle:
a) Removal and refitting of oil pressure relief valve (see Section 29)
b) Removal and refitting of timing belt and sprockets
c) Removal and refitting of camshaft housing (SOHC engines)
d) Removal and refitting of camshaft(s)
e) Removal and refitting of cylinder head
f) Removal and refitting of sump
g) Removal and refitting of oil pump
h) Removal and refitting of piston/connecting rod assemblies
i) Removal and refitting of flywheel
j) Renewal of crankshaft front oil seal
k) Removal and refitting of engine/transmission mountings

Note: It is possible to renew the crankshaft rear oil seal with the engine in the vehicle, but this requires the use of special tools, and is a difficult operation, due to the lack of working space. For this reason, this operation is described with the engine removed from the vehicle.

5 Major operations requiring engine removal

The engine must be removed from the vehicle to carry out the following operations:
a) Renewal of the crankshaft main bearings
b) Removal and refitting of the crankshaft
c) Renewal of crankshaft rear oil seal

6 Method of engine removal

An engine with the 'flat-type' flywheel, and without air conditioning, can be removed either on its own, or together with the transmission. Unless work is also necessary on the transmission, it is recommended that the engine is removed on its own, by disengaging it from the transmission and lifting it out through the top of the engine compartment, using a hoist and lifting tackle. If you wish to remove the complete engine/ transmission assembly, you need to remove the front subframe and pull it out from underneath.

An engine with a 'pot-type' flywheel or with air conditioning can only be removed together with the transmission as a complete assembly, by removing the front subframe.

The flywheel type affects the method of engine removal because of its influence on the clutch. On models with the 'flat-type' flywheel, the clutch can be removed separately from the transmission. On models with the 'pot-type' flywheel, the transmission has to be removed first to access the clutch. This affects the method of disengagement of the engine and transmission, so that on models with the 'pot-type' flywheel you cannot lift out the engine with the transmission still in place. For details of the flywheel types, see Chapter 6, Section 1.

2A

7 Engine - removal and refitting (leaving transmission in car)

Note: A hoist and lifting tackle will be required for this operation. If the torque converter is removed (even partially) from an automatic transmission, a considerable amount of fluid inside it will leak out. To prevent this, when prising the engine from the transmission and removing it, be careful to keep the torque converter pressed firmly into the transmission. If the transmission is to be removed for some time, retain the torque converter by bolting a strip of metal across the bellhousing mating surface.

7.13 Removing the fuel injection wiring harness - SOHC model

Note: *This section is inapplicable to models with 'pot-type' flywheels or air conditioning. On these models you will need to remove the engine and transmission together, as described in Section 8. For details of flywheel types, see Chapter 6, Section 1.*

Removal

1 Disconnect the battery negative lead.
2 Remove the bonnet (see Chapter 11).
3 Apply the handbrake, then jack up the front of the vehicle, and support securely on axle stands (see "*Jacking and Vehicle Support*").
4 Drain the cooling system, remove the radiator and transmission fluid cooler hoses (automatic models), as described in Chapter 3.
5 Drain the engine oil as described in Chapter 1, remove the oil filter and discard it safely.
6 Remove the air cleaner (or air cleaner cover), the air cleaner trunking, and the air box from the throttle body (as applicable), referring to Chapter 4A if necessary.
7 Remove the alternator, as described in Chapter 5.
8 Unbolt the power steering hydraulic pump from the engine block, as described in Chapter 10, and place it to one side, but do not disconnect the fluid hoses.
9 Disconnect the brake servo vacuum hose from the inlet manifold.
10 Disconnect the throttle cable from the lever and bracket on the throttle body or inlet manifold, as applicable.
11 Remove the coolant hose(s) from the inlet manifold and/or throttle body, as applicable.
12 Disconnect the fuel hoses from the fuel pipes at the right-hand side of the engine compartment.

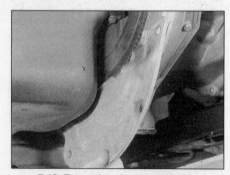

7.18 Removing the transmission bellhousing cover plate

Caution: Be prepared for fuel spillage, and take adequate fire precautions. Plug the open ends of the pipes and hoses, to prevent dirt ingress and further fuel leakage.

13 Disconnect all relevant wiring connections and plugs, and remove the fuel injection wiring harness. Pull up on the wiring harness housing, and compress the wiring plug retaining clips to release the harness housing from the fuel injectors **(see illustration)**.
14 Disconnect the heater coolant hoses from the coolant gallery at the rear of the cylinder block.
15 Disconnect the wiring from the following components (where applicable):

a) Starter motor
b) Distributor (note HT lead positions)
c) Oil pressure switch
d) Oil temperature switch
e) TDC sensor
f) Oil level sensor
g) Knock sensor
h) Coolant temperature sensor
i) Temperature gauge sender

16 Make a final check to ensure that all relevant hoses, pipes and wires have been disconnected, and that they are positioned clear of the engine.
17 Remove the front section of the exhaust system, as described in Chapter 4B, or the complete exhaust if it is more convenient.
18 Unbolt and remove the transmission bellhousing cover plate **(see illustration)**.
19 Remove the crankshaft pulley. Some pulleys are secured by four bolts, which must be unscrewed using an Allen key or hexagon bit. Unscrew each of the three bolts in turn and remove them. On other engines, the pulley is secured by a single bolt, which also secures the crankshaft sprocket. On manual transmission models, if the engine is in the vehicle, the crankshaft can be prevented from turning by having an assistant engage first gear and depress the brake pedal. Alternatively, the flywheel (or flexplate, on automatics), ring gear teeth can be jammed, through the bellhousing cover aperture using a large screwdriver, or similar tool. Access to the crankshaft pulley is most easily obtained through the right-hand wheel arch, after removing the roadwheel.
20 Remove the clutch (if applicable), as described in Chapter 6. On automatic models, use chalk or a felt-tip pen to mark the relationship of the torque converter to the flexplate before unbolting the torque converter. Refer to the note at the beginning of this Section and to Chapter 7B for further information.
21 Attach a hoist and lifting gear to the engine lifting brackets on the cylinder head, and support the weight of the engine.
22 Unscrew and remove two of the three upper engine-to-transmission bolts, accessible from the engine compartment, leaving one fastened for safety.
23 Unbolt the right-hand engine mounting from the body and from the cylinder block,

and withdraw the mounting bracket. Note that on models with serpentine belts, the belt goes through the engine mounting so that the belt and mounting come off together.
24 Unscrew and remove the four lower engine-to-transmission bolts.
25 Support the transmission using a trolley jack and interposed block of wood. Remove the last upper transmission bolt.
26 Manipulate the engine as necessary to separate it from the transmission. Note that the transmission locates on dowels in the cylinder block.
27 Carefully raise the hoist, and lift the engine from the vehicle, taking care not to damage any of the surrounding components in the engine compartment.
28 With the engine removed, the transmission can be supported by placing a length of wood between the bellhousing and the front suspension subframe. Once the wooden support is in place, remove the trolley jack from under the transmission.

Refitting

29 Clean out the threaded bores in the bodywork, where the right-hand engine mounting bolts are to be fitted (see the note at the beginning of Section 9).
30 On automatic transmissions, use an M10 x 1.25 bottoming tap to clean the threads in the torque converter's threaded bosses and ensure that new bolts are available for reassembly.

 HAYNES HiNT *If a tap is not available, cut two slots into the threads of one of the old flywheel bolts and use the bolt to remove the locking compound from the threads.*

31 Support the transmission with a trolley jack and remove the length of wood from between the bellhousing and the subframe.
32 Support the engine with the hoist and lifting tackle, and gently lower it into position in the engine compartment.
33 Mate the engine and transmission together, ensuring that the transmission locates on the dowels in the cylinder block, then refit the three upper engine-to-transmission bolts.
34 Tighten all nuts and bolts to their specified torque wrench settings. When tightening the torque converter-to-flexplate bolts on automatic transmissions, a commercially-available adapter will be required **(see illustration)**.
35 On manual transmissions, if the clutch is still bolted to the flywheel, ensure that the weight of the transmission is not allowed to hang on the input shaft as it is engaged with the clutch friction disc.
36 Refit the four lower engine-to-transmission bolts, but again do not fully tighten them at this stage.

37 Fit the right-hand engine mounting bracket to the cylinder block, and tighten the securing bolts to the specified torque.

38 Manipulate the engine and transmission as necessary to enable the right-hand engine mounting bush to be bolted to the bodywork. Fit new bolts, coated with locking fluid, and tighten them to the specified torque.

39 Tighten all the engine-to-transmission bolts to the specified torque, then disconnect the lifting tackle and hoist from the engine, and remove the trolley jack from beneath the transmission.

40 Refit the transmission bellhousing cover plate.

41 Refit the clutch, as described in Chapter 6.

42 Refit the front section of the exhaust system (or the complete exhaust), as described in Chapter 4B.

43 Refit the crankshaft pulley using a reversal of the removal procedure described earlier in paragraph 20, and tighten the securing bolt(s) to the specified torque.

44 Lower the vehicle to the ground.

45 Refit all relevant wires, pipes and hoses, etc., using a reversal of the removal procedure described earlier.

46 Refit the power steering pump, as described in Chapter 10.

47 Refit the alternator and the auxiliary drivebelt(s), as described in Chapter 5. In the case of V-belts, tension them as described in Chapter 1.

48 Refit the air cleaner components, referring to Chapter 4A if necessary.

49 Fit a new oil filter (if not already replaced), and fill the engine with oil, as described in Chapter 1.

50 Refill the cooling system, as described in Chapter 3.

51 Refit the bonnet as described in Chapter 11.

52 Reconnect the battery negative lead.

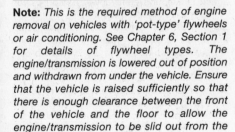

8 Engine and transmission - removal, separation, reconnection and refitting

Note: *This is the required method of engine removal on vehicles with 'pot-type' flywheels or air conditioning. See Chapter 6, Section 1 for details of flywheel types. The engine/transmission is lowered out of position and withdrawn from under the vehicle. Ensure that the vehicle is raised sufficiently so that there is enough clearance between the front of the vehicle and the floor to allow the engine/transmission to be slid out from the front.*

Removal

1 Proceed as described in Section 7, paragraphs 1 to 17 inclusive.

2 On models with air conditioning, unbolt the compressor and position it clear of the engine. **Do not** open the refrigerant circuit.

3 Working in the engine compartment, remove the gear selector linkage, as

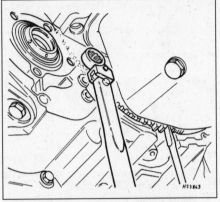

7.34 Commercially-available torque wrench adapter being used to tighten torque converter bolts

described in Chapters 7A and 7B, as appropriate.

4 On manual transmission models, remove the retaining clip, then slide the clutch cable from the release lever, pushing the release lever back towards the bulkhead if necessary to allow the cable to be disconnected. On automatic models disconnect the selector cable from the actuating lever, then either unbolt the cable bracket or release the cable from the bracket. In either case, pull the cable support from the bracket on the transmission casing, then move the cable and secure to one side out of the way, taking note of its routing.

5 Disconnect the wiring from the reversing lamp switch, located at the front of the manual transmission casing, above the left-hand mounting bracket. On automatic models, disconnect the transmission wiring by unplugging the five connector plugs from the various switches, solenoids and sensors. Release also the wiring from any clips or ties securing to the vehicle.

6 Where applicable, withdraw the automatic transmission breather hose from under the battery bracket. Disconnect the oxygen sensor wiring if fitted.

7 Unscrew the securing sleeve, and disconnect the speedometer cable from the transmission.

8 Unscrew the retaining nut, and disconnect the earth strap from the transmission endplate.

9 Remove the front section of the exhaust system, as described in Chapter 4B, or the whole exhaust system if it is more convenient.

10 Attach a hoist and lifting gear to the engine lifting brackets on the cylinder head, and support the weight of the engine.

11 Remove the front suspension subframe assembly as described in Chapter 10. You will need to undo the front suspension lower arm balljoints because the arms come away as part of the subframe assembly. You will also need to undo the two bolts connecting the rear engine/transmission mounting to the subframe. Before you undo the six subframe

securing bolts, mark the positions where the subframe meets the underbody, at the front and rear ends, for refitting.

12 Disconnect the inboard ends of the driveshafts from the differential, referring to the relevant paragraphs of Chapter 8. Be prepared for oil spillage as the driveshafts are withdrawn, and plug the apertures in the differential, to prevent further loss of oil and dirt ingress. Support the driveshafts by suspending them with wire or string - do not allow them to hang down under their own weight.

13 Make a final check to ensure that all relevant hoses, pipes, wires etc. have been disconnected, and that they are positioned clear of the engine and transmission.

14 Remove the bolts connecting the left and right-hand engine/transmission mounting bushes to the bodywork.

15 If available, place a low trolley under the engine/transmission assembly, so that it can easily be removed from under the vehicle. Lower the engine/transmission assembly, making sure that nothing is trapped, and take care not to damage the radiator/cooling fan assembly. Use the help of an assistant during this procedure, as it may be necessary to tilt the assembly slightly to clear the body panels.

16 Detach the hoist and withdraw the engine/transmission from under the vehicle.

Separation

17 With the engine/transmission assembly removed, support the assembly on blocks of wood positioned on a workbench, or failing that, on a clean area of the workshop floor.

18 Clean away any external dirt using paraffin or a water-soluble solvent and a stiff brush.

19 Unbolt and remove the transmission bellhousing cover plate, if there is one.

20 Ensure that both engine and transmission are adequately supported, then unscrew and remove the engine-to-transmission bolts.

21 Carefully withdraw the transmission from the engine, ensuring that the weight of the transmission is not allowed to hang on the input shaft while it is engaged with the clutch friction disc. Note that the transmission locates on dowels positioned in the cylinder block.

22 On automatic models unbolt the transmission bellhousing cover plate (three bolts), then use chalk or a felt-tip pen to mark the relationship of the torque converter to the flexplate before unbolting the torque converter. **Note:** *If the torque converter is removed (even partially) from the transmission, a considerable amount of the fluid inside it will leak out. To prevent this, when prising the transmission off its locating dowels and removing it, be careful to keep the torque converter pressed firmly into the transmission. If the transmission is to be removed for some time, retain the torque converter by bolting a strip of metal across the bellhousing mating surface. Applying a spanner to the crankshaft*

2A

pulley/sprocket bolt, rotate the crankshaft until the first bolt appears, then use a screwdriver or similar to jam the flexplate ring gear teeth to prevent it from rotating as the bolt is unscrewed. Unscrew each of the three bolts in turn and remove them.

Reconnection

23 Where applicable, if the clutch assembly has been removed from the flywheel, it will prove easier to refit before the transmission has been refitted.

24 On automatics, if any fluid was spilled from the torque converter, be careful to refill it as much as possible. Wipe clean the converter's spigot to prevent damage to the transmission's input shaft oil seal as the converter is installed, and ensure that the converter engages correctly on the fluid pump shaft.

25 If the transmission has been renewed, be careful to flush clean the radiator fluid cooler passages. Vauxhall recommend the use of low-pressure compressed air, but this will require great care to avoid deforming the radiator.

26 Be very careful to ensure that all components are scrupulously clean, to avoid the risk of dirt getting into the system.

27 On automatic transmissions, use an M10 x 1.25 bottoming tap to clean the threads in the torque converter's threaded bosses and ensure that new bolts are available for reassembly, where applicable.

28 Tighten all nuts and bolts to their specified torque wrench settings. When tightening the torque converter-to-flexplate bolts on automatic transmissions, a commercially available adapter will be required (see illustration 7.34).

29 On manual transmissions, if the clutch is still bolted to the flywheel, ensure that the weight of the transmission is not allowed to hang on the input shaft as it is engaged with the clutch friction disc.

30 Carefully offer the transmission to the engine until the bellhousing is located on the dowels in the cylinder block, then refit the engine-to-transmission bolts, and tighten them to the specified torque.

31 Refit the transmission bellhousing cover plate.

Refitting

32 Clean out the threaded bores in the bodywork, where the left and right-hand engine/transmission mounting bushes are to be fitted (see the note at the beginning of Section 9).

33 Slide the engine/transmission into position and reconnect the hoist and lifting tackle to the engine lifting brackets. Then, with the aid of an assistant, lift the assembly into position in the engine compartment, manipulating the hoist and lifting tackle as necessary, taking care not to trap any components.

34 Refit the left and right-hand mounting bushes to the bodywork, using new bolts coated with locking fluid. Tighten the bolts to the specified torque.

35 Refit the front subframe as described in Chapter 10. If the rear engine/transmission mounting bracket has been removed from the transmission, refit the bracket using new locking plates under the bolt heads, and tighten the bolts to torque. Then fit the two bolts connecting the rear mounting to the subframe and tighten them to torque.

36 Remove the lifting tackle and hoist from the engine.

37 Where applicable, on engines with 'flat-type' flywheels, the clutch can now be fitted, and the transmission input shaft can be pressed into engagement with the splined hub of the clutch friction disc, (see Chapter 6).

38 Reconnect the inboard ends of the driveshafts to the differential, with reference to the relevant paragraphs of Chapter 8, and using new snap rings.

39 Refit the front section of the exhaust system (or the whole exhaust), as described in Chapter 4B.

40 On automatic models, connect the wires to the various switches, solenoids and sensors. Reconnect the transmission breather hose and oxygen sensor.

41 Reconnect the transmission earth strap, and tighten the securing nut.

42 On models with air conditioning, refit the air conditioning compressor.

43 Lower the vehicle to the ground.

44 Reconnect the speedometer cable to the transmission, and tighten the securing sleeve.

45 Reconnect the reversing lamp wiring.

46 On manual transmission models, refit the clutch cable to the bracket on the transmission casing, then reconnect the cable to the release lever, and adjust the cable as described in Chapter 6. Ensure that the cable is routed as noted during removal.

47 Refit the gear selector linkage, as described in Chapter 7A, if applicable.

48 Proceed as described in Section 7, paragraphs 44 to 50 inclusive.

49 Top-up the transmission oil level, as described in Chapters 7A and 7B.

50 Adjust the selector cable on completion, and refill the transmission with fluid.

51 Reconnect the battery negative lead.

9 Engine and transmission mountings - renewal

Note: *When refitting left and right-hand engine/transmission mounting bushes, first check that the original bolts which secured the mounting bush to the body rotate freely in their threaded bores and are not fouled by old locking fluid. If necessary, re-cut the threaded bores using an M10 x 1.25 mm tap. Then use new bolts, coated with locking fluid, to secure the mounting bush to the bodywork.*

HAYNES HiNT *If a tap is not available, cut two slots into the threads of one of the old flywheel bolts and use it to clean out the threaded bores.*

1 The engine/transmission assembly is suspended in the engine compartment on three mountings, two of which are attached to the transmission, and one to the engine.

Right-hand mounting (models with V-belts)

2 If not already done, apply the handbrake, then raise the front of the vehicle, and support securely on axle stands (see *"Jacking and Vehicle Support"*).

3 Attach lifting tackle and a hoist to the engine lifting brackets on the cylinder head, and support the weight of the engine.

4 Working under the vehicle, unbolt the engine mounting bracket from the cylinder block, and unbolt the mounting bush from the body, then withdraw the bracket/mounting assembly.

5 Unbolt the mounting bush from the bracket.

6 Fit the new mounting bush to the bracket. Tighten the securing bolts to the specified torque.

7 Refit the mounting bracket to the cylinder block, and tighten the securing bolts to the specified torque.

8 Clean out the threaded bores in the bodywork, then fit new mounting bush-to-body bolts, coated with locking fluid (see the note at the beginning of this Section). Tighten the bolts to the specified torque.

9 Disconnect the lifting tackle and hoist from the engine.

10 Lower the vehicle to the ground.

Right-hand mounting (models with serpentine belts, without air conditioning)

11 On these models, a single auxiliary drivebelt passes round the crankshaft, alternator and power steering pump pulleys, and is tensioned by an automatic tensioner pulley. The belt passes through the right-hand engine mounting, so you have to remove the mounting and drivebelt together as a complete assembly.

Removal

12 For improved access, remove the air cleaner assembly and air inlet trunking (see Chapter 4A).

13 If the original drivebelt is to be removed and refitted, mark the rotational direction of the belt with chalk.

14 Using a spanner or socket on the automatic tensioning roller hexagon, turn the tensioning roller clockwise (as viewed from the right-hand side of the car) and hold it in this position. With the drivebelt tension released, slip the drivebelt off the pulleys, then allow the tensioner to return to its original position.

9.16 Right-hand mounting bracket and bush with drivebelt. The arrow on the belt gives the direction of travel

9.17 Undo the bolt and separate the mounting bush from the bracket

15 Support the front of the vehicle and the engine as described in paragraphs 2 and 3.

16 Undo the three bolts on the mounting bracket and two bolts on the mounting bush, then withdraw the bracket and bush assembly, complete with the drivebelt **(see illustration)**.

17 Undo the bolt and separate the mounting bush from the bracket **(see illustration)**.

18 If the drivebelt is to be removed, undo the three bolts and separate the two halves of the bracket. Alternatively, undo two bolts and slacken one, then rotate the two halves against each other to open up the gap **(see illustration)**.

Refitting

19 Refitting is the reverse of removal, noting the following points.

20 When refitting the same drivebelt, fit the belt in the same direction, marked by the arrow.

21 When refitting a new drivebelt, make sure you have the correct type of belt. There is a longer belt on models with air conditioning.

22 Clean out the threaded bores in the bodywork, then fit new mounting bush-to-body bolts, coated with locking fluid (see the note at the beginning of this Section). Tighten the bolts to the specified torque.

9.18 Remove the drivebelt from the mounting bracket

23 You will need an assistant to help you refit the drivebelt around the pulleys. Slacken the tensioner from underneath the car and feed the belt round the power steering pump pulley, while your assistant, working above the car, feeds the belt over the alternator pulley. Then release the tensioner.

24 Disconnect the lifting tackle and lower the vehicle to the ground.

Right-hand mounting (models with serpentine belts, with air conditioning)

Removal

25 In this case the drivebelt passes underneath the engine mounting, not through the middle of it, so there is no need to remove the drivebelt with the mounting.

26 Remove the air cleaner assembly and air inlet trunking if necessary, to give better access to the mounting bolts.

27 Support the front of the vehicle and the engine as described in paragraphs 2 and 3.

28 If you wish to remove the complete mounting assembly, undo the three bolts securing the mounting bracket to the engine block components. Alternatively, if you wish to remove just the mounting bush, undo the single bolt connecting the bush to the mounting bracket. The choice may depend on the accessibility of the bolts.

29 Working under the vehicle, undo the two bolts connecting the mounting bush to the bodywork and withdraw the bush (or the complete assembly).

Refitting

30 Fit the new mounting bush to the bracket and tighten the securing bolt to the specified torque. Refit the mounting bracket to the engine block components, if it has been removed.

31 Clean out the threaded bores in the bodywork, then fit new mounting bush-to-body bolts, coated with locking fluid (see the note at the beginning of this Section). Tighten the bolts to the specified torque.

32 Disconnect the lifting tackle and lower the vehicle to the ground.

Left-hand mounting

Removal

33 Support the front of the vehicle and the engine as described in paragraphs 2 and 3.

34 Working under the vehicle, undo the two bolts connecting the mounting bush to the mounting bracket, and the two bolts connecting the bush to the bodywork **(see illustration)**.

Refitting

35 Fit the new mounting bush to the bracket, and tighten the securing bolts to the specified torque.

36 Clean out the threaded bores in the bodywork, then fit new mounting bush-to-body bolts, coated with locking fluid (see the note at the beginning of this Section). Tighten the bolts to the specified torque.

37 Disconnect the lifting tackle and lower the vehicle to the ground.

Rear mounting

Removal

38 Support the front of the vehicle and the engine as described in paragraphs 2 and 3.

2A

9.34 Left-hand transmission mounting bush and bracket

9.39a Two bolts connecting the rear transmission mounting bush to the subframe . . .

39 Working under the vehicle, undo the two bolts connecting the mounting bush to the front subframe, and the two bolts connecting the bush to the mounting bracket **(see illustrations)**.

Refitting

40 Fit the new mounting bush to the subframe and mounting bracket, and tighten the securing bolts to the specified torque.
41 Disconnect the lifting tackle and lower the vehicle to the ground.

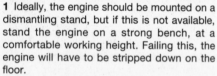

10 Engine dismantling and reassembly - general

1 Ideally, the engine should be mounted on a dismantling stand, but if this is not available, stand the engine on a strong bench, at a comfortable working height. Failing this, the engine will have to be stripped down on the floor.
2 Cleanliness is most important, and if the engine is dirty, it should be cleaned with paraffin in an upright position.
3 Avoid working with the engine directly on a concrete floor, as grit presents a real source of trouble.
4 If the engine oil appears extremely dirty or contaminated, avoid inverting the engine until the sump has been removed. This will prevent any contaminated "sludge" from entering the oilways.
5 As parts are removed, clean them in a paraffin bath. Do not immerse parts with

11.4a Remove the main outer timing belt cover . . .

internal oilways in paraffin, as it is difficult to remove, usually requiring a high pressure hose. Clean oilways with nylon pipe cleaners.
6 It is advisable to have containers available to hold small items, to prevent loss and confusion when refitting.
7 Always obtain complete sets of gaskets when the engine is being dismantled. Keep the old gaskets as they can be used as patterns to make replacements should new gaskets not be available.
8 Where possible, refit nuts, bolts and washers to their locations after removal of the relevant components, as this helps protect the threads, and will also prove helpful during reassembly.
9 Retain unserviceable components, to compare them with the new components supplied.
10 Many of the engine components are secured using socket-headed "Torx" or "Allen" bolts, and tools will be required to remove and refit such bolts.
11 Read through each relevant Section of this Chapter carefully *before beginning work,* to ensure that any special tools that may be required are available. Many components (gaskets, oil seals, and certain bolts) must be renewed on reassembly; where applicable, obtain the required new components before starting work.
12 Before beginning a complete strip of the engine, the following ancillary components can be removed once the engine has been removed from the vehicle:
a) *Inlet and exhaust manifolds (where applicable)*

9.39b . . . and two bolts connecting the bush to the mounting bracket

b) *Starter motor*
c) *Rear coolant gallery and hoses*
d) *Oil pressure switch*
e) *Oil temperature switch (where applicable)*
f) *Oil level sensor (where applicable)*
g) *Knock sensor (where applicable)*
h) *TDC sensor (where applicable)*
i) *Distributor components*
j) *Thermostat/housing*
k) *Power steering pump and mounting bracket*
l) *Alternator mounting bracket*
m) *Engine lifting brackets*
n) *Dipstick/crankcase breather tube*
o) *Inlet manifold mounting bracket (where applicable)*

13 To ensure maximum life, with minimum trouble, from a rebuilt engine, not only must everything be correctly assembled, but it must also be spotlessly clean. All oilways and coolant passages must be clear, and all washers must be fitted in their original positions. Oil all bearings and other moving surfaces thoroughly with clean engine oil during assembly.
14 Before assembly begins, renew any bolts or studs with damaged threads.
15 Obtain a torque wrench, an angle-torque gauge, sockets and bits, an oil can, clean lint-free rag, and a set of engine gaskets and oil seals, together with a new oil filter.
16 If they have been removed, new cylinder head bolts, flywheel bolts, big-end bearing cap bolts and main bearing cap bolts will also be required.
17 On completion of reassembly, refit the applicable ancillary components listed in paragraph 12.
18 Follow the procedure shown in Section 35.

11 Timing belt and sprockets (without automatic tensioner) - removal, refitting and adjustment

Note: *A two-legged puller may be required to remove the crankshaft sprocket.*

Removal

1 Disconnect the battery negative lead.
2 Remove the auxiliary drivebelts as described in Chapter 5. There may be twin V-belts driving the alternator and power steering pump, or a single serpentine belt which will also drive the air conditioning pump, if fitted.
3 Disconnect the wiring from the temperature gauge sender.
4 Release the securing clips (or hexagon-headed screws, if fitted), and remove the main outer timing belt cover, then unclip the smaller outer timing belt cover from the coolant pump. Where applicable, three screws retain the lower (small) outer cover to the rear cover, the fourth secures the tensioner **(see illustrations)**.
5 Turn the crankshaft using a socket or spanner on the crankshaft sprocket bolt, until the timing mark on the camshaft sprocket is

11.4b . . . and the smaller cover from the coolant pump

11.5a Camshaft sprocket TDC mark aligned with notch in rear timing belt cover . . .

11.5b . . . and notch in crankshaft pulley aligned with pointer on rear timing belt cover

aligned with the notch in the rear timing belt cover, and the notch in the crankshaft pulley is aligned with the pointer on the rear timing belt cover **(see illustrations)**.

6 Loosen the three coolant pump securing bolts **(see illustration)**, and turn the pump to relieve the tension in the timing belt, then slide the belt from the camshaft sprocket.

7 The crankshaft pulley must now be removed. The pulley is secured by four bolts, which must be unscrewed using an Allen key or hexagon bit. On manual transmission models, if the engine is in the vehicle, the crankshaft can be prevented from turning by having an assistant engage first gear and depress the brake pedal. Alternatively, the flywheel ring gear teeth can be jammed using a large screwdriver or similar tool.

8 With the crankshaft pulley removed, the timing belt can be withdrawn.

9 If desired, the sprockets and the rear timing belt cover can be removed as follows, otherwise go on to paragraph 19.

10 To remove the camshaft sprocket, first disconnect the breather hose(s) from the camshaft cover, then unscrew the securing bolts noting the locations of the HT lead brackets and any other wiring brackets, and remove the camshaft cover.

11 Recover the gasket. Prevent the camshaft

from turning by holding it with a spanner on the flats provided between Nos 3 and 4 camshaft lobes, and unscrew the camshaft sprocket bolt.

12 Withdraw the sprocket from the end of the camshaft.

13 To remove the crankshaft sprocket, it will be necessary to prevent the crankshaft from turning, as described in paragraph 7. Take care when unscrewing the sprocket bolt, as it is very tight. If necessary, use a two-legged puller to remove the sprocket. Recover the Woodruff key and the thrustwasher from the end of the crankshaft.

14 To remove the main rear timing belt cover, disconnect the TDC sensor wiring plug and unclip the wiring from the belt cover. Then unscrew the two upper securing bolts and the lower securing bolt. Withdraw the cover, manipulating it from the smaller rear belt cover on the coolant pump **(see illustration)**.

15 If desired, the smaller rear belt cover can be removed from the coolant pump, after unscrewing the securing bolt **(see illustration)**, by rotating it to disengage it from the retaining flange on the pump.

Refitting

16 Refit the rear timing belt covers using a reversal of the removal procedure, ensuring

11.6 Loosening a coolant pump securing bolt

that the main cover engages correctly with the smaller cover on the coolant pump, and reconnect the TDC sensor.

17 Refit the thrustwasher and the Woodruff key to the end of the crankshaft. Then refit the crankshaft sprocket, and tighten the securing bolt to the specified torque in the two stages given in the Specifications. Ensure that the washer is in place under the bolt head, and prevent the crankshaft from turning as during removal **(see illustrations)**.

18 Refit the camshaft sprocket, ensuring that the locating pin on the end of the camshaft engages with the hole in the sprocket, and

2A

11.14 Loosening the main rear timing belt cover lower securing bolt

11.15 Unscrewing the coolant pump rear belt cover securing bolt

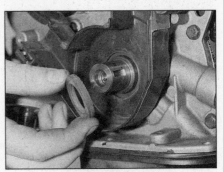

11.17a Refit the thrustwasher . . .

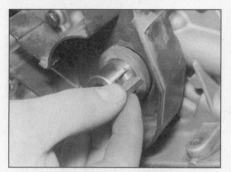

11.17b . . . the Woodruff key . . .

11.17c . . . the crankshaft sprocket . . .

11.17d . . . and the washer and bolt

11.17e Tighten the bolt to the specified torque . . .

11.17f . . . then through the specified angle

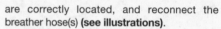

are correctly located, and reconnect the breather hose(s) **(see illustrations)**.

19 Temporarily refit the crankshaft pulley and ensure that the crankshaft pulley and camshaft sprocket timing marks are still aligned as described in paragraph 5, then refit the timing belt around the sprockets **(see illustration)**, starting at the crankshaft sprocket.

20 Refit the crankshaft pulley, and tighten the securing bolts to the specified torque **(see illustration)**. Prevent the crankshaft from turning, as during removal.

21 Adjust the timing belt tension (go to paragraph 25).

22 Refit the outer timing belt covers and reconnect the temperature gauge sender wiring.

23 Refit the auxiliary drivebelts as described in Chapter 5. If there are separate V-belts, driving

tighten the securing bolt to the specified torque. Prevent the camshaft from turning as during removal. Check the condition of the

camshaft cover gasket and renew if necessary, then refit the camshaft cover, ensuring that the HT lead brackets and any other wiring bracket

11.18a Refit the camshaft sprocket . . .

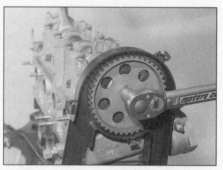

11.18b . . . and tighten the securing bolt to the specified torque

11.18c Fit the camshaft cover gasket . . .

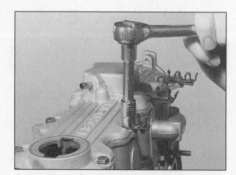

11.18d . . . fit the cover and tighten the bolts. Note position of HT lead brackets

11.19 Refitting the timing belt

11.20 Tightening a crankshaft pulley securing bolt

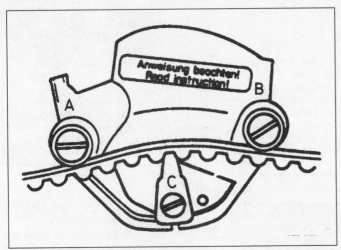

11.28 Tension blade KM-510-A correctly positioned on timing belt. Belt must pass through points A, B and C - SOHC engines

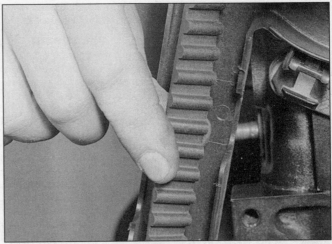

11.36 Checking timing belt tension by twisting belt through 90° between thumb and forefinger

the alternator and power steering pump, tension them as described in Chapter 1.

24 Reconnect the battery negative lead.

Adjustment

Note: *The manufacturers specify the use of a special gauge Vauxhall tool No KM-510-A for checking the timing belt tension. If access to a gauge cannot be obtained it is strongly recommended that the vehicle is taken to a Vauxhall dealer to have the belt tension checked at the earliest opportunity.*

25 The tension of a used timing belt should be checked with the engine at normal operating temperature. The tension of a new timing belt should be checked with the engine cold.

26 Release the securing clips and remove the main outer timing belt cover, then unclip the smaller outer timing belt cover from the coolant pump.

27 Turn the crankshaft through at least quarter of a turn clockwise using a socket or spanner on the crankshaft sprocket bolt.

28 If the special gauge is available, place the locked gauge at the centre of the belt run between the coolant pump and the camshaft sprocket. The gauge should locate on the timing belt **(see illustration)**.

29 Slowly release the operating lever on the gauge, then lightly tap the gauge two or three times, and note the reading on the scale.

30 If the reading is not as specified, loosen the three coolant pump securing bolts, and rotate the pump in the required direction to achieve the desired reading on the gauge. Rotate the pump clockwise to increase the belt tension, or anti-clockwise to decrease the tension.

31 Lightly tighten the coolant pump securing bolts.

32 Remove the tensioning gauge, and turn the crankshaft through one full turn clockwise.

33 Re-check the belt tension as described in paragraphs 28 and 29.

34 If the tension is not as specified, repeat paragraphs 30 to 33 inclusive until the desired, consistent reading is obtained.

35 On completion of adjustment, remove the checking gauge, tighten the coolant pump bolts to the specified torque, and refit the outer timing belt covers.

36 If the special checking gauge is not available, the timing belt tension can be checked approximately by twisting the belt between the thumb and forefinger, at the centre of the run between the coolant pump and the camshaft sprocket. It should just be possible to twist the belt through 90° using moderate pressure **(see illustration)**. If adjustment is necessary, continue as described previously in this Section, but have

the belt tension checked by a Vauxhall dealer using the special gauge at the earliest opportunity. If in doubt, err on the tight side when adjusting the tension. If the belt is too slack, it may jump on the sprockets, which could result in serious engine damage.

12 Timing belt, sprockets and tensioner - removal, refitting and adjustment

Removal

1 A spring-loaded automatic timing belt tensioner is fitted, from 1993 onward **(see illustration)**.

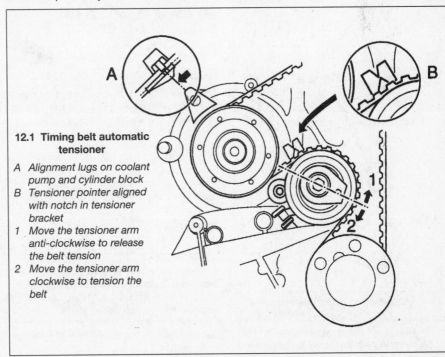

12.1 Timing belt automatic tensioner

A Alignment lugs on coolant pump and cylinder block
B Tensioner pointer aligned with notch in tensioner bracket
1 Move the tensioner arm anti-clockwise to release the belt tension
2 Move the tensioner arm clockwise to tension the belt

2 Remove the auxiliary drivebelts and timing belt main outer cover, as described in Section 11, paragraphs 1 to 4.

3 Unscrew the timing belt tensioner securing bolt slightly. Insert a tool in the slot on the tensioner arm, and turn the tensioner arm until the timing belt is slack. The belt can then be removed. If required, the timing belt sprockets can now be removed, as described in Section 11.

4 With the timing belt slackened or removed, check that the tensioner roller rotates smoothly and easily, with no noises or signs of free play, roughness or notchy movement. Undo the securing bolt and remove the tensioner, and check that there is no sign of physical wear or damage. If the tensioner is faulty in any way, or if there is any reason to doubt the continued efficiency of its spring, the complete assembly must be renewed.

Refitting

5 Refit the tensioner into position and tighten the securing bolt slightly. If removed, refit the timing belt sprockets as described in Section 11.

6 Ensure that the coolant pump is correctly positioned by checking that the lug on the coolant pump flange is aligned with the corresponding lug on the cylinder block. If this is not the case, slacken the coolant pump mounting bolts slightly and move the pump accordingly (see Chapter 3). Tighten the bolts to the specified torque on completion.

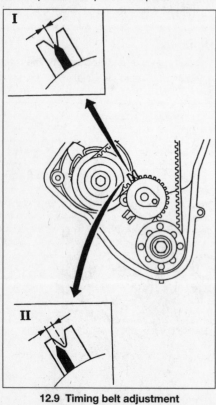

12.9 Timing belt adjustment

I *Alignment for new belts*
II *Alignment for 'run-in' belts (gap is approximately 4 mm to the left of centre)*

7 Refit the timing belt around the sprockets, then tension it as follows.

Adjustment

8 Slacken the automatic tensioner securing bolt and move the tensioner arm anti-clockwise, until the tensioner pointer lies at its stop. Tighten the tensioner securing bolt to hold the tensioner in this position.

9 Turn the crankshaft through two complete revolutions in the normal direction of rotation, and check that with the crankshaft pulley TDC mark aligned with the pointer on the rear timing belt cover, the TDC mark on the camshaft sprocket is still aligned with the notch in the timing belt rear cover. Slacken the automatic tensioner securing bolt again and move the tensioner arm clockwise, until the tensioner pointer is aligned with the notch in the tensioner bracket. In the first few hours of operation a new belt will be subjected to 'settling-in', (known as the running-in procedure). If you are refitting a used belt (one that has been 'run-in'), align the pointer to approximately 4 mm to the left of the notch **(see illustration)**.

10 Tighten the tensioner securing bolt securely. Turn the crankshaft through one complete revolution, in the normal direction of rotation, and check that the crankshaft and camshaft timing marks still align. Then refit the remainder of the components as described in Section 11.

11 With the timing belt adjustment set in this way, correct tension will always be maintained by the automatic tensioner and no further checking or adjustment will be necessary.

13 Camshaft front oil seal - removal and refitting
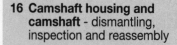

Removal

1 The camshaft front oil seal may be renewed with the engine in the vehicle without removing the camshaft as follows.

2 Remove the timing belt and the camshaft sprocket, as described in Section 11.

3 Punch or drill a small hole in the centre of the now-exposed oil seal. Screw in a self-tapping screw, and pull on the screw with pliers to extract the seal.

Refitting

4 Clean the oil seal seat with a wooden or plastic scraper.

5 Grease the lips of the new seal, and drive it into position until it is flush with the housing, using a socket or tube. Take care not to damage the seal lips during fitting.

6 Refit the camshaft sprocket and the timing belt and tension the timing belt as described in Section 11.

14 Camshaft rear oil seal - removal and refitting

Removal

1 The camshaft rear oil seal may be renewed with the engine in the vehicle without removing the camshaft as follows.

2 Remove the distributor as described in Chapter 5.

3 Prise the seal from the camshaft housing.

Refitting

4 Fit the new seal so that it is flush with the end of the housing, then refit the distributor as described in Chapter 5.

15 Camshaft housing and camshaft - general

Note: *The engine must be cold when removing the camshaft housing. **Do not** remove the camshaft housing from a hot engine. New cylinder head bolts must be used on refitting and sealer will be required when refitting the camshaft housing. Also see paragraph 3 before starting work.*

1 The camshaft can only be removed without disturbing the housing, if a special tool is available to depress the cam followers whilst the camshaft is withdrawn.

2 If such a tool is available, the camshaft can be removed, after removing the timing belt and camshaft sprocket as described in Section 11.

3 If the special tool is not available, the camshaft housing must be removed. Since the cylinder head bolts must be removed, it is strongly recommended that a new cylinder head gasket is fitted. If the gasket is not renewed, and it "blows" on reassembly, the cylinder head will have to be removed to renew the gasket, and another new set of bolts will have to be obtained for refitting. You have been warned!

4 Removal and refitting of the camshaft housing is described in Section 18, along with cylinder head removal and refitting. If it is decided not to disturb the cylinder head, the relevant paragraphs referring specifically to cylinder head removal and refitting can be ignored.

5 Removal of the camshaft from the housing is described in Section 16.

16 Camshaft housing and camshaft - dismantling, inspection and reassembly

Dismantling

1 With the camshaft housing removed from the cylinder head as described in Section 18, continue as follows.

16.3 Camshaft thrustplate and securing bolts

2 Remove the distributor and its components as described in Chapter 5 and carefully prise out the camshaft rear oil seal.

3 Working at the distributor end of the camshaft, unscrew the two camshaft thrustplate securing bolts, using an Allen key or hexagon bit **(see illustration)**.

4 Withdraw the thrustplate, noting which way round it is fitted **(see illustration)**.

5 Carefully withdraw the camshaft from the distributor end of the camshaft housing, taking care not to damage the bearing journals **(see illustration)**.

Inspection

6 With the camshaft removed, examine the bearings in the camshaft housing for signs of obvious wear or pitting. If evident, a new camshaft housing will probably be required.

7 The camshaft itself should show no marks or scoring on the journal or cam lobe surfaces. If evident, renew the camshaft. Note that if the

16.9 Prising out the camshaft front oil seal

16.10a Fitting a new camshaft front oil seal using a special tool

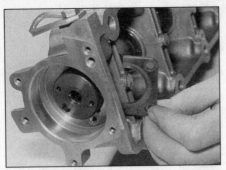

16.4 Removing the camshaft thrustplate

camshaft is renewed, all the rocker arms should also be renewed.

8 Check the camshaft thrustplate for signs of wear or grooves, and renew if evident.

9 It is advisable to renew the camshaft front oil seal as a matter of course if the camshaft has been removed. Prise out the old seal using a screwdriver **(see illustration)**.

Reassembly

10 Carefully drive in the new front seal until it is flush with the housing, using a socket or tube. Fit a new camshaft rear oil seal. Replace the distributor O-ring on other models **(see illustrations)**.

11 Begin reassembly by liberally oiling the bearings in the housing and the oil seal lip. Carefully insert the camshaft into the housing from the distributor end, taking care to avoid damage to the bearings.

12 Refit the thrustplate, and tighten the securing bolts **(see illustration)**. Check the camshaft endfloat by inserting a feeler blade between the thrustplate and the camshaft end flange. If the endfloat exceeds that specified, renew the thrustplate.

13 Refit the distributor as described in Chapter 5.

14 Refit the camshaft housing, as described in Section 18.

15 If a new camshaft has been fitted, it is important to observe the following running-in schedule (unless otherwise specified by the manufacturer) immediately after initially starting the engine:

One minute at 2000 rpm
One minute at 1500 rpm

16.10b Fitting a new camshaft rear oil seal

16.5 Withdrawing the camshaft from the housing

One minute at 3000 rpm
One minute at 2000 rpm

16 Change the engine oil (but not the filter, unless due) approximately 600 miles (1000 km) after fitting a new camshaft (see Chapter 1).

17 Camshafts, "undersize" - general

The camshafts and camshaft housings are sorted on production into one of two size groups; standard and 0.10 mm "undersize". Note that this is not intended to provide replacements for worn engines, but is to allow for production tolerances; either may be fitted to new engines.

"Undersize" components are marked with a spot of violet-coloured paint, that on the camshaft housing being applied on top at the timing belt end.

Whenever the camshaft or its housing are to be renewed, check (by direct measurement, if necessary) whether they are standard or undersize and ensure that only matching items are obtained for reassembly.

18 Cylinder head - removal and refitting (engine in vehicle)

Note 1: *The engine must be cold when the cylinder head is removed. Do not remove the cylinder head from a hot engine. New cylinder head bolts and a new cylinder head gasket*

2A

16.12 Tightening a camshaft thrustplate securing bolt

18.7 Disconnecting a camshaft cover breather hose

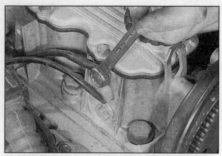

18.9 Unbolting the fuel injection wiring harness earth leads from the camshaft housing

18.17a Disconnecting the crankcase breather tube stub hose

must be used on refitting and sealer will be required when refitting the camshaft housing.
Note 2: *The torque settings stated are only applicable to latest specification head bolts, available from Vauxhall. Earlier type or alternative make, head bolts may require different torques. Consult your supplier.*

Removal

1 Disconnect the battery negative lead.
2 Drain the cooling system, (see Chapter 3).
3 Disconnect the exhaust downpipe from the manifold, referring to Chapter 4B.
4 The cylinder head can be removed complete with the manifolds, or the manifolds can be detached from the cylinder head before removal, with reference to the relevant Sections of Chapter 4A or 4B. If no work is to be carried out on the inlet manifold, it can be unbolted from the cylinder head and supported to one side out of the way, thus avoiding the need to disconnect the relevant hoses, pipes and wiring.
5 If the cylinder head is to be removed complete with the manifolds, disconnect all relevant hoses, pipes and wiring from the inlet manifold and associated components, referring to Chapter 4A. Loosen the alternator mountings, with reference to Chapter 5, then unbolt the upper alternator mounting from the inlet manifold.

6 If the inlet manifold is to be left in the engine compartment, continue as follows, otherwise go on to paragraph 13.
7 Disconnect the air cleaner trunking from the air box on the throttle body, or directly from the throttle body (as applicable), and disconnect the camshaft cover breather hose that runs to the throttle body (as applicable) **(see illustration)**.
8 Disconnect the smaller coolant hose from the top of the thermostat housing.
9 Unbolt the two wiring harnesses earth leads from the camshaft housing **(see illustration)**.
10 Loosen the alternator mountings, referring to Chapter 5, then unbolt the upper alternator mounting from the inlet manifold.
11 Make a final check to ensure that all necessary hoses, pipes and wires have been disconnected, then unscrew the securing nuts, noting the location of the engine lifting bracket, and lift the inlet manifold from the cylinder head. Ensure that the manifold is properly supported, taking care not to strain any of the hoses, pipes and wires, etc., which are still connected.
12 Recover the manifold gasket from the cylinder head.
13 If desired, remove the exhaust manifold, with reference to Chapter 4B.
14 Remove the timing belt and the camshaft sprocket, as described in Section 11.

15 Unscrew the two upper rear timing belt cover securing bolts from the camshaft housing.
16 Disconnect the HT leads from the spark plugs and the coil, labelling them if necessary to aid refitting, and remove the distributor cap, referring to Chapter 5. Where applicable, disconnect the distributor wiring plug.
17 If not already done, disconnect the stub hose that connects the crankcase breather tube to the camshaft housing. If applicable, unscrew the bolt securing the crankcase breather tube bracket to the end of the cylinder head **(see illustrations)**.
18 Disconnect the coolant hoses from the thermostat housing.
19 Make a final check to ensure that all relevant hoses, pipes and wires, etc., have been disconnected.
20 Working from the outside inwards in a spiral pattern as shown **(see illustration)**, loosen all the cylinder head bolts by a quarter of a turn. Then loosen all the bolts by half a turn, and finally loosen and remove the bolts. Recover the washers.
21 Lift the camshaft housing from the cylinder head **(see illustration)**. If necessary, tap the housing gently with a soft-faced mallet to free it from the cylinder head, but do not lever at the mating faces. Note that the camshaft housing is located on dowels.

18.17b Unbolting the crankcase breather tube bracket from the cylinder head

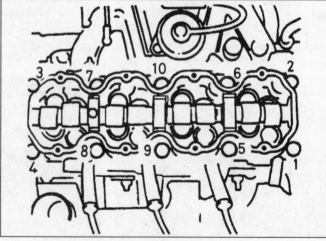

18.20 Cylinder head bolt loosening sequence - SOHC engines

18.21 Lifting the camshaft housing from the cylinder head

18.22a Lift the rocker arms . . .

18.22b . . . and their thrust pads from the cylinder head

22 Lift the rocker arms and their thrust pads from the cylinder head, keeping them in order so that they can be refitted in their original positions **(see illustrations)**.

23 Lift the hydraulic valve lifters from the cylinder head, and place them upright in an oil bath until they are to be refitted **(see illustration)**. Ensure that the depth of oil is sufficient to fully cover the valve lifters, and keep the lifters in order, so that they can be refitted in their original positions.

24 Lift the cylinder head from the cylinder block **(see illustration)**. If necessary, tap the cylinder head gently with a soft-faced mallet to free it from the block, but do not lever at the mating faces. Note that the cylinder head is located on dowels.

25 Recover the cylinder head gasket and discard it.

Refitting

26 Clean the cylinder head and block mating faces, and the camshaft housing and cylinder head mating faces by careful scraping. Take care not to damage the cylinder head and camshaft housing, which are made of light alloy and are easily scored. Cover the coolant passages and other openings with masking tape or rag to prevent dirt and carbon falling in. Mop out all the oil from the bolt holes; if oil is left in the holes, hydraulic pressure could crack the block when the bolts are refitted.

27 If desired, the cylinder head can be dismantled and inspected as described in Sections 20 and 21, and the camshaft housing can be dismantled as described in Section 16.

28 Begin refitting by locating a new gasket on the block so that the word "OBEN" or "TOP" can be read from above **(see illustrations)**.

29 With the mating faces scrupulously clean,

locate the cylinder head on the block so that the positioning dowels engage in their holes.

30 Refit the hydraulic valve lifters, thrust pads and rocker arms to the cylinder head in their original positions. Liberally oil the valve lifter bores, and if new lifters are being fitted initially immerse each one in a container of clean engine oil and compress it (by hand) several times to charge it. Lubricate the contact faces of the valve lifters, thrust pads and rocker arms with a little molybdenum disulphide grease **(see illustration)**.

31 Temporarily refit the crankshaft pulley, and ensure that the timing marks are still positioned as they were before the timing belt was removed (see Section 11).

32 Apply sealing compound (Vauxhall part No 90094714, or equivalent) to the cylinder head top mating face **(see illustration)**, then refit the camshaft housing to the cylinder head.

2A

18.23 Lift the hydraulic valve lifters from the cylinder head

18.24 Lifting the cylinder head from the cylinder block

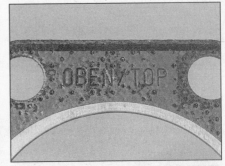

18.28a Cylinder head gasket "OBEN/TOP" markings

18.28b Cylinder head gasket correctly located over dowel in cylinder block

18.30 Lubricate the valve lifter contact faces with molybdenum disulphide grease

18.32 Apply sealing compound to the cylinder head top mating face

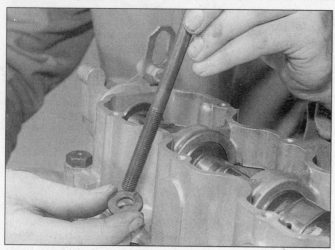

18.33 Fit new cylinder head bolts, ensuring that the washers are in place

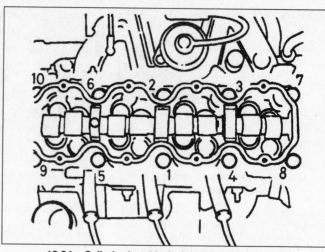

18.34a Cylinder head bolt tightening sequence - SOHC engines

33 Fit the new cylinder head bolts, ensuring that the washers are in place under their heads, and screw the bolts in *by hand* as far as possible **(see illustration)**.

34 Tighten the bolts working from the inside outwards in a spiral pattern as shown. Tighten the bolts in the four stages given in the Specifications - i.e. tighten all bolts to the Stage 1 torque, then tighten all bolts to Stage 2 and so on **(see illustrations)**.

35 Further refitting is a reversal of the removal procedure, remembering the following points.

36 Ensure that the HT leads are refitted to their correct cylinders.

37 Refit the camshaft sprocket and the timing belt and tension the timing belt as described in Section 11.

38 Where applicable, refit the manifolds to the cylinder head, with reference to Chapter 4A or 4B, using new gaskets.

39 Reconnect the exhaust downpipe to the manifold, using a new gasket, referring to Chapter 4B, if necessary.

40 Refit the upper alternator mounting to the inlet manifold, then adjust the alternator drivebelt tension (if a V-belt is used), as described in Chapter 1.

41 Refill the cooling system, (see Chapter 3).

42 On completion, check that all relevant hoses, pipes and wires, etc., have been reconnected.

43 When the engine is started, check for signs of leaks.

44 Once the engine has reached normal operating temperature, check the idle speed and mixture, with reference to Chapter 4A.

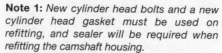

19 Cylinder head - removal and refitting (engine removed)

Note 1: *New cylinder head bolts and a new cylinder head gasket must be used on refitting, and sealer will be required when refitting the camshaft housing.*

Note 2: *The torque settings stated are only applicable to latest specification head bolts, available from Vauxhall. Earlier type or alternative make, head bolts may require different torques. Consult your supplier.*

Removal

1 The cylinder head can be removed complete with the manifolds, or the manifolds can be detached from the cylinder head

before removal, with reference to Chapter 4A or 4B.

2 Remove the timing belt and the camshaft sprocket, as described in Section 11.

3 Unscrew the two upper rear timing belt cover securing bolts from the camshaft housing **(see illustration)**.

4 Disconnect the HT leads from the spark plugs, labelling them if necessary to aid refitting, and remove the distributor cap referring to Chapter 5.

5 If not already done, disconnect the stub hose that connects the crankcase breather tube to the camshaft housing. If applicable, unscrew the bolt securing the crankcase breather tube bracket to the end of the cylinder head.

6 Make a final check to ensure that all relevant hoses, pipes and wires have been disconnected. Proceed as described in Section 18, paragraphs 20 to 25 inclusive.

Refitting

7 Proceed as described in Section 18, paragraphs 26 to 38 inclusive.

8 On completion check that all relevant hoses, pipes and wires, etc., have been reconnected.

18.34b Tighten the cylinder head bolts to the specified torque . . .

18.34c . . . then through the specified angle

19.3 Upper rear timing belt cover securing bolts (arrowed)

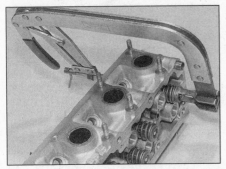

20.3 Valve spring compressor tool fitted to No 1 exhaust valve

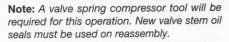

20 Cylinder head -
dismantling and reassembly

Note: *A valve spring compressor tool will be required for this operation. New valve stem oil seals must be used on reassembly.*

Dismantling

1 With the cylinder head removed as described in Sections 18 or 19, clean away all external dirt.
2 If not already done, remove the thermostat cover, complete with the thermostat, as described in Chapter 3. Remove the manifolds as described in Chapter 4A or 4B. Remove the spark plugs if not already done.
3 To remove a valve, fit a valve spring compressor tool. Ensure that the arms of the tool are securely positioned on the head of the valve and the spring cap **(see illustration)**.

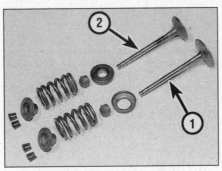

20.7 Inlet (1) and exhaust (2) valve components

4 Compress the valve spring to relieve the pressure of the spring cap acting on the collets. If the spring cap sticks on the valve stem, support the compressor tool and give the end a light tap with a hammer to help free the cap.
5 Extract the two split collets, then slowly release the compressor tool.
6 Remove the spring cap, spring, valve stem oil seal, and the spring seat, then withdraw the valve.
7 Repeat the procedure for the remaining valves, keeping all components in strict order, so that they can be refitted in their original positions **(see illustration)**.
8 The cylinder head and valves can be inspected for wear and damage (see Section 21).

Reassembly

9 Make sure all the components are clean.
10 Starting at one end of the cylinder head, fit the valve components as follows.

20.11 Inserting an exhaust valve into its guide

11 Insert the appropriate valve into its guide, ensuring that the valve stem is well lubricated with clean engine oil **(see illustration)**. Note that if the original components are being refitted, all components must be refitted in their original positions.
12 Fit the spring seat **(see illustration)**.
13 New valve stem oil seals should be supplied with a fitting sleeve, which fits over the collet groove in the valve stem, to prevent damage to the oil seal as it is slid down the valve stem **(see illustration)**. If no sleeve is supplied, wind a short length of tape round the top of the valve stem to cover the collet groove.
14 Push the valve stem oil seal down the valve stem using a tube until the seal is fully engaged with the spring seat **(see illustrations)**. Remove the fitting sleeve or tape, as applicable, from the valve stem.
15 Fit the valve spring and the spring cap **(see illustrations)**.

2A

20.12 Fit the valve seat (exhaust valve shown)

20.13 Slide the oil seal fitting sleeve down the valve stem . . .

20.14a . . . then fit the valve stem oil seal . . .

20.14b . . . and push onto the spring seat using a socket

20.15a Fit the valve spring . . .

20.15b . . . and the spring cap

20.17 Retain the split collets with a little grease

16 Fit the spring compressor tool, and compress the valve spring until the spring cap passes beyond the collet groove in the valve stem.

17 Apply a little grease to the collet groove, then fit the split collets into the groove, with the narrow ends nearest the spring **(see illustration)**. The grease should hold them in the groove.

18 Slowly release the compressor tool, ensuring that the collets are not dislodged from the groove. When the compressor is fully released, give the top of the valve assembly a sharp tap with a soft-faced mallet to settle the components.

19 Repeat the procedure for the remaining valves, ensuring that all components are refitted in their original positions, where applicable.

20 Where applicable, refit the manifolds as described in Chapter 4A or 4B, and/or the thermostat cover and thermostat as described in Chapter 3. Refit the spark plugs if desired.

21 Refit the cylinder head as described in Sections 18 or 19.

21 Cylinder head -
inspection and renovation

Note: *Refer to a dealer for advice before attempting to carry out valve grinding or valve seat resitting operations, as these operations may not be possible for the DIY mechanic. This is because hardened valve seats are fitted for use with unleaded petrol.*

21.9 Renewing the thermostat housing sealing ring

⚠️ **Warning: The exhaust valves fitted to C 20 XE (DOHC) models are fitted with sodium to improve their heat transfer. Sodium is a highly reactive metal, which will ignite or explode spontaneously on contact with water (including water vapour in the air). These must NOT be disposed of with ordinary scrap. Seek advice from a Vauxhall dealer or your Local Authority, if the valves are to be disposed of.**

Inspection

1 Remember that the cylinder head is of light alloy construction and is easily damaged, use a blunt scraper or rotary wire brush to clean all traces of carbon deposits from the combustion spaces and the ports. The valve stems and valve guides should also be freed from any carbon deposits. Wash combustion spaces and ports down with paraffin and scrape the cylinder head surface free of any foreign matter with the side of a steel rule, or a similar article.

2 If the engine is installed in the car, clean the pistons and the top of the cylinder bores. If the pistons are still in the block, it is essential that great care is taken to ensure that no carbon gets into the cylinder bores. This could scratch the cylinder walls or cause damage to the pistons and rings. To ensure this does not happen, first turn the crankshaft so that two of the pistons are at the top of their bores. Insert rag into the other two bores or seal them off with paper and masking tape. The waterways should also be covered with small pieces of masking tape, to prevent particles of carbon entering the cooling system and damaging the coolant pump.

3 Press a little grease into the gap between the cylinder walls and the two pistons that are to be worked on. With a blunt scraper, carefully scrape away the carbon from the piston crown, taking great care not to scratch the aluminium. Also scrape away the carbon from the surrounding lip of the cylinder wall. When all carbon has been removed, scrape away the grease that will now be contaminated with carbon particles, taking care not to press any into the bores. To assist prevention of carbon build-up, the piston crown can be polished with a metal polish.

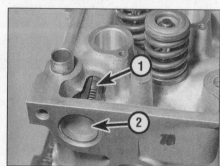

21.10 Oil pressure regulating valve (1) and plug (2)

Remove the rags or masking tape from the other two cylinders, and turn the crankshaft so that the two pistons that were at the bottom are now at the top. Place rag or masking tape in the cylinders that have been decarbonised, and continue as just described.

4 Examine the heads of the valves for pitting and burning, especially the heads of the exhaust valves. The valve seatings should be examined at the same time. If the pitting on the valve and seat is very slight, the marks can be removed by grinding the seats and valves together with coarse, and then fine, valve grinding paste.

5 Where bad pitting has occurred to the valve seats, it will be necessary to recut them and fit new valves. This latter job should be entrusted to the local dealer or engineering works. In practice it is very seldom that the seats are so badly worn. Normally it is the valve that is too badly worn for refitting, and the owner can easily buy a new set of valves and match them to the seats by valve grinding.

Renovation

6 Valve grinding is carried out as follows. Smear a trace of coarse carborundum paste on the seat face and apply a suction grinder tool to the valve head. With a semi-rotary motion, grind the valve head to its seat, lifting the valve occasionally to redistribute the grinding paste. When a dull matt even surface is produced on both the valve seat and the valve, wipe off the paste and repeat the process with fine carborundum paste, lifting and turning the valve to redistribute the paste as before. A light spring placed under the valve head will greatly ease this operation. When a smooth unbroken ring of light grey matt finish is produced, on both valve and valve seat faces, the grinding operation is complete. Carefully clean away every trace of grinding compound, taking great care to leave none in the ports or in the valve guides. Clean the valves and valve seats with a paraffin-soaked rag, then with a clean rag, and finally, if an air line is available, blow the valves, valve guides and valve ports clean.

7 Check that all valve springs are intact. If any one is broken, all should be renewed. Check the free height of the springs against new ones. If some springs are not long enough, replace them all. Springs suffer from fatigue and it is a good idea to renew them even if they look serviceable.

8 The cylinder head can be checked for warping either by placing it on a piece of plate glass or using a straight-edge and feeler blades. If there is any doubt or if its block face is corroded, have it re-faced by your dealer or motor engineering works.

9 Always renew the sealing ring between the cylinder head and the thermostat housing when the head is removed for overhaul **(see illustration)**. Reference to Chapter 2B will show that a considerable amount of work is involved if you wish to renew the sealing ring with the cylinder head installed.

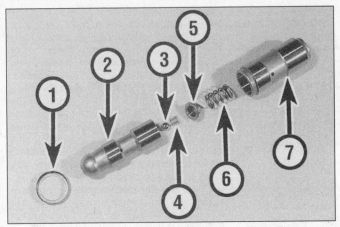

22.1 Hydraulic valve lifter components - SOHC engines

1 Collar	3 Ball	6 Large spring
2 Plunger	4 Small spring	7 Cylinder
	5 Plunger cap	

22.8 Locate the ball (1) on its seat (2) in the base of the plunger

10 If the oil pressure regulating valve in the cylinder head is to be renewed, access is gained through the circular plug covering the end of the valve **(see illustration)**. The old valve must be crushed, then its remains extracted, and a thread (M10) cut in the valve seat to allow removal using a bolt. A new valve and plug can then be driven into position. In view of the intricacies of this operation, it is probably best to have the valve renewed by a Vauxhall dealer if necessary.

22 Hydraulic valve lifters - inspection

1 On engines that have covered a high mileage, or for which the service history (particularly oil changes) is suspect, it is possible for the valve lifters to suffer internal contamination. In extreme cases this may result in increased engine top end noise and wear. To minimise the possibility of problems occurring later in the life of the engine, it is advisable to dismantle and clean the hydraulic valve lifters as follows whenever the cylinder head is overhauled. Note that no spare parts are available for the valve lifters, and if any of the components are unserviceable, the complete assembly must be renewed **(see illustration)**.

2 With the cylinder head removed as described in Sections 18 or 19, and dismantled as described in Section 20, first inspect the valve lifter bores in the cylinder head for wear. If excessive wear is evident, the cylinder head must be renewed. Also check the valve lifter oil holes in the cylinder head for obstructions.

3 Starting with number 1 valve lifter, carefully pull the collar from the top of the valve lifter cylinder. It should be possible to remove the collar by hand - if a tool is used, take care not to distort the collar.

4 Withdraw the plunger from the cylinder, and recover the spring.

5 Using a small screwdriver, carefully prise the cap from the base of the plunger. Recover the spring and ball from under the cap, taking care not to lose them as the cap is removed.

6 Carefully clean all the components using paraffin or solvent, paying particular attention to the machined surfaces of the cylinder (internal surfaces), and piston (external surfaces). Thoroughly dry all the components using a lint-free cloth. Carefully examine the springs for damage or distortion - the complete valve lifter must be renewed if the springs are not in perfect condition.

7 Lubricate the components sparingly with clean engine oil of the correct grade, then reassemble as follows.

8 Invert the plunger and locate the ball on its seat in the base of the plunger **(see illustration)**.

9 Locate the smaller spring on its seat in the plunger cap, then carefully refit the cap and spring, ensuring that the spring locates on the ball. Carefully press around the flange of the cap, using a small screwdriver if necessary, until the flange is securely located in the groove in the base of the plunger **(see illustrations)**.

2A

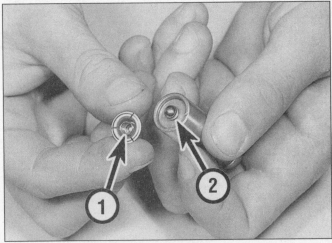

22.9a Spring (1) located in plunger cap, and ball (2) located on seat in plunger

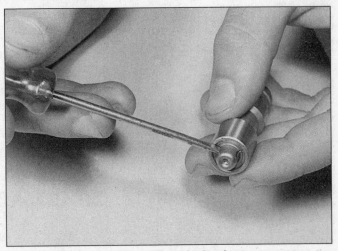

22.9b Locate the cap flange in the plunger groove

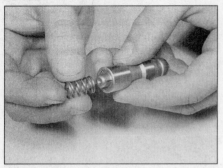

22.10a Locate the spring over the plunger cap . . .

22.10b . . . then slide the plunger and spring assembly into the cylinder

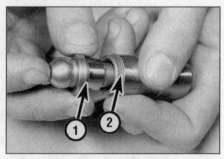

22.11 Slide the collar (1) over the top of the plunger and engage with the groove (2) in the cylinder

10 Locate the larger spring over the plunger cap, ensuring that the spring is correctly seated, and slide the plunger and spring assembly into the cylinder **(see illustrations)**.
11 Slide the collar over the top of the plunger, and carefully compress the plunger by hand, until the collar can be pushed down to engage securely with the groove in the cylinder **(see illustration)**.
12 Repeat the above procedures on the remaining valve lifters.

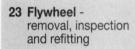

23 Flywheel -
removal, inspection and refitting

Note: *New flywheel securing bolts must he used on refitting. Certain models are fitted with a 'Pot type' flywheel. Although, it has a deeply recessed surface for the clutch disc, the operations below are the same.*

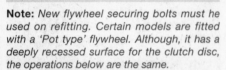

23.5 Removing the flywheel

Removal

1 If not already done, remove the clutch (see Chapter 6) and the starter motor (see Chapter 5).
2 If the engine is in the vehicle, remove the clutch release bearing and its guide sleeve, as described in Chapter 6.
3 Although the flywheel bolt holes are offset so that the flywheel can only be fitted in one position, it will make refitting easier if alignment marks are made between the flywheel and the end of the crankshaft.
4 Prevent the flywheel from turning by jamming the ring gear teeth using a large screwdriver or similar tool. Access is most easily obtained through the starter motor aperture if the engine is in the vehicle.
5 Unscrew the securing bolts, and remove the flywheel **(see illustration)**.
Caution: Take care, as the flywheel is heavy!

Inspection

6 With the flywheel removed, it can be inspected as follows.
7 If the teeth on the flywheel starter ring are badly worn, or if some are missing, then it will be necessary to remove the ring and fit a new one.
8 The old ring can be split with a cold chisel, after making a cut with a hacksaw blade between two gear teeth. Take great care not to damage the flywheel during this operation, and always use eye protectors. Once the ring has been split, it will spread apart and can be lifted from the flywheel.

9 The new ring gear must be heated to 180 to 230°C (356 to 446°F) and unless facilities for heating by oven or flame are available, leave the fitting to a dealer or motor engineering works. The new ring gear must not be overheated during this work, or the temper of the metal will be altered.
10 The ring should be tapped gently down onto its register, and left to cool naturally - the contraction of the metal on cooling will ensure that it is a secure and permanent fit.
11 If the clutch friction disc contact surface of the flywheel is scored, or on close inspection, shows evidence of small hairline cracks (caused by overheating), it may be possible to have the flywheel surface ground. This is provided that the overall thickness of the flywheel is not reduced too much. Consult a specialist engine repairer and if it is not possible, renew the flywheel complete.

Refitting

12 Refitting is a reversal of removal, remembering the following points.
13 Align the previously made marks on the flywheel and crankshaft, and fit new flywheel securing bolts. Tighten them to the specified torque in the three stages given in the Specifications, whilst preventing the flywheel from turning, as during removal **(see illustrations)**.
14 Where applicable, refit the clutch release bearing, guide sleeve and the clutch, as described in Chapter 6.

23.13a Tool for locking flywheel fitted to engine-to-transmission bolt hole

23.13b Tighten the flywheel securing bolts to the specified torque . . .

23.13c . . . and then through the specified angle

26.4 Fitting a new crankshaft rear oil seal

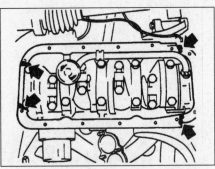

27.12a Apply sealing compound (arrowed) to oil pump and rear main bearing cap joints before refitting sump

27.12b Applying sealing compound to the joint between the oil pump and cylinder block

24 Flexplate (automatic transmission) - removal and refitting

Removal

1 Remove the transmission (see Chapter 7B).
2 Prevent the flexplate from turning by jamming its ring gear teeth using a large screwdriver or similar tool.
3 Unbolt and remove the flexplate. Examine the bolts and renew them all as a set if there is the slightest doubt about their condition.
4 The ring gear can be checked and renewed if necessary, as described in Section 23.

Refitting

5 Refitting is the reverse of the removal procedure. If the bolts are to be re-used, use a wire brush to clean their threads, apply a few drops of thread-locking compound (Vauxhall Part No 90167347, or equivalent) to the threads of each bolt on refitting. Tighten the bolts to the specified torque wrench setting.
6 Refit the transmission. Refer to Chapter 7B if necessary.

25 Crankshaft front oil seal - renewal

1 Remove the timing belt and the rear timing belt cover, as described in Section 11.
2 Ensure that the Woodruff key is removed from the end of the crankshaft.
3 Punch or drill a small hole in the centre of the now-exposed oil seal. Screw in a self-tapping screw, and pull on the screw with pliers to extract the seal. Several attempts may be necessary.
Caution: Be careful not to damage the sealing face of the crankshaft.
4 Clean the oil seal seat with a wooden or plastic scraper.
5 Before fitting the new oil seal, steps must be taken to protect the oil seal lips from damage, and from turning back on the shoulder at the front end of the crankshaft. Grease the seal lips, and then wind tape around the end of the crankshaft to form a gentle taper.

6 Tap the seal into position using a large socket or tube, until the seal is flush with the outer face of the oil pump housing.
7 Refit the rear timing belt cover and the timing belt. Tension the timing belt as described in Section 11.

26 Crankshaft rear oil seal - renewal

1 With the engine removed from the vehicle, remove the flywheel or flexplate (as applicable).
2 Punch or drill a small hole in the centre of the now-exposed oil seal. Screw in a self-tapping screw, and pull on the screw with pliers to extract the seal. Several attempts may be necessary.
Caution: Be careful not to damage the sealing face of the crankshaft.
3 Clean the oil seal seat with a wooden or plastic scraper.
4 Grease the lips of the new seal, then tap the seal into position using a tube, until flush with the outer faces of the cylinder block and rear main bearing cap **(see illustration)**.
5 Refit the flywheel or flexplate (as applicable), as described in Sections 23 or 24.

27 Sump - removal and refitting

Note: *The sump gasket(s) must be renewed on refitting and sealer will be required for use on the oil pump and rear main bearing cap-to-cylinder block joints*

Removal

1 If the engine is in the vehicle, continue as follows, otherwise go on to paragraph 7.
2 Disconnect the battery negative lead.
3 Drain the engine oil, referring to Chapter 1 if necessary, then refit and tighten the drain plug.
4 Apply the handbrake, then jack up the front of the vehicle, and support securely on axle stands (see "*Jacking and Vehicle Support*").
5 Remove the front section of the exhaust system, as described in Chapter 4B, or the whole exhaust if it is more convenient.

6 Where applicable, disconnect the wiring from the oil level sensor.
7 Unscrew the securing bolts and remove the engine-to-transmission blanking plate from the bellhousing.
8 Remove the securing bolts, and withdraw the sump. Note that on most models, the sump baffle will probably be pulled away from the cylinder block with the sump, but cannot be removed until the oil pick-up pipe has been removed.
9 To remove the sump baffle, it is necessary to unbolt the bracket securing the oil pick-up pipe to the cylinder block. The baffle can then be manipulated over the oil pick-up pipe. Prise the rubber gasket from the sump baffle.
10 If need be, the oil pick-up pipe can be removed by unscrewing the single bolt securing the support bracket to the cylinder block (if not already done). Then remove the two bolts securing the end of the pipe to the oil pump. Recover the O-ring.
11 Clean all traces of old gasket and sealing compound from the mating faces of the cylinder block, sump baffle (where applicable), and sump.

Refitting

12 Begin refitting by applying sealing compound (Vauxhall part No 90485251 or equivalent) to the joints between the oil pump and cylinder block, and the rear main bearing cap and cylinder block **(see illustrations)**.
13 Locate a new rubber gasket over the sump baffle flange, ensuring that it is seated correctly **(see illustration)**.

27.13 Locate a new rubber gasket over the sump baffle flange

2A

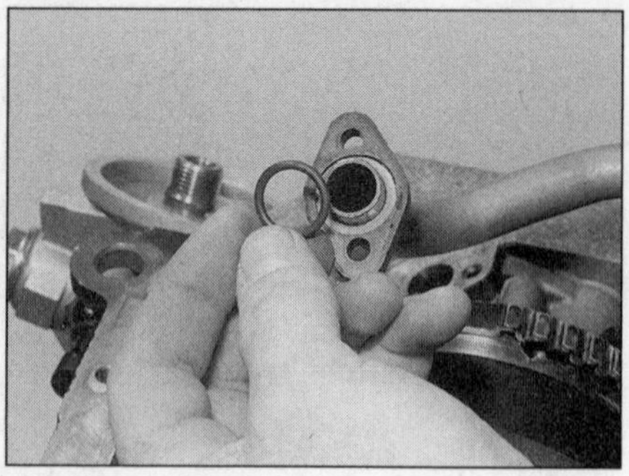

27.15a Fit a new O-ring to the oil pick-up pipe . . .

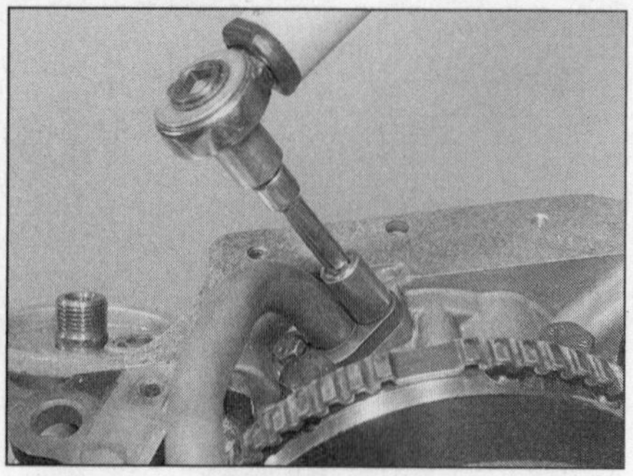

27.15b . . . and tighten the securing bolts to the specified torque

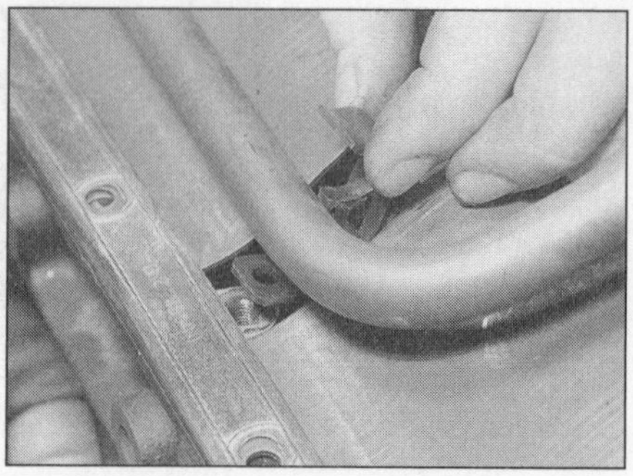

27.16 Refitting the oil pick-up pipe bracket

14 Offer the sump baffle up to the cylinder block, manipulating it over the oil pick-up pipe where applicable.

15 If the oil pick-up pipe has been removed, refit it to the oil pump using a new O-ring and tighten the bolts to the specified torque **(see illustrations)**.

16 Where applicable, refit the bracket securing the oil pick-up pipe to the cylinder block, ensuring that it passes through the relevant hole in the sump baffle, if applicable **(see illustration)**.

17 Coat the sump securing bolts with thread-locking compound (i.e. Vauxhall part No. 90167347), then refit the sump, and tighten the bolts to the specified torque **(see illustrations)**.

18 If the engine is in the vehicle, further refitting is a reversal of the removal procedure, but refit the front section of the exhaust system referring to Chapter 4B. On completion, refill the engine with oil, as described in Chapter 1.

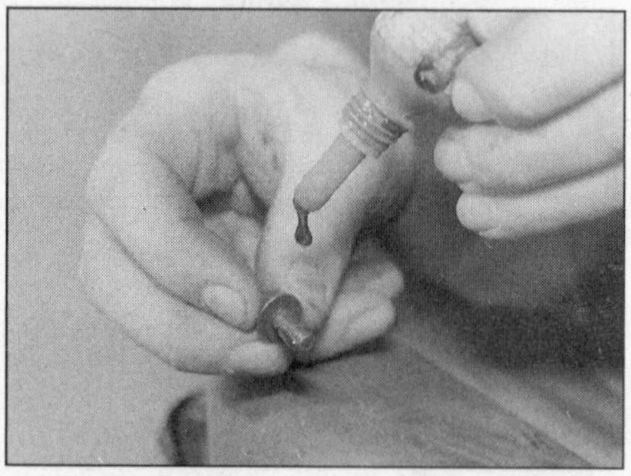

27.17a Coat the sump securing bolts with thread-locking compound before fitting

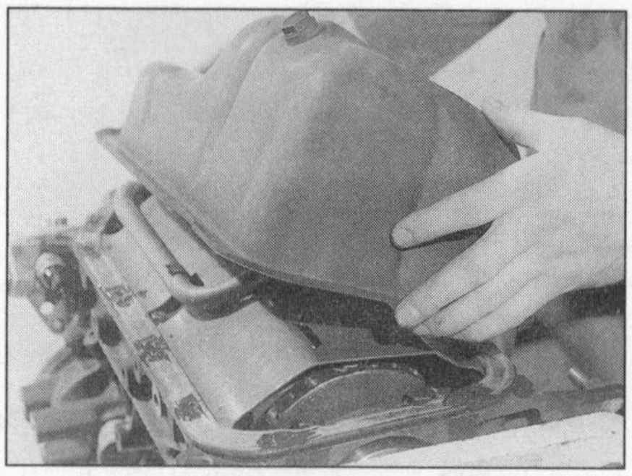

27.17b Refitting the sump

28 Oil pump - removal and refitting

Removal

1 Remove the timing belt, sprockets and the rear timing belt cover, as shown in Section 11.

2 Remove the sump, oil pick-up pipe and sump baffle (where applicable), as described in Section 27.

3 Unscrew the oil filter from its mounting on the oil pump, referring to Chapter 1, if necessary.

4 Disconnect the wiring from the oil pressure switch mounted on the oil pump.

5 Remove the securing bolts, and withdraw the oil pump from the cylinder block. Recover the gasket.

6 The oil pump can be dismantled for inspection, as described in Section 29.

Refitting

7 Thoroughly clean the mating faces of the oil pump and cylinder block, then locate a new gasket on the block **(see illustration)**.

8 Before refitting the oil pump, steps must be taken to protect the oil seal lips from damage, and from turning back on the shoulder at the front end of the crankshaft. Grease the seal lips, and then wind tape around the crankshaft to form a gentle taper.

9 Refit the oil pump, ensuring that the inner gear engages with the flats on the crankshaft, and tighten the securing bolts to the specified torque, then remove the tape from the end of the crankshaft **(see illustrations)**.

10 Reconnect the wiring to the oil pressure switch.

11 Fit a new oil filter, (see Chapter 1).

12 Refit the sump baffle (where applicable), oil pick-up tube and sump, (see Section 27).

13 Refit the rear timing belt cover and the timing belt, and tension the timing belt as described in Section 11.

29 Oil pump - dismantling, inspection and reassembly

Note: *A new crankshaft front oil seal must be used on reassembly.*

Dismantling

1 With the oil pump removed as described in Section 28, continue as follows.

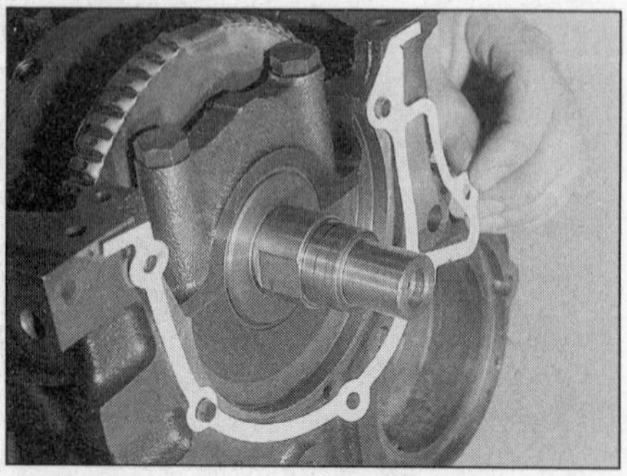

28.7 Fit a new oil pump gasket to the cylinder block

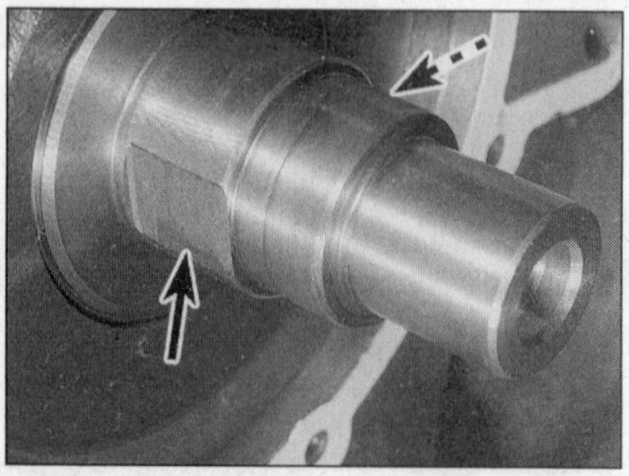

28.9a Oil pump inner gear must engage with two flats (arrowed)

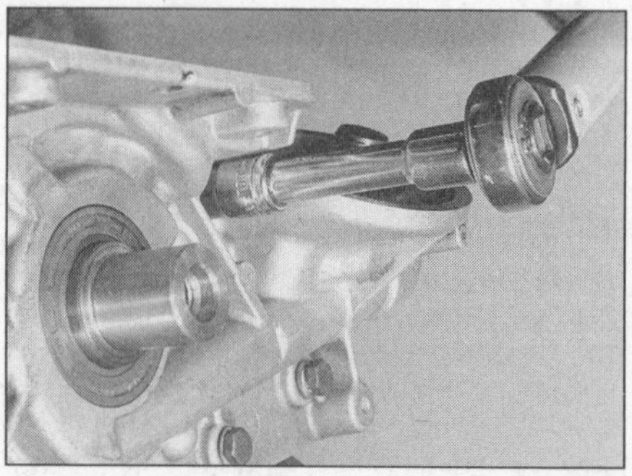

28.9b Tighten the oil pump securing bolts to the specified torque - SOHC engine

29.2 Removing an oil pump rear cover securing screw - SOHC engine

29.3 Check the clearance between the inner and outer gear teeth . . .

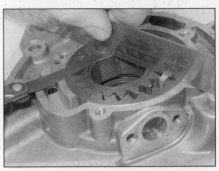

29.4 . . . and between the edges of the gears and the housing - SOHC engine

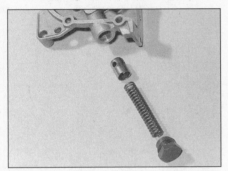

29.7 Oil pressure relief valve components - SOHC engine

29.9a Prise out the old crankshaft front oil seal . . .

29.9b . . . and fit the new seal using a socket - SOHC engine

2 Remove the securing screws and withdraw the rear cover **(see illustration)**. The screws may be very tight, in which case it may be necessary to use an impact driver to remove them.

Inspection

3 Check the clearance between the inner and outer gear teeth (backlash) using a feeler blade **(see illustration)**.

4 Check the clearance between the edges of the gears and the housing (endfloat) using a straight edge and a feeler blade **(see illustration)**.

5 If any of the clearances are outside the specified limits, renew the components as necessary.

6 Ensure that the gears and the interior of the pump body are scrupulously clean before reassembly, and note that the outer gear is marked with a punch dot to indicate the gear outer face.

7 The oil pressure relief valve components can be removed from the pump by unscrewing the cap **(see illustration)**. Examine the spring and plunger, and renew if necessary.

Reassembly

8 Thoroughly clean the components before refitting.

9 Always renew the crankshaft front oil seal at the front of the oil pump housing. Prise out the old seal using a screwdriver, and fit the new seal using a socket or tube, so that it is flush with the outer face of the housing **(see illustrations)**.

10 Ensure that the mating faces of the rear cover and the pump housing are clean, then coat the pump housing mating face with sealing compound (Vauxhall part No 90485251, or equivalent) and refit the rear cover. Refit and tighten the securing screws.

11 Refit the pump, as described in Section 28.

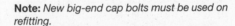

30 Pistons and connecting rods - removal and refitting

Note: *New big-end cap bolts must be used on refitting.*

Removal

1 Remove the cylinder head, as described previously in Section 18.

2 Remove the sump, oil pick-up pipe and sump baffle (where applicable), as described in Section 27.

3 If the connecting rods and big-end caps are not marked to indicate their positions in the cylinder block (i.e. cylinder numbers), centre-punch them at adjacent points either side of the cap/rod joint. Note to which side of the engine the marks face **(see illustration)**.

4 Unscrew the big-end cap bolts from the first connecting rod, and remove the cap. If the bearing shells are to be re-used, tape the cap and shell together.

5 Check the top of the piston bore for a wear ridge. If evident, carefully scrape it away with a ridge reaming tool, otherwise as the piston is pushed out of the block, the piston rings may jam against the ridge.

6 Place the wooden handle of a hammer against the bottom of the connecting rod, and push the piston/rod assembly up and out of the cylinder bore. Recover the bearing shell, and tape it to the connecting rod if it is to be re-used.

7 Remove the remaining three assemblies in a similar way. Rotate the crankshaft as necessary to bring the big-end bolts to the most accessible position.

8 The piston can be separated from the connecting rod by removing the circlips that secure the fully floating gudgeon pin. Note the orientation of the piston and connecting rod before separation, and if necessary, make alignment marks. Reassembly is a reversal of dismantling ensuring that the piston and connecting rod are correctly orientated.

9 The pistons and connecting rods can be examined for wear and damage, as described in Section 31, and the bearings can be examined as described in Section 33.

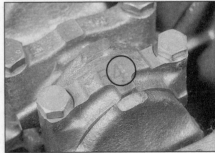

30.3 Big-end cap centre punch identification marks (circled). Note that lug on bearing cap faces flywheel end of engine

2A

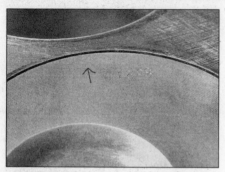

30.14a Piston crown arrow must point towards timing belt end of engine

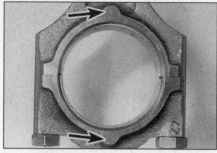

30.14b Lugs (arrowed) on connecting rod and big-end cap must point towards flywheel end of engine

30.15 Tapping a piston into its bore

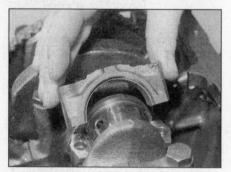

30.17 Fitting a big-end bearing cap

30.18a Tighten the big-end cap bolts to the specified torque . . .

30.18b . . . then through the specified angle

Refitting

10 Begin reassembly by laying the piston/connecting rod assemblies out in their correct order, complete with bearing shells, ready for refitting into their respective bores in the cylinder block.

11 Ensure that the seats for the bearing shells are absolutely clean, and then fit the shells into the seats.

12 Wipe out the cylinder bores and oil them. Oil the piston rings liberally, and ensure that the ring gaps are positioned as described in Section 31.

13 Fit a piston ring compressor tool to the first assembly to be installed.

14 Insert the rod and piston into the top of the cylinder bore, so that the base of the compressor stands on the block. Check that the connecting rod markings are towards the side of the engine noted during removal. Note that the arrow or notch, as applicable, on the

piston crown should point towards the timing belt end of the engine, and the lugs on the connecting rods should point towards the flywheel end of the engine **(see illustrations)**.

15 Apply the wooden handle of a hammer to the piston crown and tap the assembly into the bore, at the same time releasing the compressor **(see illustration)**.

16 Oil the relevant crankpin, then guide the big-end of the connecting rod near to the crankpin, and pull it firmly onto the crankpin. Ensure that the bearing shell remains in position in the connecting rod.

17 Fit the big-end cap, with the markings towards the side of the engine noted during removal **(see illustration)**. Note that the lug should point towards the flywheel end of the engine.

18 Fit new big-end cap bolts, and tighten them to the specified torque in the three stages given in the Specifications **(see illustrations)**.

19 Repeat the procedure on the remaining three assemblies.

20 Refit the sump baffle (where applicable), oil pick-up pipe and sump, (see Section 27).

21 Refit the cylinder head, (see Section 18).

31 Pistons and connecting rods - examination and renovation

Examination

1 Examine the mating faces of the big-end caps to see if they have ever been filed, in a mistaken attempt to take up bearing wear. This is extremely unlikely, but if evident, the offending connecting rods and caps must be renewed.

2 Check the alignment of the rods visually, and if all is not well, take the rods to a Vauxhall dealer for a more detailed check.

3 The gudgeon pins are an interference (shrink) fit in the connecting rod small ends. Separation of the pistons and rods is a job for a dealer due to the special tools required, as is any remedial action required if the gudgeon pin is no longer an interference fit in the rod.

4 Examine the pistons for ovality, scoring and scratches.

5 If new rings are to be fitted to the existing pistons, expand the old rings over the tops of the pistons. The use of two or three old feeler blades will be helpful in preventing the rings dropping into empty grooves. Note that the oil control ring is in three sections, and note which way up each ring is fitted, for use when refitting **(see illustrations)**.

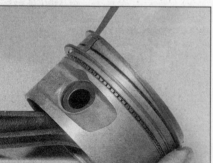

31.5a Using a feeler blade to aid removal of a piston ring

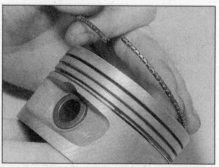

31.5b Removing the centre section of the oil control ring

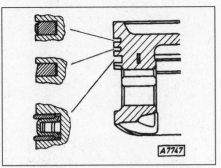

31.5c Sectional view showing correct orientation of piston rings on all engines

Renovation

6 Before fitting the new rings to the pistons, insert them into their relevant cylinder bores, and check that the ring end gaps are within the specified limits using a feeler blade **(see illustration)**. Check the ring gaps at the upper and lower limits of the piston travel in the bores.

7 If any of the ring end gaps exceed the specified tolerance, the relevant rings will have to be renewed, and if the ring grooves in the pistons are worn, new pistons may be required.

8 Clean out the piston ring grooves using a piece of old piston ring as a scraper. Take care not to scratch the surface of the pistons. Protect your fingers, piston ring edges are sharp. Also probe the groove oil return holes, to ensure that they are not blocked.

9 Check the cylinder bores for signs of wear ridges towards the top of the bores. If wear ridges are evident, and new piston rings are being fitted, the top ring must be stepped to clear the wear ridge, or the bore must be de-ridged using a scraper.

10 Fit the oil control ring sections with the lower steel ring gap offset 25 to 50 mm to the right of the spreader ring gap, and the upper steel ring gap offset by the same distance to the left of the spreader ring gap.

11 Fit the lower compression ring, noting that the ring is tapered or stepped. The ring should be fitted with the word "TOP" uppermost.

12 Fit the upper compression ring, and offset the ring gap by 180° to the lower compression ring gap. If a stepped ring is being fitted, fit the ring with the smaller diameter of the step uppermost.

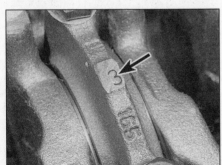

32.8 Main bearing cap identification mark (arrowed)

31.6 Measuring a piston ring end gap using a feeler blade

13 If new pistons are to be fitted, they must be selected from the grades available, after measuring the cylinder bores as described in Section 34.

14 Normally the appropriate oversize pistons are supplied by the dealer when the block is rebored.

15 Whenever new piston rings are being installed, the glaze on the original cylinder bores should be "broken", using either abrasive paper or a glaze-removing tool in an electric drill. If abrasive paper is used, use strokes at 60° to the bore centre line, to create a cross-hatching effect.

32 Crankshaft and bearings - removal and refitting

Note: *New main bearing cap bolts must be used on refitting.*

Removal

1 With the engine removed from the vehicle, continue as follows.

2 Remove the cylinder head, (see Section 18).

3 Remove the sump, oil pick-up pipe and sump baffle (where applicable), (see Section 27).

4 Remove the oil pump, (see Section 28).

5 Remove the flywheel or flexplate (as applicable), as described in Sections 23 and 24.

6 Remove the pistons and connecting rods, as described in Section 30.

7 Invert the engine so that it is standing on the top face of the cylinder block.

8 The main bearing caps are numbered 1 to 4

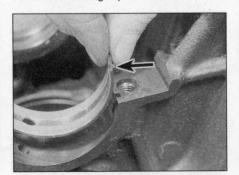

32.17 Main bearing shell tag (arrowed) engages with groove in cylinder block

from the timing belt end of the engine. The rear (flywheel end) cap is not marked. To ensure that the caps are refitted the correct way round, note that the numbers are read from the coolant pump side of the engine with the engine inverted **(see illustration)**.

9 Unscrew and remove the main bearing cap bolts, and tap off the bearing caps. If the bearing shells are to be re-used, tape them to their respective caps.

10 Note that the centre bearing shell incorporates thrust flanges to control crankshaft endfloat.

11 Lift the crankshaft (complete with timing sensor wheel, if fitted), from the crankcase.

12 Extract the upper bearing shells, and identify them for position if they are to be re-used.

13 The crankshaft, bearings and sensor wheel can be examined for wear and damage, (Section 33), and the cylinder block and bores can be examined as described in Section 34.

Refitting

14 Begin refitting by ensuring that the crankcase and crankshaft are thoroughly clean, and that all oilways are clear. If possible, blow through the oil drillings with compressed air, and inject clean engine oil into them.

> **HAYNES HINT** *A good alternative to compressed air, is to use a water dispersing lubricant spray into each hole, using the spout provided.*

15 If the crankshaft is being replaced, where applicable, transfer the timing sensor wheel and tighten to the correct torque.

16 Wipe clean the bearing shell seats in the crankcase and the bearing caps, then fit the upper bearing shells to their seats.

17 Note that there is a tag on the back of each bearing shell, which engages with a groove in the relevant seat in the crankcase or bearing cap **(see illustration)**.

18 If new bearing shells are being fitted, wipe away all traces of protective grease.

19 Note that the central bearing shells have thrust flanges which control crankshaft endfloat **(see illustration)**. Note also that the shells fitted to the crankcase all have oil duct holes, while only the centre main bearing cap shell has an oil duct hole.

2A

32.19 Fitting a central main bearing shell. Note thrust flanges

32.22 Lowering the crankshaft into the crankcase

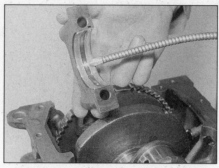

32.24 Lubricate the main bearing shells before fitting the caps

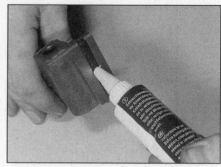

32.25a Fill the side grooves of the rear main bearing cap with RTV jointing compound . . .

32.25b . . . and the lower surfaces with sealing compound

32.27a Tighten the main bearing cap bolts to the specified torque . . .

32.27b . . . then through the specified angle

20 When the shells are firmly located in the crankcase and the bearing caps, lubricate them with clean engine oil.
21 Fill the lips of a new crankshaft rear oil seal with grease, and fit it to the end of the crankshaft.
22 Carefully lower the crankshaft into position in the crankcase **(see illustration)**.
23 If necessary, seat the crankshaft using light blows with a rubber hammer on the crankshaft balance webs.
24 Lubricate the main bearing journals and shells **(see illustration)**, and then fit numbers 2, 3 and 4 main bearing caps, and tighten the new bolts as far as possible by hand.
25 Fill the side grooves of the rear main bearing cap with RTV jointing compound (Vauxhall part No 90485251, or equivalent). Coat the lower surfaces of the bearing cap with sealing compound (Vauxhall part No 15

04 200, or equivalent), **(see illustrations)**. Fit the bearing cap, and tighten the new bolts as far as possible by hand.
26 Fit the front (No 1) main bearing cap, and tighten the new bolts as far as possible by hand, ensuring that the bearing cap is exactly flush with the end face of the cylinder block.
27 Working from the centre bearing cap outwards, tighten the bearing cap securing bolts to the specified torque in the three stages given in the Specifications; i.e. tighten all bolts to Stage 1, then tighten all bolts to Stage 2 and Stage 3 **(see illustrations)**.
28 When all bolts have been fully tightened, inject further RTV jointing compound into the side grooves of the rear main bearing cap, until it is certain that they are full.
29 Now rotate the crankshaft, and check that it turns freely, with no signs of binding or tight spots.

30 Check that the crankshaft endfloat is within the specified limits, using a dial gauge, or by inserting a feeler blade between the thrust flange of the centre main bearing shell and the machined surface of the crankshaft **(see illustrations)**. Before measuring, ensure that the crankshaft is fully forced towards one end of the crankcase, to give the widest possible gap at the measuring location. Incorrect endfloat will most likely be due to crankshaft wear or to incorrect regrinding, assuming that the correct bearing shells have been fitted.
31 Refit the previously removed components, referring to the relevant Sections of this Chapter.

33 Crankshaft and bearings - examination

1 Examine the crankpin and main journal surfaces for signs of scoring or scratches, and check the ovality and taper of the crankpins and main journals. If the bearing surface dimensions do not fall within the tolerance ranges given in the Specifications at the beginning of this Chapter, the crankpins and/or main journals will have to be reground.
2 Big-end and crankpin wear is accompanied by distinct metallic knocking, particularly noticeable when the engine is pulling from low revs, and some loss of oil pressure.
3 Main bearing and main journal wear is accompanied by severe engine vibration rumble

32.30a Check crankshaft endfloat using a dial gauge . . .

32.30b . . . or a feeler blade

- getting progressively worse as engine rev's increase - and again by loss of oil pressure.

4 If the crankshaft requires regrinding, take it to an engine reconditioning specialist, who will machine it for you and supply the correct undersize bearing shells.

5 Inspect the big-end and main bearing shells for signs of general wear, scoring, pitting and scratches. The bearings should be matt grey in colour. With leadindium bearings, should a trace of copper colour be noticed, the bearings are badly worn, as the lead bearing material has worn away to expose the indium underlay. Renew the bearings if they are in this condition, or if there are any signs of scoring or pitting.

Caution: You are strongly advised to renew the bearings - regardless of their condition at time of major overhaul. Refitting used bearings is a false economy.

6 The undersizes available are designed to correspond with crankshaft regrind sizes. The bearings are in fact, slightly more than the stated undersize, as running clearances have been allowed for during their manufacture.

7 Main and big-end bearing shells can be identified as to size by the marking on the back of the shell. Standard size shell bearings are marked STD or .00, undersize shells are marked with the undersize such as 0.020 u/s. This marking method applies only to replacement bearing shells, and not to those used during production.

8 An accurate method of determining bearing wear is by using a Plastigage. The crankshaft is located in the main bearings (and, if necessary, the big-end bearings), and the Plastigage filament is located across the journal. Vauxhall recommend that the crankshaft journal and bearing shells are lightly lubricated, to prevent the Plastigage from tearing as the bearing cap is removed. The bearing cap should be fitted, and the bolts tightened to the specified torque. The cap is then removed, and the width of the filament is checked against a scale that shows the bearing running clearance. The clearance should be compared with that given in the Specifications.

9 Where applicable, check the teeth of the crankshaft TDC sensor wheel for damage (see illustration). If evident, the crankshaft must be renewed.

10 Similarly, check the condition of the pins in the front crankshaft balance weight, which serve as detect points for the plug-in diagnostic sensor used by Vauxhall dealers (see illustration).

34 Cylinder block and bores - examination and renovation
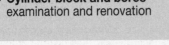

1 Examine the cylinder bores for taper, ovality, scoring and scratches. Start by carefully examining the top of the cylinder bores. If they are at all worn, a very slight

33.9 Check the condition of the TDC sensor wheel teeth at the front of the crankshaft

ridge will be found on the thrust side. This marks the top of the piston ring travel. The owner will have a good indication of the bore wear before dismantling the engine, or removing the cylinder head. Excessive oil consumption, accompanied by blue smoke from the exhaust, is a sure sign of worn cylinder bores and piston rings.

2 Measure the bore diameter across the block, and just below any ridge. This can be done with an internal micrometer or a dial gauge. Compare this with the diameter of the bottom of the bore, which is not subject to wear. If no measuring instruments are available, use a piston from which the rings have been removed, and measure the gap between it and the cylinder wall with a feeler blade. Refer to the Specifications. If the cylinder wear exceeds the permitted tolerances, then the cylinders will need reboring, in which case note the following points:

a) *Piston and cylinder bores are closely matched in production. The actual diameter of the piston is indicated by numbers on its crown; the same numbers stamped on the crankcase indicate the bore diameter.*

b) *After reboring has taken place, the cylinder bores should be measured accurately and oversize pistons selected from the grades available to give the specified piston-to-bore clearance.*

c) *For grading purposes, the piston diameter is measured across the bottom of the skirt.*

3 If the wear is marginal and within the tolerances given, new special piston rings can be fitted to offset the wear.

4 Thoroughly examine the crankcase and cylinder block for cracks and damage, and use a piece of wire to probe all oilways and waterways to ensure that they are unobstructed.

5 Note that the rubber plug located next to the bellhousing flange on the cylinder block covers the aperture for the installation of a diagnostic TDC sensor. The sensor, when connected to a monitoring unit, indicates TDC from the position of the pins set into the crankshaft balance weight.

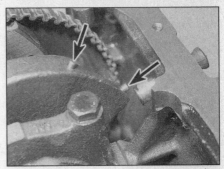

33.10 Check the condition of the pins (arrowed) in the front crankshaft balance weight

35 Examination and renovation - general

1 With the engine completely stripped, clean all components and examine them for wear. Each component should be checked, and where necessary renewed or renovated, as described in the relevant Sections of this Chapter.

2 Renew main and big-end bearing shells as a matter of course, unless it is known that they have had little wear, and are in perfect condition.

3 If in doubt whether to renew a component that is still just serviceable, consider the time and effort that will be incurred should the component fail at an early date after rebuild. Obviously, the age and expected life of the vehicle must influence the standards applied.

4 Gaskets, oil seals and O-rings must all be renewed as a matter of routine. Flywheel, cylinder head, and main and big-end bearing cap bolts must be renewed, because of the high stress to which they are subjected.

5 Renew the engine core plugs while they are easily accessible, if they show signs of leakage. Knock out the old plugs with a hammer and chisel or punch. Clean the plug seats, smear the new plugs with sealing compound, and tap them squarely into position.

36 Initial start-up after major overhaul or repair

1 Make a final check to ensure that everything has been reconnected to the engine, and that no rags or tools have been left in the engine compartment.

2 Check that oil and coolant levels are correct (see "Weekly checks").

3 Start the engine. This may take a little longer than usual, as fuel is pumped to the engine.

4 Check that the oil pressure warning lamp goes out when the engine starts. This may take a few seconds as the new oil filter fills with oil.

2A

5 Run the engine at a fast tickover, and check for leaks of oil, fuel and coolant. If a new camshaft has been fitted, pay careful attention to the running-in procedure given in Section 16, paragraphs 15 and 16. Where applicable, check the power steering and/or automatic transmission fluid cooler unions for leakage. Some smoke and odd smells may be experienced, as assembly lubricants and sealers burn off the various components.

6 Bring the engine to normal operating temperature. Check the ignition timing, idle speed and the mixture (where applicable), as described in Chapter 4A.

7 Allow the engine to cool, then recheck the oil and coolant levels. Top-up if necessary (see "*Weekly checks*").

8 If new bearings, pistons, etc., have been fitted, the engine should be run-in at reduced speeds and loads for the first 500 miles (800 km) or so. It is beneficial to change the engine oil and filter after this mileage (see Chapter 1).

Chapter 2 Part B:
DOHC engine procedures

Contents

Degrees of difficulty

Easy, suitable for novice with little experience		Fairly easy, suitable for beginner with some experience		Fairly difficult, suitable for competent DIY mechanic		Difficult, suitable for experienced DIY mechanic		Very difficult, suitable for expert DIY or professional	

Specifications

Note: *All specifications are as for SOHC engines, unless shown otherwise.*

General

Type (all models) .... Four-cylinder, in-line, water-cooled, transversely mounted. Double belt-driven overhead camshafts, acting on hydraulic valve lifters

Manufacturer's engine codes:
C20 XE .... 2.0 litre (1998 cc) + catalyst
X20 XEV .... 2.0 litre (1998 cc) + catalyst. 'Ecotec' type engine
Compression ratio:
C20 XE .... 10.5 : 1
X20 XEV .... 10.8 : 1
Maximum power:
C20 XE .... 110 kW (150 bhp) at 6000 rpm
X20 XEV .... 100 kW (136 bhp) at 5400 rpm
Maximum torque:
C20 XE
Up to model year 1993 .... 196 Nm at 4800 rpm
1993-on .... 196 Nm at 4600 rpm
X20 XEV .... 185 Nm at 4000 rpm

Cylinder head

Overall height of cylinder head (sealing surface to sealing surface):
C20 XE .... 135.58 to 135.68 mm
X20 XEV .... 134.00 mm
Installation height of valve guide:
C20 XE .... 10.70 to 11.00 mm
X20 XEV .... 13.70 to 14.00 mm

Camshaft

Camshaft bearing journal diameter (all models)	27.939 to 27.960 mm
Camshaft bearing diameter in housing (all models)	28.000 to 28.021 mm

Cam lift:
C20 XE	9.5 mm
X20 XEV	10.0 mm

Maximum permissible radial run-out:
C20 XE	0.04 mm
X20 XEV	0.06 mm
Endfloat (all models)	0.040 to 0.144 mm

Valves and guides

	Inlet	Exhaust
Overall length - production (mm):		
C20 XE	105.0	105.0
X20 XEV	102.0	92.0
Overall length - service (mm):		
C20 XE	104.6	104.6
X20 XEV	101.7	91.8
Head diameter (mm):		
C20 XE	33.0 ± 0.1	29.0 ± 0.1
X20 XEV	32.0 ± 0.1	29.0 ± 0.1
Stem diameter (mm):		
C20 XE		
Standard	6.955 to 6.970	6.945 to 6.960
0.075 mm oversize	7.030 to 7.045	7.020 to 7.035
0.150 mm oversize	7.105 to 7.120	7.095 to 7.110
0.250 mm oversize	7.205 to 7.220	7.195 to 7.210
X20 XEV		
Standard	5.955 to 5.970	5.945 to 5.960
0.075 mm oversize	6.030 to 6.045	6.020 to 6.035
0.150 mm oversize	6.105 to 6.120	6.095 to 6.110
Valve guide bore (mm):		
C20 XE		
Standard	7.000 to 7.015	
0.075 mm oversize	7.075 to 7.090	
0.150 mm oversize	7.150 to 7.165	
0.250 mm oversize	7.400 to 7.415	
X20 XEV		
Standard	6.000 to 6.012	
0.075 mm oversize	6.075 to 6.090	
0.150 mm oversize	6.150 to 6.165	
Valve seat angle (all models)	44° 40'	

Lubrication system

Lubricant capacity	See Chapter 1 Specifications

Oil pressure at idle (engine warm):
C20 XE	2.5 bar
X20 XEV	1.5 bar

Torque wrench settings

Note: *Use new bolts (or nuts, if applicable), where asterisked (*).*

	Nm	lbf ft
Alternator to cylinder block bracket	35	26
Brake servo line to inlet manifold	20	15
Camshaft bearing cap to cylinder head (M6)	10	7
Camshaft bearing cap to cylinder head (M8)	20	15
Camshaft bearing cap to head (X20 XEV)	8	6
Camshaft sprocket to camshaft:		
Stage 1	50	37
Stage 2	Angle tighten by 60°	
Stage 3	Angle tighten by 15°	
Coolant pipe to cylinder block	20	15
Cover to cylinder head (M6 bolts)	9	7
Cover to cylinder head (M8 nuts)	22	16
Cover to exhaust manifold (X20 XEV)	5	4
Crankshaft pulley to timing belt drive sprocket	20	15
Crankshaft pulse pick-up	6	4
Exhaust manifold to cylinder head *	22	16
Exhaust pipe to adapter	12	9
Inlet manifold support to cylinder block	25	18

Torque wrench settings (continued)

	Nm	lbf ft
Intermediate shaft bracket to cylinder block	55	41
Knock sensor to cylinder block	20	14
Oil cooler lines to adapter/oil cooler	30	22
Oil filter to oil pump	15	11
Oil dipstick flange to cylinder block	25	18
Oil pump safety valve	30	22
Oil pump, threaded adapter	23	17
Power steering pump to support	25	18
Spark plug lead cover to cylinder head cover:		
C20 XE	8	6
X20 XEV	6	4
Starter to cylinder block	45	33
Starter support to cylinder block	25	18
Temperature regulator plug (M20) *	30	22
Timing belt cover	8	6
Timing belt drive sprocket to crankshaft: *		
Stage 1	250	184
Stage 2	Angle tighten by between 40° and 50°	
Timing belt guide roller bracket to block	25	18
Timing belt guide roller to bracket	25	18
Timing belt guide roller to cylinder block		
Engines up to 1993:		
Stage 1	25	18
Stage 2	Angle tighten by 45°	
Stage 3	Angle tighten by 15°	
1993-on engines	25	18
Timing belt tensioner pulley securing bolt	20	15
Transfer box bracket to cylinder block	60	44
Transmission to cylinder block	60	44

1 General description

This part of Chapter 2 describes procedures that are specific to the DOHC engine. It should be read in conjunction with Part A.

The lower engine is basically the same as the 2.0 litre SOHC. However the pistons are attached to the connecting rods by gudgeon pins, which are fully floating, and are secured by circlips.

Both camshafts on these engines are driven from the crankshaft by one toothed composite rubber belt. Each cylinder has four valves (two inlet and two exhaust), operated directly from the camshafts by hydraulic self-adjusting valve lifters. One camshaft operates the inlet valves, and the other operates the exhaust valves.

The following variations exist on the upper engine:

a) *On C20 XE models, up to 1993, a Hall-effect distributor is driven by the exhaust camshaft, at the transmission end of the engine.*

b) *On C20 XE models, from 1993 onwards, a camshaft phase sensor is mounted on the exhaust camshaft, in the position previously occupied by the distributor. The spark is provided by a direct ignition system.*

c) *On X20 XEV models a camshaft phase sensor is mounted at the timing belt end of the engine, so that it picks up a signal from the exhaust side camshaft sprocket. The spark is provided by a direct ignition system.*

All C20 XE models are fitted with a remotely mounted oil cooler.

Some DOHC models are fitted with an engine undershield which needs to be removed to carry out repairs underneath the vehicle. There may be a small panel which can be removed to expose the sump bolt, for changing oil, and a large panel under everything else.

2 Engine - removal and refitting

Removal

1 Carry out procedure in Chapter 2A, noting the following differences.

2 With the car safely raised, remove the engine undershield, if there is one.

3 The fuel hoses need to be disconnected from the fuel rail.

4 Disconnect the coolant hoses from the cylinder block and cylinder head. Also disconnect the oil cooler pipe unions from the oil pump.

5 Unbolt the right-hand driveshaft centre bearing support bracket from the rear of the cylinder block.

Refitting

6 Refitting the engine is similar to the procedure in Chapter 2A. The exceptions being, replacement of the right-hand driveshaft centre bearing support bracket at the rear of the cylinder block and retightening the securing bolts.

7 Replace the undershield, if there is one.

3 Engine/transmission mountings - renewal

The procedure for replacing the engine/transmission mountings is similar to SOHC models, see Chapter 2A. However, some engines are fitted with an undershield that needs to be removed before replacing the mountings.

Note: *Do not forget to replace the undershield before lowering the car.*

4 Timing belt, sprockets, belt tensioner and idler pulleys - removal, refitting and adjustment

Note: *The timing belt should be renewed on refitting. A two-legged puller may be required to remove the crankshaft sprocket.*

Removal

1 Disconnect the battery negative lead.

2B

4.5a Camshaft sprocket TDC mark aligned with notch in camshaft cover

4.5b ... and notch in crankshaft pulley aligned with pointer on rear timing belt cover (circled)

2 Disconnect the air cleaner trunking from the airflow meter, then remove the cover and the air cleaner element from the air cleaner. If desired, for improved access, the complete air cleaner assembly can be removed, as described in Chapter 4A.

3 Remove the auxiliary drivebelts as described in Chapter 5. There may be twin V-belts driving the alternator and power steering pump, or a single serpentine belt which will also drive the air conditioning pump, if fitted.

4 Remove the three securing screws, and withdraw the outer timing belt cover. Recover the rubber grommets from the screw holes in the cover if they are loose.

5 Turn the crankshaft using a Torx socket on the crankshaft sprocket bolt, until the timing marks on the camshaft sprockets are aligned with the notches in the camshaft cover. The notch in the crankshaft pulley should also be aligned with the pointer on the rear timing belt cover **(see illustrations)**.

6 Extract the six securing bolts using a splined bit, and withdraw the crankshaft pulley **(see illustration)**. If necessary, counterhold the crankshaft using a socket on the crankshaft sprocket bolt. If the engine is in the vehicle, the crankshaft can be prevented from turning by having an assistant engage first gear and depress the brake pedal.

Alternatively, the flywheel ring gear teeth can be jammed using a large screwdriver or similar tool. Before removing the pulley, check that the timing marks are still aligned.

7 Loosen the securing bolt and release the timing belt tensioner pulley, then slide the belt from the sprockets and pulleys **(see illustration)**.

8 If desired, the sprockets, tensioner and idler pulleys, and the rear timing belt cover can be removed as follows, otherwise go on to paragraph 26.

9 To remove the camshaft sprockets, first disconnect the breather hoses from the camshaft cover **(see illustration)**.

10 Extract the two securing bolts and remove the spark plug cover **(see illustration)**, then disconnect the HT leads from the spark plugs, and unclip them from the end of the camshaft cover. If necessary, mark the HT leads for position, to avoid confusion when refitting.

11 Unscrew the twenty securing bolts and withdraw the camshaft cover **(see illustration)**.

12 Recover the one-piece rubber gasket **(see illustration)**.

13 Prevent the relevant camshaft from turning by holding it with a spanner on the flats provided in front of No 1 cam lobe, and unscrew the camshaft sprocket bolt **(see illustration)**.

4.6 Crankshaft pulley and securing bolts viewed through right-hand wheel arch

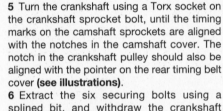

4.7 Timing belt tensioner pulley securing bolt (arrowed)

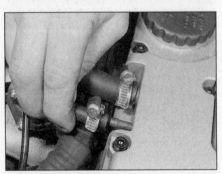

4.9 Disconnecting a breather hose from the rear of the camshaft cover

4.10 Removing the spark plug cover

4.11 Unscrewing a camshaft cover securing bolt

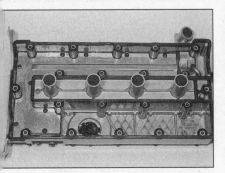

4.12 Camshaft cover removed to show one-piece rubber gasket

4.13 Spanner positioned to counterhold exhaust camshaft

14 Withdraw the sprocket from the end of the camshaft, then repeat the procedure for the remaining camshaft sprocket.

15 Remove the crankshaft sprocket. It will be necessary to prevent the crankshaft from turning by bolting a metal bar to the sprocket using two of the crankshaft pulley bolts, or by jamming the flywheel ring gear teeth. A Torx socket will be required to unscrew the sprocket bolt - take care, as the bolt is very tight. If necessary, use a two-legged puller to remove the sprocket. Recover the thrustwashers from the end of the crankshaft, and from under the bolt head.

16 To remove the belt tensioner pulley, simply unscrew the securing bolt from the

centre of the pulley, then withdraw the pulley complete with mounting plate **(see illustration)**. Recover the spacer sleeve from the pulley bolt.

17 To remove the belt idler pulley, unscrew the securing bolt from the centre of the pulley, then withdraw the pulley and recover the spacer sleeve from the pulley bolt.

18 The rear timing belt cover can now be removed after unscrewing the upper and middle studs for the timing belt outer cover screws. Note that the upper stud simply unscrews from the cylinder head, but the middle stud is secured by a bolt. Unscrew the two upper and single lower right-hand rear

belt cover securing bolts, and withdraw the rear belt cover **(see illustrations)**.

Refitting

19 Refit the rear timing belt cover using a reversal of the removal procedure.

20 Refit the belt idler and tensioner pulleys, noting that the spacer sleeves should be fitted with their smaller diameters against the pulleys **(see illustration)**. **Do not** fully tighten the tensioner pulley bolt at this stage.

21 Refit the thrustwasher to the end of the crankshaft, then refit the crankshaft sprocket. Apply a little grease to the threads of the securing bolt, and tighten it to the specified torque in the two stages given in the Specifications. Ensure that the thrustwasher is in place under the bolt head, and prevent the crankshaft from turning as during removal.

22 Refit the camshaft sprockets. Ensure that the locating pins on the ends of the camshafts engage with the holes in the sprockets and with the sprocket timing marks facing forwards. Then tighten the securing bolts to the specified torque in the three stages given in the Specifications. Prevent the camshafts from turning, same as during removal.

23 Check the condition of the camshaft cover rubber gasket and renew if necessary, then refit the camshaft cover and tighten the securing bolts **(see illustration)**.

2B

4.16 Timing belt tensioner pulley securing bolt (1), tensioner pulley mounting plate (2), and idler pulley securing bolt (3)

4.18a Timing belt outer cover screw upper stud (1) and rear belt cover upper securing bolts (2)

4.18b Rear timing belt cover lower right-hand securing bolt

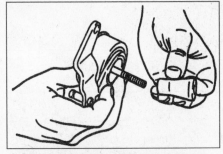

4.20 Belt tensioner pulley and spacer sleeve. Note that smaller diameter of spacer sleeve fits against pulley

4.23 Tightening a camshaft cover securing bolt

24 Refit the HT leads to the spark plugs (ensuring that they are refitted to their correct cylinders), then clip the leads to the end of the camshaft cover. Refit the spark plug cover and tighten the securing bolts.

25 Reconnect the breather hose to the camshaft cover.

26 Temporarily refit the crankshaft pulley, and ensure that the crankshaft pulley and camshaft sprocket timing marks are still aligned as described in paragraph 5. Then fit a new timing belt around the sprockets and pulleys, starting at the crankshaft sprocket.

27 Refit the crankshaft pulley, and tighten the securing bolts to the specified torque. If necessary, prevent the crankshaft from turning as during removal.

28 Adjust the timing belt tension, as described from paragraph 33 onwards.

29 Refit the outer timing belt cover, ensuring that the rubber grommets are in place in the screw holes, and tighten the securing screws.

30 Refit the auxiliary drivebelt(s), as described in Chapter 5. In the case of V-belts, tension them as described in Chapter 1.

31 Refit the air cleaner components as applicable, referring to Chapter 4A, if necessary.

32 Reconnect the battery negative lead.

Adjustment

Note: *The manufacturers specify the use of special adjustment wrench Vauxhall tool No KM-666 for adjusting the timing belt tension. If access to this tool cannot be obtained an approximate adjustment can be achieved using the method described in this Section. However it is emphasised that the vehicle should be taken to a dealer at the earliest possible opportunity to have the tension adjusted using the special tool.* **Do not** *drive the vehicle over any long distance until the belt tension has been adjusted by a dealer.*

Approximate adjustment

33 No checking of timing belt adjustment is specified, and the following adjustment

procedure applies to a newly fitted belt. The adjustment must be carried out with the engine cold.

34 With the timing belt cover removed and the tensioner pulley bolt slackened, ensure that the TDC marks on the camshaft sprockets and the crankshaft pulley are aligned as described in paragraph 5. If necessary, turn the crankshaft to achieve alignment.

35 Have an assistant press the tensioner pulley against the belt until the belt can just be twisted through 45°, using moderate pressure with the thumb and forefinger, on the longest belt run between the exhaust camshaft sprocket and the belt idler pulley.

36 Have the assistant hold the tensioner pulley in position, and tighten the tensioner pulley bolt to the specified torque as given in the Specifications.

37 Turn the crankshaft clockwise through two complete revolutions, and check that, with the crankshaft pulley TDC mark aligned with the pointer on the rear timing belt cover, the TDC marks on the camshaft sprockets are still aligned with the notches in the camshaft cover.

38 Proceed as described in paragraphs 29 to 32, inclusive.

39 Have the belt tension adjusted by a Vauxhall dealer using the manufacturer's special tool at the earliest opportunity.

Adjustment using Vauxhall special tool (KM-666)

40 Proceed as described in paragraphs 33 and 34.

41 Fit the special tool KM-666 to the belt tensioner pulley mounting plate, in accordance with the tool manufacturer's instructions.

42 Working anti-clockwise from the TDC mark on the exhaust camshaft sprocket, mark the eighth tooth on the sprocket **(see illustration)**.

43 Turn the crankshaft clockwise until this tooth is aligned with the TDC notch in the camshaft cover. The crankshaft must be

turned evenly and without jerking, to prevent the timing belt from jumping off the sprockets and pulleys.

44 Tighten the tensioner pulley bolt to the specified torque.

45 Remove the special tool.

46 Turn the crankshaft clockwise until the TDC marks on the camshaft sprockets are aligned with the notches in the camshaft cover, and check that the crankshaft pulley TDC mark is aligned with the pointer on the rear timing belt cover.

47 Proceed as described in paragraphs 29 to 32 inclusive.

---

5 Timing belt with automatic adjuster - removal, refitting and adjustment

Removal

1 The operations are essentially the same as described in Section 4, except that the tensioner pulley incorporates an automatic adjuster that simplifies the procedure as follows.

2 To release the belt tension before removal, unscrew the timing belt tensioner pulley securing bolt slightly, then with a large screwdriver (or similar tool) inserted in the slot on the tensioner arm, turn the tensioner arm until the timing belt is slack. Tighten the securing bolt slightly to hold the tensioner in this position.

Refitting

3 Before fitting the timing belt, carefully check the tensioner/idler pulleys for any signs of damage, and particularly for any signs of cracking. It may be prudent to replace these components as a matter of course, regardless of their apparent condition, to avoid any future problems.

4 To refit the timing belt, first ensure that the coolant pump is correctly positioned by checking that the lug on the coolant pump flange is aligned with the corresponding lug on the cylinder block. If this is not the case, slacken the coolant pump mounting bolts slightly and move the pump accordingly. Tighten the bolts to the specified torque on completion (see Chapter 3).

5 Refit the timing belt as described in Section 4, then tension it as follows.

Adjustment

6 Slacken the tensioner pulley securing bolt and move the tensioner arm anti-clockwise, until the tensioner pointer lies at its stop. Tighten the tensioner pulley securing bolt to hold the tensioner in this position.

7 Turn the crankshaft through two complete revolutions in the normal direction of rotation and check that with the crankshaft pulley TDC mark aligned with the pointer on the rear timing belt cover, the TDC marks on the camshaft sprockets are still aligned with the notches in the camshaft cover.

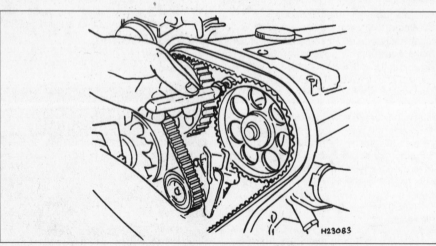

4.42 Working anti-clockwise from the TDC mark on the exhaust camshaft sprocket, mark the eighth tooth on the sprocket

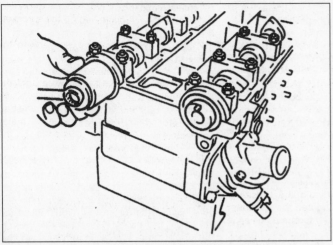

6.5 Using the camshaft sprocket bolt, washer and a tube to fit a new camshaft front oil seal

7.3 Camshaft bearing cap. Note position of identification mark (arrowed)

8 Slacken the tensioner pulley securing bolt once again and move the tensioner arm clockwise, until the tensioner pointer is aligned with the notch in the tensioner. In the first few hours of operation a new belt will be subjected to 'settling-in', (known as the running-in procedure). If you are refitting a used belt (one that has been 'run-in'), align the pointer to approximately 4 mm to the left of the notch, refer to Section 12 in Chapter 2A. Tighten the tensioner pulley securing bolt to the specified torque. Turn the crankshaft through one complete revolution in the normal direction of rotation and check that the crankshaft and camshaft timing marks still align, then refit the remainder of the components as described in Section 4.

9 With the timing belt adjustment set in this way, correct tension will always be maintained by the automatic tensioner and no further checking or adjustment will be necessary.

6 Camshaft front oil seal - removal and refitting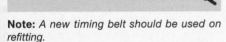

Note: A new timing belt should be used on refitting.

Removal

1 The camshaft front oil seals may be renewed with the engine in the vehicle without removing the camshafts as follows.

2 Remove the timing belt and the relevant camshaft sprocket(s), as described in Section 4.

3 Punch or drill a small hole in the centre of the now-exposed oil seal. Screw in a self-tapping screw, and pull on the screw with pliers to extract the seal.

4 Clean the oil seal seat with a wooden or plastic scraper.

5 Lubricate the lips of a new camshaft front oil seal with a little grease, and fit the oil seal, using a tube or socket of similar diameter with a washer and the camshaft sprocket bolt.

Screw the camshaft sprocket bolt into the end of the camshaft to draw the oil seal into position on its shoulder (**see illustration**).

6 Where applicable, repeat the procedure on the remaining camshaft oil seal.

Refitting

7 Refit the camshaft sprockets, the timing belt and tension the timing belt as described in Sections 4 and 5.

7 Camshafts - removal, inspection and refitting

Note: A new timing belt should be used on refitting.

Removal

1 Remove the timing belt and the relevant camshaft sprockets, as described in Section 4.

2 If the exhaust camshaft is to be removed from C20 XE engines, remove the distributor or camshaft phase sensor from the end of the cylinder head, referring to Chapter 5.

3 Check the camshaft bearing caps for identification marks, and if none are present, make corresponding marks on the bearing caps and the top surface of the cylinder head using a centre punch. Note the orientation of the bearing caps before removal, as they must be refitted in exactly the same positions from which they are removed (**see illustration**).

4 Loosen the relevant camshaft bearing cap nuts by half a turn, then loosen all the nuts by a further half turn and so on (this is necessary to slowly relieve the tension in the valve springs). Note that the exhaust camshaft rear bearing cap that also supports the distributor (if fitted) is secured by four nuts (**see illustration**).

5 Remove the bearing cap nuts and the bearing caps, then carefully lift the relevant camshaft from the cylinder head without jerking.

6 Repeat the procedure for the remaining camshaft if desired.

Inspection

7 With the camshaft(s) removed, examine the bearing surfaces in the cylinder head and bearing caps for signs of obvious wear or pitting. If evident, the cylinder head and all bearing caps must be renewed as a matched set, as there is no provision for refacing if the bearing caps cannot be renewed individually.

8 The camshaft(s) should show no marks or scoring on the journal or cam lobe surfaces. If evident, renew the camshaft(s).

9 It is advisable to renew the camshaft front oil seal(s) as a matter of course. Prise the old seal(s) from the front of the camshaft(s) and discard them.

Refitting

10 Begin refitting by liberally coating the contact faces of the hydraulic valve lifters and the camshaft(s) with molybdenum disulphide paste.

11 Coat the mating faces of the front and rear bearing caps with sealing compound and refit the bearing caps in their original positions as noted during removal.

12 Tighten the camshaft bearing cap nuts to the specified torque in half-turn stages, as when

7.4 Exhaust camshaft rear bearing cap securing nuts (arrowed)

2B

loosening the nuts. Note that when refitting the exhaust camshaft, the two smaller rear bearing cap securing nuts should be tightened after all the main camshaft bearing cap nuts have been tightened. Note also that the two smaller nuts should be tightened to a lower torque wrench setting than the main nuts.

13 Turn the camshaft until the locating peg for the camshaft sprocket is uppermost, then lubricate the lips of a rear camshaft front oil seal with a little grease, and fit the oil seal, using a tube or socket of similar diameter with a washer and the camshaft sprocket bolt. Screw the camshaft sprocket bolt into the end of the camshaft to draw the oil seal into position on its shoulder.

14 Repeat the procedure for the remaining camshaft.

15 On C20 XE models, refit the distributor or camshaft phase sensor, with reference to Chapter 5.

16 Fit a new timing belt and the camshaft sprockets, then adjust the timing belt as described in Section 4 or 5, as applicable.

8 Cylinder head - removal and refitting (engine in vehicle)

Note 1: *The engine must be cold when the cylinder head is removed.* **Do not** *remove the cylinder head from a hot engine. New cylinder head bolts, a new cylinder head gasket and a new timing belt must be used on refitting.*

Note 2: *The torque settings (as shown in Chapter 2A) are only applicable to latest specification head bolts, available from Vauxhall. Earlier type or alternative make, head bolts may require different torques. Consult your supplier.*

Removal

1 Disconnect the battery negative lead.
2 Drain the cooling system, as described in Chapter 3.

3 Remove the front section of the exhaust system, as described in Chapter 4B.
4 The cylinder head can be removed complete with the inlet manifold, or the inlet manifold can be detached from the cylinder head before removal, with reference to Chapter 4A. If no work is to be carried out on the inlet manifold, it can be unbolted from the cylinder head and supported to one side out of the way, thus avoiding the need to disconnect the relevant hoses, pipes and wiring.
5 If the cylinder head is to be removed complete with the inlet manifold, disconnect all relevant hoses, pipes and wiring from the inlet manifold and associated components, referring to Chapter 4A, and unbolt the manifold support bracket from the manifold. Loosen the alternator mountings with reference to Chapter 5, then unbolt the upper alternator mounting from the inlet manifold.
6 If the inlet manifold is to be left in the engine compartment, continue as follows, otherwise go on to paragraph 17.
7 Disconnect the wiring plug from the airflow meter, and the breather hose from the air box on the throttle body. Disconnect the air cleaner trunking and remove the airflow meter/air box assembly from the throttle body. Refer to Chapter 4A if necessary.
8 Disconnect the end of the throttle cable from the throttle valve lever, then unbolt the throttle cable support bracket and remove it from the inlet manifold.
9 Unscrew the two earth lead securing nuts from the fuel rail (one at each end of the rail) and disconnect the three earth leads.
10 Disconnect the wiring plug from the throttle position switch.
11 Pull up on the wiring harness housing, and disconnect the wiring plugs from the fuel injectors by compressing the retaining clips. Move the wiring harness housing to one side.
12 Disconnect the two breather hoses from the rear of the camshaft cover.
13 Loosen the alternator mountings, with reference to Chapter 5, then unbolt the upper

alternator mounting from the inlet manifold.
14 Unbolt the manifold support bracket from the manifold.
15 Make a final check to ensure that all necessary hoses, pipes and wires have been disconnected, then unscrew the securing nuts and lift the inlet manifold from the cylinder head. Ensure that the manifold is properly supported, taking care not to strain any of the hoses, pipes and wires, etc., which are still connected.
16 Recover the manifold gasket from the cylinder head.
17 Remove the timing belt, camshaft sprockets, and timing belt tensioner and idler pulleys, as described in Section 4.
18 Unscrew the upper and middle studs for the timing belt outer cover screws. Note that the upper stud simply unscrews from the cylinder head, but the middle stud is secured by a bolt.
19 Unscrew the two upper rear timing belt cover securing bolts from the cylinder head.
20 Remove the distributor cap or DIS unit, and the HT leads, with reference to Chapter 5.
21 Disconnect the distributor wiring plug, if applicable.
22 Disconnect the coolant hose from the left-hand end of the cylinder head.
23 Unscrew the bolt securing the crankcase breather tube bracket to the end of the cylinder head.
24 Disconnect the radiator top hose from the thermostat housing, and disconnect the wiring plugs from the temperature gauge sender and the coolant temperature sensor (both situated in the thermostat housing).
25 Make a final check to ensure that all relevant hoses, pipes and wires have been disconnected.
26 On X20 XEV models, remove the camshaft, as described in Section 7.
27 Using a Torx socket, and working in the order shown **(see illustrations)**, loosen all the cylinder head bolts by a quarter of a turn, then loosen all the bolts by half a turn, and finally

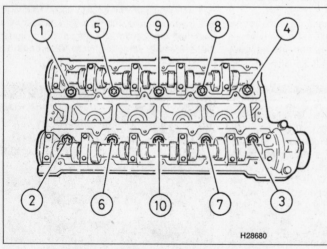

8.27a Cylinder head bolt loosening sequence - C20 XE engines

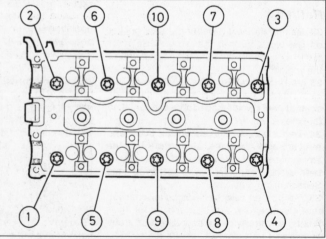

8.27b Cylinder head bolt loosening sequence - X20 XEV engines

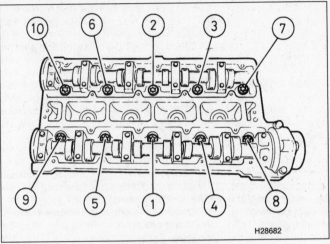

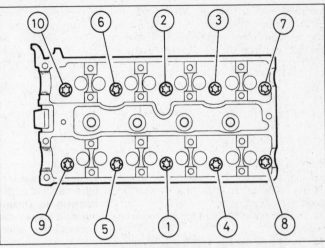

8.36a Cylinder head bolt tightening sequence - C20 XE engines

8.36b Cylinder head bolt tightening sequence - X20 XEV engines

loosen and remove the bolts. Recover the washers. Note that the loosening sequence on X20 XEV differs to other DOHC engines.

28 Lift the cylinder head from the cylinder block. If necessary, tap the cylinder head gently with a soft-faced mallet to free it from the block, but do not lever at the mating faces. Note that the cylinder head is located on dowels.

29 Recover the cylinder head gasket and discard it.

30 Clean the cylinder head and block mating faces by careful scraping. Take care not to damage the cylinder head, which is made of light alloy and is easily scored. Cover the coolant passages and other openings with masking tape or rag, to prevent dirt and carbon falling in. Mop out all the oil from the bolt holes; if oil is left in the holes, hydraulic pressure could crack the block when the bolts are refitted.

31 If desired, the cylinder head can be dismantled and inspected as described in Section 10.

Refitting

32 Begin refitting by locating a new gasket on the block so that the word "OBEN" or "TOP" is uppermost at the timing belt end of the engine.

33 With the mating faces scrupulously clean, locate the cylinder head on the block so that the positioning dowels engage in their holes.

34 Temporarily refit the crankshaft pulley and the camshaft sprockets, and ensure that the timing marks are still positioned as they were before the timing belt was removed (see Section 4).

35 Fit the new cylinder head bolts, ensuring that the washers are in place under their heads, and screw the bolts in by hand as far as possible.

36 Tighten the bolts in the order shown and in the four stages given in the Specification

(see Chapter 2A) - i.e. tighten all bolts to the Stage 1 torque, then tighten all bolts to Stage 2 and so on **(see illustrations)**.

37 Further refitting is a reversal of the removal procedure, remembering the following points.

38 Refit the timing belt tensioner and idler pulleys, camshaft sprockets and a new timing belt as described in Section 4, and tension the timing belt as described in Sections 4 and 5.

39 Where applicable, refit the inlet manifold to the cylinder head with reference to Chapter 4A, using a new gasket.

40 Refit the front section of the exhaust system as described in Chapter 4B, using a new gasket.

41 Refit the upper alternator mounting to the inlet manifold (where applicable), then adjust the alternator drivebelt tension, as described in Chapter 5.

42 Refill the cooling system (Chapter 3).

43 On completion, check that all relevant hoses, pipes and wires, etc., have been reconnected.

44 When the engine is started, check for signs of leaks.

45 Once the engine has reached normal operating temperature, check and if necessary adjust the mixture (where applicable) with reference to Chapter 4A.

9 Cylinder head - removal and refitting (engine removed)

Note: *New cylinder head bolts, a new cylinder head gasket, and a new timing belt must be used on refitting. The torque settings (as shown in Chapter 2A) are only applicable to latest specification head bolts, available from Vauxhall. Earlier type or alternative make, head bolts may require different torques. Consult your supplier.*

⚠️ **Warning: The exhaust valves fitted to C20 XE models are fitted with sodium to improve their heat transfer. Sodium is a highly reactive metal, which will ignite or explode spontaneously on contact with water (including water vapour in the air). These must NOT be disposed of with ordinary scrap. Seek advice from a Vauxhall dealer or your Local Authority, if the valves are to be disposed.**

Removal

1 The cylinder head can be removed complete with the inlet manifold, or the inlet manifold can be detached from the cylinder head before removal, with reference to Chapter 4A.

8.36c Tighten the cylinder head bolts to the specified torque . . .

8.36d . . . and then through the specified angle

2B

2 Proceed as described in Section 8, paragraphs 17 to 19 inclusive.

3 If not already done, remove the distributor cap or DIS unit, and the HT leads, referring to Chapter 5.

4 Unscrew the bolt securing the crankcase breather tube bracket to the end of the cylinder head.

5 Make a final check to ensure that all relevant hoses, pipes and wires have been disconnected.

6 Continue as described in Section 8, paragraphs 26 to 31.

Refitting

7 Proceed as described in Section 8, paragraphs 32 to 38 inclusive.

8 On completion, check that all relevant hoses, pipes and wires, etc., have been reconnected.

10 Cylinder head -
dismantling and reassembly

Dismantling

1 With the cylinder head removed as described in Section 8, clean away all external dirt.

2 If not already done, remove the thermostat housing and thermostat as described in Chapter 3, and remove the manifolds as described in Chapters 4A and 4B.

3 Remove the spark plugs (if not already done) (see Chapter 1) and remove the distributor or DIS unit, with reference to Chapter 5.

4 Remove the camshafts as described in Section 7.

5 Remove the hydraulic valve lifters from their bores using a rubber suction plunger tool - do not invert the cylinder head to remove the valve lifters. Keep the valve lifters upright at all times (oil groove at bottom) **(see illustration)**, and immerse them in order of removal in a container of clean engine oil until they are to be refitted.

6 To remove the valve components, continue as described in Chapter 2A, Section 20, paragraphs 3 to 7 inclusive.

7 The cylinder head and valves can be inspected for wear and damage as described in Chapter 2A, Section 21.

Reassembly

8 With all components cleaned, refit the valve components as described in Chapter 2A, Section 20, paragraphs 10 to 19 inclusive.

9 Refit the hydraulic valve lifters to the cylinder head in their original positions. Liberally oil the valve lifter bores, and if new lifters are being fitted, initially immerse each one in a container of clean engine oil and compress it (by hand) several times to charge it.

10 Refit the camshafts, as described in Section 7.

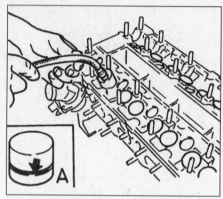

10.5 Remove the hydraulic valve lifters using a rubber plunger. Inset (A) shows valve lifter upright, with oil groove (arrowed) at bottom

11 Refit the spark plugs if desired, and refit the distributor or DIS unit, with reference to Chapters 1 and 5.

12 Where applicable, refit the manifolds and/or the thermostat and housing.

13 Refit the cylinder head, as described in Sections 8 and 9, as applicable.

11 Valve lifters -
general

Although the valve lifters on these engines cannot be dismantled they should be carefully inspected for obvious signs of wear on the contact faces. Also check the valve lifter oil holes for obstructions and for any signs of oil sludge build-up. If excessive wear is evident (this is unlikely), all the valve lifters must be renewed as a set.

12 Crankshaft front oil seal -
renewal

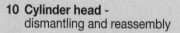

1 The procedure is similar to SOHC models (see Chapter 2A), noting the following points.

2 The spacer ring (if fitted), from the end of the crankshaft, must be removed before refitting.

13.1 Single-pan aluminium alloy sump - C20 XE engines

3 After fitting the new seal, coat the oil pump mating face of the spacer ring with sealing compound, then push the spacer ring onto the end of the crankshaft, until it is seated against the oil pump.

4 The timing belt should be renewed.

5 Refit the rear timing belt cover and the timing belt, as described in Section 4. Adjust it as described in Sections 4 and 5.

13 Sump -
removal and refitting

Note: *Sump gaskets cannot be reused. Ensure that new gaskets are obtained before removing the sump.*

C20 XE engines

Removal

1 The C20 XE engine has a single-pan aluminium alloy sump **(see illustration)**. The procedure for removal is similar to SOHC models (see Chapter 2A), with the following variations.

2 The engine undershield must be removed, if there is one.

3 Instead of having a single rubber gasket that fits around both faces of the sump baffle, there are two cork gaskets on either side of the baffle. Remove both the cork gaskets and clean all sealing surfaces, scrupulously.

Refitting

4 Locate a new gasket on the cylinder block, if necessary applying a little sealing compound to hold it in place.

5 Locate the second new gasket on the sump baffle, but do not use sealing compound.

X20 XEV engines

Note: *The sump gasket(s) must be renewed on refitting and sealer will be required for use on the oil pump and rear main bearing cap-to-cylinder block joints.*

Removal

6 The X20 XEV engine has a dual-pan sump with a steel pan underneath an aluminium alloy pan. If the engine is in the vehicle, continue as follows, otherwise go to paragraph 13.

7 Disconnect the battery negative lead.

8 Remove the engine undershield, if there is one.

9 Drain the engine oil, referring to Chapter 1 if necessary, then refit and tighten the drain plug.

10 Apply the handbrake, then jack up the front of the vehicle, and support securely on axle stands (see *"Jacking and Vehicle Support"*).

11 Remove the front section of the exhaust system, as described in Chapter 4B, or the whole exhaust if it is more convenient.

12 Disconnect the wiring from the oil level multi-plug.

13.13 Lower steel sump pan -
X20 XEV engines

13.15 Upper aluminium alloy sump pan
connected to transmission bellhousing -
X20 XEV engines

14.2 Oil cooler pipe unions at oil pump

13 Undo the Torx bolts and remove the lower steel pan (see illustration).

14 Remove the oil pick-up pipe, depending on how the bolts become accessible. If necessary, remove the pipe after the upper sump pan and baffle have been removed.

15 Undo the bolts securing the upper sump pan to the bellhousing (see illustration).

16 Undo the 15 Torx bolts securing the upper sump pan to the engine block and remove both the sump pan and baffle plate. If necessary, undo the remaining bolts on the oil pick-up pipe and remove it with the baffle plate. Recover the O-ring when disconnecting the end of the pipe from the oil pump.

17 Remove and discard all the gaskets from the mating faces between the cylinder block, baffle plate and the upper and lower pans. There may be a single rubber gasket that fits round both sides of the baffle plate, or there may be a cork gasket on either side. Clean all traces of the old gaskets and sealing compound from the mating faces.

Refitting

18 Refitting is the reverse of removal, noting the following points.

19 Use sealing compound (Vauxhall part No 90485251 or equivalent) on the joints between the oil pump and cylinder block, and the rear main bearing cap and cylinder block, same as in Chapter 2A.

20 Use new gaskets on all the mating faces between the cylinder block, baffle, and the upper and lower sump pans. If a rubber gasket is used on the sump baffle, making sure the new one is seated correctly. If cork gaskets are used, fit a new one to the cylinder block, if necessary applying a little sealing

compound to hold it in place, and fit the other new gasket to the sump baffle, but do not use sealing compound.

21 If the oil pick-up pipe has been removed, refit it to the oil pump using a new O-ring and tighten the bolts to the specified torque (see Chapter 2A).

22 Use thread-locking compound (i.e. Vauxhall part No. 90167347) on the bolts connecting the upper pan to the engine block and the lower pan to the upper pan.

14 Oil pump -
removal and refitting

Removal

1 Apart from the following variations, the procedure is the same as for SOHC models.

2 If the engine is still in the vehicle, disconnect the oil cooler pipe unions from the oil pump, and move the pipes to one side out of the way (see illustration).

3 Remove the spacer ring from the end of the crankshaft (see illustration).

Refitting

4 Coat the oil pump mating face of the spacer ring with sealing compound, then push the spacer ring onto the end of the crankshaft until it is seated against the oil pump.

14.3 Oil pump securing bolts (arrowed)
and crankshaft spacer ring (A)

5 The timing belt should be renewed (see Sections 4 and 5, for details).

6 Remember also to reconnect the oil cooler pipes to the oil pump and to tighten the unions.

15 Oil cooler -
removal and refitting

Removal

1 To gain sufficient access to remove the oil cooler, the radiator must be removed (as described in Chapter 3). Alternatively, the front bumper can be removed, as described in Chapter 11 (see illustration).

2 With the appropriate component(s) removed for access, unscrew the oil cooler pipe unions from the oil cooler. Be prepared for oil spillage, and plug the open ends of the pipes, to prevent further oil leakage and dirt ingress.

3 Unscrew the two securing nuts, and withdraw the oil cooler from its mounting brackets.

Refitting

4 Refitting is a reversal of removal, but on completion, check and if necessary top-up the engine oil level, as described in "Weekly checks".

15.1 Oil cooler viewed through front
spoiler. Securing nuts arrowed

2B

Chapter 3
Cooling, heating and ventilation systems

Contents

Degrees of difficulty

| **Easy,** suitable for novice with little experience | | **Fairly easy,** suitable for beginner with some experience | | **Fairly difficult,** suitable for competent DIY mechanic | | **Difficult,** suitable for experienced DIY mechanic | | **Very difficult,** suitable for expert DIY or professional | |

3

Specifications

System type . . . .   Pressurised, with remote expansion tank. Coolant pump driven by timing belt

Coolant
Type/specification (all models) . . . .   See "*Lubricants and fluids*"
Capacity . . . .   See Chapter 1 Specifications

Thermostat
Starts to open at (all models) . . . .   92°C
Fully open at (all models) . . . .   107°C
Operating temperature (approx.) . . . .   80°C

Expansion tank cap
Opening pressure (all models) . . . .   1.20 to 1.35 bar
Boiling point . . . .   125°C

Cooling fan switch
Switches on at (all models) . . . .   100°C
Switches off at (all models) . . . .   95°C

Torque wrench settings	**Nm**	**lbf ft**
Coolant pump bolts (M8)	25	18
Oil pipes to radiator	22	16
Outlet to thermostat housing	8	6
Temperature gauge sender	10	7
Thermostat housing to cylinder head	15	11

1 General description

HAYNES HINT *When renewing any hoses, use a little soapy water as a lubricant, or soften the hose in hot water. Do not use oil or grease, as this may attack the rubber.*

Engine cooling is achieved by a conventional pump-assisted system, in which the coolant is pressurised. The system consists of a radiator, a coolant pump driven by the engine timing belt, an electric cooling fan, a thermostat, an expansion tank, and connecting hoses. Hoses also carry coolant to and from the heater matrix, which provides heat for the ventilation and heating system.

The system works in the following way. Cold coolant from one side of the radiator, which is mounted at the front of the engine compartment, passes to the coolant pump, which forces the coolant through the coolant passages in the cylinder block and cylinder head. The coolant absorbs heat from the engine, and then returns to the radiator through the heater matrix. As the coolant flows across the radiator it is cooled, and the cycle is repeated.

Air flows through the radiator, to cool the coolant as a result of the vehicle's forward motion. However, if the coolant temperature exceeds a given figure, a temperature-sensitive switch in the radiator switches on the electric fan, to increase the airflow through the radiator. The fan only operates when necessary, with a consequent reduction in noise and energy consumption.

To reduce the time taken for the engine to warm up when starting from cold, the thermostat, located in the cylinder head outlet, prevents coolant flowing to the radiator until the temperature has risen sufficiently. Instead, the outflow from the cylinder head bypasses the radiator, and is redirected around the engine. When the temperature reaches a given figure, the thermostat opens, to allow coolant to flow to the radiator. The thermostat is operated by the expansion of a temperature sensitive wax capsule.

An expansion tank is incorporated in the system, to allow for coolant expansion. The system is topped up through a filler cap on the expansion tank.

Note that later models may be fitted with self-tensioning spring clamps to secure the cooling system (including heater) hoses. These clamps can be released by squeezing together their free ends using a large pair of self-grip pliers or similar so that the clamp can be moved up the hose, clear of the union. Check that the clamp is securely seated, and check for leaks on reassembly.

2 Cooling system - draining

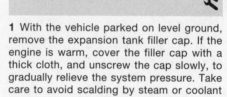

1 With the vehicle parked on level ground, remove the expansion tank filler cap. If the engine is warm, cover the filler cap with a thick cloth, and unscrew the cap slowly, to gradually relieve the system pressure. Take care to avoid scalding by steam or coolant escaping from the pressurised system.
2 On DOHC models, remove the engine undershield, with reference to Chapter 11.
3 Position a container beneath the radiator bottom hose connection, then slacken the hose clip and ease the hose from the radiator stub. If the hose joint has not been disturbed for some time, it will be necessary to manipulate the hose to break the joint. Allow the coolant to drain into the container.
4 As no cylinder block drain plug is fitted, and the radiator bottom hose may be situated halfway up the radiator, the system cannot be drained completely. Care should therefore be taken when refilling the system to maintain antifreeze strength.
5 If the coolant has been drained for a reason other than renewal, then provided it is clean and less than two years old, it can be re-used.
6 If the coolant has been drained for renewal, and is badly contaminated, the cooling system should be flushed as described in Section 3. As the system cannot be drained completely, it is advisable to flush the system whenever the coolant is renewed, to minimise the impurities remaining in the system.

3 Cooling system - flushing

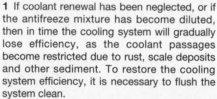

1 If coolant renewal has been neglected, or if the antifreeze mixture has become diluted, then in time the cooling system will gradually lose efficiency, as the coolant passages become restricted due to rust, scale deposits and other sediment. To restore the cooling system efficiency, it is necessary to flush the system clean.
2 The radiator should be flushed independently of the engine, to avoid unnecessary contamination.
3 To flush the radiator, disconnect the top hose at the radiator, then insert a garden hose into the radiator top inlet. Direct a flow of clean water through the radiator, and continue flushing until clean water emerges from the radiator bottom outlet (the bottom hose should have been disconnected to drain the system). If after a reasonable period, the water still does not run clear, the radiator can be flushed with a good proprietary cleaning agent. It is important that the manufacturer's instructions are followed carefully. If the contamination is particularly bad, insert the hose in the radiator bottom outlet, and flush the radiator in reverse.

4 To flush the engine, continue as follows.
5 Remove the thermostat and cover assembly, as described in Section 9.
6 With the radiator bottom hose disconnected from the radiator, insert a garden hose into the radiator bottom hose. Direct a flow of clean water through the engine, and continue flushing until clean water emerges from the thermostat housing. It is advisable to place a sheet of plastic under the thermostat housing to deflect water away from the engine and surrounding components during the flushing process.
7 On completion of flushing, refit the thermostat and cover assembly, reconnect the hoses and remove the sheet of plastic.

4 Cooling system - filling

1 Before attempting to fill the cooling system, make sure that all hoses and clips are in good condition, and that the clips are tight. Note that an antifreeze mixture must be used all year round, to prevent corrosion of the alloy engine components - refer to Section 5.
2 Remove the expansion tank cap, and fill the system by slowly pouring the coolant into the expansion tank to prevent air locks from forming.
3 If the coolant is being renewed, begin by pouring in a couple of pints of water, followed by the correct quantity of antifreeze (see Section 5), then top-up with more water.
4 Top-up the coolant level to the "COLD" (or "KALT") mark on the expansion tank, then refit the expansion tank cap.
5 Start the engine and run it until it reaches normal operating temperature, then stop the engine and allow it to cool.
6 Check for leaks, particularly around disturbed components. Check the coolant level in the expansion tank, and top-up if necessary. Note that the system must be cold before an accurate level is indicated in the expansion tank. If the expansion tank cap is removed while the engine is still warm, cover the cap with a thick cloth and unscrew the cap slowly, to gradually relieve the system pressure. Take care to avoid scalding by steam or coolant escaping from the pressurised system.
7 On DOHC models, refit the engine undershield on completion (see Chapter 11).

5 Coolant mixture - general

It is important to use an antifreeze mixture in the cooling system all year round, to prevent corrosion of the alloy engine components. The coolant mixture should be made up from clean, preferably soft, tap water, and a good quality antifreeze containing corrosion inhibitor. Ensure that the antifreeze is ethylene glycol based, as the cheaper methanol based types evaporate over a period of time.

The proportions of water and antifreeze used will depend on the degree of protection required. A coolant mixture containing 25% antifreeze should be regarded as the minimum strength required to maintain good anti-corrosion properties. Details of the degree of protection provided against freezing will be supplied with the antifreeze by the manufacturers. For absolute protection, use a 50% antifreeze mixture.

The coolant mixture should be renewed every two years, as the corrosion inhibitors will deteriorate with time.

Before filling the system with fresh coolant, drain and flush the system, as described in Sections 2 and 3, and check that all hoses are secure and that the clips are tight. Antifreeze has a searching action, and will leak more rapidly than plain water.

Refill the system as described in Section 4. All future topping-up should be carried out using a coolant mixture of the same proportions as that used to initially fill the system.

Caution: Do not use antifreeze in the windscreen wash system, as it will attack the vehicle paintwork.

![warning triangle] *Warning: Antifreeze is poisonous, and must be handled with due care.*

6 Radiator (manual transmission) - removal and refitting

Removal

1 The radiator can be removed complete with the coolant fan and shroud if there is no need to disturb the fan. If desired, the fan and its shroud can be removed from the radiator,

with reference to Section 12.
2 Drain the cooling system, as described in Section 2.
3 Disconnect the radiator top hose and the expansion tank hose at the radiator.
4 Disconnect the battery negative lead, then disconnect the wiring from the cooling fan switch, located at the bottom right-hand side of the radiator.
5 Disconnect the cooling fan wiring connector, noting its location for use when refitting.
6 Compress and remove the two radiator securing clips, located at the top corners of the radiator **(see illustration)**.
7 Pull the top of the radiator back towards the engine to free it from the top mountings, then lift the radiator to disengage the lower securing lugs. Move the radiator clear of the vehicle, taking care not to damage the cooling fins **(see illustration)**.

Refitting

8 The radiator can be inspected and cleaned as described in Section 8.
9 Refitting is a reversal of removal, bearing in mind the following points.
10 Ensure that the radiator rubber mountings are in good condition and renew if necessary, and ensure that the lower securing lugs engage correctly as the radiator is refitted.
11 Refill the cooling system (see Section 4).

7 Radiator (automatic transmission) - removal and refitting

Removal

1 On models with automatic transmission, the radiator left-hand side tank incorporates a heat exchanger to cool the transmission fluid. It is connected to the transmission by a pair of flexible hoses, with a metal pipe at each end.
2 When removing the radiator, either clamp

the transmission fluid cooler flexible hoses, or slacken their clamps, work them off their unions and swiftly plug or cap each hose end and union to minimise the loss of fluid and to prevent the entry of dirt.

Refitting

3 On refitting, reverse the removal procedure and do not forget to check the transmission fluid level, topping-up as necessary to replace the lost fluid, as described in Chapter 1.

8 Radiator - inspection and cleaning

1 If the radiator has been removed due to suspected blockage, reverse-flush it as described in Section 3.
2 Clean dirt and debris from the radiator fins, using an air jet or a soft brush. Take care, as the fins are easily damaged and are sharp.
3 If necessary, a radiator specialist can perform a "flow test" on the radiator, to establish whether an internal blockage exists.
4 A leaking radiator must be referred to a specialist for permanent repair. Do not attempt to weld or solder a leaking radiator, as damage to the plastic components may result.
5 In an emergency, minor leaks from the radiator can be cured by using a radiator sealant.

9 Thermostat - removal and refitting

Note 1: *A new O-ring should be used when refitting the thermostat.*
Note 2: *If it is necessary to renew the thermostat, the complete cover and thermostat must be renewed as an assembly, as the two cannot be separated.*

3

6.6 Compressing a radiator securing clip - SOHC model

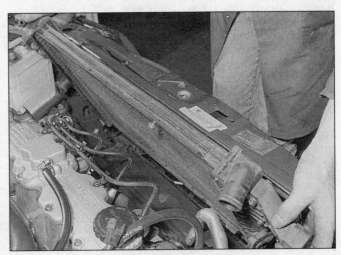

6.7 Withdrawing the radiator - SOHC model

9.3a Withdraw the thermostat cover complete with thermostat . . .

9.3b . . . and recover the O-ring - SOHC model

Removal

1 Remove the engine undershield, if fitted. Partially drain the cooling system, as described in Section 2.

2 Disconnect the radiator top hose from the thermostat cover.

3 Unscrew and remove the thermostat cover securing bolts, and withdraw the cover complete with the thermostat. Recover the O-ring **(see illustrations)**.

4 If desired, the thermostat can be tested, as described in Section 10.

Refitting

5 Refitting is a reversal of removal, but use a new O-ring, and on completion refill the cooling system, as described in Section 4.

11.4 Coolant pump securing bolt (arrowed) - SOHC model

10 Thermostat - testing

1 A rough test of the thermostat may be made by suspending it with a piece of string in a container full of water. Heat the water to bring it to the boil - the thermostat must open by the time the water boils. If not, renew it.

2 If a thermometer is available, the precise opening temperature of the thermostat may be determined, and compared with the figures given in the Specifications. The opening temperature is also marked on the thermostat.

3 A thermostat that fails to close as the water cools must also be renewed.

11 Coolant pump - removal and refitting

SOHC models

Removal

1 If the engine is in the vehicle, drain the cooling system as described in Section 2.

2 Remove the timing belt as described in Chapter 2A.

3 Remove the timing belt tension roller from the oil pump, where applicable.

4 Unscrew and remove the coolant pump securing bolts **(see illustration)**.

5 Withdraw the coolant pump from the cylinder block, and recover the O-ring **(see**

illustrations). It may be necessary to tap the pump lightly with a plastic-faced hammer to free it from the cylinder block.

6 If desired, the rear timing belt cover can be removed from the pump by rotating the cover to release it from the flange on the pump.

7 No overhaul of the coolant pump is possible, and if faulty, the unit must be renewed.

Refitting

8 Refitting is a reversal of removal, bearing in mind the following points.

9 Use a new O-ring when refitting the pump. Before refitting the pump, smear the pump mounting face in the cylinder block and the O-ring with a silicone grease or petroleum jelly.

10 Do not fully tighten the pump securing bolts until the timing belt has been fitted and tensioned.

11 Refit and tension the timing belt, as described in Chapter 2A.

12 If the engine is in the vehicle, refill the cooling system, as described in Section 4.

DOHC models

Removal

13 Remove the engine undershield (see Chapter 11).

14 If the engine is in the vehicle, drain the cooling system as described in Section 2.

15 Remove the timing belt, camshaft sprockets, crankshaft sprocket, timing belt tensioner and idler rollers, and the timing belt rear cover, as described in Chapter 2B.

16 Proceed as described in paragraphs 4 and 5.

17 No overhaul of the coolant pump is possible, and if faulty, the unit must be renewed.

Refitting

18 Refitting is a reversal of removal, bearing in mind the following points.

19 Always use a new O-ring. Before fitting the pump, smear the pump mating face in the cylinder block and the O-ring with a silicone grease or petroleum jelly.

20 Refit the pump, and ensure that the lugs on the pump and the cylinder block are aligned before tightening the pump securing bolts to the specified torque **(see illustration)**.

11.5a Withdraw the coolant pump . . .

11.5b . . . and recover the O-ring - SOHC model

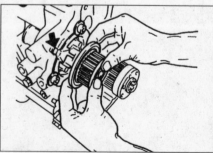

11.20 Lugs (arrowed) on coolant pump and cylinder block must be aligned - DOHC models

12.3 Withdrawing the fan shroud assembly - SOHC model

21 Refit the remaining components, and tension the timing belt, as described in Chapter 2B.

22 If the engine is in the vehicle, refill the cooling system, as described in Section 4. Replace the undershield (see Chapter 11).

12 Cooling fan - removal and refitting

Removal

1 Disconnect the battery negative lead.

2 Disconnect the wiring from the cooling fan, noting the location of the wiring connector for use when refitting.

3 Unscrew the two upper fan shroud securing bolts from the top corners of the shroud, then tilt the assembly back slightly towards the engine, and withdraw it upwards away from the radiator (see illustration).

4 To separate the fan motor from the shroud, unscrew the three securing nuts. If desired, the fan blades can be separated from the motor by removing the securing spring clip from the end of the motor shaft.

5 No spare parts are available for the motor, and if the unit is faulty, it must be renewed.

Refitting

6 Reassembly (where applicable), and refitting are reversals of the dismantling and removal procedures, but ensure that the lower end of the fan shroud locates correctly on the radiator.

7 On completion, start the engine and run it until it reaches normal operating temperature, then continue to run the engine and check that the cooling fan cuts in and functions correctly.

13 Expansion tank and coolant level sensor - removal and refitting

Expansion tank

Removal

1 The expansion tank is secured by a single screw at its front edge. If the tank is to be moved for access purposes, it should be possible to move it sufficiently within the confines of the hoses once the securing screw has been removed. If the tank is to be removed completely, continue as follows.

2 Disconnect the two hoses from the top of the expansion tank, and suspend them above the height of the engine to prevent coolant loss.

3 Remove the tank securing screw, then manipulate the tank from its location, holding it as high as possible above the engine.

4 Position a container beneath the tank, then disconnect the bottom hose and allow the contents of the tank to drain into the container. Suspend the bottom hose as high as possible above the engine to prevent coolant loss.

Refitting

5 Refitting is a reversal of removal, but on completion check and if necessary top-up the coolant level, as described in Section 4. The coolant drained from the expansion tank during removal can be re-used, provided it has not been contaminated.

Coolant level sensor

6 The coolant level sensor, where fitted, is an integral part of the expansion tank cap. If the level sensor is faulty, the complete cap assembly must be renewed.

14 Temperature gauge sender - removal and refitting

Note: *See Chapter 5 for details of the coolant temperature sensor which provides a signal for the ECU. On C20 XE and X20 XEV models, the coolant temperature sensor is mounted alongside the temperature gauge sender.*

Removal

1 On C20 NE and C20 XE models, the temperature gauge sender is screwed into the thermostat housing. On X20 XEV models, it is in front of the DIS unit mounting flange (see illustrations).

2 Partially drain the cooling system, as described in Section 2, to minimise coolant spillage.

3 Disconnect the battery negative lead.

4 Disconnect the wiring from the sender, then unscrew the sender from its location.

Refitting

5 Refitting is the reverse of removal, remembering the following points.

6 Coat the sender threads with sealant before fitting, and tighten to the specified torque.

7 Top-up the cooling system, as described in Section 4.

8 On completion, start the engine and check the operation of the temperature gauge. Also check for coolant leaks.

15 Cooling fan switch - removal and refitting

Note: *A new sealing ring should be used when refitting the switch.*

Removal

1 The cooling fan switch is located at the bottom right-hand corner of the radiator (see illustration).

2 If a faulty switch is suspected, the circuit to the fan motor can be tested by temporarily bridging the terminals in the switch wiring plug, and switching on the ignition. If the cooling fan now operates, the switch is faulty

3

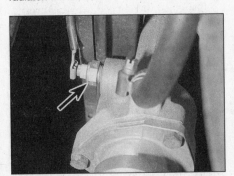

14.1a Temperature gauge sender location (arrowed) - C20 NE model

14.1b Temperature gauge sender location (arrowed) - C20 XE model

14.1c Temperature gauge sender location (arrowed) - DIS unit removed - X20 XEV model

15.1 Cooling fan switch location - SOHC model viewed from below

16.4a Remove the two heater control panel securing screws from the clock/trip computer aperture . . .

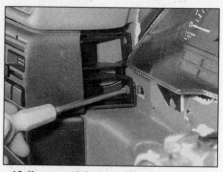

16.4b . . . and the remaining screw from the right-hand end of the panel

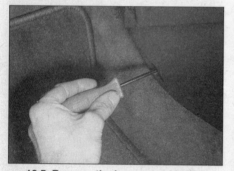

16.5 Remove the lower panel by the passenger footwell

16.6 Heater control cables disconnected, showing cable end securing clips

16.7 Withdraw the heater control panel from the facia

and should be renewed. To remove the switch, continue as follows. .

3 Disconnect the battery negative lead, then disconnect the switch wiring plug if not already done.

4 Drain the cooling system, as described in Section 2.

5 Unscrew the switch from the radiator and recover the sealing ring.

Refitting

6 Refitting is a reversal of removal, but use a new sealing ring, and refill the cooling system as described in Section 4.

7 On completion, start the engine and run it until it reaches normal operating temperature, then continue to run the engine and check that the cooling fan cuts in and functions correctly.

16 Heater control panel -
removal and refitting

Removal

1 Disconnect the battery negative lead.

2 Remove the steering column shrouds, and the instrument panel lower and upper trim panels, as described in Chapter 11.

3 Remove the clock or trip computer, as applicable, from the facia, referring to Chapter 12 if necessary.

4 Remove the two heater control panel securing screws from the clock/trip computer

aperture, and the remaining securing screw from the right-hand end of the panel (exposed by removing the instrument panel lower trim panel) **(see illustrations)**.

5 Remove the lower panel by the passenger footwell **(see illustration)**.

6 Reach up behind the facia, and disconnect the bowden cables from the control levers at the rear of the heater control panel. Note that each cable is secured by a plastic clip, and in some cases, by an additional metal clip, which must be released before the cable end can be disconnected from the control lever **(see illustration)**. This is a tricky operation, and some patience will be required. Mark the cables to ensure that they are refitted in their original positions.

7 Withdraw the heater control panel from the facia **(see illustration)**, and disconnect the wiring plugs from the rear of the panel.

17.4 Removing the plastic cover from the heater matrix

Refitting

8 Refitting is a reversal of removal, but on completion, move all the control levers through their full extent of travel, and check the heater mechanism for correct operation.

17 Heater matrix -
removal and refitting

Removal

1 Drain the cooling system (see Section 2).

2 Working in the engine compartment, disconnect the coolant hoses from the heater matrix pipes at the bulkhead.

3 Working inside the vehicle, remove the front centre console section (see Chapter 11).

4 Extract the two front and two rear securing screws, and remove the plastic cover from under the heater matrix **(see illustration)**.

5 Remove the two front retaining screws from the heater matrix securing straps, then lower the securing straps and withdraw the heater matrix from the facia **(see illustration)**. The pipes at the rear of the matrix must be fed through the bulkhead, and the grommets in the heater matrix housing may be displaced as the matrix is withdrawn. Where applicable, recover the grommets.

Refitting

6 Refitting is a reversal of removal, remembering the following points.

7 Ensure that the coolant pipe grommets are seated correctly in the heater matrix housing, as shown **(see illustration)**.

8 Ensure that the rubber mounting strips are correctly seated between the mounting straps and the matrix.

9 On completion, refill the cooling system, as described in Section 4.

18 Heater blower motor - removal and refitting

Removal

1 The heater blower motor is situated under the windscreen cowl panel.

2 Remove the windscreen cowl panel, as described in Chapter 11.

3 Remove the windscreen wiper motor and linkage, as described in Chapter 12.

4 Unclip the cover from the top of the motor **(see illustration)**.

5 Disconnect the motor wiring plug.

6 Remove the two clamp screws, then lift off the clamp and withdraw the motor assembly from its housing **(see illustration)**.

7 It is possible to renew the motor resistor by pressing the retaining clips together to release the resistor bracket. Fit the new resistor, ensuring that the retaining clips lock it into position **(see illustration)**.

8 No overhaul of the motor assembly is possible, and if faulty, the unit must be renewed.

18.4 Unclip the cover from the heater blower motor

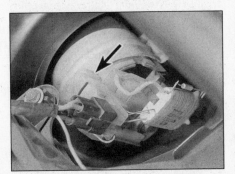

18.7 Heater blower motor resistor retaining clip (arrowed)

17.5 Unscrewing a heater matrix securing strap screw

Refitting

9 Refitting is a reversal of removal, ensuring that the mounting rubber is correctly seated between the clamp and the motor.

19 Facia ventilation nozzles - removal and refitting

Centre facia ventilation nozzles

Removal

1 Using a screwdriver, carefully prise the cap from the hazard warning flasher switch.

2 Carefully prise the nozzle assembly from the facia, using a screwdriver with a piece of card under the blade, to avoid damage to the facia trim **(see illustrations)**.

18.6 Unscrewing a heater blower motor clamp screw

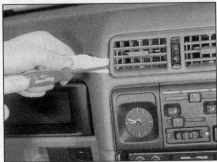

19.2a Using a screwdriver with protected blade . . .

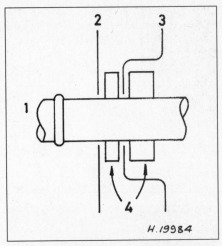

17.7 Heater matrix coolant pipe grommet location

1 Coolant pipe
2 Engine compartment bulkhead
3 Heater matrix housing
4 Grommet

3 If desired, the nozzle housing can be removed as follows.

4 Move the knurled airflow adjuster wheel to the "O" position, then pull the actuating rod sideways from its carrier.

5 Release the two lower securing clips by levering with a screwdriver and pull the housing from the facia.

Refitting

6 Refitting is the reverse of removal, but note that if the housing has been removed, the airflow adjuster actuating rod must be pulled out to its stop, then pressed into its carrier with the adjuster wheel in the "O" position.

Passenger side facia ventilation nozzle

Removal

7 Carefully prise the nozzle from the facia, using a screwdriver with a piece of card under the blade, to avoid damage to the facia trim.

8 If desired, the nozzle housing can be removed as follows.

9 Move the knurled airflow adjuster wheel to the "O" position, then pull the actuating rod sideways from its carrier.

19.2b . . . to release the centre facia ventilation nozzles

3

10 Extract the single screw securing the housing to the facia, then release the securing clips and pull the housing from the facia.

Refitting

11 Refitting is the reverse of removal, with reference to paragraph 6.

Driver's side facia ventilation nozzle

12 The procedure is as described for the passenger side nozzle, except that there is no screw securing the housing to the facia.

Side window demister nozzles

Removal

13 Simply prise the nozzle from the facia, taking care not to damage the facia trim.

Refitting

14 To refit, push the nozzle into position until it locks.

Chapter 4 Part A:
Fuel and exhaust systems - fuel injection

Contents

Degrees of difficulty

Easy, suitable for novice with little experience	**Fairly easy,** suitable for beginner with some experience	**Fairly difficult,** suitable for competent DIY mechanic	**Difficult,** suitable for experienced DIY mechanic	**Very difficult,** suitable for expert DIY or professional

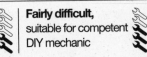

Specifications

4A

General

Injection system type:
  C20 NE . . . . Motronic M1.5
  C20 XE (up to 1993) . . . . Motronic M2.5
  C20 XE (from 1993) . . . . Motronic M2.8
  X20 XEV (up to 1997) . . . . Simtec 56.1
  X20 XEV (from 1997) . . . . Simtec 56.5
Fuel tank capacity:
  All models . . . . 63.0 ± 2 litres
Fuel octane rating (use unleaded petrol only on all models):
  C20 NE . . . . 91 RON (Regular) or 95 RON (Premium) depending on setting of
                                  coding plug
  C20 XE* . . . . 91 RON (Regular) to 98 RON (Premium)
  X20 XEV* . . . . 91 RON (Regular) to 98 RON (Premium). Avoid high engine loads with
                                  low octane petrol (91 RON).

*Note: *Knock control system automatically adjusts ignition timing according to octane number. See Chapter 5.*

Idle settings

Idle speed:
  C20 NE . . . . 800 ± 80 rpm
  C20 XE . . . . 940 ± 80 rpm
  X20 XEV . . . . 850 ± 160 rpm
Idle mixture (CO content):
  All models . . . . 0.3 % (at 2800 to 3200 rpm)
Note: *Idle speed and CO adjustment is not possible on these models, for information only.*

Fuel pressure (regulator vacuum hose connected)

Motronic 1.5:
Feed	1.8 to 2.2 bar
Return	0.3 to 1.5 bar
Motronic 2.5	2.0 to 2.2 bar
Motronic 2.8	2.2 to 2.7 bar
Simtec 56.1, 56.5	not available

Torque wrench settings

	Nm	lbf ft
Bracket, tank vent valve to coolant flange	8	6
Exhaust manifold nuts	22	16
Exhaust downpipe-to-manifold bolts	25	18
Exhaust fixings except flexible joint bolts	25	18
Exhaust flexible joint bolts	12	9
Fuel distributor pipe to inlet manifold	8	6
Fuel flow damper	20	15
Fuel injector retainer	3	2
Fuel pressure regulator	2.5	2
Fuel pump clamp	4	3
Fuel tank mounting strap bolts	20	15
Idle air control stepper motor	2.5	2
Inlet manifold nuts	22	16
Oxygen sensor	30	22
Throttle body mounting	20	15
Throttle body upper-to-lower section	6	4.5
Throttle potentiometer	2	1.5
Throttle valve housing to inlet manifold	9	7

1 General description

All models within the Calibra range have electronic fuel injection and ignition systems. Signals from a variety of sensors are processed by an electronic control unit (ECU) to determine the amount of fuel to be injected and the spark ignition timing. A single ECU controls both the injection and ignition. This chapter describes only the fuel injection system. For details of the ignition system, see Chapter 5.

Fuel is supplied from a roller-vane pump, through a fuel filter and pressure regulator to the fuel rail. The fuel rail acts as a reservoir for the four fuel injectors, which inject fuel into the cylinder inlet tracts, upstream of the inlet valves.

The ECU controls the injectors by sending electrical pulses of varying duration, causing them to open. The amount of fuel injected depends on the duration of the pulse.

On a simultaneous multi-point injection system, all four fuel injectors open simultaneously in response to an electrical pulse that occurs once per crankshaft revolution.

On a sequential multi-point injection system, the fuel injectors operate independently of each other, injecting fuel upstream of each inlet valve as it opens.

The ECU receives signals about the throttle position and inlet air mass in a variety of ways, depending on the model. All models have either a throttle potentiometer or a throttle switch. In addition, they have either a mechanical vane-type air flow meter or a more accurate air mass meter based on a hot wire or film. The ECU processes the data from these sensors and calculates the amount of fuel required. In some cases, the rate of change is calculated, so that extra fuel is injected for acceleration when the throttle is opened suddenly. Information from the throttle potentiometer is also used to cut off the fuel supply on the overrun, thus improving fuel economy and reducing exhaust gas emissions.

Idle speed is controlled by a variable-orifice solenoid valve, which regulates the amount of air bypassing the throttle valve. The solenoid valve is controlled by the ECU and there is no provision for direct adjustment of the idle speed.

Additional sensors inform the ECU of the engine coolant temperature and in some cases the inlet air temperature.

All Calibra models are fitted with catalytic converters and must only be operated on unleaded petrol. Do not use leaded petrol because it will contaminate the catalytic converter. A variety of grades of unleaded petrol can be used (see Specifications) and on C20 NE models which use the Motronic M1.5 system you need to set a coding plug to achieve the correct ignition timing for the grade of petrol being used. See Chapter 5 for details.

An oxygen sensor, screwed into the front section of the exhaust system, provides the ECU with a measurement of the amount of oxygen in the exhaust gases. This enables the ECU to adjust the mixture strength, which in turn affects the oxygen measurement, creating a closed-loop system. Until the oxygen sensor is fully warmed up it gives no feedback, and the ECU uses pre-programmed values (open-loop control) to determine the correct injector pulse width. When the sensor reaches its normal operating temperature, its tip (which is sensitive to oxygen) sends the ECU a varying voltage depending on the oxygen measurement. If the inlet air/fuel mixture is too rich, the exhaust gases are low in oxygen and the sensor sends a low-voltage signal. The voltage rises as the mixture weakens and the amount of oxygen rises in the exhaust gases. Peak conversion efficiency of all major pollutants occurs if the inlet air/fuel mixture is maintained at the chemically correct ratio for the complete combustion of petrol of 14.7 parts (by weight) of air to 1 part of fuel (the "stoichiometric" ratio). The sensor output voltage alters in a large step at this point and the ECU uses the signal change as a reference point, correcting the inlet air/fuel mixture accordingly by altering the fuel injector pulse width. The correct control of mixture strength is important not just for the operation of the engine and the exhaust gas emissions, but also to protect the catalytic converter from being contaminated by unburnt fuel.

Motronic M1.5

This version of the Motronic system is fitted to the C20 NE (SOHC) engine and has the following sensors:
a) Crankshaft speed/position sensor
b) Throttle potentiometer
c) Air flow meter (vane type)
d) Engine coolant temperature sensor mounted in the thermostat housing
e) Octane number plug
f) Oxygen sensor mounted in the exhaust system

Simultaneous multi-point fuel injection is used, so that the fuel injectors receive an electrical pulse once per crankshaft revolution, which operates all four injectors simultaneously.

Inlet air passes from the air cleaner, through the vane type airflow meter, then through the throttle valve to the cylinder inlet tracts. A flap in the airflow meter is deflected in proportion to the airflow. This deflection is converted into an electrical signal and passed to the Motronic module.

A coding plug needs to set to RON 91 (Regular) or RON 95 (Premium) to achieve the correct ignition timing for the grade of petrol being used. See Chapter 5 for details.

A fuel pump cut-off relay is controlled by the Motronic module, which cuts the power to the fuel pump should the engine stop with the ignition switched on, if there is an accident.

Motronic M2.5

This version of the Motronic system was fitted to the C20 XE (DOHC) engine until 1993. Sequential multi-point fuel injection is used, whereby each injector receives an individual electrical pulse allowing the four injectors to operate independently, giving fine control of the fuel supply to each cylinder.

Inlet air passes from the air cleaner, through a hot wire type air mass meter, then through a two-stage throttle body assembly to the cylinder inlet tracts. The electrical current required to maintain the temperature of the hot wire in the air mass meter is directly proportional to the mass flow rate of the air trying to cool it. The current is converted into a signal, which is passed to the Motronic module.

The throttle body contains two throttle valves that open progressively, allowing high torque at part throttle, and high-speed "breathing" capacity at full-throttle.

There is no throttle potentiometer. Instead there is a throttle valve switch with contacts for the full-load and idling positions.

The ignition timing is adjusted automatically by the knock control system to correspond to the grade of petrol being used, and there is no coding plug. See Chapter 5.

A Hall-effect distributor is used, which incorporates a camshaft phase sensor in the distributor body. See Chapter 5.

Motronic M2.8

This version of the Motronic system was fitted to the C20 XE (DOHC) engine from 1993 onwards. It is the basically the same as the earlier M2.5 system except for the following:

A hot film mass airflow meter replaces the hot wire type used on the M2.5 system. The operation is the same except that a thin, electrically heated plate is used instead of a wire, making it more robust and less vulnerable to failure.

An inlet air temperature sensor is located in the hose between the hot film mass airflow meter and the air cleaner for precise monitoring of the inlet air temperature. Signals from the sensor are used in conjunction with other sensors to indicate the occurrence of a hot start condition. The Motronic module then interprets these signals to alter the injector duration accordingly.

The throttle valve switch is discarded and the throttle potentiometer is re-introduced.

The Hall-effect distributor is replaced by a Direct Ignition System (DIS) with two ignition coils, each providing a spark for two cylinders, and there is a separate camshaft phase sensor. For details see Chapter 5.

Simtec 56.1

This system is used on X20 XEV models up to 1997 and the fuel injection features are similar to the Motronic M2.8, although it is a different system and is not a development of Motronic. The sensors are as follows:

a) Crankshaft speed/position sensor
b) Camshaft phase sensor, mounted on the timing side of the engine
c) Throttle potentiometer
d) Hot film mass airflow meter
e) Engine coolant temperature sensor
f) Air inlet temperature sensor, fitted to the inlet duct between the air cleaner and the air mass meter
g) Knock sensor
h) Oxygen sensor mounted in the exhaust system
i) Wheel speed sensor

A Direct Ignition System (DIS) is used and there is no distributor. For details see Chapter 5.

The system is fitted with exhaust gas recirculation (EGR) and secondary air injection (AIR) for emission control purposes. For details see Chapter 4B.

Simtec 56.5

This system is used on X20 XEV models from 1997 onwards and is the same as Simtec 56.1 but with the following modifications.

There is a switched intake system with four air inlet tracts, one for each cylinder, that go round in a loop. Four switchover valves are mounted on a single shaft so that they all operate together. The valves open and close to send the inlet air round a long or short path. The switchover valves are regulated, depending on the engine speed and load. At engine speeds above 3,600 rpm the valves are generally open, sending the air round the short path. The result is smoother and higher torque progression, especially in the lower engine speed range.

The secondary air injection system has been modified. See Chapter 4B.

The control unit hardware has been modified.

2 Fuel injection system - precautions

⚠ **Warning: Many of the procedures in this sub-Section require the removal of fuel lines and connections that may result in some fuel spillage. Before carrying out any operation on the fuel system, refer to the precautions given in Safety first! at the beginning of this Manual and follow them implicitly. Petrol is a highly dangerous and volatile liquid, and the precautions necessary when handling it cannot be overstressed.**

⚠ **Warning: The fuel injection system is pressurised, therefore extra care must be taken when disconnecting fuel lines. When disconnecting a fuel line union, loosen the union slowly, to avoid a sudden release of pressure that may cause fuel to spray out. Fuel pressure checking must be entrusted to a Vauxhall dealer, or other specialist, who has the necessary special equipment.**

3 System testing - general

1 The fuel system can be tested using a simple hand-held device called TECH 1, connected to a plug on the engine wiring harness. For details, see the Reference Section of this manual. If you do not have TECH 1, you cannot test the individual fuel system components except for basic electrical tests. However, you can continue as follows.

2 If a fault arises, check first that it is not due to poor maintenance. Check that the air filter element is clean, and the spark plugs are in good condition and correctly gapped. Check also that the engine breather hoses are clear and undamaged and that the throttle cable is correctly adjusted. If the engine is running very roughly, check the compression pressures (see Chapter 2A) and remember the possibility that one of the hydraulic tappets might be faulty, producing an incorrect valve clearance.

3 If the fault is thought to be due to a dirty injector, it is worth trying one of the established injector-cleaning treatments before renewing, perhaps unnecessarily, the injector.

4 If the fault persists, check the ignition system components (as far as possible).

5 If the fault is still not eliminated, work methodically through the system, checking all fuses, wiring connectors and wiring, looking for any signs of poor connections, dampness, corrosion, dirt or other faults.

6 Once the system components have been checked for signs of obvious faults, take the vehicle to a Vauxhall dealer for the full system to be tested on special equipment.

4A

4.2 Disconnect the air trunking from the airflow meter - SOHC models

4.3 Disconnect the air trunking from the air cleaner cover - DOHC models

4.7 Remove the air cleaner housing

7 Do not attempt to "test" any component, and particularly the ECU, with anything other than the correct test equipment, available at a Vauxhall dealer. If any of the wires to be checked lead to a component such as the ECU, always first unplug the relevant connector from the system components so that there is no risk of the component being damaged by the application of incorrect voltages from test equipment.

4 Air cleaner housing - removal and refitting

Note: *This section describes complete removal of the air cleaner, including the cover element and housing. For removal of the element during regular servicing, see Chapter 1.*

Removal

1 Unclip the coolant expansion tank hose from the air cleaner cover, and move it to one side out of the way.
2 On SOHC models, there is a vane-type airflow meter connected directly to the air cleaner cover, so that the cover and meter have to be removed together. Disconnect the battery negative lead, then disconnect the wiring plug from the meter. Loosen the clamp screw and disconnect the meter from the air trunking at the downstream end **(see illustration)**.
3 On DOHC models, there is a mass airflow meter, separated from the air cleaner cover by a length of air trunking. Loosen the clamp screw and disconnect the air trunking from the air cleaner cover **(see illustration)**.
4 Release the two securing clips from the left-hand side of the air cleaner cover, and undo the two captive securing screws from the

right-hand side, then lift off the cover. On SOHC models, lift off the cover and airflow meter as a complete assembly.
5 Lift out the air cleaner element.
6 Slacken the three rubber mounting nuts on the air cleaner housing.
7 Lift up the air cleaner housing to release it from the air intake pipe, then remove it from the vehicle **(see illustration)**.

Refitting

8 Refitting is the reverse of removal.

5 Air intake resonance box - removal and refitting

Removal

1 The resonance box is connected to the air cleaner inlet, to reduce induction noise. It is located under the right front wing, between the bumper and the wheel arch.
2 Remove the front bumper trim (Chapter 11).
3 Remove the plastic moulding from the right of the box **(see illustration)**.
4 Remove two vertical screws holding lower flap to wheel arch liner **(see illustration)**.
5 Remove one horizontal screw holding the box onto the plastic mounting on the inner wing **(see illustration)**.
6 Disengage the bottom of the box from the lug and pull the box down so that the front pipe detaches from the air inlet.
7 Remove the screw holding the plastic moulding to the inner wing **(see illustration)**.

5.3 Remove the plastic moulding from the right of the resonance box

5.4 Remove two vertical screws holding lower flap to wheel arch liner

5.5 Remove the horizontal screw holding the box to the plastic mounting

5.7 Remove the screw holding the plastic moulding to the inner wing

5.8 Disengage the lug and push the moulding upward

5.9 Pull the resonance box down

8 Disengage the lug and push the moulding upward **(see illustration)**.
9 Pull the resonance box down and remove it from the vehicle **(see illustration)**.

Refitting

10 Refitting is the reverse of removal.

6 Air box -
removal and refitting

Removal

1 The air box, if fitted, is secured by two or three bolts to the top of the throttle body. Take note of the routing and connections of the inlet air temperature control system vacuum pipes.
2 Disconnect the engine breather hose from

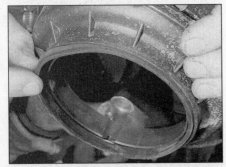

6.4a Ensure the sealing ring is located in the air box groove

6.4b Do not overtighten the air box screws

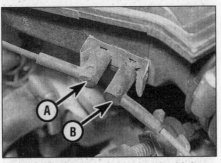

6.2 Vacuum pipe connections to air box

A To throttle body   B To air cleaner

the air box and the vacuum pipe from the rearmost of the throttle body's three unions **(see illustration)**.
3 Do not lose the sealing ring as the air box is withdrawn.

Refitting

4 On refitting, ensure that the sealing ring is seated correctly in the slot in the underside of the air box, tighten the screws (but do not overtighten them), and reconnect the vacuum pipe and breather hose **(see illustrations)**.

7 Air temperature sensor
(later models) -
removal and refitting

1 The inlet air temperature sensor is fitted to the inlet air trunking, alongside the mass airflow meter, on the following models:
 a) C20 XE models from 1993 onwards with Motronic M2.8.
 b) X20 XEV models with Simtec.

Removal

2 Disconnect the battery negative lead.
3 Disconnect the wiring plug at the inlet air temperature sensor.
4 Release the hose clips and remove the air trunking then remove the inlet air temperature sensor from the trunking.

Refitting

5 Refitting is the reverse of removal. Ensure that the air trunking is correctly fitted to the mass airflow meter.

9.1a Fuel filter (arrowed) - 'out-of-tank' fuel pump models

8 Depressurising the fuel
system -
general

⚠ *Warning: The following procedures will merely relieve the pressure in the fuel system. Remember that fuel will still be present in the system components, so take precautions before disconnecting any of them. Refer to Section 2.*

1 The fuel system consists of the fuel pump, the fuel filter, the fuel injectors and the pressure regulator in the throttle body. Metal pipes and flexible hoses of the fuel lines connect these components. All these contain fuel that will be under pressure while the engine is running and/or while the ignition is switched on.
2 The pressure will remain for some time after the ignition has been switched off and must be relieved before any of these components are disturbed.
3 Remove either the fuel pump fuse (number 11) or the fuel pump relay and start the engine. Allow the engine to idle until it cuts out. Turn the engine over once or twice on the starter to ensure that all pressure is released, then switch off the ignition.
4 Do not forget to refit the fuse or relay when work is complete.

9 Fuel filter ('Out-of-tank'
fuel pump models) -
removal and refitting

Note: *Refer to Section 2 before proceeding.*

Removal

1 The fuel filter is located on the fuel pump bracket under the rear of the vehicle, either on the right-hand side of the spare wheel well or in front of the fuel tank, depending on model **(see illustrations)**.
2 Disconnect the battery negative lead.
3 Have a container to hand, to catch the fuel that will be released as the filter is removed.
4 Clamp the fuel hoses on either side of the filter, to minimise fuel loss when the hoses are disconnected.

4A

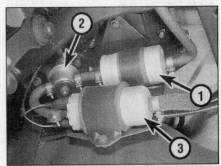

9.1b Fuel filter (1), fuel flow damper (2) and pump (3) - 'out-of-tank' fuel pump models)

10.6 Fuel filter - 'in-tank' fuel pump type

5 Loosen the clamp screws, and disconnect the fuel hoses from the filter. Be prepared for fuel spillage, and take adequate fire precautions.

6 Loosen the clamp bolt(s), and withdraw the fuel filter from its bracket. Note the orientation of the flow direction arrow on the body of the filter, and the position of the "AUS" (out) marking on the filter end face.

Refitting

7 Refitting is a reversal of removal, ensuring that the flow direction markings are correctly orientated.

8 Run the engine and check for leaks on completion. If leakage is evident, stop the engine immediately, and rectify the problem without delay.

10 Fuel filter ('In-tank' fuel pump models) - removal and refitting

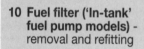

Note: *Refer to Section 2 before proceeding.*

Removal

1 Depressurise the fuel system (Section 8).

2 Chock the front wheels, jack up the rear of the vehicle and support it on axle stands placed under the body side members (see *"Jacking and Vehicle Support"*). The fuel filter is located at the rear of the fuel tank, on the right-hand side.

3 Unclip the fuel hose from the filter mounting bracket.

4 Note carefully any markings on the fuel filter

12.4 Disconnecting a fuel pump wiring plug - 'out-of-tank' fuel pump model

casing. There should be at least an arrow (showing the direction of fuel flow) pointing in the direction of the fuel supply hose leading to the engine compartment. There may also be the words "EIN" (in) and "AUS" (out) embossed in the appropriate end of the casing.

5 Clamp the fuel filter hoses, then slacken the clips and disconnect the hoses.

6 Undo the single screw to release the mounting bracket, then open the clamp with a screwdriver to remove the fuel filter **(see illustration)**.

Refitting

7 Fit the new fuel filter using the reverse of the removal procedure, but ensure that the fuel flow direction arrow or markings point in the correct direction. Switch on the ignition and check carefully for leaks; if any signs of leakage are detected, the problem must be rectified before the engine is started.

11 Fuel pump - testing

5

1 If the fuel pump is functioning, it should be possible to hear it "buzzing" by listening under the rear of the vehicle when the ignition is switched on. Unless the engine is started, the fuel pump should switch off after approximately one second. If the noise produced is excessive, this may be due to a faulty fuel flow damper. The damper can be renewed referring to Section 18, if necessary.

2 If the pump appears to have failed completely, check the appropriate fuse and relay.

3 To test the fuel pump, special equipment is required, and it is recommended that any suspected faults are referred to a Vauxhall dealer.

12 Fuel pump ('Out-of-tank' fuel pump models) - removal and refitting

Note: *Refer to Section 2 before proceeding.*

Removal

1 The fuel pump is located on a bracket under the rear of the vehicle, either on the right-hand side of the spare wheel well or in front of the fuel tank on other models.

2 Disconnect the battery negative lead.

3 Have a container to hand, to catch the fuel that will be released as the damper is removed.

4 Disconnect the wiring plug(s) from the fuel pump **(see illustration)**.

5 Clamp the fuel hoses on either side of the damper, to minimise fuel loss when the hoses are disconnected.

6 Loosen the clamp screws, and disconnect the fuel hoses from the pump. Be prepared for spillage, and take adequate fire precautions.

7 Loosen the clamp bolt, and slide the pump from its bracket.

Refitting

8 Refitting is a reversal of removal, ensuring that the pump is fitted the correct way round in its bracket. Push the pump into the rubber clamping sleeve as far as the rim on the pump body **(see illustration)**.

9 Run the engine and check for leaks on completion. If leakage is evident, stop the engine immediately, and rectify the problem without delay.

13 Fuel pump ('In-tank' fuel pump models) - removal and refitting

Removal

1 Remove the fuel tank, as described in Section 16.

2 Undo the fuel pipe unions and disconnect the wiring multi-plug.

3 Unscrew the plastic cap, then withdraw the mounting bracket and pump assembly from the tank.

4 Recover the gasket and discard it.

5 Cover the tank opening, as a safety measure and to prevent the entry of dirt.

6 If the pump is to be renewed, first move it to a clean working area and carry out the following.

7 Prise off the filter at the base of the pump assembly, then release the clips and separate the pump bracket from the damper ring.

8 Disconnect the fuel hose from the upper flange.

9 Make your own marks or notes to ensure that they can be reconnected the same way round, and unsolder the wires connecting the pump to the flange.

10 Press the pump out of the rubber sleeve.

Refitting

11 Reassembly and refitting are the reverse of removal and dismantling, noting the following points.

12 Ensure that the pump is seated correctly in the sleeve and that the hose is securely fastened.

13 Ensure that the wires are correctly reconnected and securely soldered.

14 Fit a new gasket.

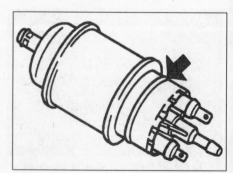

12.8 Fuel pump clamping sleeve should rest against rim (arrowed)

14 Fuel pump relay - renewal

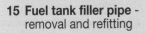

The relay is mounted in the engine compartment relay box (Chapter 12). Where more than one relay is fitted, the fuel pump relay is the one with the black base.

15 Fuel tank filler pipe - removal and refitting

Removal

1 If the vehicle has an anti-syphon device, run the vehicle until the tank level is low. Otherwise, siphon out the fuel through the filler pipe into a clean metal container that can be sealed.

2 Raise the bottom edge of the seal surrounding the filler neck and undo the single securing screw beneath **(see illustration)**.

3 Chock the front wheels, jack up the rear of the vehicle and support it securely on axle stands (see *"Jacking and Vehicle Support"*) placed under the body side members.

4 Unscrew the single filler pipe mounting bolt from the underbody, then work along the length of the pipe, cutting or releasing any clips or ties securing other pipes or hoses to it. Releasing their clips, disconnect the filler and vent hoses from the pipe's lower end and the small-bore vent hoses from the unions at its upper end.

5 Having ensured that all components have been removed or disconnected which might prevent its removal, manoeuvre the pipe away from the vehicle's underside.

6 To check the operation of the pipe's anti-leak valve, invert the filler pipe and fill the lower union (now uppermost) with petrol. If the valve is functioning correctly, no petrol will leak from the other union. If petrol leaks from the other union the valve is faulty and the complete filler pipe must be renewed.

Refitting

7 Refitting is the reverse of the removal procedure, noting the following.

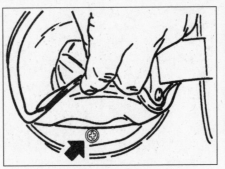

15.2 Fuel filler pipe securing screw (arrowed)

8 Check the condition of all hoses and clips, renewing any components that are found to be worn or damaged.

9 When reconnecting the small-bore vent hoses to the unions at the pipe's upper end, connect the hose from the charcoal canister to the uppermost union and the vent hose from the tank itself to the lower union **(see illustration)**.

10 Replacing any that were cut on removal use the clips or ties provided to secure any other pipes or hoses to the filler pipe.

11 Check carefully for signs of leaks on refilling the tank; if any signs of leakage are detected, the problem must be rectified immediately.

16 Fuel tank - removal, examination and refitting

Note: *Refer to Section 2 before proceeding.*

Removal

1 If the vehicle has an anti-syphon device, run the vehicle until the tank level is low. Otherwise, siphon out the fuel through the filler pipe into a clean metal container that can be sealed.

2 Disconnect the battery negative lead.

3 Chock the front wheels, then jack up the rear of the vehicle, and support on axle stands placed under the body side members (see *"Jacking and Vehicle Support"*).

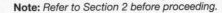

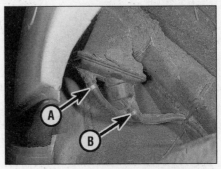

15.9 Vent hose connections at fuel tank filler pipe

A Charcoal canister hose
B Tank vent hose

4 Disconnect the fuel lines as follows:
a) On models with 'in-tank' fuel pumps, disconnect the pipe union from the fuel filter.
b) On models with 'out-of-tank' fuel pumps, disconnect the pipe union from the fuel pump.
c) Disconnect the fuel return line on the underbody where the flexible hose meets the metal pipe.

Caution: Be prepared for fuel spillage, and take adequate fire precautions. Plug the open ends of the hoses, to prevent dirt ingress and further fuel loss.

5 Disconnect the multi-plugs on all wiring harnesses that lead to the fuel tank. On models with 'in-tank' fuel pumps there are two plugs on the underbody, adjacent to the road spring **(see illustration)**.

6 Detach all accessible breather hoses from their clips on the side of the tank **(see illustration)**.

7 Undo the four nuts and remove the plastic tray from behind the fuel tank **(see illustration)**.

8 Undo the fuel filler neck clip **(see illustration)**.

9 Support the weight of the fuel tank on a jack, with an interposed block of wood.

10 Unscrew the securing bolts from the tank mounting straps **(see illustration)**. Then remove the straps and lower the tank sufficiently to enable the vent hoses and breather hoses to be disconnected. Note the positions of all hoses for refitting.

4A

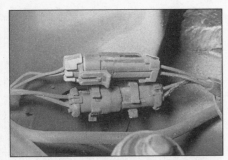

16.5 Fuel tank wiring multi-plugs on vehicle underbody - models with 'in-tank' fuel pumps

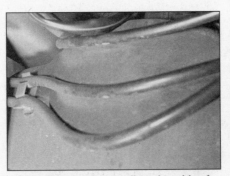

16.6 Breather hoses clipped to side of tank

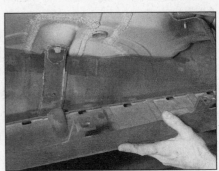

16.7 Remove the plastic tray from behind the fuel tank

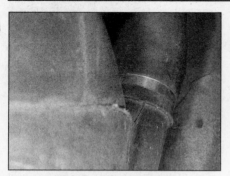

16.8 Fuel filler neck clip

16.10 Fuel tank mounting strap

18.1 Fuel flow damper

11 Lower the fuel tank and withdraw it from under the vehicle.

Examination

12 If the tank contains sediment or water, it may be cleaned out using two or three rinses with clean fuel. Shake vigorously using several changes of fuel, but before doing so, remove the fuel tank sender unit, as described in Section 17. This procedure should be carried out in a well-ventilated area, and it is vital to take adequate fire precautions - refer to the *"Safety first!"* Section at the beginning of this manual for further details.
13 Any repairs to the fuel tank should be carried out by a professional, and removal of all residual fuel vapour requires several hours of specialist cleaning.

Refitting

14 Refitting is the reverse of removal, ensuring that all hoses are reconnected to their correct locations as noted during removal.
15 On completion, fill the fuel tank, then run the engine and check for leaks. If leakage is evident, stop the engine immediately, and rectify the problem without delay.

17 Fuel tank sender unit - removal and refitting

Note: *Refer to Section 2 before proceeding.*

Models with 'in tank' fuel pump

1 The sender unit is integrated into the fuel pump assembly, which is removed as described in Section 13.

Models with 'out of tank' fuel pump

Removal

2 Remove the fuel tank, (see Section 16).
3 Undo the fuel pipe unions and disconnect the wiring multi-plug.
4 Make alignment marks on the sender unit and the fuel tank so that the sender unit can be refitted in its original position.
5 Unscrew the plastic cap and withdraw the sender unit, taking care to avoid bending the float arm.

6 Recover the gasket and discard it.
7 Cover the tank opening, as a safety measure and to prevent the entry of dirt.

Refitting

8 Refitting is the reverse of removal, noting the following points:
9 Ensure that the marks that have been made on the sender unit and fuel tank are correctly aligned.
10 Fit a new gasket.

18 Fuel flow damper - removal and refitting

Note: *Refer to Section 2 before proceeding.*

Removal

1 The fuel flow damper, if fitted, is located in front of the fuel tank, in the feed line between the fuel pump and the fuel filter **(see illustration)**. Its purpose is to reduce pressure fluctuations in the fuel return line, thus reducing noise levels.
2 Disconnect the battery negative lead.
3 Have a container to hand, to catch the fuel that will be released as the damper is removed.
4 Clamp the fuel hoses on either side of the damper, to minimise fuel loss when the hoses are disconnected.
5 Loosen the clamp screws, and disconnect the fuel hoses from the damper. Be prepared for fuel spillage, and take adequate fire precautions.

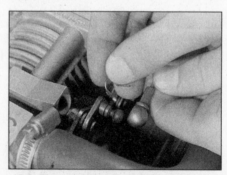

19.2 Disconnecting the throttle cable end from the throttle valve lever - SOHC model

6 Unscrew the securing nut, and withdraw the damper from the bracket.

Refitting

7 Refitting is the reverse of removal. Tighten the damper securing nut to the specified torque setting.
8 Run the engine and check for leaks on completion. If leakage is evident, stop the engine immediately, and rectify the problem without delay.

19 Throttle cable - removal, refitting and adjustment

Removal

1 Remove the air box, if fitted (see Section 6).
2 Remove the throttle cable end from the throttle valve linkage. If it is connected to the linkage by a balljoint and wire spring clip **(see illustration)**, remove the clip with a pair of needle-nosed pliers and prise the cable end off the linkage.
3 The outer seating grommet is held by a clip to a bracket on the inlet manifold. Withdraw the clip and pull the grommet out of the bracket, then release the cable as far as the bulkhead **(see illustration)**.
4 Working inside the passenger compartment, remove the driver's footwell trim panel. Refer to Chapter 11, if necessary.
5 Release the end of the cable's inner wire from the "keyhole" fitting at the top of the

19.3 Throttle cable end grommet in bracket on inlet manifold

throttle pedal by easing back the spring and prising the cable end out of the slot.

6 Prise the grommet out of the bulkhead and tie a length of string to the cable.

7 Noting carefully its routing, withdraw the cable through the bulkhead into the engine compartment; untie the string, leaving it in place, when the pedal end of the cable appears.

Refitting

8 Refitting is the reverse of the removal procedure, noting the following points:

a) *First ensure that the cable is correctly routed, then draw it through the bulkhead aperture using the string.*

b) *Ensure that the bulkhead grommet is correctly seated.*

c) *Connect the cable end to the throttle linkage. Seat the cable outer grommet in the bracket and pull it through so that the cable inner wire is just taut when the throttle linkage is held fully closed. Fit the clip to secure the cable outer in that position.*

d) *Check the throttle operation and cable adjustment, as described below, then refit the airbox if applicable.*

Adjustment

9 First check that the pedal is at a convenient height for the driver. This setting can be adjusted by turning the pedal stop screw (it will be necessary to remove the footwell trim panel to reach the screw). Remember that the pedal must be left with enough travel for the throttle valve to open fully. Also check that the pedal pivot bushes are in good condition.

10 Returning to the engine compartment, check that the linkage pivots and balljoints are unworn and operate smoothly throughout their full travel. When the throttle valve is fully closed and the throttle pedal is released, there should be hardly any free play in the cable inner wire.

11 If adjustment is required, extract the clip securing the cable outer seating grommet in the cable bracket and replace it in the appropriate groove, so that the cable outer is repositioned correctly.

12 With an assistant operating the throttle pedal from the driver's seat. Check that when the pedal is fully depressed, the throttle valve is fully open. If there is insufficient pedal travel to permit this, unscrew the pedal stop screw, then reset the cable at the throttle linkage.

13 When cable adjustment is correct, refit all disturbed components.

20 Throttle pedal - removal and refitting

Removal

1 Working inside the vehicle, remove the lower trim panel from the driver's footwell (see Chapter 11).

2 Slide the cable retainer from the bracket on the top of the pedal, and disconnect the cable end from the pedal.

3 Extract the circlip from the right-hand end of the pedal pivot shaft, then slide out the pivot shaft from the left-hand side of the pivot bracket **(see illustration)**. Recover the pivot bushes and the pedal return spring.

4 Examine the pivot bushes for wear, and renew if necessary.

Refitting

5 Refitting is the reverse of removal, but on completion check the throttle mechanism for satisfactory operation, and check the throttle cable adjustment, as described in Section 19.

21 Idle mixture - checking

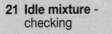
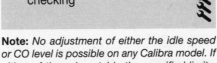

Note: *No adjustment of either the idle speed or CO level is possible on any Calibra model. If either of these is outside the specified limits, there is a system fault and the problem should be referred to a dealer. There is a CO adjustment screw on the vane-type airflow meter on C20 NE models, but it is not used and has no effect.*

1 In order to check the idle mixture, the following conditions must be met:

a) *The engine must be at normal operating temperature*

b) *All electrical consumers (cooling fan, heater blower, headlamps etc.) must be switched off*

c) *The spark plug gaps must be correctly adjusted (see Chapter 1)*

d) *The throttle cable free play must be correctly adjusted - see Section 19*

e) *The air inlet trunking must be free from leaks, and the air filter must be clean*

2 Connect a tachometer and an exhaust gas analyser to the vehicle in accordance with the equipment manufacturer's instructions.

3 Start the engine and turn it at 2000 rpm for approximately 30 seconds, then allow it to idle. Check that the idle speed is within the specified limits, then check the CO level in the exhaust gas.

22.12 Fuel pressure regulator (arrowed) - DOHC model

20.3 Throttle pedal pivot assembly. Circlip arrowed

22 Fuel pressure regulator - removal and refitting

Note: *Refer to Section 2 before proceeding.*

Removal

SOHC models

1 Disconnect the battery negative lead.

2 For improved access, remove the idle speed adjuster as described in Section 23. Disconnect the wiring harness housing from the fuel injectors and move it to one side, taking care not to strain the wiring. Pull up on the wiring harness housing, and compress the wiring plug retaining clips to release the harness housing from the injectors.

3 Position a wad of rag beneath the pressure regulator, to absorb the fuel that will be released as the regulator is removed.

4 Loosen the clamp screws and disconnect the fuel hoses from the regulator. Be prepared for fuel spillage, and take adequate fire precautions.

5 Disconnect the vacuum pipe from the top of the pressure regulator and withdraw the regulator.

DOHC models

6 Disconnect the battery negative lead.

7 Disconnect the wiring plug from the air mass meter. Recover the sealing ring.

8 Loosen the clamp screw securing the air trunking to the right-hand end of the air mass meter.

9 Using an Allen key or hexagon bit, unscrew the four bolts securing the air box to the throttle body. Lift the air box from the throttle body and disconnect the hose from the base of the air box, then withdraw the air box/air mass meter assembly.

10 Disconnect the two breather hoses from the rear of the camshaft cover, and move them to one side.

11 Disconnect the wiring plug from the throttle potentiometer.

12 Disconnect the vacuum pipe from the top of the pressure regulator **(see illustration)**.

13 Position a wad of rag beneath the regulator, to absorb the fuel that will be released as the regulator is removed.

4A

23.2 Disconnecting the idle speed adjuster wiring plug - C20 NE model

23.4 Withdrawing the idle speed adjuster complete with hoses - C20 NE model

23.10 Idle speed adjuster (arrowed) viewed from underneath vehicle - C20 XE model

14 Using a spanner or socket, and working underneath the regulator, unscrew the four Torx type securing bolts, then withdraw the regulator. Be prepared for fuel spillage, and take adequate fire precautions.

Refitting

15 Refitting is the reverse of removal, ensuring that all wires, pipes and hoses are correctly reconnected. Note that on DOHC models, the regulator vacuum pipe should be routed over the top of the camshaft cover breather hoses.
16 On completion, check the regulator for leaks, pressurising the system by switching the ignition on and off several times, before the engine is started.

23 Idle speed adjuster - removal and refitting

Note: *The idle speed adjuster is controlled by the ECU, and manual adjustment of the idle speed is not possible. If the idle speed is not correct, there is a system fault and you will need to consult a Vauxhall dealer.*

C20 NE models

Removal

1 Disconnect the battery negative lead.
2 Disconnect the wiring plug from the idle speed adjuster **(see illustration)**.
3 The adjuster can be removed complete with its connecting hoses, or separately, leaving the hoses in place.

23.16 Idle speed adjuster alongside throttle body - X20 XEV model

4 Loosen the relevant clamp screws, then disconnect the hoses, and withdraw the idle speed adjuster **(see illustration)**.

Refitting

5 Refitting is the reverse of removal.

C20 XE models

Removal

6 Disconnect the battery negative lead.
7 Loosen the clamp screw, and disconnect the hose from underneath the air box on the throttle body. Remove the clamp from the hose.
8 Apply the handbrake, then jack up the front of the vehicle, and support securely on axle stands placed under the body side members (see "*Jacking and Vehicle Support*").
9 Remove the engine undershield, as described in Chapter 11, if there is one.
10 Working underneath the vehicle, disconnect the wiring plug from the idle speed adjuster, which is located underneath the inlet manifold above the starter motor **(see illustration)**.
11 Loosen the clamp screw and disconnect the remaining idle speed adjuster hose from the inlet manifold, then withdraw the adjuster downwards complete with the hoses.
12 If the hoses are to be removed from the adjuster, mark their locations before removal so that they can be correctly reconnected. Once the adjuster has been refitted, it is impossible to swap the hose positions.

Refitting

13 Refitting is the reverse of removal. Ensure

24.2 Disconnect the wiring plug from the throttle potentiometer on rear of throttle

that the idle speed adjuster rests horizontally, with the wiring routed over the top of the coolant hose. If the wiring is routed under the coolant hose, this may cause the idle speed adjuster to be bent downwards, resulting in a restriction or fracture in the air hose to the inlet manifold.

X20 XEV models

Removal

14 Disconnect the battery negative lead.
15 Disconnect the wiring plug from the air mass meter and recover the sealing ring. Disconnect the wiring plug from the inlet air temperature sensor.
16 Loosen the clamp screw at the right-hand end of the air mass meter. Disconnect the air trunking from the throttle body and remove it with the air mass meter to access to the idle speed adjuster underneath **(see illustration)**.
17 Disconnect the wiring plug from the idle speed adjuster. Undo the appropriate bolt and hoses, then withdraw the adjuster.

Refitting

18 Refitting is the reverse of removal.

24 Throttle potentiometer - removal and refitting

Removal

Potentiometer on rear of throttle

1 Disconnect the battery negative lead.
2 Disconnect the wiring plug from the throttle potentiometer **(see illustration)**.
3 Remove the two securing screws and withdraw the potentiometer from the throttle body **(see illustration)**.

Potentiometer on upper throttle trunking

4 Disconnect the battery negative lead.
5 Disconnect the wiring plug from the air mass meter. Recover the sealing ring.
6 Loosen the clamp screw securing the air trunking to the right-hand end of the air mass meter.
7 Using an Allen key or hexagon bit, unscrew the four bolts securing the air box to the

throttle body. Lift the air box from the throttle body, and disconnect the hose from the base of the air box, then withdraw the air box/air mass meter assembly.

8 Disconnect the wiring plug from the throttle potentiometer **(see illustration)**.

9 Remove the two securing screws and withdraw the potentiometer from the throttle body.

Refitting

10 Refitting is the reverse of removal, noting the following points.

a) *Install the potentiometer when the throttle valve is fully closed, and ensure that its adapter seats correctly on the throttle valve spindle.*

b) *Tighten the screws carefully to the specified torque.*

25 Throttle switch (Motronic M2.5) - removal and refitting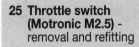

The early C20 XE engines up to 1993, fitted with Motronic M2.5 injection/ignition systems, have a throttle switch instead of a throttle potentiometer. Removal and refitting is the same as for a throttle potentiometer.

26.2 Airflow meter securing bolt (arrowed) - SOHC model

24.3 Remove the two securing screws from the throttle potentiometer on rear of throttle

26 Airflow meter (Motronic M1.5) - removal and refitting

Note: *If the air funnel is removed, a new gasket must be used on refitting. The airflow meter securing bolts must be coated with thread-locking compound on refitting.*

Removal

1 Remove the air cleaner cover and airflow meter as an assembly, as described in Section 4, paragraphs 1, 2 and 4.

2 Unscrew the single bolt securing the airflow meter to the front of the air cleaner cover **(see illustration)**.

3 Unscrew the four securing bolts from inside the air cleaner cover, recover the two reinforcing plates, and withdraw the airflow meter **(see illustration)**.

4 If desired, the air funnel can be unclipped from inside the air cleaner cover.

Refitting

5 Refitting is the reverse of removal, remembering the following points.

24.8 Disconnect the wiring plug from the throttle potentiometer on upper throttle trunking

6 If the air funnel has been removed, refit it using a new gasket.

7 Coat the threads of the four airflow meter securing bolts that fit inside the air cleaner cover with thread-locking compound.

27 Air mass meter - hot wire (Motronic M2.5) - removal and refitting

Removal

1 Disconnect the battery negative lead.

2 Disconnect the wiring plug from the air mass meter. Recover the sealing ring **(see illustration)**.

3 Loosen the clamp screws from the air trunking on either side of the air mass meter, then disconnect the air trunking and withdraw the meter.

Refitting

4 Refitting is the reverse of removal, but inspect the air mass meter wiring plug sealing ring and renew if necessary.

4A

26.3 Airflow meter securing bolts, reinforcing plates and air funnel - SOHC model

27.2 Recover the sealing ring from the air mass meter wiring plug - DOHC model

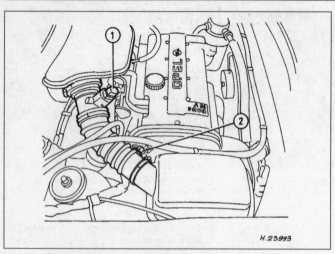

28.5a Hot film mass airflow meter attachments - Motronic M2.8

1 Hot film mass airflow meter wiring plug
2 Inlet air temperature sensor wiring plug

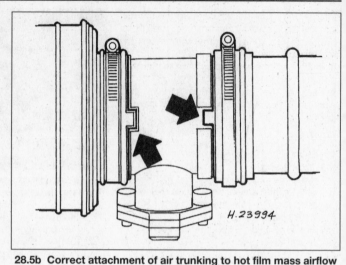

28.5b Correct attachment of air trunking to hot film mass airflow meter - Motronic M2.8

Arrows indicate air trunking to airflow meter alignment notches

28 Air mass meter - hot film (Motronic M2.8 and Simtec) - removal and refitting

Removal

1 Disconnect the battery negative lead.
2 Disconnect the wiring plug at the hot film air mass meter and at the inlet air temperature sensor.
3 Remove the upper part of the air cleaner together with the inlet air trunking and air mass meter.
4 Release the hose clamps and separate the air mass meter from the inlet air trunking, noting the position of the trunking with the air mass meter. If there is any external damage replace the unit.

Refitting

5 Refitting is the reverse of removal but ensure that the air trunking is connected to the air mass meter as shown. Also ensure that the marks on the air trunking and air box are aligned as shown **(see illustrations)**.

29 Fuel injectors - removal and refitting

Note: *Refer to Section 2 before proceeding. New O-rings must be used when refitting the injectors. Where applicable, a tachometer and an exhaust gas analyser will be required to check the idle mixture on completion.*

SOHC models

Removal

1 Disconnect the battery negative lead.
2 Unscrew the union nut, and disconnect the brake servo vacuum hose from the inlet manifold.
3 Remove the idle speed adjuster, complete with hoses, referring to Section 23 if necessary.
4 Disconnect the vacuum pipe from the top of the fuel pressure regulator.
5 Disconnect the wiring harness housing from the fuel injectors, and move it to one side, taking care not to strain the wiring. Pull up on the wiring harness housing, and compress the wiring plug retaining clips to release the harness housing from the injectors.
6 Remove the four bolts from the brackets securing the fuel rail to the inlet manifold, then lift the fuel rail complete with fuel injectors sufficiently to enable the injector(s) to be removed **(see illustrations)**. Take care not to strain the fuel hoses.
7 To remove an injector from the fuel rail, prise out the metal securing clip using a screwdriver, then pull the injector from the fuel rail **(see illustrations)**.

Refitting

8 Overhaul of the fuel injectors is not possible, as no spares are available. If faulty, an injector must be renewed.
9 Begin refitting by fitting new seals to both ends of each fuel injector **(see illustration)**. Even if only one injector has been removed, new seals should be fitted to all four injectors.
10 Refitting is the reverse of removal, ensuring that all hoses, pipes and wires are correctly reconnected.
11 On completion, check the idle mixture as described in Section 21.

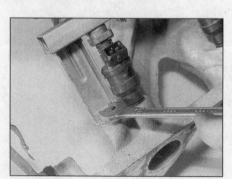

29.6a Remove the outer . . .

29.6b . . . and inner fuel rail securing bolts . . .

29.6c . . . and lift the fuel rail from the inlet manifold (inlet manifold removed for clarity) - SOHC model

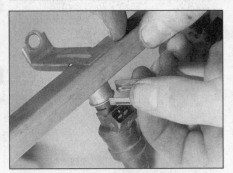

29.7a Withdraw the securing clip . . .

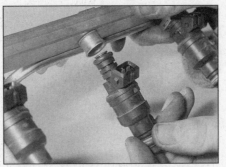

29.7b . . . then pull the injector from the fuel rail - SOHC model

29.9 Fit new seals to the injectors

DOHC models

Removal

12 Disconnect the battery negative lead.

13 Loosen the clamp screw securing the air trunking to the left-hand end of the air mass meter.

14 Using an Allen key or hexagon bit, unscrew the four bolts securing the air box to the throttle body. Lift the air box from the throttle body, and disconnect the hose from the base of the air box, then withdraw the air box.

15 Position a wad of rag beneath one of the fuel hose unions on the fuel rail, to absorb the fuel that will be released as the union is disconnected.

16 Slowly loosen the fuel hose union to relieve the pressure in the fuel line, then disconnect the hose from the fuel rail. Be prepared for fuel spillage, and take adequate fire precautions. Plug the end of the fuel hose, to prevent dirt ingress and further fuel leakage.

17 Repeat paragraphs 15 and 16 for the remaining fuel hose-to-fuel rail union.

18 Disconnect the two breather hoses from the rear of the camshaft cover. Disconnect the larger hose from the throttle body, and remove the hose completely.

19 Disconnect the vacuum pipe from the top of the fuel pressure regulator.

20 Disconnect the wiring plug from the air mass meter. Recover the sealing ring.

21 Disconnect the wiring plug from the throttle potentiometer.

22 Slide the end of the throttle cable from the throttle valve lever on the throttle body, then unbolt the cable bracket from the inlet manifold, and move it to one side (see illustration).

23 Disconnect the wiring harness housing from the fuel injectors, and move it to one side, taking care not to strain the wiring. Pull up on the wiring harness housing, and compress the wiring plug retaining clips to release the housing from the injectors.

24 Unscrew and remove the two fuel rail securing nuts, and withdraw the fuel rail complete with fuel injectors from the inlet manifold. Note the position of the earth leads on the fuel rail securing studs (see illustration).

25 To remove an injector from the fuel rail, prise out the metal securing clip using a screwdriver, then pull the injector from the fuel rail

Refitting

26 Refitting is as described in paragraphs 8 to 11 inclusive.

30 Throttle body - removal and refitting

Note: *Refer to Section 2 before proceeding. A new throttle body gasket must be used on refitting*

SOHC models

Removal

1 Disconnect the battery negative lead.

2 Loosen the clamp screws securing the air trunking to the throttle body and the airflow meter, then withdraw the air trunking.

3 Loosen the clamp screw, and disconnect the idle speed adjuster hose from the throttle body.

4 Disconnect the camshaft cover breather hose from the throttle body.

5 Disconnect the coolant hoses from the throttle body. Be prepared for coolant spillage, and clamp or plug the open ends of the hoses, to prevent further coolant loss.

6 Disconnect the wiring plug from the throttle potentiometer.

7 Release the securing clip, then disconnect the throttle cable end balljoint from the throttle valve lever.

4A

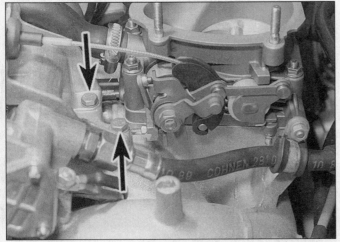

29.22 Throttle cable bracket securing bolts (arrowed) - DOHC model

29.24 Earth leads secured to fuel rail stud (arrowed) - DOHC model

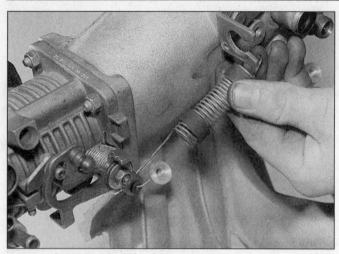

30.8 Unhook the throttle return spring from the bracket on the inlet manifold (inlet manifold removed for clarity)

30.10a Unscrew the securing nuts . . .

8 Slide the throttle cable grommet from the bracket on the inlet manifold, then unhook the throttle return spring from the bracket **(see illustration)**.

9 Make a final check to ensure that all relevant hoses and wires have been disconnected and moved clear of the throttle body.

10 Unscrew the four securing nuts, and withdraw the throttle body from the inlet manifold **(see illustrations)**. Access to the lower nuts is difficult and it may be necessary to move the two fuel hoses to one side for improved access. Take care not to strain the hoses.

11 Recover the gasket.

12 If desired, the throttle potentiometer can be removed from the throttle body, with reference to Section 24.

Refitting

13 Refitting is the reverse of removal, remembering the following points.

14 Where applicable, refit the throttle potentiometer, as described in Section 24.

15 Refit the throttle body, using a new gasket **(see illustration)**.

16 Ensure that all hoses and wires are correctly reconnected and routed.

17 Check and if necessary top-up the coolant level, as described in *"Weekly checks"*.

18 Check and if necessary adjust the throttle cable free play, as described in Section 19.

DOHC models

Removal

19 Disconnect the battery negative lead.

20 Loosen the clamp screw securing the air trunking to the left-hand side of the air mass meter.

21 Using an Allen key or hexagon bit, unscrew the four bolts securing the air box to the throttle body. Lift the air box from the throttle body, and disconnect the hose from the base of the air box, then withdraw the air box.

22 Disconnect the wiring plug from the throttle potentiometer.

23 Unscrew the retaining nut, and remove the fuel hose bracket from the left-hand side of the throttle body **(see illustration)**.

24 Slide the throttle cable end from the throttle valve lever.

25 Disconnect the breather hose from the front of the throttle body.

26 Disconnect the vacuum pipe from the top

of the fuel pressure regulator.

27 Make a final check to ensure that all relevant hoses, pipes and wires have been disconnected and moved clear of the throttle body.

28 Unscrew the four securing nuts, and withdraw the throttle body from the inlet manifold. Recover the gasket.

29 If desired, the throttle potentiometer can be removed from the throttle body, referring to Section 24, if necessary.

30 **Do not** under any circumstances attempt to adjust the throttle valve linkage. If the throttle valve linkage is faulty, refer the problem to a Vauxhall dealer.

Refitting

31 Refitting is the reverse of removal, remembering the following points.

32 Where applicable, refit the throttle potentiometer, as described in Section 24.

33 Refit the throttle body, using a new gasket.

34 Ensure that all hoses, pipes and wires are correctly reconnected and routed.

35 On completion, check and if necessary adjust the throttle cable free play, as described in Section 19.

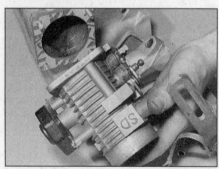

30.10b . . . and withdraw the throttle body (inlet manifold removed for clarity) - SOHC models

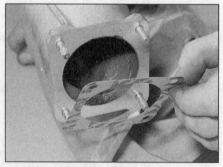

30.15 Refit the throttle body, using a new gasket

30.23 Remove the fuel hose bracket (arrowed) from the throttle body - DOHC models

31 Inlet manifold (SOHC) - removal and refitting

Note: *Refer to the warning in Section 2, before proceeding. Use a new gaskets when refitting.*

Removal

1 Disconnect the battery negative lead.
2 Remove the idle speed adjuster and its hoses, referring to Section 23, if necessary.
3 Release the securing clip, then disconnect the throttle cable and balljoint from the throttle valve lever. Slide the throttle cable grommet from the bracket on the inlet manifold, and move the throttle cable to one side out of the way.
4 Loosen the clamp screw and disconnect the air trunking from the throttle body.
5 Unscrew the union nut and disconnect the brake servo vacuum hose from the inlet manifold **(see illustration)**.
6 Disconnect the camshaft cover breather hose from the throttle body.
7 Disconnect the coolant hoses from the throttle body. Be prepared for coolant spillage, and clamp or plug the open ends of the hoses, to prevent further coolant loss.
8 Disconnect the wiring plug from the throttle potentiometer.
9 Disconnect the vacuum pipe from the top of the fuel pressure regulator.
10 Disconnect the wiring harness housing from the fuel injectors and move it to one side, taking care not to strain the wiring. Pull up on the wiring harness housing, and compress the wiring plug retaining clips to release the harness housing from the injectors.
11 Disconnect the fuel hoses from the fuel rail. Be prepared for fuel spillage, and take adequate fire precautions. Clamp or plug the open ends of the hoses, to prevent dirt ingress and further fuel leakage.
12 Unscrew and remove the top alternator mounting nut and bolt.
13 Make a final check to ensure that all relevant hoses, pipes and wires have been disconnected.
14 Unscrew the securing nuts, and withdraw the manifold from the cylinder head. Recover the gasket **(see illustrations)**.
15 It is possible that some of the manifold studs may be unscrewed from the cylinder head when the manifold securing nuts are unscrewed. In this event, the studs should be screwed back into the cylinder head once the manifold has been removed, using two manifold nuts locked together.
16 If desired, the ancillary components can be removed from the manifold, referring to the relevant Chapter.

Refitting

17 Refitting is the reverse of removal, remembering the following points.

18 Where applicable refit any ancillary components to the manifold, with reference to the relevant Sections of this Chapter.
19 If the alternator mounting bracket has been unbolted from the manifold, refit it before refitting the manifold, as access to the securing bolt is extremely limited once the manifold is in place.
20 Refit the manifold using a new gasket, and tighten the securing nuts to the specified torque.
21 Ensure that all relevant hoses, pipes and wires are correctly reconnected.
22 On completion, check and if necessary top-up the coolant level (see *"Weekly checks"*).
23 Check and if necessary adjust the throttle cable free play, as described in Section 19.
24 If any of the fuel system components have been disturbed or renewed, check the idle mixture as described in Section 21.

32 Inlet manifold (DOHC) - removal and refitting

Note: *On X20 XEV models from 1997 onwards with Simtec 56.5 there is a switched intake system with a switchover valve and solenoid which needs to be disconnected.*

Removal

1 Disconnect the battery negative lead.
2 Disconnect the wiring plug from the air mass meter. Recover the sealing ring. On C20 XE models from 1993 onwards with Motronic 2.8, and on X20 XEV models, disconnect the wiring plug from the inlet air temperature sensor.
3 Loosen the clamp screw securing the air trunking to the right-hand end of the air mass meter.
4 On C20 XE models, use an Allen key or hexagon bit to unscrew the four bolts securing the air box to the throttle body. Lift the air box from the throttle body, and disconnect the hose from the base of the air box then withdraw the air box/air mass meter assembly. On X20 XEV models, disconnect the air intake hose from the

31.5 Disconnecting the brake servo vacuum hose - SOHC models

throttle body and remove it with the air mass meter.
5 Disconnect the wiring plug from the throttle valve switch or the throttle potentiometer.
6 Slide the throttle cable end from the throttle valve lever. Then pull the cable end grommet from the bracket on the inlet manifold and move the throttle cable to one side out of the way.
7 Disconnect the two breather hoses from the rear of the camshaft cover. Disconnect the larger hose from the throttle body, and remove the hose completely.
8 Position a wad of rag beneath one of the fuel hose unions on the fuel rail, to absorb the fuel that will be released as the union is disconnected.
9 Slowly loosen the fuel hose union, to gradually relieve the pressure in the fuel feed line, then disconnect the hose from the fuel rail. Be prepared for fuel spillage, and take adequate fire precautions. Plug the end of the fuel hose, to prevent dirt ingress and further fuel leakage.
10 Repeat paragraphs 8 and 9 for the remaining fuel hose-to-fuel rail union.
11 Disconnect the vacuum pipe from the top of the fuel pressure regulator.
12 Disconnect the wiring harness housing from the fuel injectors and move it to one side, taking care not to strain the wiring. Pull up on the wiring harness housing, and compress the wiring plug retaining clips to release the housing from the injectors.
13 Unscrew the union nut, and disconnect the brake servo vacuum hose from the left-

31.14a Unscrew the securing nuts . . .

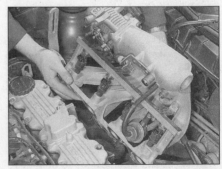

31.14b . . . and withdraw the inlet manifold - SOHC models

4A

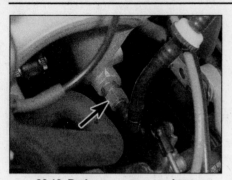

32.13 Brake servo vacuum hose connection at inlet manifold (arrowed) - DOHC models

hand side of the inlet manifold **(see illustration)**. On X20 XEV models from 1997 onwards with Simtec 56.5, disconnect the secondary air system vacuum hose from the inlet manifold.

14 Unscrew the retaining nut, and remove the fuel hose bracket from the left-hand side of the throttle body.

15 Unscrew the securing nuts, and disconnect the earth leads from the fuel rail securing studs at either end of the fuel rail.

16 Unscrew the securing bolt, and remove the cable/hose bracket from the left-hand end of the inlet manifold.

17 On X20 XEV models, disconnect the wiring plug from the idle speed adjuster alongside the throttle body. On C20 XE models, remove the idle speed adjuster as described in Section 23.

18 Unscrew and remove the top alternator mounting nut and bolt.

19 Make a final check to ensure that all relevant hoses, pipes and wires have been disconnected.

20 Unscrew the securing nuts, and withdraw the manifold from the cylinder head. Recover the gasket.

21 It is possible that some of the manifold studs may be unscrewed from the cylinder head when the manifold securing nuts are unscrewed. In this event, the studs should be screwed back into the cylinder head once the manifold has been removed, using two manifold nuts locked together.

22 If desired, the ancillary components can be removed from the manifold, with reference to the relevant Sections of this Chapter.

Refitting

23 Refitting is the reverse of removal.

Chapter 4 Part B:
Fuel and exhaust systems - exhaust and emissions

Contents

Degrees of difficulty

Easy, suitable for novice with little experience	Fairly easy, suitable for beginner with some experience	Fairly difficult, suitable for competent DIY mechanic	Difficult, suitable for experienced DIY mechanic	Very difficult, suitable for expert DIY or professional

Specifications

Torque wrench settings	Nm	lbf ft
AIR non-return valve to pipe	30	22
AIR pipe support bracket to manifold	8	6
AIR pipe to manifold	20	15
AIR pipe to support bracket	8	6
AIR pump bracket to protective shield	10	7
AIR pump to wheel arch	20	15
AIR pump to insulator	10	7
AIR valves to bracket	4	3
Carbon canister	4	3
EGR valve	20	15
Exhaust manifold*	22	16
Exhaust rear section clamp bolt	17.5	13
Heat shield	8	6
Oxygen sensor	30	22

Use new nuts for DOHC models

1 Emission control systems - general

General

1 All Calibra models are fitted with an evaporative emission control system to minimise the escape of fuel tank vapours into the atmosphere.

2 X20 XEV models with the Simtec injection/ignition system are additionally fitted with the following emission control systems, to conform to the European exhaust emission limits which came into effect in 1996.

a) Exhaust gas recirculation (EGR)
b) Secondary air injection (AIR - Air Injection Reactor)

Evaporative emission control - all models

3 To prevent the escape of unburnt fuel vapours to the atmosphere, the fuel tank filler cap is sealed and a carbon canister collects the fuel vapours generated in the tank when the vehicle is parked. When the engine is running under suitable conditions, a vent valve opens and releases the vapours from the carbon canister to the inlet manifold.

4 The vent valve operates under the control of the fuel injection/ignition system. To ensure that the engine runs correctly when it is cold and/or idling, and to protect the catalytic converter from the effects of an over-rich mixture, the valve is not opened by the control module until the engine is under partial or full load. The valve solenoid is then modulated on and off to allow the stored vapour to pass into the inlet tract.

5 The carbon canister is mounted under the right-hand front wing, behind the wheel arch, and is removed and refitted as described in Section 9.

6 The vent valve is in a variety of locations on different models, and is removed and refitted as described in Section 2.

7 On Simtec systems, the tank ventilation is monitored closely with the Lambda control (or oxygen sensor) and is subject to adaptive control by the ECU.

Exhaust gas recirculation (EGR) - X20 XEV models with Simtec

8 The EGR system returns a specific amount of exhaust gas into the combustion process, to reduce the formation of nitrogen oxides (NO_x).

2.1 Fuel tank vent valve - Simtec system with DIS module removed

Secondary air injection (AIR) - X20 XEV models with Simtec

9 The secondary air injection system has an electrically driven pump that injects air into the exhaust manifold, reducing the amount of CO and HC emissions. The pump is mounted under the left-hand front wing, in front of the wheel arch.

10 Simtec 56.5, introduced in 1997, is a development of the earlier version 56.1 and includes the following modifications to the secondary air system:

a) *A vacuum connection has been added to the upper part of the intake manifold to supply the secondary air system with vacuum. Previously the vacuum was supplied from a connection in the vacuum line, but now there is a throttle in that position.*

b) *The secondary air non-return valve has*

4.3 Remove the plastic panel from the bodywork in front of the nearside wheel

4.4 Undo the two horn plugs

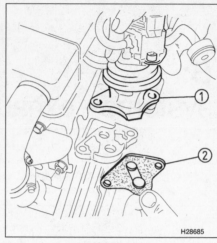

3.6 EGR valve

1 *Valve*   2 *Gasket*

been eliminated due to the re-design of the secondary air cut-off valve.

2 Fuel tank vent valve - removal and refitting

Removal

1 The fuel tank vent valve is in a variety of locations on different models:

a) *On C20 NE engines, it is mounted above the injectors for cylinders 2 and 4;*

b) *On C20 XE engines, it is mounted on the left-hand end of the engine, underneath the end of the fuel injector wiring harness housing;*

c) *On X20 XEV engines, it is fitted to the rear of the DIS module mounting bracket (see illustration).*

2 Disconnect the battery negative lead and the valve wiring plug, then disconnect the two vent hoses, having made a note of their connections. Either remove the valve from its mounting bracket, or unbolt the bracket, as required.

Refitting

3 Refitting is the reverse of removal.

4.5 Undo the bottom air pipe

---

3 EGR valve (Simtec system) - removal and refitting

Note: *A new gasket will be required when refitting the valve.*

Removal

1 Disconnect the battery negative lead.
2 Remove the wiring harness and vacuum hose.
3 Mark the position of the valve, to ensure correct relocation.
4 Undo the three bolts, and remove the valve from the dual spark ignition coil's coolant flange.

Refitting

5 Clean the sealing surfaces of the valve and flange.
6 Refit the valve with a new gasket and line up the marks made before removal **(see illustration)**.

4 AIR pump assembly (Simtec system) - removal and refitting

Removal

1 Disconnect the battery negative lead.
2 Remove the front bumper trim (Chapter 11).
3 Remove the plastic panel from the bodywork in front of the nearside wheel **(see illustration)**.
4 Undo the two horn plugs **(see illustration)**.
5 Undo the bottom air pipe **(see illustration)**.
6 Slacken the two nuts under the wing and the nut behind the bracket **(see illustrations)**.
7 Push the whole pump and horn assembly back and pull it down, then disconnect the multi-plug.
8 Remove the assembly from the vehicle **(see illustration)**.
9 To separate the components, continue as follows.
10 Remove the securing bracket from the air pickup filter **(see illustration)**.
11 Mark the position of the blower motor on its mounting, to refit in the same position, then

4.6a Slacken the two nuts under the wing . . .

4.6b . . . and the nut behind the bracket

4.8 AIR pump and horn assembly

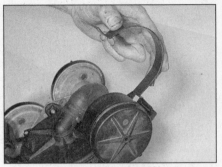

4.10 Remove the securing bracket from the air pickup filter

4.11 Undo the three bolts securing the blower to the mounting

4.12 Separate the air expansion chamber from the blower outlet

4.13 Separate the air pickup filter from the blower inlet

undo the three bolts **(see illustration)**. Detach the multi-plug from the bracket, then remove the motor.

12 Mark the position of the air expansion chamber on the blower outlet, to refit in the same position so that the horn can fit in the recess. Undo the clip and separate the expansion chamber from the blower **(see illustration)**.

13 Undo the clip and separate the air pickup filter from the blower inlet **(see illustration)**. If you wish, you can remove both the expansion chamber and filter without separating the pump from its mounting.

14 If required, undo the three remaining nuts and separate the pump mounting from the bracket.

Refitting

15 Refitting is the reverse of removal. Ensure correct alignment of the components.

---

5 AIR cut-off valve - removal, testing and refitting

Removal

1 Before removal, mark on the cut-off valve the direction of flow towards the non-return valve **(see illustration)**.

2 Disconnect and remove the air duct and vacuum hoses.
3 Undo the switchover valve's bolts and move to one side.
4 The cut-off valve can now be removed from the bracket.

Testing

5 To test the cut-off valve a vacuum hand pump with gauge will be required. If available, connect to the cut-off valve and ensure that air through-flow aperture is fully open when a vacuum is applied.

Refitting

6 Refitting is the reverse of removal. Ensure that the valve is fitted in the correct direction.

---

6 AIR switchover valve - removal and refitting

Removal

1 Disconnect the battery negative lead.
2 Disconnect wiring plug from the valve.
3 Mark the location of the vacuum hoses before removing them from the valve.
4 After disconnecting the hoses undo the two bolts, and remove them from its bracket.

Refitting

5 Refitting is the reverse of removal. Ensure that the hoses are fitted correctly **(see illustration)**.

4B

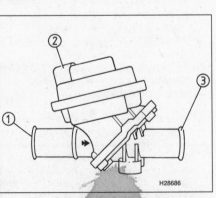

5.1 AIR cut-off valve

1 *Connection to AIR pump*
2 *Connection to AIR switchover valve*
3 *Connection to AIR non-return valve*

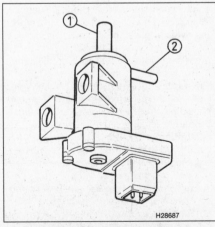

H28687

6.5 AIR switchover valve

1 *Connection to brake servo vacuum hose*
2 *Connection to cut-off valve*

7 AIR pipe and non-return valve - removal and refitting

Note: *New air pipe washers will be required when refitting.*

Removal

1 Remove the non-return valve air duct hose.
2 Undo the bolts from the engine lifting eye bracket, and turn the bracket onto its left-hand side.
3 Remove the pipe support bracket by releasing its three bolts.
4 Remove the heat shield that is secured by two bolts.
5 The air pipe can now be removed by releasing the two securing bolts.
6 If necessary, the non-return valve can now be disconnected.
7 Carefully clamp the pipe using a vice with protective jaws. Unbolt the valve from the pipe, then clean and inspect for damage.

Refitting

8 Before refitting, coat the threads of the non-return valve with suitable sealing compound (available from your Vauxhall dealer).
9 Use new washers when refitting the pipe (take care as the washers have sharp edges). Coat the pipe mounting bolts with suitable assembly paste (available from your Vauxhall dealer), before refitting.
10 Refitting is the reverse of removal. Retighten to the correct torque as shown in the Specifications.

8 Catalytic converter - description, general and precautions

Description

1 The purpose of the catalytic converter, fitted to all Calibra models, is to change potentially harmful hydrocarbon and carbon monoxide exhaust gases into harmless gases and water vapour. The converter consists of a stainless steel canister containing a catalyst-coated honeycomb ceramic. The catalyst is a mixture of three precious metals, platinum, palladium and rhodium.
2 The exhaust gases pass freely through the honeycomb, where the catalyst speeds up the chemical change of the exhaust gases, without being permanently altered itself.
3 To avoid damage to the catalyst, the engine must be kept properly tuned, and unleaded petrol must always be used. Normal leaded petrol will "poison" the catalyst, and must not be used.
4 To enable the engine management system to achieve complete combustion of the fuel mixture, and thus to minimise exhaust emissions, an oxygen sensor is fitted in the exhaust gas stream. The sensor monitors the oxygen level in the exhaust gas, and sends a signal to the electronic control unit, which constantly alters the fuel/air mixture within a narrow band to reduce emissions, and to allow the catalytic converter to operate at maximum efficiency. No adjustment of idle mixture is therefore possible on models fitted with a catalytic converter.

General and precautions

5 Ninety-nine per cent of exhaust gases from a petrol engine (however efficient or well tuned), consists of nitrogen (N_2), carbon dioxide (CO_2), oxygen (O_2), other inert gases and water vapour (H_2O). The remaining 1% is made up of the noxious pollutants, including carbon monoxide (CO), unburned hydrocarbons (HC), oxides of nitrogen (NO_x) and some solid matter, including a small lead content.
6 The device most commonly used to clean up vehicle exhausts is the catalytic converter. It is fitted into the vehicle's exhaust system and uses precious metals (platinum and palladium or rhodium) as catalysts to speed up the reaction between the pollutants and the oxygen in the exhaust gases. CO and HC are oxidised to form CO_2 and H_2O, and in the three-way type of catalytic converter, NO_x is reduced to N_2.
7 The converter consists of an element of ceramic honeycomb, coated with a combination of precious metals in such a way as to produce a vast surface area over which the exhaust gases must flow. The three-way closed-loop type converter fitted to these models can remove over 90% of pollutants.
8 The catalytic converter is a reliable and simple device that needs no maintenance. However there are some facts that an owner should be aware if the converter is to function properly for its full service life **(see illustration)**.

  a) DO NOT use leaded petrol in a vehicle equipped with a catalytic converter. The lead will coat the precious metals, reducing their converting efficiency and will eventually destroy the converter.
  b) Always keep the ignition and fuel systems well maintained according to the manufacturer's schedule (see "Routine maintenance" and the relevant Chapter). In particular, ensure that the air cleaner filter element, the fuel filter and the spark plugs are renewed at the correct intervals. If the inlet air/fuel mixture is allowed to become too rich due to neglect, the unburned surplus will enter and burn in the catalytic converter, overheating the element, eventually destroying the converter.
  c) If the engine develops a misfire, do not drive the vehicle at all (or at least as little as possible) until the fault is cured. The misfire will allow unburned fuel to enter the converter, which will result in its overheating, as noted above.
  d) The engine control indicator (the outline of an engine with a lightning symbol superimposed), will light when the ignition is switched on and the engine is started, then it will go out. While it may light briefly while the engine is running, it should go out again immediately and stays unlit. If it lights and stays on while the engine is running, seek the advice of a Vauxhall dealer as soon as possible. A fault has occurred in the fuel injection/ignition system that, apart from increasing fuel consumption and impairing the engine's performance, may damage the catalytic converter.
  e) DO NOT push or tow-start the vehicle. This will soak the catalytic converter in unburned fuel causing it to overheat when the engine does start see (b) above.
  f) DO NOT switch off the ignition at high engine speeds. If the ignition is switched off at anything above idle speed, unburned fuel will enter the (very hot) catalytic converter, with the possible risk of its igniting on the element and damaging the converter.
  g) DO NOT use fuel or engine oil additives. These may contain substances harmful to the catalytic converter.
  h) DO NOT continue to use the vehicle if the engine burns oil to the extent of leaving a visible trail of blue smoke. The unburned carbon deposits will clog the converter passages and reduce its efficiency. In severe cases the element will overheat.
  i) Remember that the catalytic converter operates at very high temperatures and the heat shields on the vehicle's underbody and the casing will become hot enough to ignite combustible materials that brush against it. DO NOT, therefore, park the vehicle in dry undergrowth, over long grass or over piles of dead leaves.
  j) Remember that the catalytic converter is FRAGILE. Do not strike it with tools during servicing work. Take great care when working on the exhaust system. Ensure that the converter is well clear of any jacks or other lifting gear used to raise the vehicle. Do not drive the vehicle over rough ground, road humps, etc., in such a way as to ground the exhaust system.
  k) In some cases, particularly when the vehicle is new and/or is used for

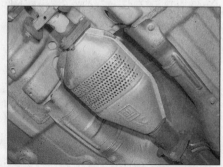

8.8 The catalytic converter is protected by heat shields

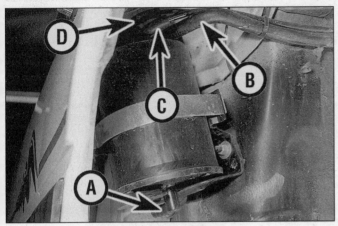

9.3 Carbon canister

A Vent to atmosphere
B Vapour feed hose from filler pipe
C Vapour exhaust hose to inlet tract
D Control valve vacuum pipe from throttle body

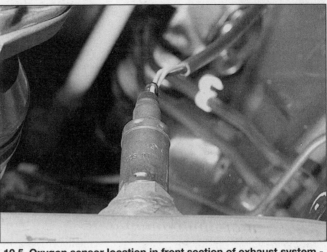

10.5 Oxygen sensor location in front section of exhaust system - DOHC models

stop/start driving, a sulphurous smell (like that of rotten eggs) may be noticed from the exhaust. This is common to many catalytic converter-equipped vehicles and seems to be due to the small amount of sulphur found in some grades of petrol. The sulphur reacts with hydrogen in the exhaust to produce hydrogen sulphide (CS) gas. While this gas is toxic, it is not produced in sufficient amounts to be a problem. Once the vehicle has covered a few thousand miles the problem should disappear. In the meanwhile a change of driving style or of the brand of petrol may effect a solution.

l) The catalytic converter, used on a well-maintained and well-driven vehicle, should last for between 50,000 and 100,000 miles. From this point on, careful checks should be made at all specified service intervals of the CO level to ensure that the converter is still operating efficiently. If the converter is no longer effective it must be renewed.

9 Carbon canister - removal and refitting
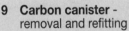

Removal

1 Apply the handbrake, then jack up the front of the vehicle, and support securely on axle stands placed under the body side members (see "Jacking and Vehicle Support").
2 Remove the front right-hand wheel and wheel arch liner.
3 Note the hose and pipe connections to the canister, or label them, to ensure that they are reconnected to their original unions, then disconnect them (see illustration). Unscrew the two nuts securing the canister mounting bracket to the vehicle body.

Refitting

4 Refitting is the reverse of removal. Ensure correct fitting of hoses and pipes.

10 Oxygen sensor - removal and refitting

Note: This sensor is also known as a Lambda sensor.

Removal

1 Disconnect the battery negative lead.
2 Disconnect the oxygen sensor wiring plug, which is located behind the coolant expansion tank.
3 Apply the handbrake, then jack up the front of the vehicle, and support securely on axle stands placed under the body side members (see "Jacking and Vehicle Support").
4 On DOHC models, remove the engine undershield, as described in Chapter 11.
5 Unscrew the oxygen sensor from the front section of the exhaust system (see illustration).
Caution: It is advisable to wear gloves, as the exhaust system could be extremely hot.
6 Withdraw the oxygen sensor and its wiring, taking care not to burn the wiring on the exhaust system. If the sensor is to be re-used, take care that the sealing ring is not lost, and that the sensor is not dropped.

Refitting

7 If a new sensor is being fitted, it will be supplied with the threads coated in a special grease to prevent it seizing in the exhaust system.
8 If the original sensor is being refitted, ensure that the screw thread is clean. Coat the thread with a lithium based copper grease.

9 Refitting is the reverse of removal. Check the exhaust system for leakage when the engine is re-started.

11 Exhaust manifold - removal and refitting

Note: New manifold-to-cylinder head, and manifold-to-downpipe, gaskets must be used on refitting.

SOHC models

Removal

1 Disconnect the battery negative lead.
2 Disconnect the HT leads from the spark plugs, if necessary labelling them to ensure refitting to the correct cylinders.
3 Loosen the clamp screw and disconnect the air cleaner hot air tube from the shroud on the manifold, if fitted. Remove the securing screws and withdraw the hot air shroud from the manifold.
4 Working under the manifold, unscrew and remove the four bolts securing the exhaust downpipe to the manifold.
5 Disconnect the oxygen sensor wiring.
6 Separate the downpipe from the manifold, and support with wire or string. Do not allow the front section of the exhaust system to hang under its own weight. Recover the gasket.
7 Unscrew the securing nuts, and withdraw the manifold from the cylinder head (see illustration). Recover the gasket.
8 It is possible that some of the manifold studs may be unscrewed from the cylinder head when the manifold securing nuts are unscrewed. In this event, the studs should be screwed back into the cylinder head once the manifold has been removed, using two manifold nuts locked together.

4B

Refitting

9 Refit the manifold using a new gasket, and tighten the securing nuts to the specified torque.

10 Reconnect the exhaust downpipe to the manifold, using a new gasket and tighten the securing bolts to the specified torque.

11 Further refitting is the reverse of removal.

DOHC models

12 Exhaust manifolds on DOHC models are of tubular design and form part of the front section of the exhaust. See Section 12 for details of removal and refitting

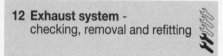

12 Exhaust system - checking, removal and refitting

Note: *All relevant gaskets and/or sealing rings should be renewed on refitting.*

Checking

1 Periodically, the exhaust system should be checked for signs of leaks or damage. Also inspect the exhaust system rubber mountings, and renew if necessary.

2 Small holes or cracks can be repaired using proprietary exhaust repair products, but where more serious corrosion or damage is evident, renewal will be necessary.

3 The manufacturers do not specify any renewal intervals for the catalytic converter.

4 The exhaust system consists of four separate sections, all of which can be renewed individually.

12.9 Exhaust front section flexible joint - SOHC models

12.10 Exhaust front section support bracket - SOHC models

11.7 Unscrewing an exhaust manifold securing nut - SOHC models

5 Before renewing an individual section of the exhaust system, it is wise to inspect the remaining sections. If corrosion or damage is evident on more than one section of the system, it may prove more economical to renew the entire system.

6 Individual sections of the exhaust system can be removed as follows.

Front section - SOHC models

Removal

7 Disconnect the battery negative lead, and disconnect the oxygen sensor wiring plug, which is located behind the coolant expansion tank.

8 Raise the vehicle, and support securely on axle stands placed under the body side members (see *"Jacking and Vehicle Support"*).

9 Unscrew the two securing bolts, and disconnect the exhaust front section from the catalytic converter at the flexible joint. Recover the sealing ring and the springs **(see illustration)**.

10 Unbolt the exhaust front section from the bracket on the cylinder block **(see illustration)**.

11 Unscrew and remove the four bolts securing the downpipe to the exhaust manifold, and withdraw the exhaust front section **(see illustration)**. Recover the downpipe-to-manifold gasket.

Refitting

12 Refitting is the reverse of removal, but use a new gasket when reconnecting the downpipe to the manifold, and a new sealing

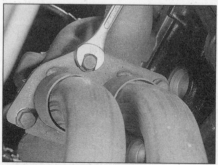

12.11 Unscrewing a downpipe-to-exhaust manifold bolt - SOHC models

ring when connecting the flexible joint. Tighten all fixings to the specified torque.

Front section - DOHC models

Removal

13 Proceed as described in paragraphs 7 and 8.

14 Remove the engine undershield, as described in Chapter 11, if there is one.

15 Proceed as described in paragraphs 9 and 10.

16 Working in the engine compartment, remove the bolts securing the exhaust manifold heat shield to the cylinder head.

17 Unscrew the two lower exhaust manifold securing nuts that also secure the heat shield brackets, and withdraw the heat shield **(see illustration)**.

18 Unscrew the remaining manifold securing nuts, then withdraw the manifold/exhaust front section from the vehicle. Recover the manifold gasket.

19 It is possible that some of the manifold studs may be unscrewed from the cylinder head when the manifold securing nuts are unscrewed. In this event, the studs should be screwed back into the cylinder head once the manifold has been removed, using two manifold nuts locked together.

Refitting

20 Refitting is the reverse of removal, but use a new manifold gasket, and use a new sealing ring when reconnecting the flexible joint. Tighten all fixings to the specified torque.

Catalytic converter

Removal

21 Proceed as described in paragraphs 8 and 9.

22 Unscrew the three securing nuts and bolts, and disconnect the catalytic converter from the exhaust centre section flanged joint. Recover the gasket.

23 Withdraw the catalytic converter from the vehicle.

Refitting

24 Refitting is the reverse of removal, but use a new sealing ring when reconnecting the flexible joint, and a new gasket when reconnecting the flanged joint. Tighten all fixings to the specified torque.

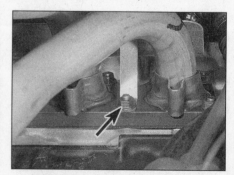

12.17 Exhaust manifold nut (arrowed) securing exhaust heat shield - DOHC models

Centre section

Removal

25 Raise the vehicle, and support securely on axle stands placed under the body side members (see "*Jacking and Vehicle Support*").

26 Unscrew the clamp bolt, and disconnect the exhaust centre section from the rear section **(see illustration)**. If necessary, tap around the joint with a hammer to break the seal, and gently prise the two sections apart. Note that the end of the centre section fits inside the rear section, to form a sleeve joint.

27 Proceed as described in paragraph 22.

28 Release the exhaust centre section from its rubber mountings on the underbody, and withdraw it from the vehicle **(see illustration)**.

Refitting

29 Refitting is the reverse of removal, but use a new gasket when reconnecting the flanged joint, and lubricate the pipes with exhaust assembly paste when connecting the centre

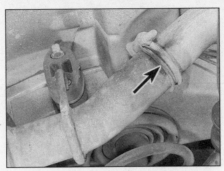

12.26 Exhaust centre section-to-rear section clamp (arrowed) - SOHC model

12.28 Exhaust centre section forward rubber mountings - DOHC models

section to the rear section. Tighten all fixings to the specified torque.

Rear section

Removal

30 Proceed as described in paragraphs 25 and 26.

31 Release the exhaust rear section from its

rubber mountings on the underbody, and withdraw it from the vehicle.

Refitting

32 Refitting is the reverse of removal, but lubricate the pipes with exhaust assembly paste when connecting the rear section to the centre section. Tighten the clamp bolt to the specified torque.

4B

Chapter 5
Engine electrical systems

Contents

Degrees of difficulty

Easy, suitable for novice with little experience		**Fairly easy,** suitable for beginner with some experience		**Fairly difficult,** suitable for competent DIY mechanic		**Difficult,** suitable for experienced DIY mechanic		**Very difficult,** suitable for expert DIY or professional	

Specifications

System type .... 12 volt, negative earth

Battery capacity .... 36, 44, 55 or 66 Ah

Alternator
Type .... Bosch or Delco-Remy
Output .... 55 or 70 A, depending upon model
Minimum brush length:
  Bosch type alternator .... 5.0 mm protrusion
  Delco-Remy type alternator .... 11.0 mm overall length

Starter motor
Type .... Pre-engaged, Bosch or Delco-Remy
Minimum brush length:
  Bosch DF type starter motor .... 11.5 mm
  Bosch DM type starter motor .... 3.0 mm
  Bosch DW type starter motor .... 4.5 mm
  Delco-Remy type starter motor .... 4.0 mm

System type
C20 NE .... Motronic M1.5
C20 XE (up to 1993) .... Motronic M2.5
C20 XE (from 1993) .... Motronic M2.8
X20 XEV (up to 1997) .... Simtec 56.1
X20 XEV (from 1997) .... Simtec 56.5

Coil
Output .... 16.0 to 20.0 kilovolts
Primary winding resistance (DOHC models only) .... 0.2 to 0.34 ohms
Secondary winding resistance (DOHC models only) .... 7.2 to 8.2 ohms

Distributor

Direction of rotor arm rotation .... Anti-clockwise (viewed from cap)
Firing order .... 1-3-4-2 (No 1 cylinder at timing belt end of engine)
Dwell angle .... Automatically controlled by electronic module (not adjustable)

Ignition timing ....

8 to 12° BTDC, automatically controlled by electronic module (not adjustable)

Spark plugs ....

See Chapter 1 Specifications

Torque wrench setting

	Nm	lbf ft
Alternator mounting	25	18
Camshaft phase sensor disc	8	6
Camshaft phase sensor	15	11
'Compact' series alternator lower mounting bolt	35	26
'Compact' series alternator upper mounting bolts	20	15
Coolant temperature sensor		
SOHC engine	10	7
DOHC engine	11	8
DIS module	7	5
Inductive pulse pick-up to block	8	6
Knock sensor (C20 XE and X20 XEV engines)	20	15
Spark plugs	25	18
Starter motor mounting bracket-to-cylinder block	25	18
Starter motor mounting:		
Engine side	45	33
Transmission side	75	55

1 Electrical system - general

Caution: Before carrying out any work on the vehicle electrical system, read through the precautions given in the "Safety first!" Section at the beginning of this manual, and in Section 3 of this Chapter.

The electrical system is the 12 volt negative earth type, and consists of a 12 volt battery, alternator with integral voltage regulator, starter motor, and related electrical accessories, components and wiring.

The battery is the maintenance-free "sealed for life" type, and is charged by an alternator, which is belt-driven from the crankshaft pulley.

The starter motor is the pre-engaged type, incorporating an integral solenoid. On starting, the solenoid moves the drive pinion into engagement with the flywheel ring gear before the starter motor is energised. Once the engine has started, a one-way clutch prevents the motor armature being driven by the engine until the pinion disengages from the flywheel.

2 Ignition system - general

1 The ignition system is responsible for igniting the air/fuel mixture in each cylinder at the correct moment, in relation to engine speed and load. All Calibra models have a fully integrated engine management system controlling both ignition and fuel injection systems. The fuel injection system is described in Chapter 4A.

2 The ignition system is based on feeding low tension voltage from the ignition switch to the primary coil, where it is converted to high tension voltage in a secondary coil. The high tension voltage is powerful enough to jump the spark plug gap in the cylinders many times a second under high compression pressures, provided the system is in good condition. The primary coil is connected to the electronic control module or a separate switching amplifier so that it can be switched on and off. The secondary coil is part of a separate circuit which sends a high tension voltage to the spark plugs, either directly or through a distributor. In the case of direct ignition, there are two sets of coils, each providing a spark to two cylinders.

3 The system functions as follows. Current flowing through the low tension coil produces a magnetic field around the high tension coil. As the engine rotates, a sensor produces an electrical impulse that is amplified and switches off the low tension circuit.

4 The subsequent collapse of the magnetic field over the high tension coil produces a high tension voltage, suitable for firing a spark. The low tension circuit is then switched on again by the electronic module, to allow the magnetic field to build up, ready for the next spark. The ignition is advanced and retarded automatically, to ensure that the spark occurs at the correct instant with respect to the engine speed and load.

MSTS-i (Microprocessor-controlled spark timing system with inductive triggering)

5 MSTS-i is a generic term for any ignition system that uses a microprocessor and a system of sensors, including inductive triggers, to control the timing and dwell of a spark. The sensors collect data on the crankshaft position, engine speed, load and temperature, and use the data to calculate the optimum timing to achieve maximum efficiency without knocking. The spark on any cylinder has to occur at an appropriate angle before top-dead centre on the ignition stroke.

6 The ignition advance angle is calculated by the microprocessor, based primarily on the engine speed and load, using a table of values known as a "timing map". Where the engine speed and load do not correspond to any pre-programmed values, the system interpolates between the nearest values as required.

7 On some systems, the ignition timing is corrected to correspond to a specific grade of petrol, and a coding plug has to be set to the correct octane rating of the petrol being used. On other systems, there are knock sensors instead of a coding plug, and ignition timing is automatically retarded if knocking (or pre-ignition) occurs.

8 Having calculated the precise timing and dwell duration of a spark, the microprocessor sends an amplified signal to the low-tension (primary) coil, switching it off, causing a high-tension voltage to occur in the secondary coil.

9 An "inductive trigger" is a type of sensor that returns electrical signals when mechanical components are passed through a magnetic field.

Distributed ignition system

10 In a distributed ignition system, the high-tension voltage is fed to the appropriate cylinder through a distributor. On Calibra models, the distributor is mounted on the camshaft (the exhaust camshaft on 16-valve models) at the transmission end of the engine. It consists of a rotor arm which passes in front of four stators, each connected to a spark plug. The arrival of the rotor arm in front of a stator is timed to coincide with the high-tension pulse that arrives from the coils, so that it sends the pulse to the appropriate plug. Since the ignition timing has already been calculated by the microprocessor, there is no need for a set of points. This type of distributor is known as a "breakerless distributor".

11 Distributed ignition is used on all C20 NE models, and on C20 XE models up to 1993.

Direct ignition system (DIS)

12 On a four-cylinder engine, the cylinders are brought to top dead centre (TDC) in pairs as the engine rotates. When the crankshaft angle is zero, cylinders 1 and 4 are at TDC with cylinder 1 on the ignition stroke and cylinder 4 on the exhaust stroke. At 180°, cylinders 2 and 3 are at TDC with cylinder 3 on the ignition stroke and cylinder 2 on the exhaust stroke. The cycle is repeated, bringing the same cylinders to TDC in pairs, but with the ignition/exhaust functions reversed.

13 In a direct ignition system, there is no distributor. Instead, there are two sets of coils, each feeding a spark directly to a pair of cylinders. Both cylinders receive the spark at the same time, regardless of which one is on the ignition stroke. The cylinder on the exhaust stroke receives a "wasted spark", but this is of no consequence. The DIS system actually uses less energy than a distributed system, because the energy used by the wasted spark is less than the energy that would be required to get the high-tension current across a distributor. It also has the advantage that it has no moving parts and is largely maintenance-free.

14 Direct ignition is used on all X20 XEV models, and on C20 XE models from 1993 onwards.

Engine speed and position sensors

15 On all Calibra models, a speed/position sensor is activated by a toothed wheel on the crankshaft. The toothed wheel has 35 equally spaced teeth, with a gap in the 36th position. The sensor is an inductive magnet signal generator, containing a permanent magnet which radiates a magnetic field onto the toothed wheel. As the teeth pass through the magnetic field, they generate an AC waveform which is picked up by the sensor, giving the engine speed. When the gap left by the missing tooth passes the sensor, the waveform is modulated, giving the crankshaft position relative to TDC on No 1 piston. Some engines have additional sensors as follows:

16 On C20 XE models, up to 1993, a Hall effect generator is mounted in the distributor. This has four cut-outs on the distributor rotor, one for each cylinder, and sends a small voltage signal to the control module whenever a cut-out passes through a magnetic field. The purpose of the Hall generator is to send a timing signal to the microprocessor at each phase of the engine cycle. It is mounted in the distributor as a matter of convenience and has nothing to do with the distribution of the high-tension voltage. The use of a Hall-effect generator is sometimes referred to as "MSTS-h".

17 On models that use direct ignition, there is no distributor in which a Hall-effect generator could be mounted. On C20 XE models from 1993 onwards, a camshaft phase sensor is attached to the cylinder head in the position normally occupied by the distributor. On X20 XEV models the camshaft phase sensor is mounted at the timing belt side of the engine and picks up a signal from a step on the exhaust camshaft sprocket.

Motronic M1.5

18 The Motronic M1.5 system is fitted to C20 NE models and has the following sensors:
  a) *Crankshaft speed/position sensor*
  b) *Throttle potentiometer*
  c) *Air flow meter (vane type)*
  d) *Engine coolant temperature sensor mounted in the thermostat housing*
  e) *Octane number plug*
  f) *Oxygen sensor mounted in the exhaust system (see Chapters 4A and 4B)*

19 A breakerless distributor is used to feed the high-tension voltage to the plugs.

20 The octane coding plug can be set to 91 or 95 RON to match the grade of petrol being used, and the microprocessor adjusts the ignition timing to prevent knocking. The factory-set value is 95 RON. If you wish to use a lower grade of petrol, you will need to reverse the plug, to prevent damage to the engine (see Section 21).

Motronic M2.5

21 This system is used on C20 XE models up to 1993 and is similar to the Motronic M1.5 but with the following differences.

22 A "Hall-effect" generator is mounted in the distributor to send an ignition trigger signal to the microprocessor for each phase of the engine cycle.

23 An ignition amplifier receives a signal from the control module and sends an amplified signal to the primary coil, switching it off and triggering the HT pulse from the secondary coil. The amplifier is mounted on the ignition coil's bracket/baseplate.

24 Instead of the vane-type air flow meter, there is a mass air meter consisting of a wire that is heated by an electrical current. The mass of air passing through the meter is measured from its cooling effect on the wire. This type of meter is independent of air temperature and gives an accurate measurement of the air flow.

25 The throttle potentiometer is replaced by a throttle valve switch with contacts for the idling and full-load positions.

26 A knock sensor is mounted on the cylinder block, to detect knocking just as it begins to occur, and the control module makes the appropriate correction to retard the ignition timing. The octane coding plug is discarded because it is unnecessary. You can fill the tank with any grade of unleaded petrol within the specified range, without having to empty it first, and the ignition timing will be adjusted automatically.

Motronic M2.8

27 This system is used on C20 XE models from 1993 onwards and is similar to the Motronic M2.5 but with the following differences.

28 A direct ignition system (DIS) is used and there is no distributor.

29 A camshaft phase sensor is mounted on the cylinder block, in the place that was previously occupied by the distributor.

30 The control module uses the signal from the camshaft phase sensor, in combination with the knock sensor, to identify the cylinder that is knocking and applies adaptive knock control to that cylinder.

31 A hot film air mass meter is used instead of a hot wire air mass meter. It operates on the same principle but is more robust and less vulnerable to failure.

32 The throttle switch is discarded and the throttle potentiometer, previously used on the M1.5 system, is re-introduced.

33 The ignition amplifier is incorporated into the control module so that it no longer exists as a separate unit.

Simtec 56.1

34 This system is used on X20 XEV models up to 1997 and the ignition features are similar to the Motronic M2.8, although it is a different system and is not a development of Motronic. It has a DIS module mounted on the cylinder block on the transmission side of the engine where the distributor or camshaft phase sensor would be mounted on the other engines.

35 The sensors are as follows:
  a) *Crankshaft speed/position sensor*
  b) *Camshaft phase sensor, mounted on the timing side of the engine*
  c) *Throttle potentiometer*
  d) *Hot film mass air meter*
  e) *Engine coolant temperature sensor*
  f) *Air inlet temperature sensor, fitted to the inlet duct between the air cleaner and the air mass meter*
  g) *Knock sensor*
  h) *Oxygen sensor mounted in the exhaust system (see Chapters 4A and 4B)*
  i) *Wheel speed sensor (odometer)*

36 The system is fitted with exhaust gas recirculation (EGR) and secondary air injection (AIR) for emission control purposes. For details see Chapter 4B.

5

Simtec 56.5

37 This system is used on X20 XEV models from 1997 onwards and is the same as Simtec 56.1 but with the following modifications.

38 There is a switched intake system with four air inlet tracts, one for each cylinder, that go round in a loop. Four switchover valves are mounted on a single shaft so that they all operate together. The valves open and close to send the inlet air round a long or short path. The switchover valves are regulated, depending on the engine speed and load. At engine speeds above 3,600 rpm the valves are generally open, sending the air round the short path. The result is smoother and higher torque progression, especially in the lower engine speed range.

39 The secondary air injection system has been modified. See Chapter 4B.

40 The control unit hardware has been modified.

3 Electrical system - precautions

⚠️ **Warning: The HT voltage generated by an electronic ignition system is extremely high and, in certain circumstances, could prove fatal. Take care to avoid receiving electric shocks from the HT side of the ignition system. Do not handle HT leads, or touch the distributor or coil, when the engine is running. If tracing faults in the HT circuit, use well-insulated tools to manipulate live leads.**

1 It is necessary to take extra care when working on the electrical system, to avoid damage to semi-conductor devices (diodes and transistors), and to avoid the risk of personal injury. Along with the precautions given in the *"Safety first!"* Section at the beginning of this manual, take note of the following points when working on the system.

2 *Always remove rings, watches, etc. before working on the electrical system.* Even with the battery disconnected, discharge could occur if a component live terminal is earthed through a metal object. This could cause a shock or nasty burn.

3 *Do not reverse the battery connections.* Components such as the alternator, or any other component having semi-conductor circuitry, could be irreparably damaged.

4 If the engine is being started using jump leads and a slave battery, connect the batteries *positive to positive* and *negative to negative.* This also applies when connecting a battery charger.

5 Never disconnect the battery terminals, or alternator multi-plug connector, when the engine is running.

6 The battery leads and alternator wiring must be disconnected before carrying out any electric welding on the vehicle.

7 Never use an ohmmeter of the type incorporating a hand-cranked generator for circuit or continuity testing.

Electronic control units

8 The Calibra has a variety of electronic control units, for the fuel/ignition system, anti-lock braking, central locking, airbags and other components depending on the options fitted. These are very sensitive and certain precautions must be taken to avoid damage, as follows.

9 When carrying out welding operations on the vehicle using electric welding equipment, the battery and alternator should be disconnected.

10 Although underbonnet-mounted control units will tolerate normal underbonnet conditions, they can be adversely affected by excess heat or moisture. If using welding equipment or pressure washing equipment, take care not to direct heat, or jets of water or steam, at the unit. If this cannot be avoided, remove the unit from the vehicle, and protect its wiring plug with a plastic bag.

11 Before disconnecting any wiring, or removing components, always ensure that the ignition is switched off.

12 Do not attempt to improvise fault diagnosis procedures using a test lamp or multimeter, as irreparable damage could be caused to the control unit.

13 After working on ignition/engine management system components, ensure that all wiring is correctly reconnected before reconnecting the battery or switching on the ignition.

14 On an ignition system that uses a "Hall-effect" distributor, do not connect test equipment that uses its own power source (e.g. an ohmmeter), directly to the distributor or the Hall-effect generator, as the test equipment will be damaged.

4 Ignition system testing - general

Note: *Refer to Section 3 before proceeding. Always switch off the ignition before disconnecting or connecting any component and when using a multi-meter to check resistances. Any voltmeter or multi-meter used to test ignition system components must have an impedance of 10 meg ohms or greater.*

1 Electronic ignition system components are normally very reliable. Most faults are far more likely to be due to loose or dirty connections, or to "tracking" of HT voltage due to dirt, dampness or damaged insulation than to component failure.

2 The simplest way to check for ignition system faults is to use a hand-held instrument called TECH 1, which connects to a diagnostic plug on the wiring harness in the engine compartment. If you do not have TECH 1, you should take your vehicle to a Vauxhall dealer and they will be able to find the fault, using TECH 1, much quicker than you would be able to find it yourself. See the Reference Chapter for further information about fault finding and test equipment.

3 A limited amount of system testing can be performed without the use of TECH 1. If you are in any doubt as to your skill and ability to test an ignition system component, or if you do not have the required equipment, take the vehicle to a Vauxhall dealer, to avoid the risk of damage to the system or to yourself. If you are sure you know what you are doing, continue with the rest of this Section.

4 If you suspect that a component is faulty, check all wiring thoroughly and work methodically to eliminate all other possibilities before condemning the component.

5 The old practice of checking for a spark by holding the live end of a HT lead a short distance away from the engine is not recommended. Not only is there a high risk of a powerful electric shock, but the ignition coil or amplifier module will be damaged. Similarly, never try to "diagnose" misfires by pulling off one HT lead at a time. Note also that the ECU is at risk if the system is triggered with an open (i.e., not properly earthed) HT circuit; ECU's are very expensive to replace, so take care!

6 If the engine either will not turn over at all, or only turns very slowly, check the battery and starter motor. Connect a voltmeter across the battery terminals (meter positive probe to battery positive terminal) and disconnect the ignition coil HT lead from the distributor cap and earth. Note the voltage reading obtained while turning over the engine on the starter for (no more than) ten seconds. If the reading obtained is less than approximately 9.5 volts, check the battery, battery connections, starter motor and charging system.

7 If the engine turns over at normal speed but will not start, check the HT circuit by connecting a timing light and turning the engine over on the starter motor. If the light flashes, voltage is reaching the spark plugs, so these should be checked first. If the light does not flash, check the HT leads themselves followed by the distributor cap, carbon brush and rotor arm.

8 If there is a spark, check the fuel system for faults as far as possible (Chapter 4A).

9 If there is still no spark, check the voltage at the ignition coil "+" or "15" terminal; it should be the same as the battery voltage (i.e., at least 11.7 volts). If the voltage at the coil is more than 1 volt less than that at the battery, check the connections back through the ignition switch to the battery and its earth until the fault is found. Note, however, that the ECU controls the coil's feed; do not attempt to "test" the ECU with anything other than the correct test equipment. If any of the wires are to be checked which lead to the ECU, always first unplug the relevant connector from the ECU so that there is no risk of the ECU being damaged by the application of incorrect voltages from test equipment.

10 If the feed to the ignition coil is sound, check the coil's primary and secondary windings (refer to Section 16). Renew the coil if faulty, but check the condition of the LT connections themselves before doing so, to ensure that the fault is not due to dirty or poorly fastened connectors.

11 An irregular misfire suggests either a loose connection or intermittent fault on the primary circuit, or a HT fault on the coil side of the rotor arm.

12 With the ignition switched off, check carefully through the system ensuring that all connections are clean and securely fastened. If the equipment is available, check the LT circuit as described in paragraphs 9 and 10 above.

13 Check that the HT coil, the distributor cap and the HT leads are clean and dry. Check the leads and the spark plugs (by substitution, if necessary), then check the distributor cap, carbon brush and rotor arm.

14 Regular misfiring is almost certainly due to a fault in the distributor cap, HT leads or spark plugs. Use a timing light (paragraph 7, above) to check whether HT voltage is present at all leads.

15 If HT voltage is not present on any particular lead, the fault will be in that lead or in the distributor cap. If HT is present on all leads, the fault will be in the spark plugs; check and renew them if there is any doubt about their condition.

16 If no HT voltage is present, check the ignition coil; its secondary windings may be breaking down under load.

17 If all components have been checked for signs of obvious faults but the system is still thought to be faulty, take the vehicle to a Vauxhall dealer for testing with TECH 1 or other special equipment.

5 Battery -
testing and charging

Note: *Refer to Section 3 before proceeding.*

Testing

1 Topping-up and testing of the electrolyte in each cell is not possible. The condition of the battery can therefore only be tested by observing the battery condition indicator.

2 The battery condition indicator is fitted in the top of the battery casing, and indicates the condition of the battery from its colour. If the indicator shows green, then the battery is in a good state of charge. If the indicator turns darker, eventually to black, then the battery requires charging, as described later in this Section. If the indicator shows clear/yellow, then the electrolyte level in the battery is too low to allow further use, and the battery should be renewed.

Charging

3 Do not attempt to charge, load or jump start a battery when the indicator shows clear/

yellow. If the battery is to be charged, remove it from the vehicle and charge it as follows.

4 The maintenance-free type battery takes considerably longer to fully recharge than the standard type, the time taken being dependent on the extent of discharge.

5 A constant-voltage type charger needs to be set, when connected, to 13.9 to 14.9 volts with a charger current below 25 amps.

6 If the battery is to be charged from a fully discharged state (less than 12.2 volts output), have it recharged by a Vauxhall dealer or battery specialist, as the charge rate will be high and constant supervision during charging is necessary.

6 Battery -
removal and refitting

Note: *Refer to Section 3 before proceeding.*

Removal

1 The battery is located at the left-hand front corner of the engine compartment.

2 Disconnect the lead(s) at the negative (earth) terminal by unscrewing the retaining nut and removing the terminal clamp.

3 Disconnect the positive terminal lead(s) in the same way.

4 Unscrew the clamp bolt sufficiently to enable the battery to be lifted from its location. Keep the battery in an upright position, to avoid spilling electrolyte on the bodywork.

Refitting

5 Refitting is the reverse of removal, but smear petroleum jelly on the terminals when reconnecting the leads, and always connect the positive lead first and the negative lead last.

7 Alternator -
description

1 A Delco-Remy or Bosch alternator may be fitted, depending on the model.

2 The alternator is belt-driven from the crankshaft pulley. Cooling is provided by a fan, mounted outside the casing on the end of the rotor shaft. An integral voltage regulator is incorporated, to control the output voltage.

3 The alternator provides a charge to the battery even at very low engine speed, and consists of a coil-wound stator in which a rotor rotates. The rotor shaft is supported in ball-bearings, and slip rings are used to conduct current to and from the field coils through the carbon brushes.

4 The alternator generates ac (alternating current), which is rectified by an internal diode circuit to dc (direct current) for supply to the battery.

5 Later models are fitted with Delco-Remy, 'compact' series alternators **(see illustration)**. They use a serpentine drivebelt with automatic tensioner, and are rigidly mounted to the engine.

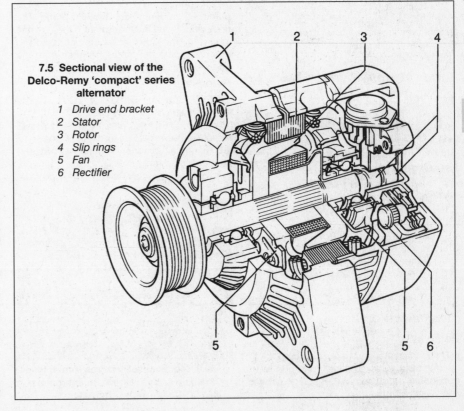

7.5 Sectional view of the Delco-Remy 'compact' series alternator

1 Drive end bracket
2 Stator
3 Rotor
4 Slip rings
5 Fan
6 Rectifier

5

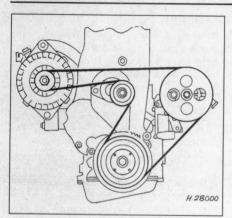

8.15 Routing of serpentine belt on models without air conditioning

8 Auxiliary drivebelts - removal and refitting

General

1 Early Calibra models, up to 1993, are fitted with twin V-belts, one for the alternator and one for the power steering pump. From 1993 onwards, these were replaced by a single serpentine belt, driving the alternator, power steering pump, and also the air conditioning pump if fitted. The serpentine belt is tensioned by an automatic tensioning roller and needs no adjustment.
2 The belts should be inspected regularly, and if found to be worn, frayed or cracked, they should be renewed as a precaution against breakage in service. It is advisable to always carry spare drivebelts of the correct type in the vehicle.

Power steering pump V-belt

Removal

3 Slacken the power steering pump mounting and adjuster bolts, as described in Chapter 10, then turn the adjuster to slacken the belt and remove it from the pulleys.

Refitting

4 Refitting is the reverse of removal, noting the following points.
5 Ensure that the correct type of belt is used, if it is being renewed.
6 Adjust the belt tension as described in Chapter 1, and tighten the bolts to the specified torque as described in Chapter 10.
7 New belts might stretch slightly and the tension should be rechecked and if necessary adjusted after approximately 250 miles (400 km).

Alternator V-belt

Removal

8 Disconnect the air inlet trunking from the air cleaner, and the air box or throttle body, as applicable, and remove it for improved access.

9 Remove the power steering pump V-belt as described in paragraph 3.
10 Slacken the two alternator mounting nuts and bolts sufficiently to allow the alternator to be pivoted in towards the engine, then slide the belt from the pulleys.

Refitting

11 Refitting is the reverse of removal, noting the following points.
12 Ensure that the correct type of belt is used, if it is being renewed.
13 Adjust the belt tension as described in Chapter 1, and tighten the bolts to the specified torque.
14 New belts might stretch slightly and the tension should be rechecked and if necessary adjusted after approximately 250 miles (400 km).

Serpentine-belt (models without air conditioning)

15 On these models, a single auxiliary drivebelt passes round the crankshaft, alternator and power steering pump pulleys, and is tensioned by an automatic tensioner pulley **(see illustration)**. The belt passes through the right-hand engine mounting, on its way from the power steering pump to the crankshaft pulley. To remove the drivebelt, you have to remove the engine mounting and drivebelt as a complete assembly, as described in Chapter 2A.

Serpentine-belt (models with air conditioning)

16 The routing of this auxiliary drivebelt is the same as in paragraph 15, except that there is an additional pulley for the air conditioning pump, below the power steering pump. The drivebelt passes underneath the engine mounting, instead of going through it, so you can disengage the mounting bush from the bodywork and feed the belt through the gap.

Removal

17 For improved access, remove the air cleaner assembly and air inlet trunking.
18 If the original drivebelt is to be refitted, mark the rotational direction on the belt with chalk.
19 Using a spanner or socket on the automatic tensioning roller hexagon, turn the tensioning roller clockwise (as viewed from

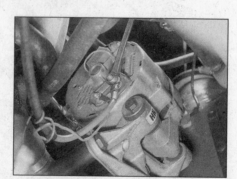

9.3 Disconnect the wires from the terminals on the rear of the alternator - Delco-Remy alternator

the right-hand side of the car) and hold it in this position. With the drivebelt tension released, slip the drivebelt off the pulleys, then allow the tensioner to return to its original position.
20 Support the engine under the sump with a jack, and place a block of wood on top of the front subframe, under the sump.
21 Undo the bolts connecting the mounting bush to the bodywork but leave the bush and bracket assembly attached to the engine. Then lower the engine just enough to allow the drivebelt to be withdrawn from between the mounting bush and the body.

Refitting

22 Refitting is the reverse of removal, noting the following points.
23 When refitting the same drivebelt, fit the belt in the same direction, marked by the arrow.
24 When refitting a new drivebelt, make sure you have the correct type of belt. There is a longer belt on models with air conditioning.
25 When refitting the engine mounting bush to the bodywork, first check that the original bolts rotate freely in their threaded bores and are not fouled by the old locking fluid. If necessary, re-cut the threaded bores using an M10 x 1.25 mm tap. Then use new bolts, coated with locking fluid, and tighten them to the torque specified in Chapter 2A.

> **HAYNES HiNT**
> *If a tap is not available, cut two slots into the threads of one of the old flywheel bolts and use it to clean out the threaded bores.*

26 You will need an assistant to help you refit the drivebelt around the pulleys. Slacken the tensioner from underneath the car and feed the belt round the power steering pump pulley, while your assistant, working above the car, feeds the belt over the alternator pulley. Then release the tensioner.

9 Alternator - removal and refitting

Note: *Refer to Section 3 before proceeding.*

Except 'compact' series alternators

Removal

1 Disconnect the battery leads.
2 Disconnect the air trunking from the air cleaner, and the air box or throttle body, as applicable, and remove it for improved access.
3 Disconnect the wiring plug, or disconnect the wires from their terminals on the rear of the alternator, noting their locations **(see illustration)**.

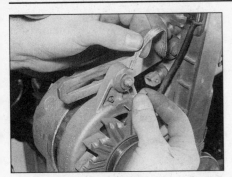

9.5 Disconnect the earth lead from the top alternator mounting bolt

4 Slacken the mounting nuts and bolts, and tilt the alternator towards the engine to release the belt tension, then slip the belt off the alternator pulley.

5 Remove the mounting nuts and bolts and recover any washers and insulating bushes, noting their locations. Note the earth strap attached to the top mounting bolt **(see illustration)**.

6 Withdraw the alternator, taking care not to knock or drop it, as this can cause irreparable damage.

Refitting

7 Refitting is the reverse of removal, remembering the following points.

8 Ensure that the earth lead is in place on the top mounting bolt.

9 Slip the drivebelt over the pulley, then tension it as described in Chapter 1.

10 Tighten the bolts to the specified torque.

'Compact' series alternators

Removal

11 Disconnect the battery negative lead.

12 Remove the air inlet trunking and, if necessary for improved access, the air cleaner assembly.

13 Using a spanner or socket on the automatic tensioning roller hexagon turn the tensioning roller clockwise (as viewed from the right-hand

side of the car) and hold it in this position. With the drivebelt tension released, slip the drivebelt off the alternator pulley, then allow the tensioner to return to its original position.

14 Disconnect the electrical cable connections at the rear of the alternator.

15 Undo and remove the alternator lower mounting bolt, and slacken both upper bolts that secure the alternator mounting brackets to the engine.

16 Undo and remove both bolts that secure the alternator to its mounting brackets, noting the location of the different length bolts. Swing the brackets clear and remove the alternator from the engine.

Refitting

17 Refitting is the reverse of removal, noting the following points.

18 Tighten the mounting bolts to the specified torque.

19 Rotate the automatic tensioner roller clockwise and slip the belt over the alternator pulley, then release the tensioner so that the correct tension is applied to the belt.

10 Alternator - testing

Due to the specialist knowledge and equipment required to test or service an alternator, it is recommended that if a fault is suspected, the vehicle is taken to a dealer or a specialist. Information is limited to the inspection and renewal of the brushes. Should the alternator not charge, or the system be suspect, the following points may be checked before seeking further assistance:

a) *If a V-belt is fitted, check the belt tension, as described in Chapter 1*

b) *Check the condition of the battery and its connections - see Section 5*

c) *Inspect all electrical cables and connections for condition and security*

11.3 Separate the drive end housing from the slip ring end housing - Delco-Remy alternator

Note that if the alternator is found to be faulty, it may prove more economical to buy a factory-reconditioned unit, rather than having the existing unit overhauled.

11 Alternator brushes - removal, inspection and refitting

Delco-Remy type (except 'compact' series)

Removal

1 Remove the alternator, as described in Section 9.

2 Draw a line across the drive end housing and the slip ring end housing, to ensure correct alignment when reassembling.

3 Unscrew the three through-bolts, and prise the drive end housing and rotor away from the slip ring end housing and stator **(see illustration)**.

4 Check the condition of the slip rings, and if necessary clean with a rag or very fine glass paper **(see illustration)**.

5 Remove the three nuts and washers securing the stator leads to the rectifier, and lift away the stator assembly **(see illustration)**.

5

11.4 Alternator slip rings (arrowed) - Delco-Remy alternator

11.5 Delco-Remy alternator with stator lead securing nuts (A) and brush holder/voltage regulator securing screws (B)

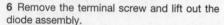

11.15 Withdrawing the twist drill used to retain the brushes - Delco-Remy alternator

11.20a Remove the securing screws . . .

11.20b . . . and withdraw the brush holder/voltage regulator assembly - Bosch alternator

6 Remove the terminal screw and lift out the diode assembly.

7 Extract the two screws securing the brush holder and voltage regulator to the slip ring end housing, and remove the brush holder assembly. Note the insulation washers under the screw heads.

Inspection

8 Check that the brushes move freely in their guides, and that the brush lengths are within the limits given in the Specifications. If any doubt exists regarding the condition of the brushes, the best policy is to renew them.

9 To fit new brushes, unsolder the old brush leads from the brush holder, and solder on the new leads in exactly the same place.

10 Check that the new brushes move freely in the guides.

Refitting

11 Before refitting the brush holder assembly, retain the brushes in the retracted position using a stiff piece of wire or a twist drill.

12 Refit the brush holder assembly so that the wire or drill protrudes through the slot in the slip ring end housing, and tighten the securing screws.

13 Refit the diode assembly and the stator assembly to the housing, ensuring that the stator leads are in their correct positions, and refit the terminal screw and nuts.

14 Assemble the drive end housing and rotor to the slip ring end housing, ensuring that the previously made marks are aligned. Insert and

tighten the three through-bolts.

15 Pull the wire or drill, as applicable, from the slot in the slip ring end housing so that the brushes rest on the rotor slip rings **(see illustration)**.

16 Refit the alternator, as described in Section 9.

Bosch type alternator

Removal

17 Disconnect the air trunking from the air cleaner, and the air box or throttle body, as applicable, and remove it for improved access.

18 Disconnect the battery leads.

19 If desired, to improve access further, the alternator can be removed, as described in Section 9.

20 Remove the two securing screws, and withdraw the brush holder/voltage regulator assembly **(see illustrations)**.

Inspection

21 Check that the brushes move freely in their guides, and that the brush lengths are within the limits given in the Specifications **(see illustration)**. If any doubt exists regarding the condition of the brushes, the best policy is to renew them as follows.

22 Hold the brush wire with a pair of pliers, and unsolder it from the brush holder. Lift away the brush. Repeat for the remaining brush.

Refitting

23 Note that whenever new brushes are fitted, new brush springs should also be fitted.

24 With the new springs fitted to the brush holder, insert the new brushes, and check that they move freely in their guides. If they bind, lightly polish with a very fine file or glass paper.

25 Solder the brush wire ends to the brush holder, taking care not to allow solder to pass to the stranded wire.

26 Check the condition of the slip rings, and if necessary clean with a rag or very fine glass paper **(see illustration)**.

27 Refit the brush holder/voltage regulator assembly, and tighten the securing screws.

28 Where applicable, refit the alternator, as described in Section 9.

29 Reconnect the battery leads.

30 Refit the air trunking.

Delco-Remy "compact" series

Removal

31 Remove the alternator as described in Section 9.

32 Remove the plastic cover from the rear of the alternator.

33 Undo the two bolts securing the brush holder to the rear of the alternator, noting that one of the bolts also secures the suppression capacitor.

34 Remove the suppression capacitor then withdraw the brush holder, noting the flat plug on the side.

Inspection

35 Check that the brushes move freely in their holder and that the brush lengths are within the limits given in the Specifications. If any doubt exists regarding the condition of the brushes, the best policy is to renew them.

36 Check the condition of the slip rings, and if necessary clean with a rag or very fine glass paper.

Refitting

37 Refitting the brushes is the reverse of removal.

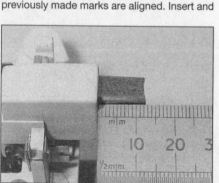

11.21 Measuring the length of an alternator brush - Bosch alternator

11.26 Alternator slip rings (arrowed) - Bosch alternator

12 Starter motor - general

The starter motor is mounted at the rear of the cylinder block, and may be of either Delco-Remy or Bosch manufacture. Both makes are of the pre-engaged type, i.e. the drive pinion is brought into mesh with the starter ring gear on the flywheel before the main current is applied.

When the starter switch is operated, current flows from the battery to the solenoid that is mounted on the starter body. The plunger in the solenoid moves inwards, so causing a centrally pivoted lever to push the drive pinion into mesh with the starter ring gear. When the solenoid plunger reaches the end of its travel, it closes an internal contact and full starting current flows to the starter field coils. The armature is then able to rotate the crankshaft, so starting the engine.

A special freewheel clutch is fitted to the starter driven pinion, so that when the engine fires and starts to operate on its own it does not drive the starter motor.

When the starter switch is released, the solenoid is de-energised, and a spring moves the plunger back to its rest position. This operates the pivoted lever to withdraw the drive pinion from engagement with the starter ring.

13 Starter motor - testing

Note: *Refer to Section 3 before proceeding.*

1 If the starter motor fails to turn the engine when the switch is operated, and engine seizure is not the problem, there are several other possible reasons:

  a) *The battery is faulty*
  b) *The electrical connections between the switch, solenoid battery and starter motor are somewhere failing to pass the necessary current from the battery through the starter to earth*
  c) *The solenoid switch is faulty*
  d) *The starter motor is mechanically or electrically defective*
  e) *The starter motor pinion and/or flywheel ring gear is badly worn, and in need of replacement*

2 To check the battery, switch on the headlamps. If they dim after a few seconds, then the battery is in a discharged state. If the lamps glow brightly, operate the starter switch and see what happens to the lamps. If they dim, then power is reaching the motor, but failing to turn it. If the starter turns slowly, go on to the next check.

3 If, when the starter switch is operated, the lamps stay bright, then insufficient power is reaching the motor. Disconnect the battery and the starter/solenoid power connections,

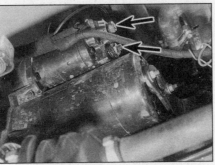

14.4 Starter motor and solenoid viewed from underneath the vehicle. Solenoid wiring connections arrowed

and the engine earth strap, then thoroughly clean them and refit them. Smear petroleum jelly around the battery connections to prevent corrosion. Corroded connections are the most frequent cause of electrical system malfunctions.

4 If the preceding checks and cleaning tasks have been carried out without success, a clicking noise will probably have been heard each time the starter switch was operated. This indicates that the solenoid switch was operating, but it does not necessarily follow that the main contacts were closing properly (if no clicking has been heard from the solenoid, it is certainly defective). The solenoid can be checked by connecting a voltmeter across the main cable connection on the solenoid and earth. When the switch is operated, these should be a reading on the voltmeter. If there is no reading, the solenoid unit is faulty, and should be renewed.

5 If the starter motor operates, but does not turn the engine, then it is likely that the starter pinion and/or flywheel ring gear are badly worn. If this is the case, the starter motor will normally be noisy in operation.

6 Finally, if it is established that the solenoid is not faulty, and 12 volts are reaching the starter, then the motor itself is faulty, and should be removed for inspection.

14 Starter motor - removal and refitting

Note: *Refer to Section 3 before proceeding.*

Removal

1 Disconnect the battery negative lead.
2 Apply the handbrake, then jack up the front of the vehicle, and support securely on axle stands positioned under the body side members (see *"Jacking and Vehicle Support"*).
3 On DOHC models, remove the engine undershield, as described in Chapter 11, if there is one.
4 Note the wiring connections on the solenoid, then disconnect them **(see illustration)**.

14.5 Starter motor mounting bracket/exhaust bracket securing bolt (arrowed)

5 Where applicable, unscrew the bolt securing the exhaust bracket and the starter motor mounting bracket to the cylinder block **(see illustration)**.
6 Unscrew the two starter motor mounting bolts. Note that the top bolt on some models is fitted from the transmission side, and secures a wiring harness bracket **(see illustration)**.
7 Withdraw the starter motor.

Refitting

8 Refitting is the reverse of removal, but where applicable, ensure that the wiring harness bracket is in place on the top mounting bolt, and tighten all bolts to the specified torque.

15 Starter motor - overhaul

If the starter motor is thought to be suspect, it should be removed from the vehicle and taken to an auto-electrician for testing. Most auto-electricians will be able to supply and fit brushes at a reasonable cost. However, check on the cost of repairs before continuing as it may prove more economical to obtain a new or exchange motor.

5

14.6 Starter motor securing bolts (arrowed) - engine removed

16.3 Disconnecting the coil LT wiring plug

16 Ignition coil (Motronic M1.5 and M2.5) - removal, testing and refitting

Note 1: *Motronic M1.5 is used on all C20 NE models, and Motronic M2.5 is used on C20 XE models up to May 1993. All other models use a direct ignition system, incorporating dual spark-ignition coils within the DIS module so that there are no separate coils. See Section 25 for details of removing and refitting the DIS module.*
Note 2: *Refer to Section 3 before proceeding.*
Note 3: *An ohmmeter will be required to test the coil.*

Removal

1 The ignition coil is clamped or bolted to the left-hand inner wing panel, near the power steering fluid reservoir.

17.4 Unscrew the distributor cap securing screw

17.5 Remove the plastic shield from the rotor arm housing

2 Disconnect the battery negative lead.
3 Carefully note the LT wiring connections before disconnecting them **(see illustration)**.
4 Note that one of the coil securing bolts also secures the power steering fluid reservoir bracket.
5 Remove the coil.
6 If required, remove the mounting clamp from the coil by loosening the clamp nut.

Testing

7 To test the coil, first disconnect the LT wiring and the HT lead. Test the coil's primary windings by connecting a multi-meter across the LT terminals ("+" or "15" and "-" or "1"). Then the secondary windings by testing across the HT terminal ("4") and one of the LT terminals (usually the "-/1" terminal, although in some cases, either terminal may serve). Typical primary resistances are less than 1 ohm, while secondary resistances can be expected to be in the 4,000 to 12,000 ohms range.
8 If the results obtained differ significantly from those given, showing windings that are shorted or open circuit, the coil must be renewed.

Refitting

9 Refitting is the reverse of removal. Ensure that the connections are correct. Usually they are physically different to prevent incorrect refitting. If not, use the terminal marks or numbers in conjunction with the relevant wiring diagram at the back of this manual to ensure that the connections are correctly remade. If the connections are reversed, so will the coil's polarity. While the engine may still run, spark plug life will be reduced and poor starting and/or misfiring may follow.
10 Ensure that the coil suppresser is in position before refitting the coil securing bolts.

17 Distributor cap and rotor arm (Motronic M1.5 and M2.5) - removal and refitting

Note 1: *Motronic M1.5 is used on all C20 NE models, and Motronic M2.5 is used on C20 XE models up to May 1993. All other models use*

17.6a Extract the two securing screws . . .

a direct ignition system and there is no distributor.
Note 2: *Refer to Section 3 before proceeding.*

Removal

1 Disconnect the battery negative lead.
2 On C20 XE models, unscrew the two securing bolts and withdraw the spark plug cover from the camshaft cover.
3 Identify each HT lead for position, so that the leads can be refitted to their correct cylinders, then disconnect the leads from the spark plugs by pulling on the connectors, not the leads. Similarly, disconnect the HT lead from the coil. Pull the leads from the clips on the camshaft cover.
4 Using a Torx socket, unscrew the three captive securing screws and withdraw the distributor cap **(see illustration)**.
5 Withdraw the plastic shield from the rotor arm housing. The shield is fitted in the housing, with an O-ring seal located in a groove in its periphery. Ease out the shield, taking care not to damage the rotor arm **(see illustration)**.
6 Using an Allen key or hexagon bit, extract the two securing screws and withdraw the rotor arm, leaving the metal rotor hub in the housing **(see illustrations)**.
7 Examine the O-ring on the plastic shield, and renew if necessary.

Refitting

8 Refitting is the reverse of removal, noting that the rotor arm can only be fitted in one position. If necessary, turn the metal rotor hub so that the screw holes align with those in the rotor arm and the end of the camshaft. Ensure that the HT leads are correctly reconnected.

18 Distributor (C20 NE models) - removal and refitting

Note: *Refer to Section 3 before proceeding.*

Removal

1 Disconnect the battery negative lead.
2 Remove the distributor cap, as described in Section 17.
3 Disconnect the distributor wiring plug.

17.6b . . . and withdraw the rotor arm

18.5 TDC arrow on the Lucas distributor body

4 If the original distributor is to be refitted, make alignment marks between the distributor body and the camshaft housing, so that the distributor can be refitted in its original position.

5 Turn the crankshaft. This can be done by either using a socket or spanner on the crankshaft pulley bolt, or by engaging top gear and pushing the vehicle backwards or forwards. Bring No 1 cylinder to the firing point. No 1 cylinder is at the firing point when:

a) *The relevant timing marks are aligned.*

b) *The tip of the rotor arm is pointing to the position occupied by the No 1 cylinder HT lead terminal in the distributor cap.*

c) *On the Bosch distributor, the rotor arm is aligned with the notch in the distributor body (remove the rotor arm and plastic shield, then refit the rotor arm to check the alignment with the notch). On the Lucas distributor, the rotor arm is approximately aligned with the TDC arrow stamped in the distributor body (see illustration).*

6 Unscrew the clamp nut and remove the clamp plate, then withdraw the distributor from the camshaft housing (see illustrations).

7 Check the condition of the O-ring on the rear of the distributor body, if there is one, and renew it if necessary.

Refitting

8 Begin refitting by checking that No 1 cylinder is still at the firing point. The relevant timing marks should be aligned. If the engine has been turned whilst the distributor has been removed, check that No 1 cylinder is on its firing stroke by removing No 1 cylinder

18.6b ... remove the clamp plate ...

18.6a Unscrew the clamp nut ...

spark plug and placing a finger over the plug hole. Turn the crankshaft until compression can be felt, which indicates that No 1 piston is rising on its compression stroke. Continue turning the crankshaft until the relevant timing marks are in alignment.

9 Turn the rotor arm to the position noted in paragraph 5c, and hold the rotor arm in this position as the distributor is fitted. Note that the distributor driveshaft will only engage with the camshaft in one position. If the original distributor is being refitted, align the marks made on the distributor body and camshaft housing before removal.

10 Refit the clamp plate and nut, but do not fully tighten the nut at this stage.

11 On the Bosch distributor, remove the rotor arm, then refit the plastic shield and the rotor arm.

12 Reconnect the distributor wiring plug.

13 Refit the distributor cap as described in Section 17.

14 Reconnect the battery negative lead.

15 Check the ignition timing, as described in Section 20.

19 Distributor (C20 XE models up to 1993) - removal and refitting

Note: *From May 1993 onwards, C20 XE models were fitted with direct ignition systems and there is no distributor.*

Removal

1 Disconnect the battery negative lead.

18.6c ... and withdraw the distributor

2 Remove the distributor cap, (see Section 17).

3 Disconnect the distributor wiring plug.

4 Unscrew the two securing bolts, and remove the distributor from the cylinder head.

5 Examine the O-ring on the rear of the distributor, and renew if necessary.

Refitting

6 Refitting is the reverse of removal. However, note that the distributor should be fitted so that the wiring plug is positioned on the upper left-hand side of the distributor body, when viewed from the distributor cap end.

20 Ignition timing - checking

1 No manual adjustment of the ignition timing is possible, except for the octane rating adjustment on C20 NE models. The ignition timing adjustment is carried out automatically by the electronic control module.

2 The ignition timing can be checked using a hand-held device called TECH 1, connected to a diagnostic plug on the wiring harness in the engine compartment. If you suspect that there is a fault and you do not have TECH 1, take the vehicle to a Vauxhall dealer for testing.

21 Ignition timing - adjustment for octane rating

C20 NE models

1 The octane coding plug can be set to 91 or 95 RON to match the grade of unleaded petrol being used, and the control module adjusts the ignition timing to prevent knocking. The factory-set value is 95 RON. If you wish to use a lower grade of petrol, you will need to reverse the plug to 91 RON. Do not use a lower grade of petrol than the value specified by the plug, otherwise knocking will occur, causing damage to the engine. No harm will be done if you use petrol with a higher grade than the setting of the plug.

2 The octane coding plug is located in a clip at the left-hand rear of the engine compartment (see illustration).

5

21.2 Octane coding plug (arrowed)

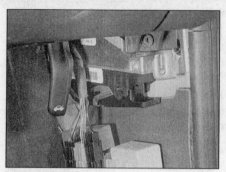

22.3 Electronic control unit above relays - Simtec

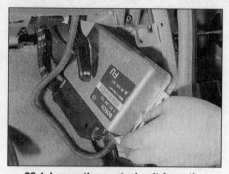

22.4 Lower the control unit from the footwell - Motronic

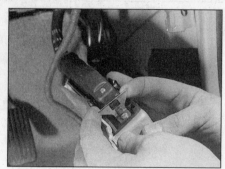

22.5 Release the control unit wiring plug clip - Motronic

3 The plug is reversible in its connector, and is marked with "95" on one side and "91" on the other, corresponding to the two grades of petrol.

4 To change the coding for use with a different type of petrol, first allow the fuel tank to become practically empty.

5 Fill the fuel tank with the required type of petrol.

6 Ensure that the ignition is switched off, then remove the coding plug from its clip and disconnect the wiring connector.

7 Rotate the plug through 180°, so that the appropriate octane rating is uppermost, then reconnect the wiring connector and refit the plug to its clip.

C20 XE and X20 XEV models

8 The ignition coding plug found on these models is **not** an octane coding plug (although its method of operation is similar) and must not be altered from its factory setting. Its purpose is to ensure that the control module uses the correct information, pre-programmed (or "mapped") into its memory, to enable the vehicle to comply with the relevant national noise and exhaust emission legislation.

9 On these models, the knock sensor circuit allows the control module to compensate for differences in the octane value of the petrol used, without the need for manual intervention. This means that these models can use any grade of unleaded petrol on sale in the UK without the need for adjustment.

22 Electronic control unit (ECU) - removal and refitting

Note: *Refer to Section 3 for precautions to be observed when working with electronic modules.*

Removal

1 Disconnect the battery negative lead.

2 Remove the driver's footwell side trim panel, as described in Chapter 11.

3 The control unit is behind the trim panel, above the relays **(see illustration)**.

4 Remove the securing screws and lower the control unit from the footwell **(see illustration)**.

5 Release the retaining clip, and disconnect the control unit wiring plug **(see illustration)**.

6 Withdraw the control unit from the vehicle.

Refitting

7 Refitting is the reverse of removal. If there is an insulating sheet on the rear face of the control unit, make sure it goes back in place correctly.

23 Coolant temperature sensor - removal and refitting

Note: *Refer to Section 3 before proceeding.*

Removal

1 The coolant temperature sensor is similar to the temperature gauge sender, described in Chapter 3, except that it provides a signal for use by the ECU. The sensor is located as follows **(see illustrations):**

a) On C20 NE models, in the end of the thermostat housing, on the inlet side of the engine;

b) On C20 XE models, in the thermostat housing, alongside the temperature gauge sender, on the exhaust side of the engine.

c) On X20 XEV models, in front of the DIS unit mounting flange, alongside the temperature gauge sender, at the transmission end of the cylinder head.

2 Disconnect the battery negative lead.

3 Partially drain the cooling system, as described in Chapter 3.

4 Disconnect the sensor wiring plug.

5 Using a spanner, unscrew the sensor and withdraw it from the thermostat housing.

Refitting

6 Refitting is the reverse of removal, remembering the following points.

7 Coat the sensor threads with sealant before fitting, and tighten to the specified torque.

8 On completion, top-up the cooling system, as described in Chapter 3, then start the engine and check for leaks.

23.1a Coolant temperature sensor wiring plug (alternator removed) - C20 NE engine

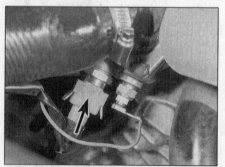

23.1b Coolant temperature sensor location (arrowed) - C20 XE engine

23.1c Coolant temperature sensor location (arrowed) - DIS unit removed - X20 XEV engine

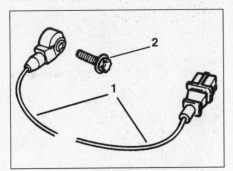

24.15 Knock sensor and wiring (Simtec system)

1 Sensor   *2 Securing bolt*

24 Knock sensor (C20 XE and X20 XEV engines) - removal and refitting

C20 XE (Motronic)

Removal

1 The sensor is located at the lower inlet manifold side of the cylinder block, below the idle speed adjuster, and is only accessible from below the vehicle.
2 Disconnect the battery negative lead.
3 Apply the handbrake, then jack up the front of the vehicle, and support securely on axle stands placed under the body side members (see "*Jacking and Vehicle Support*").
4 Remove the engine undershield, as described in Chapter 11.
5 Disconnect the sensor wiring plug.
6 Unscrew the securing bolt, and withdraw the sensor from the cylinder block.

Refitting

7 Refitting is the reverse of removal, but note that the mating faces of the sensor and cylinder block must be cleaned thoroughly before fitting the sensor.

X20 XEV (Simtec)

Removal

8 Disconnect the battery negative lead.
9 Disconnect the wiring harness plugs from the inlet air temperature sensor and hot film air mass meter.

25.4a Undo the four Torx bolts . . .

25.2a Disconnect the HT leads from the DIS module. The leads are numbered . . .

10 Remove the crankcase ventilation hoses.
11 Remove the coolant hoses from the air inlet hoses. Remove the air mass meter, complete with the air inlet hoses, from the upper part of the air cleaner and throttle body.
12 Use a screwdriver to press the retaining clip for the 1st and 4th cylinder injectors in the plug strip towards the fuel distributor pipe - lifting the plug strip at the same time. On the underside of the plug strip there are a total of 6 plug connections, 4 of which are for the injectors.
13 Disconnect the wiring harness plug for the knock sensor from the plug strip.
14 Connect a 1 metre length of separate cable to the knock sensor wiring harness plug (note routing).
15 Remove the knock sensor from the cylinder block **(see illustration)**.
16 Disconnect the knock sensor cable from the separately attached cable which remains in the engine compartment.

Refitting

17 Refitting is the reverse of removal, but note the following.
18 Before refitting, ensure that the sensor is spotlessly clean. The entire contact surface of the sensor must lie directly on the cylinder block. Do not use any form of washers.
19 Carefully refit the sensor into the block and tighten it to the correct torque.
20 Guide the knock sensor cable between the ridges on the inlet manifold using a separate cable - ensure correct routing.
21 Remove the cable.
22 Insert the wiring harness plug for the knock sensor, into the plug strip.

25.4b . . . and remove the DIS module - X20 XEV engine

25.2b . . . and the DIS module is also numbered - X20 XEV engine

23 Correctly align the spring clips for the injectors as they may prevent engagement of the plug strip. Correct contact between the plug strip and the injector is essential.
24 When connecting the plug strip, an audible 'click' should be heard.
25 Ensure that the hoses are in good condition and installed securely with the two clamps.

25 DIS module (Motronic M2.8 and Simtec) - removal and refitting

Note 1: DIS modules were fitted to C20 XE engines from 1993 onwards when Motronic M2.8 was introduced. The earlier models with Motronic M2.5 had a Hall-effect distributor.
Note 2: Refer to Section 3 before proceeding.

Removal

1 Disconnect the battery negative lead.
2 Disconnect the HT leads from the module terminals noting their locations to ensure correct refitting. The HT leads are all labelled with the cylinder numbers, and the corresponding numbers are stamped on the module, next to each terminal **(see illustrations)**.
3 Disconnect the module wiring plug.
4 On X20 XEV engines, undo the four Torx bolts and remove the DIS module from the mounting bracket **(see illustrations)**.
5 On C20 XE engines, the DIS module is fitted to a mounting bracket on the end of the cylinder head so that it faces sideways **(see illustration)**. Undo the bolts securing the

5

25.5 The DIS module is mounted sideways on C20 XE engines

26.6 The camshaft phase sensor detects a step in the thickness of the camshaft sprocket perimeter - X20 XEV engine

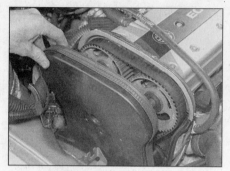

26.9 Remove the timing cover - X20 XEV engine

26.10 Remove the spark plug cover - X20 XEV engine

mounting bracket to the cylinder head and remove the module and bracket. Note the installed position of the module on the bracket, undo the four securing screws and separate the module from the bracket.

Refitting

6 Refitting is the reverse of removal.

26 Camshaft phase sensor - removal and refitting

Note: *Refer to Section 3 before proceeding.*

C 20 XE engine, 1993 onwards

Removal

1 The camshaft phase sensor is mounted on the end of the cylinder head, on the exhaust side, in front of the DIS unit.
2 Disconnect the battery negative lead.
3 Disconnect the wiring plug, then undo the phase sensor securing bolts.

4 Withdraw the phase sensor from the cylinder head, then undo the bolt and remove the phase sensor disc from the end of the camshaft.

Refitting

5 Refitting is the reverse of removal.

X 20 XEV engine

6 The camshaft phase sensor detects a step in the thickness of the camshaft sprocket perimeter **(see illustration)**.

Removal

7 Remove the air cleaner housing, as described in Chapter 4A.
8 Remove the auxiliary drivebelt from the alternator pulley. Using a spanner or socket on the automatic tensioning roller hexagon, turn the tensioning roller clockwise (as viewed from the right-hand side of the car) and hold it in this position. With the drivebelt tension released, slip the drivebelt off the alternator, then allow the tensioner to return to its original position.

9 Undo the three bolts and remove the timing cover **(see illustration)**. Two of the bolts have rubber grommets.
10 Undo the two bolts and remove the spark plug cover **(see illustration)**.
11 Disconnect the camshaft phase sensor plug **(see illustration)**. You will need to use a screwdriver to push the wire clip in and release the plug. Do not lose rubber grommet from inside the plug.
12 Undo the bolt from the timing assembly backplate, between the two camshaft sprockets, and withdraw the phase sensor upwards **(see illustrations)**.

Refitting

13 Refitting is the reverse of removal. Make sure that the lower edge of the timing cover fits correctly behind the crankshaft pulley without bending the rubber sealing strip inwards. It may be easier to remove and refit the crankshaft pulley, accessible by removing the wheel arch and inner wing.

26.11 Disconnect the camshaft phase sensor plug - X20 XEV engine

26.12a Undo the bolt from the timing assembly backplate . . .

26.12b . . . and withdraw the phase sensor - X20 XEV engine

Chapter 6
Clutch

Contents

Degrees of difficulty

Easy, suitable for novice with little experience	**Fairly easy,** suitable for beginner with some experience	**Fairly difficult,** suitable for competent DIY mechanic	**Difficult,** suitable for experienced DIY mechanic 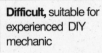	**Very difficult,** suitable for expert DIY or professional

Specifications

System type .... Single dry plate, operated by cable

Friction disc diameter
SOHC models .... 216 mm
DOHC models .... 228 mm

Clutch adjustment dimension (pedal movement)
All models .... 134.0 to 141.0 mm

Torque wrench settings	**Nm**	**lbf ft**
Clutch bellhousing cover plate:		
Steel type	12	9
Alloy type	6	4
Clutch cover to flywheel	15	11
Clutch release fork to pivot shaft clamp	35	26
Input shaft socket headed screw	15	11
Roadwheel bolts	110	81
Thrust bearing guide to transmission	5	4
Transmission endplate:		
M7 bolts	15	11
M8 bolts	20	15

6

1 General description

1 The clutch is of single dry plate type, and consists of five main components: friction disc, pressure plate, diaphragm spring, cover and release bearing.
2 The friction disc is free to slide along the splines of the transmission input shaft. This is held in position between the flywheel and the pressure plate by the pressure exerted on the pressure plate by the diaphragm spring. Friction lining material is riveted to both sides of the friction disc. Spring cushioning between the friction linings and the hub absorbs transmission shocks, and helps to ensure a smooth take-up of power as the clutch is engaged.

3 The diaphragm spring is mounted on pins, and is held in place in the cover by annular fulcrum rings.
4 The release bearing is located on a guide sleeve at the front of the transmission. The bearing is free to slide on the sleeve, under the action of the release arm that pivots inside the clutch bellhousing.
5 The release arm is operated by the clutch pedal, by way of a cable. As wear takes place on the friction disc over a period of time, the clutch pedal will rise progressively, in relation to its original position. No periodic adjustment of the clutch cable is specified by the manufacturers.
6 When the clutch pedal is depressed, the release arm is actuated by means of the cable. The release arm pushes the release bearing forwards, to bear against the centre of the diaphragm spring, thus pushing the centre

of the diaphragm spring inwards. The diaphragm spring acts against the fulcrum rings in the cover. When the centre of the spring is pushed in, the outside of the spring is pushed out, so allowing the pressure plate to move backwards away from the friction disc.
7 When the clutch pedal is released, the diaphragm spring forces the pressure plate into contact with the friction linings on the friction disc. This simultaneously pushes the friction disc forwards on its splines, forcing it against the flywheel. The friction disc is now firmly sandwiched between the pressure plate and the flywheel, and drive is taken up.
8 An unusual feature of this layout (except for pot-type flywheels) is that the clutch assembly, release bearing and guide sleeve oil seal can be renewed without removing the engine or transmission from the vehicle.

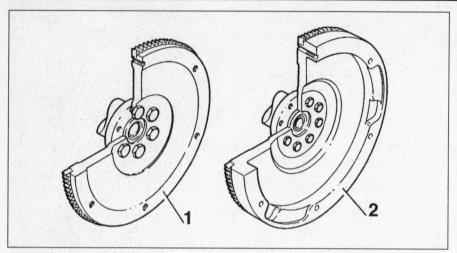

1.9 Flywheel types

1 *Earlier 'flat type'*   2 *Later 'pot type'*

Flat and pot-type flywheels

9 During 1992 the 'flat-type' flywheel was gradually replaced by the 'pot-type' flywheel on new models **(see illustration)**. This design gives smoother running and reduces transmission rattle. On these vehicles, the transmission must be removed to replace the clutch.

10 You can find out what type of flywheel has been fitted by removing the cover plate, if it exists, from the base of the clutch bellhousing **(see illustration)**. After the introduction of the pot flywheel, the cover plate became a redundant feature because no useful work

could be done on the clutch without first removing the transmission. On F18 transmissions, which were introduced in 1994, there is no cover plate on the clutch bellhousing.

2 Clutch cable - removal and refitting

Removal

1 Working in the engine compartment, measure the length of the threaded rod protruding through the plastic block at the release arm end of the cable. This will enable approximate pre-setting of the cable when refitting.
2 Remove the clip from the threaded rod at the release arm, then slide the rod from the release arm **(see illustration)**. Push the release arm towards the bulkhead, and if necessary slacken the cable adjuster, to aid removal.
3 Pull the cable assembly from the lug on the clutch bellhousing **(see illustration)**.
4 Working inside the vehicle, remove the lower trim panel from the driver's footwell, then unhook the return spring from the clutch pedal, and disconnect the cable end from the

1.10 Cover plate on clutch bellhousing

pedal. Note that the end of the return spring retains the cable end in the pedal. Access is limited, and it may prove easier to remove the clutch pedal, as described in Section 4, before disconnecting the cable.
5 The cable assembly can now be withdrawn into the engine compartment, by pulling it through the bulkhead. Take care not to damage the bulkhead grommet as the cable is withdrawn.

Refitting

6 Refitting is the reverse of removal. Position the threaded rod so that the length of thread protruding through the plastic block is as noted before removal, then adjust the cable as described in Section 3.
7 Ensure that the bulkhead grommet is correctly seated.

3 Clutch cable - adjustment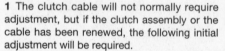

1 The clutch cable will not normally require adjustment, but if the clutch assembly or the cable has been renewed, the following initial adjustment will be required.
2 Using a tape measure or similar, measure the distance from the centre of the clutch pedal's rubber pad to a fixed point on the steering wheel rim. The pedal must be hanging in its normal resting position. Repeat the measurement with the pedal fully depressed **(see illustrations)**.

2.2 Remove the clip from the threaded rod at the clutch release arm

2.3 Clutch cable attachment to lug on bellhousing

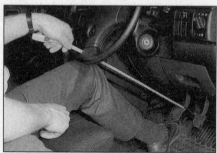

3.2a Checking clutch adjustment - measure distance from steering wheel rim to centre of pedal rubber (pedal at rest) . . .

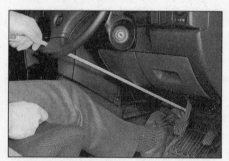

3.2b . . . depress pedal fully and repeat measurement from same point on steering wheel to pedal's new position

4.3 Clutch pedal pivot locking clip (arrowed)

4.5a Clutch pedal components assembled as when in place in vehicle

A   Clutch cable is retained by return spring

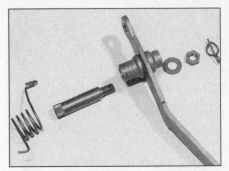

4.5b Clutch pedal pivot components

3 Subtract the first measurement from the second to calculate the pedal movement. This should be within the specified range. If the pedal movement is approximately as that specified, the cable may be adjusted as follows.

4 Working in the engine compartment, remove the clip from the threaded rod at the release arm on the transmission, then turn the adjuster as required. Turn the adjuster clockwise to increase pedal movement, or anti-clockwise to decrease pedal movement. Recheck the pedal movement, and then refit the clip to the threaded rod on completion.

5 On a vehicle in which the clutch has covered a high mileage, it may no longer be possible to adjust the cable. This indicates that the clutch friction disc requires renewal. Note that when correctly adjusted, the clutch pedal will rest slightly higher than the brake pedal - it is incorrect for the two pedals to be in alignment. If the pedals are aligned, the cable requires adjustment. Note also that there should be no play in the clutch pedal.

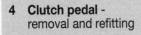

4 Clutch pedal - removal and refitting

Removal

1 Remove the clutch cable, as described in Section 2, paragraphs 1 and 2.
2 Working inside the vehicle, remove the lower trim panel from the driver's footwell.
3 Remove the locking clip from the right-hand end of the pedal pivot shaft, then unscrew the pedal retaining nut and recover the washer(s) **(see illustration)**.
4 Push the pivot shaft out of the pedal bracket, towards the centre of the vehicle, then lower the pedal and return spring. Note the position of any washers and/or spacers on the pivot shaft, so that they can be refitted in their original positions.
5 Disconnect the cable end of the pedal by releasing the return spring, and withdraw the pedal and return spring from the vehicle **(see illustrations)**.

Refitting

6 Refitting is the reverse of removal, but before inserting the pedal pivot shaft, smear the surface with a little molybdenum disulphide grease.
7 On completion, adjust the clutch cable if necessary, as described in Section 3.

5 Clutch (engine and transmission in vehicle) - removal, inspection and refitting

Note 1: *The manufacturers recommend the use of special tools for this procedure, although alternatives can be improvised as described in the text. It is suggested that this Section is read thoroughly before work begins, so tools can be made available as required.*
Note 2: *This section is inapplicable to models with 'pot-type' flywheels because you cannot remove the clutch while the transmission is connected to the engine. First you will need to separate the transmission from the engine, as described in Chapters 2A or 7A, then remove the clutch as described in Section 6 of this Chapter. See Section 1 for details of the flat and pot-type flywheels.*

Removal

1 Where applicable, remove the left-hand front wheel trim, then loosen the roadwheel bolts. Apply the handbrake, jack up the front

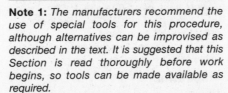

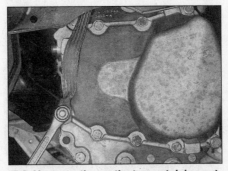

5.3 Unscrew the earth strap retaining nut

of the vehicle and support on axle stands (see *"Jacking and Vehicle Support"*). Remove the roadwheel for improved access. On DOHC models, remove the engine undershield, with reference to Chapter 11.
2 Unscrew the securing bolts and remove the cover plate from the base of the clutch bellhousing **(see illustration 1.10)**.
3 Unscrew the retaining nut, and disconnect the earth strap from the transmission endplate **(see illustration)**.
4 Place a container beneath the transmission endplate, to catch the oil that will be released, then unscrew the securing bolts and remove the endplate **(see illustration)**. Note the location of the studded bolt that retains the earth strap. For improved access, remove the wheel arch liner, as described in Chapter 11.
5 Recover the gasket.
6 Extract the circlip from inside the end of the input shaft, using a pair of circlip pliers.
7 Using a twelve-point splined key, unscrew the socket-headed screw from the end of the input shaft.
8 The input shaft can now be pulled out of engagement with the splined hub of the clutch friction disc. The manufacturers specify the use of special tools for this operation (tools KM-556-1-A and KM-556-4), but an alternative can be improvised as shown **(see illustration)**. The tool bolts into place on the end of the transmission, using the endplate securing bolts **(see illustration 5.25)**. Tool dimensions will vary according to transmission type.
9 Alternatively, screw an M7 bolt into the end

5.4 Removing the transmission endplate (wheel arch liner removed)

6

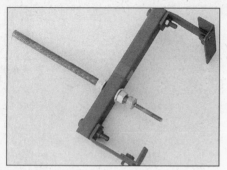

5.8 Improvised tool for disengaging transmission input shaft from clutch

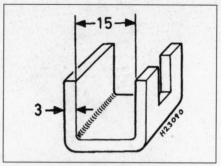

5.11 Clutch pressure plate retaining clamp dimensions (in mm)

5.12 Clamp fitted to compress clutch pressure plate prior to removal

of the input shaft, and use the bolt to pull the shaft out to its stop. It is likely that the input shaft will be a very tight fit, in which case it may prove difficult to withdraw, without using the special tool previously described. In certain cases, a slide hammer can be attached to the end of the shaft to enable it to be withdrawn.

10 Before the clutch assembly can be removed, the pressure plate must be compressed against the tension of the diaphragm spring. Otherwise the assembly will be too thick to be withdrawn through the space between the flywheel and the edge of the bellhousing.

11 Three special clamps are available from the manufacturers for this purpose (tool No KM-526-A), but alternatives can be made up from strips of metal. The clamps should be U-shaped, and conform to the dimensions given below **(see illustration)**. Bevel the edges of the clamps to ease fitting, and cut a slot in one of the U-legs, to clear the pressure plate rivets.

a) *Thickness of metal strip - 3.0 mm (0.12 in)*
b) *Distance between U-legs - 15.0 mm (0.59 in)*

12 Have an assistant depress the clutch pedal fully, then fit each clamp securely over the edge of the cover/pressure plate, engaging the clamps in the apertures around the rim of the cover **(see illustration)**. Turn the crankshaft using a spanner on the sprocket bolt, to bring each clamp location into view.

13 Once the clamps have been fitted, have the assistant release the clutch pedal.

14 Progressively loosen and remove the six

5.15 Withdraw the clutch assembly from the bellhousing

bolts and spring washers that secure the clutch cover to the flywheel. As previously, turn the crankshaft to bring each bolt into view. Note the position of the mark on the flywheel that aligns with the notch in the rim of the clutch cover.

15 The clutch assembly can now be withdrawn downwards from the bellhousing **(see illustration)**. Be prepared to catch the friction disc, which may drop out of the cover as it is withdrawn, and note which way round the friction disc is fitted. The greater projecting side of the hub should face away from the flywheel.

16 The pressure plate can be compressed against the tension of the diaphragm spring, in a vice fitted with soft jaw protectors, in order to remove the clamps.

17 The clutch components can be inspected for wear and damage.

Inspection

18 With the clutch assembly removed, clean off all traces of dust using a dry cloth. Although most friction discs now have asbestos-free linings, some do not, and it is wise to take precautions; asbestos dust is harmful, and must not be inhaled.

19 Examine the linings of the friction disc for wear and loose rivets, distortion, cracks, broken torsion springs and worn splines. The surface of the friction linings may be highly glazed, but, as long as the friction material pattern can be clearly seen, this is satisfactory. If there is any sign of oil contamination, indicated by a continuous, or patchy, shiny black discoloration, the plate must be renewed, and the source of the contamination traced and rectified. This will be either a leaking crankshaft oil seal or transmission input shaft oil seal - or both. Renewal procedures are given in Chapters 2A, 2B and 7, as applicable. The friction disc must also be renewed if the lining thickness has worn down to, or just above, the level of the rivets heads.

20 Check the machined faces of the flywheel and pressure plate. If either is grooved, or heavily scored, renewal is necessary. The pressure plate must also be renewed if any cracks are apparent, or if the diaphragm spring is damaged or its pressure suspect.

21 With the clutch removed, it is advisable to check the condition of the release bearing, as described in Section 7.

Refitting

Note: *The circlip in the end of the input shaft, and the transmission endplate gasket, should be renewed on reassembly*

22 Some replacement clutch assemblies are supplied with the pressure plate already compressed using the three clamps described in paragraph 11. If this is not the case, the pressure plate should be compressed against the tension of the diaphragm spring. Use a vice fitted with soft jaw protectors, and the clamps used during removal should be fitted **(see illustration)**.

23 It is important to ensure that no oil or grease gets on the friction disc linings, or the pressure plate and flywheel faces. It is advisable to refit the clutch assembly with clean hands, and to wipe down the pressure plate and flywheel faces with a clean rag before assembly begins.

24 Apply a smear of molybdenum disulphide grease to the splines of the friction disc hub. Then offer the disc to the flywheel, with the greater projecting side of the hub facing away from the flywheel. Hold the friction disc against the flywheel while the cover/pressure plate assembly is offered into position.

25 The input shaft must now be pushed through the hub of the friction disc, until its end engages in the spigot bearing in the end

5.22 Clamp fitted to compress clutch pressure plate prior to installation

(Note slot cut in clamp to clear pressure plate rivet)

5.25 Use the improvised tool to engage the input shaft with the clutch friction disc

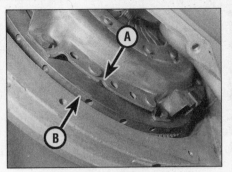

5.26a Clutch alignment marks

A *Notch in clutch cover*
B *Paint mark on flywheel*

5.26b Tighten the clutch cover-to-flywheel bolt to the specified torque .

of the crankshaft. Under no circumstances must the shaft be hammered home, as transmission damage may result. If the input shaft cannot be pushed home by hand, steady pressure should be exerted on the end of the shaft. The manufacturers specify the use of a special tool for this operation (tool No KM-564). The improvised tool used earlier to withdraw the shaft can also be used, by repositioning the nut as shown **(see illustration)**.

26 With the input shaft pushed fully home, position the cover/pressure plate assembly so that the mark on the flywheel is in alignment with the notch in the rim of the clutch cover. Then refit and progressively tighten the six clutch cover-to-flywheel bolts and spring washers in a diagonal sequence **(see illustrations)**. Turn the crankshaft, using a spanner on the sprocket bolt, to gain access to each bolt in turn, and finally tighten all bolts to the specified torque.

27 Have an assistant depress the clutch pedal, then remove the three clamps from the edge of the cover/pressure plate, again turning the crankshaft for access to each clamp.

28 Once the clamps have been removed, have the assistant release the clutch pedal.

29 Screw the socket-headed screw into the end of the input shaft, then fit a new circlip.

30 Using a new gasket, refit the transmission endplate, and tighten the securing bolts to the specified torque. Ensure that the studded bolt that retains the earth strap is fitted to its correct location, as noted during removal.

31 Reconnect the transmission earth strap, and fit the retaining nut.

32 Refit the cover plate to the base of the clutch bellhousing, and tighten the securing bolts to the specified torque. Where applicable, refit the wheel arch liner, and on DOHC models, refit the engine undershield (see Chapter 11).

33 Refit the roadwheel, then lower the vehicle to the ground, and finally tighten the roadwheel bolts to the specified torque setting. Refit the wheel trim, where applicable.

34 Check the clutch cable adjustment, as described in Section 3.

35 Check and if necessary top-up the transmission oil level, as described in Chapter 7.

6 Clutch (transmission removed) - removal and refitting

Removal

1 After obtaining access to the clutch by removing the transmission, or by removing and separating the engine/transmission assembly, continue as follows.

2 Note the position of the mark on the flywheel that aligns with the notch in the rim of the clutch cover. Then progressively unscrew the six bolts and spring washers that secure the clutch cover to the flywheel.

3 With all the bolts removed, lift off the clutch assembly. Be prepared to catch the friction disc as the cover assembly is lifted from the flywheel, and note which way round the friction disc is fitted. The greater projecting side of the hub should face away from the flywheel.

4 The clutch components can be inspected for wear and damage, as described in Section 5.

Refitting

5 It is important to ensure that no oil or grease gets on the friction disc linings, or the pressure plate and flywheel faces. It is advisable to refit the clutch assembly with clean hands, and to wipe down the pressure plate and flywheel faces with a clean rag before assembly begins.

6 Place the friction disc against the flywheel, ensuring that it is fitted the correct way round. The greater projecting side of the hub should face away from the flywheel.

7 Fit the clutch cover assembly, aligning the mark on the flywheel with the notch in the rim of the clutch cover **(see illustration)**. Insert the six bolts and spring washers, and tighten them finger-tight, so that the friction disc is gripped, but can still be moved.

8 The friction disc must now be centralised, so that when the engine and transmission are mated, the transmission input shaft splines will pass through the splines in the friction disc hub.

9 Centralisation can be carried out by inserting a round bar or a long screwdriver through the hole in the centre of the friction disc, so that the

end of the bar rests in the spigot bearing in the centre of the crankshaft. Where possible, use a blunt instrument, but if a screwdriver is used, wrap tape around the blade to prevent damage to the bearing surface. Moving the bar sideways or up and down will move the friction disc in whichever direction is necessary to achieve centralisation. With the bar removed, view the friction disc hub, in relation to the hole in the end of the crankshaft and the circle created by the ends of the diaphragm spring fingers. When the hub appears exactly in the centre, all is correct. Alternatively, if a clutch aligning tool can be obtained, this will eliminate all the guesswork, and obviate the need for visual alignment.

10 Tighten the cover retaining bolts gradually in a diagonal sequence, to the specified torque. Remove the alignment tool.

11 The engine and transmission can now be mated together, as described in Chapters 2A or 7A, as applicable.

12 On completion, check the clutch cable adjustment, as described in Section 3.

7 Clutch release bearing and arm - removal and refitting

Note: *If the release bearing guide sleeve is removed, a new O-ring should be used on refitting.*

Removal

1 Access to the release bearing can be obtained by removing the clutch assembly as

6.7 Notch (arrowed) in clutch cover must align with flywheel mark

6

7.4a Pull the release bearing from the guide sleeve . . .

7.4b . . . then pull out the release arm pivot shaft, and withdraw the release fork

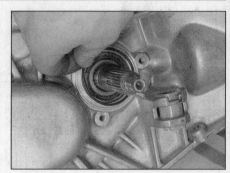

7.6a Fit a new guide sleeve O-ring . . .

described in Section 5 or by removing the transmission as described in Chapter 7A.

2 Unscrew the clamp bolt securing the release fork to the release arm pivot shaft.

3 If not already done, disconnect the clutch cable from the release arm, by removing the clip from the threaded rod, and then sliding the threaded rod from the release arm.

4 Pull the release bearing from the guide sleeve, then pull the release arm pivot shaft up and out of the bellhousing, and withdraw the release fork **(see illustrations)**. Where applicable, pull the bearing from the plastic collar.

5 Spin the release bearing, and check it for roughness. Hold the outer race, and attempt to move it laterally against the inner race. If any excessive movement or roughness is evident, renew the bearing. If a new clutch has been fitted, it is wise to renew the release

bearing as a matter of course.

6 If desired, the release bearing guide sleeve can be removed by unscrewing the three securing bolts, and then the input shaft oil seal can be renewed. Recover the O-ring that fits between the guide sleeve and the bellhousing. Prise the old oil seal from the guide sleeve, and fit a new seal using a tube drift or socket. Fill the space between the lips of the oil seal with lithium-based grease, then refit the guide sleeve, using a new O-ring. The O-ring should be fitted dry **(see illustrations)**.

7 The nylon bushes supporting the release arm pivot shaft can be renewed if necessary, by tapping them from their lugs in the bellhousing using a drift. Drive the new bushes into position, ensuring that their locating tabs engage with the slots in the bellhousing lugs **(see illustration)**.

Refitting

8 Refitting the release bearing and arm is the reverse of removal, remembering the following points.

9 Lightly smear the inner surfaces of the release arm pivot bushes, and the outer surface of the release bearing guide sleeve, with molybdenum disulphide grease.

10 Where applicable, fit the release bearing to the plastic collar, then fit the release bearing and fork together, and tighten the release fork clamp bolt to the specified torque **(see illustration)**.

11 Refit the clutch assembly as described in Section 5.

12 If the engine and transmission have been separated, reconnect them as described in Chapters 2A or 7A.

13 On completion, check the clutch cable adjustment as described in Section 3.

7.6b . . . followed by the guide sleeve

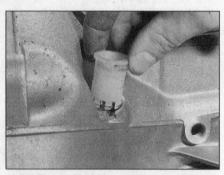

7.7 Renew the release arm pivot shaft nylon bush

7.10 Tighten the release fork clamp bolt

Chapter 7 Part A:
Manual transmission

Contents

Degrees of difficulty

| Easy, suitable for novice with little experience | | Fairly easy, suitable for beginner with some experience | | Fairly difficult, suitable for competent DIY mechanic | | Difficult, suitable for experienced DIY mechanic | | Very difficult, suitable for expert DIY or professional | |

Specifications

General

Transmission type (all models) .... Five forward speeds and one reverse, synchromesh on all forward gears. Integral differential.

Transmission type:	Code	Wide Ratio (WR) or Close Ratio (CR) *
C20 NE		
Up to 1994	F16	CR
From 1994	F18	CR
C20 XE		
Up to 1994	F20	CR
1994	F18+	CR
1995	F20	CR
X20 XEV		
1994	F18	WR or CR
From 1995	F18	WR

* Refer to transmission number identification or production option codes

Lubrication

Oil type/specification .... See "Lubricants and fluids"
Oil capacity .... See Chapter 1 Specifications

Torque wrench settings

	Nm	lbf ft
5th gear selector fork to intermediate plate	22	16
5th gear selector interlock pawl to intermediate plate	7	5
Clutch bellhousing cover plate	7	5
Differential cover plate to transmission:		
Alloy cover plate	18	13
Steel cover plate	30	22
Endplate to transmission:		
M7 bolts	15	11
M8 bolts	20	15
Engine to transmission	75	55
Gearchange lever housing to floor pan	6	4
Gear selector cover to transmission	15	11
Gear selector tube clamp	15	11
Input shaft socket head	15	11
Interlock bridge piece to intermediate plate	7	5
Intermediate plate to transmission	15	11
Left-hand transmission mounting to body	75	55
Left-hand transmission mounting to transmission	65	48
Rear transmission mounting to front subframe	40	30
Reversing lamp switch to transmission	20	15
Roadwheel bolts	110	81
Speedometer drivegear retaining plate	4	3

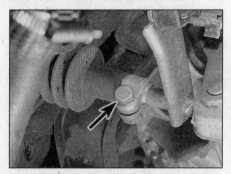

2.1 Gear selector tube-to-linkage clamp bolt (arrowed)

2.2 Extract the plug from the adjuster hole . . .

2.3 . . . and insert a twist drill to engage with the selector lever

1 General description

A five speed gearbox is fitted to all manual transmission models. A variety of transmission types are used, depending on the engine and year. For details see the Specifications.

To determine the final drive ratio refer to the 'transmission number'. This can be found on the transmission's end cover. This number will also identify whether a close or wide ratio transmission has been fitted. Production codes, found on the bonnet support panel, can also be translated by a Vauxhall dealer, to give this information.

Drive from the clutch is picked up by the input shaft, which runs in parallel with the mainshaft. The input shaft and mainshaft gears are in constant mesh, and selection of gears is by sliding synchromesh hubs, which lock the appropriate mainshaft gear to the mainshaft.

The 5th speed components are located in an extension housing at the end of the transmission, which allows some component commonality with the four speed transmissions used in other Vauxhall front-wheel-drive vehicles.

Reverse gear is obtained by sliding an idler gear into mesh with two straight cut gears on the input shaft and mainshaft.

All the forward gear teeth are helically cut, to reduce noise and improve wear characteristics.

The F18 and F18+ transmission includes a 'gear set brake', to enable silent engaging of reverse gear.

The differential is mounted in the main transmission casing, and drive is transmitted to the differential by a pinion gear on the end of the mainshaft. The inboard ends of the driveshafts locate directly into the differential.

Gear selection is by a floor mounted gearchange lever, through a remote control linkage.

2 Gear selector linkage - adjustment

Note: *On completion of adjustment, a new plug must be fitted to the adjuster hole in the gear selector cover. Obtain a new plug before starting work.*

1 Working in the engine compartment, loosen the clamp bolt securing the gear selector tube to the linkage **(see illustration)**. On models from 1993, the clamp has been repositioned slightly and is now more easily accessible from below the car.

2 Extract the plug from the adjuster hole in the gear selector cover **(see illustration)**.

3 Looking towards the front of the vehicle, grip the gear selector tube, and twist it in an anti-clockwise direction until a 4.5 mm (0.18 in) diameter twist drill can be inserted through the adjuster hole in the gear selector cover, to engage with the hole in the selector lever **(see illustration)**.

4 Working inside the vehicle, pull back on the front edge of the gearchange lever gaiter, and free its lower end from the centre console, to allow access to the base of the lever.

5 The help of an assistant will now be required, to hold the gearchange lever in neutral in the 1st/2nd gear plane. The lever should be resting against the reverse stop, and the arrow and notch should be aligned as shown **(see illustration)**.

6 On later models (1993 on), with the

gearchange lever in its correct position for adjustment, a second 4.5 mm (0.18 in) diameter twist drill should be inserted into the holes in the gearchange lever and lever base provided for this purpose. This means that the lever can be positively locked for adjustment, and an assistant will not be required to hold the lever in the correct position.

7 Without moving the gearchange lever, tighten the clamp bolt securing the gear selector tube to the linkage in the engine compartment.

8 On pre-1993 models, check that the free play between the hook (A) and the stop (B) at the base of the gearchange lever is as specified **(see illustration)**.

9 Refit the gearchange lever gaiter to the centre console.

10 Remove the twist drill from the adjuster hole in the gear selector cover, and seal the hole with a new plug.

11 Finally, check that all gears can be engaged easily with the vehicle at rest, engine running, and clutch pedal depressed.

2.5 Arrow on gearchange lever aligned with notch in reverse stop

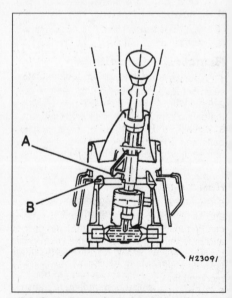

2.8 Gearchange lever free play between hook (A) and stop (B) should be a maximum of 3.0 mm (0.12 in)

3 Gearchange lever housing assembly - removal and refitting

Removal

1 Working in the engine compartment, loosen the clamp bolt securing the gear selector tube to the linkage.

2 Remove the gearchange lever (Section 5).

3 Remove the front section of the centre console, as described in Chapter 11.

4 Unscrew the four bolts securing the gearchange lever housing to the floor pan.

5 The housing and selector tube can now be withdrawn. Pull the assembly towards the rear of the vehicle, to feed the selector tube through the bulkhead. As the selector tube is fed through the bulkhead, have an assistant remove the clamp from the end of the selector tube in the engine compartment, to avoid damage to the rubber boot on the bulkhead.

6 If desired, the rubber boot can be renewed by pulling the old boot from the bulkhead, and pushing the new boot into position, ensuring that it is correctly seated.

Refitting

7 The selector tube bush in the gearchange lever housing can be renewed after sliding the selector tube from the housing. Prise the bush insert from the front of the housing, then prise the bush from the insert. Refitting is the reverse of removal, but lubricate the inside of the bush with a little silicone grease.

8 Refitting of the assembly is the reverse of removal, but before tightening the selector tube clamp bolt, adjust the gear selector linkage as described in Section 2.

4 Gear selector linkage - removal and refitting

Removal

1 Loosen the clamp bolt securing the gear selector tube to the linkage.

2 Prise off the securing clip, then withdraw the pivot pin from the linkage universal joint.

3 Release the spring clip, then pull the bellcrank pivot pin from the bracket on the rear engine/transmission mounting.

4 Withdraw the linkage from the vehicle.

Refitting

5 Check the linkage components for wear, and renew as necessary. The pivot bushes can be renewed by prising out the old bushes and pressing in the new, and the link rod can be renewed by pulling it from the balljoints **(see illustration)**. Further dismantling is not recommended.

6 Refitting is the reverse of removal, but before tightening the selector tube clamp bolt, adjust the gear selector linkage as described in Section 2.

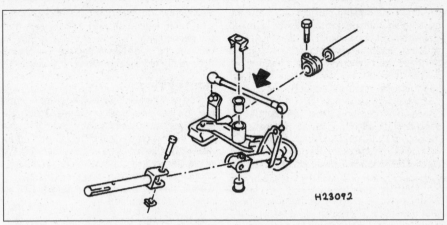

4.5 Gear selector linkage components - link rod arrowed

5 Gearchange lever - removal and refitting

Removal

1 Pull back on the front edge of the gearchange lever gaiter, and free its lower end from the centre console to allow access to the base of the lever **(see illustration)**.

2 Release the clip from the base of the lever shaft, then withdraw the pivot pin, and lift out the lever **(see illustration)**.

Refitting

3 Refitting is the reverse of removal.

6 Gearchange lever gaiter - removal and refitting

Removal

1 Remove the gearchange lever, as described in Section 5.

2 Immerse the gearchange lever knob in hot water (approximately 80°C/176°F) for a few minutes, then twist the knob and tap it from the lever. There is a strong possibility that the knob will be destroyed during removal.

5.1 Free the gearchange lever gaiter from the centre console

3 Slide the old gaiter from the lever, and fit the new one. Use a little liquid detergent to aid fitting if necessary.

Refitting

4 Refit the knob, preheating it in hot water as during removal, and driving it on with a soft faced mallet. Ensure that the knob is fitted the correct way round.

5 Refit the gearchange lever, as described in Section 5.

7 Differential bearing oil seals - removal and refitting

Note: *A balljoint separator tool will be required for this operation. The driveshaft snap ring(s) and lower arm to suspension strut balljoint locking pin(s) must be renewed on reassembly.*

Removal

1 The differential bearing oil seals can be renewed with the transmission in situ as follows.

2 Where applicable, remove the wheel trim from the relevant front roadwheel, then loosen the roadwheel bolts. Apply the handbrake, jack up the front of the vehicle, and support on axle stands (see *"Jacking and Vehicle Support"*) positioned under the body side members. Remove the roadwheel.

7A

5.2 Lifting out the gearchange lever with pivot pin and clip

3 Extract the locking pin, then unscrew the castellated nut from the lower arm to suspension strut balljoint.

4 Using a balljoint separator tool, disconnect the lower arm to suspension strut balljoint.

5 The inboard end of the driveshaft (or intermediate shaft) must now be disconnected, referring to Chapter 8, if necessary. Support the driveshaft by suspending it with string or wire. **Do not** allow the driveshaft to hang under its own weight.

6 Prise the oil seal from the differential, using a screwdriver or similar instrument.

Refitting

7 Smear the sealing lip of the new oil seal with transmission oil, then using a tool of the same diameter, drive the new seal into the differential, until it sits flush on its seat.

8 Reconnect the inboard end of the driveshaft, referring to Chapter 8, if necessary. Use a new snap-ring.

9 Reconnect the lower arm to suspension strut balljoint, then fit the castellated nut and tighten to the specified torque (see Chapter 10). Secure the nut with a new locking pin.

10 Refit the roadwheel, then lower the vehicle to the ground, and finally tighten the roadwheel bolts to the specified torque setting. Refit the wheel trim, where applicable.

11 Top-up the transmission oil level, as described in Chapter 1.

8 Input shaft (clutch) oil seal - removal and refitting

Note: *A new clutch release bearing guide sleeve O-ring must be used on refitting.*

Removal

1 Remove the clutch release bearing and fork, as described in Chapter 6.

2 Unscrew the securing bolts and withdraw the clutch release bearing guide sleeve from the bellhousing. Recover the O-ring that fits between the guide sleeve and the bellhousing.

3 Drive the old seal from the guide sleeve.

Refitting

4 Fit a new seal using a socket or tube. Press the new seal into position evenly. Take care, as the seal can be easily damaged.

5 Fill the space between the lips of the new seal with lithium based grease, then refit the guide sleeve, using a new O-ring. The O-ring should be fitted dry.

6 Refit the clutch release bearing and fork, as described in Chapter 6.

9 Transmission - removal and refitting (leaving engine in vehicle)

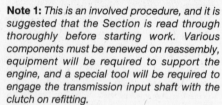

Note 1: *This is an involved procedure, and it is suggested that the Section is read through thoroughly before starting work. Various components must be renewed on reassembly, equipment will be required to support the engine, and a special tool will be required to engage the transmission input shaft with the clutch on refitting.*

Note 2: *There are different transmission removal procedures for models with 'flat-type' and 'pot-type' flywheels, because only the 'flat-type' allows separate removal of the clutch. For details of the two flywheel types, see Chapter 6, Section 1.*

Removal

All transmissions

1 Disconnect the battery negative lead.

2 Working in the engine compartment, loosen the clamp bolt securing the gear selector tube to the linkage. Pull the selector tube towards the engine compartment bulkhead to separate it from the linkage.

3 Remove the retaining clip, then slide the clutch cable from the release lever, pushing the release lever back towards the bulkhead if necessary, to allow the cable to be disconnected. Pull the cable support from the bracket on the transmission casing, then move the cable to one side out of the way, taking note of its routing.

4 Disconnect the wiring from the reversing lamp switch, which is located at the front of the transmission casing, above the left-hand mounting bracket.

5 Unscrew the securing sleeve, and disconnect the speedometer cable from the transmission.

6 Unscrew and remove the three upper engine to transmission bolts.

7 The engine must now be supported from its left-hand lifting bracket. Ideally, the engine should be supported using a strong wooden or metal beam, resting on blocks positioned securely in the channels at the sides of the engine compartment. The Vauxhall special tool designed specifically for this purpose is shown **(see illustration)**. Alternatively, the engine can be supported using a hoist and lifting tackle. However in this case, the hoist must be of such a design to enable the engine to be supported with the vehicle raised off the ground, leaving sufficient clearance to withdraw the transmission from under the front of the vehicle.

8 Where applicable, remove the wheel trims, then loosen the front roadwheel bolts on both sides of the vehicle. Apply the handbrake, then jack up the front of the vehicle, and support securely on axle stands (see *"Jacking and Vehicle Support"*) positioned under the body side members. Note that the vehicle must be raised sufficiently high to enable the transmission to be withdrawn from under the front of the vehicle. Remove the front roadwheels.

9 Ensure that the engine is adequately supported as described in paragraph 7, then remove the front subframe, as described in Chapter 10.

10 Disconnect the inboard ends of the driveshafts. Refer to Chapter 8, if necessary. Be prepared for oil spillage as the driveshafts are withdrawn, and plug the apertures in the differential to prevent further oil loss and dirt ingress. Support the driveshafts by suspending them with wire or string - do not allow the driveshafts to hang down under their own weight.

11 Unscrew the retaining nut, and disconnect the earth strap from the transmission endplate.

12 Place a container beneath the transmission endplate to catch the oil that will be released, then unscrew the securing bolts and remove the endplate. Note the location of the studded bolt that retains the earth strap. For improved access, remove the wheel arch liner, as described in Chapter 11.

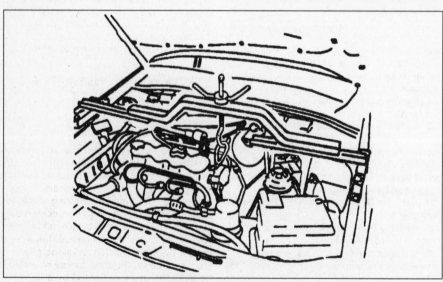

9.7 Vauxhall special tool No KM-263 used to support engine

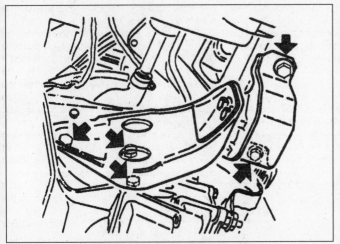

9.18 Remove the left-hand transmission mounting by unscrewing the five bolts (arrowed)

9.19 Cover plate on clutch bellhousing - all transmissions except F18

13 Recover the gasket.

14 Extract the circlip from inside the end of the input shaft, using a pair of circlip pliers.

15 Using a twelve point splined key, unscrew the socket headed screw from the end of the input shaft.

16 The input shaft must now be pulled out of engagement from the splined hub of the clutch friction disc, as described in Chapter 6. Note that there is no need to remove the clutch assembly (flat-type flywheels only), unless renewal of the clutch components is required.

17 Support the transmission with a trolley jack, with an interposed block of wood to spread the load.

18 Remove the left-hand transmission mounting completely, by unscrewing the two bolts securing the rubber mounting to the vehicle body, and the three bolts securing the mounting bracket to the transmission **(see illustration)**.

Transmissions with flat-type flywheels

19 Unscrew the securing bolts, and remove the cover plate from the base of the clutch bellhousing **(see illustration)**.

All transmissions

20 Ensure that the transmission is adequately supported, then unscrew and remove the remaining engine to transmission bolts.

21 The transmission can now be lowered and withdrawn from under the front of the vehicle. The help of an assistant will greatly ease this operation.

Refitting

22 Before beginning the refitting operations, check that the two original bolts that secured the left-hand transmission rubber mounting to the vehicle body rotate freely in their threaded bores in the body. If necessary, re-cut the threaded bores, using an M10 x 1.25 mm tap.

23 On models with a flat-type flywheel, clutch reassembly will be easier after the transmission has been refitted.

24 Begin refitting by positioning the transmission under the front of the vehicle, and support with a trolley jack and interposed block of wood, as during removal.

25 Raise the transmission sufficiently to enable the lower engine to transmission bolts to be fitted, then refit the bolts, but do not fully tighten them at this stage.

26 Refit the left-hand transmission mounting, using two new bolts to secure the rubber mounting to the vehicle body. Tighten all bolts to the specified torque.

27 Tighten the previously fitted lower engine to transmission bolts to the specified torque, then withdraw the trolley jack from under the transmission.

28 Where applicable, the clutch can now be fitted, and the transmission input shaft can be pressed into engagement with the splined hub of the clutch friction disc, as described in Chapter 6.

29 Screw the socket headed screw into the end of the input shaft, then fit a new circlip.

30 Using a new gasket, refit the transmission endplate, and tighten the securing bolts to the specified torque. Ensure that the studded bolt that retains the earth strap is fitted to its correct location, as noted during removal.

31 Reconnect the transmission earth strap, and fit the retaining nut.

32 Refit the cover plate to the base of the clutch bellhousing, where applicable and tighten the securing bolts.

33 Reconnect the inboard ends of the driveshafts. Refer to Chapter 8, for details, and use new snap-rings.

34 Refit the front subframe, as described in Chapter 10.

35 Refit the front roadwheels, but do not fully tighten the roadwheel bolts yet.

36 If a hoist and lifting tackle has been used to support the engine, either disconnect the lifting tackle, or lower the hoist sufficiently to enable the vehicle to be lowered to the ground.

37 Lower the vehicle to the ground, then tighten the roadwheel bolts to the specified torque, and refit the wheel trims (where applicable).

38 Disconnect and remove the equipment used to support the engine, if not already done.

39 Refit the three upper engine to transmission bolts, and tighten them to the specified torque.

40 Reconnect the speedometer cable, and tighten the securing sleeve.

41 Reconnect the reversing lamp switch wiring.

42 Refit the clutch cable support to the bracket on the transmission casing, then reconnect the cable to the release lever, and adjust the cable as described in Chapter 6. Ensure that the cable is routed as noted during removal.

43 Reconnect the gear selector tube to the linkage, then adjust the linkage as described in Section 2 before tightening the clamp bolt.

44 Top-up the transmission oil level, as described in Chapter 1.

45 Reconnect the battery negative lead.

10 Transmission overhaul - general

Overhauling a transmission is a difficult and involved job for the DIY home mechanic. Besides dismantling and reassembling many small parts, clearances must be precisely measured and, if necessary, changed by selecting shims and spacers. Internal transmission components are also often difficult to obtain, and in many instances, extremely expensive. Because of this, if the transmission develops a fault or becomes noisy, the best course of action is to have the unit overhauled by a specialist repairer, or to obtain an exchange reconditioned unit.

7A

Nevertheless, it is not impossible for the more experienced mechanic to overhaul the transmission, provided the special tools are available. The job is done in a deliberate step-by-step manner, so that nothing is overlooked.

The tools necessary for an overhaul include internal and external circlip pliers, bearing pullers, a slide hammer, a set of pin punches, a dial test indicator, and possibly a hydraulic press. In addition, a large, sturdy workbench and a vice will be required.

During dismantling of the transmission, make careful notes of how each component is fitted, to make reassembly easier and more accurate.

Before dismantling the transmission, it will help if you have some idea what area is malfunctioning. Certain problems can be closely related to specific areas in the transmission, which can make component examination and replacement easier. Refer to the Fault finding at the end of this manual, for more information.

11 Differential overhaul - general

Before considering overhaul of the differential assembly, compare the price of the new components required with the cost of a new or reconditioned unit, as it may prove more economical to fit a complete new assembly.

Note that if the crownwheel, or the pinion gear on the transmission mainshaft are to be renewed, they must be renewed as a matched pair.

Due to the requirement for special tools to set the differential bearings preload it is recommended that overhaul of the differential is entrusted to a Vauxhall dealer, who will have the necessary expertise to complete the task effectively.

12 Speedometer drive - removal and refitting

Removal

1 Trace the speedometer cable down to the transmission and disconnect the cable.
2 Disconnect the wiring connector for the odometer frequency sensor, if applicable.
3 Unbolt the retaining plate and withdraw the drive assembly **(see illustration)**.

Refitting

4 On refitting, always renew the sealing O-ring, and coat the splines with molybdenum disulphide grease. Tighten the retaining plate bolt to its specified torque wrench setting. Reconnect the speedometer cable and wiring (if applicable).

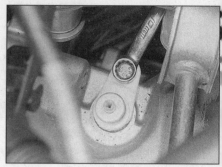

12.3 Unbolt the speedometer drive retaining plate

13 Reversing lamp switch - removal and refitting

Removal

1 The reversing lamp switch is located at the front of the transmission casing, and is accessible from the engine compartment.
2 To remove the switch, first disconnect the battery negative lead, then disconnect the wiring from the switch and unscrew the switch from the transmission.

Refitting

3 Refitting is the reverse of removal. Tighten the switch to its specified torque wrench setting.

Chapter 7 Part B:
Automatic transmission

Contents

Degrees of difficulty

| Easy, suitable for novice with little experience | | Fairly easy, suitable for beginner with some experience | | Fairly difficult, suitable for competent DIY mechanic | | Difficult, suitable for experienced DIY mechanic | | Very difficult, suitable for expert DIY or professional | 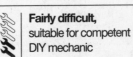 |

Specifications

General

Type (all models) .... Hydrodynamic torque converter with electrically controlled mechanical lock-up system, two epicyclic gearsets giving four forward gears (including overdrive) and reverse, integral final drive; gear changing under full electronic control, with three driving "modes" selectable

Manufacturer .... Aisin AW Co, Ltd
Code:
  C20 NE
    All model years .... AF 20
    1992 .... AF14
  C20 XE .... No automatic gearboxes
  X20 XEV AF20

Lubrication

Recommended fluid .... See "Lubricants and fluids"
Capacity - at fluid change .... See Chapter 1 Specifications

Torque wrench settings

	Nm	lbf ft
Actuating lever to selector lever shaft	16	12
Bellhousing cover plate	7	5
Dipstick/filler tube nut	20	15
Engine/transmission left-hand mounting to subframe	65	48
Engine/transmission left-hand mounting to transmission	60	44
Fluid cooler banjo union	22	16
Fluid drain plug	45	33
Fluid temperature sensor	25	19
Fluid temperature sensor cover	25	19
Input/output speed sensor Torx	6	5
Selector cable clamp	6	5
Selector console mounting	10	8
Starter inhibitor switch to selector lever shaft	8	6
Starter inhibitor switch/filler tube fastener to transmission ...	25	19
Torque converter to flexplate (using adapter - see text)	50	37
Transmission to engine	75	55

7B

1 General description

Note: *If the vehicle has to be towed and the transmission is operational, it can be towed FORWARDS ONLY (transmission in position N) on all four wheels for a distance of no more than 62 miles (100 km), at speeds of no more than 50 mph (80 km/h). If the transmission is thought to* be faulty, or if either the distance or the towing speed is likely to exceed the maximum stated, the vehicle MUST be towed with the front wheels off the ground. Refer also to the "towing" section at the front of this manual.

1 The transmission comprises a hydrodynamic torque converter and a pair of epicyclic gearsets that are controlled hydraulically by multi-plate clutches and a servo-assisted band brake to produce three forward ratios with an overdrive fourth, and reverse. The final drive differential is similar to that described in Chapter 7A. Fluid temperature is controlled by a fluid cooler built into the radiator **(see illustration)**.

2 Gear changing is electrically controlled, with a mechanical lock-up on third and fourth gears, and three driving "modes" selectable according to need or preference.

3 Gear shift points are varied, according to "mode" and gear selected. This happens after information concerning transmission fluid temperature and input versus output speed, throttle pedal and valve position, and engine coolant temperature has been fed, from various sensors, to the electronic control unit (ECU) **(see illustration)**.

4 The ECU controls the transmission through four solenoids regulating hydraulic pressure to either select gears (solenoids 1 and 2), to control converter clutch lock-up (solenoid 3), or to control main fluid pressure according to throttle valve opening angle, thus altering shift quality (solenoid 4).

5 The ECU also retards the ignition timing during gearchanges to improve shift quality, and has a self-diagnosis function that flashes a warning lamp if there is a system failure. It can also bring a backup operation that uses predetermined values, so that the car can be driven for repair. It will also cut out the air conditioning (where fitted), if its operation will affect the vehicle's driving performance.

6 The modes (selected from position "D") are as follows:

7 "Economy" mode is switched on automatically, when the engine is started. The facia warning lamp will light, when switching on the ignition and starting, and then it goes out. It uses all four gears including overdrive/4th with gearchanges being made at low engine speeds for maximum smoothness and economy.

8 "Sport" mode is switched on by pressing the button "S" in the top of the selector lever (the facia warning lamp will light). It makes gearchanges at higher engine speeds and locks out (electrically) 4th gear. It is switched off (to return to "Economy") by pressing the button again, by switching the ignition on and off, by driving with the backup activated, or by switching to "Winter" mode.

9 "Winter" mode (also known as the "Starting-off Aid" or "Start-Up Assistance"), is switched on by pressing the button with a "snowflake" symbol at the base of the selector lever. This mode locks out 1st and 2nd gears so that the vehicle can start off smoothly (in 3rd gear) on slippery roads. Switching to "Economy" mode can be achieved in several ways - by pressing the button again, by moving the selector lever to another position, by switching the ignition on and off, by holding the accelerator pedal fully depressed (to the kick-down position) for more than two seconds, by driving with the backup activated or by exceeding 50 mph (80 km/h).

10 The transmission and its control system is complex but, if not abused, will prove reliable and durable. Repair and overhaul of the

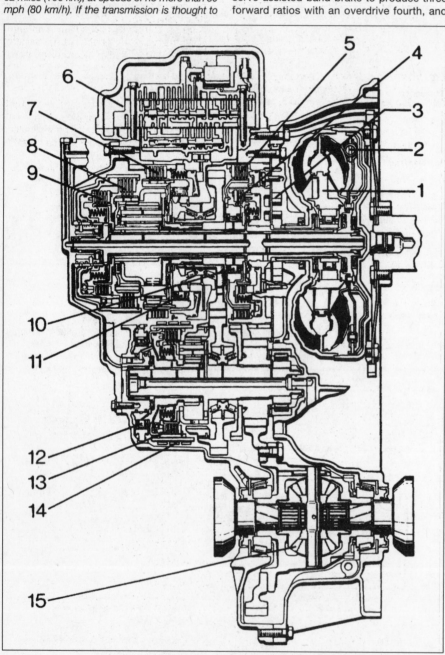

1.1 Cutaway through AF 14/20 automatic transmission

1 *Torque converter*	6 *Valve body assembly*
2 *Converter clutch*	7 *Multi-plate brake B3*
3 *Fluid pump*	8 *Multi-plate clutch C1*
4 *Multi-plate brake B1*	9 *Multi-plate clutch C2*
5 *Multi-plate brake B2*	10 *Free-wheel mechanism F1*

11 *Free-wheel mechanism F2*
12 *Free-wheel mechanism F3*
13 *Multi-plate clutch C3*
14 *Brake band B4*
15 *Final drive differential*

transmission itself are beyond the scope of many dealers, let alone the home mechanic, while the electrical control system can only be checked thoroughly using special Vauxhall test equipment. This Section is therefore restricted to those servicing procedures that can be carried out by the home mechanic. Any fault diagnosis, overhaul or repair work must be entrusted only to a suitably equipped Vauxhall dealer or to an automatic transmission specialist who has the facilities and skill required to undertake such work.

11 On models fitted with the X20 XEV engine, a modified ECU is fitted. One of the modifications is a 'downshift lockout', which prevents changing down from "D" to "3", at speeds above 121 mph (194 km/h).

2 Transmission fluid - renewal

1 This operation is much quicker and more efficient if the vehicle is first taken on a journey of sufficient length to warm the engine/transmission up to normal operating temperature.
2 Park the vehicle on level ground, switch off the ignition, and apply the handbrake firmly. For improved access, jack up the front of the car and support it securely on axle stands (see "*Jacking and Vehicle Support*").
3 Withdraw the dipstick, then position a container under the drain plug at the rear right-hand side of the transmission, below the driveshaft, and unscrew the plug.
4 Allow the fluid to drain completely into the container. If the fluid is hot, take precautions against scalding.
5 When the fluid has finished draining, clean the drain plug threads and those of the transmission casing, fit a new sealing washer and refit the drain plug, tightening it to the specified torque wrench setting. Where applicable, lower the vehicle to the ground.
6 Refill the transmission with the specified amount and type of fluid, then check the fluid level (see "*Lubricants and fluids*" and Chapter 1).
7 Dispose of the old fluid safely; do not pour it down a drain.

3 Kickdown switch - adjustment

1 Remove the air box, air cleaner or inlet ducting, as required, to see the throttle valve (refer to Chapter 4A if necessary).
2 Have an assistant depress the throttle pedal until it contacts the switch on the vehicle's floor. Check that the throttle valve is fully open at this point, and that the pedal acts squarely on the centre of the switch button.
3 If the contact point requires adjustment, it must be made by resetting the throttle pedal stop screw and then adjusting the cable (see

Chapter 4A or 7A) as required. If necessary, set the cable so that only the barest minimum of free play is left.
4 If the throttle pedal does not contact the switch button correctly, check that the pedal pivot bushes are in good condition and either reposition the switch on its retainer or bend the pedal carefully.

4 Kickdown switch - removal and refitting

Removal

1 Loosen the carpet retainer located under the throttle pedal and raise the carpet. Disconnect the switch wiring (the cable runs to the centre of the instrument panel) and unclip the switch from its retainer.

Refitting

2 On refitting, guide the switch through the carpet aperture to reconnect the wiring; press the switch onto the retainer as far as the stop, then check its adjustment (see above).

5 Starter inhibitor switch - removal and refitting

Removal

1 With the handbrake firmly applied, select position "N".
2 Disconnect the battery negative lead.
3 Unscrew its retaining nut and withdraw the dipstick/filler tube.
4 Prising off the retaining clamp and withdrawing the washer, disconnect the selector cable from the actuating lever on the transmission.
5 Disconnect the switch wiring at its connector plugs.
6 Using pliers to counterhold the shaft, unscrew the nut securing the actuating lever to the selector lever shaft; prise off the locking plate, and unscrew the large nut and washer securing the switch to the shaft.
7 Unscrew the fastener securing the switch to the transmission.

Refitting

8 On refitting, ensure that the selector lever

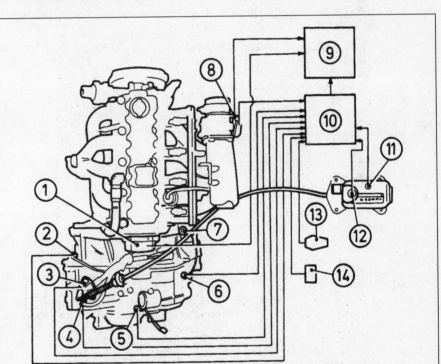

**1.3 Electrical control system of AF 14/20 automatic transmission -
Motronic fuel injection/ignition system**

1 Distributor
2 Transmission fluid temperature sensor
3 Starter inhibitor switch
4 Connection for pressure-regulating solenoids
5 Transmission input speed sensor
6 Transmission output speed sensor
7 Speedometer cable connection
8 Throttle position sensor
9 Motronic module
10 Automatic transmission ECU
11 "Winter" mode button
12 "Economy/Sport" mode button
13 Kickdown switch
14 Brake lamp switch

7B

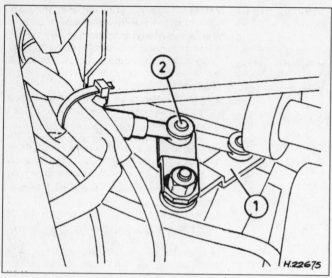

6.1 Transmission actuating lever position "P" (1) and position "N" (2)

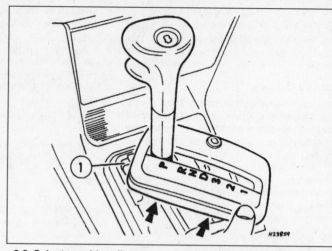

6.2 Selector cable adjustment - release clips (arrowed) to allow centre console top cover to be moved aside

1 Box spanner inserted through aperture to slacken cable clamp bolt

shaft is in position "N" (the third detent from the front). Lower the switch onto the shaft and rotate it until the shaft's flattened surface is aligned with the outline on the switch housing, then secure the switch by tightening the switch/filler tube fastener to the specified torque wrench setting.

9 Next tighten (very carefully, noting its specified torque wrench setting) the large nut retaining the switch on the selector lever shaft; do not forget the washer. Refit the locking plate to secure the nut.

10 When tightening the actuating lever on the selector lever shaft, use pliers to counterhold the shaft; again tighten the nut to its specified torque wrench setting.

11 When refitting the dipstick/filler tube, always renew the sealing O-ring, greasing it to aid installation, and tighten the nut to its specified torque wrench setting.

12 Connect the switch wiring and the selector cable, then check the cable adjustment (see below).

6 Selector cable - adjustment

1 With an assistant operating the selector lever, check that the actuating lever on the transmission moves into the appropriate detent. Detent "P" is at the front and marked, as is position "N"; none of the other detents are marked **(see illustration)**. Check also that the parking pawl actually locks the roadwheels in this position.

2 If adjustment is required, check carefully that the selector lever is in position "P", then unclip the cover (two clips on each side) from the top of the centre console and rotate it to one side **(see illustration)**. Using a box spanner through the aperture exposed, slacken the cable clamp bolt.

3 Returning to the engine compartment, press the transmission actuating lever fully forwards and to the right (i.e., towards the battery holder), ensuring that it meets the stop.

4 Have the assistant hold the actuating lever in position while the cable clamp bolt is tightened, to its specified torque wrench setting.

5 Refit the cover and recheck the selector operation.

7 Selector cable - removal and refitting

Removal

1 With the handbrake firmly applied, select position "P".

2 Disconnect the battery negative lead.

3 Prising off the retaining clamp and withdrawing the washer, disconnect the selector cable from the actuating lever on the transmission.

4 Unscrew the retaining nuts and withdraw the cable mounting bracket from the transmission.

5 Working in the passenger compartment, unclip the cover (two clips on each side) from the top of the centre console and remove the ashtray assembly. Then withdraw the centre console rear section (refer to Chapter 11) until the selector lever cover can be removed. Check that the handbrake is still applied and move the selector lever to position "2".

6 Slacken the cable clamp bolt and unscrew the cable locknut, then withdraw the cable from the centre console and pull it into the engine compartment, prising out the bulkhead grommet to do so.

Refitting

7 Refitting is the reverse of the removal procedure; adjust the cable (see above) on completion.

8 Selector lever - removal and refitting

Removal

1 Disconnect the rear end (only) of the selector cable, as described in Section 7, paragraphs 1, 2, 5 and 6. Then disconnect the wiring from the driving mode switches and unplug the illuminating bulb's socket from the panel.

2 Unscrew the nut securing the lever to its pivot **(see illustration)** and withdraw the lever, manoeuvring it sideways to do so.

Refitting

3 Refitting is the reverse of removal. Adjust the cable (see above) on completion.

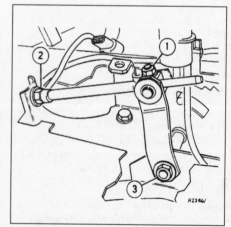

8.2 Selector cable attachment at lever end

1 Cable clamp bolt   3 Lever pivot nut
2 Cable locknut

9 Selector lever console - removal and refitting

Removal

1 Remove the selector lever (see above).
2 Unscrew the four hexagon-headed screws securing the console to the floor panel and withdraw it.

Refitting

3 Refitting is the reverse of removal. Tighten the screws to their specified torque wrench setting.

10 Driving "mode" switches - removal and refitting

"Economy/Sport" mode button

Removal

1 Disconnect the battery negative lead.
2 Remove the selector lever (see Section 8).
3 Using a length of welding rod or similar inserted into the lever's lower end, press out the switch.
4 Having made a careful note of the wiring connections, unsolder the wires from the switch.

Refitting

5 On refitting, solder the wires onto the new switch's terminals, ensuring that they are correctly reconnected, then press the switch into the lever.
6 Refit the selector lever, as described in Section 8.

"Winter" mode button

Removal

7 Disconnect the battery negative lead.
8 Unclip the cover (two clips on each side) from the top of the centre console and move it to one side until the switch wiring plug can be disconnected.
9 Prise the switch out of the cover, taking care not to mark the finish.

Refitting

10 Refitting is the reverse of removal.

11 Electronic Control Unit (ECU) - removal and refitting

Removal

1 Disconnect the battery negative lead.
2 Remove the glovebox assembly (Chapter 11) to access the control unit, mounted on the bulkhead.
3 Disconnect the wiring harness plug from the control unit.

4 Release the control unit from its bracket and withdraw it from the vehicle.

Refitting

5 Refitting is the reverse of removal. Ensure that the wiring plug is correctly reconnected and the unit is located securely.

12 Selector illumination bulb - renewal

Removal

1 Disconnect the battery negative lead.
2 Unclip the cover (two clips on each side) from the top of the centre console and move it to one side until the bulbholder can be unplugged.
3 The bulb is a push fit in the bulbholder.

Refitting

4 Refitting is the reverse of removal.

13 Cooler hoses and pipes - general

1 Check the hoses at regular intervals and renew them if there is the slightest doubt about their condition.
2 Always take note of the pipe and hose connections before disturbing them; also note the hose routing.
3 To minimise the loss of fluid, and to prevent the entry of dirt into the system, clamp (using self-locking pliers or clamping tools) the hoses before disconnecting them. Then slacken their securing clamps. Work each hose in turn off its union and swiftly plug or cap the hose and union. If plugs are used, take care to remove them on refitting.
4 Discard the clamp(s) and fit new ones as a matter of course whenever a hose is disconnected.

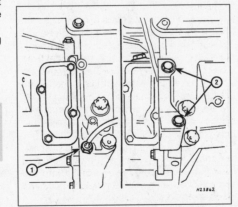

15.2 Transmission fluid temperature sensor replacement

1 Temperature sensor
2 Sensor cover bolts

5 Refit the hoses, ensuring that they are connected to their original unions and route them as noted on removal so that they are not kinked or twisted. This should ensure that the movement of the engine on its mountings will not cause the hoses to stretch or rub against other components.
6 Align the new hose clamps so that they cannot foul any other component and tighten them securely.
7 Always renew the sealing washers if the banjo union bolts are disturbed, and tighten the bolts to their specified torque wrench setting. Be particularly careful when tightening the bolt or union into the plastic radiator/cooler body.

14 Differential bearing oil seals - renewal

Removal

1 Drain the transmission fluid (see Section 2).
2 Work as described in Chapter 7A, using transmission fluid to lubricate the new seals on installation.

Refitting

3 Refill the transmission with clean fluid and check the fluid level, as described in Chapter 1, on completion.

15 Temperature sensor - removal and refitting

Removal

1 Disconnect the battery negative lead.
2 Unbolt the sensor cover from the front of the transmission (see illustration).
3 Disconnect the sensor wiring at its connector plug.
4 Unscrew the sensor; swiftly plug the aperture to prevent the loss of fluid and the entry of dirt.

Refitting

5 Refitting is the reverse of removal. Always renew the sensor sealing ring; tighten the sensor (if possible) and the cover bolts to their specified torque wrench settings.

16 Input/output speed sensors - removal and refitting

Removal

1 The speed sensors are fitted into the transmission casing's upper surface. They are similar in appearance and can be identified by their wiring connectors. The input speed sensor is the unit closer to the transmission's left-hand end.

7B

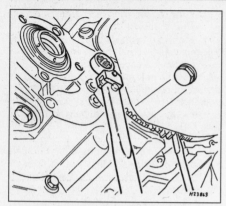

17.13 Commercially available torque wrench adapter being used to tighten torque converter bolts

2 Disconnect the battery negative lead.
3 Disconnect the sensor wiring at its connector plug.
4 Unscrew the sensor's securing (Torx-type) screw and withdraw the sensor; swiftly plug the aperture to prevent the loss of fluid and the entry of dirt.

Refitting

5 Refitting is the reverse of removal. Always renew the sensor sealing ring and tighten the securing screw to its specified torque wrench setting.

---

17 Transmission - removal and refitting

Note: *If the transmission is being removed for repair, ensure first that the fault is genuinely in the transmission, rather than in the control system (see "Fault finding"). The following procedure, being essentially the same as the removal/refitting of a manual transmission, is based on that given in Chapter 7A. Before starting work, read that Section as well as the following text and ensure that you have all the tools and facilities required.*

Removal

1 Disconnect the battery negative lead.
2 Drain the transmission fluid (see Section 2).
3 Disconnect the transmission wiring by unplugging the five connector plugs from the various switches, solenoids and sensors, then release the wiring from any clips or ties securing it to the vehicle.
4 Disconnect the selector cable from the transmission actuating lever, then either unbolt the cable bracket or release the cable from the bracket. Secure the cable clear of the transmission.
5 Releasing it from any clips or ties securing it, withdraw the transmission breather hose from under the battery bracket.
6 Disconnect the oxygen sensor wiring (where fitted).
7 Disconnect the speedometer drive cable.
8 Working as described above, disconnect the fluid cooler hoses (either at the transmission or at the radiator, as convenient).
9 Support the engine/transmission, remove the front suspension subframe and disconnect the driveshafts, working as described in Chapter 7A, Section 9, paragraphs 7 to 10, referring where necessary to Chapters 8 and 10.
10 Unbolt the transmission bellhousing cover plate (three bolts), then use chalk or a felt-tip pen to mark the relationship of the torque converter to the flexplate before unbolting the torque converter. Applying a spanner to the crankshaft pulley/sprocket bolt, rotate the crankshaft until the first bolt appears, then use a screwdriver or similar to jam the flexplate ring gear teeth to prevent it from rotating as the bolt is unscrewed. Unscrew each of the three bolts in turn and discard them.
11 Working as described in Chapter 7A, Section 9, paragraphs 17 to 21 (ignoring paragraph 19), remove the transmission.
12 If the torque converter is removed (even partially) from the transmission, a considerable amount of the fluid inside it will leak out. To prevent this, when prising the transmission off its locating dowels and removing it, be careful to keep the torque converter pressed firmly into the transmission. If the transmission is to be removed for some time, retain the torque converter by bolting a strip of metal across the bellhousing mating surface.

Refitting

13 Refitting is the reverse of removal, noting the following points.

a) *If any fluid was spilled from the torque converter, be careful to refill it as much as possible. Wipe clean the converter's spigot to prevent damage to the transmission's input shaft oil seal as the converter is installed, and ensure that the converter engages correctly on the fluid pump shaft.*

b) *If the transmission has been renewed, be careful to flush clean the radiator fluid cooler passages. Vauxhall recommend the use of low-pressure compressed air, but this will require great care to avoid deforming the radiator.*

c) *Be very careful to ensure that all components are scrupulously clean, to avoid the risk of dirt getting into the system.*

d) *Use an M10 x 1.25 bottoming tap to clean the threads in the torque converters threaded bosses and ensure that new bolts are available for reassembly.*

e) *Check the threads of the engine/transmission left-hand mounting (Chapter 7A, Section 9, paragraph 22) and ensure that new bolts are available for reassembly.*

f) *Tighten all nuts and bolts to their specified torque wrench settings.*

g) *When tightening the torque converter-to-flexplate bolts to their specified torque wrench settings, a commercially available adapter will be required (see illustration).*

h) *Adjust the selector cable on completion, and refill the transmission with fluid (see Section 2).*

Chapter 8
Driveshafts

Contents

Degrees of difficulty

Easy, suitable for novice with little experience	Fairly easy, suitable for beginner with some experience	Fairly difficult, suitable for competent DIY mechanic	Difficult, suitable for experienced DIY mechanic	Very difficult, suitable for expert DIY or professional

Specifications

General
Type (all models) . . . .   Unequal-length open shafts, with constant velocity joint at each end. Certain models have vibration damper fitted to right-hand shaft

Torque wrench settings

	Nm	lbf ft
Front hub nut *		
Stage 1	130	96
Stage 2	Loosen nut fully	
Stage 3	20	15
Stage 4	Angle-tighten a further 80° *	
Intermediate shaft support bearing:		
Bracket to cylinder block	55	40
Bearing flange to bracket	18	13
Lower arm to suspension strut balljoint nut	70	52
Roadwheel bolts	110	81

* Refer to text in Section 2

1 General description

Drive from the differential is taken to the roadwheels by two open driveshafts with a constant velocity joint at each end. On some models, the right-hand driveshaft consists of two parts, with two constant velocity joints, and a plain intermediate shaft. The driveshaft's inboard joint fits over splines on the intermediate shaft's outer end. The intermediate shaft is supported at this point by a bearing that is secured in a bracket bolted to the rear of the engine's cylinder block. Refer to Section 3 for details.

The driveshafts are splined at both ends. The inner ends fit into the differential, and are retained by snap-rings, while the outer ends fit into the front hubs, and are retained by the front hub nuts.

The right-hand driveshaft is longer than the left-hand one, due to the position of the differential. Certain models have a two-piece vibration damper fitted to the right-hand driveshaft.

2 Driveshaft - removal and refitting

Note: *The following **must** be renewed when refitting the driveshaft: hub nut, washer and split pin, driveshaft retaining snap-ring, and lower arm to suspension strut balljoint nut locking pin. A balljoint separator tool will be required for this operation. For models with an intermediate shaft, refer also to Section 3.*

Removal

1 Where applicable, remove the wheel trim from the relevant front roadwheel, then loosen the roadwheel bolts. Apply the handbrake, jack up the front of the vehicle, and support on axle stands (see "*Jacking and Vehicle Support*") positioned under the body side members. Remove the roadwheel.

2 Extract the split pin from the castellated hub nut on the end of the driveshaft.

3 The hub nut must now be loosened. The nut is extremely tight, and an extension bar will be required to loosen it. To prevent the driveshaft from turning, insert two roadwheel bolts, and insert a metal bar between them to counterhold the hub. Remove the hub nut and washer from the driveshaft **(see illustration)**.

2.3 Remove the hub nut and washer from the driveshaft

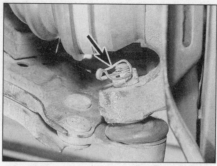

2.4a Extract the locking pin (arrowed) . . .

2.4b . . . then remove the balljoint castellated nut

2.5 Use a balljoint separator tool to disconnect the balljoint

2.6 Use a square-section bar to release the left-hand driveshaft

2.7 Withdraw the left-hand driveshaft from the differential . . .

4 Extract the locking pin, then unscrew the castellated nut from the lower arm to suspension strut balljoint (see illustrations).

5 Using a balljoint separator tool, disconnect the lower arm-to-suspension strut balljoint (see illustration).

6 A lever will now be required to release the inner end of the driveshaft from the differential or, as applicable, the intermediate shaft. To release the right-hand driveshaft, a flat steel bar with a good chamfer on one end can be used. The left-hand driveshaft is more difficult to release, and a square or rectangular-section bar will be required (see illustration).

7 Lever between the driveshaft and the differential housing to release the driveshaft snap-ring from the differential. If necessary, use the bar as a drift to drive out the left-hand driveshaft. Have a container available, to catch the oil that will be released as the

driveshaft is withdrawn from the differential. Support the driveshaft, and do not allow it to hang under its own weight (see illustration).

8 Plug the opening in the differential, to prevent further oil loss and dirt ingress.

9 Withdraw the outer end of the driveshaft from the hub, and remove the driveshaft from the vehicle (see illustration). It should be possible to pull the driveshaft from the hub by hand, but if necessary tap the end of the shaft with a soft-faced mallet to release it.

Caution: Do not use heavy blows, as damage to the driveshaft joints may result.

Caution: Do not allow the vehicle to rest on its wheels with one or both driveshafts removed, as damage to the wheel bearings(s) may result.

10 If moving the vehicle is unavoidable, temporarily insert the outer end of the driveshaft(s) in the hub(s) and tighten the hub nut(s). In this case, the inner end(s) of the

driveshaft(s) must be supported, for example by suspending with string from the vehicle underbody.

Caution: Do not allow the driveshaft to hang down under its own weight

11 Certain models have a two-piece vibration damper fitted to the right-hand driveshaft. If the damper is removed for any reason, it is important to refit it so that the distance between the inner end of the outer joint gaiter and the outer face of the damper is as shown (see illustrations).

Refitting

12 Before refitting a driveshaft, make sure that the contact faces of the shaft and wheel bearing are clean (see illustration).

2.9 . . . and the hub

2.11a Vibration damper fitted to right-hand driveshaft

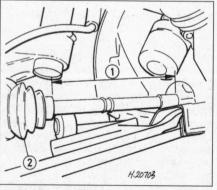

2.11b Driveshaft damper weight distance from outer joint gaiter

1 268.0 to 270.0 mm (10.5 to 10.56 in)
2 Outer joint

13 Begin refitting by applying a little molybdenum disulphide grease to the driveshaft splines, then insert the outer end of the shaft into the hub. Fit a new washer, and screw on a new hub nut finger tight.

14 Fit a new snap-ring to the inboard end of the driveshaft, then remove the plug from the opening in the differential, and push the driveshaft into the differential as far as possible **(see illustration)**.

15 Place a screwdriver or similar tool on the weld bead of the inner driveshaft joint, **not** the metal cover, and drive the shaft into the differential (or over the intermediate shaft) until the retaining snap-ring engages positively. Pull on the **outer** circumference of the joint to check the engagement.

16 Reconnect the lower arm-to-suspension strut balljoint, then fit the castellated nut, and tighten to the specified torque. Secure the nut with a new locking pin.

17 Tighten the new hub nut to the specified torque, in the stages given in the Specifications. Prevent the driveshaft from turning, as during removal **(see illustrations)**. If in this position none of the grooves in the nut line up with the pin hole, turn the nut up to a further 9°, and secure with a split pin.

18 Refit the roadwheel, then lower the vehicle to the ground, and finally tighten the roadwheel bolts to the specified torque wrench setting. Refit the wheel trim, where applicable.

19 Check and if necessary top-up the transmission oil level, as described in Chapter 1.

---

3 Intermediate shaft (where fitted) - removal, overhaul and refitting

Note: *A press may be required to remove and refit the intermediate shaft support bearing.*

Removal

1 First remove the right-hand outer driveshaft as described in Section 2.

2 Unbolt the support bearing's bracket from the cylinder block.

3 Placing a container to catch the oil that will

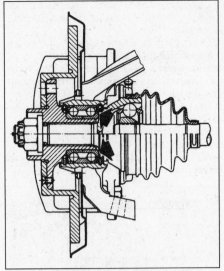

2.12 Sectional view of front hub assembly

Clean the contact faces (arrowed) of the driveshaft and wheel bearing

be released, pull the intermediate shaft out of the differential, and plug the aperture to minimise oil loss and to prevent the entry of dirt.

Overhaul

4 Turn the bearing by hand, feeling for signs of roughness, notchy movement or free play. If there is any doubt about the condition of the bearing it must be renewed.

5 Unscrew the two bolts securing the flange to the bearing bracket; withdraw the bracket.

6 Remove the snap-ring from the intermediate shaft's outer end, followed by the O-ring and the larger (bearing retaining) circlip.

7 Remove the bearing and flange from the shaft. If the bearing is a very tight fit, use a hydraulic puller or a press; be careful to support the bearing's inner race during removal if the bearing is to be re-used.

8 Support the flange on two wooden blocks placed on the work surface and drive out the bearing.

2.14 Fit a new snap-ring (arrowed) to the driveshaft

9 To fit the new bearing, heat it evenly if necessary using a hair dryer, paint-stripping heat gun or similar until it can be pressed onto the shaft. Using a hammer and a tubular drift that bears only on the bearing's inner race, tap the bearing fully onto the shaft until it seats against the shaft shoulder. Fit the flange over the other end of the shaft and onto the bearing outer race, then refit the retaining circlip, followed by a new O-ring and a new snap-ring.

10 Refit the bracket to the shaft assembly.

11 To ensure correct alignment, do not tighten the flange bolts until the shaft is refitted to the differential and the bearing bracket is correctly secured to the cylinder block (see below). When this has been done, apply a few drops of thread-locking compound to their threads, and tighten the bolts to the specified torque wrench setting.

Refitting

12 Refitting is the reverse of removal, noting the following points **(see illustration)**.

a) Grease the shaft splines to prevent damage to the seal lip as the shaft is refitted.

b) Offer up the bracket to the cylinder block and tighten the bolt to its specified torque wrench setting.

c) If the support bearing assembly was dismantled, refit the flange to the bracket and tighten the two bolts (see above).

d) Refit the outer driveshaft (Section 2).

2.17a Tighten the hub nut to the specified torque . . .

2.17b . . . then through the specified angle (see Specifications)

3.12 Right-hand driveshaft support bearing is bolted to the rear of the cylinder block

8

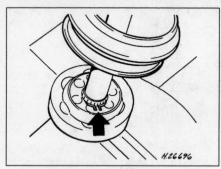

4.3 Driveshaft joint retaining circlip (arrowed)

4 Driveshaft joint - renewal

Note: *Ensure that a new securing circlip is supplied when ordering a new driveshaft joint.*

1 A worn driveshaft joint must be renewed, as it cannot be overhauled. If driveshaft joint wear is apparent on a vehicle in which the driveshaft has covered more than 48 000 miles (80 000 km), the manufacturers recommend that the complete driveshaft is renewed.

2 With the driveshaft removed, as described in Section 2, release the metal securing band and slide the rubber gaiter from the worn joint.

3 Using circlip pliers, expand the circlip that secures the joint to the driveshaft **(see illustration)**.

4 Using a soft-faced mallet, tap the joint from the driveshaft **(see illustration)**.

5 Ensure that a new circlip is fitted to the new joint, then tap the new joint onto the driveshaft until the circlip engages in its groove.

6 Pack the joint with the type of grease specified by your Vauxhall dealer.

7 Refit the rubber gaiter to the new joint, referring to Section 5, if necessary.

8 Refit the driveshaft to the vehicle, as described in Section 2.

5 Driveshaft joint gaiter - renewal

1 With the driveshaft removed as described in Section 2, remove the relevant joint as described in Section 4. Note that if both gaiters on a driveshaft are to be renewed it is only necessary to remove one joint.

2 Release the remaining securing band and slide the gaiter from the driveshaft.

3 Clean the old grease from the joint, then re-pack the joint with the type of fresh grease specified by your Vauxhall dealer. If excessively worn or damaged, the driveshaft joint should be renewed, referring to Section 4 if necessary.

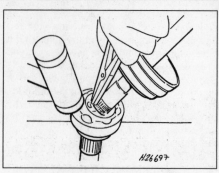

4.4 Tapping joint from driveshaft

4 Slide the new gaiter onto the driveshaft so that the smaller diameter opening is located in the groove in the driveshaft.

5 Refit the joint, using a new securing circlip. Tap the joint onto the driveshaft until the circlip engages in its groove.

6 Slide the gaiter over the joint, then squeeze the gaiter to expel as much air as possible.

7 Secure the gaiter using new securing bands. To fit a securing band, wrap it around the gaiter, and while pulling on the band as tight as possible, engage the lug on the end of the band with one of the slots. Use a screwdriver if necessary to push the band as tight as possible before engaging the lug and slot. Finally tighten the band by compressing the raised square portion of the band with pliers, taking care not to cut the gaiter.

Chapter 9
Braking system

Contents

Degrees of difficulty

Easy, suitable for novice with little experience		Fairly easy, suitable for beginner with some experience		Fairly difficult, suitable for competent DIY mechanic	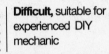	Difficult, suitable for experienced DIY mechanic		Very difficult, suitable for expert DIY or professional	

Specifications

System type
All models . . . . Anti-lock Braking System (ABS). Front and rear discs, with vacuum servo assistance, operated via hydraulic modulator, dual hydraulic circuit split front/rear, pressure-proportioning valves in rear hydraulic circuit. Cable-operated handbrake on rear wheels

Front discs
Type . . . . Ventilated
Diameter . . . . 256 mm
Maximum disc run-out . . . . 0.1 mm
Minimum pad friction material thickness (including backing plate) . . . . 7.0 mm
Minimum disc thickness after machining* . . . . 22.0 mm
*When this dimension is reached, only one further new set of brake pads is permissible, then renew the discs

Rear discs
Type . . . . Solid
Diameter . . . . 260 mm
Maximum disc run-out . . . . 0.1 mm
Minimum pad friction material thickness (including backing plate) . . . . 7.0 mm
Minimum disc thickness after machining* . . . . 8.0 mm
*When this dimension is reached, only one further new set of disc pads is permissible, then renew the discs
Minimum handbrake shoe friction material thickness (lining only) . . . . . 1.0 mm

Rear drums
Internal diameter . . . . 200 mm
Minimum shoe friction material thickness . . . . 0.5 mm above rivet heads

Brake fluid type/specification
All models . . . . See "Lubricants and fluids"

9

Torque wrench settings

	Nm	lbf ft
ABS hydraulic modulator mounting	8	6
ABS wheel sensor mounting	8	6
ABS control unit	1.5	1
Brake fluid line unions	16	12
Caliper and wheel cylinder bleed screws	9	7
Front brake disc securing screw	4	3
Front brake fluid hose to caliper union	40	30
Front caliper bracket to hub carrier	95	70
Front caliper guide	30	22
Front caliper to mounting bracket	30	22
Handbrake lever securing	20	15
Master cylinder mounting	22	16
Pressure proportioning valve to master cylinder:		
ATE type	12	9
GMF type	40	30
Rear brake backplate/stub axle spring:		
Stage 1	50	37
Stage 2	Angle-tighten a further 30°	
Stage 3	Angle-tighten a further 15°	
Rear brake disc securing screw	8	6
Rear caliper mounting	80	59
Rear drum securing screw	4	3
Rear wheel cylinder mounting	9	7
Roadwheel bolts	110	81
Vacuum servo support bracket to bulkhead	22	16
Vacuum servo to support bracket	20	15

1 General description

The footbrake operates on all four wheels. Ventilated disc brakes are fitted at the front, and solid disc brakes are fitted at the rear. Actuation is hydraulic, with vacuum servo assistance. The handbrake is cable-operated, and acts on a drum brake fitted to the rear wheels only.

Anti-lock braking (ABS) is fitted as standard on all models.

The hydraulic system is split front and rear. If there is a hydraulic fluid leak in one circuit, the remaining circuit will still function, so that some braking capability remains.

The hydraulic fluid supply to the rear brakes is regulated so that the front brakes are always applied first under heavy braking. The fluid pressure to the rear brakes is controlled by two valves, one for each brake, which are either screwed into the master cylinder or mounted on the rear underbody of the vehicle, depending on model.

The brake servo is the direct-acting type, fitted between the pedal and the master cylinder. The servo is powered by vacuum developed in the inlet manifold. Should the servo fail, the brakes will still operate, but increased pedal pressure will be required.

2 Anti-lock braking system (ABS) - general

ABS is fitted as standard to all Calibra models. When the ignition is switched on, an 'ABS' symbol illuminates in the instrument panel for a short time.

The system comprises an electronic control unit, roadwheel sensors, hydraulic modulator, and the necessary valves and relays. Disc brakes are fitted to all four wheels. The purpose of the system is to stop the wheels locking during heavy brake applications. This is achieved by automatic release of the brake on the locked wheel, followed by re-application of the brake. This procedure is carried out several times a second by the hydraulic modulator.

The modulator is controlled by the ABS electronic control unit, which itself receives signals from the wheel sensors, which monitor the locked or unlocked state of the wheels. The two front brakes are modulated separately, but the two rear brakes are modulated together.

The ABS unit is fitted between the brake master cylinder and the brakes.

If the 'ABS' symbol, in the instrument panel stays lit after approximately 4 seconds, or if it comes on sporadically or stays on whilst driving, there is a fault in the system. Should this occur, it is recommended that a complete test is carried out by a Vauxhall dealer, who will have the necessary specialist diagnostic equipment. Due to the special equipment required, it is not practical for the DIY mechanic to carry out the test procedure.

To prevent possible damage to the electronic control unit, always disconnect the control unit wiring plug before carrying out electrical welding work.

It is recommended that the control unit is removed if the vehicle is being subjected to high temperatures, like for instance, during certain paint-drying processes.

If using steam cleaning equipment, do not aim the water/steam jet directly at the control unit.

Do not disconnect the control unit wiring plug with the ignition switched on.

Do not use a battery booster to start the engine.

After working on the ABS components, ensure that all wiring plugs are correctly reconnected, and have the complete system tested by a Vauxhall dealer, at the earliest opportunity.

All models up to 1991 use the ABS-2E system which has the electronic control module under a cover in the passenger side sill trim panel. From 1992 onwards the ABS-2EH system was fitted, which has the control module bolted to the hydraulic modulator.

The main differences between the two systems are in the electrical components and circuits, the most obvious of these being the omission of the surge arrester relay on the 2EH system.

3 Hydraulic system - bleeding

Caution: If brake fluid is spilt on the paintwork, the affected area must be washed down with cold water immediately. Brake fluid is an effective paint stripper!

General

1 If any of the hydraulic components in the braking system have been removed or disconnected, or if the fluid level in the reservoir has been allowed to fall appreciably, it is certain that air will have entered into the system. The removal of all this air from the hydraulic system is essential if the brakes are to function correctly, and the process of removing it is known as bleeding.

2 Where an operation has only affected one circuit of the hydraulic system, which is split front and rear, then it will only be necessary to bleed the relevant circuit. If the master cylinder has been disconnected and reconnected, or the fluid level has been allowed to fall appreciably, then the complete system must be bled. When bleeding the complete system, the front brakes must be bled before the rear brakes.

3 One of three methods can be used to bleed the system, although Vauxhall recommend the use of a pressure bleeding kit.

Bleeding - two-man method

4 Obtain a clean jar, and a length of rubber or plastic bleed tubing that will fit the bleed screws tightly. The help of an assistant will be required.

5 Remove the dust cap and clean around the bleed screw on the relevant brake caliper (see illustration), then attach the bleed tube to the screw.

6 Check that the fluid reservoir is topped up, and then destroy the vacuum in the brake servo by giving several applications of the brake pedal.

7 Immerse the open end of the bleed tube in the jar, which should contain two or three inches of hydraulic fluid. The jar should be positioned about 300 mm (12.0 in) above the bleed screw to prevent any possibility of air entering the system down the threads of the bleed screw when it is slackened.

8 Open the bleed screw half a turn, and have the assistant depress the brake pedal slowly to the floor. With the brake pedal still depressed, retighten the bleed screw, and then have the assistant quickly release the pedal. Repeat the procedure.

9 Observe the submerged end of the tube in the jar. When air bubbles cease to appear, tighten the bleed screw when the pedal is being held fully down by the assistant.

10 Top-up the fluid reservoir. It must be kept topped up throughout the bleeding operations. If the connecting holes to the master cylinder are exposed at any time due to low fluid level, the air will be drawn into the system, and the whole bleeding process will have to start again.

11 If the complete system is being bled, the procedure should be repeated on the remaining front brake and then on the rear brakes.

12 On completion, remove the bleed tube, and discard the fluid that has been bled from the system, unless it is required to make up the level in the bleed jar. Never re-use old fluid.

13 On completion of bleeding, top-up the fluid level in the reservoir. Check the action of the brake pedal, which should be firm, and free from any "sponginess" that would indicate that air is still present in the system.

Bleeding - with one-way valve

14 There are a number of one-man brake bleeding kits currently available from motor accessory shops. It is recommended that one of these kits should be used whenever possible, as they greatly simplify the bleeding operations. They also reduce the risk of expelled air or fluid being drawn back into the system.

15 Proceed as described in paragraphs 5 and 6.

16 Open the bleed screw half a turn, then depress the brake pedal to the floor, and slowly release it. The one-way valve in the bleeder device will prevent expelled air from returning to the system at the completion of each stroke. Repeat the operation until clear hydraulic fluid, free from air bubbles, can be seen coming through the tube. Tighten the bleed screw.

17 Proceed as described in paragraphs 11 to 13 inclusive.

Bleeding - with pressure bleeding kit

18 These are also available from motor accessory shops, and are usually operated by air pressure from the spare tyre.

19 By connecting a pressurised container to the master cylinder fluid reservoir, bleeding is then carried out by simply opening each bleed screw in turn and allowing the fluid to run out. Like turning on a tap, until no air bubbles are visible in the fluid being expelled.

4.6 Withdraw the pad wear sensor from the inboard pad

3.5 Remove the dust cap from a rear caliper bleed screw

20 Using this method, the large reserve of fluid provides a safeguard against air being drawn into the master cylinder during the bleeding operations.

21 This method of bleeding is recommended by Vauxhall.

22 Begin bleeding with reference to paragraphs 5 and 6, and continue as described in paragraphs 11 to 13 inclusive.

4 Front disc pads - inspection, removal and refitting

⚠ **Warning: When working on the brake components, take care not to disperse brake dust into the air, or to inhale it, since it may contain asbestos, which can damage your health.**

Inspection

1 Where applicable, remove the wheel trims, then loosen the front roadwheel bolts and apply the handbrake. Jack up the front of the vehicle, and support on axle stands (see "*Jacking and Vehicle Support*") positioned under the body side members.

2 Remove the roadwheels. Turn the steering to full right-hand lock, and check the wear of the friction material on the right-hand brake pads. Check that the thickness of the friction material (including the backing plate) is not less than the minimum given in the Specifications.

3 Turn the steering to full left-hand lock, and check the left-hand brake pads in the same way.

4 If any brake pad is worn below the specified minimum thickness, renew all the front pads as a set.

5 If the pads require renewal, continue as follows.

Removal

6 Where applicable, pull the pad wear sensor from the inboard pad, and disconnect the wiring at the connector under the wheel arch, next to the suspension strut (see illustration). Note the wire routing.

7 Using a screwdriver, prise the pad retaining clip from the outboard edge of the caliper, noting how it is located (see illustration).

9

4.7 Prise out the disc pad retaining clip

4.8a Remove a caliper guide bolt dust cap

4.8b Withdraw the caliper, inboard and outboard pad

8 Prise out the two guide bolt dust caps from the inboard edge of the caliper, then using an Allen key or hexagon bit, unscrew the guide bolts, and lift the caliper and inboard pad from the bracket. Recover the outboard brake pad **(see illustrations)**. Suspend the caliper body with wire or string, to avoid straining the brake fluid hose.

9 Pull the inboard pad from the caliper piston, noting that it is retained by a clip attached to the pad backing plate **(see illustration)**.

Refitting

10 Brush the dust and dirt from the caliper, but take care not to inhale it. Carefully remove any rust from the edge of the brake disc.

11 To accommodate the new thicker pads, the caliper piston must be depressed fully into its cylinder bore, using a flat bar of metal such as a tyre lever. The action of depressing the piston will cause the fluid level in the reservoir

4.9 Remove the inboard pad from the caliper piston

4.12 Caliper piston cutaway recess (arrowed) correctly positioned

to rise, so to avoid spillage, syphon out some fluid using an old hydrometer or a teat pipette. Refer to the warning at the beginning of Section 3. Do not lever between the piston and disc to depress the piston.

12 Check that the cutaway recesses in the piston are positioned vertically **(see illustration)**. If necessary, carefully turn the piston to its correct position.

13 Apply a little brake grease to the contact surfaces of the new brake pads.

14 Fit the new inboard pad to the caliper piston, ensuring that the piston is correctly located.

15 Locate the outboard pad on the caliper bracket, with the friction material facing the disc.

16 Refit the caliper to the bracket, and tighten the guide bolts to the specified torque **(see illustration)**.

17 Refit the guide bolt dust caps.

18 Refit the pad retaining clip, locating it as noted before removal.

19 Where applicable, fit a new pad wear sensor to the inboard pad, and connect the wiring at the connector under the wheel arch. Route the wiring as noted during removal.

20 Repeat the operations on the remaining side of the vehicle.

21 Refit the roadwheels and lower the vehicle to the ground. **Do not** tighten the roadwheel bolts to the specified torque until the vehicle is resting on its wheels.

22 Apply the footbrake hard several times to position the pads against the discs.

23 Check and if necessary top-up the brake fluid level (see "Weekly checks").

4.16 Tightening a caliper guide bolt

24 New brake pads should be carefully bedded in and, where possible, heavy braking should be avoided during the first 100 miles (160 km) or so after fitting new pads.

5 Rear disc pads - inspection, removal and refitting

> **Warning: When working on the brake components, take care not to disperse brake dust into the air, or to inhale it, since it may contain asbestos, which can damage your health.**

Inspection

1 Where applicable, remove the wheel trims, then loosen the rear roadwheel bolts and chock the front wheels. Jack up the rear of the vehicle, and support on axle stands (see "Jacking and Vehicle Support") positioned under the body side members. Remove the roadwheels.

2 Check the wear of the friction material on the brake pads, on both sides of the vehicle. Check that the thickness of the friction material (including the backing plate) is not less than the minimum given in the Specifications.

3 If any brake pad is worn below the specified minimum thickness, renew all the rear pads as a set as follows.

Removal

4 Note how the anti-rattle spring is located, then drive out the upper and lower pad retaining pins from the outside of the caliper using a pin punch **(see illustration)**.

5.4 Driving out a rear disc pad retaining pin

5 Remove the anti-rattle spring **(see illustration)**.

6 Push the pads away from the disc slightly, then using a pair of pliers, withdraw the outboard pad and anti-squeal shim that fits between the pad and the caliper body.

7 Withdraw the inboard pad and anti-squeal shim.

Refitting

8 Proceed as described in Section 4, paragraphs 10 and 11.

9 Check that the cutaway recesses in the pistons are positioned downwards, at approximately 23° to the horizontal. A template made of card may be used to check the setting **(see illustration)**. If necessary, carefully turn the pistons to their correct positions.

10 Apply a little brake grease to the top and bottom edges of the backplates on the new brake pads.

11 Locate the new pads and the anti-squeal shims in the caliper. Ensure that the friction material faces the disc, and check that the pads are free to move slightly.

12 Locate the anti-rattle spring on the pads, then insert the pad retaining pins from the inside edge of the caliper, while depressing the spring. Tap the pins firmly into the caliper.

13 Repeat the operations on the remaining side of the vehicle.

14 Proceed as described in Section 4, paragraphs 21 to 24 inclusive.

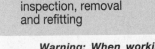

6 Rear handbrake shoes - inspection, removal and refitting

⚠️ **Warning: When working on the brake components, take care not to disperse brake dust into the air, or to inhale it, since it may contain asbestos, which can damage your health.**

Inspection

1 Although rear disc brakes are fitted, the handbrake operates independently of the footbrake, using drum brakes on the inside of the disc.

2 To inspect the handbrake shoes it will be necessary to remove the brake disc, as described in Section 9.

3 With the disc removed, check that the friction material has not worn down to less than the specified minimum.

4 If any one of the shoes has worn below the specified limit, all four handbrake shoes must be renewed as a set, as follows.

Removal

5 Clean the dust and dirt from the various components, but take care not to inhale it.

6 Disconnect the handbrake cable and the return spring from the handbrake operating lever at the brake backplate. If necessary, slacken the handbrake cable adjustment, with reference to Section 21.

5.5 Removing a rear disc pad retaining pin anti-rattle spring

7 Remove the shoe hold-down pins, springs and cups by turning the cups through 90° using a pair of pliers. Note that the hold-down pins are removed through the rear of the brake backplate. Note also the position and orientation of all components, then unhook the upper and lower return springs from the shoes, and recover the handbrake operating lever and the adjuster.

Refitting

8 Apply a little brake grease to the threads of the adjuster, then screw it together to its minimum length. Also apply a little brake grease to the shoe rubbing areas on the lockplate.

9 Fit one of the new brake shoes, and secure it to the backplate with the hold-down pin, spring and cup.

10 Fit the handbrake operating lever in position.

11 Fit the remaining brake shoe, and secure with the hold-down pin, spring and cup.

12 Hook the lower return spring onto the shoes.

13 Fit the adjuster between the upper ends of the shoes, as noted before dismantling, then fit the upper return spring **(see illustration)**.

14 Reconnect the handbrake cable and the return spring to the handbrake operating lever.

15 Refit the brake disc as described in Section 9, but do not refit the roadwheel at this stage.

16 Repeat the operations on the remaining side of the vehicle.

17 Check the handbrake cable adjustment, as described in Section 21.

6.13 Handbrake shoe adjuster and upper return spring correctly fitted

5.9 Checking a rear caliper piston cut away recess angle with a card template

18 Refit the roadwheels and lower the vehicle to the ground. **Do not** tighten the roadwheel bolts to the specified torque until the vehicle is resting on its wheels.

7 Front disc caliper - removal, overhaul and refitting

Note: *Refer to the warning at the beginning of Section 4 before proceeding. Before dismantling a caliper, check that replacement parts can be obtained, and retain the old components to compare them with the new ones. New sealing rings must be used on the fluid hose union bolt on refitting.*

Removal

1 Where applicable, remove the wheel trims, then loosen the relevant front roadwheel bolts and apply the handbrake. Jack up the front of the vehicle, and support securely on axle stands (see "*Jacking and Vehicle Support*") positioned under the body side members. Remove the roadwheel.

2 Remove the brake disc pads, as described in Section 4.

3 Working under the bonnet, remove the brake fluid reservoir cap, and secure a piece of polythene over the filler neck with a rubber band, or by refitting the cap. This will reduce the loss of fluid during the following procedure.

4 Unscrew the brake fluid hose union bolt from the rear of the caliper, and disconnect the hose. Recover the two sealing rings from the union bolt (one either side of the hose end fitting). Be prepared for fluid spillage, and plug the open ends to prevent dirt ingress and further fluid loss.

5 Withdraw the caliper body from the vehicle.

6 If desired, the caliper bracket can be removed from the hub carrier by unscrewing the two securing bolts **(see illustration)**.

Overhaul

7 To overhaul the caliper, continue as follows. Otherwise, go on to paragraph 22 for details of refitting.

8 Brush the dirt and dust from the caliper, but take care not to inhale it.

9

7.6 Caliper bracket securing bolts (arrowed)

9 Using a screwdriver, carefully prise the dust seal from the end of the piston and the caliper body, and remove it.

10 Place a thin piece of wood in front of the piston to prevent it from falling out of its bore and sustaining damage. Then apply low air pressure - e.g. from a foot pump - to the hydraulic fluid union hole in the rear of the caliper body, to eject the piston from its bore.

11 Remove the wood and carefully withdraw the piston.

12 Carefully prise the seal from the groove in the caliper piston bore, using a plastic or wooden instrument.

13 Inspect the surfaces of the piston and its bore in the caliper for scoring, or evidence of metal-to-metal contact. If evident, renew the complete caliper assembly.

14 If the piston and bore are in good condition, discard the seals and obtain a repair kit, which will contain all the necessary renewable items.

15 Clean the piston and cylinder bore with brake fluid or methylated spirit, nothing else!

16 Begin reassembly by fitting the seal into the caliper bore.

17 Locate the dust seal in its groove in the piston. Dip the piston in clean brake fluid and insert it squarely into the cylinder. Check that the cutaway recesses in the piston are positioned vertically. If necessary, carefully turn the piston to its correct position.

18 When the piston has been partially depressed, engage the dust seal with the rim of the caliper bore.

19 Push the piston further into its bore, but not as far as the stop, ensuring that it does not jam.

20 If desired, the guide bolt sleeves can be renewed. Extract the nylon compression sleeve from within each rubber, then carefully compress the rubber shoulder, and push the rubber through the hole in the caliper body to remove it from the inboard end.

21 Fit the new sleeves using a reversal of the removal procedure.

Refitting

22 Where applicable, refit the caliper bracket to the hub carrier, and tighten the securing bolts to the specified torque.

23 Reconnect the brake fluid hose union, using new sealing rings on the union bolt.

24 Refit the disc pads, as described in Section 4.

25 Remove the polythene from the brake fluid reservoir filler neck, and bleed the relevant brake hydraulic circuit, as described in Section 3.

26 Refit the roadwheel and lower the vehicle to the ground. **Do not** tighten the roadwheel bolts to the specified torque wrench setting until the vehicle is resting on its wheels.

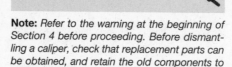

8 Rear disc caliper - removal, overhaul and refitting

Note: *Refer to the warning at the beginning of Section 4 before proceeding. Before dismantling a caliper, check that replacement parts can be obtained, and retain the old components to compare them with the new ones.*

Removal

1 Where applicable, remove the wheel trim, then loosen the relevant rear roadwheel bolts and chock the front wheels. Jack up the rear of the vehicle, and support on axle stands (see *"Jacking and Vehicle Support"*) positioned under the body side members. Remove the roadwheel.

2 Remove the disc pads, as described in Section 5.

3 Working under the bonnet, remove the brake fluid reservoir cap and secure a piece of polythene over the filler neck with a rubber band, or by refitting the cap. This will reduce the loss of fluid during the following procedure.

8.5a Withdrawing a rear caliper mounting bolt . . .

4 Unscrew the brake fluid pipe union nut from the rear of the caliper, and disconnect the pipe. Take care not to strain the pipe. Be prepared for fluid spillage, and plug the open ends to prevent dirt ingress and further fluid loss.

5 Unscrew the two mounting bolts and withdraw the caliper from the vehicle, noting that the caliper securing bolts also secure the ABS sensor bracket **(see illustrations)**. Take care not to strain the ABS sensor wiring.

Overhaul

6 If desired, the caliper can be overhauled as follows. Otherwise, go on to paragraph 20 for details of refitting.

7 Brush the dirt and dust from the caliper, but take care not to inhale it.

8 Note that no attempt must be made to separate the two halves of the caliper.

9 Using a screwdriver, prise the dust seal retaining clips from the piston dust seals, then carefully prise off the dust seals.

10 Using a clamp, secure one of the pistons in its fully retracted position. Then apply low air pressure (e.g. from a foot pump), to the hydraulic fluid union hole in the rear of the caliper body, to eject the remaining piston from its bore.

Caution: Take care not to drop the piston, which may result in damage.

11 Temporarily close off the bore of the removed piston, using a flat piece of wood or similar improvised tool. Then remove the clamp from the remaining piston, and again apply air pressure to the caliper union to eject the piston.

12 Carefully prise the seals from the grooves in the caliper piston bores, using a plastic or wooden instrument.

13 Inspect the surfaces of the pistons and their bores in the caliper for scoring, or evidence of metal-to-metal contact. If evident, renew the complete caliper assembly.

14 If the pistons and bores are in good condition, discard the seals and obtain a repair kit, which will contain all the necessary renewable items. Also obtain a tube of brake cylinder paste.

15 Clean the piston and cylinder bore with brake fluid or methylated spirit - nothing else!

16 Apply a little brake cylinder paste to the pistons, cylinder bores and piston seals.

17 Begin reassembly by fitting the seals to the grooves in the caliper bores.

18 Locate the dust seals in their grooves in the pistons, then insert the pistons carefully into their bores until they enter the seals. It may be necessary to rotate the pistons to prevent them from jamming in the seals.

19 When the pistons have been partially depressed, engage the dust seals with the rims of the caliper bores, and fit the retaining clips.

Refitting

20 Refit the caliper and tighten the securing bolts to the specified torque, ensuring that the ABS sensor bracket is in position.

8.5b . . . which also secures the ABS sensor bracket

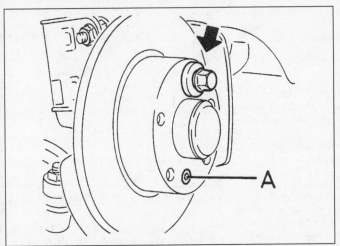

9.2 Refit a wheel bolt and spacer (arrowed) opposite the disc securing screw (A) before checking brake disc run-out

9.16 Withdraw the rear brake disc

21 Reconnect the brake fluid pipe to the caliper, and tighten the union nut.

22 Refit the disc pads, as described in Section 5.

23 Remove the polythene from the brake fluid reservoir filler neck and bleed the relevant brake hydraulic circuit, as described in Section 3.

24 Refit the roadwheel and lower the vehicle to the ground. **Do not** tighten the roadwheel bolts to the specified torque wrench setting until the vehicle is resting on its wheels.

9 Brake disc - inspection, removal and refitting

Inspection

1 Where applicable, remove the wheel trim, then loosen the relevant roadwheel bolts. If checking a front disc, apply the handbrake, and if checking a rear disc, chock the front wheels, then jack up the relevant end of the vehicle and support on axle stands (see "*Jacking and Vehicle Support*") positioned under the body side members. Remove the roadwheel.

2 Where applicable, check that the brake disc securing screw is tight. Then fit a spacer approximately 10.0 mm (0.4 in) thick to one of the roadwheel bolts, and refit and tighten the bolt in the hole opposite the disc securing screw **(see illustration)**.

3 Rotate the brake disc, and examine it for deep scoring or grooving. Light scoring is normal, but if excessive, the disc should be removed and either renewed or machined (within the specified limits) by an engineering works.

4 Using a dial gauge, or a flat metal block and feeler blades, check that the disc run-out does not exceed the figure given in the

Specifications. Measure the run-out 10.0 mm (0.4 in) in from the outer edge of the disc.

5 If the disc run-out is excessive, remove the disc as described later in this Section. Check that the disc-to-hub surfaces are perfectly clean. Refit the disc and check the run-out again.

6 If the run-out is still excessive, the disc should be renewed.

7 To remove a disc, continue as follows.

Front disc

Removal

8 Where applicable, remove the roadwheel bolt and spacer used when checking the disc.

9 Remove the disc pads (Section 4).

10 Unscrew the two securing bolts and remove the caliper bracket.

11 Remove the securing screw and withdraw the disc from the hub, where applicable tilting it to clear the brake caliper.

Refitting

12 Refitting is the reverse of removal, but make sure that the mating faces of the disc and hub are perfectly clean, and apply a little locking fluid to the threads of the securing screw. Refit the disc pads (Section 4).

Rear disc

Removal

13 Where applicable, remove the roadwheel bolt and spacer used when checking the disc.

14 Remove the disc pads, as described in Section 5.

15 Remove the brake caliper with reference to Section 8, but leave the hydraulic fluid pipe connected. Move the caliper to one side, and suspend it using wire or string to avoid straining the pipe.

16 Remove the securing screw and withdraw the disc from the hub **(see illustration)**. If the disc is tight, collapse the handbrake shoes by

inserting a screwdriver through the adjuster hole in the disc and turning the adjuster wheel.

Refitting

17 Refitting is the reverse of removal, but make sure that the mating faces of the disc and hub are perfectly clean, and apply a little locking fluid to the threads of the securing screw. Refit the disc pads, as described in Section 5.

10 Rear brake backplate - removal and refitting

Removal

1 Where applicable, remove the wheel trim, then loosen the relevant rear roadwheel bolts and chock the front wheels. Jack up the rear of the vehicle, and support on axle stands (see "*Jacking and Vehicle Support*") positioned under the body side members. Remove the roadwheel.

2 Remove the brake disc, as described in Section 9.

3 Remove the rear hub, as described in Chapter 10.

4 Remove the handbrake shoes, as described in Section 6.

5 Using a screwdriver, prise out the lockplate that secures the handbrake cable in the backplate.

6 Using a splined key, unscrew the four securing bolts and withdraw the backplate.

Refitting

7 Refitting is the reverse of removal. Before refitting the roadwheel and lowering the vehicle to the ground, check and if necessary adjust the handbrake, as described in Section 21.

9

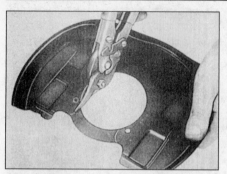

11.5 Cutting a section of metal from a new front brake disc shield prior to fitting

11 Front brake disc shield - removal and refitting

Removal

1 Where applicable, remove the wheel trim, then loosen the relevant front roadwheel bolts and apply the handbrake. Jack up the front of the vehicle, and support on axle stands (see *"Jacking and Vehicle Support"*) positioned under the body side members. Remove the roadwheel.

2 Remove the brake disc, as described in Section 9.

3 Using a screwdriver inserted through the holes in the hub flange, extract the three screws securing the disc shield to the hub carrier.

4 Using plate shears or an alternative tool, cut a section of metal from the rear edge of the shield to enable the shield to be withdrawn over the hub, then remove the shield.

Refitting

5 If a new shield is to be fitted, cut out a section of metal, as during removal of the old shield, to enable the shield to be fitted **(see illustration)**. Smooth the cut edges, and coat them with anti-corrosion paint.

6 Further refitting is the reverse of removal, remembering the following points.

7 Refit the brake disc, (see Section 9).

8 **Do not** tighten the roadwheel bolts to the specified torque wrench setting until the vehicle is resting on its wheels.

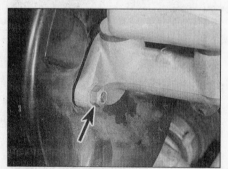

12.7 Master cylinder securing nut (arrowed)

12 Master cylinder - removal and refitting

Note 1: *All Calibra models are fitted with ABS as standard. The master cylinder cannot be dismantled, and no attempt should be made at overhaul. If faulty, the complete unit must be renewed.*
Note 2: *Refer to the warning at the beginning of Section 4 before proceeding.*

Removal

1 Disconnect the battery negative lead.

2 Depress the footbrake pedal several times to dissipate the vacuum in the servo unit.

3 Disconnect the wiring plug from the brake fluid level sensor in the reservoir filler cap.

4 If possible, use a teat pipette or an old hydrometer to remove the brake fluid from the reservoir. This will reduce the loss of fluid later in the procedure.

5 Locate a container beneath the master cylinder, to catch the brake fluid that will be released.

6 Identify the brake fluid pipes for position, then unscrew the union nuts and disconnect the pipes from the master cylinder.

7 Unscrew the two securing nuts, and withdraw the master cylinder from the studs on the vacuum servo unit **(see illustration)**.

8 Clean the external surfaces of the cylinder, then using a screwdriver carefully prise the fluid reservoir and its seals from the top of the cylinder.

Refitting

9 Refitting is the reverse of removal, but use new seals when fitting the brake fluid reservoir, and on completion, bleed the complete brake hydraulic system, as described in Section 3.

13 Vacuum servo - description and testing

Description

1 The vacuum servo is fitted between the brake pedal and the master cylinder, and provides assistance to the driver when the pedal is depressed, reducing the effort required to operate the brakes. The unit is operated by vacuum from the inlet manifold. With the brake pedal released, vacuum is channelled to both sides of the internal diaphragm. However, when the pedal is depressed, one side of the diaphragm is opened to atmosphere, resulting in assistance to the pedal effort. Should the vacuum servo develop a fault, the hydraulic system is not affected, but greater effort will be required at the pedal.

Testing

2 The operation of the servo can be checked as follows.

3 With the engine stopped, destroy the vacuum in the servo by depressing the brake pedal several times.

4 Hold the brake pedal depressed and start the engine. The pedal should sink slightly as the engine is started.

5 If the pedal does not sink, check the servo vacuum hose for leaks.

6 If no defects are found in the vacuum hose, the fault must lie in the servo itself.

7 No overhaul of the servo is possible, and if faulty, the complete unit must be renewed.

14 Vacuum servo - removal and refitting

Removal

1 Disconnect the battery negative lead.

2 Working inside the vehicle, remove the lower trim panel from the driver's footwell.

3 Disconnect the wiring plug from the brake lamp switch, then twist the switch anti-clockwise and remove it from its bracket.

4 Pull the spring clip from the right-hand end of the servo fork-to-pedal pivot pin.

5 Using a pair of pliers, pull back the end of the pedal return spring from the pedal, to enable the servo fork-to-pedal pivot pin to be removed. Withdraw the pivot pin.

6 Remove the windscreen cowl panel, as described in Chapter 11, then remove the windscreen wiper motor and linkage as described in Chapter 12.

7 Remove the coolant expansion tank as described in Chapter 3.

8 Pull the vacuum pipe from the brake servo.

9 Unscrew the two securing nuts, and carefully withdraw the brake master cylinder from the studs on the servo. Move the master cylinder forwards slightly, taking care not to strain the brake pipes.

10 Remove the two plugs covering the servo securing bolts from the cowl panel **(see illustrations)**.

11 Using an Allen key or hexagon bit, unscrew the servo securing bolts and remove

14.10a Remove the plugs . . .

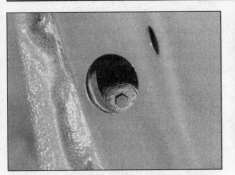

14.10b . . . to expose the servo securing bolts

14.11a Unscrew the securing bolts . . .

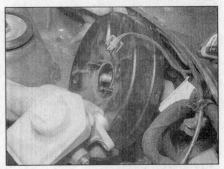

14.11b . . . and withdraw the servo

them completely, then lift the servo from the bulkhead **(see illustrations).**

12 If desired, the mounting bracket can be removed from the servo by unscrewing the four securing nuts. Note that the bracket will stick to the servo, as it is fitted with sealing compound.

13 The servo cannot be overhauled, and if faulty, the complete unit must be renewed.

Refitting

14 Before refitting the servo, check that the operating fork dimension is correct as follows.

15 Measure the distance from the end face of the servo casing to the centre of the pivot pin hole in the end of the operating fork. The distance should be 144.0 mm (5.6 in). To make accurate measurement easier, insert a bolt or bar of similar diameter through the pivot pin hole, and measure to the centre of the bolt or bar **(see illustration).**

16 If adjustment is necessary, slacken the locknut, turn the fork to give the specified dimension, then tighten the locknut.

17 Where applicable, coat the contact faces of the servo and the mounting bracket with sealing compound, then refit the bracket to the servo, and tighten the securing nuts to the specified torque.

18 Coat the threads of the servo securing bolts with locking fluid, then fit the servo to the bulkhead and tighten the securing bolts.

19 Refit the securing bolt cover plugs to the cowl panel.

20 Refit the master cylinder to the servo, and tighten the securing nuts to the specified torque.

21 Reconnect the vacuum pipe to the servo.

22 Refit the coolant expansion tank, as described in Chapter 3.

23 Refit the windscreen wiper motor and linkage as described in Chapter 12, then refit the windscreen cowl panel (see Chapter 11).

24 Further refitting is the reverse of removal. On completion, test the operation of the servo, as described in Section 13.

15 ABS hydraulic modulator - removal and refitting

Note: Refer to Section 2, and the warning at the beginning of Section 4, before proceeding.

Removal

1 Disconnect the battery negative lead.

2 Remove the brake fluid reservoir cap, and secure a piece of polythene over the filler neck with a rubber band, or by refitting the cap. This will reduce the loss of fluid during the following procedure.

3 Remove the securing screw, and withdraw the plastic cover from the hydraulic modulator.

4 Remove the two clamp screws, and lift off the modulator wiring harness clamp **(see illustration).**

5 Disconnect the modulator wiring plug, levering it from the socket with a screwdriver if necessary.

6 Unscrew the brake fluid pipe union nuts, and disconnect the pipes from the modulator.

Be prepared for fluid spillage, and plug the open ends to prevent dirt ingress and further fluid loss. Move the pipes just clear of the modulator, taking care not to strain them.

7 Unscrew the three modulator securing nuts **(see illustration),** then tilt the modulator slightly, and withdraw it upwards from its bracket, sufficiently to gain access to the earth lead securing nut at the front lower edge of the modulator.

8 Unscrew the securing nut and disconnect the earth lead, then withdraw the modulator from the vehicle, taking care not to spill brake fluid on the vehicle paintwork.

9 If a new modulator is to be fitted, pull the two relays from the top of the old modulator, and transfer them to the new unit. No attempt must be made to dismantle the modulator.

Refitting

10 Before refitting the modulator, check that the bolts securing the mounting bracket to the body panel are tight, and that the modulator rubber mountings are in good condition. Renew the rubber mountings if necessary.

11 Refitting is a reversal of removal, remembering the following points.

12 Make sure that the earth lead is reconnected before fitting the modulator to its mounting bracket.

13 On completion, remove the polythene sheet from the brake fluid reservoir filler neck, and bleed the complete brake hydraulic system, as described in Section 3.

14.15 Measuring the servo operating fork dimension using a bolt inserted through the pivot pin hole

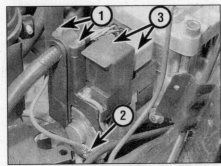

15.4 ABS hydraulic modulator (cover removed)

1 Wiring harness clamp screws	*2 Earth lead*
	3 Relays

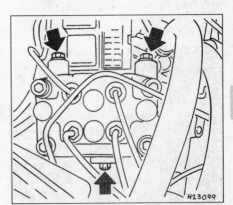

15.7 ABS hydraulic modulator securing nuts (arrowed)

9

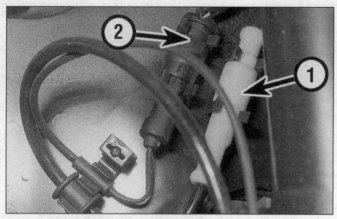

16.3 Front wheel sensor wiring under wheel arch

1 ABS sensor connector
2 Disc pad wear sensor wiring connector

16.4 ABS front wheel sensor securing bolt (arrowed)

14 Check that the ABS warning lamp extinguishes when first starting the engine after the modulator has been removed. At the earliest opportunity, take the vehicle to a Vauxhall dealer, and have the complete system tested, using the dedicated ABS test equipment.

16 ABS wheel sensors - removal and refitting

Note: *Refer to Section 2 before proceeding.*

Front wheel sensor

Removal

1 Disconnect the battery negative lead.
2 Where applicable, remove the wheel trim, then loosen the relevant front roadwheel bolts and apply the handbrake. Jack up the front of the vehicle, and support on axle stands (see *"Jacking and Vehicle Support"*) positioned under the body side members. Remove the roadwheel.
3 Unclip the sensor wiring connector from the retaining clip under the wheel arch, then separate the two halves of the wiring connector, prising them apart with a screwdriver if necessary **(see illustration)**.

4 Using an Allen key or hexagon bit, unscrew the bolt securing the wheel sensor to its mounting bracket, then carefully lever the sensor from the bracket using a screwdriver **(see illustration)**. Recover the seal ring.

Refitting

5 Examine the condition of the seal ring, and renew if necessary.
6 Refitting is the reverse of removal, remembering the following points.
7 Smear a little grease on the sensor casing before fitting it to the bracket.
8 Do not tighten the roadwheel bolts to the specified torque until the vehicle is resting on its wheels.
9 Check that the ABS warning lamp extinguishes when first starting the engine after a wheel sensor has been removed. At the earliest opportunity, take the vehicle to a Vauxhall dealer, and have the complete system tested, using the dedicated ABS test equipment.

Rear wheel sensor

Removal

10 Disconnect the battery negative lead.
11 Where applicable, remove the wheel trim, then loosen the relevant rear roadwheel bolts and chock the front wheels. Jack up the rear

of the vehicle, and support on axle stands (see *"Jacking and Vehicle Support"*) positioned under the body side members. Remove the roadwheel.
12 Unclip the sensor wiring connector from the retaining clip on the rear underbody, then separate the two halves of the wiring connector, prising them apart with a screwdriver if necessary **(see illustration)**.
13 Note the routing of the sensor wiring, and, where applicable, release it from the clips on the underbody.
14 Using an Allen key or hexagon bit, unscrew the bolt securing the wheel sensor to the mounting bracket, then carefully lever the sensor from its location using a screwdriver **(see illustration)**. Recover the seal ring.

Refitting

15 Proceed as described in paragraphs 5 to 9 inclusive.

17 ABS electronic control module - removal and refitting

Note: *Refer to Section 2 before proceeding.*

ABS-2E systems

Removal

1 Ensure that the ignition is switched off, then disconnect the battery negative lead.
2 The control module is located under a cover in the passenger sill, to the left-hand side of the seat.
3 Extract the three securing screws, and lift the cover from the control module. Note that two of the screws are covered by plastic trim plugs.
4 Lift the control module from its recess, then release the retaining clip and disconnect the module wiring plug. Withdraw the module **(see illustrations)**.

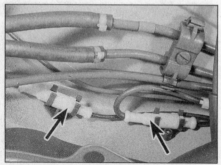

16.12 ABS rear wheel sensor wiring connectors (arrowed) on rear underbody

16.14 ABS rear wheel sensor (arrowed)

17.4a Lift out the ABS control module . . .

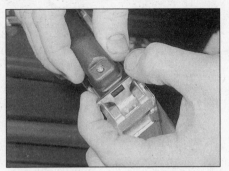

**17.4b . . . and release the wiring plug
retaining clip - ABS-2E system**

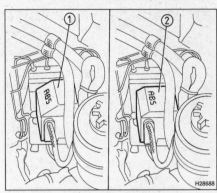

17.11 ABS-2EH control unit

1 Slanted cover type
2 Flat cover type

Refitting

5 Refitting is the reverse of removal.
6 Check that the ABS warning lamp extinguishes when first starting the engine after the module has been removed. At the earliest opportunity, take the vehicle to a Vauxhall dealer, and have the complete system tested, using the dedicated ABS test equipment.

ABS-2EH systems

7 On this system, introduced in 1992 as a modification of the previous ABS-2E, the control unit is mounted directly onto the hydraulic modulator, within the engine compartment.

Removal

8 Ensure that the ignition is switched off, then disconnect the battery negative lead.
9 Remove the cover from the hydraulic modulator.
10 Disconnect both the wiring harness and solenoid valve connectors.
11 Relays can only be removed from the control units that have slanted covers (see illustration). The relays for the solenoid valve and pump motor, if removable, can now be removed. If the unit has a flat cover, and is faulty, the whole unit will have to be replaced.
12 Undo the fixing bolts and remove the control unit.

Refitting

13 Refitting is the reverse of removal. Refer also to paragraph 6.

---

18 ABS relays (ABS-2E systems only) - removal and refitting

Note: *Refer to Section 2 before proceeding. For ABS-2EH system relays, refer to Section 17, paragraphs 7 to 13.*

Solenoid valve and pump motor relays

Removal

1 The solenoid valve and pump motor relays are mounted on the hydraulic modulator.
2 Disconnect the battery negative lead.

3 Remove the securing screw and withdraw the plastic cover from the hydraulic modulator.
4 Pull out the appropriate relay. The small relay is for the solenoid valve, and the large relay is for the pump motor.

Refitting

5 Refitting is the reverse of removal.
6 Check that the ABS warning lamp extinguishes when first starting the engine after a relay has been removed. At the earliest opportunity, take the vehicle to a Vauxhall dealer, and have the complete system tested, using the dedicated ABS test equipment.

Surge arrester relay

Removal

7 The surge arrester relay is located in the relay box at the left rear of the engine compartment.
8 Disconnect the battery negative lead.
9 Unclip the lid and open the relay box, then pull out the relay (see illustration).

Refitting

10 Refitting is the reverse of removal, with reference to paragraph 6.

---

19 Rear brake pressure-proportioning valves - removal and refitting

Note: *Refer to the warning at the beginning of Section 4 before proceeding. Note also that the valves must only be renewed in pairs, and both valves must be of the same calibration. Ensure that correct type of valves are fitted. The bodies have been stamped for easier identification.*

Master cylinder-mounted valves

Removal

1 Remove the brake fluid reservoir cap, and secure a piece of polythene over the filler neck with a rubber band, or by refitting the cap. This will reduce the loss of fluid during the following procedure.
2 Locate a container beneath the master cylinder, to catch the brake fluid that will be released.

3 Identify the two lower brake pipes for position, then unscrew the union nuts and disconnect the pipes from the proportioning valves in the base of the master cylinder. Plug the open ends of the pipes to prevent dirt ingress.
4 Unscrew the proportioning valves from the master cylinder, and plug the open ends of the cylinder to prevent dirt ingress.

Refitting

5 Refitting is the reverse of removal, but on completion, remove the polythene from the brake fluid reservoir filler neck, and bleed the complete hydraulic system, as described in Section 3.

Rear underbody-mounted valves

Removal

6 Proceed as described in paragraph 1.
7 Chock the front wheels, then jack up the rear of the vehicle, and support securely on axle stands (see "*Jacking and Vehicle Support*") positioned under the body side members.
8 Working under the rear of the vehicle, unscrew the union nut and disconnect the brake pipe from one of the valves. Be prepared for fluid spillage, and plug the open end of the pipe to prevent dirt ingress and further fluid spillage.
9 Similarly, disconnect the flexible hose from the valve.

18.9 ABS surge arrester relay (arrowed)

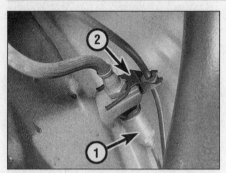

19.10 Brake pressure-proportioning valve on rear underbody

1 *Valve*
2 *Retaining clip*

10 Pull the valve retaining clip from the bracket on the underbody, noting that on certain models, the retaining clip also secures the ABS sensor wiring, and withdraw the valve **(see illustration)**.

11 Repeat the procedure for the other valve.

Refitting

12 Proceed as described in paragraph 5.

20 Brake fluid pipes and hoses - general, removal and refitting

Note: *Refer to the warning at the beginning of Section 4, before proceeding.*

General

1 When checking the condition of the system's pipes and/or hoses, carefully check that they do not foul other components such as the power steering gear pipes (where applicable), so that there is no risk of the pipes chafing. If necessary use clips or ties to secure braking system pipes and hoses well clear of other components.

Rigid pipes

Removal

2 Some of the commonly used brake pipes can be obtained from Vauxhall parts dealers, ready-formed and complete with unions, but other brake pipes must be prepared using

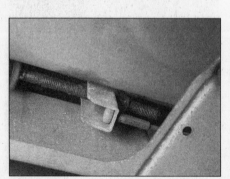

21.4 Handbrake lever operating rod connected to equaliser yoke

4.75 mm (0.19 in) diameter brake pipe. Kits for making the brake pipes can be obtained from certain motor accessory shops.

3 Before removing a brake pipe, remove the brake fluid reservoir cap, and secure a piece of polythene over the filler neck with a rubber band, or by refitting the cap. This will reduce the loss of fluid when the pipe is disconnected.

4 Jack up the vehicle, and support securely on axle stands (see "*Jacking and Vehicle Support*") positioned under the body side members.

5 To remove a brake pipe, unscrew the unions at each end, and release the pipe from the retaining clips.

Refitting

6 Refitting is the reverse of removal, taking care not to overtighten the unions.

7 On completion, remove the polythene from the brake fluid reservoir filler neck, and bleed the relevant hydraulic circuit(s), as described in Section 3.

Flexible hoses

Removal

8 Proceed as described previously for the rigid pipes, but note that a flexible pipe must never be installed twisted, although a slight "set" is permissible to give it clearance from adjacent components.

Refitting

9 When reconnecting a flexible hose to a front brake caliper, note that the sealing rings on the union bolt must be renewed.

21 Handbrake - adjustment

1 Where applicable, remove the wheel trims, then loosen the rear roadwheel bolts and chock the front wheels. Jack up the rear of the vehicle, and support securely on axle stands (see "*Jacking and Vehicle Support*") positioned under the body side members. Remove the roadwheels.

2 Pull the handbrake lever as far as the second notch on the ratchet.

21.5 Use a screwdriver to turn the handbrake adjuster wheel

3 If necessary, to access the handbrake lever operating rod, unscrew the four securing nuts and withdraw the exhaust centre box heat shield by carefully sliding it round the centre box.

4 Loosen the nut securing the cable equaliser yoke to the handbrake lever operating rod **(see illustration)**.

5 Using a screwdriver inserted through the adjuster hole in one of the discs/hubs **(see illustration)**, turn the adjuster wheel until the brake shoes can just be heard to rub when the disc/hub is turned by hand in the normal direction of rotation.

6 Turn the adjuster wheel back until the disc/hub is just free to turn.

7 Repeat paragraphs 5 and 6 on the other side of the vehicle.

8 Tighten the nut on the cable adjuster or the equaliser, as applicable, until the brake shoes just begin to operate. Check that the shoes operate equally on both wheels.

9 Fully release the handbrake, then apply it again.

10 The discs/hubs must lock when the handbrake lever reaches the sixth notch on the ratchet. If necessary, turn the nut on the cable adjuster or equaliser, as applicable, to achieve this.

11 Where applicable, refit the exhaust heat shield.

12 Refit the roadwheels and lower the vehicle to the ground. **Do not** tighten the roadwheel bolts to the specified torque wrench setting until the vehicle is resting on its wheels.

22 Handbrake cable - removal and refitting

Removal

1 The left and right-hand handbrake cables, and the equaliser yoke, are removed as an assembly.

2 Loosen the rear roadwheel bolts, then chock the front wheels, jack up the rear of the vehicle, and support securely on axle stands (see "*Jacking and Vehicle Support*") positioned under the body side members. Remove the roadwheels.

3 Note the routing of the handbrake cables, as an aid to refitting.

4 If necessary, to access the handbrake lever operating rod, unscrew the four securing nuts and withdraw the exhaust centre box heat shield by carefully sliding it round the centre box.

5 Note the length of exposed thread at the cable equaliser yoke, then unscrew the securing nut and disconnect the equaliser yoke from the handbrake lever operating rod **(see illustration 21.4)**.

6 Unhook the cable ends from the brake shoe operating levers and the return springs **(see illustration)**.

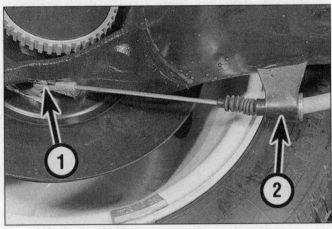

22.6 Handbrake cable end fitting at brake shoe

    1 *Operating lever*
    2 *Cable bracket on semi-trailing arm*

23.8 Handbrake lever securing bolts
(arrowed)

7 Detach the cable from the guides on the underbody and the semi-trailing arms. Note that the cables can be fed through certain guides, but in some cases, the guide brackets may have to be bent away from the underbody to allow the cables to be withdrawn.
8 Withdraw the cables and equaliser assembly from the vehicle.

Refitting

9 Refitting is the reverse of removal, remembering the following points.
10 Use a new self-locking nut to secure the equaliser yoke to the handbrake lever operating rod, and screw the nut onto the rod to the position noted before removal.
11 Ensure that the cables are routed as noted before removal.
12 Before refitting the roadwheels and lowering the vehicle to the ground, adjust the handbrake, as described in Section 21.

23 Handbrake lever - removal and refitting

Removal

1 Disconnect the battery negative lead.
2 Jack up the vehicle, and support on axle stands (see "*Jacking and Vehicle Support*") positioned securely under the body side members.
3 If necessary, to access the handbrake lever operating rod, unscrew the four securing nuts and withdraw the exhaust centre box heat shield by carefully sliding it round the centre box.
4 Note the length of exposed thread at the handbrake cable equaliser yoke, then unscrew the securing nut and disconnect the equaliser yoke from the handbrake lever operating rod **(see illustration 21.4)**. Slide the rubber sealing grommet from the underbody

and operating rod.
5 Remove the front passenger seat, as described in Chapter 11.
6 Remove the rear section of the centre console, as described in Chapter 11.
7 Access to the handbrake lever-to-floor mounting bolts is provided by slits in the carpet. If no slits are provided, either carefully cut some, or release and fold back the carpet.
8 Unscrew the mounting bolts, and withdraw the handbrake lever sufficiently to disconnect the handbrake "on" warning lamp switch wiring **(see illustration)**.
9 Disconnect the wiring and withdraw the handbrake lever and operating rod from the vehicle.
10 A worn ratchet segment can be renewed by driving the securing sleeve from the handbrake lever, using a metal rod or a bolt of similar diameter **(see illustration)**.
11 Drive the new sleeve supplied with the new segment into the lever to permit a little play between the segment and lever.
12 If desired, a new pawl can be fitted if the original pivot rivet is drilled out **(see illustration)**.
13 Rivet the new pawl so that the pawl is still free to move.

14 The handbrake "on" warning lamp switch can be removed from the lever assembly after unscrewing the securing bolt.

Refitting

15 Refitting is the reverse of removal, remembering the following points.
16 Use a new self-locking nut to secure the equaliser yoke to the handbrake lever operating rod, and screw the nut onto the rod to the position noted before removal.
17 Before lowering the vehicle to the ground, adjust the handbrake (see Section 21).

24 Brake pedal - removal and refitting

Removal

1 Disconnect the battery negative lead.
2 Remove the lower trim panel from the driver's footwell.
3 Disconnect the wiring plug from the brake lamp switch, then twist the switch anti-clockwise and remove it from its bracket.

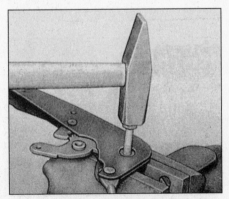

23.10 Driving out the handbrake lever ratchet segment securing sleeve

23.12 Drilling out the handbrake lever pawl pivot pin

9

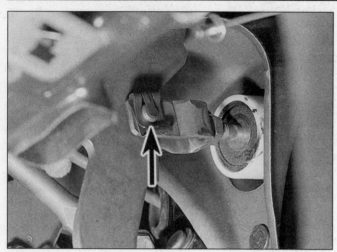

24.4 Brake servo fork-to-pedal pivot pin spring clip (arrowed)

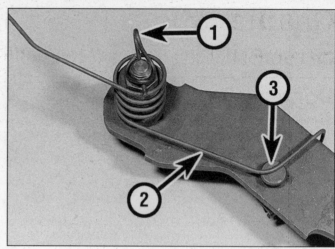

24.5 Brake pedal assembly removed from vehicle

1   Locking clip   3   Pedal pivot pin
2   Pedal return spring

4 Pull the spring clip from the right-hand end of the servo fork-to-pedal pivot pin **(see illustration)**.

5 Using a pair of pliers, pull back the end of the pedal return spring from the pedal, to enable the servo fork-to-pedal pivot pin to be removed. Withdraw the pivot pin **(see illustration)**.

6 Pull the locking clip from the left-hand end of the pedal pivot pin.

7 Unscrew the nut from the left-hand end of the pivot pin, then slide the pivot pin from the right-hand end of the pedal mounting bracket. If necessary, tap the end of the pivot pin with a soft-faced hammer to free the splines from the mounting bracket. Recover any washers that may be positioned on the pivot pin, noting their locations.

8 Withdraw the pedal and return spring.

Refitting

9 Refitting is the reverse of removal, remembering the following points.

10 Ensure that the pedal return spring is correctly located on the pedal before refitting.

11 Coat the pedal pivot pin with a little molybdenum disulphide grease.

12 Ensure that any washers on the pedal pivot pin are positioned as noted before removal.

Chapter 10
Suspension and steering

Contents

Degrees of difficulty

Easy, suitable for novice with little experience		Fairly easy, suitable for beginner with some experience		Fairly difficult, suitable for competent DIY mechanic		Difficult, suitable for experienced DIY mechanic		Very difficult, suitable for expert DIY or professional	

Specifications

General

Front suspension type	Independent, with MacPherson struts and anti-roll bar
Rear suspension type	Fully independent, with semi-trailing arms, coil springs, telescopic shock absorbers and anti-roll bar
Steering type	Rack and pinion power steering.
Vehicle condition for "laden" measurements	70 kg in each front seat, fuel tank half full

Front suspension (laden):
Camber	-40' ± 40'
Castor	+2° ± 1°
Toe in	+15' ± 10'
Toe out on turns	1° 30' ± 45'
Max. deviation between wheels on toe out	40'

Rear suspension (laden, after depressing rear of vehicle several times):
Camber	-2° 10' ± 40'
Toe in	+25' + 30'/-20'

Steering

Ratio	18 : 1
Power steering fluid type	See "Lubricants and fluids"

Power steering drivebelt tension (measured with Vauxhall gauge):
New belt	250 to 300 N
Used belt	450 N

Wheels and tyres

Wheel size	5½J x 14 or 6J x 15

Tyre size:
5½J x 14 wheels	195/60 R14-85 H or V, 175/70 R14-84 Q M+S
6J x 15 wheels	195/60 R15-87 H or V, 205/55 R15-87 H or V

Temporary spare wheel:
Wheel size	4J x 15
Tyre size	T 125/85 R 15-95 M or F

10

Torque wrench settings

	Nm	lbf ft

Front suspension

	Nm	lbf ft
Anti-roll bar to subframe	20	15
Balljoint to lower arm	60	44
Lower arm to suspension strut balljoint *	70	52
Lower arm to subframe front (horizontal) pivot: *		
Stage 1	100	74
Stage 2	Angle-tighten a further 60°	
Stage 3	Angle-tighten a further 15°	
Lower arm damper weight (where applicable)	20	15
Subframe to underbody bolts: *		
Front	115	85
Centre	170	125
Rear:		
Stage 1	100	74
Stage 2	Angle-tighten a further 75°	
Stage 3	Angle-tighten a further 15°	
Suspension strut upper mounting	55	41
Suspension strut piston rod	55	41
Suspension strut ring	200	148

Rear suspension

	Nm	lbf ft
Anti-roll bar	22	16
Crossmember mounting bracing bracket to underbody	65	48
Crossmember rear tube to body	60	44
Forward crossmember to body	125	92
Rear hub *	300	221
Semi-trailing arm to crossmember	100	74
Shock absorber lower mounting	110	81
Shock absorber upper mounting	20	15

* Use new nuts/locking pins or bolts (as applicable)

Steering

	Nm	lbf ft
Steering gear mounting (to bulkhead)	22	16
Steering wheel retaining nut	25	18
Tie-rod to steering gear	95	70
Tie-rod end clamp	20	15
Tie-rod end to suspension strut balljoint	60	44
Steering shaft to flexible coupling	22	16
Steering gear pinion to flexible coupling	22	16
Steering gear pinion	40	30
Steering gear damper adjuster	60	44
Fluid pipe to power steering gear unions	42	31
Fluid pipe to power steering pump union	28	21
Union nut, expandable hose to pressure line	28	21
Power steering pump mounting:		
Models with V-belts:		
Bolts "A" and "C" (refer to text)	25	18
Bolt "B" (refer to text)	40	30
SOHC models with serpentine belts:		
Bolts "1", "2", "3" and "4" (refer to text)	20	15
DOHC models with serpentine belts:		
Bolts "1" and "2" (refer to text)	25	18
Bolts "3" and "4" (refer to text)	18	13
Steering column to dashboard mounting bracket	22	16
Steering column upper right hand mounting	22	16

Roadwheels

	Nm	lbf ft
Roadwheel	110	81

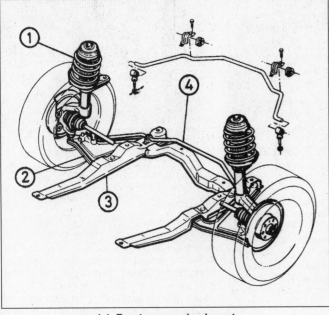

1.1 Front suspension layout

1 MacPherson strut 3 Subframe
2 Lower arm 4 Anti-roll bar

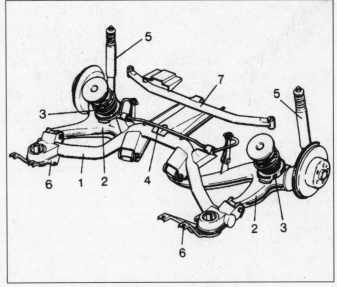

1.4 Rear suspension layout

1 Crossmember 5 Shock absorber
2 Semi-trailing arm 6 Crossmember mounting
3 Coil springs bracing bracket
4 Anti-roll bar 7 Crossmember rear tube

1 General description

1 The front suspension consists of MacPherson struts, lower arms, and an anti-roll bar. The lower arms and the anti-roll bar are mounted on a detachable U-shaped front subframe, which also carries the rear engine/transmission mounting **(see illustration)**.

2 Each lower arm is attached to the subframe by a horizontal front bush and a vertical rear bush. In conjunction with the steering geometry, this arrangement allows the front wheels to steer themselves against any imbalance in the braking forces. This would maintain stability when braking with one side of the vehicle on a slippery surface, and the other on dry tarmac.

3 The hub carriers are mounted between the lower ends of the MacPherson struts, and the lower arms, and carry the double row ball type wheel bearings and the brake assemblies.

4 The rear suspension is the fully independent type, consisting of semi-trailing arms, with double-conical coil springs, telescopic shock absorbers and an anti-roll bar. The front end of each semi-trailing arm is attached to a suspension crossmember by two horizontal bushes, and the rear ends are located by the shock absorbers, which are bolted to the underbody at their upper ends. The coil springs are mounted independently of the shock absorbers, and act directly between the semi-trailing arms and the underbody. The anti-roll bar is located on the suspension crossmember, and is attached to each semi-trailing arm by a vertical link. The suspension crossmember is bolted directly to the vehicle underbody at its forward end **(see illustration)**.

5 The steering gear is the rack-and-pinion type. Movement is transmitted to the front wheels through tie-rods, which are connected to the rack through a sliding sleeve at their inner ends, and to the suspension struts through balljoints at their outer ends.

6 The steering column consists of an outer column that incorporates a collapsible section, and a shaft connected to a flexible coupling at its lower end.

7 Power steering is fitted as standard on all models. The power steering is hydraulically operated, and pressure is supplied by a fluid pump driven by a drivebelt from the engine crankshaft. Fluid cooler pipes are mounted beneath the radiator to keep the temperature of the hydraulic fluid within the operating limits.

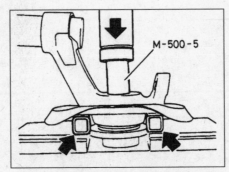

2.3 Press the front hub from the wheel bearing

2 Front wheel bearing - renewal

HAYNES HiNT *The bearing will probably be destroyed during the removal operation. The use of a puller will greatly ease the procedure.*

Removal

1 Remove the relevant suspension strut/hub carrier assembly, as described in Section 4.

2 Unscrew the securing screw, and remove the brake disc from the hub.

3 Support the hub carrier on two metal bars positioned as shown **(see illustration)**, then using a metal bar or tube of similar diameter, press or drive the hub from the wheel bearing. Alternatively, screw two roadwheel bolts into the hub and, using progressively thicker packing pieces, tighten the bolts to force the hub from the bearing. Note that one half of the inner bearing race will remain on the hub.

4 Using a puller, pull the half inner bearing race from the hub. Alternatively, support the bearing race on suitably thin metal bars, and press or drive the hub from the bearing race **(see illustration)**.

5 Remove the three securing screws, and lift the brake disc shield from the hub carrier **(see illustration)**.

6 Extract the inner and outer bearing retaining circlips **(see illustration)**.

10

2.4 Remove the half inner bearing race from the hub

2.5 Remove the brake disc shield securing screws

2.6 Extract the outer bearing retaining circlip

7 Using a puller, pull the bearing from the hub carrier, applying pressure to the outer race. Alternatively, support the hub carrier, and press or drive out the bearing.

Refitting

8 Before installing the new bearing, thoroughly clean the bearing location in the hub carrier, and fit the outer bearing retaining

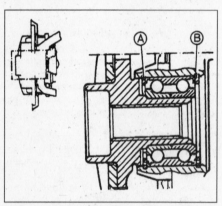

2.8 Cross sectional view of front wheel bearing/hub assembly

A Outer bearing retaining circlip
B Inner bearing retaining circlip

circlip, "A" **(see illustration)**. Note that the circlip tabs should be positioned towards the bottom of the hub carrier.

9 Press or drive the new bearing into position until it contacts the outer circlip, applying pressure to the outer race **(see illustration)**.

10 Fit the inner bearing retaining circlip, with the tabs positioned towards the bottom of the hub carrier.

11 Fit the brake disc shield.

12 Press or draw the hub into the bearing. The bearing inner track must be supported during this operation. This can be achieved using a socket, long bolt, washers and a length of bar as shown **(see illustration)**.

13 Refit the brake disc.

14 Refit the suspension strut/hub carrier assembly, as described in Section 4.

3 Front subframe - removal and refitting

Note: *Suitable equipment will be required to support the engine during this procedure. A balljoint separator tool will be required. The lower arm to suspension strut balljoint nut locking pins must be renewed on refitting.*

Removal

1 The subframe is removed complete with the lower arms and the anti-roll bar as an assembly.

2 Before removing the subframe, the engine must be supported from its left hand lifting bracket. Ideally, the engine should be supported using a strong wooden or metal beam resting on blocks positioned securely in the channels at the sides of the engine compartment. The Vauxhall special tool designed specifically for this purpose is shown in Chapter 7A. Alternatively, the engine can be supported using a hoist and lifting tackle. However in this case, the hoist must be of such a design as to enable the engine to be supported with the vehicle raised off the ground, leaving sufficient clearance to withdraw the subframe from under the front of the vehicle.

3 Where applicable, remove the wheel trims, then loosen the front roadwheel bolts on both sides of the vehicle. Apply the handbrake, then jack up the front of the vehicle, and support securely on axle stands (see *"Jacking and Vehicle Support"*) positioned under the body side members. Remove the front roadwheels.

2.9 Fit a new front wheel bearing using a socket, nut, bolt, washers and length of bar

2.12 Draw the hub into the bearing using improvised tools

3.8 Rear mounting securing nuts

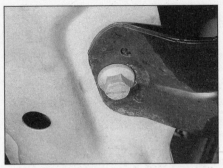

3.11a Front subframe front securing bolt

3.11b Front subframe rear securing bolt which also secures rear end of lower arm

4 Remove the front section of the exhaust system, with reference to Chapter 4B, or the complete exhaust if it is more convenient. On DOHC models, unbolt the oil cooler hose bracket from the right hand side of the subframe.

5 Working on one side of the vehicle, extract the locking pin, then unscrew the castellated nut from the lower arm to suspension strut balljoint.

6 Using a balljoint separator tool, disconnect the lower arm to suspension strut balljoint.

7 Repeat paragraphs 5 and 6 for the remaining lower arm.

8 Ensure that the engine is adequately supported, then unscrew and remove the two nuts and washers securing the rear engine/transmission mounting to the subframe **(see illustration)**.

9 Support the subframe on a trolley jack, with an interposed wooden beam to prevent the subframe from tipping as it is withdrawn.

10 Mark the positions where the subframe meets the underbody, at the front and rear ends, for refitting.

11 Unscrew and remove the six bolts securing the subframe to the vehicle underbody. Note that the rear bolts also secure the lower arms to the subframe **(see illustrations)**. The bolts are very tight, and an extension bar will probably be required to loosen them.

12 Lower the jack supporting the subframe, and withdraw the assembly from under the front of the vehicle.

13 If desired, the anti-roll bar and/or the lower arms can be removed from the subframe, with reference to Sections 8 and 5 respectively.

Refitting

14 Refitting is the reverse of removal, remembering the following points.

15 If the anti-roll bar and/or the lower arms have been removed from the subframe, refit them with reference to Section 8 and/or 5, as applicable.

16 Refit the subframe to the underbody in exactly the right position, according to the marks that have been made.

17 Tighten all nuts and bolts to the specified torques, noting that the rear subframe to underbody bolts must be tightened in stages (see Specifications).

18 Secure the lower arm to suspension strut balljoint nuts with new locking pins.

19 Refit the front section of the exhaust system, with reference to Chapter 4B. On models with oil coolers, refit the oil cooler hose bracket to the right hand side of the subframe.

20 Finally tighten the roadwheel bolts to the specified torque wrench setting when the vehicle has been lowered to the ground, and where applicable, refit the wheel trims.

---

4 Front suspension strut - removal, overhaul and refitting

Note: *A balljoint separator tool will be required during this procedure, and a spring compressor tool will be required if the strut is to be overhauled. The tie-rod end balljoint self-locking nut, the driveshaft retaining snap ring, and the hub nut must be renewed on refitting.*

Removal

1 Where applicable, remove the wheel trim, then loosen the relevant front roadwheel bolts. Apply the handbrake, then jack up the front of the vehicle, and support securely on axle stands (see "*Jacking and Vehicle Support*") positioned under the body side members. Remove the relevant front roadwheel.

2 Remove the ABS wheel sensor from the hub carrier, referring to Chapter 9, and disconnect the wiring from the strut.

3 Remove the brake caliper from the hub carrier, as described in Chapter 9. The caliper can be suspended out of the way, using wire or string, to avoid the need to disconnect the hydraulic fluid hose.

4 Unscrew and remove the self-locking nut from the tie-rod end to suspension strut balljoint.

5 Using a balljoint separator, disconnect the tie-rod end to suspension strut balljoint.

6 Disconnect the outboard end of the driveshaft from the hub carrier, as described in Chapter 8. Support the driveshaft by suspending with wire or string. Do not allow the driveshaft to hang down under its own weight.

7 Working in the engine compartment, unscrew the nut securing the suspension strut to the suspension turret. To unscrew the nut, it will be necessary to counterhold the suspension strut piston rod using a splined key **(see illustration)**. Support the suspension strut as the nut is unscrewed, as once the nut has been removed, the strut is free to drop from the vehicle.

8 Withdraw the suspension strut/hub carrier assembly from the vehicle **(see illustration)**.

9 If desired, the suspension strut can be overhauled as follows, otherwise go on to paragraph 30 for details of the refitting procedure.

Overhaul

10 The hub, wheel bearing and brake disc shield can be removed, as described in Section 2.

4.7 Unscrew the suspension strut top mounting nut

4.8 Withdraw the suspension strut

10

4.13a Lift off the strut upper mounting rubber . . .

4.13b . . . and the bearing

4.14 Lift off the upper spring seat and damper ring

11 With the suspension strut resting on a bench or clamped in a vice, fit a spring compressor tool, and compress the coil spring to relieve the pressure on the upper spring seat. Ensure that the compressor tool is securely located on the spring, according to the tool manufacturer's instructions.

12 Hold the strut piston rod with the splined key used during strut removal, and unscrew the piston rod nut.

13 Lift off the strut upper mounting rubber and the bearing **(see illustrations)**.

14 Lift off the upper spring seat and damper ring, then carefully release the spring compressor and remove the spring **(see illustration)**. Note which way up the spring is fitted.

15 Slide the bellows and the rubber buffer that fits inside the bellows from the strut **(see illustration)**.

16 To remove the shock absorber cartridge,

the ring nut must be unscrewed from the top of the strut tube. This nut is extremely tight. One method that can be used to unscrew the nut is to invert the strut and clamp the nut in a vice, then lever the strut round using a long bar and a bolt passed through the tie-rod bracket.

17 With the ring nut removed, the shock absorber cartridge can be withdrawn **(see illustrations)**.

18 The shock absorber can be tested by clamping the lower end in a vice, then fully extending and contracting the shock absorber several times. Any evidence of jerky movement or lack of resistance indicates the need for renewal.

19 Examine all components for wear or damage and renew as necessary. Pay particular attention to the mounting rubber and the bearing.

20 Begin reassembly by sliding the shock

absorber cartridge into the strut, and refitting the ring nut.

21 Clamp the strut in a vice, and tighten the ring nut to the specified torque, using a suitably large long reach socket.

22 Refit and compress the coil spring, ensuring that the lower end of the spring rests against the lug on the lower spring seat **(see illustration)**.

23 Refit the rubber buffer and the bellows.

24 Refit the upper spring seat and the damper ring, ensuring that the mark on the damper ring is aligned with the hole in the spring seat, as shown **(see illustration)**. The spring seat should be positioned with the hole at right angles to (i.e. 90° away from) the end of the spring.

25 Lubricate the bearing with a little grease, then refit it with the visible part of the bearing race uppermost.

26 Refit the strut upper mounting rubber.

4.15 Slide off the bellows and the rubber buffer

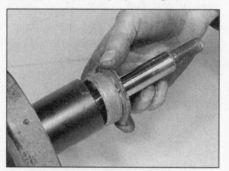

4.17a Remove the ring nut . . .

4.17b . . . and withdraw the shock absorber cartridge

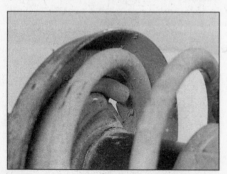

4.22 Lower end of spring rests against lug on lower spring seat

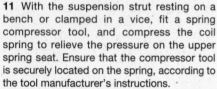

4.24 Mark on suspension strut damper ring aligned with hole in spring seat

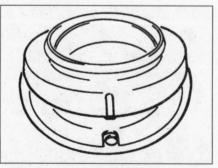

4.27 Tighten the piston rod nut

27 Counterhold the strut piston rod, and tighten the piston rod nut to the specified torque. This can be achieved by holding the piston rod using the splined key fitted to a torque wrench, and tightening the nut using a spanner until the specified torque is reached **(see illustration)**.

28 Carefully release and remove the spring compressor tool, ensuring that the spring seats correctly at top and bottom. Ensure that the lower end of the spring still rests against the lug on the lower spring seat.

29 The strut can now be refitted to the vehicle as follows.

Refitting

30 Locate the top end of the strut in the suspension turret, then refit the securing nut and tighten it to the specified torque using the method described in paragraph 27.

31 Reconnect the outboard end of the driveshaft to the hub carrier (see Chapter 8).

32 Reconnect the tie-rod end balljoint to the suspension strut, and tighten a new self locking nut to the specified torque.

33 Refit the brake caliper to the hub carrier, as described in Chapter 9.

34 Refit the ABS wheel sensor to the hub carrier, with reference to Chapter 9, and reconnect the wiring to the strut.

35 Refit the roadwheel, and lower the vehicle to the ground. Finally tighten the roadwheel bolts to the specified torque setting with the vehicle resting on its wheels, and where applicable, refit the wheel trim.

36 Check and if necessary adjust the front wheel alignment, as described in Section 32.

---

5 Front suspension lower arm - removal and refitting

Note 1: *A new lower arm to suspension strut balljoint nut locking pin, and a new anti-roll bar to lower arm nylock nut must be used on refitting.*

Note 2: *Regular inspection of the front suspension lower arms is recommended in order to detect damage or distortion which could eventually lead to failure. Any sign of cracking, creasing or other damage should be investigated and the arm renewed if necessary. If in doubt, consult your Vauxhall dealer for advice.*

Removal

1 Where applicable, remove the wheel trim, then loosen the relevant front roadwheel bolts. Apply the handbrake, then jack up the front of the vehicle, and support securely on axle stands (see "*Jacking and Vehicle Support*") positioned under the body side members. Remove the relevant front roadwheel.

2 Unscrew and remove the nut securing the end of the anti-roll bar to the lower arm. Recover the dished washers and mounting rubbers.

5.5 Lower arm front pivot bolt

3 Extract the locking pin, then unscrew the castellated nut from the lower arm to suspension strut balljoint.

4 Using a balljoint separator tool, disconnect the lower arm to suspension strut balljoint.

5 Unscrew and remove the two pivot bolts securing the lower arm to the subframe **(see illustration)**. Note that the rear pivot bolt also secures the subframe to the underbody. Both bolts are very tight, and an extension bar will probably be required to loosen them.

6 Pull the lower arm from the subframe, and withdraw it from the vehicle.

7 Note that the metal sleeves in the rear mounting bush can be discarded as they are not required for refitting.

8 There was a change in the design of the lower arm in mid-1993, with a strengthening flange along the seam on the forward facing side of the arm, and a modified inner profile **(see illustration)**. The new design gives greater strength to the area around the front pivot bolt. If you have an arm of the old design, and there is any sign of damage or distortion around the front pivot bolt, you should obtain a replacement arm of the new design from a Vauxhall dealer.

9 Some models have a damper weight bolted to the right hand lower arm. In this case, if the arm is to be replaced with a new arm of the same design, it is important to ensure that the damper weight is transferred to the new arm. However, you should not transfer the damper weight from an arm of the old design to a replacement arm of the new design.

Refitting

10 Start refitting by pushing the lower arm into position in the subframe.

11 Fit the two pivot bolts, then hold the lower arm in a horizontal position, and tighten the bolts to the specified torque. Note that the rear bolt must be tightened in stages, see Specifications.

12 Reconnect the lower arm to suspension strut balljoint, and tighten the castellated nut to the specified torque. Secure the nut with a new locking pin.

13 Reconnect the end of the anti-roll bar to the lower arm, noting that the dished washers that retain the mounting rubbers should be fitted with their concave sides facing towards

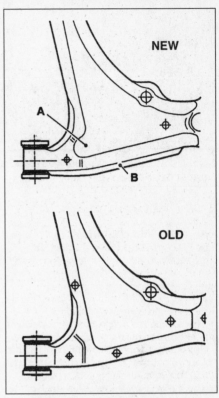

5.8 Front suspension lower arm

A Modified inner profile
B Strengthening flange along seam

the lower arm. Note that on certain models, nylock type nuts are used to secure the anti-roll bar to the lower arms, these nuts should be renewed on refitting.

14 Tighten the anti-roll bar to lower arm nuts to give the specified rubber bush compression shown **(see illustration)**. If necessary, renew the rubber bushes.

15 Refit the roadwheel and lower the vehicle to the ground. Finally tighten the roadwheel bolts to the specified torque with the vehicle resting on its wheels, and where applicable, refit the wheel trim.

16 Check and if necessary adjust the front wheel alignment, as described in Section 32.

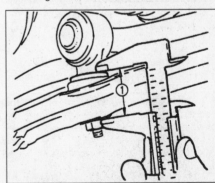

5.14 Front anti-roll bar rubber bush compression

1 38.0 to 39.0 mm

10

8.10a Front anti-roll bar damper weight

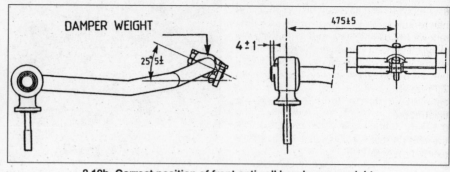

8.10b Correct position of front anti-roll bar damper weight

(All dimensions in mm)

6 Front suspension lower arm bushes - renewal

Removal

1 Remove the lower arm (Section 5).
2 The bushes are a tight fit in the lower arm, and must be pressed out.
3 If a press is not available, the bushes can be drawn out using a long bolt, nut, washers and a socket or length of metal tubing.
4 The vertical bush should be pressed out through the top of the lower arm, from below, and the horizontal bush should be pressed out towards the front of the lower arm, from the rear.

Refitting

5 Lubricate the new bushes using soapy water, then fit them to the lower arm, reversing the method described in paragraph 3.
6 The new vertical bush should be pressed into the lower arm from below, and the new horizontal bush should be pressed into the lower arm from front to rear. The horizontal bush should project from the lower arm equally at both ends.
7 Refit the lower arm, as described in Section 5.

7 Front suspension lower arm balljoint - renewal

Removal

1 Remove the lower arm, as described in Section 5.
2 Mount the lower arm in a vice, then drill the heads from the three rivets that secure the balljoint to the lower arm, using a 12.0 mm (0.47 in) diameter drill.
3 If necessary, tap the rivets from the lower arm, then remove the balljoint.

Refitting

4 The new balljoint should be fitted using three special bolts, spring washers and nuts, available from a Vauxhall parts centre.

5 Ensure that the balljoint is fitted the correct way up, noting that the securing nuts should be positioned on the underside of the lower arm.
6 Tighten the balljoint to lower arm nuts to the specified torque.
7 Refit the lower arm, as described in Section 5.

8 Front anti-roll bar - removal and refitting

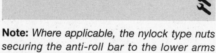

Note: *Where applicable, the nylock type nuts securing the anti-roll bar to the lower arms must be renewed on refitting.*

Removal

1 Support the engine, and raise the vehicle as described in Section 3, paragraphs 2 and 3.
2 If desired, remove the front section of the exhaust system, with reference to Chapter 4B.
3 Working under the vehicle, unscrew and remove the locknuts securing the ends of the anti-roll bar to the lower arms. Recover the dished washers and mounting rubbers.
4 Ensure that the engine is adequately supported, then unscrew and remove the two nuts and washers securing the engine/transmission rear mounting to the subframe.
5 Support the subframe on a trolley jack, with an interposed wooden beam to spread the load.
6 Unscrew and remove the two rear and two centre bolts securing the subframe to the vehicle underbody. Note that the rear bolts also secure the lower arms to the subframe. The bolts are very tight, and an extension bar will probably be required to loosen them.
7 Loosen, but do not remove the two front subframe to underbody securing bolts.
8 Carefully lower the subframe until the anti-roll bar to subframe bolts are accessible, then unscrew and remove the bolts.
9 Lift the anti-roll bar from the subframe and the lower arms, and withdraw it from the vehicle.

Refitting

10 On some models, a damper weight is fitted to the centre of the anti-roll bar. If the anti-roll bar is to be renewed, the damper weight (where applicable) must be transferred to the new component, and positioned as shown **(see illustrations)**.
11 If desired, the anti-roll bar mounting bushes can be renewed (Section 9).
12 Refitting is the reverse of removal, remembering the following points.
13 Reconnect the ends of the anti-roll bar to the lower arm, noting that the dished washers that retain the mounting rubbers should be fitted with their concave sides facing towards the lower arm. Note that on certain models, nylock type nuts are used to secure the anti-roll bar to the lower arms, these nuts should be renewed on refitting.
14 Tighten the anti-roll bar to lower arm nuts to give the specified rubber bush compression, as described in Section 5, paragraph 14. If necessary, renew the rubber bushes.
15 Tighten all nuts and bolts to the specified torques, noting that the rear subframe to underbody bolts must be tightened in stages, see Specifications.
16 Where applicable, refit the front section of the exhaust with reference to Chapter 4B.
17 Finally tighten the roadwheel bolts when the vehicle is resting on its wheels to the specified torque, and where applicable, refit the wheel trims.

9 Front anti-roll bar bushes - renewal

1 Remove the anti-roll bar (Section 8).
2 To renew an anti-roll bar end mounting bush, mount the anti-roll bar in a vice, then with light hammer blows on a drift, drive the end link from the anti-roll bar.
3 The bush can now be prised from the end link, using a screwdriver or similar tool.
4 Lubricate the new bush with a little soapy water to aid fitting, then press it into place in the end link.
5 If necessary, repeat the procedure on the remaining end link.

6 With either end link removed, the anti-roll bar to subframe mounting bushes can be renewed if desired, by sliding the bushes along the bar and manipulating them until they can be withdrawn from the end of the bar. Fit the new bushes in the same way.

7 Press or drive the end link(s) onto the anti-roll bar to the position shown **(see illustration)**.

8 Before refitting the anti-roll bar, examine the anti-roll bar to lower arm bushes, and renew if necessary.

9 Refit the anti-roll bar (Section 8).

10 Rear shock absorber - removal and refitting

Removal

1 Note that shock absorbers should be renewed in pairs.

2 Working in the luggage compartment, open the storage boxes at the left and right. One of these is marked as a first aid box.

3 Prise off the cap that covers the shock absorber top mounting **(see illustration)**.

4 Counterhold the shock absorber piston rod, and unscrew the shock absorber top mounting nut. Remove the washer and the upper mounting rubber.

5 Drive the rear wheels up onto ramps, and chock the front wheels. Alternatively, chock the front wheels, then jack up the rear of the vehicle, and support securely on axle stands (see "*Jacking and Vehicle Support*") placed under the body side members. If the vehicle is jacked up, the relevant semi-trailing arm must be supported with a jack as the vehicle is raised.

6 Unscrew and remove the bolt and washer securing the lower end of the shock absorber to the semi-trailing arm **(see illustration)**.

7 Withdraw the shock absorber from under the vehicle, and recover the lower mounting rubber.

8 The shock absorber can be tested by clamping the lower mounting eye in a vice, then fully extracting and contracting the shock absorber several times. Any evidence of jerky movement or lack of resistance indicates the need for renewal.

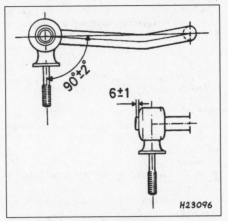

9.7 Correct position of end link on front anti-roll bar

(Dimensions in mm)

Refitting

9 Before refitting the shock absorber, examine the mounting rubbers for wear or damage, and renew if necessary.

10 Refitting is the reverse of removal, remembering the following points.

11 Where applicable, ensure that the shock absorber is fitted with the air line union facing the correct way round.

12 Tighten the shock absorber lower mounting bolt to the specified torque.

11 Rear shock absorber mounting rubbers - renewal

1 The shock absorber top mounting rubbers can be renewed without removing the shock absorber as follows.

2 Proceed as described in Section 10, paragraphs 2 to 4 inclusive.

3 Keeping the roadwheels resting on the ground, jack up the rear of the vehicle slightly, to enable the shock absorber to be compressed sufficiently by hand to release the top mounting from the body.

4 Remove the lower mounting rubber from the top of the shock absorber.

5 Fit the new mounting rubbers using a reversal of the removal procedure.

12 Rear wheel bearing - renewal

Note: *This is a difficult operation, and it is suggested that this Section is read carefully before beginning work. A torque wrench capable of measuring the high torque of the rear hub nut and a puller will be required. A new hub nut and locking collar must be used on reassembly.*

Removal

1 Loosen the relevant rear roadwheel bolts, chock the front wheels, then jack up the rear of the vehicle, and support securely on axle stands (see "*Jacking and Vehicle Support*") positioned under the body side members. Remove the roadwheels.

2 Remove the locking clip and release the brake fluid line from the bracket on the semi-trailing arm. Note that the locking clip also supports the ABS sensor wire.

3 Unscrew the securing bolts, and withdraw the brake caliper and the ABS sensor bracket from the brake backplate. Support the caliper and the ABS sensor bracket out of the way, by suspending with string or wire from the vehicle underbody.

4 Remove the securing screw and withdraw the brake disc. If necessary, retract the handbrake shoes to enable the disc to be removed, by turning the adjuster with a screwdriver inserted through one of the unthreaded holes in the disc, see Chapter 9.

5 Using a splined key inserted through one of the unthreaded holes in the hub flange, unscrew the four brake backplate securing bolts. Note that the upper bolts are shorter than the lower bolts, and are fitted with locking plates.

6 Prise out the plastic cover from the rear of the ABS toothed sensor wheel, to expose the rear hub nut **(see illustrations)**.

7 Relieve the staking on the hub nut locking collar, then prise the locking collar from the ABS sensor wheel.

8 Screw two wheel bolts into the hub flange, and use a long metal bar between the bolts to hold the hub stationary, then unscrew the hub nut using a socket and extension bar. Note that the hub nut is extremely tight.

10.3 Remove the cap from the rear shock absorber top mounting

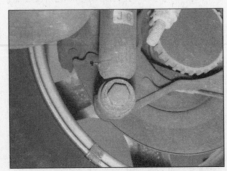

10.6 Rear shock absorber lower mounting bolt

12.6a Prise out the plastic cover (arrowed) . . .

10

12.6b ... for access to the rear hub nut

9 Pull the ABS sensor wheel from the hub, if necessary using a three legged puller.

10 Press the rear hub outwards from the bearing, using a puller attached to the semi-trailing arm. Note that the inner bearing track may stay on the hub as it is removed.

11 Extract the bearing retaining circlip from the outer edge of the semi-trailing arm **(see illustration)**. Then press or drive out the bearing, applying pressure to the bearing outer race. If desired, the bearing can be removed in the same way as the rear hub using a puller, again noting that pressure must be applied to the bearing outer race.

12 If the inner bearing race has remained on the hub, remove it using a puller.

Refitting

13 Clean all components, and examine them for wear and damage.

14 Begin reassembly by pressing the new bearing into the semi-trailing arm, using pressure on the bearing outer track. If necessary, a tube or socket with a long bolt, nut and washers may be used to draw the bearing into position. Press the bearing into the semi-trailing arm until it rests against the shoulder.

15 Fit the bearing retaining circlip, ensuring that it seats correctly in its groove.

16 Have an assistant support the bearing inner track at the inner end of the semi-trailing arm using a metal tube, then carefully drive in the rear hub from outside.

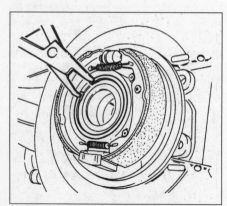

12.11 Extract the rear hub bearing retaining circlip

Caution: Do not use excessively sharp blows, as the bearing is easily damaged.

17 Fit the ABS sensor wheel to the inner end of the hub. If necessary, have an assistant support the outer end of the hub, and drive the sensor wheel fully home from the inside. Take care not to damage the teeth on the sensor wheel.

18 Fit a new hub nut and tighten it to the specified torque, holding the hub stationary as during removal.

19 Fit a new locking collar to the hub nut, and stake it to the ABS sensor wheel.

20 Refit the plastic cover to the rear of the ABS sensor wheel.

21 Refit the brake backplate securing bolts, and tighten them to the specified torque. Ensure that the shorter bolts are fitted to the top of the plate, and make sure that the locking plates are fitted.

22 Refit the brake disc and tighten its securing screw, then operate the handbrake several times to operate the adjuster mechanism and bring the shoes to their correct seat position.

23 Refit the brake caliper and the ABS sensor bracket to the bracket backplate, and tighten the securing bolts to the specified torque.

24 Reconnect the brake fluid line to its bracket on the semi-trailing arm, and secure with the locking clip.

25 Refit the roadwheel, then lower the vehicle to the ground. Finally tighten the roadwheel bolts to the specified torque with the vehicle resting on its wheels.

13 Rear hub -
removal and refitting

Removal

1 Removal and refitting of the rear hub is described in Section 12, as part of the wheel bearing renewal procedure.

2 Note that the wheel bearing will almost certainly be destroyed during removal of the hub, and must therefore be renewed.

Refitting

3 Refer to the note at the beginning of Section 12 before proceeding.

14 Rear suspension coil spring
- removal and refitting

Removal

1 Note that the rear springs should be renewed in pairs, and if the springs are to be renewed, it is advisable to renew the spring damping rubbers at the same time.

2 Chock the front wheels, jack up the rear of the vehicle, and support securely on axle

stands positioned under the body side members.

3 Working under the rear of the vehicle, remove the locking clips and release the brake fluid lines from their brackets on either side of the vehicle underbody. Note that the locking clips also support the ABS sensor wires.

4 Working on each side of the vehicle in turn, support the semi-trailing arm with a trolley jack, then unscrew and remove the bolt and washer securing the lower end of the shock absorber to the semi-trailing arm. Carefully lower the trolley jack, and withdraw it once the shock absorber has been disconnected from the semi-trailing arm.

5 Disconnect the fuel outlet hose from the fuel filter, located on the right hand side of the underbody in front of the fuel tank.

Caution: Be prepared for fuel spillage, and take adequate fire precautions. Plug the open ends of the filter and hose, to prevent further fuel spillage and dirt ingress.

6 Support the rear plate of the rear suspension crossmember with a trolley jack, then unscrew and remove the two securing bolts from the crossmember rear tube.

7 Carefully lower the trolley jack supporting the crossmember rear plate, taking care not to strain any of the hoses, pipes or wires, until the coil springs and their rubber dampers can be withdrawn. Note the orientation of the springs as they are removed.

Refitting

8 Begin refitting by positioning the springs and their seats between the semi-trailing arms and the underbody as noted during removal.

9 Carefully raise the jack supporting the crossmember rear plate, then refit the crossmember rear tube to underbody bolts, and tighten them to the specified torque.

10 Reconnect the fuel outlet hose to the fuel filter, and tighten the clamp screw.

11 Reconnect the shock absorbers to the semi-trailing arms, support the semi-trailing arms with a trolley jack as during removal. Tighten the securing bolts to the specified torque.

12 Refit the brake lines to the brackets on the underbody, and secure with the locking clips.

13 Lower the vehicle to the ground.

15 Rear suspension assembly -
removal and refitting

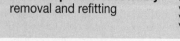

Removal

1 Loosen the rear roadwheel bolts, chock the front wheels, then jack up the rear of the vehicle, and support securely on axle stands (see *"Jacking and Vehicle Support"*) positioned under the body side members. Remove the roadwheels.

2 Remove the rear half of the exhaust system (from the front expansion box rearwards), as described in Chapter 3.

3 Disconnect the handbrake cables and their return springs from the handbrake operating levers, with reference to Chapter 9.

4 Withdraw the handbrake cables from the brackets on the semi-trailing arms.

5 Remove the locking clips and release the brake fluid lines from their brackets on the semi-trailing arms. Note that the locking clips also support the ABS sensor wires **(see illustration)**.

6 Unscrew the securing bolts, and withdraw the brake calipers and the ABS sensor brackets from the brake backplates. Support the calipers and the ABS sensor brackets out of the way by suspending with string or wire from the vehicle underbody.

7 Working on each side of the vehicle in turn, support the semi-trailing arm with a trolley jack, then unscrew and remove the bolt and washer securing the lower end of the shock absorber to the semi-trailing arm. Carefully lower the trolley jack, and withdraw it once the shock absorber has been disconnected from the semi-trailing arm.

8 Disconnect the fuel outlet hose from the fuel filter, located on the right hand side of the underbody in front of the fuel tank.

Caution: Be prepared for fuel spillage, and take adequate fire precautions. Plug the open ends of the filter and hose, to prevent further fuel spillage and dirt ingress.

9 Support the rear plate of the rear suspension crossmember with a trolley jack, then unscrew and remove the two securing bolts from the crossmember rear tube **(see illustration)**.

10 Carefully lower the trolley jack supporting the crossmember rear plate, until the coil springs and their rubber dampers can be withdrawn. Note the orientation of the springs as they are removed.

11 Make a check to ensure that all relevant hoses, pipes, cables and wires are clear of the rear suspension assembly.

12 With the weight of the rear suspension assembly supported on the trolley jack positioned under the crossmember rear plate, unscrew and remove the two forward crossmember securing bolts. Note that the bolts also pass through the crossmember mounting bracing brackets.

13 Unscrew and remove the two bolts in each case securing the crossmember mounting bracing brackets to the underbody. Then with the help of an assistant, carefully lower the rear suspension assembly and withdraw it from under the vehicle **(see illustration)**.

14 If desired, the assembly can be dismantled with reference to the relevant Sections of this Chapter.

15 The crossmember front mounting bushes can be renewed using a tube or socket, nut, bolt, washers and distance pieces as necessary to draw out the old bushes and fit the new ones. Lubricate the rear bushes with a little soapy water to aid fitting.

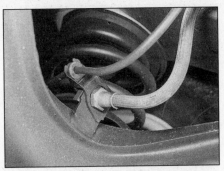

15.5 Brake fluid line/ABS sensor wire bracket and locking clip on semi-trailing arm

Refitting

16 Begin refitting by positioning the rear suspension assembly under the rear of the vehicle, and raising it (with the aid of an assistant) using a trolley jack positioned under the crossmember rear plate as during removal.

17 Refit the two forward crossmember securing bolts, ensuring that they also pass through the crossmember mounting bracing brackets, but do not fully tighten them at this stage.

18 Refit the crossmember mounting bracing bracket to underbody bolts and tighten them to the specified torque, then tighten the two forward crossmember securing bolts to the specified torque.

19 If necessary, lower the trolley jack supporting the crossmember rear plate, and refit the coil springs and their dampers between the semi-trailing arms and the underbody, as noted during removal.

20 Carefully raise the trolley jack supporting the crossmember rear plate, then fit the two crossmember rear tube securing bolts, and tighten them to the specified torque. Withdraw the trolley jack.

21 Reconnect the fuel outlet hose to the fuel filter, and tighten the clamp screw.

22 Working on each side of the vehicle in turn, raise the semi-trailing arm with a trolley jack to allow the lower shock absorber securing bolt and washer to be fitted. Tighten the bolts to the specified torque, then withdraw the trolley jack.

23 Refit the brake calipers and the ABS sensor brackets to the brake backplates, and tighten the securing bolts to the specified torque.

24 Reconnect the brake fluid lines to their brackets on the semi-trailing arms, and secure with the locking clips.

25 Refit the handbrake cables to their brackets on the semi-trailing arms, and reconnect the cable ends and return springs to the handbrake operating levers, then check the handbrake cable adjustment, as described in Chapter 9.

26 Refit the rear half of the exhaust system, with reference to Chapter 3.

27 Refit the roadwheels and lower the vehicle

15.9 Rear suspension crossmember rear tube

to the ground. Finally tighten the roadwheel bolts to the specified torque with the vehicle resting on its wheels.

16 Rear suspension semi-trailing arm - removal and refitting

Removal

1 Loosen the relevant rear roadwheel bolts, chock the front wheels, then jack up the rear of the vehicle, and support securely on axle stands positioned under the body side members (see *"Jacking and Vehicle Support"*). Remove the roadwheel.

2 Working under the rear of the vehicle, remove the locking clip and release the brake fluid line from its bracket on the semi-trailing arm. Note that the locking clip also supports the ABS sensor wire.

3 Unscrew the two securing bolts, and withdraw the brake caliper and the ABS sensor bracket from the brake backplate. Support the caliper and the ABS sensor bracket out of the way by suspending with string or wire from the vehicle underbody.

4 Disconnect the handbrake cable and its return spring from the handbrake operating lever, with reference to Chapter 9.

5 Withdraw the handbrake cable from the bracket on the semi-trailing arm.

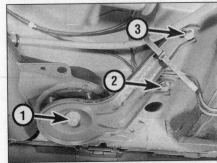

15.13 Forward crossmember fixings

1   Securing bolt
2 and 3   Crossmember mounting bracing bracket bolts

10

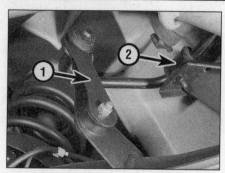

18.7 Rear anti-roll bar fixings

1 End link *2 Clamp bracket*

6 Disconnect the anti-roll bar end link from the semi-trailing arm, by unscrewing the single securing nut and bolt. Recover the rubber bush and the spacer sleeve.

7 Support the semi-trailing arm with a trolley jack, then unscrew and remove the bolt and washer securing the lower end of the shock absorber to the semi-trailing arm.

8 Carefully lower the trolley jack sufficiently to enable the coil spring and its rubber dampers to be withdrawn. Note the orientation of the spring as it is removed. Once the spring has been removed, withdraw the jack.

9 Check that all relevant hoses, pipes, cables and wires have been positioned clear of the semi-trailing arm.

10 Unscrew and remove the two self locking nuts and bolts securing the forward end of the semi-trailing arm to the suspension crossmember, then withdraw the semi-trailing arm from under the vehicle.

11 Refer to Section 12 for details of removal and refitting of the rear hub components.

12 The semi-trailing arm mounting bushes can be renewed using a tube or socket, nut, bolt, washers and distance pieces as necessary to draw out the old bushes and fit the new ones. To aid removal of the old bushes, the protruding ends of the bushes can be cut off using a sharp knife. Lubricate the new bushes with a little soapy water to aid fitting.

Refitting

13 Begin refitting by manipulating the forward end of the semi-trailing arm into position in the suspension crossmember brackets.

14 Fit the semi-trailing arm securing bolts, with new self-locking nuts, but do not fully tighten them at this stage. Note that the bolt heads must face each other.

15 Support the semi-trailing arm with a trolley jack, then refit the coil spring and its rubber dampers as noted during removal.

16 Carefully raise the trolley jack to allow the lower shock absorber securing bolt and washer to be fitted. Tighten the bolt to the specified torque then withdraw the trolley jack.

17 Refit the rubber bush and the spacer sleeve, and reconnect the anti-roll bar end link to the semi-trailing arm. Tighten the securing nut to the specified torque while counter-holding the bolt using a spanner.

18 Refit the handbrake cable to the bracket on the semi-trailing arm, and reconnect the cable end and return spring to the handbrake operating lever, then check the handbrake cable adjustment, as described in Chapter 9.

19 Refit the brake caliper and the ABS sensor bracket to the brake backplate, and tighten the securing bolts to the specified torque.

20 Reconnect the brake fluid line to its bracket on the semi-trailing arm, and secure with the locking clip.

21 Refit the roadwheel, then lower the vehicle to the ground. Finally tighten the roadwheel bolts with the vehicle resting on its wheels.

22 With the vehicle resting on its wheels, release the handbrake, and "bounce" the rear of the car to settle the suspension components.

23 Chock the front wheels, and load each front seat with the equivalent of 70 kg. Working under the rear of the vehicle, tighten the semi-trailing arm securing nuts (self-locking) to the specified torque, while counter-holding the bolts using a spanner.

17 Rear suspension crossmember - removal and refitting

Removal and refitting of the rear suspension crossmember is described in Section 15, where the crossmember is removed as part of the complete rear suspension assembly.

The relevant components can then be removed from the crossmember, with reference to the relevant Sections of this Chapter.

18 Rear anti-roll bar - removal and refitting

Removal

1 Chock the front wheels, then jack up the rear of the vehicle, and support securely on axle stands positioned under the body side members (see "*Jacking and Vehicle Support*").

2 Working under the rear of the vehicle, remove the locking clips and release the brake fluid lines from their brackets on either side of the vehicle underbody. Note that the locking clips also support the ABS sensor wires.

3 Disconnect the fuel outlet hose from the fuel filter, located on the right hand side of the underbody in front of the fuel tank.

Caution: Be prepared for fuel spillage, and take adequate fire precautions. Plug the open ends of the filter and hose, to prevent further fuel loss and dirt ingress.

4 Support the rear plate of the rear suspension crossmember using a trolley jack, then unscrew and remove the two securing bolts from the crossmember rear tube.

5 Carefully lower the trolley jack, taking care

not to strain any of the hoses, pipes or wires, to allow access to the anti-roll bar to crossmember securing brackets.

6 Disconnect the anti-roll bar end links from the semi-trailing arms by unscrewing the single securing nut and bolt in each case. Recover the rubber bushes and the spacer sleeves.

7 Unscrew and remove the two bolts securing the anti-roll bar clamp brackets to the suspension crossmember, and withdraw the anti-roll bar from the vehicle **(see illustration)**.

8 With the anti-roll bar removed from the vehicle, the end links can be removed by sliding them from the ends of the bar.

9 Examine the anti-roll bar mounting bushes for wear or damage, and renew as necessary.

10 If desired, the rubber bushes can be removed from the end links for renewal by pressing them out using a length of bar, or tube, nut, bolt and washers.

11 The mounting bushes that locate in the clamp brackets can be slid from the end of the anti-roll bar, after removal of one of the end links.

12 Lubricate the new bushes with soapy water to aid fitting.

13 Where applicable, refit the end links to the anti-roll bar.

Refitting

14 Begin refitting by positioning the anti-roll bar under the rear of the vehicle, and securing the end links. Use new rubber bushes and spacer sleeves, and tighten the nuts to the specified torque while counter-holding the bolts using a spanner.

15 Refit the clamps securing the anti-roll bar to the suspension crossmember, and tighten the securing bolts to the specified torque.

16 Carefully raise the jack supporting the crossmember, then refit the bolts securing the crossmember rear tube to the underbody, and tighten them to the specified torque.

17 Reconnect the fuel outlet hose to the fuel filter, and tighten the clamp screw.

18 Reconnect the brake lines to their brackets on the underbody, and secure with the locking clips.

19 Lower the vehicle to the ground.

19 Steering wheel - removal and refitting

Note: *A two legged puller will be required for this operation.*

Steering wheel without airbag

Removal

1 Disconnect the battery negative lead.

2 Set the front wheels in the straight ahead position, and unless unavoidable, do not move them until the steering wheel has been refitted.

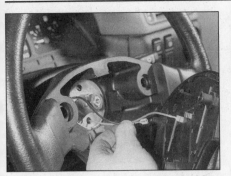

19.3 Disconnect the horn push pad wiring

19.4 Prise back the tabs on the steering wheel retaining nut lockwasher

19.7 Two legged puller fitted to remove steering wheel

3 Prise the horn push pad from the centre of the steering wheel, and disconnect the wiring **(see illustration)**.

4 Using a screwdriver, prise back the tabs on the lockwasher securing the steering wheel retaining nut **(see illustration)**.

5 Unscrew and remove the steering wheel retaining nut and the lockwasher.

6 Make alignment marks between the steering wheel and the end of the column shaft.

7 A small two legged puller must now be fitted to the steering wheel to pull it from the column shaft **(see illustration)**. Note that the steering wheel is a very tight fit on the shaft.

Refitting

8 Begin refitting by gently tapping the steering wheel into position on the column shaft, using a metal tube or socket, and ensuring that the marks made during removal are aligned. Before tapping the wheel fully home, check the centralisation, as described in Section 20.

9 Refit the lockwasher and the steering wheel retaining nut, and tighten the nut to the specified torque. Bend up the lockwasher tabs to secure the nut.

10 Refit the horn push pad, ensuring that the wiring is securely connected, and reconnect the battery negative lead.

Steering wheel with airbag

11 See Chapter 12 for details of how to remove and refit a steering wheel with an airbag.

20 Steering wheel - centralising

1 The steering straight ahead position is achieved when the reference dimension between the centre of the tie-rod to steering gear bolt locking plate(s), and the centre of the rib on the right hand steering gear mounting clamp, is as shown. In this position, the flexible rubber coupling upper pinch bolt should lie horizontally on top of the steering shaft **(see illustrations)**.

2 Check that the steering wheel is centralised.

3 If the steering wheel is off centre by more than 5°, it should be removed, then moved the required number of splines on the column shaft to achieve centralisation, and refitted as described in Section 19.

21 Steering shaft flexible rubber coupling - renewal

1 Position the front roadwheels in the straight ahead position.

2 Working in the engine compartment, loosen the steering gear mounting bolts.

3 Working in the driver's footwell, remove the lower trim panel by releasing the retaining clips.

4 Unscrew and remove the two pinch bolts

from the flexible coupling **(see illustration)**.

5 Push the coupling upwards, remove it from the steering gear pinion shaft, then tilt it and withdraw it from the steering shaft.

6 Before refitting, ensure that the steering gear and the steering wheel are centralised, with reference to Section 20.

7 Fit the coupling, and refit the pinch bolts, but do not tighten them at this stage.

8 Push downwards on the coupling, and tighten the lower pinch bolt.

9 Tighten the steering gear mounting bolts to the specified torque.

10 Pull the steering shaft upwards until it contacts the bearing stop, then tighten the coupling upper pinch bolt.

11 Refit the driver's footwell lower trim panel.

22 Steering column - removal and refitting

Note 1: *A bolt extractor will be required during this operation. A new shear head bolt and (where applicable) a new self-locking nut must be used to secure the column on refitting.*

Note 2: *When removing and refitting the steering column on models equipped with an air bag, read the contents of the following Sections carefully and follow the instructions implicitly. Note that two additional bracing struts, to cater for the additional weight of the air bag assembly, are bolted between the column and centre floor tunnel.*

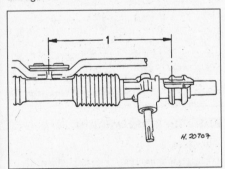

20.1a Steering centralised for setting of steering wheel straight ahead position

1 = 325.0 mm (12.8 in)

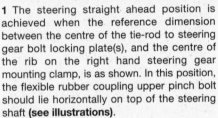
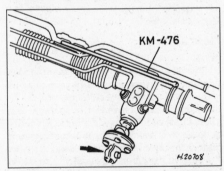

20.1b Flexible coupling upper pinch-bolt alignment (arrowed) with steering gear centralised

21.4 Steering shaft flexible rubber coupling. Upper pinch-bolt arrowed

10

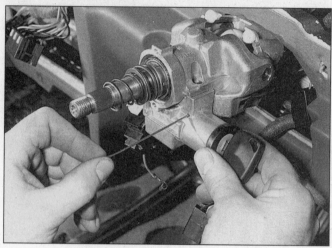

22.11 Removing the lock cylinder - adjustable tilt steering column

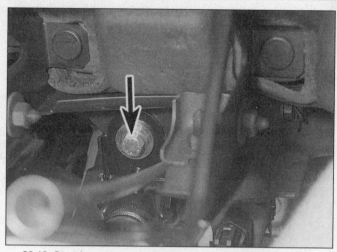

22.13 Steering column to dashboard mounting bracket bolt (arrowed)

 Warning: If an airbag is fitted, read the warning in Chapter 12, before starting work.

Removal

1 Disconnect the battery negative lead.

2 Set the front wheels in the straight ahead position.

3 Working in the driver's footwell, remove the lower trim panel by releasing the retaining clips.

4 On models with an adjustable tilt steering column, move the column to its fully raised position, then unscrew the adjuster lever.

5 Remove the steering wheel, for improved access. See Section 19 for models without airbags, and Chapter 12 for models with airbags.

6 Prise out the screw covers from the front face of the steering column shrouds, then remove the two column shroud securing screws.

7 Remove the three securing screws from the underside of the lower column shroud, then remove both the upper and lower shrouds.

8 Disconnect the wiring plugs from the ignition switch and the indicator and wiper switches, and where applicable, disconnect the horn push wires from the switch housing.

9 On models with a fixed steering column and without an airbag, depress the indicator switch and wiper switch retaining clips and withdraw

22.14 Column upper mounting shear head bolt (arrowed)

the switches. On models with an adjustable tilt steering column or an airbag, unscrew the two Torx screws securing the indicator/wiper switch assembly to the steering column, and remove the switch assembly.

10 Insert the ignition key into the ignition switch, and turn it to position "II".

11 Insert a thin rod into the hole in the lock housing, then press the rod to release the detent spring, and pull out the lock cylinder using the key **(see illustration)**.

12 Working at the lower end of the steering shaft, unscrew and remove the upper pinch bolt securing the steering shaft to the flexible rubber coupling.

13 Unscrew and remove the bolt securing the column to the dashboard mounting bracket **(see illustration)**.

14 Two fixings must now be extracted from the column upper mounting bracket. The right hand bolt is of the shear head type, and must be centre punched, drilled and removed using a bolt extractor **(see illustration)**. A conventional bolt, or a self-locking nut, is used on the left hand side.

15 Withdraw the column assembly into the vehicle interior, and then remove it from the vehicle. Handle the column carefully, avoiding knocks or impact of any kind, which may damage the collapsible section of the column.

16 If desired, the column can be overhauled, as described in Section 23.

Refitting

17 Start refitting by ensuring that the roadwheels are still in the straight ahead position, and that the flexible coupling is positioned so that the upper pinch bolt will be horizontal on top of the steering shaft.

18 If a new column assembly is to be fitted, a large plastic washer will be found at the base of column tube. This washer is used to centre the shaft in the tube, and should be removed when fitting is complete.

19 Offer the column into position, and reconnect the flexible coupling. Refit the pinch bolt, but do not fully tighten it at this stage.

20 Loosely fit the upper mounting fixings, using a new shear head bolt, and (where applicable) a new self-locking nut.

21 Refit the bolt securing the column to the dashboard mounting bracket, and tighten the bolt to the specified torque.

22 Tighten the upper mounting fixings. The shear head bolt should be tightened until the head breaks off, and the conventional bolt or self-locking nut, as applicable, should be tightened to the specified torque.

23 Pull upwards on the steering shaft until the shaft contacts the bearing stop, then tighten the flexible coupling upper pinch bolt.

24 Prise the plastic centring washer from the base of the column tube and remove it from the steering shaft.

25 Further refitting is the reverse of removal. Refit the steering wheel, as described in Section 19.

26 On completion, carry out a test drive along a route with several corners, and check that the steering mechanism operates smoothly.

23 Steering column - overhaul

Note: *On models equipped with an airbag, the steering column must be removed from the vehicle for overhaul. The steering column is fixed, but has a lock housing similar to the adjustable column.*

 Warning: If an airbag is fitted, read the warning in Chapter 12, before starting work.

Fixed steering column

Overhaul

1 If the steering column is in position in the vehicle, continue as described in Section 22, paragraphs 1 to 11 inclusive.

2 Prise out the ignition switch housing safety plugs **(see illustration)**, then turn the housing anti-clockwise, and pull it from the steering column.

3 The bearing can be removed from the ignition switch housing by prising apart the two bearing fixing catches, and pressing or driving out the bearing with a piece of tubing on the bearing outer race. When pressing in the new bearing, make sure that the thrustwasher and contact springs are correctly located (see illustration).

4 The ignition switch is secured to the steering lock housing by two grub screws. Remove the screws to extract the switch. It is recommended that the switch and the lock cylinder are not both removed at the same time, so that their mutual alignment is not lost.

5 If the steering column is in position in the vehicle, unscrew and remove the upper pinch bolt from the steering shaft flexible rubber coupling in the driver's footwell.

6 Withdraw the steering shaft from the steering column tube.

7 Begin reassembly by fitting the temporary plastic centring washer, which will be supplied with a new column or steering shaft, into the base of the column tube.

8 Insert the shaft into the column tube. If the column is in position in the vehicle, engage the bottom end of the shaft with the flexible coupling and refit the upper pinch bolt, but do not tighten it at this stage.

9 Where applicable, refit the ignition switch, and tighten the grub screws.

10 Refit the ignition switch housing, using new safety plugs.

11 If the column is in position in the vehicle, pull upwards on the steering shaft until the shaft contacts the bearing stop, then tighten the flexible coupling upper pinch bolt. Ensure that the roadwheels are still in the straight ahead position, and that the flexible coupling is positioned so that the upper pinch bolt is horizontal on top of the steering shaft.

12 Where applicable, further reassembly is the reverse of dismantling. Refit the steering wheel, as described in Section 19.

13 On completion, carry out a test drive along a route with several corners, and check that the steering mechanism operates smoothly.

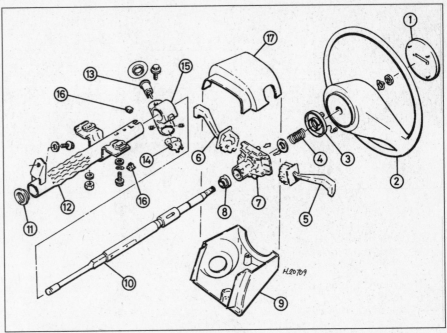

23.2 Exploded view of fixed type steering column and associated components

1 Horn push pad	7 Switch housing	13 Lock barrel
2 Steering wheel	8 Bearing	14 Ignition switch
3 Cam assembly	9 Lower column shroud	15 Lock housing
4 Spring	10 Steering shaft	16 Switch housing safety
5 Lighting switch	11 Centralising plastic discs	plugs
6 Wash/wipe switch	12 Column tube	17 Upper column shroud

Adjustable tilt steering column

Note: New shear head bolts must be used to secure the lock housing on reassembly.

Overhaul

14 If the steering column is in position in the vehicle, continue as described in Section 22, paragraphs 1 to 11 inclusive.

15 The tilt adjuster spring can be removed by simply prising it free using a screwdriver. Be careful, as the spring may fly out.

16 The ignition switch is secured to the lock housing by two grub screws. Access to the "hidden" grub screw is virtually impossible with the steering column installed. For this, and further dismantling, the column must therefore be removed, as described in Section 22.

17 The lock housing is secured to the bearing housing by two shearhead bolts, which must be centre punched, drilled and removed using a bolt extractor, if the two housings are to be separated (see illustration).

18 The column bearing upper race can be renewed after removing the retaining ring, pressure rings and spring. Note that it may be necessary to compress the spring to remove the retaining ring. Take care, as the spring may fly out as the retaining ring is removed.

19 To remove the bearing housing from the column, the fulcrum pins must be extracted, using a nut and bolt to draw them out. Vauxhall special tool KM-585 is available for this purpose (see illustration).

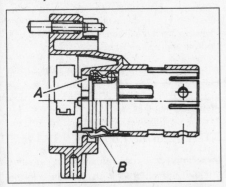

23.3 Sectional view of ignition switch housing

A Thrustwasher   B Contact springs

23.17 Lock housing shear head bolt location (arrowed) - adjustable tilt steering column

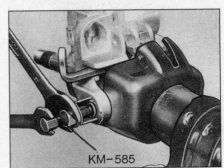

23.19 Extracting the bearing housing fulcrum pins using special tool KM-585 - adjustable tilt type steering column

10

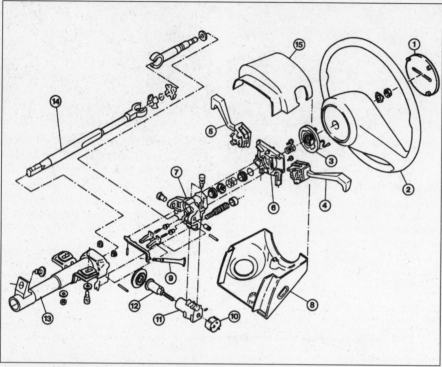

23.23 Exploded view of adjustable tilt type steering column and associated components

1 Horn push pad	6 Switch housing	11 Lock housing
2 Steering wheel	7 Bearing housing	12 Lock barrel
3 Cam assembly	8 Lower column shroud	13 Column tube
4 Lighting switch	9 Tilt adjuster lever	14 Steering shaft
5 Wash/wipe switch	10 Ignition switch	15 Upper column shroud

20 The column bearing lower race can be driven from the upper shaft using a hammer and a drift or chisel. Press or drive the new race onto the shaft.

21 The column bearings themselves can only be renewed complete with the housing.

22 The shaft universal joint and the tilt mechanism detent components can be dismantled for component renewal if necessary.

23 Reassembly is the reverse of dismantling, noting the following points **(see illustration)**.

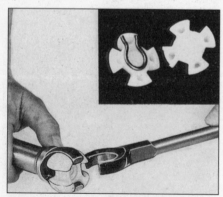

23.24 Steering shaft universal joint, adjustable tilt type steering column

Inset Spring clip location

24 When reconnecting the steering shaft universal joint, note that the spring clips should be located in the recesses of each half of the joint **(see illustration)**.

25 If the lock housing and bearing housing have been separated, clean out the securing bolt holes with a tap. Apply thread locking compound to new shear head bolts, and tighten the bolts until their heads break off.

26 After fitting the bearing housing fulcrum pins, stake them both in three equidistant places.

27 If the bearings have been renewed, the gaps between the bearing housing and the buffers that limit the movement in the upper position should be checked to ensure that they are equal. Check the gap with a feeler blade. A kit containing different thicknesses of buffer, with instructions, is available if required.

24 Steering gear bellows - renewal

Note: *New bellows securing clips will be required for refitting.*

1 Remove the steering gear, as described in Section 25.

2 Remove the mounting clamp and rubber from the left hand end of the steering gear.

3 Disconnect the power steering fluid pipe unions from the left hand end of the steering gear.

4 Remove the outer bellows securing clips from each end of the steering gear, then slide off the bellows/tube assembly.

5 Remove the inner bellows securing clips, and separate the bellows from the tube.

6 Fit the new bellows to the tube, using new clips. The clips should be positioned so that when the steering gear is fitted to the vehicle, the ends of the clips point upwards.

7 Fit the bellows/tube assembly to the steering gear, and secure with new clips, again positioned with the ends of the clips pointing upwards. Ensure that the bellows are not twisted.

8 Reconnect the power steering fluid pipe unions, using new O-rings.

9 Refit the mounting clamp and rubber, then refit the steering gear (Section 25).

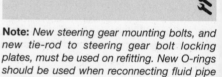

25 Steering gear assembly - removal, overhaul and refitting

Note: *New steering gear mounting bolts, and new tie-rod to steering gear bolt locking plates, must be used on refitting. New O-rings should be used when reconnecting fluid pipe unions.*

Removal

1 Disconnect the battery negative lead.

2 Unbolt and move the brake servo to gain access to the right hand steering gear mounting clamp. It may also be necessary to unbolt the coolant expansion tank and/or the brake master cylinder.

3 Set the front wheels in the straight ahead position.

4 Disconnect the power steering fluid hoses from the pipes at the left hand end of the steering gear.

Caution: Be prepared for fluid spillage, and plug the open ends of the pipes and hoses, to prevent dirt ingress and further fluid loss.

5 Where applicable, to provide space for the steering gear to be withdrawn, remove the relay box from the left hand side of the engine compartment, referring to Chapter 12, if necessary.

6 Prise the locking plate(s) from the tie-rod to steering gear bolts, then unscrew and remove the bolts and recover the washers and spacer plate **(see illustrations)**.

7 Working in the driver's footwell, remove the lower trim panel by releasing the retaining clips.

8 On models with an adjustable tilt steering column, move the column to its fully raised position.

9 Unscrew and remove the lower pinch bolt securing the steering shaft to the flexible rubber coupling.

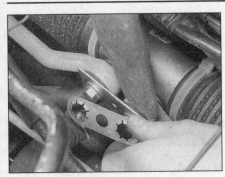

25.6a Prise off the locking plate . . .

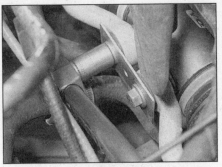

25.6b . . . then unscrew and remove the tie-rod to steering gear bolts

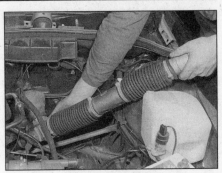

25.10 Remove the steering gear

10 Working in the engine compartment, unbolt the two clamps securing the steering gear to the bulkhead, then manipulate the steering gear out from the left hand side of the engine compartment **(see illustration)**. The help of an assistant may be required to release the flexible rubber coupling from the steering shaft as the steering gear is withdrawn. Note that on some models, various wires and hoses may be secured to the steering gear with cable-ties. Ensure that, where applicable, all wires and hoses are free before the steering gear is removed.

Overhaul

11 Overhaul of the power steering gear is not recommended by the manufacturers.
12 Fluid leaks from the hydraulic fluid pipe unions can normally be corrected by renewing the unions seals with the rack installed.
13 Bellows renewal is covered in Section 24.
14 Adjustment of the power steering gear should not be attempted.
15 Any faults with the steering gear should be referred to a Vauxhall dealer, although renewal of the complete assembly will probably be the only course of action available.

Refitting

16 Refitting is the reverse of removal, remembering the following points.
17 Before refitting, centralise the steering gear by counting the number of turns of the pinion shaft required to move the rack from lock to lock. Then set the rack by turning the pinion shaft from the full lock position through half the number of turns counted. Note that

fluid may be ejected from the steering gear pipes as the rack is turned, and it may be necessary to remove the plugs from the ends of the pipes to allow the rack to turn.
18 Use new mounting bolts to secure the steering gear clamps to the bulkhead **(see illustration)**.
19 The tie-rod to steering gear bolt locking plate(s) must be renewed on refitting.
20 Reconnect the flexible rubber coupling to the steering shaft (with the rack and steering wheel centralised) so that the upper pinch bolt lies horizontally on top of the steering shaft, as described in Section 20, paragraph 1.
21 Renew the O-ring when reconnecting the fluid hose to pipe union.
22 On completion, top-up the power steering fluid level (see "Weekly checks") and bleed the fluid circuit as described in Section 26.

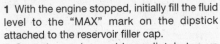

26 Power steering fluid circuit - bleeding

1 With the engine stopped, initially fill the fluid level to the "MAX" mark on the dipstick attached to the reservoir filler cap.
2 Start the engine and immediately top-up the fluid level to the "MIN" mark on the dipstick. Do not allow the reservoir to run dry at any time. The help of an assistant will ease this operation.
3 With the engine running at idle speed, turn the steering wheel slowly two or three times approximately 45° left and right of the centre,

then turn the wheel twice from lock to lock. **Caution: Do not hold the wheel on either lock, as this imposes strain on the hydraulic system.**
4 Stop the engine, and check the fluid level. With the fluid at operating temperature (80°C/176°F) the level should be on the "MAX" mark, and with the fluid cold (20°C/68°F), the level should be on the "MIN" mark. Top-up if necessary.

27 Power steering pump - removal and refitting

Note: A new fluid pipe union O-ring must be used on refitting.

Removal

1 Slacken the drivebelt and remove it from the power steering pump pulley. On models with V-belts, you will need to slacken the pump mounting and adjuster bolts, then adjust the length of the threaded rod **(see illustration)**. On models with serpentine belts, use a spanner or socket on the automatic tensioning roller hexagon, turn the tensioning roller clockwise (as viewed from the right-hand side of the car) and hold it in this position. Slip the drivebelt off the pulley, then allow the tensioner to return to its original position.
2 Disconnect the fluid pipe union and the flexible fluid hose from the pump **(see illustration)**.

25.18 Tightening a steering gear mounting bolt

27.1 Adjusting the length of the power steering pump threaded rod

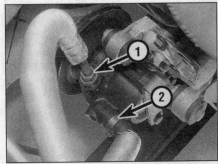

27.2 Power steering pump connections

1 *Fluid pipe union*
2 *Flexible hose connection*

10

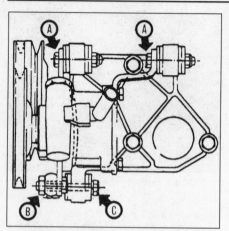

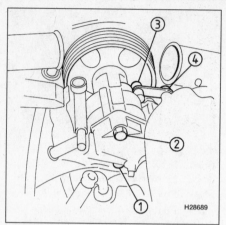

27.8 Mounting and adjuster bolts (arrowed) must be loosened to adjust drivebelt tension - models with V-belts

For A, B and C see "Torque wrench settings" in Specifications

27.9 Power steering pump mounting (tightening torques shown in Specifications) - models with serpentine belts

1 Pump to support
2 Pump to support
3 Shackle to pump*
4 Shackle to engine*

* The shackle is not present on some models

Caution: Be prepared for fluid spillage, and plug the open ends of the pump, pipe and hose, to prevent dirt ingress and further fluid loss.

3 Unscrew and remove the mounting bolts. Recover the nuts, and take care not to lose the rubber insulators that fit into the mounting bracket.

4 Withdraw the pump from the vehicle.

5 No overhaul of the pump is possible, and if faulty, a new unit must be fitted.

Refitting

6 Refitting is the reverse of removal, noting the following points.

7 Renew the O-ring when reconnecting the fluid pipe union.

8 On models with V-belts, tension the power steering drivebelt as described in Chapter 1, then tighten the pump mountings to the torque wrench setting **(see illustration)**.

9 On models with serpentine belts, tighten the pump mountings to the torque wrench setting **(see illustration)**, then refit the belt around all the pulleys and release the automatic tensioner.

10 On completion, top-up the fluid level (see *"Weekly checks"*) and bleed the fluid circuit (Section 26).

28 Power steering fluid reservoir - removal and refitting

Removal

1 The reservoir can be removed from the mounting bracket by unscrewing the clamp screw and removing the clamp.

2 Have a container ready to catch the fluid, then disconnect the fluid hoses from the reservoir and drain the fluid. Plug the open ends of the hoses, to prevent dirt ingress and further fluid loss.

3 If desired, the mounting bracket can be unbolted from the body panel, but note that on certain models, the bolts securing the bracket also secure the ignition coil and suppressor, refer to Chapter 5. Where applicable, unclip the brake fluid pipes and any wiring from the bracket before removal.

Refitting

4 Refitting is the reverse of removal, but on completion, bleed the fluid circuit (Section 26).

29 Power steering fluid cooler pipes - removal and refitting

Note: *New fluid pipe union O-rings must be used on refitting.*

Removal

1 Remove the radiator (Chapter 3).

2 Working at the left hand side of the engine compartment, disconnect the fluid cooler pipe unions **(see illustration)**.

Caution: Be prepared for fluid spillage, and plug the open ends of the pipes to prevent dirt ingress and further fluid loss.

3 Release the three plastic clips securing the pipes to the lower body panel, then manipulate the pipes from the engine compartment **(see illustration)**.

Refitting

4 Refitting is the reverse of removal, but renew the O-rings when reconnecting the fluid pipe unions, and refit the radiator as described in Chapter 3.

5 On completion, top-up the fluid level (see *"Weekly checks"*), and bleed the fluid circuit as described in Section 26.

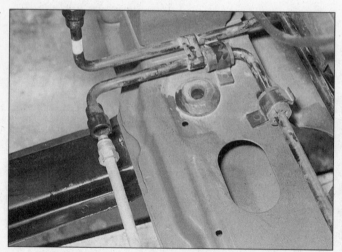

29.2 Power steering fluid cooler pipe unions in engine compartment - SOHC model

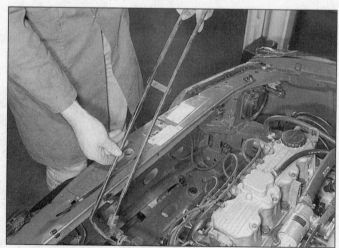

29.3 Removing the power steering fluid cooler pipes - SOHC model

30 Tie-rod end -
removal and refitting

Note: *A balljoint separator tool will be required for this operation. A new tie-rod end balljoint self-locking nut must be used on refitting.*

Removal

1 Where applicable, remove the wheel trim, then loosen the relevant front roadwheel bolts. Apply the handbrake, then jack up the front of the vehicle, and support securely on axle stands (see *"Jacking and Vehicle Support"*) positioned under the body side members. Remove the relevant front roadwheel.

2 Loosen the tie-rod end clamp bolt, which secures the tie-rod end to the threaded adjuster pin on the tie-rod **(see illustration)**.

3 Unscrew the self-locking nut from the tie-rod end to suspension strut balljoint.

4 Using a balljoint separator, disconnect the tie-rod end to suspension strut balljoint **(see illustration)**.

5 Note the position of the tie-rod end on the adjuster pin, either by marking the pin with paint or tape, or by counting the number of threads exposed, then unscrew the tie-rod end from the tie-rod.

6 Note that the tie-rod ends are handed. The right hand tie-rod end is marked "R" but the left hand tie-rod end has no marking.

Refitting

7 Start refitting by screwing the tie-rod end onto the adjuster pin to approximately the same position as was noted during removal.

8 Reconnect the tie-rod end balljoint to the suspension strut, and tighten a new self-locking nut to the specified torque.

9 Tighten the tie-rod end clamp bolt.

10 Refit the roadwheel, and lower the vehicle to the ground. Finally tighten the roadwheel bolts to the specified torque with the vehicle resting on its wheels, and where applicable, refit the wheel trim.

11 Check the front wheel alignment, as described in Section 32, and adjust if necessary. No harm will result from driving the vehicle a short distance to have the alignment checked.

31 Tie-rod -
removal and refitting

Note: *A new tie-rod to steering gear bolt locking plate, and where applicable, a new tie-rod end balljoint self-locking nut, must be used on refitting. If the tie-rod is to be removed complete with the tie-rod end, a balljoint separator tool will be required.*

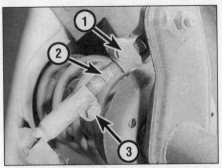

30.2 Tie-rod end viewed from underneath

1 Tie-rod end clamp bolt
2 Threaded adjuster pin
3 Tie-rod clamp bolt

Removal

1 The tie-rod can either be removed leaving the tie-rod end in place, or as an assembly with the tie-rod end.

2 Proceed as described in Section 30, paragraph 1.

3 If the tie-rod is to be removed complete with the tie-rod end, continue as described in Section 30, paragraphs 3 and 4.

4 If the tie-rod is to be removed independently of the tie-rod end, loosen the tie-rod clamp bolt, which secures the tie-rod to the threaded adjuster pin on the tie-rod end.

5 Prise the locking plate(s) from the tie-rod to steering gear bolts, then unscrew and remove the bolts, and recover the washers and spacer plate **(see illustration)**.

6 If the tie-rod is being removed complete with the tie-rod end, the assembly can now be withdrawn from the vehicle.

7 If the tie-rod is to be removed independently of the tie-rod end, note the position of the tie-rod end on the adjuster pin. Do this either by marking the pin with paint or tape, or by counting the number of threads exposed, then unscrew the tie-rod from the tie-rod end and withdraw it from the vehicle.

Refitting

8 Refitting is the reverse of removal, remembering the following points.

9 The tie-rod to steering gear bolt locking plate(s) must be renewed on refitting.

10 If the tie-rod is being refitted complete with the tie-rod end, reconnect the tie-rod end balljoint to the suspension strut, and tighten a new self-locking nut to the specified torque.

11 If the tie-rod is being refitted with the tie-rod end already in place on the vehicle, screw the tie-rod onto the adjuster pin to approximately the same position as noted during removal, and tighten the clamp bolt.

12 Finally tighten the roadwheel bolts with the vehicle resting on its wheels, and where applicable, refit the wheel trim.

13 On completion, check the front wheel alignment, as described in Section 32 and adjust if necessary. No harm will result from driving the vehicle a short distance to have the alignment checked.

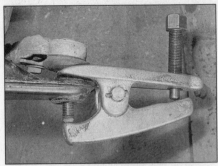

30.4 Disconnecting the tie-rod end to suspension strut balljoint

32 Front wheel alignment -
general

Accurate front wheel alignment is essential for precise steering and handling, and for even tyre wear. Before carrying out any checking or adjusting operations, make sure that the tyres are correctly inflated. Check also that all steering and suspension joints and linkages are in sound condition and that the wheels are not buckled or distorted, particularly around the rims. It will also be necessary to have the car positioned on flat level ground, with enough space to push the car backwards and forwards through about half its length.

Front wheel alignment consists of four factors:

a) *Camber is the angle at which the roadwheels are set from the vertical when viewed from the front or rear of the vehicle. Positive camber is the angle (in degrees) that the wheels are tilted outwards at the top from the vertical.*

b) *Castor is the angle between the steering axis and a vertical line when viewed from each side of the vehicle. Positive castor is indicated when the steering axis is inclined towards the rear of the vehicle at its upper end.*

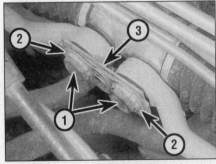

31.5 Tie-rod to steering gear fixings

1 Fixing bolts   3 Spacer plate
2 Locking plates

10

c) Steering axis inclination is the angle, when viewed from the front or rear of the vehicle, between the vertical and an imaginary line drawn between the upper and lower front suspension strut mountings.

d) Toe setting is the amount by which the distance between the front inside edges of the roadwheels differs from that between the rear inside edges, when measured at hub height. If the distance between the front edges is less than that at the rear, the wheels are said to "toe-in". If it is greater than at the rear, the wheels "toe-out."

Camber, castor and steering axis inclination are set during manufacture, and are not adjustable. Unless the vehicle has suffered accident damage, or there is gross wear in the suspension mountings or joints, it can be assumed that these settings are correct. If for any reason it is believed that they are not correct, the task of checking them should be left to a Vauxhall dealer, who will have the necessary special equipment needed to measure the small angles involved.

It is, however, within the scope of the home mechanic to check and adjust the front wheel toe setting. To do this, a tracking gauge must first be obtained. Two types of gauges are available, and can be obtained from motor accessory shops. The first type measures the distance between the front and rear inside edges of the roadwheels, as previously described, with the car stationary. The second type, known as a scuff plate, measures the actual position of the contact surface of the tyre, in relation to the road surface, with the vehicle in motion. This is achieved by pushing or driving the front tyre over a plate, which then moves slightly according to the scuff of the tyre, and shows this movement on a scale. Both types have their advantages and disadvantages, but either can give satisfactory results if used correctly and carefully. Alternatively, a tracking gauge can be fabricated from a length of steel tubing, suitably cranked to clear the sump and clutch bellhousing, with a set-screw and a locknut at one end.

Many tyre specialists will also check toe settings free, or for a nominal charge.

Make sure that the steering is in the straight ahead position when making measurements.

If adjustment is found to be necessary, clean the ends of the tie-rods in the area of the adjustment pin and clamp bolts.

Slacken the clamp bolts (one on each tie-rod balljoint and one on each tie-rod), and turn the adjustment pin on each tie-rod by the same amount in the same direction. Only turn each pin by a quarter turn at a time before rechecking.

When adjustment is correct, tighten the clamp bolts to the specified torque. Check that the tie-rod lengths are equal to within 5 mm (0.2 in), and that the steering wheel spokes are in the correct straight ahead position.

Chapter 11
Bodywork and fittings

Contents

Degrees of difficulty

Easy, suitable for novice with little experience	**Fairly easy,** suitable for beginner with some experience	**Fairly difficult,** suitable for competent DIY mechanic	**Difficult,** suitable for experienced DIY mechanic	**Very difficult,** suitable for expert DIY or professional

Specifications

Torque wrench setting	Nm	lbf ft
Front seat rails to floor	20	15
Seat belt fixings	35	26

1 General description

The bodyshell and floorpan are of pressed steel, and form an integral part of the vehicle's structure, without the need for a separate chassis.

Various areas are strengthened, to provide for suspension, steering and engine mounting points, and load distribution.

Extensive corrosion protection is applied to all new vehicles. Various anti-corrosion preparations are used, including galvanising and PVC under-sealing. Protective wax is injected into the box sections and other hollow cavities.

Extensive use is made of plastic for peripheral components, such as the radiator grille, bumpers and wheel trims, and for much of the interior trim.

Interior fittings are to a high standard on all models, and a wide range of optional equipment is available throughout the range.

Except for the rear quarter windows, all fixed glass is bonded in position, using a special adhesive. Any work in this area should be entrusted to a Vauxhall dealer or glass replacement specialist.

2 Bodywork and underframe - maintenance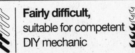

The general condition of a vehicle's bodywork is the one thing that significantly affects its value. Maintenance is easy but needs to be regular. Neglect, particularly after minor damage, can lead quickly to further deterioration and costly repair bills. It is important also to keep watch on those parts of the vehicle not immediately visible, for

instance the underside, inside all the wheel arches and the lower part of the engine compartment.

The basic maintenance routine for the bodywork is washing preferably with a lot of water, from a hose. This will remove all the loose solids that may have stuck to the vehicle. It is important to flush these off in such a way as to prevent grit from scratching the finish. The wheel arches and underframe need washing in the same way to remove any accumulated mud that will retain moisture and tend to encourage rust. Oddly enough, the best time to clean the underframe and wheel arches is in wet weather when the mud is thoroughly wet and soft. In very wet weather the underframe is usually cleaned of large accumulations automatically and this is a good time for inspection.

Periodically, except on vehicles with a wax-based underbody protective coating, it is a good idea to have the whole of the underframe of the vehicle steam cleaned, engine compartment included, so that a thorough inspection can be carried out to see what minor repairs and renovations are necessary. Steam cleaning is available at many garages and is necessary for removal of the accumulation of oily grime that sometimes is allowed to become thick in certain areas. The dirt can then be simply hosed off. Note that these methods should not be used on vehicles with wax-based underbody protective coating or the coating will be removed. Such vehicles should be inspected annually, preferably just before winter, when the underbody should be washed down and any damage to the wax coating repaired. Ideally, a completely fresh coat should be applied. It would also be worth considering the use of such wax-based protection for injection into door panels, sills, box sections, etc., as an additional safeguard against rust damage where such protection is not provided by the vehicle manufacturer.

After washing paintwork, wipe off with a chamois leather to give an unspotted clear finish. A coat of clear protective wax polish, will give added protection against chemical pollutants in the air. If the paintwork sheen has dulled or oxidised, use a cleaner/polisher combination to restore the brilliance of the shine. This requires a little effort, but such dulling is usually caused because regular washing has been neglected. Care needs to be taken with metallic paintwork, as special non-abrasive cleaner/polisher is required to avoid damage to the finish.

Always check that the door and ventilator opening drain holes and pipes are completely clear so that water can be drained out. Bright work should be treated in the same way as paint work. Windscreens and windows can be kept clear of the smeary film that often appears, by using a glass cleaner. Never use any form of wax or other body or chromium polish on glass.

3 Upholstery and carpets - maintenance

Mats and carpets should be brushed or vacuum cleaned regularly to keep them free of grit. If they are badly stained remove them from the vehicle for scrubbing or sponging and make quite sure they are dry before refitting. Seats and interior trim panels can be kept clean by wiping with a damp cloth. If they do become stained (which can be more apparent on light coloured upholstery) use a little liquid detergent and a soft nail brush to scour the grime out of the grain of the material. Do not forget to keep the headlining clean in the same way as the upholstery. When using liquid cleaners inside the vehicle do not over-wet the surfaces being cleaned. Excessive damp could get into the seams and padded interior causing stains, offensive odours or even rot. If the inside of the vehicle gets wet accidentally it is worthwhile taking some trouble to dry it out properly, particularly where carpets are involved. **Do not** leave oil or electric heaters inside the vehicle for this purpose.

4 Minor body damage - repair

Repairs of minor scratches in bodywork

If the scratch is very superficial, and does not penetrate to the metal of the bodywork, repair is very simple. Lightly rub the area of the scratch with a paintwork renovator, to remove loose paint from the scratch and to clear the surrounding bodywork of wax polish. Rinse the area with clean water.

Apply touch-up paint to the scratch using a fine paint brush; continue to apply fine layers of paint until the surface of the paint in the scratch is level with the surrounding paintwork. Allow the new paint at least two weeks to harden: then blend it into the surrounding paintwork by rubbing the scratch area with a paintwork renovator or a very fine cutting paste and apply wax polish.

Where the scratch has penetrated right through to the metal of the bodywork, causing the metal to rust, a different repair technique is required. Remove any loose rust from the bottom of the scratch with a penknife, then apply rust inhibiting paint, to prevent the formation of rust in the future. Using a rubber or nylon applicator fill the scratch with bodystopper paste. If required, this paste can be mixed with cellulose thinners to provide a very thin paste that is ideal for filling narrow scratches. Before the stopper-paste in the scratch hardens, wrap a piece of smooth cotton rag around the top of a finger. Dip the finger in cellulose thinners and then quickly sweep it across the surface of the stopper-paste in the scratch; this will ensure that the surface of the stopper-paste is slightly hollowed. The scratch can now be painted over as described earlier in this Section.

Repair of dents in bodywork

When deep denting of the vehicle's bodywork has taken place, the first task is to pull the dent out, until the affected bodywork almost attains its original shape. There is little point in trying to restore the original shape completely, as the metal in the damaged area will have stretched on impact and cannot be reshaped fully to its original contour. It is better to bring the level of the dent up to a point that is about 8 in (3 mm) below the level of the surrounding bodywork. In cases where the dent is very shallow anyway, it is not worth trying to pull it out at all. If the underside of the dent is accessible, it can be hammered out gently from behind, using a mallet with a wooden or plastic head. Whilst doing this, hold a block of wood firmly against the outside of the panel to absorb the impact from the hammer blows and thus prevent a large area of the bodywork from being "belled-out".

Should the dent be in a section of the bodywork that has a double skin or some other factor making it inaccessible from behind, a different technique is called for. Drill several small holes through the metal inside the area particularly in the deeper section. Then screw long self-tapping screws into the holes just sufficiently for them to gain a good purchase in the metal. Now the dent can be pulled out by pulling on the protruding heads of the screws with a pair of pliers.

The next stage of the repair is the removal of the paint from the damaged area, and from an inch or so of the surrounding "sound" bodywork. This is accomplished most easily by using a wire brush or abrasive pad on a power drill, although it can be done just as effectively by hand using sheets of abrasive paper. To complete the preparation for filling, score the surface of the bare metal with a screwdriver or the tang of a file, or alternatively, drill small holes in the affected area. This will provide a good "key" for the filler paste.

To complete the repair see the Section on filling and re-spraying.

Repair of rust holes or gashes in bodywork

Remove all paint from the affected area and from an inch or so of the surrounding "sound" bodywork, using an abrasive pad or a wire brush on a power drill. If these are not available a few sheets of abrasive paper will do the job just as effectively. With the paint removed you will be able to gauge the severity of the corrosion and therefore decide whether to renew the whole panel (if this is possible) or to repair the affected area. New body panels are not as expensive as most people think and it is often quicker and more satisfactory to fit a new panel than to attempt to repair large areas of corrosion.

Remove all fittings from the affected area except those which will act as a guide to the original shape of the damaged bodywork (e.g. headlamp shells, etc.). Then, using tin snips or a hacksaw blade, remove all loose metal and any other metal badly affected by corrosion. Hammer the edges of the hole inwards to create a slight depression for the filler paste.

Wire brush the affected area to remove the powdery rust from the surface of the remaining metal. Paint the affected area with rust inhibiting paint. If the back of the rusted area is accessible treat this also.

Before filling can take place it will be necessary to block the hole in some way. This can be achieved by using aluminium or plastic mesh, or aluminium tape.

Aluminium or plastic mesh, or glass fibre matting, is probably the best material to use for a large hole. Cut a piece to the approximate size and shape of the hole to be filled, then position it in the hole so that its edges are below the level of the surrounding bodywork. It can be retained in position by several blobs of filler paste around its periphery.

Aluminium tape should be used for small or very narrow holes. Pull a piece off the roll and trim it to the approximate size and shape required. Then pull off the backing paper (if used) and stick the tape over the hole. It can be overlapped if the thickness of one piece is insufficient. Burnish down the edges of the tape with the handle of a screwdriver or similar, to ensure that the tape is securely attached to the metal underneath.

Bodywork repairs filling and re-spraying

Before using this Section, see the Sections on dent, deep scratch, rust holes and gash repairs.

Many types of bodyfiller are available, but generally those proprietary kits that contain a tin of filler paste and a tube of resin hardener are best for this type of repair. These can be used directly from the tube. A wide, flexible plastic or nylon applicator will be found invaluable for imparting a smooth and well-contoured finish to the surface of the filler.

Mix up a little filler on a clean piece of card or board - measure the hardener carefully (follow the maker's instructions on the pack) otherwise the filler will set too rapidly or too slowly. Using the applicator apply the filler paste to the prepared area; draw the applicator across the surface of the filler to achieve the correct contour and to level the filler surface. When a contour that approximates to the correct one is achieved, stop working the paste - if you carry on too long the paste will become sticky and begin to "pick up" on the applicator. Continue to add thin layers of filler paste at twenty-minute intervals until the level of the filler is just proud of the surrounding bodywork.

Once the filler has hardened, excess can be removed using a metal plane or file. From then on, progressively finer grades of abrasive paper should be used, starting with a 40 grade production paper and finishing with 400 grade wet-and-dry paper. Always wrap the abrasive paper around a flat rubber, cork, or wooden block otherwise the surface of the filler will not be completely flat. During the smoothing of the filler surface the wet-and-dry paper should be periodically rinsed in water. This will ensure that a very smooth finish is imparted to the filler at the final stage.

At this stage the "dent" should be surrounded by a ring of bare metal, which in turn should be encircled by the finely "feathered" edge of the good paintwork. Rinse the repair area with clean water, until all the dust produced by the rubbing-down operation has gone.

Spray the whole repair area with a light coat of primer. This will show up any imperfections in the surface of the filler. Repair these imperfections with fresh filler paste or bodystopper, and again smooth the surface with abrasive paper. If bodystopper is used, it can be mixed with cellulose thinners to form a thin paste that is ideal for filling small holes. Repeat this spray and repair procedure until you are satisfied that the surface of the filler, and the feathered edge of the paintwork are perfect. Clean the repair area with clean water and allow to dry fully.

The repair area is now ready for final spraying. Paint spraying must be carried out in a warm, dry, windless and dust free atmosphere. This condition can be created artificially if you have access to a large indoor working area, but if you are forced to work in the open, you will have to pick your day very carefully. If you are working indoors, dousing the floor in the work area with water will help to settle the dust that would otherwise be in the atmosphere. If the repair area is confined to one body panel, mask off the surrounding panels; this will help to minimise the effects of a slight miss-match in paint colours. Bodywork fittings (e.g. chrome strips, door handles, etc.), will also need to be masked off. Use genuine masking tape and several thicknesses of newspaper for the masking operations.

Before beginning to spray, agitate the aerosol can thoroughly, then spray a test area (an old tin, or similar) until the technique is mastered. Cover the repair area with a thick coat of primer; the thickness should be built up using several thin layers of paint rather than one thick one. Using 400 grade wet-and-dry paper, rub down the surface of the primer until it is smooth. While doing this, the work area should be thoroughly doused with water, and the wet-and-dry paper periodically rinsed in water. Allow to dry before spraying on more paint.

Spray on the top coat, again building up the thickness by using several thin layers of paint. Start spraying in the centre of the repair area and then work outwards, with a side-to-side motion, until the whole repair area and about 2 inches of the surrounding original paintwork is covered. Remove all masking material 10 to 15 minutes after spraying on the final coat of paint.

Allow the new paint at least two weeks to harden, then using a paintwork renovator or a very fine cutting paste, blend the edges of the paint into the existing paintwork. Finally, apply wax polish.

Plastic components

With the use of more and more plastic body components (e.g. bumpers, spoilers, and in some cases major body panels), repair of more serious damage to such items has become a matter of either entrusting repair work to a specialist in this field, or renewing complete components. Repair of such damage by the DIY owner is not feasible owing to the cost of the equipment and materials required for effecting such repairs. The basic technique involves making a groove along the line of the crack in the plastic using a rotary burr in a power drill. The damaged part is then welded back together by using a hot air gun to heat up and fuse a plastic filler rod into the groove. Any excess plastic is then removed and the area rubbed down to a smooth finish. It is important that a filler rod of the correct plastic is used, as body components can be made of a variety of different types (e.g. polycarbonate, ABS, polypropylene).

Damage of a less serious nature (abrasions, minor cracks, etc.), can be repaired by the DIY owner using a two-part epoxy filler repair material. Once mixed in equal proportions this is used in similar fashion to the bodywork filler used on metal panels. The filler is usually cured in twenty to thirty minutes, ready for sanding and painting.

If the owner is renewing a complete component himself, or if he has repaired it with epoxy filler, he will have a problem of finding a paint for finishing which is compatible with the type of plastic used. At one time the use of a universal paint was not possible owing to the complex range of plastics come across in body component applications. Standard paints, generally, will not bond to plastic or rubber satisfactorily, but special paints are available to match any plastic or rubber finish can be obtained from dealers. However, it is now possible to obtain a plastic body parts finishing kit that consists of a pre-primer treatment, a primer and coloured top coat. Full instructions are normally supplied with a kit, but the method of use is to first apply the pre-primer to the component concerned and allow it to dry for up to 30 minutes. Then the primer is applied and left to dry for about an hour before finally applying the special coloured top coat. The result is a correctly coloured component where the paint will flex with the plastic or rubber, a property that standard paint does not normally possess.

5 Major body damage - repair

Major impact or rust damage should only be repaired by a Vauxhall dealer or other competent specialist. Alignment jigs are needed for successful completion of such work, superficially effective repairs may leave dangerous weaknesses in the structure. Distorted components can also impose severe stresses on steering and suspension components with consequent premature failure.

11

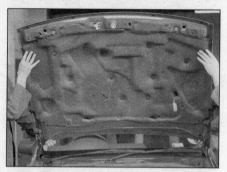

6.5 Lifting the bonnet from the vehicle

6 Bonnet - removal and refitting

HAYNES HiNT To aid refitting mark the position of the bonnet before removal.

Removal

1 Open the bonnet, and support it in the fully open position.
2 On models fitted with an underbonnet lamp, disconnect the battery negative lead, then prise the lamp from the bonnet and disconnect the wiring. If the bonnet is to be refitted, to aid routing of the wiring on refitting, tie a length of string to the end of the wiring. Then withdraw the wiring through the bonnet and untie the string, leaving it in position in the bonnet.
3 Similarly, disconnect the windscreen washer fluid hose from the connector in the bonnet, but tie the string to the connector, to prevent it from slipping into an inaccessible position in the bonnet.
4 Mark the position of the hinges on the bonnet.
5 With the help of an assistant, support the weight of the bonnet, then unscrew the securing bolts from the hinges, and lift the bonnet from the vehicle (see illustration). If the bonnet is to be refitted, rest it carefully on rags or cardboard, to avoid damaging the paint.
6 If a new bonnet is to be fitted, transfer all the serviceable fittings (rubber buffers, lock striker, etc.) to it.
7 If desired, the bonnet hinges can be removed from the vehicle, after unscrewing the three bolts in each case securing them to the upper flanges of the front wings.

Refitting

8 Refitting is the reverse of removal, remembering the following points.
9 Align the hinges with the previously made marks on the bonnet.
10 If the original bonnet is being refitted, draw the windscreen washer fluid hose, and where applicable, the underbonnet lamp wiring, through the bonnet using the string.

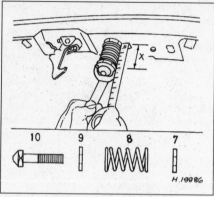

6.11 Bonnet lock striker adjustment

  7 Locknut   9 Washer
  8 Spring   10 Striker pin

  X = 40.0 to 45.0 mm (1.57 to 1.77 in) measured from bonnet panel to washer (9)

11 If the lock striker has been disturbed, adjust it to the dimension shown (see illustration), then tighten the locknut.
12 If necessary, adjust the hinge bolts and the front rubber buffers until a good fit is obtained with the bonnet shut.

7 Bonnet lock components - removal and refitting

Removal

1 Open the bonnet, and support it in the fully open position.
2 The lock hook is fitted to a pair of brackets under the bonnet, and is secured by a rivet with a flattened end (see illustration). File off the flattened end and remove the rivet, then withdraw the hook.
3 To remove the bonnet lock striker from the bonnet, loosen the locknut, then unscrew the striker and recover the washers and spring.
4 To remove the locking spring, disconnect the end of the bonnet release cable from the spring. Then unhook the end of the spring from the slot in the front body panel, and manipulate the spring out through the top of the panel, taking care not to damage the paint.

7.2 Bonnet lock hook and striker

Refitting

5 Refitting is the reverse of removal, noting the following points.
6 When refitting the lock hook, use a new rivet and flatten the end with pliers.
7 When refitting the lock striker, adjust it as described in Section 6, paragraph 11, then tighten the locknut.
8 On completion, close the bonnet and check that the lock and the bonnet release mechanism operate satisfactorily.

8 Bonnet lock release cable - removal and refitting

Removal

1 Open the bonnet, and support it in the fully open position.
2 Unscrew the release cable clip from the front body panel.
3 Disconnect the end of the release cable from the locking spring under the front body panel.
4 Remove the driver's side lower facia panel, as described in Section 34, then disconnect the release cable from the release handle. If necessary, remove the release handle from its retainer for access to the cable end.
5 Pull the cable assembly through the grommet in the engine compartment bulkhead into the engine compartment.
6 Release the cable from any remaining clips and cable-ties, and withdraw it from the engine compartment.

Refitting

7 Refitting is the reverse of removal, but ensure that the cable is correctly routed, and on completion check the release mechanism for satisfactory operation.

9 Tailgate - removal and refitting

Removal

1 Open the tailgate fully.
2 Disconnect the battery negative lead.
3 Remove the securing screws, and withdraw the tailgate trim panels.
4 Disconnect all the relevant wiring now exposed (see illustration).
5 If the original tailgate is to be refitted, tie string to the ends of all the relevant wires, then feed the wiring through the top edge of the tailgate. Untie the string, leaving it in position in the tailgate to assist refitting.
6 Prise off the rear roof trim panel, taking care not to break the securing clips, and lower the rear of the headlining slightly for access to the tailgate hinge securing screws (see illustrations). Mark the hinge positions on the body.

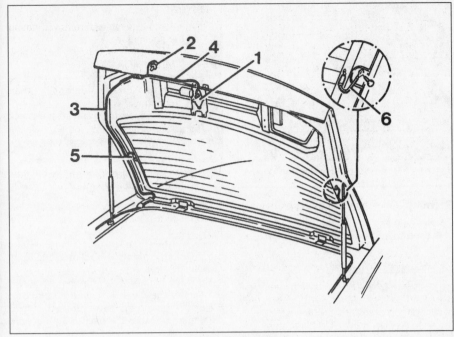

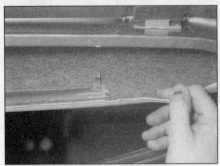

9.6a Prise off the rear roof trim panel . . .

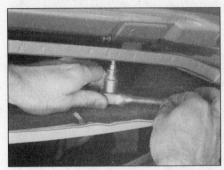

9.6b . . . for access to the tailgate hinge screws

9.4 Tailgate and wiring

1 Rear screen wiper motor
2 Tailgate courtesy lamp switch
3 Tailgate wiring harness
4 Rear wiper wiring harness
5 Rear screen heater connection
6 Ground lead

7 Have an assistant support the weight of the tailgate, then disconnect the tailgate struts from their mounting balljoints, with reference to Section 12.

8 Ensure that the tailgate is adequately supported, then remove the hinge securing screws and withdraw the tailgate from the vehicle. If the tailgate is to be refitted, rest it carefully on rags or cardboard, to avoid damaging the paint.

9 If desired, the hinges can be removed from the tailgate by driving out the hinge pins.

10 If the tailgate can be moved up and down on its hinges due to wear in the hinge pins or their holes, it may be possible to drill out the holes and fit slightly oversize pins. Consult a Vauxhall dealer for further advice.

11 If a new tailgate is to be fitted, transfer all serviceable components to it.

Refitting

12 Refitting is the reverse of removal, remembering the following points.

13 Align the hinges with the previously made marks on the body.

14 If the original tailgate is being refitted, draw the wiring through the tailgate, using the string.

15 If necessary, adjust the hinge bolts and the rubber buffers, to obtain a good fit when the tailgate is shut.

16 If necessary, adjust the position of the lock striker on the body, to achieve satisfactory lock operation.

10 Tailgate lock - removal and refitting

Removal

1 Open the tailgate and remove the luggage compartment rear trim panel (see Section 33).

2 Undo the two bolts on the tailgate lock **(see illustration)**.

3 Withdraw the lock and disconnect the adjustable catch rod **(see illustration)**.

Refitting

4 Refitting is the reverse of removal, but if necessary adjust the position of the lock to achieve satisfactory operation.

10.2 Undo the two bolts on the tailgate lock

11 Tailgate lock cylinder and central locking motor - removal and refitting

Lock cylinder

Removal

1 The tailgate lock cylinder is mounted in the right tail lamp, but can be withdrawn without removing the lamp. Open the tailgate and remove the luggage compartment rear trim panel (see Section 33).

2 Pull away the additional trim panel at the right, behind the tail lamp.

3 Disconnect the main catch rod and central locking rod.

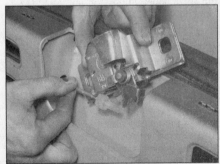

10.3 Disconnect the adjustable operating rod from the tailgate lock

11

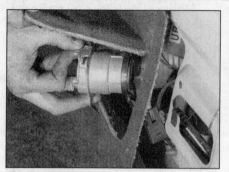

11.7 Tailgate lock housing and cylinder

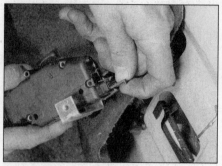

11.10 Tailgate central locking motor and bracket

12.2 Prise the spring clip from the tailgate strut balljoint

4 Undo the three nuts on the tailgate lock cylinder housing. Two of them also hold the central locking motor.

5 Undo the remaining bolt on the central locking bracket.

6 Slide the central locking motor away, still on its wiring, and disconnect the central locking multi-plug.

7 Withdraw the lock and cylinder through the aperture **(see illustration)**. Keep the wiring with the lock and disconnect the other end from the loom behind the panel.

8 To remove the lock cylinder from the housing, release the tabs on the spring plate and withdraw the cylinder.

Refitting

9 Refitting is the reverse of removal, but check the operation of the lock on completion.

Central locking motor

Removal

10 If required, the lock and central locking motor can be removed together. First remove the lock (see paragraphs 1 to 7), then withdraw the central locking motor **(see illustration)**.

11 To remove the central locking motor by itself, proceed as in paragraphs 1 to 4, but do not remove all three nuts from the lock cylinder housing. Just undo the two nuts that hold the central locking motor. Then proceed as in paragraphs 5 and 6, and withdraw the motor.

Refitting

12 Refitting is the reverse of removal, but check the operation of the lock on completion.

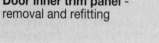

12 Tailgate strut - removal and refitting

Removal

1 Open the tailgate fully, and have an assistant support it.

2 Release the strut from its mounting balljoints by prising the spring clips a little way out **(see illustration)**, and pulling the strut off the balljoints. If the strut is to be re-used, do not remove the spring clips completely, and do not prise them out further than 6.0 mm (0.24 in).

Refitting

3 Refitting is the reverse of removal.

13 Door - removal and refitting

Removal

1 The door hinges are welded onto the door-frame and the body pillar, so that there is no provision for adjustment or alignment.

2 To remove a door, open it fully and support it under its lower edge on blocks covered with pads of rag.

3 Disconnect the battery negative lead, and disconnect the wiring connector from the front edge of the door. To release the connector, twist the locking collar, then pull the connector from the socket in the door **(see illustration)**.

4 Undo the nut and bolt from the check arm pivot above the lower hinge **(see illustration)**.

5 Remove the plastic covers from the hinge pins, then drive out the pins using a punch. Have an assistant support the door as the pins are driven out, then withdraw the door from the vehicle.

Refitting

6 Refitting is the reverse of removal, using a new check link roll pin.

7 If the door can be moved up and down on its hinges due to wear in the hinge pins or their holes, it may be possible to drill out the holes and fit slightly oversize pins. Consult a Vauxhall dealer for further advice.

8 Door closure may be adjusted by altering the position of the lock striker on the body pillar, using an Allen key or hexagon bit.

14 Door inner trim panel - removal and refitting

Removal

1 Disconnect the battery negative lead.

2 Remove the two plugs from inside the tidy bin and remove the screws from behind them **(see illustration)**.

13.3 Disconnect the wiring connector from the front edge of the door

13.4 Check arm and lower hinge

14.2 Remove the screws from inside the tidy bin

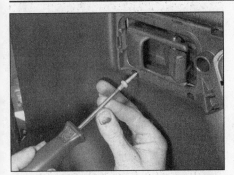

14.6 Remove the screws from the door handle surround

3 Remove the screw from underneath the panel.
4 Remove the screw from under the grab handle.
5 Unclip the door handle cover.
6 Remove the two screws from the door handle surround moulding **(see illustration)**.
7 Release the plastic clips securing the trim panel to the door frame. This can be done using a wide blade screwdriver, but it is preferable to use a forked tool to minimise the possibility of damage to the trim panel and the clips.
8 Once the clips have been released, pull the trim panel away from the door.
9 Disconnect the two multi-plugs for the mirror switch and the small speaker **(see illustration)**.
10 Remove any remaining clips from the door with the forked tool and put them in the trim panel for refitting **(see illustration)**.
11 Unplug the wiring harness clips **(see illustration)**.
12 Carefully pull away the plastic sheet and keep it intact for refitting **(see illustration)**.

Refitting

13 Refitting is the reverse of removal, remembering the following points.
14 If the plastic insulating sheet has been removed from the door, make sure that it is refitted intact and securely glued to the door. If the sheet is damaged or detached, rainwater may leak into the vehicle or damage the door trim.
15 Renew any clips that were broken during removal of the trim panel, and mount them in the panel together with the other clips. Refit the

14.9 Disconnect the two multi-plugs for the mirror switch and small speaker

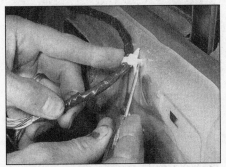

14.11 Unplug the wiring harness clips

panel by pressing all the clips into the holes and make sure they engage correctly.

15 Door interior handle - removal and refitting

Removal

1 Remove the door inner trim panel, as described in Section 14.
2 Slide the handle forward in the slots and pull it out slightly **(see illustration)**.
3 Manipulate the rods to the rearmost position in the handle mechanism and disengage them **(see illustration)**.

Refitting

4 Refitting is the reverse of removal, but check the mechanism for satisfactory operation before refitting the door inner trim panel.

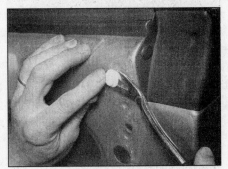

14.10 Remove the clips from the door with the forked tool

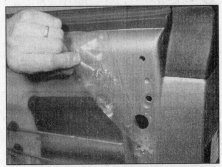

14.12 Pull away the plastic sheet

16 Door exterior handle - removal and refitting

Removal

1 Remove the door inner trim panel, as described in Section 14.
2 Peel back the plastic insulating sheet sufficiently to gain access to the exterior handle **(see illustration)**.
3 Unscrew the two nuts securing the exterior handle to the door.
4 Unclip the central locking microswitch from the rear edge of the exterior handle assembly.
5 Release the two lower retaining clips, then manipulate the exterior handle assembly through the outside of the door, and disconnect the operating rods.

15.2 Slide the door handle forward in the slots and pull it out slightly

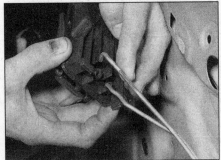

15.3 Disengage the rods from the door handle

16.2 Door exterior handle assembly

11

17.2 Extract the circlip from the end of the lock cylinder . . .

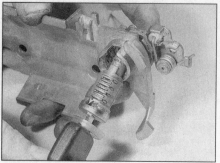

17.3a . . . then withdraw the lock cylinder using the key . . .

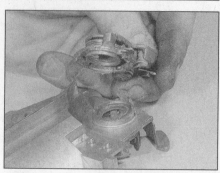

17.3b . . . and recover the lever assembly

Refitting

6 Refitting is the reverse of removal, but check the operation of the mechanism before refitting the door inner trim panel, then refit the trim panel with reference to Section 14.

17 Door lock barrel - removal and refitting

Removal

1 Remove the door exterior handle, as described in Section 16.
2 Insert the key into the lock, then extract the circlip from the end of the lock cylinder (**see illustration**).
3 Withdraw the lock cylinder using the key, and recover the lever assembly (**see illustrations**).

Refitting

4 Refitting is the reverse of removal, but check the operation of the door lock, handle and window regulator mechanisms before refitting the door trim panel, and refit the trim panel with reference to Section 14.

18 Door lock and central locking motor - removal and refitting

Removal

1 Remove the door inner trim panel and the plastic insulating sheet, as described in Section 14.
2 Wind the window upwards.
3 Slide the inner door handle forward and pull it out, then disengage it from the rods as described in Section 15.

4 Detach the upper rod from the lock and withdraw it (**see illustration**).
5 Remove the upper plastic cover and lower grommet, undo the bolts and remove the rear window guide, as described in Section 22.
6 Remove the deadlocking cover (**see illustration**). This is an anti-theft device which prevents a screwdriver or piece of wire from being inserted behind the weather shield to open the lock.
7 Pull off the vertical rod from the exterior handle to the linkage (**see illustration**).
8 Detach the lower rod from the lock and withdraw it. You will need to tilt the rod up and press a clip down to disengage it (**see illustration**).
9 Depress the clips and disconnect the multi-plug from the bottom of the central locking motor (**see illustration**).
10 Undo the three Torx screws from the locking mechanism (**see illustration**).

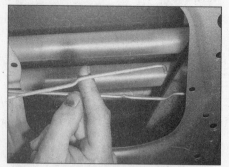

18.4 Detach the upper rod from the lock and withdraw it

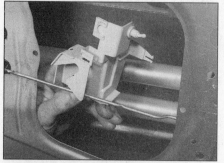

18.6 Remove the deadlocking cover

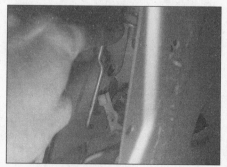

18.7 Pull off the rod from the exterior handle to the linkage

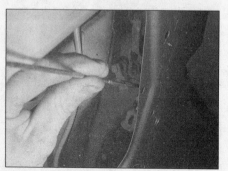

18.8 Detach the lower rod from the lock

18.9 Disconnect the multi-plug from the central locking motor

18.10 Undo the three Torx screws from the locking mechanism

18.12 Withdraw the locking mechanism and central locking motor

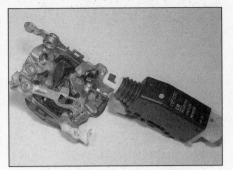

18.13 Lock and motor assembly

18.14 Exterior handle operating rod adjuster wheel (arrowed) at lock end of rod

11 Drop the locking mechanism down to disengage it from the second vertical rod to the exterior handle.
12 Withdraw the locking mechanism and central locking motor through the aperture (see illustration).
13 The locking mechanism and central locking unit are screwed together as a single assembly (see illustration).

Refitting

14 Refitting is the reverse of removal, but check the operation of the door lock, handle, and window regulator mechanisms before refitting the door trim panel. If the lock operation is not satisfactory, the exterior handle operating rod can be adjusted by turning the knurled plastic adjuster wheel at the end of the rod (see illustration).

19 Door check arm - removal and refitting

Removal

1 Open the door fully, then using a punch, drive the roll pin from the door check arm pivot.
2 Remove the door inner trim panel, as described in Section 14.
3 Working at the front edge of the door, unscrew the two bolts securing the check arm to the door, then withdraw the check arm through the inside of the door.

Refitting

4 Refitting is the reverse of removal, but use a new roll pin to secure the check arm to the pivot.

20 Windscreen and rear window - removal and refitting

1 Except for the rear quarter windows, all fixed glass is bonded in position, using a special adhesive.
2 Special tools, adhesives and expertise are required for successful removal and refitting of glass fixed by this method. Such work must therefore be entrusted to a Vauxhall dealer or a windscreen specialist.
3 The same remarks apply if sealing of the windscreen or other glass surround is necessary.

21 Rear quarter windows - removal and refitting

Removal

1 Remove the trim panels, as described in Section 33, in the following order:
a) Sill trim panel;
b) Rear quarter trim panel;
c) Centre body trim panel;

d) Rear quarter window trim and parcel shelf panel.
2 Have an assistant support the rear quarter window from outside the vehicle, then unscrew the ten plastic securing nuts and push the window out from the body (see illustration).

Refitting

3 Refitting is the reverse of removal, but ensure that the seal around the edge of the window glass is correctly seated against the body as the window is fitted.

22 Door windows - removal and refitting

Sash window

Removal

1 Remove the door inner trim panel and the plastic insulating sheet, as described in Section 14.
2 Wind the window fully upwards.
3 Remove the two upper bolts from the regulator lever (see illustration).
4 Remove the inner weather strip from the top of the door (see illustration).
5 Remove the plastic cover from the upper rear corner of the door, then remove the upper bolt that secures the rear guide rail (see illustrations).

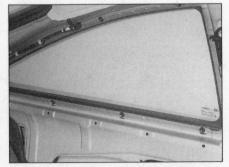

21.2 Trim panels removed, exposing rear quarter window securing nuts

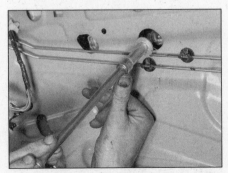

22.3 Remove the two upper bolts from the window regulator lever

22.4 Remove the inner weather strip from the top of the door

11

22.5a Remove the plastic cover from the upper rear corner of the door . . .

6 Remove the plastic grommet from the lower rear corner of the door, then remove the lower bolt that secures the rear guide rail **(see illustration)**.

7 Remove the rear guide rail **(see illustration)**.

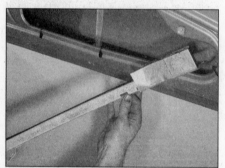

22.7 Remove the rear guide rail

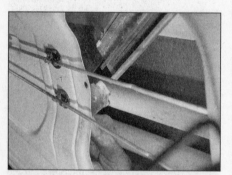

22.9 Manipulate the window away from the lifting guide

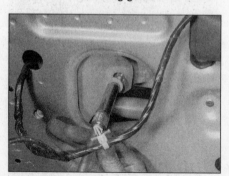

22.16b . . . and the one middle bolt

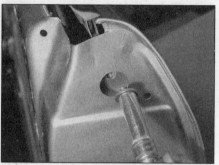

22.5b . . . then remove the upper bolt that secures the rear guide rail

8 Lower the window half way while supporting the window. Be careful to keep your fingers away from the mechanism while it is moving.

9 Manipulate the window away from the lifting guide **(see illustration)**.

10 Lift the window out, back end upwards **(see illustration)**.

Refitting

11 Refitting is the reverse of removal, but note the following points:

12 The window is frameless, so make sure it fits correctly and does not foul against the upper weatherstrip when the door is closed. If the front guide rail has not been moved, the window should fit correctly, although you can adjust the upper and lower bolts on the rear guide rail if necessary.

13 If the battery has been disconnected, the electric windows need to be re-programmed.

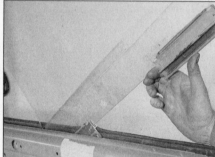

22.10 Lift the window out

22.17a Remove the top bolt from the front window guide . . .

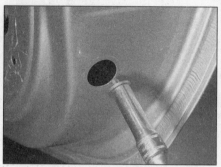

22.6 Remove the lower bolt that secures the rear guide rail

Close all the doors, switch on the ignition, then close each window in turn using the relevant switch. When the window has fully closed, continue to keep the switch depressed for at least five seconds.

Front quarter window

Removal

14 Remove the door inner trim panel and the plastic insulating sheet, as described in Section 14.

15 Remove the mirror, as described in Section 24. Hold onto the mirror as you undo the bolts so it doesn't fall.

16 Remove the two upper bolts and the one middle bolt **(see illustrations)**.

17 Remove the top and bottom guide bolts from the front window guide. The window has to be up to get the bottom bolt out **(see illustrations)**.

22.16a Remove the two upper bolts . . .

22.17b . . . and remove the bottom bolt

18 Lower the window.

19 Remove the inner weatherstrip from the top of the door, as described in paragraph 4.

20 Manipulate the front quarter window and tilt it backwards, then pull it out complete with the front window guide **(see illustration)**.

Refitting

21 Refitting is the reverse of removal, but note the following points:

22 The front window guide affects the fitting of both the front quarter window and the sash window. Make sure it is adjusted correctly, using the upper and lower bolts, so that the frameless windows do not foul against the upper weatherstrip when the door is closed. The upper and lower bolts on the rear guide rail **(see illustrations 22.5b and 22.6)** are also available for sash window adjustment.

23 Do not tighten the two upper bolts and the one middle bolt **(see illustrations 22.16a and 22.16b)** until the window adjustment is correct.

24 When refitting the mirror, remember to fit the weatherstrip under mirror. Make sure the mirror is not too far forward, otherwise it might foul against the bodywork when closing the door.

25 If the battery has been disconnected, the electric windows need to be re-programmed. Close all the doors, switch on the ignition, then close each window in turn using the relevant switch. When the window has fully closed, continue to keep the switch depressed for at least five seconds.

24.3 Removing the mirror glass (mirror removed)

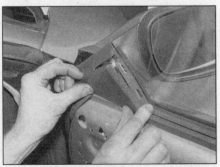

24.6 Remove the plastic cover from the mirror bracket

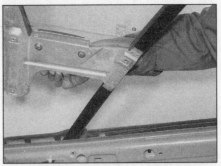

22.20 Remove the front quarter window complete with the window guide

23 Door window regulator - removal and refitting

Removal

1 Remove the door inner trim panel and the plastic insulating sheet, as described in Section 14.

2 Wind the window fully upwards and remove the two upper bolts from the regulator lever, as described in Section 22.

3 Wind the window down half way, pushing it at the same time because the mechanism will not bring it down with the bolts removed. Support the window in the half-open position by placing a wooden prop under it, ensuring that the prop is clear of the regulator mechanism.

4 Remove the plastic cover and grommet to access the bolts, then remove the rear guide rail, as described in Section 22.

5 Drill out the four rivets securing the regulator mechanism to the door, using an 8.5 mm (0.34 in) diameter drill **(see illustration)**. Take care not to damage the door panel.

6 Manipulate the regulator backwards to disengage it from the window guides, then withdraw it through the lower aperture.

7 Disconnect the battery negative lead (if not already done), then disconnect the multi-plug.

Refitting

8 Refitting is the reverse of removal, remembering the following points.

24.7 Disconnect the wiring multi-plug

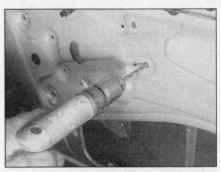

23.5 Drill out the four rivets securing the window regulator to the door

9 Ensure that the regulator arms are correctly positioned in the guide rails before securing the regulator assembly to the door.

10 Secure the regulator assembly to the door, using new rivets.

11 On completion, the electronic control system must be programmed, as described in Section 22.

24 Door mirror - removal and refitting

Glass renewal

1 If desired, the mirror glass can be removed for renewal without removing the mirror.

2 Disconnect the battery negative lead.

3 Carefully prise the glass from its balljoints using a screwdriver and disconnect the heater wires from the glass. Take care, as the glass is easily broken if forced **(see illustration)**.

4 To refit, simply push the glass onto the balljoints, ensuring that the heater wires are connected.

Mirror - removal and refitting

5 Disconnect the battery negative lead.

6 Remove the plastic cover from the mirror bracket on the inside front edge of the door **(see illustration)**.

7 Disconnect the wiring multi-plug **(see illustration)**.

8 Remove the three bolts and remove the mirror with the weatherstrip **(see illustrations)**.

24.8a Remove the three bolts . . .

11

24.8b ... and withdraw the mirror

Hold onto the mirror as you undo the bolts so it doesn't fall.

9 Refitting is the reverse of removal, but ensure that the rubber weather seal is correctly fitted under the mirror housing. Make sure the mirror is not too far forward, otherwise it might foul against the bodywork when closing the door.

Electric motor removal and refitting

Removal

10 Remove the mirror glass, as described previously in this Section.

11 Extract the three motor securing screws, and disconnect the wiring plug, then withdraw the motor **(see illustration)**.

Refitting

12 Refitting is the reverse of removal, but

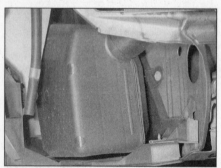

25.9 Air intake resonance box under right wing in front of wheel arch

25.11 Pull the front bumper mounting bracket forward and detach the lighting cable from the four clips

24.11 Mirror motor securing screws (arrowed)

ensure that the wiring is routed behind the motor, to avoid interfering with the adjustment mechanism.

25 Bumpers - removal and refitting

Front bumper trim

Removal

1 Undo the ambient air temperature sensor from under the front left-hand side of the bumper.

2 Undo the wheel arch screws, one on each side.

3 Working underneath the front bumper trim, remove the horizontal screws at each end, one on the nearside and one on the offside.

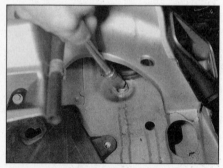

25.10 Remove the front bumper mounting bolts from the inner wing

25.12 When refitting the front bumper mounting bracket, make sure the two lugs go in the slots correctly

Remove the vertical screw, second from the end on the offside, but ignore the other screws.

4 Remove the three expanding grommets from under the trim. Punch the expanders through the grommets and retrieve them afterwards.

5 Remove the three screws at the top of the trim, under the bonnet closure.

6 Remove the trim by pulling it forward, and detach the headlamp washer hoses if fitted.

Refitting

7 Refitting is the reverse of removal.

Front bumper bracket

Removal

8 Remove the front bumper trim (see paragraphs 1 to 6).

9 Remove the air intake resonance box (see Chapter 4A), located under the wing in front of the right wheel arch **(see illustration)**.

10 Remove the bolts from the left and right inner wing, one on each side **(see illustration)**.

11 Pull the bracket forward, with the styrofoam padding, and detach the lighting cable from the four clips behind the bracket **(see illustration)**.

Refitting

12 Refitting is the reverse of removal. Make sure the two lugs in the bracket go in the slots correctly, one left, one right **(see illustration)**.

Rear bumper trim

Removal

13 Remove and disconnect the number plate lights (see Chapter 12).

14 Remove the two plastic grommets from under the rear of the bumper **(see illustration)**.

15 Remove the screws from under the left and right side of the bumper, one on each side **(see illustration)**.

16 Remove the screws from under the left and right wheel arches, one on each side **(see illustration)**.

17 Slide the bumper trim backwards **(see illustration)**.

25.14 Remove the two plastic grommets from under the rear bumper

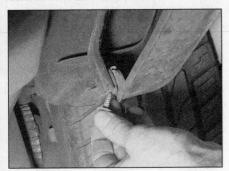

25.15 Remove the screws from under the left and right side of the rear bumper

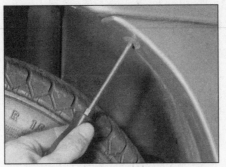

25.16 Remove the screws from under the rear wheel arches

25.17 Slide the rear bumper trim backwards

Refitting

18 Refitting is the reverse of removal.

Rear bumper complete assembly

Removal

19 The complete rear bumper assembly can be removed without separating the trim from the bracket. Remove and disconnect the number plate lights and remove the screws from the left and right hand side of the bumper and under the wheel arches (see paragraphs 13, 15 and 16) but do not remove the two plastic grommets.

20 Undo the bolts from the bumper supporting brackets under the car, then slide the complete assembly backwards so that the brackets come away from the bodywork **(see illustration)**.

21 Undo the number plate wiring clip from the support bracket.

Refitting

22 Refitting is the reverse of removal.

26 Radiator grille panel and V-grille - removal and refitting

Removal

1 Remove the front bumper trim (see Section 25).

2 To remove the plastic grille panel from the trim, remove the two screws **(see illustration)**, release the plastic clips and pull the panel backward.

3 To remove the V-grille from the trim, remove the screw from underneath **(see illustration)**,

undo the four clips at the top, and pull the V-grille forward.

4 You can remove the plastic panel and V-grille separately. You don't need to remove one before the other.

Refitting

5 Refitting is the reverse of removal.

27 Windscreen cowl panel - removal and refitting

Removal

1 Remove the bonnet sealing strip from the front of the cowl panel **(see illustration)**.

2 Remove the wiper arms, referring to Chapter 12 if necessary.

3 Undo the plastic nuts securing the cowl to the wiper mechanism.

4 Working from one end of the cowl panel, pull the cowl off its clips and move it aside **(see illustration)**. Take care as it is easily damaged. **Do not** tension the washer hose, or the cables for the underbonnet lamp if fitted.

5 If required, the cowl can be left in this position to access the components underneath. If you wish to remove the cowl completely, continue as follows:

6 Disconnect the hose from the washer reservoir and note its route for refitting.

7 If there is an underbonnet lamp, disconnect the battery negative lead, then disconnect the lamp wiring from the bulkhead and note its route for refitting.

25.20 Detach the rear bumper mounting brackets from the bodywork

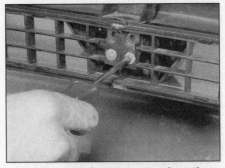

26.2 Remove the two screws from the plastic grille panel

26.3 Remove the screw from under the V-grille

27.1 Remove the bonnet sealing strip from the front of the cowl panel

27.4 Pull the windscreen cowl panel off its clips and move it aside

11

8 Feed the hose and wiring through the hole in the cowl, then remove the cowl.

Refitting

9 Refitting is the reverse of removal. Make sure that the panel is correctly seated along its length, that the washer fluid hose, and where applicable the underbonnet lamp wiring, is correctly routed.

28 Wheel arch liners - general

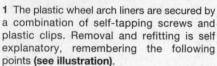

1 The plastic wheel arch liners are secured by a combination of self-tapping screws and plastic clips. Removal and refitting is self explanatory, remembering the following points (see illustration).
2 Some of the securing clips may be held in place using a central pin, which must be tapped out to release the clip.
3 The clips are easily broken during removal, and it is advisable to obtain a few spare clips for possible use when refitting.
4 Certain models may have additional underbody shields and splashguards fitted, which may be attached to the wheel arch liners.

29 Engine undershield - where fitted (DOHC models) - removal and refitting

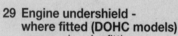

Removal

1 Apply the handbrake, then jack up the front of the vehicle, and support on axle stands (see "*Jacking and Vehicle Support*").
2 Extract the two securing screws, and remove the oil filter access panel.
3 Working around the edges of the splash shield, remove the self tapping screws that secure the shield to the body, noting that some of the screws also secure the wheel arch liners.
4 With the help of an assistant, pull the shield from the vehicle, and place it to one side to avoid damage.

Refitting

5 Refitting is the reverse of removal.

32.2 Forked tool being used to remove a clip from a trim panel

28.1 Removing a wheel arch liner

30 Fuel filler flap - removal and refitting

Removal

1 Open the flap for access to the four screws securing the flap to the rear wing.
2 Remove the securing screws, and withdraw the flap.

Refitting

3 Refitting is the reverse of removal.

31 Sunroof components

The sunroof is a complex piece of equipment consisting of a large number of components. It is strongly recommended that the sunroof mechanism is not disturbed unless necessary. If the sunroof mechanism is faulty, or requires overhaul, consult a dealer for advice.

32 Interior trim panels - general

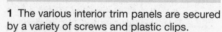

1 The various interior trim panels are secured by a variety of screws and plastic clips.
2 Where press-fit plastic fasteners are used, it is advisable to use a forked tool similar to that

33.2 Remove the screws from the sill trim panel

shown to remove them, to avoid damage to the clips and the trim panel (see illustration).
3 Removal and refitting of most of the trim panels is self-explanatory but in all cases, care must be taken, as the panels are easily damaged by careless handling and the use of sharp instruments to release clips.

33 Interior trim panels - removal and refitting

Sill trim panel

Removal

1 On early models, before 1992, the ABS-2E control module is located under a cover in the passenger side sill trim panel. When removing the panel, first extract the three securing screws and remove the cover from the ABS control module. Note that two of the screws are covered by plastic caps, which must be prised out to expose the screws. In 1992, the ABS-2EH system was introduced, which does not have the control module under the sill trim panel. Instead it is bolted to the hydraulic modulator in the engine compartment.
2 Undo the screws from the sill trim panel and remove it (see illustration).

Refitting

3 Refitting is the reverse of removal, but ensure that the panel is correctly seated with its top edge located under the sill weatherstrip.

Footwell side trim panel

Removal

4 Remove the screws from the front end of the sill trim panel so that it can be pulled away slightly from the footwell side trim panel.
5 Remove the two tabs from the footwell side trim panel and pull it off, releasing it from under the weatherstrip on the door aperture (see illustration).

Refitting

6 Refitting is the reverse of removal, but ensure that the trim panel is correctly seated under the weatherstrip.

33.5 Removing the driver's footwell side trim panel

Front body pillar trim panel

Removal

7 If a grab handle is fitted, prise off the end caps and undo the bolts securing the handle to the roof frame.

8 Remove the screw from the trim panel. Prise the trim panel from the body pillar to release the retaining clips. If necessary, pull the weatherstrip from the edge of the pillar.

Refitting

9 Refitting is the reverse of removal, but ensure that the trim panel is correctly seated under the weatherstrip.

Rear quarter trim panel

Removal

10 Pull the two tabs at the front of the rear seat cushion to release it from the catches on the vehicle floor, then lift the cushion and push the seat belt buckles through the holes. Remove the cushion from the vehicle.

11 Remove the sill trim panel, as described earlier in this Section.

12 Undo one screw at the top front corner of the rear quarter trim panel and peel back the weatherstrip (see illustration).

13 Grip the panel at the front top and bottom, and pull it out to release the studs. Then pull the panel forwards to release it from the remaining studs and withdraw it from the vehicle (see illustration).

Refitting

14 Refitting is the reverse of removal, but

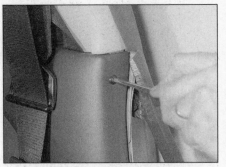
33.12 Undo the screw from the rear quarter trim panel and peel back the weatherstrip

ensure that the trim panel is correctly seated under the weatherstrip.

Centre body pillar trim panel

Removal

15 Remove the rear quarter trim panel, as described earlier in this Section.

16 Push upwards on the coat hanger clip at the top of the centre body pillar trim panel and remove the clip, then remove the screw from the panel underneath it (see illustrations).

17 Unclip the seat belt from the lower end of the trim panel and move it aside, then remove the screw from the panel (see illustration).

18 Prise off the clip to expose the upper mounting bolt on the front seat belt, then undo the bolt and recover the spacer (see illustration).

19 Pull off the trim panel.

33.13 Release the rear quarter trim panel from its studs and remove it

Refitting

20 Refitting is the reverse of removal.

Rear quarter window trim and parcel shelf panel

21 This component is a single plastic moulding which provides the trim panel above the rear quarter window and the cover for the parcel shelf behind the rear seat.

22 Remove the rear quarter trim panel, as described earlier in this Section.

23 Remove the centre body pillar trim panel, as described earlier in this Section.

24 Prise off the clip to expose the upper mounting bolt on the rear seat belt, then undo the bolt and recover the spacer (see illustration).

25 Remove the four screws from the panel. Three of them are covered by plastic caps. Two screws are on the section above the rear quarter window and two are on the parcel shelf cover (see illustrations).

26 Remove the panel carefully, taking care not to break it, and place it on the floor.

27 To remove the panel completely from the vehicle, undo the rear seat belt lower bolt (see illustration), and remove the panel and seat belt together.

28 To separate the seat belt from the panel, undo the bolt securing the seat belt reel to the parcel shelf cover, undo the clip at the front corner of the cover and open up the gap between the two parts of the moulding, taking care not to break it, then pass the seat belt through the gap.

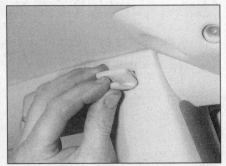
33.16a Remove the coat hanger clip on the centre body pillar trim panel . . .

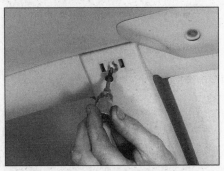
33.16b . . . then remove the screw from underneath it

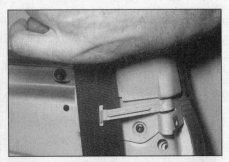
33.17 Unclip the seat belt to expose the lower screw on the centre body pillar trim panel

33.18 Undo the front seat belt upper mounting bolt

33.24 Undo the rear seat belt upper mounting bolt

11

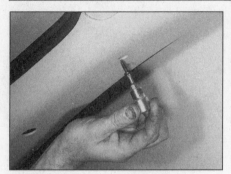

33.25a Remove two screws from the panel above the rear quarter window ...

29 Refitting is the reverse of removal. Note that you can remove and refit the seat belt while the panel is in place, as described in Section 38.

Luggage compartment rear trim panel

30 Undo the three nuts and five studs on the rear trim panel. One of the nuts is in the hazard warning sign compartment.
31 Release the top of the trim panel from the clips on the bodywork and remove the panel **(see illustration)**.
32 Refitting is the reverse of removal. Make sure the clips at the top of the panel are attached correctly.

Tailgate trim panels

33 The tailgate trim panels are secured by screws, and removal and refitting are self-explanatory. Note that the lower side panel securing screws also secure the rear panel.

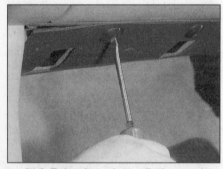

34.2 Releasing a footwell trim panel securing clip

34.5a Remove the four securing screws from the fusebox aperture ...

33.25b ... one screw from the side of the parcel shelf cover ...

33.27 Undo the rear seat belt lower bolt

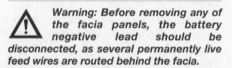

34 Facia panels -
removal and refitting

⚠️ *Warning: Before removing any of the facia panels, the battery negative lead should be disconnected, as several permanently live feed wires are routed behind the facia.*

Footwell trim panels

Removal

1 The lower footwell trim panels on the driver's and passenger sides are secured by turnbuckle type plastic clips.
2 To remove a panel, use a screwdriver to turn the heads of the clips through 90° **(see illustration)**, then withdraw the panel from the facia.

34.5b ... then withdraw the lower facia panel

33.25c ... and one screw from the front corner of the parcel shelf cover

33.31 Release the rear trim panel from its upper securing clips

Refitting

3 Refitting is the reverse of removal.

Driver's side lower facia panel

Removal

4 Open the flap covering the fusebox to expose the four lower facia panel securing screws.
5 Remove the four screws, then lower the panel and pull it towards the driver's door to release the two securing clips. Withdraw the panel from the facia **(see illustrations)**.

Refitting

6 Refitting is the reverse of removal.

Steering column shrouds

Removal

7 On models with an adjustable tilt steering column, move the column to its fully raised position, then unscrew the adjuster lever **(see illustration)**.

34.7 Removing the column adjuster lever

34.9a Prise out the covers . . .

34.9b . . . then remove the front column shroud securing screws

34.10a Remove the three lower column shroud securing screws . . .

8 Turn the steering wheel as necessary to expose one of the front steering column shroud securing screw covers.

9 Prise out the cover, and remove the column shroud securing screw, then turn the steering wheel to enable the remaining cover and screw to be removed **(see illustrations)**.

10 Remove the three securing screws from the underside of the lower column shroud, then remove the lower and upper shrouds **(see illustrations)**.

Refitting

11 Refitting is the reverse of removal, but make sure that the column switch gaiters engage in the cut-outs in the upper shroud.

Instrument panel lower trim panel

Removal

12 Remove the steering column shrouds, as

described previously in this Section.

13 The panel is secured by clips at either end, which must be released by pulling the ends of the panel from the facia **(see illustration)**. This is a tricky operation, as to release both ends, the panel must be bent slightly at its centre.

Caution: Take great care, as the panel is easily broken.

Refitting

14 Refitting is the reverse of removal.

Instrument panel upper trim panel

Removal

15 Remove the instrument panel lower trim panel, as described previously in this Section.

16 Extract the two now-exposed upper trim panel securing screws, one from each end of the panel, noting that the left-hand screw also

secures the heater control panel **(see illustration)**.

17 Withdraw the panel from the facia **(see illustration)**.

Refitting

18 Refitting is the reverse of removal.

Lighting switch panel

Removal

19 Remove the instrument panel upper and lower trim panels, as described previously in this Section.

20 Remove the remaining securing screw from the left-hand side of the lighting switch panel **(see illustration)**.

21 Pull the lighting switch panel from the facia, to release the securing clips at the right-hand end.

22 Ensure that the battery negative lead has been disconnected, then disconnect the

34.10b . . . then remove the lower . . .

34.10c . . . and upper shrouds (steering wheel removed)

34.13 Removing the instrument panel lower trim panel

34.16 Unscrewing the left-hand instrument panel upper trim panel securing screw

34.17 Withdrawing the instrument panel upper trim panel

34.20 Removing the lower left-hand lighting switch panel securing screw

11

34.22 Disconnecting the wiring plugs from the lighting switches

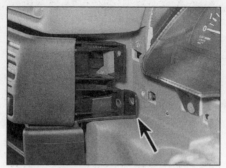

34.29a Right-hand securing lug (arrowed) behind heater control panel

34.29b Manipulating the radio/oddments tray from the facia

wiring plugs from the switches, and withdraw the switch panel **(see illustration)**.

Refitting

23 Refitting is the reverse of removal.

Radio/oddments tray panel

Removal

24 Remove the radio, as described in Chapter 12.
25 Remove the lower and upper instrument panel trim panels, as described previously in this Section.
26 Remove the lower securing screw from the right-hand side of the heater control panel.
27 Remove the clock or trip computer, as applicable, from the facia referring to Chapter 12, if necessary.
28 Remove the two now-exposed heater control panel securing screws from the

clock/trip computer aperture.
29 Carefully manipulate the heater control panel forwards within the limits of the control cable travel, then manipulate the radio/oddments tray out from the facia. This is a tricky operation, as the radio/oddments tray securing lugs rest behind the heater control panel securing lugs **(see illustrations)**. Take care not to strain the heater control cables.
30 With the radio/oddments tray removed, the radio support tray can be removed if desired by unscrewing the two securing screws, then sliding the tray forwards to disconnect the wiring and aerial plugs **(see illustrations)**.

Refitting

31 Refitting is the reverse of removal, taking care not to damage the heater control components as the radio/oddments tray is manipulated into position.

Glovebox assembly

> ⚠ **Warning: If an airbag is fitted, read the warning in Chapter 12, before starting work.**

Removal

32 Carefully prise the side trim panels from the passenger's oddments tray, using a screwdriver **(see illustration)**.
33 Open the glovebox, then using a screwdriver, release the two lower retaining clips at the rear of the oddments tray, and withdraw the oddments tray from the facia **(see illustrations)**.
34 Where applicable, prise out the glovebox lamp, and disconnect the wiring **(see illustration)**.
35 Extract the two upper and two lower securing screws, then withdraw the glovebox assembly from the facia **(see illustrations)**.

34.30a Slide the radio support tray from the facia . . .

34.30b . . . then disconnect the wiring and aerial plugs

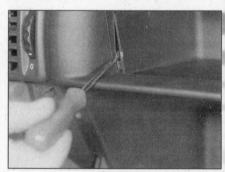

34.32 Prise the side trim panels from the oddments tray . . .

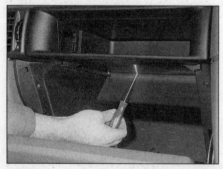

34.33a . . . then release the lower retaining clips . . .

34.33b . . . and withdraw the oddments tray

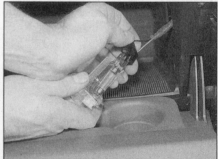

34.34 Prise out the glovebox lamp and disconnect the wiring

34.35a Extract the upper . . .

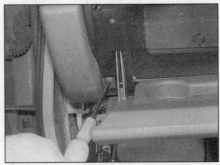

34.35b . . . and lower glovebox securing screws . . .

34.35c . . . then withdraw the glovebox

Refitting

36 Refitting is the reverse of removal, but where applicable, feed the wiring through the glovebox lamp aperture as the assembly is offered into position.

35.1a Prise the trim panel from the centre console . . .

35 Centre console - removal and refitting

Rear section

Removal

1 Prise the trim panel from the front of the rear centre console, under the handbrake grip, to expose the front securing screw, then remove the screw **(see illustrations)**.
2 Remove the rubber mat from the bottom of the cassette tray at the rear of the centre console, to expose the two rear securing screws, then remove the screws **(see illustrations)**.

3 Remove the screw that secures the handbrake gaiter **(see illustration)**.
4 Disconnect the battery negative lead, if not already done.
5 Pull up on the metal clamp on the wiring block to release it, then pull it backwards to disengage it from the wiring harness connector **(see illustrations)**.
6 Lift out the rear centre console, switches and wiring block as a complete unit, pulling it up over the handbrake **(see illustration)**.

Refitting

7 Refitting is the reverse of removal, but make sure the tabs on the console go into the slots in the moulding next to the connector block, otherwise the console will not go forward far enough **(see illustration)**.

35.1b . . . then remove the front securing screw

35.2a Remove the rubber mat from the cassette tray . . .

35.2b . . . then remove the two rear securing screws

35.3 Remove the screw that secures the handbrake gaiter

35.5a Pull up on the metal clamp on the wiring block to release it . . .

35.5b . . . then pull the wiring block backwards

11

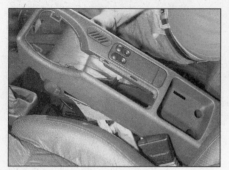

35.6 Lift out the rear centre console

Front section

Removal

8 Remove the rear centre console section, as described previously in this Section.
9 Remove the gearchange lever, as described in Chapters 7A or 7B, as applicable.
10 Disconnect the battery negative lead, if not already done.
11 Pull the ashtray assembly from the centre console, and disconnect the wiring plugs from the cigarette lighter **(see illustration)**.
12 Extract the two now-exposed screws securing the centre console to the facia **(see illustration)**.
13 Working at either side of the centre console, remove the two lower centre console-to-facia securing screws, and the two centre console-to-floor bracket securing screws **(see illustration)**.

35.12 Extract the two centre console-to-facia securing screws

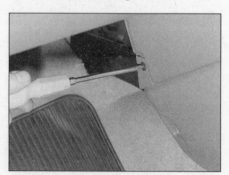

35.13 Unscrewing a side centre console-to-facia securing screw

35.7 Make sure the tabs go into the slots when refitting the rear centre console

14 The front centre console section can now be withdrawn.

Refitting

15 Refitting is the reverse of removal, but feed the cigarette lighter wiring through the aperture in the centre console as the centre console is offered into position.

---

36 Headlining -
removal and refitting

Models with sunroofs

1 The sunroof is a complex piece of equipment and should not be disturbed unless necessary. It is recommended that you should consult a dealer for advice if the headlining has to be removed from a model with a sunroof. You can, however, detach the headlining from the rear of the roof for the purpose of accessing the tailgate hinges (Section 9) and the radio aerial (Chapter 12).

Models without sunroofs

Removal

2 Disconnect the battery negative lead.
3 Remove the grab handle from the front body pillar trim panel, where fitted.
4 Remove the sunvisors. On models with illuminated sunvisor vanity mirrors, pull the lamp wiring from the roof as the sunvisor is withdrawn and disconnect the wiring plugs.
5 Prise the courtesy lamp and its trim panel from the roof and disconnect the wiring.

37.1 Withdraw the outer seat rail trim

35.11 Disconnecting the wiring plugs from the cigarette lighter

6 On models with anti-theft warning systems, release the ultrasonic sensor trim panels from the headlining and withdraw them downwards.
7 Remove the front body pillar and centre body pillar trim panels, as described in Section 33.
8 Loosen the upper edge of the rear quarter window trim panels, referring to Section 33 if necessary.
9 Open the tailgate, and prise the rear trim panel from the roof.
10 With the help of an assistant, lower the headlining from the roof, and withdraw it through the tailgate.

Refitting

11 Refitting is the reverse of removal.

---

37 Seats (without tensioners) -
removal and refitting

⚠️ **Warning: Refer to Section 40, if seat belt tensioners are fitted.**

Front seats

Removal

1 Remove the single securing screw from the front edge of the outer seat rail trim, then withdraw the trim **(see illustration)**.
2 Unclip the trim from the rear edge of the inner seat rail **(see illustration)**.
3 Remove the four bolts that secure the seat

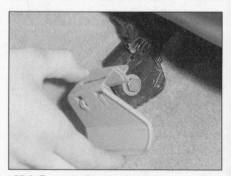

37.2 Remove the trim from the rear edge of the inner seat rail

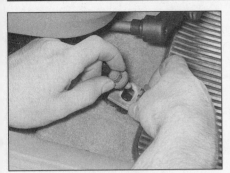

37.3 Removing a front seat rail securing bolt, washer and backplate

rails to the floor, and recover the washers and backplates **(see illustration)**.

4 If the front seats are heated, undo the multi-plug under the seat.

5 Withdraw the seat, complete with rails.

6 If required, the seat can be separated from the rails for attention to the adjustment mechanism.

Refitting

7 Refitting is the reverse of removal. Note that the manufacturers recommend the use of new bolts to secure the seat rails to the floor.

Rear seat cushion

Removal

8 Pull the two tabs at the front of the cushion to release it from the catches on the vehicle floor.

9 Lift up the cushion and feed the two centre

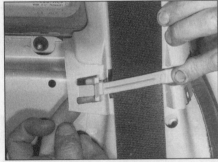

38.2 Unclip the front seat belt from the centre body pillar trim panel

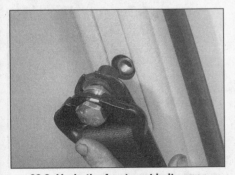

38.3 Undo the front seat belt upper mounting bolt

37.9 Feed the two centre seat belt buckles through the holes in the rear seat cushion

seat belt buckles through the holes **(see illustration)**.

10 Withdraw the cushion from the vehicle.

Refitting

11 Refitting is the reverse of removal. Push the seat cushion into position until the securing catches lock.

Rear seat back

Removal

12 Pull the two tabs at the front of the rear seat cushion, to release it from the catches, and pull the cushion away from the seat back.

13 Undo the bolts connecting the rear seat hinges to the left and right body panels. Recover the washers and shims **(see illustration)**.

14 Undo the nut and bolt connecting the two parts of the split rear seat to the central hinge, and recover the washer **(see illustration)**.

Refitting

15 Refitting is the reverse of removal.

---

38 Seat belts -
removal and refitting

Note: *For details on mechanical seat belt tensioners, refer to Section 39.*

Front seat belt

Removal

1 Remove the rear quarter trim panel, as

38.4 Undo the lower bolt and remove the front seat belt inertia reel unit

37.13 Bolt connecting rear seat hinge to body panel

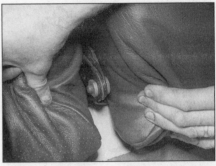

37.14 Nut and bolt connecting split rear seat to central hinge

described in Section 33.

2 Unclip the seat belt from the bottom of the centre body pillar trim panel **(see illustration)**.

3 Prise off the trim to expose the upper seat belt mounting bolt, then remove the bolt and recover the spacer **(see illustration)**.

4 Undo the lower bolt from the body panel and remove the inertia reel unit **(see illustration)**.

5 Remove the plastic caps from the two bolts securing the lower seat belt rail to the floor. Slacken one bolt and remove the other, then detach the belt from the rail and remove it from the vehicle **(see illustration)**.

6 If required, you can remove the upper mounting height adjuster. Remove the centre body pillar trim panel, as described in Section 33, then undo the two bolts and withdraw the adjuster **(see illustration)**.

7 If required, you can unbolt the seat belt stalk from the seat frame, but see Section 40

38.5 Remove the front seat belt from the lower rail

11

38.6 Undo the bolts and remove the front seat belt height adjuster

38.10 Undo the rear seat belt upper mounting bolt

38.11 Undo the rear seat belt lower bolt

for important safety procedures on models with seat belt tensioners.

Refitting

8 Refitting is the reverse of removal, but note that, when refitting the height adjuster, the arrows should be uppermost, pointing towards the roof. Ensure that the belt is fitted untwisted.

Rear seat belt

Removal

9 Remove the rear quarter trim panel, as described in Section 33.

38.12 Undo the bolt and remove the rear seat belt inertia reel unit from the parcel shelf box

10 Prise off the trim to expose the upper seat belt mounting bolt, then remove the bolt and recover the spacer **(see illustration)**.
11 Undo the lower seat belt mounting bolt **(see illustration)**.
12 Undo the rear seat belt mounting bolt from inside the parcel shelf box. Remove the inertia reel unit and place it on the floor **(see illustration)**.
13 Remove the screw from the front corner of the parcel shelf box, then undo the clip from inside the box and slightly separate the two parts of the plastic moulding around the seat belt hole, taking care not to damage it

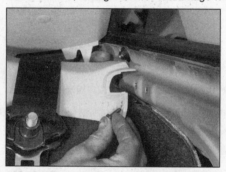

38.13a Remove the screw from the front corner of the parcel shelf cover . . .

(see illustrations). Feed the seat belt buckle and bracket through the enlarged hole, then withdraw the belt through the parcel shelf box.
14 If required, you can undo the two bolts on the floor and remove the central seat belt stalk **(see illustration)**.

Refitting

15 Refitting is the reverse of removal. Ensure that the belt is fitted untwisted.

---

39 Seat belt tensioners - general

1 All 1993-onwards Calibra models are equipped with mechanical front seat belt tensioners which automatically tighten the front seat belts in the event of a head-on collision. The mechanically operated device ensures that the seat belt remains close to the body, thus preventing the wearer from sliding out, under the belt, during impact **(see illustration)**.
2 The tensioner system consists of a powerful preloaded spring, contained in a cylinder, which is released in the event of severe impact. The spring pulls back the seat belt by means of a bowden cable and fulcrum

38.13b . . . and undo the clip from inside the parcel shelf cover

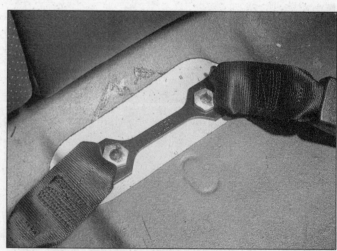

38.14 Central seat belt stalk on floor under rear seat cushion

mechanism attached to the belt stalk, mounted on the seat frame.

3 The tensioner assembly, fitted to the underside of the front seat, is maintenance free and, once triggered, must be replaced as a complete unit.

4 Due to the specialist safety related nature of the seat belt tensioner system, replacement must be entrusted to a suitably equipped Vauxhall dealer.

40 Seats, front (with seat belt tensioners) - removal and refitting

⚠️ *Warning: The seat belt tensioners fitted to the front seat assemblies may cause injury if triggered inadvertently. Before carrying out any work on the front seats, a safety fork must be inserted into the seat belt tensioner cylinder, to prevent the possibility of the tensioner being triggered (see paragraphs 3 and 4 below). Seats should always be transported and installed with the safety fork in place. If a seat is to be disposed of, the tensioner must be triggered before the seat is removed from the vehicle, by inserting the safety fork, and striking the tensioner cylinder sharply with a hammer. If the tensioner has been triggered due to a sudden impact or accident, the unit must be renewed, as it cannot be reset. Due to safety considerations, tensioner renewal should be entrusted to a Vauxhall dealer.*

Removal

1 Remove the single securing screw from the front edge of the outer seat rail trim, release the rear retaining lug and remove the trim rearwards.

2 Unclip the trim from the rear edge of the inner seat rail.

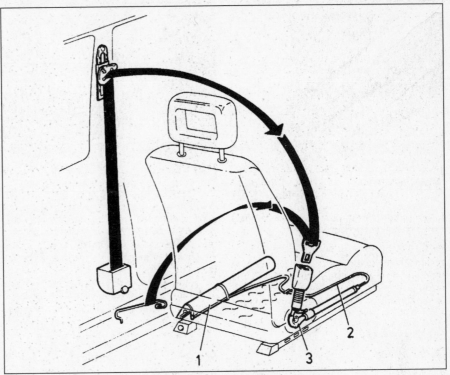

39.1 Mechanical seat belt tensioner system

1 Spring   *2 Bowden cable*   *3 Fulcrum mechanism*

3 Locate the plastic safety fork for the seat belt tensioner, which is usually taped to the outside of the tensioner spring cylinder.

4 Insert the fork into the aperture provided at the rear of the spring cylinder, ensuring that the fork engages securely **(see illustration)**.

5 Remove the four bolts which secure the seat rails to the floor **(see illustration)**. Recover the washers and backplates.

6 If the front seats are heated, undo the multi-plug under the seat.

7 Withdraw the seat complete with rails.

8 Seek the advice of a Vauxhall dealer if there is any doubt about the condition of the seat belt tensioner assembly.

Refitting

9 Refitting is the reverse of removal. Note that the manufacturers recommend the use of new bolts to secure the seat rails to the floor. Tighten the bolts to the specified torque wrench settings (see Specifications) in the order - rear inner, front inner, rear outer, front outer.

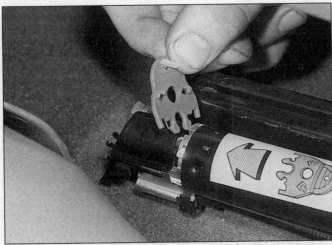

40.4 Insert the safety fork into the aperture in the seat belt tensioner spring cylinder

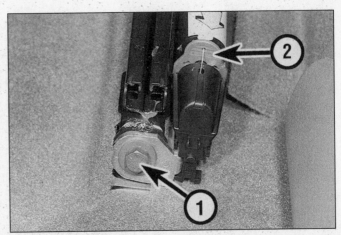

40.5 Front outer seat rail fixings

1 Securing bolt
2 Seat belt tensioner safety fork (inserted in the spring cylinder)

11

Chapter 12
Body electrical systems

Contents

Degrees of difficulty

Easy, suitable for novice with little experience	**Fairly easy,** suitable for beginner with some experience	**Fairly difficult,** suitable for competent DIY mechanic	**Difficult,** suitable for experienced DIY mechanic	**Very difficult,** suitable for expert DIY or professional

Specifications

Wiper blades
Type . . . . 19 ins. Champion X-48

Fuses
Rating:
Red	10 A
Blue	15 A
Yellow	20 A
Green	30 A

Torque wrench settings

	Nm	lbf ft
Airbag unit to steering wheel	10	7
Airbag control unit	10	7
Brackets, passenger airbag	22	16
Passenger airbag to bracket	8	6
Steering wheel to column	25	18

12

1 General information and precautions

⚠️ **Warning: Before carrying out any work on the electrical system, read through the precautions given in "Safety first!" at the beginning of this manual, and in Chapter 5.**

The electrical system is the 12-volt negative earth type. Power for the lights and all electrical accessories is supplied by a lead/acid type battery, which is charged by the alternator.

This Chapter covers repair and service procedures for the various electrical components not associated with engine. Information on the battery, alternator and starter motor can be found in Chapter 5.

It should be noted that, before working on any component in the electrical system, the battery negative terminal should first be disconnected, to prevent the possibility of electrical short-circuits and/or fires.

Whenever the occasion arises, carefully check the routing of the wiring harness, ensuring that it is correctly secured by the clips or ties provided so that it cannot chafe against other components. Carefully check points such as the clutch cable bracket, clutch housing and harness support bracket, the inlet manifold, the horn mounting bracket, the starter motor terminals, and the rear bumper and number plate lamp.

If evidence is found of the harness having chafed against other components, repair the damage and ensure that the harness is secured or protected so that the problem cannot occur again.

Caution: If the radio/cassette player fitted to the vehicle is one with an anti-theft security code, as the standard unit is, refer to "Radio/cassette player anti-theft system - precaution" in the Reference Section of this manual before disconnecting the battery.

2 Electrical fault-finding - general information

Note: *Refer to the precautions given in "Safety first!" (at the beginning of this manual) and to Section 1 of this Chapter before starting work. The following tests relate to testing of the main electrical circuits, and should not be used to test delicate electronic circuits (such as anti-lock braking systems), particularly where an electronic control module is used.*

A typical electrical circuit consists of an electrical component, any switches, relays, motors, fuses, fusible links or circuit breakers related to that component, and the wiring and connectors that link the component to both the battery and the chassis. To help to pinpoint a problem in an electrical circuit, wiring diagrams are included at the end of this Chapter.

Before attempting to diagnose an electrical fault, first study the appropriate wiring diagram, to obtain a complete understanding of the components included in the particular circuit concerned. The possible sources of a fault can be narrowed down by noting whether other components related to the circuit are operating properly. If several components or circuits fail at one time, the problem is likely to be related to a shared fuse or earth connection.

Electrical problems usually stem from simple causes, such as loose or corroded connections, a faulty earth connection, a blown fuse, a melted fusible link, or a faulty relay (refer to Section 3 for details of testing relays). Visually inspect the condition of all fuses, wires and connections in a problem circuit before testing the components. Use the wiring diagrams to determine which terminal connections will need to be checked, to pinpoint the trouble-spot.

The basic tools required for electrical fault-finding include the following:

a) a circuit tester or voltmeter (a 12-volt bulb with a set of test leads can also be used for certain tests).
b) a self-powered test light (sometimes known as a continuity tester).
c) an ohmmeter (to measure resistance).
d) a battery.
e) a set of test leads.
f) a jumper wire, preferably with a circuit breaker or fuse incorporated, which can be used to bypass suspect wires or electrical components.

Before attempting to locate a problem with test instruments, use the wiring diagram to determine where to make the connections.

To find the source of an intermittent wiring fault (usually due to a poor or dirty connection, or damaged wiring insulation), a "wiggle" test can be performed on the wiring. This involves wiggling the wiring by hand, to see if the fault occurs as the wiring is moved. It should be possible to narrow down the source of the fault to a particular section of wiring. This method of testing can be used in conjunction with any of the tests described in the following sub-Sections.

Apart from problems due to poor connections, two basic types of fault can occur in an electrical circuit - open-circuit, or short-circuit.

Open-circuit faults are caused by a break somewhere in the circuit, which prevents current from flowing. An open-circuit fault will prevent a component from working, but will not cause the relevant circuit fuse to blow.

Short-circuit faults are caused by a "short" somewhere in the circuit, which allows the current flowing in the circuit to "escape" along an alternative route, usually to earth. Short-circuit faults are normally caused by a breakdown in wiring insulation, which allows a feed wire to touch either another wire, or an earthed component such as the bodyshell. A short-circuit fault will normally cause the relevant circuit fuse to blow.

Finding an open-circuit

To check for an open-circuit, connect one lead of a circuit tester or voltmeter to either the negative battery terminal or a known good earth.

Connect the other lead to a connector in the circuit being tested, preferably nearest to the battery or fuse.

Switch on the circuit, remembering that some circuits are live only when the ignition switch is moved to a particular position.

If voltage is present (indicated either by the tester bulb lighting or a voltmeter reading, as applicable), this means that the section of the circuit between the relevant connector and the battery is problem-free.

Continue to check the remainder of the circuit in the same fashion.

When a point is reached at which no voltage is present, the problem must lie between that point and the previous test point with voltage. Most problems can be traced to a broken, corroded or loose connection.

Finding a short-circuit

To check for a short-circuit, first disconnect the load(s) from the circuit (loads are the components that draw current from a circuit, such as bulbs, motors, heating elements, etc.).

Remove the relevant fuse from the circuit, and connect a circuit tester or voltmeter to the fuse connections.

Switch on the circuit, remembering that some circuits are live only when the ignition switch is moved to a particular position.

If voltage is present (indicated either by the tester bulb lighting or a voltmeter reading, as applicable), this means that there is a short-circuit.

If no voltage is present, but the fuse still blows with the load(s) connected, this indicates an internal fault in the load(s).

Finding an earth fault

The battery negative terminal is connected to "earth" (the metal of the engine/transmission and the car body), and most systems are wired so that they only receive a positive feed. The current returns through the metal of the car body. This means that the component mounting and the body form part of that circuit. Loose or corroded mountings can therefore cause a range of electrical faults, ranging from total failure of a circuit, to a puzzling partial fault. In particular, lights may shine dimly (especially when another circuit sharing the same earth point is in operation). Motors (e.g. wiper motors or the radiator cooling fan motor) may run slowly, and the operation of one circuit may have an affect on another. Note that on many vehicles, earth straps are used between certain components, such as the engine/transmission and the body, usually where there is no metal-to-metal contact between components, due to flexible rubber mountings, etc.

To check whether a component is properly earthed, disconnect the battery, and connect

3.2 Main fuses and relays in facia panel

3.5 Removing a fuse

3.11 Relays in engine compartment box

one lead of an ohmmeter to a known good earth point. Connect the other lead to the wire or earth connection being tested. The resistance reading should be zero; if not, check the connection as follows.

If an earth connection is thought to be faulty, dismantle the connection, and clean back to bare metal both the bodyshell and the wire terminal or the component earth connection mating surface. Be careful to remove all traces of dirt and corrosion, then use a knife to trim away any paint, so that a clean metal-to-metal joint is made. On reassembly, tighten the joint fasteners securely; if a wire terminal is being refitted, use serrated washers between the terminal and the bodyshell, to ensure a clean and secure connection. When the connection is remade, prevent the onset of corrosion in the future by applying a coat of petroleum jelly or silicone-based grease.

3 Fuses and relays - general

Fuses

1 Fuses are designed to break a circuit when a predetermined current is reached, to protect the components and wiring which could be damaged by excessive current flow. Any excessive current flow will be due to a fault in the circuit, usually a short-circuit (Section 2).
2 The main fuses and relays are located in a panel at the lower right-hand side of the facia, under a hinged cover **(see illustration)**.
3 The circuits protected by the fuses and relays in the main fuse panel are marked on the inside of the panel cover.
4 A blown fuse can be recognised from its melted or broken wire.
5 To remove a fuse, first ensure that the relevant circuit is switched off. Then open the cover and pull the relevant fuse or relay from the panel **(see illustration)**. If desired, the lower end of the panel can be tilted forwards, after releasing the retaining clips to improve access.
6 Before renewing a blown fuse, trace and rectify the cause, and always use a fuse of the

correct rating. Never substitute a fuse of a higher rating, or make temporary repairs using wire or metal foil, as more serious damage or even fire could result.
7 Spare fuses are provided in the blank terminal positions in the fusebox.
8 Note that the fuses are colour-coded, see Specifications. Refer to the wiring diagrams for details of the fuse ratings and the circuits protected.
9 Additional fuses may exist among the relays behind the fuse panel and in the relay box in the engine compartment.

Relays

10 A relay is an electrically operated switch, used for the following reasons:
a) *A relay can switch a heavy current remotely from the circuit in which the current is flowing, allowing the use of lighter-gauge wiring and switch contacts.*
b) *A relay can receive more than one control input, unlike a mechanical switch.*
c) *A relay can have a timer function - for example, the intermittent wiper relay.*
11 Relays are situated in a variety of locations.
a) *In the main fuse panel.*
b) *Behind the main fuse panel. Remove the securing screws and pull the fuse panel forwards to improve access.*
c) *In the relay box at the left-hand rear of the engine compartment (see illustration).*
12 If a circuit or system controlled by a relay develops a fault, and the relay is suspect, operate the system. If the relay is functioning, it should be possible to hear it "click" as it is energised. If this is the case, the fault lies with the components or wiring of the system. If the relay is not being energised, then either the relay is not receiving a main supply or a switching voltage, or the relay itself is faulty. Testing is by the substitution of a known good unit, but be careful - while some relays are identical in appearance and in operation, others look similar but perform different functions.
13 To remove a relay, first ensure that the relevant circuit is switched off. The relay can then simply be pulled out from the socket, and pushed back into position.

4 Ignition switch and lock cylinder - removal and refitting

Removal

1 Disconnect the battery negative lead.
2 Turn the steering wheel as necessary to expose the two front steering column shroud securing screws, which are covered by plastic caps. Prise out the caps and remove the screws.
3 Remove the three securing screws from the underside of the lower column shroud, then remove both the upper and lower shrouds.
4 To remove the lock cylinder, insert the ignition key and turn it to position "II".
5 Insert a thin rod into the hole in the lock housing, then press the rod to release the detent spring, and pull out the lock cylinder using the key.
6 The ignition switch is secured to the steering lock housing by two grub screws. Disconnect the wiring plug, and remove the screws to extract the switch **(see illustration)**. Removal of the steering wheel, may aid removal. Refer to Chapter 10 or Section 53, as applicable. It is recommended that the switch and the lock cylinder are not both removed at the same time, so that their mutual alignment is not lost.

Refitting

7 Refitting is the reverse of removal.

4.6 Removing an ignition switch securing screw

12

7.2 Use a thin rod to depress the lighting switch knob retaining clip

7.3a Press the switch securing clips towards the switch spindle . . .

7.3b . . . then pull the switch from the facia

5 Direction indicator/lighting switch - removal and refitting

Removal

1 Disconnect the battery negative lead.
2 Turn the steering wheel as necessary to expose the two front steering column shroud securing screws, which are covered by plastic caps. Prise out the caps and remove the screws.
3 Remove the three securing screws from the underside of the lower column shroud, then remove both the upper and lower shrouds.
4 Disconnect the wiring plug from the switch.
5 Depress the switch retaining clip, and withdraw the switch from the housing.

Refitting

6 Refitting is the reverse of removal.

6 Wash/wipe switch - removal and refitting

Proceed as described in Section 5.

7 Facia panel switches - removal and refitting

1 Disconnect the battery negative lead.

Lighting switch

Removal

2 Pull the switch out slightly and insert a small screwdriver or rod through the hole in the bottom of the switch knob to depress the knob retaining clip. Pull the knob from the switch (**see illustration**).
3 Press the two now-exposed switch securing clips towards the switch spindle, then pull the switch from the facia and disconnect the wiring plug (**see illustrations**).
4 Note that the switch assembly cannot be dismantled, and if any part of the switch is faulty, the complete assembly must be renewed.

Refitting

5 Refitting is the reverse of removal.

Push-button switches

Removal

6 First check beneath the switch, if there is a small hole in the facia, insert a slim screwdriver or metal rod into it. Release the switch retaining spring clip by pressing it upwards against the switch, then remove the switch and disconnect its wiring. If there is no hole, remove the switch by prising it out of the facia using a small screwdriver. Lever gently under the switch's lower edge (use adhesive tape or a piece of card to protect the facia's finish). Disconnect the switch wiring plug and withdraw the switch (**see illustration**).

Refitting

7 Refitting is the reverse of removal.

Headlamp aim adjustment switch

8 The procedure is as described for push-button switches.

Hazard warning switch

Removal

9 Using a screwdriver, carefully prise the cap from the switch (**see illustration**).
10 Using a screwdriver with a piece of card under the blade to avoid damage to the facia trim, prise the ventilation nozzle from the facia.
11 Prise the switch from the facia and disconnect the wiring (**see illustration**).

Refitting

12 Refitting is the reverse of removal.

Heater blower motor switch

Removal

13 Remove the heater control panel, as described in Chapter 11.
14 Disconnect the wiring plug from the switch, if not already done.
15 Prise the switch out from the rear of the heater control panel.

Refitting

16 Refitting is the reverse of removal, but refer to Chapter 11, when refitting the heater control panel.

7.6 Prise the push-button switch from the facia

7.9 Prise the cap from the hazard warning flasher switch

7.11 Withdraw the hazard warning flasher switch from the facia

9.2 Prise the sunroof switch housing from the roof trim panel, triggering the four clips

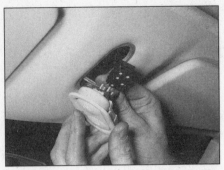

9.3 Disconnect the sunroof switch multi-plug

9.4 Separate the sunroof switch from its housing

8 Electric door mirror switch - removal and refitting

Removal

1 Disconnect the battery negative lead.
2 Prise the plastic surround from the door interior handle.
3 Free the trim panel from the top edge of the door by releasing the securing clips. This can be done using a screwdriver, but it is preferable to use a forked tool, to minimise the possibility of damage to the trim panel and the clips.
4 Note the position of the mirror switch wiring connector in the bracket at the top of the door, then separate the two halves of the connector.
5 Insert a screwdriver into the two slots and prise the switch from the door trim panel, then feed the wiring through the panel.

Refitting

6 Refitting is the reverse of removal, but ensure that the wiring is correctly routed, so as not to foul the door interior handle mechanism.

9 Sunroof operating switch - removal and refitting

Removal

1 Disconnect the battery negative lead.
2 Using a thin-bladed screwdriver, prise the switch housing from the roof trim panel, triggering the four clips **(see illustration)**. *Caution: Be careful not to break the clips, otherwise you will need to buy a new switch.*
3 Disconnect the multi-plug **(see illustration)**.
4 If required, separate the switch from its housing by pushing it out **(see illustration)**.

Refitting

5 Refitting is the reverse of removal.

10 Courtesy lamp switch - removal and refitting

HAYNES HiNT *Tape the wiring to the door pillar, to prevent it falling back into the door pillar. Alternatively, tie a piece of string to the wiring to retrieve it.*

Removal

1 Disconnect the battery negative lead.
2 Open the door and remove the switch securing screw.
3 Withdraw the switch from the door pillar, and pull the wiring out sufficiently to prevent it from springing back into the pillar.
4 Disconnect the wiring and remove the switch.

Refitting

5 Refitting is the reverse of removal.

11 Luggage compartment lamp switch - removal and refitting

Removal

1 Disconnect the battery negative lead.
2 Open the tailgate and remove the switch securing screw. The screw is behind the trim

11.2 Remove the luggage compartment lamp switch

panel, but you do not need to remove the panel to reach it **(see illustration)**.
3 Withdraw the switch from the body panel, and pull the wiring out sufficiently to prevent it from springing back into the body.
4 Disconnect the wiring and remove the switch.

Refitting

5 Refitting is the reverse of removal.

12 Brake lamp switch - removal and refitting

Removal

1 Disconnect the battery negative lead.
2 Remove the lower trim panel from the driver's footwell.
3 Disconnect the wiring plug from the brake lamp switch, then twist the switch anti-clockwise and remove it from its bracket.

Refitting

4 Refitting is the reverse of removal.

13 Handbrake "on" warning lamp switch - removal and refitting

For access to the switch, the handbrake lever must be removed. Removal and refitting of the switch is described as part of the handbrake lever removal and refitting procedure, in Chapter 9.

14 Oil pressure warning lamp switch - removal and refitting

Removal

1 Disconnect the battery negative lead.
2 The switch is screwed into the oil pump, on the inlet manifold side of the engine **(see illustration)**.
3 In most cases the switch can be reached quite easily from above. However, on some models access will be easier if the front of the

12

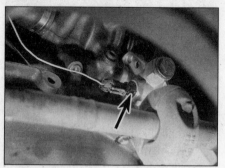

14.2 Oil pressure warning lamp switch (arrowed) viewed from underneath vehicle - SOHC model

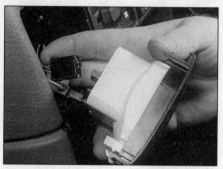

16.3 Disconnect the wiring plugs from the clock

18.4 Unscrewing a lower instrument panel securing screw

vehicle is jacked up and supported on axle stands (see "*Jacking and Vehicle Support*") (ensure that the handbrake is securely applied) and the front right-hand roadwheel is removed.

4 Disconnect the switch wire and use a spanner to unscrew the switch. As you withdraw the switch, swiftly plug the hole in the oil pump to minimise the loss of oil and to prevent the entry of dirt.

Refitting

5 Refitting is the reverse of the removal procedure; tighten the switch securely but do not overtighten it, reconnect its wire, then check and if necessary top-up the oil level, as described in "*Weekly checks*". Wash off any spilt oil and check for leaks when the engine is restarted.

15 Cigarette lighter - removal and refitting

Removal

1 Disconnect the battery negative lead.
2 Slide the ashtray/cigarette lighter assembly from the facia, then disconnect the wiring and slide the illumination bulb from the cigarette lighter.
3 To remove the cigarette lighter assembly, simply pull it from the illumination ring

assembly. If desired, the illumination ring assembly can be removed, by pulling it from the housing after depressing the retaining clips.

Refitting

4 Refitting is the reverse of removal.

16 Clock or trip computer - removal and refitting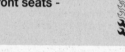

Removal

1 Disconnect the battery negative lead.
2 Using a thin-bladed screwdriver, carefully prise the clock or trip computer from the facia panel.
3 Disconnect the wiring plugs and withdraw the clock or trip computer (**see illustration**).

Refitting

4 Refitting is the reverse of removal.

17 Heated front seats - general

Heating pads are fitted to the front seats of some models. Before attempting to remove a seat so equipped, disconnect the battery and the leads from the heating pad.

18 Instrument panel - removal and refitting

Removal

1 Disconnect the battery negative lead.
2 Remove the steering wheel (see Chapter 10 or Section 53, where applicable).
3 Remove the steering column shrouds, and the instrument panel upper and lower trim panels (see Chapter 11).
4 Remove the single upper, and two lower, instrument panel securing screws (**see illustration**).
5 Carefully withdraw the instrument panel, and disconnect the speedometer cable and the two wiring plugs. Note that the speedometer cable is retained by a clip, which must be pressed towards the speedometer to release the cable (**see illustration**).
6 If desired, the instrument panel can be dismantled, with reference to Section 19.

Refitting

7 Refitting is the reverse of removal, but ensure that the speedometer cable is not kinked or twisted between the instrument panel and the bulkhead as the panel is refitted.

19 Instrument panel components - removal and refitting

1 With the instrument panel removed, as described in Section 18, continue as follows.

Panel illumination and warning lamp bulbs

Removal

2 Twist the relevant bulbholder clockwise, and withdraw it from the printed circuit board on the rear of the instrument panel (**see illustration**).
3 The bulbs are integral with the bulbholders, and must be renewed as a unit.

Refitting

4 Refitting is the reverse of removal.

18.5 Disconnecting an instrument panel wiring plug. Note speedometer cable retaining clip

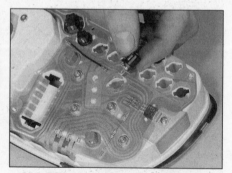

19.2 Withdrawing an instrument panel illumination lamp bulb

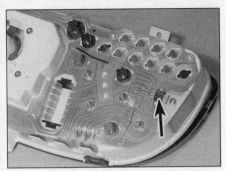

19.5 Instrument panel voltage stabiliser (arrowed)

19.8 Removing the instrument panel shroud

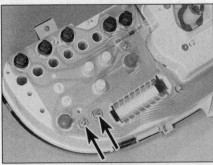

19.12 Tachometer securing nuts (arrowed)

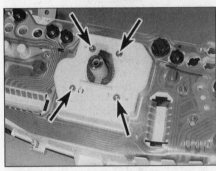

19.14 Speedometer securing screws (arrowed)

Voltage stabiliser

Removal

5 Remove the single securing screw from the rear of the instrument panel, then pull the voltage stabiliser from the contacts on the printed circuit board **(see illustration)**.

Refitting

6 Refitting is the reverse of removal.

Fuel and temperature gauges - "low series" models

Removal

7 Pull the trip meter reset pin from the front of the panel.
8 Release the two retaining clips at the top of the panel, and remove the panel shroud **(see illustration)**.
9 Unscrew the two securing nuts, and withdraw the relevant gauge through the front of the instrument panel.

Refitting

10 Refitting is the reverse of removal.

Fuel and temperature gauge assembly - "high series" models

11 The procedure is as described in paragraphs 7 to 10 inclusive, except that the gauge assembly is secured by four nuts.

Tachometer

12 The procedure is as described in paragraphs 7 to 10 inclusive except that the tachometer is secured by three nuts **(see illustration)**.

Speedometer

Removal

13 Proceed as described in paragraphs 7 and 8.
14 Extract the four securing screws from the rear of the panel **(see illustration)**.

Refitting

15 Refitting is the reverse of removal.

Printed circuit board

Removal

16 Remove all bulbs and instruments, and the voltage stabiliser, as described previously in this Section.

17 Carefully peel the printed circuit board from the instrument panel.

Refitting

18 Refitting is the reverse of removal, but ensure that the printed circuit board is seated correctly on the rear of the instrument panel.

20 Trip computer components - removal and refitting

1 Disconnect the battery lead.

Display module

Removal

2 Using a thin-bladed screwdriver, carefully prise the module from the facia panel.
3 Disconnect the wiring plug and withdraw the module.

Refitting

4 Refitting is the reverse of removal.

Display module illumination bulb

Removal

5 Remove the display module, as described in paragraphs 2 and 3.
6 Using a length of rubber sleeving of similar diameter, or an alternator tool, extract the bulb by inserting the tool through the hole in the side of the display module **(see illustration)**.

Refitting

7 Refitting is the reverse of removal.

20.6 Removing the trip computer display module illumination bulb

Operating switch

Removal

8 Remove the rear section of the centre console, as described in Chapter 11.
9 Release the wiring plug from the switch using a screwdriver.
10 Lift the switch, then pull it down and out from the centre console.

Refitting

11 Refitting is the reverse of removal.

Outside air temperature sensor

Removal

12 The sensor is located at the left-hand end of the front bumper **(see illustration)**.
13 Prise the cover cap from the bumper, then unclip the sensor, and disconnect the wiring plug.

20.12 Trip computer outside air temperature sensor location (arrowed)

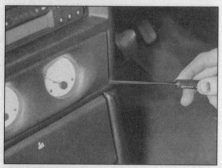

21.1 Prise out the oil pressure and battery gauge panel with a screwdriver

Refitting

14 Refitting is the reverse of removal.

21 Oil pressure and battery condition gauges - removal and refitting

Removal

1 Prise out the panel with a screwdriver **(see illustration)**.
2 Remove the panel from the facia and disconnect the multi-plug **(see illustration)**.

Refitting

3 Refitting is the reverse of removal.

22 Check control system components - removal and refitting

1 Disconnect the battery negative lead.

Warning lamp bulbs

2 The warning lamp bulbs are located in the instrument panel, and removal and refitting are described in Section 19.

Control module

Removal

3 The control module is located behind the passenger side of the facia, above the glovebox.
4 Remove the glovebox assembly, as

22.18 Engine oil level sensor - C20 XE model

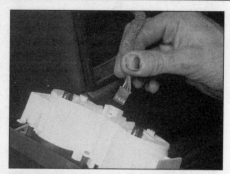

21.2 Remove the panel from the facia and disconnect the multi-plug

described in Chapter 11.
5 Disconnect the control module wiring plug, then release the control module from its mounting and withdraw the unit.

Refitting

6 Refitting is the reverse of removal.

Coolant level sensor

Removal

7 The coolant level sensor is integral with the coolant expansion tank cap.
8 Disconnect the wiring from the top of the cap, then unscrew the cap and withdraw it from the expansion tank.
9 If faulty, the complete cap assembly must be renewed.

Refitting

10 Refitting is the reverse of removal.

Washer fluid level sensor

Removal

11 The sensor is mounted in the side of the fluid reservoir.
12 Disconnect the wiring from the sensor, then unscrew the sensor from the fluid reservoir. If the fluid level is above the level of the sensor, be prepared for fluid spillage.

Refitting

13 Refitting is the reverse of removal.

Brake fluid level sensor

14 The procedure is as described for the coolant level sensor in paragraphs 7 to 10 inclusive.

23.5 Undo the bolt and remove the horns

Engine oil level sensor

Removal

15 Apply the handbrake, jack up the front of the vehicle, and support securely on axle stands (see "*Jacking and Vehicle Support*") positioned under the body side members.
16 On DOHC models, remove the engine undershield, as described in Chapter 11, if there is one.
17 Disconnect the sensor wiring plug.
18 Unscrew the three or four sensor securing screws, as applicable, and withdraw the sensor, manipulating the float through the hole in the sump **(see illustration)**. Recover the sealing ring. Be prepared for some oil spillage.
19 Examine the condition of the sealing ring, and renew if necessary.

Refitting

20 Refitting is the reverse of removal. On completion, check, and if necessary top-up, the engine oil level (see "*Weekly checks*").

Bulb failure sensor

Removal

21 The bulb failure sensor is mounted behind the fuse/relay panel in the facia.
22 Release the retaining clips from the lower end of the fuse/relay panel, and tilt it forwards.
23 Reach up behind the fuse/relay panel, and pull the sensor from its socket.

Refitting

24 Refitting is the reverse of removal.

23 Horns - removal and refitting

1 The twin horns are mounted under the left wing, between the front bumper and the wheel arch. Other components may be mounted above the horns, as follows:
a) *The AIR pump, on models with a pulsair system;*
b) *The headlamp washer tank, on models with headlamp washers.*

Removal

2 Disconnect the battery negative lead.
3 Remove the front bumper trim (see Chapter 11).
4 Disconnect the horn wiring connectors.
5 Undo the bolt and remove the horns with their mounting bracket **(see illustration)**.
6 If required, undo the two nuts and separate the horns from the bracket.

Refitting

7 Refitting is the reverse of removal.

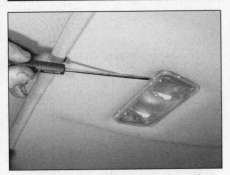

24.3 Prise the courtesy lamp from the headlining

24 Interior lamps -
removal and refitting

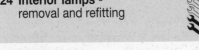

Overhead courtesy and map reading lamp

1 On models with sunroofs, the overhead lamp is in the headlining to the rear of the sunroof. On models without sunroofs, it is at the front of the headlining above the windscreen.

Removal

2 Disconnect the battery negative lead.
3 Using a thin-bladed screwdriver, carefully prise the lamp out of the headlining **(see illustration)**.
4 Detach the four wiring spade connectors **(see illustration)**.

25.5 Prise out the luggage compartment lamp

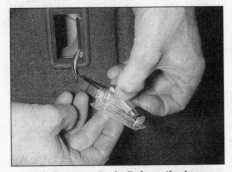

25.6 Remove the bulb from the lamp

24.4 Detach the four wiring spade connectors

Refitting

5 Refitting is the reverse of removal. The wiring spade connectors are all different, so they cannot be wrongly connected.

Other interior lamps

6 Remove the lamp or bulbholder as described in Section 25, then disconnect the wiring. Refitting is the reverse of removal.

25 Interior lamp bulbs -
renewal

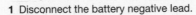

1 Disconnect the battery negative lead.

Overhead courtesy and map reading lamp

Removal

2 Using a thin-bladed screwdriver, prise off the lens at either the front or back, in line with the switches **(see illustration)**.
3 Remove the courtesy lamp bulb by pulling it downwards. Remove the map reading bulbs by pulling them sideways out of the bulbholders.

Refitting

4 Refitting is the reverse of removal.

Luggage compartment, under-bonnet and glovebox lamps

Removal

5 Using a thin-bladed screwdriver, prise the lamp from its location **(see illustration)**.

25.12 Removing the clock illumination lamp bulbholder

25.2 Prise off the courtesy lamp lens in line with the switches

6 Carefully prise the bulb from the lamp **(see illustration)**.

Refitting

7 Refitting is the reverse of removal.

Cigarette lighter illumination lamp

Removal

8 Slide the ashtray/cigarette lighter assembly from the facia, then disconnect the wiring and pull the bulbholder from the rear of the cigarette lighter housing.
9 The bulb is a push fit in the bulbholder.

Refitting

10 Refitting is the reverse of removal.

Clock illumination lamp

11 Remove the clock (Section 16).
12 Twist the bulbholder and pull it from the rear of the clock **(see illustration)**.
13 The bulb is a push fit in the bulbholder.

Trip computer display module illumination lamp

14 Refer to Section 20.

Heater control panel illumination lamp

Removal

15 Remove the heater control panel, as described in Chapter 11.
16 Pull the bulbholder from the rear of the control panel **(see illustration)**.
17 The bulb is a push fit in the bulbholder.

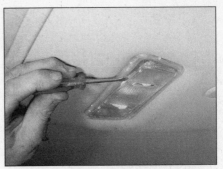

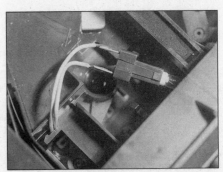

25.16 Heater control panel illumination lamp bulbholder withdrawn

25.20 Prise out the vanity mirror and lamp panel

25.21 Remove the vanity mirror bulbs

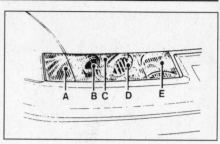

26.1 Headlamp unit

A Indicator	D Fog lamp
B Dipped beam	E Main beam
C Parking lamp	

Refitting

18 Refitting is the reverse of removal.

Facia panel switch illumination lamp

19 If a bulb fails in one of the facia panel switches, the complete switch assembly must be renewed, as described in Section 7, as no individual spare parts are available.

Vanity mirror illumination lamp

Removal

20 Lower the sunvisor and, using a thin-bladed screwdriver, prise out the whole mirror panel including both lamps **(see illustration)**.
21 Pull the bulbs from the spring contacts **(see illustration)**.

Refitting

22 Refitting is the reverse of removal.

26 Headlamp unit - removal and refitting

1 The headlamps (low and high beam), indicators, fog lamps and parking lamps are all housed in a single unit **(see illustration)**.

Removal

2 Disconnect the battery negative lead.
3 Remove the front bumper trim, (Chapter 11).
4 Remove the foam padding but leave the bumper bracket in place **(see illustration)**.
5 Remove the three securing screws from around the headlamp, two at the top and one at the bottom.
6 Withdraw the headlamp unit and disconnect the indicator bulbholder, the main multi-plug and the adjustment motor plug **(see illustrations)**.

7 If required, the headlamp lens can be removed by releasing the spring clips around its edge.

Refitting

8 Refitting is the reverse of removal.
9 On completion, have the headlamp alignment checked, with reference to Section 28.

27 Headlamp aim adjustment motor - removal and refitting

Removal

1 Remove the headlamp (Section 26).
2 Twist the motor one quarter turn (clockwise on the right headlamp, anticlockwise on the left headlamp) to release it from the headlamp, then carefully disconnect the motor spindle balljoint and remove the motor **(see illustrations)**.

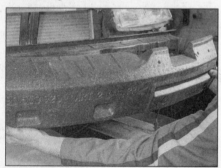

26.4 Remove the foam padding from the bumper bracket

26.6a Withdraw the headlamp unit and disconnect the indicator bulbholder . . .

26.6b . . . disconnect the main headlamp multi-plug . . .

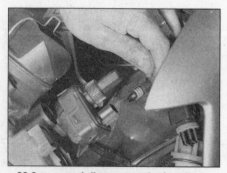

26.6c . . . and disconnect the headlamp aim adjustment motor plug

27.2a Twist the headlamp aim adjustment motor one quarter turn . . .

27.2b . . . then disconnect the motor spindle balljoint and remove the motor

28.3 Headlamp aim vertical adjustment switch for load compensation

Refitting

3 Refitting is the reverse of removal, but ensure that the motor is correctly engaged with the balljoint.

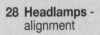

28 Headlamps - alignment

1 Correct alignment of the headlamp beams is most important, not only to ensure good vision for the driver, but also to protect other drivers from being dazzled.
2 Accurate alignment should be carried out using optical beam setting equipment.
3 The headlamp aim can be vertically adjusted to compensate for vehicle load using a motor mounted behind the headlamp (see Section 27). The motor is operated by a facia-

30.3a Undo the six screws from behind the rear lamp unit . . .

30.3b . . . and withdraw the unit

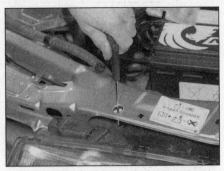

28.4 Adjusting the horizontal headlamp aim

mounted switch **(see illustration)**.
a) Position '0', is for correct alignment if just the driving seat is occupied.
b) Position '1', if all seats are occupied.
c) Position '2', if all seats occupied and luggage.
d) Position '3', for just driver and luggage.
4 In an emergency, the following adjustments can be made. Set the facia-mounted switch to position '0' and turn the knob on the adjustment motor until the vertical alignment is correct with just the driver's seat occupied. Then insert a screwdriver into the hole above the headlamp and turn the adjustment screw until the horizontal aim is correct **(see illustration)**. After making adjustments, the alignment should be checked using beam setting equipment at the earliest opportunity.

29 Side repeater lamp - removal and refitting

Removal

1 Disconnect the battery negative lead.
2 Remove the wheel arch liner, as described in Chapter 11.
3 Working in the engine compartment, disconnect the wiring plug, and detach the earth lead from the body panel.
4 Working under the wheel arch, depress the retaining tabs and manipulate the lamp through the outside of the wing, pulling the wiring and the grommet from the inner wing panel.

30.4 Disconnect the rear lamp unit multi-plug

5 The lens can be removed from the lamp by twisting it to release the retaining clips.
6 Check the condition of the rubber sealing ring, and renew if necessary.

Refitting

7 Refitting is the reverse of removal.

30 Rear lamp unit - removal and refitting

Right rear lamp with tailgate lock

Removal

1 Disconnect the battery negative lead.
2 The tailgate lock housing and cylinder are mounted in the right rear lamp. Disconnect the main catch rod and central locking rod, and detach the central locking motor from the lock housing, but leave the lock housing and cylinder in place (see Chapter 11).
3 Undo the six screws from behind the lamp unit and withdraw the unit **(see illustrations)**.
4 Disconnect the lamp unit multi-plug **(see illustration)**.
5 Disconnect the central locking detector wire from behind the body panel, but leave it attached to the lamp unit.

Refitting

6 Refitting is the reverse of removal.

Left rear lamp

7 Removal and refitting is the same as for the right rear lamp except that there are no locking components to be detached and everything is accessible by opening the flap in the trim panel behind the lamp unit.

31 Number plate lamp, rear - removal and refitting

Removal

1 Disconnect the battery negative lead.
2 Using a thin-bladed screwdriver, carefully prise the lamp surround from the bumper **(see illustration)**.

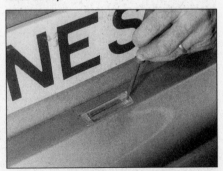

31.2 Prise the number plate lamp surround from the bumper

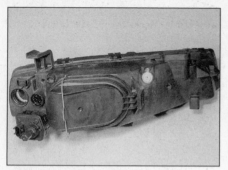

32.1 Rear view of the left headlamp unit, removed from the vehicle

3 Pull the lamp from the bumper and disconnect the wiring.

Refitting

4 Refitting is the reverse of removal.

---

32 Exterior lamp bulbs - renewal

Caution: The glass envelopes of the headlamp and foglamp bulbs must not be touched with the fingers. If the glass is accidentally touched, it should be washed with methylated spirits and dried with a soft cloth. Failure to observe this procedure may result in premature bulb failure.

1 The headlamps (low and high beam), indicators, fog lamps and parking lamps are all housed in a single unit **(see illustration)**.

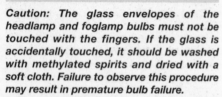

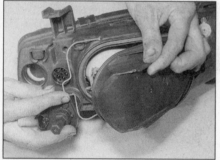

32.6 Release the retaining clip and remove the cover from behind the headlamp

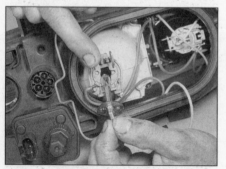

32.7b . . . then lift the retaining clip and withdraw the bulb

---

32.3 Remove the cover from above the headlamp

This illustration shows the rear view of the left headlamp unit, removed from the vehicle, but all the bulbs are accessible with the unit in the vehicle.

2 Disconnect the battery negative lead.

Headlamp main beam

Removal

3 Remove the cover from above the headlamp **(see illustration)**.
4 Pull the wiring plug from the base of the bulb, then release the two spring clips by pushing them outwards. Grasp the bulb by its contacts and carefully withdraw it **(see illustration)**. **Do not** touch the bulb glass.

Refitting

5 Refitting is the reverse of removal. Make sure the fixing lugs on the bulb holder engage in the reflector.

32.7a Remove the connector from the dipped beam bulb . . .

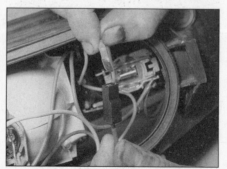

32.8a Undo the foglamp bulb connector . . .

32.4 Withdraw the headlamp main beam bulb

Headlamp dipped beam, foglamp and parking lamp

Removal

6 Working in the engine compartment, release the retaining clip, and remove the cover from behind the headlamp **(see illustration)**.
7 To remove the dipped beam bulb, remove the connector from the bulb base, press together the two ends of the retaining clip and swivel it upwards, then grasp the bulb by its contacts and carefully withdraw it **(see illustrations)**. **Do not** touch the bulb glass.
8 To remove the foglamp bulb, undo the connector, press apart the two ends of the retaining clip and swivel it upwards, then carefully withdraw the bulb and its connecting cable **(see illustrations)**. **Do not** touch the bulb glass.
9 To remove the parking lamp bulb, press the bulb holder in and give it a quarter turn anti-clockwise, then withdraw it. Remove the bulb from the holder **(see illustration)**.

Refitting

10 Refitting is the reverse of removal.

Front indicator lamp

Removal

11 The front indicator lamp is accessed from the rear of the headlamp unit, above the adjustment motor and alongside the main headlamp multi-plug. Working in the engine compartment, twist the bulbholder anti-clockwise and pull it from the lamp unit **(see illustration)**.
12 Remove the bulb from the holder.

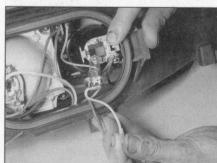

32.8b . . . then lift the retaining clip and withdraw the bulb and its connecting cable

32.9 Remove the parking lamp holder and bulb

32.11 Disconnect the indicator bulbholder

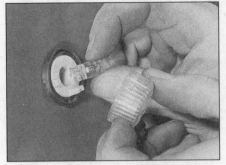

32.14 Removing a front indicator side repeater lamp bulb

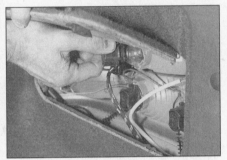

32.17 Lift the flap behind the rear lamp and unscrew a bulbholder

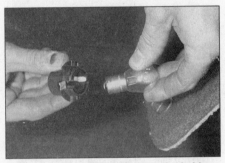

32.18 Remove the bulb from the holder

32.21 Unclip the lens from the rear number plate lamp

Refitting

13 Refitting is the reverse of removal.

Front indicator side repeater lamp

Removal

14 Twist the lamp lens anti-clockwise and pull it from the lamp, then remove the bulb **(see illustration)**.

Refitting

15 Refitting is the reverse of removal, but ensure that the rubber sealing ring is correctly seated between the lens and the body panel.

Rear lamp unit

Removal

16 The rear lamp unit contains the following lamps, all mounted in the same type of bulb holder:
 a) *Indicator, at outside top;*
 b) *Reverse lamp, at inside top;*
 c) *Tail lamp and brake lamp, at outside bottom;*
 d) *Fog lamp, at inside bottom.*
17 Working in the luggage compartment, lift the flap in the trim panel behind the lamp unit and unscrew the appropriate bulbholder **(see illustration)**.
18 Remove the bulb from the holder by pressing and turning **(see illustration)**.

Refitting

19 Refitting is the reverse of removal.

Rear number plate lamp

Removal

20 Using a thin-bladed screwdriver, carefully prise the lamp surround from the bumper.

21 Pull the lamp from the bumper, taking care not to strain the wiring, and unclip the lens **(see illustration)**.
22 Remove the bulb from the holder.

Refitting

23 Refitting is the reverse of removal.

---

33 Wiper blades - renewal

Removal

1 The wiper blades should be renewed when they no longer clean the glass effectively.
2 Lift the wiper arm away from the glass. On some models it may be more convenient to do this with the bonnet open.
3 With the blade at 90° to the arm, depress the spring clip and slide the blade from the hook **(see illustration)**.

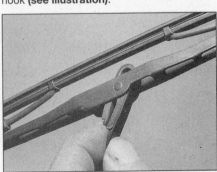

33.3 Removing a wiper blade

4 If necessary, extract the two metal inserts and unhook the wiper rubber.

Refitting

5 Refitting is the reverse of removal, but where applicable, make sure that the cut-outs in the metal inserts securing the rubber to the blade face each other.

---

34 Wiper arms - removal and refitting

Removal

1 The wiper motor should be in its parked position before removing the wiper arm. Mark the position of the blade on the glass with adhesive tape as a guide to refitting.
2 Lift the hinged covers, and remove the nuts and washers securing the arms to the spindles **(see illustration)**.

34.2 Lift the hinged cover and remove the nut and washer - tailgate wiper

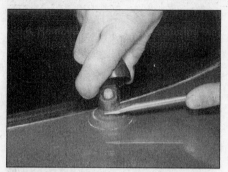

34.3 Prise the wiper arm from the spindle

3 Prise the arms from the spindles, using a screwdriver if necessary **(see illustration)**. Take care not to damage the paintwork.

Refitting

4 Refitting is the reverse of removal. Note that the passenger side wiper arm is longer than that fitted to the driver's side. Ensure that the arms are fitted to their correct locations, as incorrect installation can cause the blades to foul one another when being used **(see illustration)**.

35 Washer nozzles - removal and refitting

1 The nozzles on all models from 1991 onwards are fitted with twin jets.

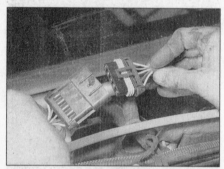

36.5 Disconnect the wiper motor wiring multi-plug

36.6 Remove the three bolts securing the wiper motor/linkage assembly

34.4 Windscreen wiper arms - 1992-on models

Removal

2 To remove a nozzle, carefully prise it from its location using a thin-bladed screwdriver. Take care not to damage the paintwork.
3 Disconnect the washer hose and withdraw the nozzle.

Refitting

4 To refit, reconnect the washer hose to the nozzle, and push the nozzle into its locating hole.
5 The nozzles can be adjusted by inserting a pin into the jet, and swivelling it to the required position.

36 Windscreen wiper motor and linkage - removal and refitting

Removal

1 Disconnect the battery negative lead.
2 Remove the wiper arms, as described in Section 34.
3 Detach the windscreen cowl panel and move it aside, as described in Chapter 11.
4 Undo the clips and remove the pollen filter **(see illustration)**.
5 Disconnect the motor wiring multi-plug **(see illustration)**.
6 Remove the three bolts securing the motor/linkage assembly to the bodywork **(see illustration)**, then withdraw the assembly.
7 To separate the motor from the linkage, continue as follows:

36.8 Remove the nut from the wiper motor/linkage centre shaft

36.4 Undo the clips and remove the pollen filter

8 Remove the nut from the centre shaft **(see illustration)** and prise off the tapered spline. Take care not to turn the motor, otherwise the position needs to be reset with the motor in the vehicle.
9 Remove the three flange bolts **(see illustration)** and separate the motor from the linkage. Note that the two arrows on the flange mark the parked position of the linkage (but not the position of the motor, which has to be on its splines correctly).
10 Do not attempt to dismantle the linkage.

Refitting

11 Refitting is the reverse of removal. Use a new pollen filter if necessary.

37 Tailgate wiper motor, linkage and spindle - removal and refitting

Motor and linkage

Removal

1 Disconnect the battery negative lead.
2 Extract the securing screws, and remove the rear tailgate trim panel.
3 The wiper and spindle are mounted at the edge of the tailgate, but the motor is at the centre. A linkage arm connects the motor to a lever on the spindle. Prise off the linkage arm balljoint, where it connects to the lever **(see illustration)**.
4 Disconnect the motor wiring plug and release the wiring harness.

36.9 Remove the three flange bolts. The two arrows on the flange mark the parked position

37.3 Lever off the tailgate wiper linkage arm balljoint

37.5 Tailgate wiper motor assembly. Note earth lead under one of the securing bolts

37.6 Arrows on mounting bracket indicate parked position

5 Undo the four bolts that secure the motor mounting bracket to the tailgate, noting that one of them secures an earth lead **(see illustration)**.
6 Remove the motor, complete with the mounting bracket and linkage arm. Note that the parked position is between the two arrows on the bracket **(see illustration)**.

Refitting

7 Refitting is the reverse of removal.

Spindle

Removal

8 Remove the tailgate trim panel and prise off the linkage arm balljoint where it connects to the spindle lever (see paragraphs 2 and 3). Move the wiper arm slightly to move the ball away from the linkage.
9 Remove the wiper arm, as described in Section 34.
10 Remove the two bolts and withdraw the spindle from underneath the tailgate **(see illustration)**.
11 Remove the rubber grommet from above the tailgate, noting the position of the off-centre hole **(see illustration)**.

Refitting

12 Refitting is the reverse of removal. Make sure the rubber grommet is in the correct position. Make sure the parked position of the arm corresponds to the parked position of the motor, as indicated by the arrows on the bracket.

---

38 Washer fluid reservoirs -
removal and refitting

1 All Calibra models have a washer fluid reservoir and pump, located at the left-hand side of the engine compartment, to supply fluid to the windscreen and tailgate washer nozzles.
2 Models fitted with headlamp washers have an additional reservoir and high-pressure pump. This reservoir is in two sections, split between the engine compartment and the left wing. The upper section, with the filler cap, is alongside the windscreen and tailgate reservoir **(see illustration)**.

37.10 Remove tailgate wiper spindle

Windscreen and tailgate washer reservoir

Removal

3 Disconnect the battery negative lead.
4 Disconnect the wiring from the washer pump and level sensor.
5 Disconnect the washer fluid hose(s) from the pump. There may be a single hose, or separate hoses for the windscreen and tailgate. Be prepared for fluid spillage.
6 Remove the screw(s) securing the reservoir to the body, and withdraw the reservoir.

Refitting

7 Refitting is the reverse of removal. Refill the reservoir with water and screenwash additive.

Headlamp washer reservoir

Removal

8 Disconnect the battery negative lead.
9 Remove the screw securing the upper section of the reservoir to the wing panel.
10 Loosen the plastic collar securing the upper section of the reservoir to the lower section, then withdraw the upper section of the reservoir from the engine compartment.
11 To remove the lower section of the reservoir, continue as follows.
12 Remove the front bumper trim (see Chapter 11).
13 If necessary, to access the reservoir fittings, remove the plastic panel from the bodywork in front of the wheel arch.

37.11 Remove rubber grommet, noting the position of the off-centre hole

14 Undo the bolts that secure the reservoir to its mountings above the horns, and gently pull it away. Alternatively, disconnect the wiring plugs from the horns and remove the reservoir and horns as a complete assembly. Be prepared for fluid spillage.
15 Disconnect the wiring and the fluid hose from the washer pump. Be prepared for fluid spillage if the reservoir still contains fluid.
16 Separate the reservoir from the horns, if they have been removed as an assembly.

Refitting

17 Refitting is the reverse of removal. Refill the reservoir with water and screenwash additive.

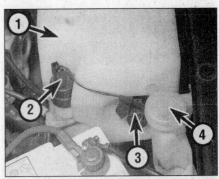

38.2 Washer fluid reservoirs

1 Windscreen/tailgate fluid reservoir
2 Windscreen/tailgate fluid pump
3 Windscreen/tailgate fluid level sensor
4 Headlamp fluid reservoir (upper section)

12

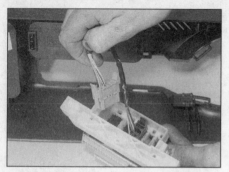

41.4 Remove the connectors from the centre console switch wiring block

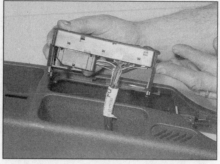

41.5 Release the clips and withdraw the switch assembly from the centre console

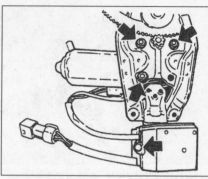

41.8 Electric window motor securing nuts and pulse pick-up securing screw (arrowed)

39 Washer fluid pumps - removal and refitting

1 Disconnect the battery negative lead.

Windscreen and tailgate washer pump

Removal

2 Disconnect the wiring and the fluid hose(s) from the pump. Be prepared for fluid spillage.
3 Pull the pump from the reservoir, being prepared for fluid spillage if the reservoir still contains fluid.
4 Examine the condition of the sealing grommet, and renew it if necessary, and clean the gauze filter at the end of the pump pick-up tube.

Refitting

5 Refitting is the reverse of removal. Refill the reservoir with water and screenwash additive.

Headlamp washer pump

Removal

6 Apply the handbrake, then jack up the front of the vehicle, and support on axle stands (see *"Jacking and Vehicle Support"*) positioned under the body side members.
7 Remove the left wheel arch liner, as described in Chapter 11, to expose the head-lamp washer pump which is at the rear corner of the lower reservoir, next to the inner wing.
8 Disconnect the wiring and the fluid hose from the pump. Be prepared for fluid spillage.
9 Pull the pump from the reservoir, being

43.4 Unscrewing a central door locking control module securing nut

prepared for fluid spillage if the reservoir still contains fluid.
10 Examine the condition of the gasket and renew it if necessary.

Refitting

11 Refitting is the reverse of removal. Refill the reservoir with water and screenwash additive.

40 Headlamp washer fluid non-return valve - removal and refitting

Removal

1 The headlamp washer system includes a non-return valve in the fluid line between the pump and the washer nozzles. The valve has a single inlet hose and two outlet hoses, one for each headlamp. Locate the valve and undo the hoses. Be prepared for fluid spillage.
2 Remove the valve from its mounting.

Refitting

3 Refitting is the reverse of removal. Refill the reservoir with water and screenwash additive.

41 Electric window components - removal and refitting

Note: *Whenever any of the electric window components are removed, after refitting the components, the electric window controls must be programmed, as described in Section 42.*
1 Disconnect the battery negative lead.

Switches

Removal

2 The switches are mounted on the centre console. They must be removed as a complete assembly, and cannot be dismantled. If one of the switches is faulty, the complete assembly must be renewed.
3 Remove the rear section of the centre console, as described in Chapter 11.
4 Release the tabs and pull the connectors out of the wiring block **(see illustration)**.
5 Release the securing clips, and withdraw the switch assembly through the top of the centre console **(see illustration)**.

Refitting

6 Refitting is the reverse of removal.

Operating motors

7 Remove the door window regulator, as described in Chapter 11.
8 To remove the motor assembly from the front door window regulator, unscrew the three motor securing nuts, and the single screw securing the pulse pick-up unit to the regulator assembly. Withdraw the motor, complete with the pulse pick-up unit. Note that if the motor or pick-up unit is/are faulty, the two components must be renewed as an assembly, as no spare parts are available **(see illustration)**.

42 Electric window controls - programming

1 Whenever the battery is disconnected, or any of the electric window components are removed, on completion of work, the electric window controls must be programmed as follows.
2 Close all doors, and switch on the ignition.
3 Close one of the windows by pressing the relevant operating switch. Press and hold the switch for a further five seconds after the relevant window has fully closed.
4 Repeat the procedure for the remaining window(s).

43 Central door locking components - removal and refitting

1 Disconnect the battery negative lead.

Electronic control module

Removal

2 The module is mounted in the driver's footwell, behind the side trim panel.
3 Remove the driver's footwell side trim panel, as described in Chapter 11.
4 Unscrew the two securing nuts, and lift the module from the body panel **(see illustration)**.

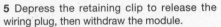

43.10 Central door locking operating microswitch (arrowed) in driver's door

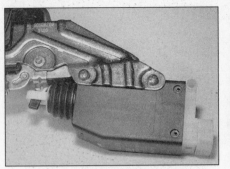

43.13 Remove the two screws and separate the central locking motor from the lock

43.17 Disconnecting the wiring plug from the tailgate lock operating motor

5 Depress the retaining clip to release the wiring plug, then withdraw the module.

Refitting

6 Refitting is the reverse of removal.

Operating switch

Removal

7 The operating switch takes the form of a microswitch, mounted inside the door at the rear of the exterior handle assembly.
8 Remove the door inner trim panel, as described in Chapter 11.
9 Peel back the plastic insulating sheet sufficiently to gain access to the exterior handle.
10 Unclip the microswitch from the rear edge of the exterior handle assembly, and disconnect the switch wiring plug from the door wiring harness, then withdraw the switch **(see illustration)**.

Refitting

11 Refitting is the reverse of removal.

Door lock operating motor

Removal

12 Remove the door lock and central locking motor, as described in Chapter 11.
13 Remove the two securing screws and separate the motor from the lock **(see illustration)**.

Refitting

14 Refitting is the reverse of removal.

Tailgate lock operating motor

Removal

15 Extract the securing screws and remove the rear tailgate trim panel.
16 Remove the two securing screws, and manipulate the motor to disconnect the lock operating rod.
17 Withdraw the motor and disconnect the wiring plug **(see illustration)**.

Refitting

18 Refitting is the reverse of removal.

Fuel filler flap lock operating motor

Removal

19 Remove the right-hand rear quarter trim panel, as described in Chapter 11.
20 Disconnect the wiring plug from the rear of the motor **(see illustration)**.
21 Unscrew the two screws securing the motor to the mounting bracket, then manipulate the motor to disconnect the lock operating rod. Withdraw the motor.

Refitting

22 Refitting is the reverse of removal.

43.20 Disconnecting the wiring plug from the fuel filler flap operating motor

44 Aerial - removal and refitting

Removal

1 Disconnect the battery negative lead.
2 You can remove the aerial and nozzle unit with the aerial attached, or you can unscrew the aerial **(see illustration)**.
3 Open the tailgate, detach the weatherstrip and pull down the headlining.
4 Pull down the aerial and amplifier cables and the nozzle hose and disconnect them **(see illustration)**.
5 Undo the nut and leave it hanging on the cables **(see illustration)**.

44.2 The aerial can be unscrewed from its mounting

44.4 Aerial and amplifier cables and nozzle hose under upper shroud

44.5 Undo the aerial mounting nut

12

44.6 Remove the aerial and nozzle unit

6 Lift the aerial and nozzle unit upwards and remove it **(see illustration)**.

Refitting

7 Refitting is the reverse of removal, but remember the following points.
8 Make sure the rubber grommet goes correctly round the foot of the aerial.
9 The hose goes through the round hole in the roof, and the wires go through the square hole.
10 Have an assistant hold the aerial/nozzle unit while tightening the nut underneath.

45 Speakers -
removal and refitting

1 The Calibra has six speakers, three on each side **(see illustration)**. These consist of:

45.5 Treble speaker removed from door trim panel

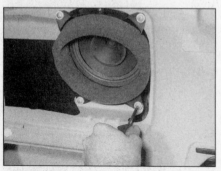

45.9 Remove the four screws from the rear speaker

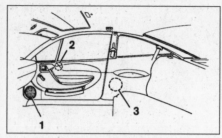

45.1 Speaker locations in body trim panels

1   *Front wide band speaker*
2   *Treble speaker*
3   *Rear wide band speaker*

a) *Wide-band speakers (50 to 18,000 Hz) behind the door trim panels and rear quarter trim panels;*
b) *Treble speakers (3000 to 22,000 Hz) behind the door trim panels.*

Door-mounted speakers

Removal

2 Disconnect the battery negative lead.
3 Remove the door inner trim panel, as described in Chapter 11.
4 The front wide band speaker is attached to the door **(see illustration)**. Remove the three securing screws, and withdraw the speaker, then disconnect the wiring plug.
5 The treble speaker is attached to the trim panel **(see illustration)**. Unclip the speaker and disconnect the plug on the wiring harness.

Refitting

6 Refitting is the reverse of removal, but note that the wide-band speaker can only be fitted one way up, so that the lug on the bottom of the speaker rim engages with the corresponding hole in the door skin.

Rear speakers

Removal

7 Disconnect the battery negative lead.
8 Remove the rear quarter trim panel, as described in Chapter 11.
9 Remove the four securing screws and withdraw the speaker **(see illustration)**.

46.3 Unscrew the grub screws . . .

45.4 Front wide band speaker attached to the door

10 Disconnect the wiring multi-plug.

Refitting

11 Refitting is the reverse of removal.

46 Radio/cassette player -
removal and refitting

Removal

1 All the radio/cassette players fitted to the Calibra range have DIN standard fixings. Two special tools, obtainable from in-car entertainment specialists, are required for removal.
2 Disconnect the battery negative lead.
3 Unscrew the four grub screws from the corners of the radio cassette player, using an Allen key or hexagon bit **(see illustration)**.
4 Insert the tools into the holes exposed by removal of the grub screws, and push them until they snap into place. Pull the tools outwards to release the unit **(see illustration)**.
5 Pull the unit forwards, and withdraw it from the facia.

Refitting

6 To refit the radio/cassette player, simply push the unit into the facia until the retaining lugs snap into place, then refit the grub screws.

46.4 . . . and withdraw the radio/cassette player using the special tools

47 Sunroof motor - general

The sunroof is a complex piece of equipment consisting of a large number of components. It is strongly recommended that the sunroof motor and other components are not disturbed unless necessary. If the motor is faulty, consult a dealer for advice.

48 Speedometer cable - removal and refitting

Removal

1 Remove the instrument panel, as described in Section 18.
2 Pull the cable through the bulkhead into the engine compartment, noting its routing.
3 Working in the engine compartment, unscrew the securing sleeve and disconnect the speedometer cable from the top of the transmission **(see illustration)**. A variety of fittings are available at the transmission end, depending on the model and accessories.

4 The cable can now be withdrawn from the vehicle, noting its routing so that it can be refitted in the same position.

Refitting

5 Refitting is the reverse of removal, ensuring that the cable is correctly routed. Make sure that the cable is not kinked or twisted between the instrument panel and the bulkhead as the instrument panel is refitted. Note that the cable should be routed to the right of the steering column support bracket.

49 Anti-theft alarm - general

1 Some models are fitted with an anti-theft alarm system **(see illustration)**. It operates in conjunction with the central locking system so that it becomes active when the vehicle is locked with a key from the driver's door. When active, it will give an audible alarm and the indicator lights will flash in any of the following circumstances:
a) A door is opened without the key;
b) The tailgate is opened without the key;
c) The bonnet is opened;

48.3 Speedometer cable securing sleeve (arrowed) at transmission

d) There is movement inside the vehicle, for example by breaking a window;
e) An attempt is made to manipulate the alarm system wiring.

The system includes an immobiliser which is activated when the ignition is switched off. The immobiliser operates a relay which prevents the starter motor from operating. It can be de-activated by turning on the ignition with the key.

2 When an alarm event occurs, an alarm code is stored in memory giving information about which sensor has triggered the alarm, and you can read the code using a hand-held device

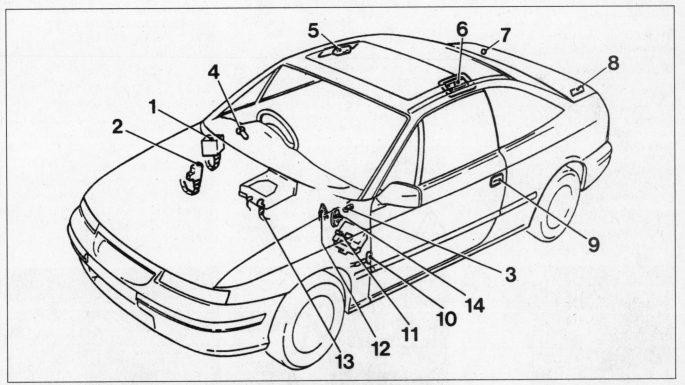

49.1 Anti-theft alarm system component locations

1 *Anti-theft alarm system control unit*	3 *Alarm system diagnostic plug*	7 *Tailgate lock*	11 *Immobiliser relay*
2 *Central locking system control unit*	4 *Ignition lock*	8 *Tailgate contact*	12 *Bonnet contact*
	5 *Ultrasonic sensor with LED*	9 *Door lock*	13 *Radio contact*
	6 *Ultrasonic sensor with button*	10 *Door contact*	14 *Siren*

12

called TECH 1 connected to the alarm system diagnostic plug **(see illustration)**. You can also use TECH 1 to obtain information about alarm system faults, although the servicing of alarms is a specialist activity and should be referred to a Vauxhall dealer.

3 Some vehicles are provided with additional security by having a second alarm siren, with its own built-in power supply, under the windscreen cowl panel. If an attempt is made to silence or de-activate the anti-theft alarm system by disconnecting the battery, the siren will sound.

4 For details of how to operate the alarm system, see the Calibra Owner's Manual.

50 Anti-theft alarm system components - removal and refitting

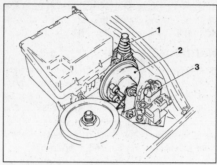

49.2 Alarm system diagnostic plug

1 *Bonnet contact*   3 *Diagnostic*
2 *Siren*   *plug*

Control unit

Removal

1 Disconnect the battery negative lead.
2 Remove the driver's side lower facia panel as described in Chapter 11.
3 If necessary, remove the footwell side trim panel as described in Chapter 11.
4 Undo the control unit retaining bolt, disconnect the wiring plug and remove the unit from its location.

Refitting

5 Refitting is the reverse of removal.

Ultrasonic sensor

Removal

6 Disconnect the battery negative lead.
7 Carefully release the ultrasonic sensor trim panel and withdraw it downwards **(see illustration)**.
8 Undo the two screws holding the sensor unit to its bracket, then disconnect the wiring plug and remove the unit from the car **(see illustration)**.

Refitting

9 Refitting is the reverse of removal.

Bonnet contact unit

Removal

10 Disconnect the battery negative lead.
11 Using a screwdriver, depress the catch at the base of the contact unit and withdraw the contact from its location.
12 Disconnect the contact wiring and remove the unit.

Refitting

13 Refitting is the reverse of removal.

Secondary alarm siren

Removal

14 Disconnect the battery negative lead.
15 Detach the windscreen cowl panel, as described in Chapter 11, and lift it up to expose the secondary alarm siren **(see illustration)**.
16 Undo the nut holding the siren to its bracket, then pull the siren forward and disconnect the multi-plug.

Refitting

17 Refitting is the reverse of removal.

51 Airbag - general

 Warning: Before starting any work on airbag or related components,

disconnect the battery. Cover the battery's terminals and wait a minimum of 1 minute as a precaution against accidental firing of the airbag unit. This period ensures that any stored energy in the back-up capacitor is dissipated. Handle the airbag unit with extreme care as a precaution against personal injury, and always hold it with the cover facing away from the body. If in doubt concerning any proposed work involving the airbag unit or its control circuitry, consult a Vauxhall dealer or other qualified specialist.

Airbags are available as optional extras for the driver (from 1993 onwards) and for the front seat passenger (from 1994 onwards), to prevent serious chest and head injuries during an accident. Sensors under the centre console measure the vehicle deceleration rate and pass these signals to a microprocessor. This unit analyses the sensor data and compares the information with pre-programmed values stored in its memory, triggering the airbag if the deceleration is severe. The airbag is inflated in 50 milliseconds by a gas generator that forces the bag out of the module cover in the centre of the steering wheel or the passenger side facia panel.

No repairs are possible on the airbag unit or its associated parts. The contents of the following Sections are confined to removal and refitting of the airbag, purely for access to other non-related components.

Should a fault be suspected on the airbag unit, indicated by the warning light on the instrument panel, or if the car has been involved in an accident, however minor, consult a Vauxhall dealer immediately. Do not attempt to dismantle any of the airbag components or carry out any work whatsoever, other than the procedures described in the following Sections.

On vehicles fitted with a passenger side airbag, **do not** fit accessories in the airbag zone. Items like telephones, cassette storage boxes, additional mirrors, etc., can be ripped off and cause serious injury, if the airbag inflates.

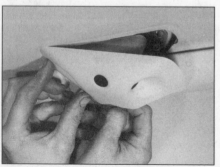

50.7 Remove the ultrasonic sensor trim panel

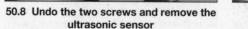

50.8 Undo the two screws and remove the ultrasonic sensor

50.15 Secondary alarm siren under windscreen cowl panel

52 Airbag unit, driver's side - removal and refitting

Warning: Read the warning at the beginning of Section 51, before starting work.

Note: *On power steering models in particular, it will be advantageous to jack up the front of the car and support it on axle stands placed under the body side members, so that the steering wheel can be turned more easily (see "Jacking and Vehicle Support").*

Removal

1 Disconnect the battery negative lead and cover the battery terminal. Wait a minimum of 1 minute.

2 With the steering wheel positioned in the straight-ahead position, turn it 90° clockwise so that the left-hand spoke is accessible from the rear.

3 Using a Torx type socket, undo the first airbag retaining bolt from the rear of the steering wheel **(see illustration)**.

4 Turn the steering wheel 180° anti-clockwise so that the right-hand spoke is accessible from the rear.

5 Undo the second retaining bolt from the rear of the steering wheel.

6 Return the steering wheel to the straight-ahead position, then carefully lift up the airbag unit.

7 Disconnect the wiring plug and remove the airbag from the car.

Warning: Stand the unit with the cover uppermost and do not expose it to heat sources in excess of 90°C. Do not attempt to open or repair the airbag unit, or apply any voltage to it. Do not use any airbag unit that is visibly damaged or has been tampered with.

Refitting

8 Refitting is the reverse of removal.

53 Steering wheel (with airbag) - removal and refitting

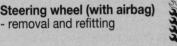

Note 1: *Read the warning at the beginning of Section 51, before starting work.*

Note 2: *A two-legged puller will be required for this operation, as the steering wheel is a very tight fit on the shaft.*

Note 3: *See Chapter 10 for details of steering wheel removal without an airbag.*

Removal

1 Remove the airbag unit as described previously.

2 Ensure that the steering wheel is in the straight ahead position.

3 From the centre of the steering wheel

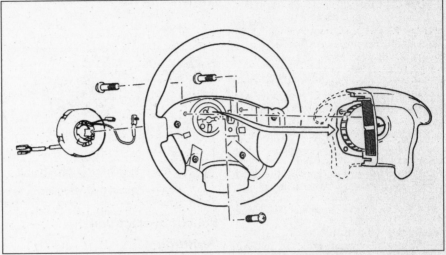

52.3 Airbag, steering wheel and contact unit details

unscrew the two screws securing the airbag contact unit.

4 Using a screwdriver, prise back the tabs on the lockwasher securing the steering wheel retaining nut.

5 Unscrew and remove the steering wheel retaining nut and the lockwasher.

6 Make alignment marks between the steering wheel and the end of the column shaft.

7 A suitably small two-legged puller must now be fitted to the steering wheel in order to pull it from the column shaft.

8 Once the steering wheel has been released from the column shaft, disconnect the horn wiring and remove the steering wheel.

Refitting

9 Begin refitting by positioning the steering wheel on the column shaft, ensuring that the marks made on removal are aligned, and that the wheel correctly engages with the airbag contact unit. It may be necessary to tap the steering wheel fully home on the column shaft using a metal tube and socket.

10 Reconnect the horn wiring.

11 Refit the lockwasher and the steering wheel retaining nut, and tighten the nut to the specified torque. Bend up the lockwasher to secure.

12 Refit the two screws securing the airbag contact unit.

13 Refit the airbag as described previously.

54 Airbag contact unit - removal and refitting

Note: *Read the warning at the beginning of Section 51, before starting work.*

Removal

1 Remove the airbag and the steering wheel as described previously.

2 Remove the steering column upper and lower shrouds, referring to Chapter 10, if necessary.

3 Disconnect the contact unit wiring plug below the steering column and withdraw the contact unit from the column, noting its fitted position as a guide to reassembly **(see illustration)**.

Refitting

4 Before refitting the contact unit, ensure that the front wheels are in the straight-ahead position.

5 Place the contact unit on the column in the correct position as noted during removal.

6 Route the wiring harness under the steering column lock/ignition switch and connect the wiring plug.

7 Refit the steering column shrouds, referring to Chapter 10, if necessary.

8 Refit the steering wheel and airbag as described previously.

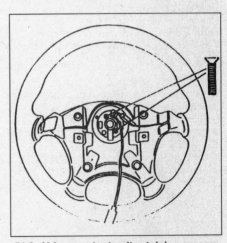

54.3 Airbag contact unit retaining screws

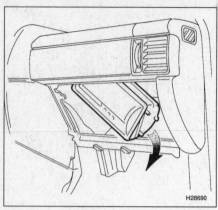

55.6 Removing the passenger side airbag

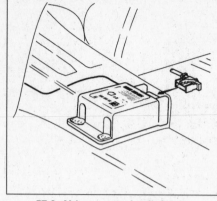

57.3 Airbag control unit details

55 Airbag unit, passenger side - removal and refitting

> **Warning: Read the warning at the beginning of Section 51, before starting work.**

Removal

1 Disconnect the battery, cover the terminals and wait at least 1 minute.
2 Remove the glovebox assembly. Refer to Chapter 11, for further details if necessary.
3 Remove the right hand ventilation air duct.
4 Disconnect the plug connections.
5 Unbolt the six M6 nuts from the two side brackets.
6 Remove the airbag unit **(see illustration)**.

Refitting

7 Refitting is the reverse of removal.

56 Bracket, passenger airbag unit - removal and refitting

Note 1: *Read the warning at the beginning of Section 51, before starting work.*
Note 2: *This process involves removal of the windscreen, refer to Chapter 11, before starting work.*

Removal

1 Remove the passenger side airbag unit as described in Section 55.
2 Remove the airbag unit cover.
3 Remove the water deflector from in front of the windscreen.
4 Remove the windscreen (see Chapter 11).
5 The brackets can now be unbolted.

Refitting

6 Refitting is the reverse of removal. Tighten the brackets to the specified torque setting.

57 Airbag control unit - removal and refitting

Note: *Read the warning at the beginning of Section 51, before starting work.*

Removal

1 Disconnect the battery negative lead and cover the battery terminal to prevent accidental reconnection.
2 Remove the centre console rear section as described in Chapter 11.
3 Disconnect the control unit wiring plug, then undo the three nuts and remove the unit from the car **(see illustration)**.

Refitting

4 Refitting is the reverse of removal. Tighten the control unit nuts to the specified torque setting.

58 Wiring diagrams - general

The wiring diagrams are of the current flow type, each circuit being shown in the simplest possible fashion. Note that since the diagrams were originally written in German (to the DIN standard), all wire colours and abbreviations used on the diagrams themselves are in German. Refer to the information given overleaf for clarification.

The bottom line of the diagram represents the "earth" or negative connection; the numbers below this line are track numbers, enabling circuits and components to be located using the key.

The lines at the top of the diagram represent "live feed" or positive connection points. The line marked "30" is live at all times. The line marked "15" is live only when the ignition is switched on.

Numbers on the diagram that are framed in square boxes at the end of a wire show the track reference number in which that wire is continued. At the point indicated will be another framed number referring back to the circuit just left.

As an example of how to use the diagrams, trace with the help of the following text the reversing lamp switch circuit located between track reference numbers 496 and 498 on the 1991 model year diagram.

Starting at the top of track 497, the supply for the circuit comes from the line "15", showing that the circuit is fed only when the ignition is switched on, through fuse 22 (F22, rated at 10 amps). Note that this fuse can also protect the feed for several other circuits, some of which may not be applicable to the vehicle being worked on.

If the vehicle in question has a manual transmission (MT), the circuit continues along a black wire of 0.75 mm cross-section (as shown by "SW 0.75" in the wire path), through terminal 12 of connector X5 to the reversing lamp switch S7. From the switch the circuit continues along a white wire, with a black tracer and of 0.75 mm cross-section (WSSW 0.75), through terminal 2 of connector X5 and terminal 1 of connector X6, to the reversing lamp bulbs (E17 and E18). The circuit is completed by a brown wire from each bulbholder to earth; in this case the "earth" wire simply attaches the component to the nearest piece of metal bodywork, but in other cases earthing is achieved by the component mounting and no wire is needed. The diagram shows, as simply as possible, that when the switch contacts (which are normally open) are closed by the driver selecting reverse gear, current is allowed to flow to earth through the switch and bulbs causing the reversing lamps to light.

If the vehicle in question has automatic transmission (AT), the circuit differs in that the "live feed" goes from fuse 22 to terminal "F" of the transmission selector lever position switch connector X46 (track reference number 773). When position "R" is selected, terminals "F" and "G" are connected so that the circuit feed continues (back to track reference number 496, the "RFS/reversing lamp" circuit) along the same route described above for manual transmission models.

Explanations of abbreviations used in wiring diagrams

ABS	Anti-lock braking system	LWR	Headlamp aim adjustment
AC	Air conditioning	M1.5	Bosch Motronic M1.5 engine management system
AZV	Trailer hitch	M2.5	Bosch Motronic M2.5 engine management system
AT	Automatic transmission	MOT	Motronic (general)
ATC	Automatic temperature control	MT	Manual gearbox
BR	Trip (on-board) computer	MUL	Multec fuel injection system
CC	Check control system	N	Norway
CRC	Cruise control	NS	Front foglamps
D	Diesel	NSL	Rear foglamps
DS	Theft protection	OEL	Oil level/pressure check system
DT	Turbo Diesel	OPT	Optional equipment
DWA	Anti-theft warning system	PBSL	Park and brake shift block (automatic transmission, selector lever in position 'P')
DZM	Tachometer		
EFC	Electric folding roof (Convertible)	P/N	Park/neutral (automatic transmission)
EKS	Pinch guard (electric windows)	POT	Potentiometer
EMP	Radio	RC	Rear suspension level control system
EUR	Euronorm (emission control standard) engine	RFS	Reversing lamps
EZ +	El Plus ignition system (with self- diagnosis)	RHD	Right-hand drive
EZV	Ecotronic	S	Sweden
FH	Electric windows	SD	Sunroof
GB	Great Britain	SH	Heated seats
HS	Heated rear window	SRA	Headlamp washers and wipers
HW	Rear window wiper	TANK	Fuel level sender unit
HZG	Heating	TD	Turbo Diesel
HRL	Luggage compartment lamp	TEMP	Temperature gauge
INS	Instrument panel	TFL	Daytime driving lamps
IRL	Courtesy lamps	TKS	Courtesy lamp (door pillar) switches
KAT	Catalytic converter	TSZI	Transistorised ignition (inductive-triggered) system
KBS	Wiring harness	VGS	Carburettor
KV	Contact breaker distributor	WEG	Odometer frequency/roadspeed sensor
L3.1	Bosch Jetronic fuel injection system	WHR	Rear suspension level control system
LCD	Liquid crystal display (LCD) instruments	WS	Warning buzzer
LHD	Left-hand drive	ZV	Central locking
4WD	Four-wheel-drive	ZYL	Cylinder

Colour codes

BL	Blue	RT	Red
HBL	Light blue	WS	White
BR	Brown	SW	Black
GE	Yellow	LI	Lilac
GR	Grey	VI	Violet
GN	Green		

Wiring identification

Example: GEWS 1.5
GE - Wire basic colour
WS -Wire tracer colour
1.5 - Wire cross-section in mm^2

Note: *Not all items shown are fitted to all models. Refer to Section 58 (Chapter 12) for details of diagram usage.*

Wiring diagrams for early models

Location of applicable circuits	Track	Location of applicable circuits	Track
Air conditioning system	800 to 850	Headlamp aim adjustment system	758 to 766
Alternator	111	Headlamp dim-dip	427 to 431
Anti-lock braking system (ABS)	701 to 722	Headlamp washers	519 to 532
Anti-theft alarm system	633 to 647	Headlamps	437 to 442
Automatic transmission control system	773 to 799	Headlamps "ON" warning buzzer	493 to 495
Battery	100	Heated front seats	560 to 566
Brake lamps	461 to 462	Heated rear window	549 to 556
Carburettor	118 to 121	Heater blower motor	853 to 862
Central locking system	600 to 627	Horn(s)	592 to 596
Check control system	347 to 371	Ignition (HEI) - 14 NV engine	121 to 128
Cigarette lighter	597 to 598	Ignition (MSTS/EZ+) - 16 SV, 18 SV engines	236 to 256
Clock	661 to 663	Instruments	301 to 344
Courtesy lamps - front	487 to 494	Luggage compartment lamp	485
Courtesy lamps - rear	569 to 573	Radiator cooling fan	113, 115
Direction indicator and hazard warning lamps	467 to 482	Radio/cassette player	586 to 591
Door mirrors	536 to 548	Rear number plate lamp	413
Electric windows	665 to 699	Reversing lamps	496 to 498
Engine compartment lamp	415	Side and tail lamps	401 to 410
Foglamps - front	444 to 452	Starter motor	102 to 110
Foglamps - rear	444 to 457	Sunroof	863 to 870
Fuel injection and ignition (Multec) - C16 NZ engine	129 to 164	Tailgate wiper	510 to 516
Fuel injection and ignition (Multec) - C18 NZ engine	972 to 997	Trip computer	650 to 662
Fuel injection/ignition (Motronic M1.5) - 2.0 litre SOHC	168 to 199	Windscreen and tailgate washers	511 to 529
Fuel injection/ignition (Motronic M2.5) - 2.0 litre DOHC	261 to 299	Windscreen wipers	501 to 506
Glovebox lamp	599		

Key to wiring diagrams for early models

No	Description	Track	No	Description	Track
E1	Side lamp - left	406	E39	Rear foglamp - right	455
E2	Tail lamp - left	356, 374, 407	E41	Courtesy lamp (with delay)	488 to 490
E3	Number plate lamp	413	E50	Kerb lamp - driver's door	666
E4	Side lamp - right	409	E51	Kerb lamp - passenger door	684
E5	Tail lamp - right	358, 376, 410	F1 on	Fuses	Various
E6	Engine compartment lamp	415	G1	Battery	101
E7	Headlamp main beam - left	437	G2	Alternator	111
E8	Headlamp main beam - right	438	G3	Battery - (Diesel models)	882, 901
E9	Headlamp dipped beam - left	360, 378, 439	G6	Alternator - (Diesel models)	884 to 886, 909 to 911
E10	Headlamp dipped beam - right	362, 380, 440	H1	Radio/cassette player	589 to 590, 634
E11	Instrument illumination lamps	328 to 329	H2	Horn	592
E12	Selector lever illumination lamp (automatic transmission)	799	H3	Direction indicator warning lamp	315 to 320
E13	Luggage compartment lamp	485	H4	Oil pressure warning lamp	310
E14	Courtesy lamp	487	H5	Brake fluid level warning lamp	313
E15	Glovebox lamp	599	H6	Hazard warning flasher lamp	470
E16	Cigarette lighter illumination lamp	596	H7	Alternator charge warning lamp	310
E17	Reversing lamp - left	497	H8	Headlamp main beam warning lamp	322
E18	Reversing lamp - right	498	H9	Brake lamp - left	364, 382, 461
E19	Heated rear window	552	H10	Brake lamp - right	366, 384, 462
E20	Front foglamp - left	448	H11	Direction indicator lamp - front left	472
E21	Front foglamp - right	447	H12	Direction indicator lamp - rear left	473
E24	Rear foglamp - left	454	H13	Direction indicator lamp - front right	461
E25	Driver's seat heater	580	H14	Direction indicator lamp - rear right	482
E27	Courtesy lamp - rear left	569 to 570	H15	Fuel level warning lamp	305
E28	Courtesy lamp - rear right	572 to 573	H16	Glow plug warning lamp (Diesel models)	323
E30	Passenger front seat heater	564	H17	Trailer direction indicator warning lamp	321
E32	Clock illumination lamp	663	H18	Horn	593
E38	Trip computer illumination lamp	654	H19	Headlamps-on warning buzzer	494 to 495

No	Description	Track
H21	Handbrake-on warning lamp	315
H25	Door mirror warning lamp	542, 952
H26	ABS warning lamp	319
H30	Engine fault warning lamp	324
H33	Direction indicator side repeater lamp - left	476
H34	Direction indicator side repeater lamp - right	478
H42	Automatic transmission warning lamp	325
H45	Four-wheel-drive warning lamp	327
H46	Catalytic converter temperature warning lamp	329
H47	Anti-theft alarm horn	638
H48	Horn	594
K3	Relay - starter motor (anti-theft alarm)	109 to 110
K5	Relay - front foglamps	448 to 450
K6	Relay - air conditioning	801 to 802
K7	Relay - air conditioning blower	804 to 805
K8	Relay - intermittent windscreen wipe	503 to 506
K9	Relay - headlamp wash	519 to 520
K10	Relay - direction indicator/hazard warning flashers	467 to 469
K20	Ignition amplifier module	122 to 124, 236 to 237, 975 to 976
K25	Relay - glow plugs (Diesel models)	889 to 892
K30	Relay - intermittent rear window wipe	513 to 515
K35	Relay - door mirror heater	550 to 552
K37	Central locking control unit	606 to 612
K47	Relay - surge arrester (ABS)	702 to 703, 735 to 736
K50	ABS control unit	707 to 721, 740 to 754
K51	Relay - cooling fan	829 to 830, 842 to 843, 837 to 838
K57	Multec electronic control unit (ECU)	139 to 161
K58	Relay - fuel pump	163 to 164, 996 to 997
K59	Relay - daytime running lamps	420 to 426
K62	Dim-dip control unit	427 to 431
K63	Relay - horn	594 to 595
K64	Relay - air conditioning blower	802 to 803
K67	Relay - cooling fan	825 to 826, 849 to 850
K68	Relay - fuel injection system	196 to 199
K69	Motronic M2.5 module	267 to 297
K73	Relay - headlamp main beam relay	432 to 433
K76	Glow plug control unit (Turbo diesel models)	916 to 921
K77	Relay - glow plugs (Turbo diesel models)	923 to 924
K78	Relay - pre-resistor (Turbo diesel models)	926 to 927
K79	Alternator charge warning lamp relay	911 to 913
K80	Relay - fuel filter heater (Diesel models)	898 to 899, 931 to 932
K82	Relay - engine revolution	895 to 896
K83	Four-wheel-drive control unit	725 to 731
K84	MSTS ignition module	242 to 256
K85	Automatic transmission control unit	774 to 797
K86	Check control unit	347 to 368
K87	Relay - auxiliary cooling fan	832 to 833, 839 to 840, 940 to 941
K88	Catalytic converter temp. control unit	758 to 760, 966 to 968
K89	Relay - rear foglamps	444 to 447
K90	Relay - air conditioning compressor	820 to 821
K91	Motronic M1.5 module	170 to 194
K94	Anti-theft alarm control unit	633 to 647
K97	Relay - headlamp washer pump time delay	530 to 532
K101	Relay - electric mirror parking position	961 to 964
K102	Parking brake control unit (automatic transmission)	769 to 771
K103	Relay - cooling fan	845 to 847
K107	Multec electronic control unit (ECU)	978 to 996
L1	Ignition coil	121 to 122, 133 to 134, 173, 174, 237 to 238, 974 to 975
M1	Starter motor	105 to 106
M2	Windscreen wiper motor	501 to 504

No	Description	Track
M3	Heater blower motor	854 to 856
M4	Radiator cooling fan motor	113, 115, 829, 847, 935
M6	Headlamp wiper motor - left	522 to 524
M7	Headlamp wiper motor - right	526 to 528
M8	Rear window wiper motor	511 to 513
M10	Air conditioning blower motor	805 to 808
M11	Cooling fan motor	840, 941
M12	Starter motor (Diesel models)	887 to 888, 905 to 906
M13	Sunroof motor assembly	865 to 869
M13.1	Sunroof motor	866 to 868
M13.2	Sunroof travel microswitch	866
M13.3	Sunroof travel microswitch	868
M18	Central locking motor - driver's door	607 to 610
M19	Central locking motor - left rear door	621 to 623
M20	Central locking motor - right rear door	625 to 627
M21	Fuel pump	164, 197, 229, 997
M24	Headlamp washer pump	532
M26	Electric aerial motor	588 to 589
M30	Door mirror motor and heater - driver's door	538 to 541
M31	Door mirror motor and heater - passenger door	544 to 547
M32	Central locking motor - passenger door	613 to 616
M33	Idle speed adjuster/idle air control stepper motor	146 to 149, 185 to 186, 277 to 278, 985 to 988
M39	Headlamp aim adjuster motor - driver's side	759 to 762
M40	Headlamp aim adjuster motor - passenger side	763 to 766
M41	Central locking motor - fuel filler	623 to 624
M47	Electric window motor - front left	667 to 671
M48	Electric window motor - front right	685 to 689
M49	Electric window motor - rear left	673 to 677
M50	Electric window motor - rear right	691 to 695
M55	Windscreen and rear window washer pump	516
M60	Central locking motor	627 to 628
M61	Sunroof assembly	872 to 880
M61.1	Sunroof motor	873 to 876
M61.2	Relay 1 - sunroof motor	872 to 873
M61.3	Relay 2 - sunroof motor	878 to 880
M62	Door mirror motor - driver's door	947 to 953
M63	Door mirror motor - passenger door	956 to 962
P1	Fuel gauge	304
P2	Coolant temperature gauge	306
P3	Clock	662
P4	Fuel level sender unit	304
P5	Coolant temperature gauge sender	306
P7	Tachometer	308
P8	Oil pressure gauge	341
P9	Voltmeter	339
P10	Oil pressure sensor	341
P11	Airflow meter (Motronic M1.5)	185 to 189
P12	Coolant temperature sensor	182, 272
P13	Trip computer outside air temperature sensor	655 to 656
P14	Distance sensor	336 to 337, 915 to 916
P17	ABS wheel sensor - front left	707, 740
P18	ABS wheel sensor - front right	710, 742
P19	ABS wheel sensor - rear left	712, 744
P20	ABS wheel sensor - rear right	713, 746
P21	Speedometer frequency sensor	332
P23	Pressure sensor	152 to 154, 984 to 986
P24	Automatic transmission fluid temperature sensor	252, 795
P25	Bulb failure sensor	373 to 386
P27	Brake pad wear sensor - front left	351, 396
P28	Brake pad wear sensor - front right	351, 396

12

Key to wiring diagrams for early models (continued)

No	Description	Track
P30	Coolant temperature sensor	150, 982
P32	Oxygen sensor - heated	194 to 195, 291 to 292
P33	Oxygen sensor	157, 991
P34	Throttle position sensor/potentiometer	158 to 160, 180 to 181, 777 to 778, 987 to 989
P35	Crankshaft speed/position sensor	189 to 191, 281 to 282, 982 to 984
P39	Trailer bulb failure sensor	368 to 370, 387 to 389
P43	Electronic speedometer	336
P44	Air mass meter (Motronic M2.5)	294 to 298
P45	Automatic transmission input speed sensor	791 to 792
P46	Knock sensor	284 to 285
P47	Distributor "Hall-effect" sensor (Motronic M2.5)	287 to 288
P48	Automatic transmission output speed sensor	789 to 790
P50	Catalytic converter temperature sensor	759 to 760, 977 to 978
P53	Anti-theft alarm sensor - driver's side	639 to 642
P54	Anti-theft alarm sensor - passenger side	644 to 647
P55	Coolant temperature sensor (Turbo diesel models)	919
R2	Carburettor preheating	121
R3	Cigarette lighter	597
R5	Glow plugs (Diesel models)	891 to 892, 922 to 924
R12	Automatic choke	118
R13	Heated windscreen washer nozzle - left	526
R14	Heated windscreen washer nozzle - right	528
R15	Mixture adjustment potentiometer	155 to 157
R19	Cooling fan motor resistor	115, 832, 935
R22	Glow plugs resistor (Turbo diesel models)	927
S1	Ignition switch	105 to 106, 885 to 886, 905 to 906
S1.2	Key contact switch	586
S2.1	Lighting switch	404 to 407
S2.2	Courtesy lamp switch	487
S2.3	Instrument illumination lamp dimmer	328
S3	Heater blower switch	853 to 860
S4	Heated rear window and mirror switch	554 to 556
S5.2	Dipped beam switch	438 to 439
S5.3	Direction indicator switch	480 to 482
S5.4	Sidelamp switch	401 to 402
S7	Reversing lamp switch	497
S8	Brake lamp switch	462
S9.2	Windscreen wiper interval switch	501 to 504
S9.5	Rear window washer/wiper switch	514 to 516
S10	Automatic transmission starter inhibitor switch	773 to 779
S11	Brake fluid level warning sensor	31
S13	Handbrake-on warning switch	315
S14	Oil pressure switch	310
S15	Luggage compartment lamp switch	485
S17	Passenger door courtesy lamp switch	490
S21	Front fog lamp switch	450 to 452
S22	Rear foglamp switch	455 to 457
S24	Air conditioning blower motor switch	804 to 811
S27	Air conditioning compressor low-pressure switch	821
S28	Air conditioning compressor high-pressure switch	821
S29	Cooling fan switch	113
S30	Driver's seat heater switch	560 to 562
S31	Rear door courtesy lamp switch - left	491
S32	Rear door courtesy lamp switch - right	491
S37	Driver's door electric window switch assembly	668 to 694
S37.1	Electric window switch - front left	668 to 670
S37.2	Electric window switch - front right	686 to 688
S37.3	Electric window switch - rear left	674 to 676
S37.4	Electric window switch - rear right	692 to 694
S37.5	Electric window safety cut-out switch	672 to 673
S37.6	Electric window anti-jam switch	690
S37.7	Electric window automatic control	677 to 682
S39	Electric window switch - rear left door	678 to 680
S40	Electric window switch - rear right door	696 to 698
S41	Central locking switch - driver's door	601 to 603
S42	Central locking switch - passenger door	605
S44	Throttle position sensor	278 to 279
S47	Driver's door courtesy lamp switch	493 to 494
S52	Hazard warning flasher switch	469 to 474
S55	Passenger seat heater switch	564 to 566
S57	Sunroof switch	864 to 869, 872 to 877
S63.1	Trip computer function reset switch	656
S63.2	Trip computer clock hours adjustment switch	657
S63.3	Trip computer function select switch	658
S63.5	Trip computer clock minutes adjustment switch	659
S64	Horn switch	592, 595
S68.1	Door mirror adjustment switch	538 to 540, 945 to 950
S68.3	Door mirror left/right selector switch	537 to 541, 946 to 950
S68.4	Door mirror parking position switch	952

No	Description	Track
S76	Air conditioning compressor switch - high-pressure fan	827
S82	Washer pump switch	347, 392
S88	Cooling fan switch	115 to 116, 935 to 936
S93	Coolant level sensor	348, 393
S95	Oil level sensor	349, 394
S98	Headlamp aim adjustment switch	758 to 760
S99	Electric window switch - driver's door	685
S100	Electric window switch - passenger door	683
S101	Air conditioning compressor switch	822 to 824
S102	Air conditioning circulation switch	816 to 818
S104	Automatic transmission kickdown switch	794
S105	Automatic transmission "Winter" mode button	796 to 798
S106	Automatic transmission "Economy/Sport" mode button	793
S109	Air conditioning compressor switch	818
S115	Automatic transmission coolant temperature switch	788 to 789
S116	Brake lamp switch	464 to 465
S117	Four-wheel-drive hydraulic pressure switch	729
S119	Air conditioning refrigerant temperature switch	829, 843
S120	Anti-theft alarm bonnet switch	635
S127	Central locking switch - tailgate	630
S128	Air conditioning refrigerant temperature cooling switch	825 to 826
S131	Air conditioning defroster lever limit switch	815
U2	Trip computer	651 to 662
U4	ABS hydraulic modulator assembly	705 to 718, 738 to 751
U4.1	ABS hydraulic pump relay	706 to 709, 739 to 742
U4.2	ABS solenoid valves relay	715 to 718, 747 to 751
U4.3	ABS hydraulic pump	705, 738
U4.4	ABS diode	717
U4.5	ABS solenoid valve - front left	710, 743
U4.6	ABS solenoid valve - front right	711, 744
U4.7	ABS solenoid valve - rear left	712, 745
U4.8	ABS solenoid valve - rear right	713
U5	Check control display	347 to 355
U5.1	Check control washer fluid level warning lamp	352
U5.2	Check control oil level warning lamp	351
U5.3	Check control coolant level warning lamp	350
U5.4	Check control tail lamp and dipped beam bulb failure warning lamp	349
U5.5	Check control brake lamp bulb failure warning lamp	348

No	Description	Track
U5.6	Check control brake wear warning lamp	347
U6	LCD instruments	
U6.1	Check control washer fluid level warning lamp	392
U6.2	Check control oil level warning lamp	394
U6.3	Check control coolant level warning lamp	393
U6.4	Check control tail lamp and dipped beam bulb failure warning lamp	391
U6.5	Check control brake lamp bulb failure warning lamp	395
U6.6	Check control brake pad wear warning lamp	396
U12.1	Temperature switch (Diesel models)	898, 931
U12.2	Fuel filter heater (Diesel models)	899, 932
U13	AF 14/20 automatic transmission	782 to 786
U13.1	Solenoid - 1/2 and 3/4 shift up	782
U13.2	Solenoid - 2/3 shift up	783
U13.3	Solenoid - converter lock-up control	784
U13.4	Solenoid - main fluid pressure control	785
V1	Brake fluid level warning lamp test diode	312
V8	Air conditioning compressor diode	820
Y1	Air conditioning compressor clutch	821
Y4	Headlamp washer solenoid valve	520
Y5	Fuel solenoid valve (Diesel models)	893, 928
Y7	Fuel injectors	187 to 194, 280 to 287
Y10	Distributor (Hall-effect)	246 to 251
Y23	Distributor (inductive discharge)	123 to 127
Y24	Distributor (inductive discharge)	129 to 136
Y25	Idle-up solenoid valve (automatic transmission)	242
Y30	Cold start valve (Diesel models)	896
Y32	Fuel injector	140, 979
Y33	Distributor	170, 262, 972 to 974
Y34	Fuel tank vent valve	193, 292
Y35	Air conditioning circulation solenoid valve	816
Y44	Four-wheel-drive solenoid valve	731
Y47	Parking brake lock lifting magnet (automatic transmission)	769
X13	Diagnostic equipment connector	149, 170 to 171, 254 to 255, 269 to 270, 325, 339 to 340, 752 to 753, 774 to 775, 992 to 993
X15	Octane coding plug	160, 184 to 185, 248 to 249, 990 to 991
X54	Ignition coding plug	270 to 271
X1 on	Wiring connectors	Various

12

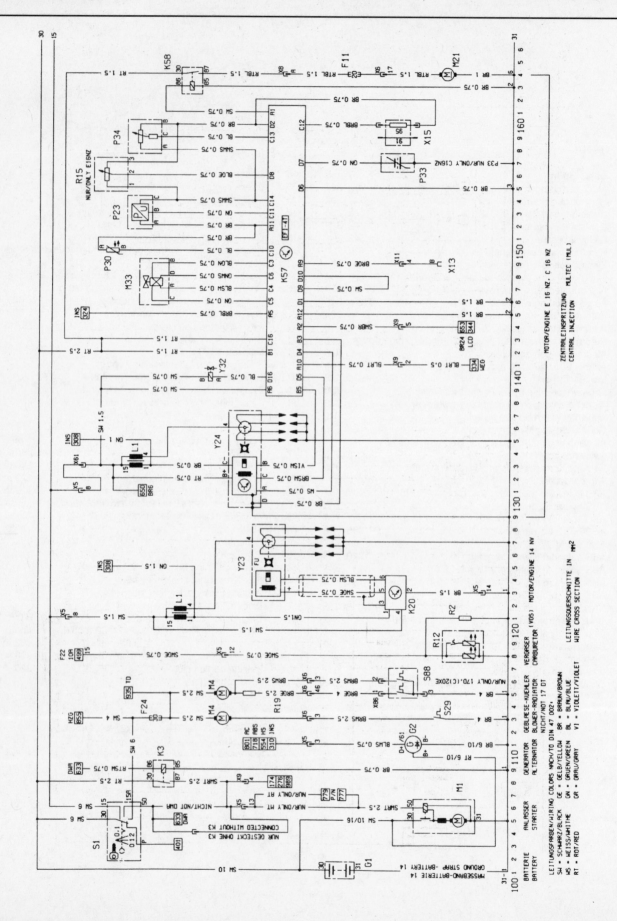

Wiring diagram for early models – Current track 0100 - 0166

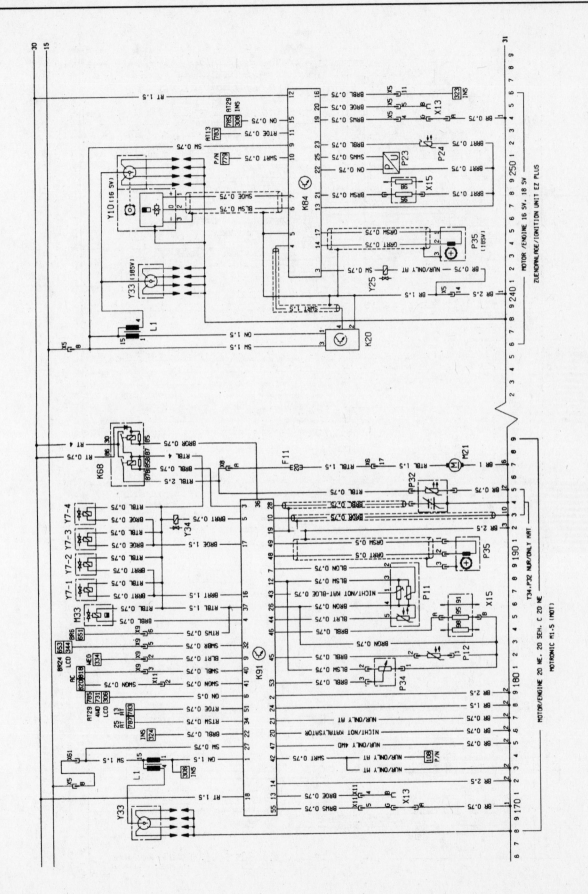

Wiring diagram for early models - Current track 0166 - 0260

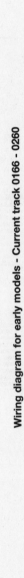

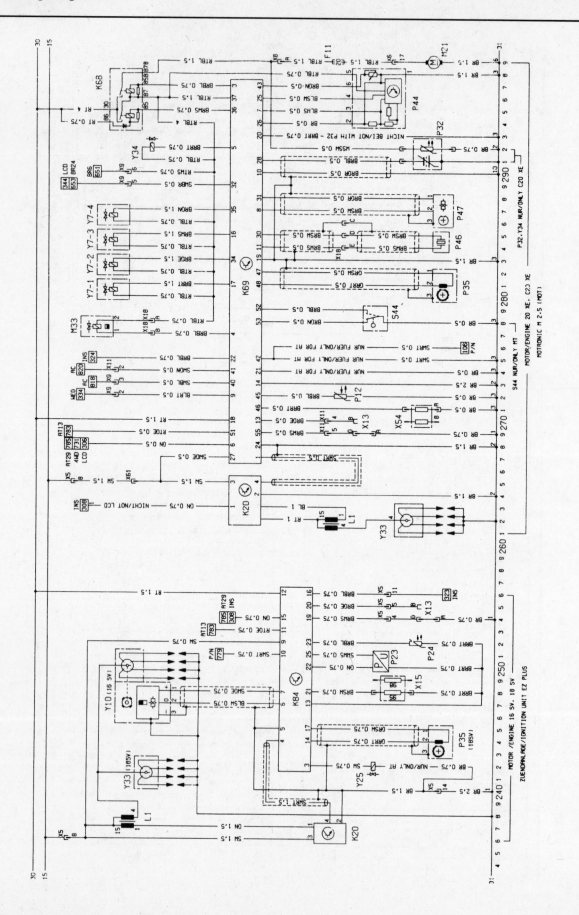

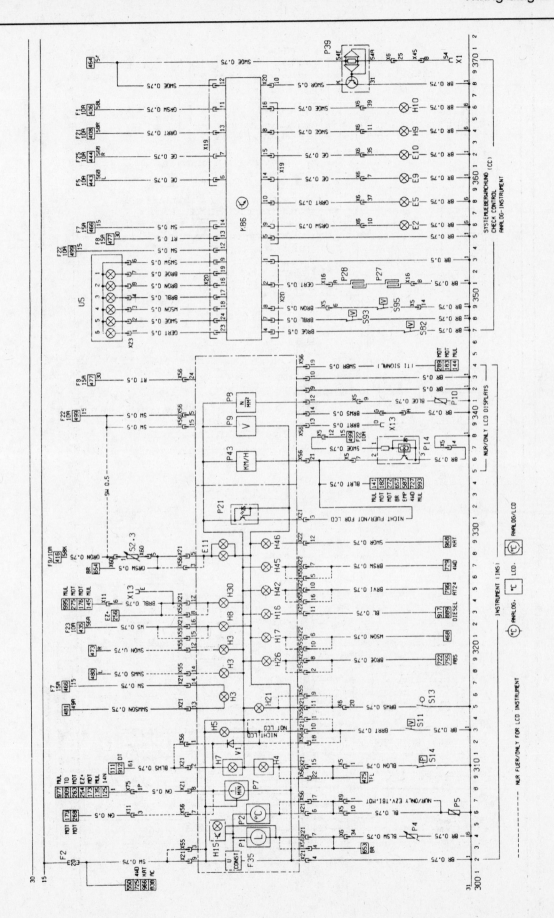

Wiring diagram for early models – Current track 0300 – 0370

12

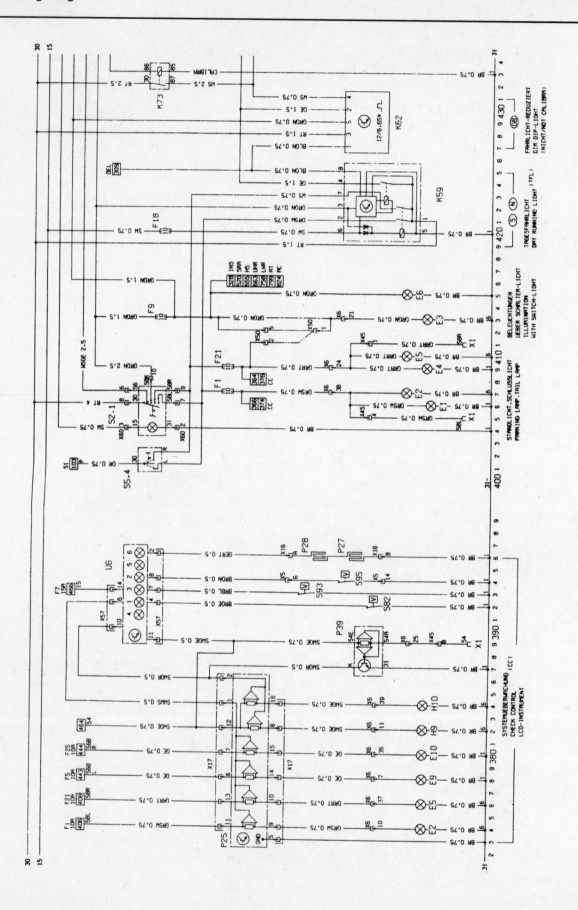

Wiring diagram for early models - Current track 0372 - 0434

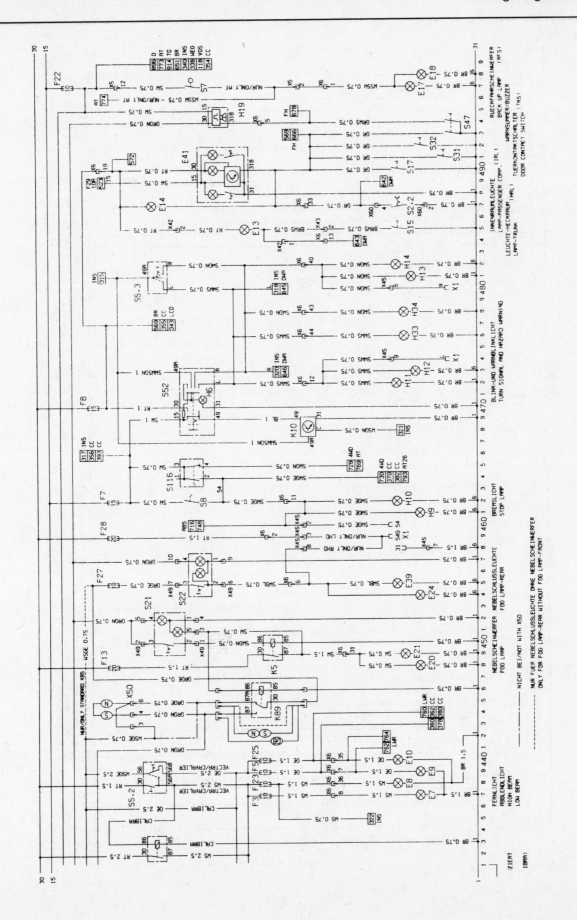

Wiring diagram for early models - Current track 0423 - 0499

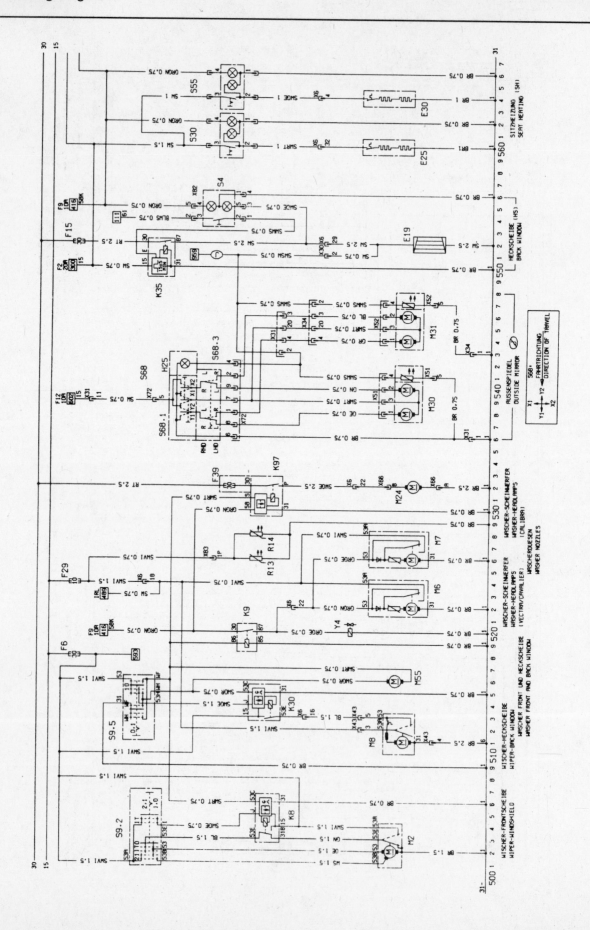

Wiring diagram for early models – Current track 0500 – 0567

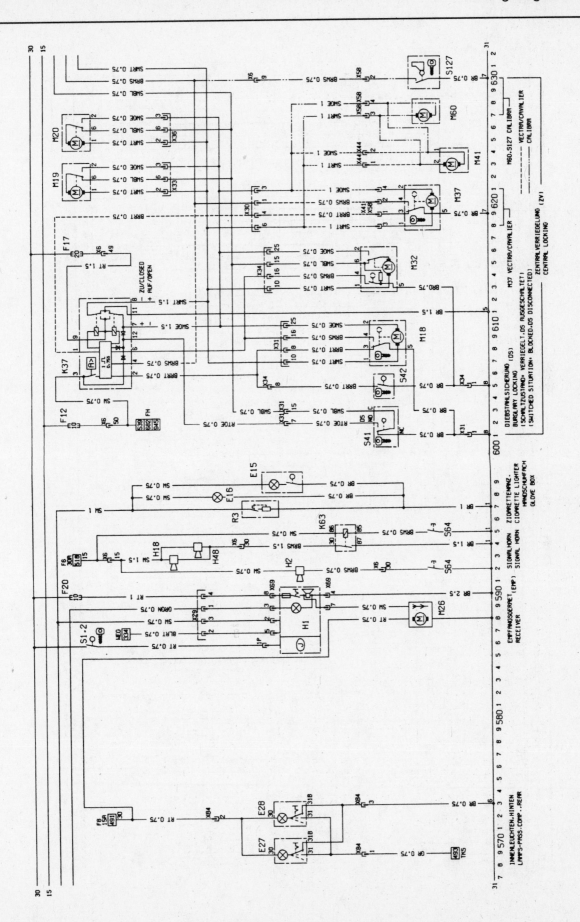

Wiring diagram for early models – Current track 0567 – 0632

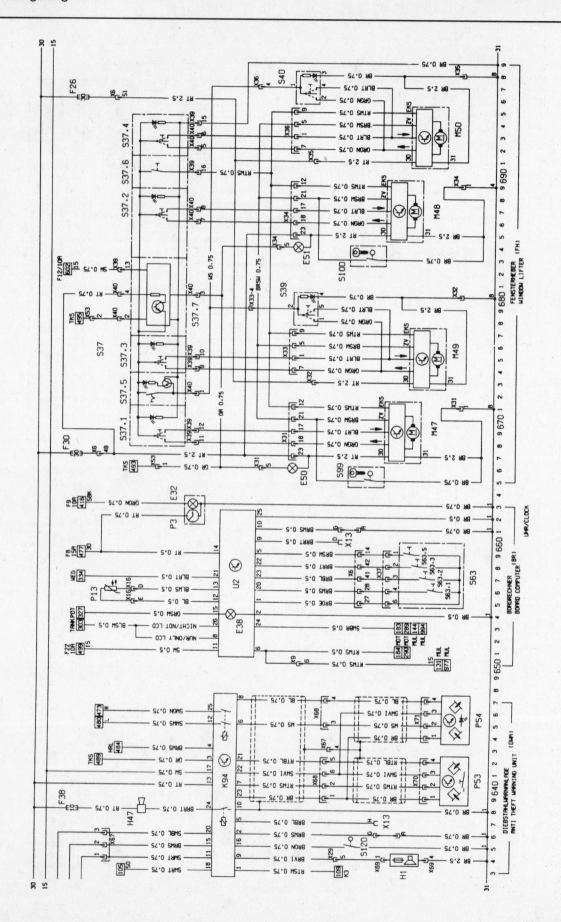

Wiring diagram for early models - Current track 0633 - 0699

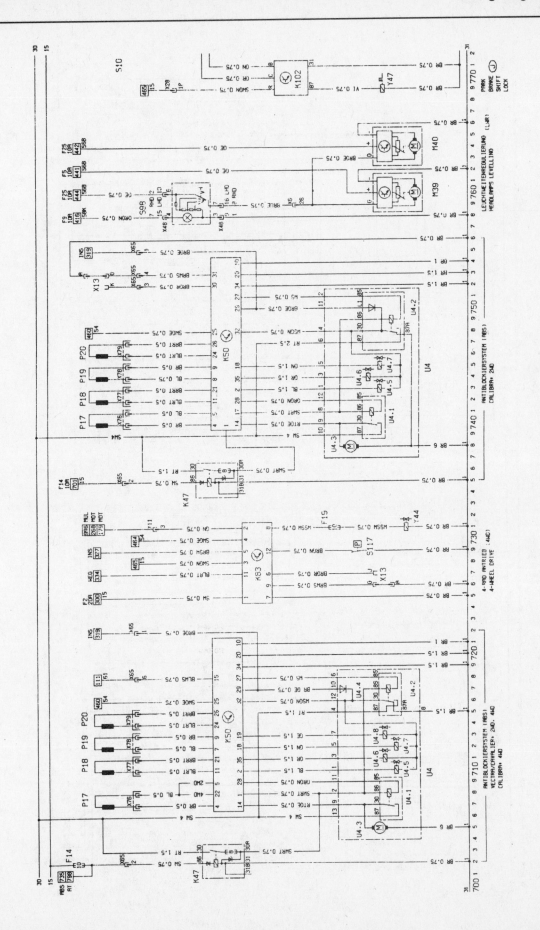

Wiring diagram for early models - Current track 0700 - 0772

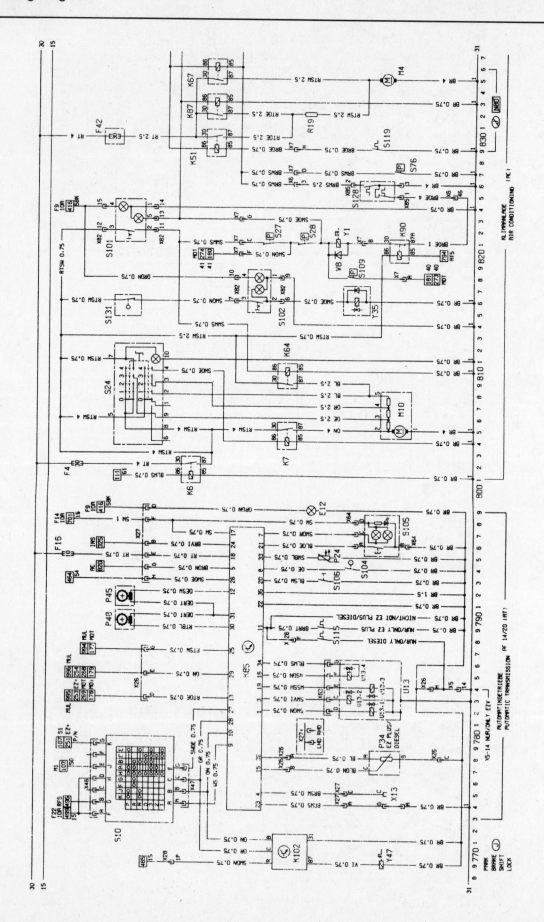

Wiring diagram for early models – Current track 0768 – 0837

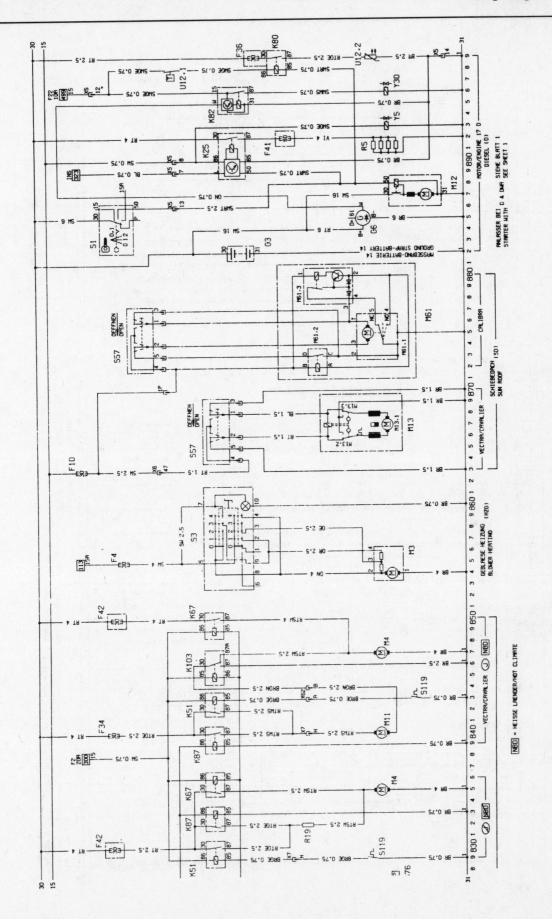

Wiring diagram for early models - Current track 0828 - 0899

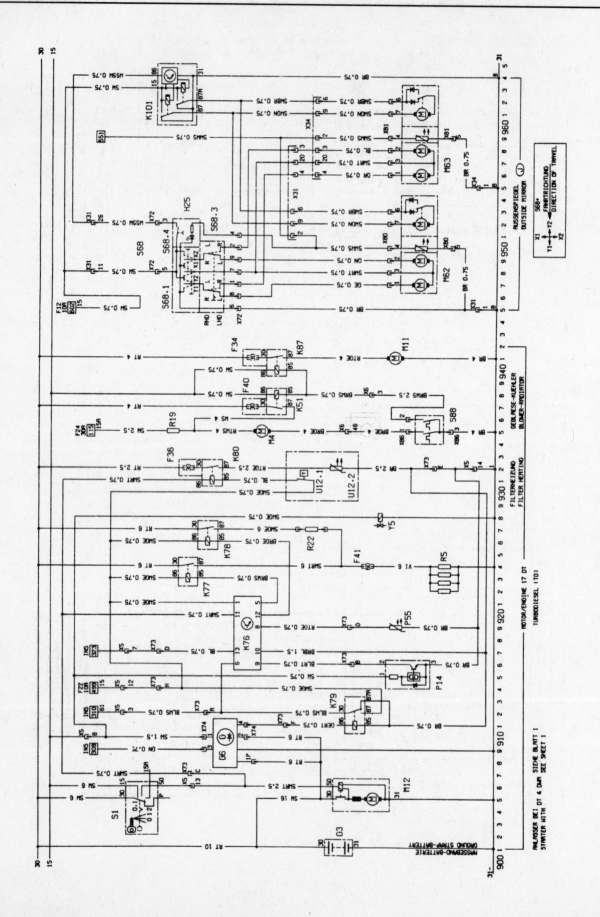

Wiring diagram for early models - Current track 0900 - 0965

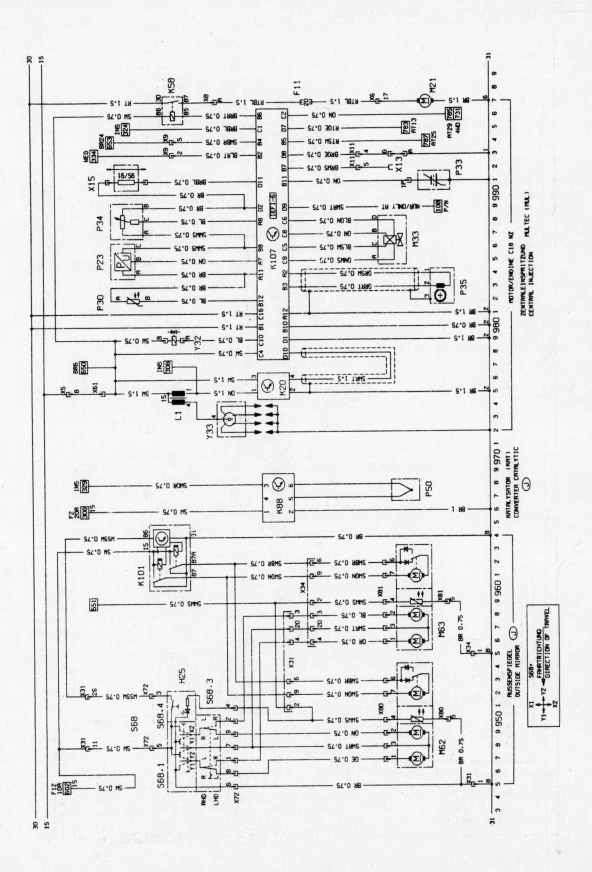

Wiring diagram for early models - Current track 0943 - 0999

Key to wiring diagrams for later models

No	Description	Track
E1	Sidelight, left	406
E2	Tail light, left	407, 657
E3	Number plate light	413, 414
E4	Sidelight, right	409
E5	Tail light, right	410, 658
E7	Headlight main beam, left	435
E8	Headlight main beam, right	436
E9	Headlight dipped beam, left	437, 659
E10	Headlight dipped beam, right	438, 660
E11	Instrument lighting	628, 629
E12	Automatic transmission selector illumination	390
E13	Luggage compartment light	486
E15	Glovebox light	577
E16	Cigarette lighter illumination	576
E17	Reversing light, left	497
E18	Reversing light, right	498
E19	Heated rear window	552
E20	Foglight, front left	453
E21	Foglight, front right	454
E24	Foglight, rear left	448
E25	Seat heating, right	560
E30	Seat heating, left	564
E37	Sun visor lamp, left	530
E38	Info display lamp	350
E39	Foglight, rear right	449
E40	Sun visor lamp, right	532
E41	Passenger compartment light delay	488 to 490
E63	Info display unit lamp	671 to 675
F1	Fuse	407
F2	Fuse	602
F3	Fuse	435
F5	Fuse	437
F6	Fuse	518
F7	Fuse	462
F8	Fuse	470
F9	Fuse	413
F10	Fuse	584
F11	Fuse	181, 247
F12	Fuse	702
F13	Fuse	453
F14	Fuse	949
F15	Fuse	552
F16	Fuse	394
F17	Fuse	716
F18	Fuse	420
F19	Fuse	342
F20	Fuse	571
F21	Fuse	409
F22	Fuse	497
F23	Fuse	436
F25	Fuse	438
F27	Fuse	449
F29	Fuse	524
F30	Fuse	768
F34	Fuse, radiator fan	274, 861, 979
F35	Fuse	602
F42	Fuse, radiator fan	854, 876, 892, 990
F46	Fuse, heating	121
F47	Fuse, air conditioning	802
F48	Fuse, TC	940
F49	Fuse, secondary air induction	245

No	Description	Track
G1	Battery	101
G2	Alternator	114
H1	Radio	315 to 329
H3	Direction indicator warning light	616
H4	Oil pressure warning light	610
H5	Brake fluid warning light	612
H6	Hazard flashers warning light	471
H7	Alternator/no-charge warning light	610
H8	Headlight main beam warning light	614
H9	Stop-light, left	462, 661
H10	Stop-light, right	463, 662
H11	Direction indicator light, front left	472
H12	Direction indicator light, rear left	473
H13	Direction indicator light, front right	481
H14	Direction indicator light, rear right	482
H15	Low fuel/fuel reserve warning light	605, 606
H17	Trailer direction indicator warning light	616
H18	Horn (twin-tone)	570
H19	Headlights 'on' warning light	494, 495
H23	Airbag warning light	619
H24	Anti-theft warning siren	732 to 734
H25	Heated mirror and rear window warning light	542, 684 to 686
H26	ABS warning light	621
H28	Seatbelt warning light	623
H30	Engine warning light	624
H33	Direction indicator side repeater light left	476
H34	Direction indicator side repeater light right	478
H36	Stop-light, centre	461
H37	Loudspeaker, front left	319, 321
H38	Loudspeaker, front right	325, 327
H39	Loudspeaker, rear left	319, 320
H40	Loudspeaker, rear right	322, 323
H42	Automatic transmission warning light	625
H45	Four-wheel-drive warning light	627
H46	Catalytic converter temperature warning light	629
H47	Anti-theft alarm horn	741
H48	Horn (twin-tone)	571
H51	Electronic traction control (ETC) warning light	620
H52	Tweeter, front left	319, 321
H53	Tweeter, front right	327
K5	Front foglight relay	454, 455
K6	Air conditioning relay	801, 802
K7	Air conditioning fan relay	804, 805
K8	Inermittent windscreen wiper relay	518
K10	Flasher relay	467, 469
K12	Secondary air induction relay	184 to 186, 253 to 255
K20	Ignition coil	204 to 240
K22	Coolant pump relay	269, 858, 859, 975
K26	Radiator fan relay	861 to 863, 978 to 980
K27	Radiator fan relay	273
K30	Intermittent rear wiper relay	503 to 506
K31	Airbag control unit	790 to 796
K35	Heated mirror and rear window relay	550 to 553
K37	Central door locking control unit	705 to 712
K43	Injection valves relay	173, 174
K44	Fuel pump relay	167, 168
K51	Radiator fan relay	282, 845 to 846, 883, 884
K52	Radiator fan relay	294, 849 to 851, 888 to 890, 987 to 989
K59	Day running light relay	420 to 425
K60	Air conditioning compressor relay	831, 832
K61	Motronic control unit	212 to 245

No	Description	Track
K63	Twin-tone horn relay	571, 572
K64	Air conditioning fan relay	813, 814
K67	Radiator fan relay	298, 853, 854, 896, 897, 995, 996
K68	Fuel injection unit realy	242 to 246
K69	Simtec control unit	137 to 178
K73	High beam relay	429, 430
K83	Four-wheel-drive control unit	335 to 342
K85	Automatic transmission control unit	373 to 396
K86	Check control control unit	648 to 664
K87	Radiator fan relay	866, 867, 880, 881, 982, 983
K88	Catalytic converter temperature control unit	364 to 366
K89	Rear foglight relay	443 to 445
K94	Anti-theft alarm control unit	736 to 752
K95	TC system control unit	925 to 940
K97	Headlight washer delay relay	513 to 515
K101	Mirror parking position mirror	695 to 698
K102	Handbrak shift lock control unit	369 to 371
K108	Radiator fan relay	891, 892, 991, 992
K109	Radiator fan relay	892, 893, 992, 993
K117	Immobiliser control unit	756 to 760
L2	Ignition coil	135 to 138, 203 to 207
M1	Starter motor	105
M2	Windscreen wiper motor	501 to 504
M3	Heater fan motor	120 to 125
M4	Radiator fan motor	276, 285, 296, 851, 873, 890, 989
M8	Tailgate wiper motor	511 to 513
M10	Air conditioning fan motor	805 to 808
M11	Radiator fan motor	291, 843, 869, 881, 984
M18	Central locking motor, driver's door	707 to 710
M21	Fuel pump	181, 247
M23	Alternator/starter fan motor	271, 863, 980
M24	Headlight washer pump	524
M27	Secondary air induction pump	185, 154
M30	Electric mirror (driver's side)	538 to 541
M31	Electric mirror (passenger side)	544 to 547
M32	Central locking motor, front passenger door	713 to 716
M33	Idle speed actuator	155, 156, 224, 225
M39	Headlight levelling motor, left	592 to 594
M40	Headlight levelling motor, right	596 to 598
M41	Central locking motor, fuel filler flap	718, 719
M47	Electric window motor, driver's door	768 to 771
M48	Electric window motor, passenger's door	779 to 782
M55	Windscreen/tailgate washer pump	217
M57	Coolant pump	270, 859, 976
M41	Central locking motor, tailgate	722, 723
M61	Sunroof motor	583 to 585
M62	Electric window motor, driver's door	681 to 687
M63	Electric window motor, passenger's door	690 to 696
M65	TC throttle valve actuator	930 to 934
P1	Fuel gauge	604
P2	Coolant temperature gauge	606
P4	Fuel level sensor	604
P5	Coolant temperature sensor	606
P7	Tachometer	608
P10	Oil pressure sensor	641
P13	Ambient air temperature sensor	352, 673
P17	Wheel sensor, front left	910, 911, 954, 955
P18	Wheel sensor, front right	913, 914, 957, 958
P19	Wheel sensor, rear left	916, 917, 960, 961
P20	Wheel sensor, rear right	919, 920, 963, 964
P21	Distance sensor	621
P27	Brake pad wear sensor, front left	652
P28	Brake pad wear sensor, front right	652
P29	Inlet manifold temperature sensor	145, 221
P30	Coolant temperature sensor	147, 222
P32	Exhaust gas oxygen sensor (heated)	167 to 170, 242, 243
P34	Throttle valve potentiometer	149 to 151, 223 to 225
P35	Crankshaft impulse sensor	158 to 160, 234, 235
P38	Automatic transmission fluid temperature sensor	386
P43	Speedometer	633
P44	Air mass meter	172 to 175, 245, 246
P45	Automatic transmission engine speed sensor	378 to 379
P46	Knock sensor	153 to 154, 227
P47	Camshaft sensor	163 to 165, 237, 238
P48	Automatic transmission distance sensor	376, 377
P50	Catalytic converter temperature sensor	365, 366
P53	Anti-theft sensor, driver's side	744 to 752
P54	Anti-theft sensor, passenger's side	744 to 752
P56	Knock sensor	229
P57	Aerial	328
P61	Oil temperature sensor, hang-on transmission	340
R3	Cigarette lighter	575
R19	Pre-resistor, radiator cooling fan motor	283, 892, 991
S1	Ignition/starter switch	103 to 105
S2	Light switch assembly	
S2.1	Light switch	404 to 407
S2.2	Light switch, passenger compartment	487
S2.3	Instrument lights dimmer	628
S3	Heater fan switch	120 to 126
S4	Rear window & mirror switch	555 to 557
S5	Direction indicator switch assembly	
S5.2	Headlight dipped beam switch	430, 431
S5.3	Direction indicator switch	480, 482
S5.4	Sidelight switch	401, 402
S7	Reversing light switch	497
S8	Stop-light switch	462
S9	Wiper switch assembly	
S9.2	Intermittent windscreen wiper switch	501 to 504
S9.5	Tailgate wash/wipe switch	514 to 516
S10	Automatic transmission selector switch	372 to 378
S11	Brake fluid level switch	612
S13	Handbrake 'on' switch	613
S14	Oil pressure sender/switch	610
S15	Luggage compartment light switch	485
S17	Courtesy light switch, passenger's door	490
S20	Pressure switch	825
S20.1	Compressor low pressure switch	825
S20.2	Compressor high pressure switch	825
S20.3	Compressor high pressure fan switch	839, 887, 986
S21	Fog lamp switch	455 to 457
S22	Fog lamp switch, rear	449 to 451
S24	Air conditioning fan switch	804 to 811
S29	Coolant temperature switch	273, 846, 861, 884, 978
S30	Seat heating switch, front left	560 to 562
S33	TC system switch	930, 931
S37	Electric window switch assembly	769 to 783
S37.1	Electric window switch, left	769, 770
S37.2	Electric window switch, right	780 to 783
S37.3	Electric window switch, automatic	774 to 777
S41	Central locking switch, driver's door	700 to 702
S42	Central locking switch, passenger's door	705
S47	Courtesy light switch, driver's door	493, 494

Key to wiring diagrams for later models (continued)

S52	Hazard warning light (hazard flashers) switch	469 to 473
S55	Seat heating switch, front left	564 to 566
S57	Sunroof switch	581 to 587
S63	Info display switch	351 to 356
S63.1	Switch reset	352
S63.2	Clock hours adjustment switch	353
S63.3	Function select switch	354
S63.4	Clock minutes adjustment switch	355
S64	Horn switch	572, 787, 788
S68	Electric mirror switch assembly	679 to 686
S68.1	Electric mirror adjustment switch	536 to 542, 679 to 682
S68.3	Electric mirror left/right switch	536 to 542, 680 to 684
S68.4	Electric mirror parking position switch	684 to 686
S82	Washer fluid level switch	648
S88	Coolant temperature switch	279, 282, 290
S89	Seat belt switch	362
S93	Coolant level switch	649
S95	Engine oil level switch	650
S98	Headlamp levelling switch	591 to 593
S99	Electric window switch, driver's	773
S100	Electric window switch, passenger's	777
S101	Air conditioning compressor switch	826 to 828
S102	Air recirculation switch	818 to 820
S104	Automatic transmission kickdown switch	393
S105	Automatic transmission Winter switch	395 to 397
S106	Automatic transmission Economy/Sport switch	392
S109	Revolution acceleration pressure switch	821
S116	Stop-light switch	464, 465
S117	Hydraulic pressure switch	338
S120	Anti-theft alarm bonnet switch	738
S121	Temperature lever limit switch	816
S127	Central locking switch, tailgate	726
S128	Coolant temperature switch	836, 837, 895, 896, 994, 995
S131	Defroster lever limit switch	818
U2	Info display	347 to 358
U4	ABS hydroaggregrate system	902
U4.1	Pump relay	904, 946
U4.2	Solenoid valve relay	902, 948
U4.3	Pump motor	905, 946
U4.4	Diode	949
U4.5	Solenoid valve relay, front left	909, 953

U4.6	Solenoid valve relay, front right	911, 955
U4.7	Solenoid valve relay, rear axle	913, 957
U4.8	ABS control unit	906 to 922, 950 to 964
U4.9	Solenoid valve plug	953
U5	Check control display assembly	648 to 654
U5.1	Washer fluid level warning light	653
U5.2	Oil level warning light	652
U5.3	Coolant level warning light	651
U5.4	Rear lights and dipped beam warning light	650
U5.5	Stop-light failure warning light	649
U5.6	Front brake pad wear warning light	648
U13	Automatic transmission solenoid valve block	380 to 385
U13.1	2/3 shift solenoid valve	381
U13.2	1/2, 3/4 shift solenoid valve	382
U13.3	Converter clutch solenoid valve	383
U13.4	Hydraulic pressure control solenoid valve	384
U13.5	Neutral control solenoid valve	380
U14	Info display unit	671 to 675
U20	Airbag contact	787 to 792
U21	Airbag, driver's side	790 to 792
U21.1	Airbag, driver's side squib	790 to 792
U22	Airbag, passenger's side	794 to 796
U22.1	Airbag, passenger's side squib	794 to 796
U25	Auxiliary instrument assembly	637 to 641
U25.1	Voltmeter	637
U25.2	Oil pressure gauge	641
U25.3	Instrument lights	639
V1	Brake system test bulb diode	611
V8	Air conditioning compressor diode	826
V21	Anti-theft warning diode	739
X1 to X96	Wiring connectors	Various
Y1	Air conditioning compressor clutch	825
Y7	Fuel injectors	164 to 171, 227 to 238
Y14	Coolant solenoid valve	816
Y15	Secondary air induction solenoid valve	183, 184, 251
Y18	EGR solenoid valve	157, 158
Y19	Inlet manifold solenoid valve	161, 162
Y34	Fuel tank ventilation valve	159, 160, 241
Y35	Air recirculation solenoid valve	818
Y44	Four-wheel-drive solenoid valve	342
Y47	Selector lever lifting magnet	369

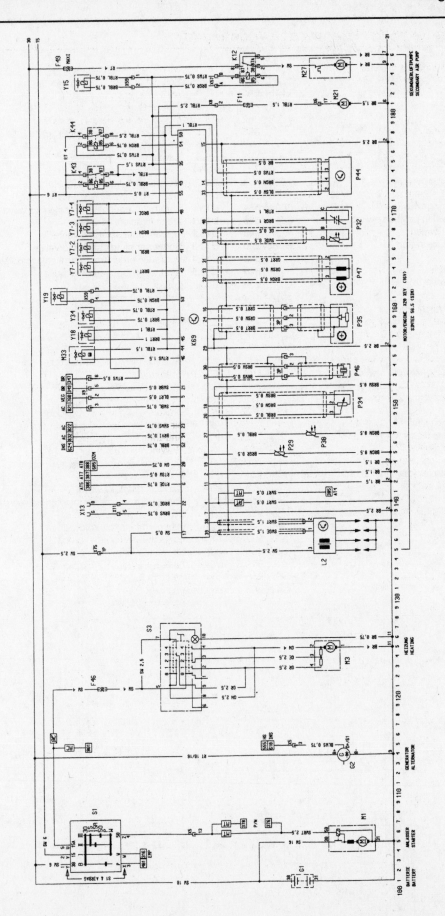

Wiring diagram for later models – Current track 0100 - 0199

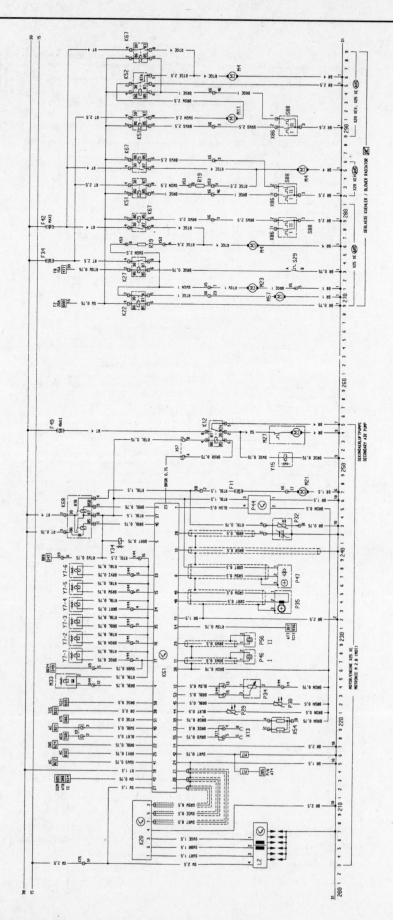

Wiring diagram for later models - Current track 0200 - 0299

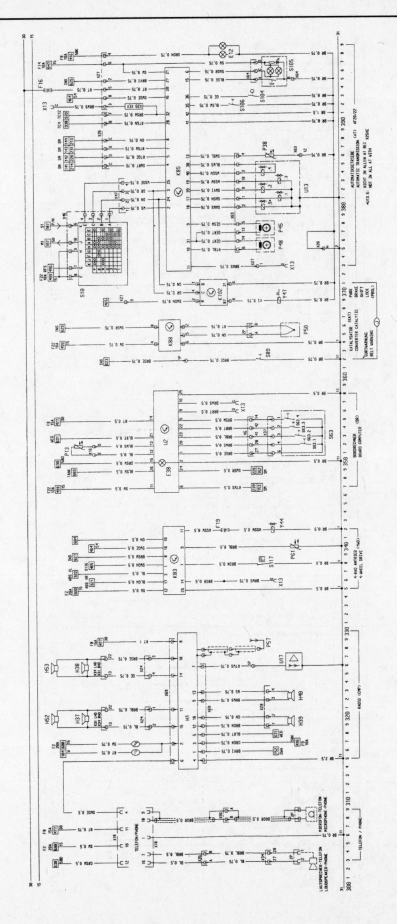

Wiring diagram for later models - Current track 0300 - 0399

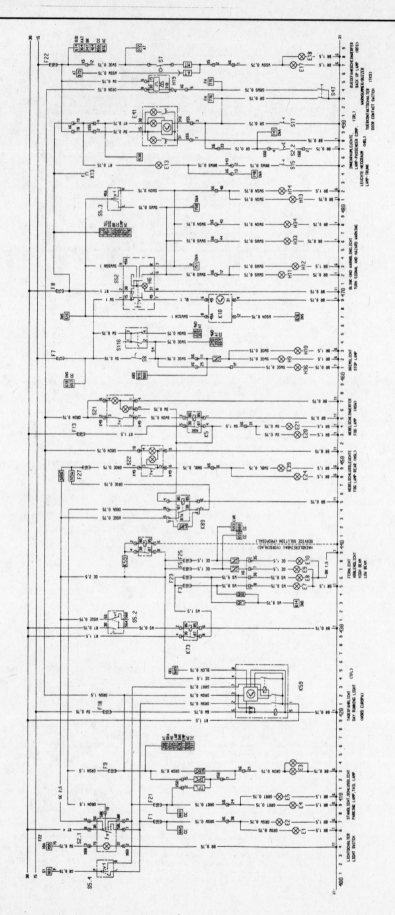

Wiring diagram for later models - Current track 0400 - 0499

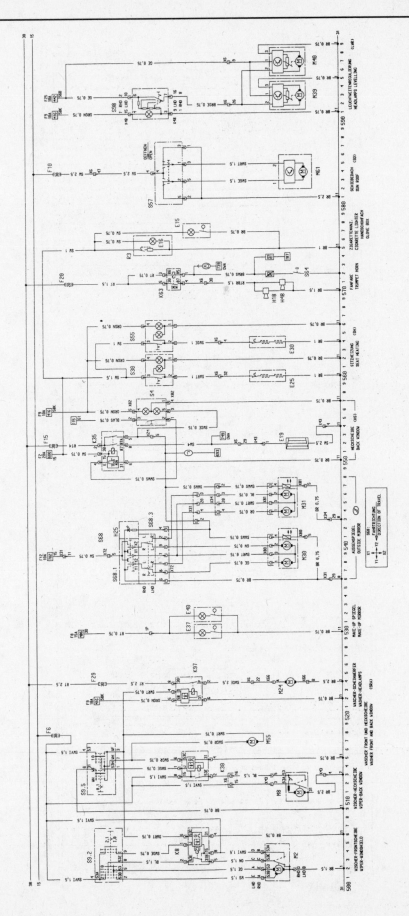

Wiring diagram for later models - Current track 0500 - 0599

12

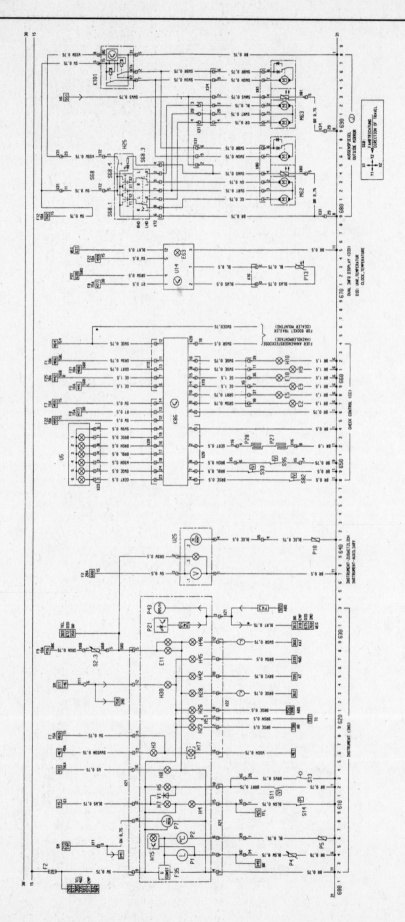

Wiring diagram for later models - Current track 0600 - 0699

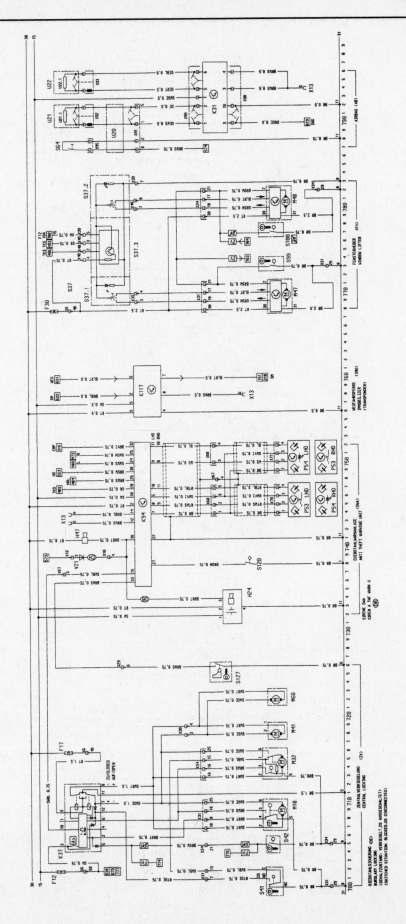

Wiring diagram for later models – Current track 0700 – 0799

12

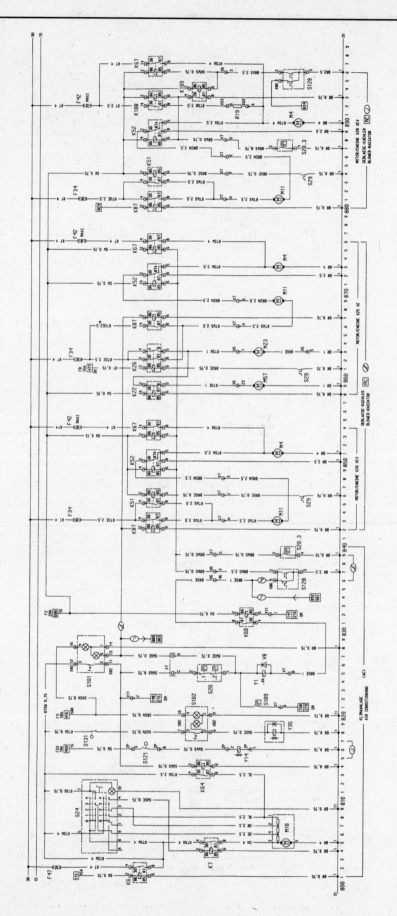

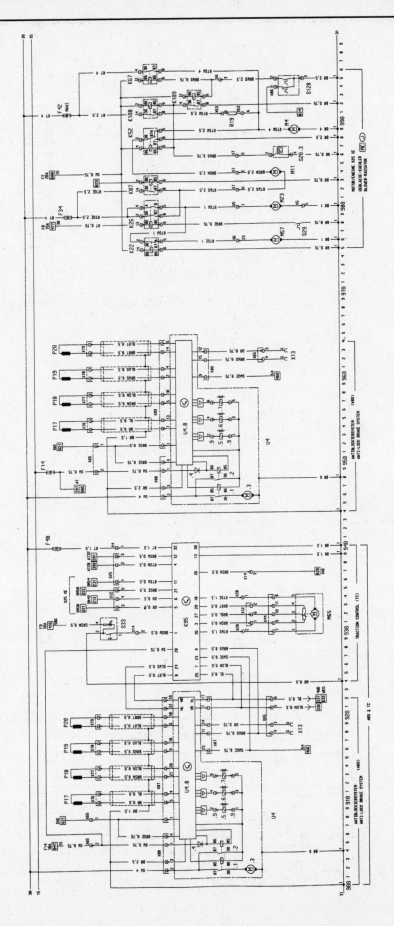

Wiring diagram for later models - Current track 0900 - 0999

12

Notes

Reference REF•1

Dimensions and Weights

Overall length
All models .... .4492 mm

Overall width
All models .... .1688 mm
Including door mirrors .... .1906 mm

Overall height (unladen)
All models .... .1320 mm
With antenna .... .1604 mm

Wheelbase
All models .... .2600 mm

Track
Front (All models) .... .1426 mm
Rear (All models) .... .1446 mm

Ground clearance (measured from exhaust)
All models except DTM .... .126 mm
DTM .... .102 mm

Weights

Kerb weight*
Dependent on model .... .1240 ± 70 kg

Maximum gross vehicle weight*
Dependent on model (see VIN plate) .... .1660 ± 70 kg

Maximum roof rack load
All models .... .100 kg

Maximum towing hitch downward load
All models .... .75 kg

Maximum towing weight*
Trailer with brakes .... .1275 ± 75 kg
Trailer without brakes .... .580 kg

Note: *For towing weights, see the vehicle papers, or calculate the difference between the gross combination weight and gross vehicle weight, specified on the VIN plate*
* *Exact details depend upon model and specification. Refer to owner's handbook.*

Conversion factors

Length (distance)

Inches (in)	x 25.4	= Millimetres (mm)	x 0.0394	=	Inches (in)
Feet (ft)	x 0.305	= Metres (m)	x 3.281	=	Feet (ft)
Miles	x 1.609	= Kilometres (km)	x 0.621	=	Miles

Volume (capacity)

Cubic inches (cu in; in³)	x 16.387	= Cubic centimetres (cc; cm³)	x 0.061	=	Cubic inches (cu in; in³)
Imperial pints (Imp pt)	x 0.568	= Litres (l)	x 1.76	=	Imperial pints (Imp pt)
Imperial quarts (Imp qt)	x 1.137	= Litres (l)	x 0.88	=	Imperial quarts (Imp qt)
Imperial quarts (Imp qt)	x 1.201	= US quarts (US qt)	x 0.833	=	Imperial quarts (Imp qt)
US quarts (US qt)	x 0.946	= Litres (l)	x 1.057	=	US quarts (US qt)
Imperial gallons (Imp gal)	x 4.546	= Litres (l)	x 0.22	=	Imperial gallons (Imp gal)
Imperial gallons (Imp gal)	x 1.201	= US gallons (US gal)	x 0.833	=	Imperial gallons (Imp gal)
US gallons (US gal)	x 3.785	= Litres (l)	x 0.264	=	US gallons (US gal)

Mass (weight)

Ounces (oz)	x 28.35	= Grams (g)	x 0.035	=	Ounces (oz)
Pounds (lb)	x 0.454	= Kilograms (kg)	x 2.205	=	Pounds (lb)

Force

Ounces-force (ozf; oz)	x 0.278	= Newtons (N)	x 3.6	=	Ounces-force (ozf; oz)
Pounds-force (lbf; lb)	x 4.448	= Newtons (N)	x 0.225	=	Pounds-force (lbf; lb)
Newtons (N)	x 0.1	= Kilograms-force (kgf; kg)	x 9.81	=	Newtons (N)

Pressure

Pounds-force per square inch (psi; lbf/in²; lb/in²)	x 0.070	= Kilograms-force per square centimetre (kgf/cm²; kg/cm²)	x 14.223	=	Pounds-force per square inch (psi; lbf/in²; lb/in²)
Pounds-force per square inch (psi; lbf/in²; lb/in²)	x 0.068	= Atmospheres (atm)	x 14.696	=	Pounds-force per square inch (psi; lbf/in²; lb/in²)
Pounds-force per square inch (psi; lbf/in²; lb/in²)	x 0.069	= Bars	x 14.5	=	Pounds-force per square inch (psi; lbf/in²; lb/in²)
Pounds-force per square inch (psi; lbf/in²; lb/in²)	x 6.895	= Kilopascals (kPa)	x 0.145	=	Pounds-force per square inch (psi; lbf/in²; lb/in²)
Kilopascals (kPa)	x 0.01	= Kilograms-force per square centimetre (kgf/cm²; kg/cm²)	x 98.1	=	Kilopascals (kPa)
Millibar (mbar)	x 100	= Pascals (Pa)	x 0.01	=	Millibar (mbar)
Millibar (mbar)	x 0.0145	= Pounds-force per square inch (psi; lbf/in²; lb/in²)	x 68.947	=	Millibar (mbar)
Millibar (mbar)	x 0.75	= Millimetres of mercury (mmHg)	x 1.333	=	Millibar (mbar)
Millibar (mbar)	x 0.401	= Inches of water (inH₂O)	x 2.491	=	Millibar (mbar)
Millimetres of mercury (mmHg)	x 0.535	= Inches of water (inH₂O)	x 1.868	=	Millimetres of mercury (mmHg)
Inches of water (inH₂O)	x 0.036	= Pounds-force per square inch (psi; lbf/in²; lb/in²)	x 27.68	=	Inches of water (inH₂O)

Torque (moment of force)

Pounds-force inches (lbf in; lb in)	x 1.152	= Kilograms-force centimetre (kgf cm; kg cm)	x 0.868	=	Pounds-force inches (lbf in; lb in)
Pounds-force inches (lbf in; lb in)	x 0.113	= Newton metres (Nm)	x 8.85	=	Pounds-force inches (lbf in; lb in)
Pounds-force inches (lbf in; lb in)	x 0.083	= Pounds-force feet (lbf ft; lb ft)	x 12	=	Pounds-force inches (lbf in; lb in)
Pounds-force feet (lbf ft; lb ft)	x 0.138	= Kilograms-force metres (kgf m; kg m)	x 7.233	=	Pounds-force feet (lbf ft; lb ft)
Pounds-force feet (lbf ft; lb ft)	x 1.356	= Newton metres (Nm)	x 0.738	=	Pounds-force feet (lbf ft; lb ft)
Newton metres (Nm)	x 0.102	= Kilograms-force metres (kgf m; kg m)	x 9.804	=	Newton metres (Nm)

Power

Horsepower (hp)	x 745.7	= Watts (W)	x 0.0013	=	Horsepower (hp)

Velocity (speed)

Miles per hour (miles/hr; mph)	x 1.609	= Kilometres per hour (km/hr; kph)	x 0.621	=	Miles per hour (miles/hr; mph)

Fuel consumption*

Miles per gallon (mpg)	x 0.354	= Kilometres per litre (km/l)	x 2.825	=	Miles per gallon (mpg)

Temperature

Degrees Fahrenheit = (°C x 1.8) + 32   Degrees Celsius (Degrees Centigrade; °C) = (°F - 32) x 0.56

It is common practice to convert from miles per gallon (mpg) to litres/100 kilometres (l/100km), where mpg x l/100 km = 282

Spare parts are available from many sources, for example: Vauxhall dealers, other garages and accessory shops, and motor factors. Our advice regarding spare part sources is as follows.

Officially appointed Vauxhall dealers

This is the best source of parts that are peculiar to your car and are otherwise not generally available (e.g. complete cylinder heads, transmission components, badges, interior trim, etc.). It is also the only place at which you should buy parts if your vehicle is still under warranty - use of non-Vauxhall components may invalidate the warranty. To be sure of obtaining the correct parts it will always be necessary to give the storeman your car's vehicle identification number, and if possible, to take the "old" parts along for positive identification. Remember that many parts are available on a factory exchange scheme - any parts returned should always be clean! It obviously makes good sense to go straight to the specialists on your car for this type of part for they are best equipped to supply you.

Other garages and accessory shops

These are often very good places to buy materials and components needed for the maintenance of your car (e.g. oil filters, spark plugs, bulbs, drivebelts, oils and greases, touch-up paint, filler paste, etc.). They also sell general accessories, usually have convenient opening hours, charge lower prices and can often be found not far from home.

Motor factors

Good factors will stock all the more important components that wear out relatively quickly (e.g. clutch components, pistons, valves, exhaust systems, brake cylinders/pipes/hoses/seals/shoes and pads, etc.). Motor factors will often provide new or reconditioned components on a part exchange basis - this can save considerable amount of money.

Vehicle Identification

Modifications are a continuing and unpublished process in vehicle manufacture, quite apart from major model changes. Spare parts manuals and lists are compiled upon a numerical basis, the individual vehicle numbers being essential to correct identification of the component required.

When ordering spare parts, always give as much information as possible. Quote the car model, year of manufacture and vehicle identification and/or engine numbers as appropriate.

The *vehicle identification plate* is riveted on top of the front body panel and includes the Vehicle Identification Number (VIN), vehicle weight information and paint and trim colour codes.

The *Vehicle Identification Number (VIN)* is given on the vehicle identification plate and is also stamped into the body floor panel between the driver's seat and the door sill panel; lift the flap in the carpet to see it **(see illustrations)**.

The *engine number is* stamped on a horizontal flat located on the exhaust manifold side of the cylinder block, at the distributor end.

During 1995, Vauxhall introduced 'Car pass' with all vehicles fitted with an electronic immobiliser. This contains important information, e.g. VIN number, key number and radio code. It also includes a special code for diagnostic equipment, therefore it must be kept in a secure place and not in the vehicle.

The Vehicle Identification Number (VIN) plate (1) and engine number (2)

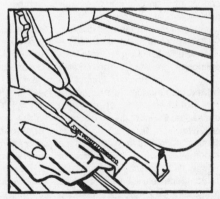

The VIN number is also stamped on the floor next to the driver's seat

Whenever servicing, repair or overhaul work is carried out on the car or its components, observe the following procedures and instructions. This will assist in carrying out the operation efficiently and to a professional standard of workmanship.

Joint mating faces and gaskets

When separating components at their mating faces, never insert screwdrivers or similar implements into the joint between the faces in order to prise them apart. This can cause severe damage which results in oil leaks, coolant leaks, etc upon reassembly. Separation is usually achieved by tapping along the joint with a soft-faced hammer in order to break the seal. However, note that this method may not be suitable where dowels are used for component location.

Where a gasket is used between the mating faces of two components, a new one must be fitted on reassembly; fit it dry unless otherwise stated in the repair procedure. Make sure that the mating faces are clean and dry, with all traces of old gasket removed. When cleaning a joint face, use a tool which is unlikely to score or damage the face, and remove any burrs or nicks with an oilstone or fine file.

Make sure that tapped holes are cleaned with a pipe cleaner, and keep them free of jointing compound, if this is being used, unless specifically instructed otherwise.

Ensure that all orifices, channels or pipes are clear, and blow through them, preferably using compressed air.

Oil seals

Oil seals can be removed by levering them out with a wide flat-bladed screwdriver or similar implement. Alternatively, a number of self-tapping screws may be screwed into the seal, and these used as a purchase for pliers or some similar device in order to pull the seal free.

Whenever an oil seal is removed from its working location, either individually or as part of an assembly, it should be renewed.

The very fine sealing lip of the seal is easily damaged, and will not seal if the surface it contacts is not completely clean and free from scratches, nicks or grooves. If the original sealing surface of the component cannot be restored, and the manufacturer has not made provision for slight relocation of the seal relative to the sealing surface, the component should be renewed.

Protect the lips of the seal from any surface which may damage them in the course of fitting. Use tape or a conical sleeve where possible. Lubricate the seal lips with oil before fitting and, on dual-lipped seals, fill the space between the lips with grease.

Unless otherwise stated, oil seals must be fitted with their sealing lips toward the lubricant to be sealed.

Use a tubular drift or block of wood of the appropriate size to install the seal and, if the seal housing is shouldered, drive the seal down to the shoulder. If the seal housing is unshouldered, the seal should be fitted with its face flush with the housing top face (unless otherwise instructed).

Screw threads and fastenings

Seized nuts, bolts and screws are quite a common occurrence where corrosion has set in, and the use of penetrating oil or releasing fluid will often overcome this problem if the offending item is soaked for a while before attempting to release it. The use of an impact driver may also provide a means of releasing such stubborn fastening devices, when used in conjunction with the appropriate screwdriver bit or socket. If none of these methods works, it may be necessary to resort to the careful application of heat, or the use of a hacksaw or nut splitter device.

Studs are usually removed by locking two nuts together on the threaded part, and then using a spanner on the lower nut to unscrew the stud. Studs or bolts which have broken off below the surface of the component in which they are mounted can sometimes be removed using a stud extractor. Always ensure that a blind tapped hole is completely free from oil, grease, water or other fluid before installing the bolt or stud. Failure to do this could cause the housing to crack due to the hydraulic action of the bolt or stud as it is screwed in.

When tightening a castellated nut to accept a split pin, tighten the nut to the specified torque, where applicable, and then tighten further to the next split pin hole. Never slacken the nut to align the split pin hole, unless stated in the repair procedure.

When checking or retightening a nut or bolt to a specified torque setting, slacken the nut or bolt by a quarter of a turn, and then retighten to the specified setting. However, this should not be attempted where angular tightening has been used.

For some screw fastenings, notably cylinder head bolts or nuts, torque wrench settings are no longer specified for the latter stages of tightening, "angle-tightening" being called up instead. Typically, a fairly low torque wrench setting will be applied to the bolts/nuts in the correct sequence, followed by one or more stages of tightening through specified angles.

Locknuts, locktabs and washers

Any fastening which will rotate against a component or housing during tightening should always have a washer between it and the relevant component or housing.

Spring or split washers should always be renewed when they are used to lock a critical component such as a big-end bearing retaining bolt or nut. Locktabs which are folded over to retain a nut or bolt should always be renewed.

Self-locking nuts can be re-used in non-critical areas, providing resistance can be felt when the locking portion passes over the bolt or stud thread. However, it should be noted that self-locking stiffnuts tend to lose their effectiveness after long periods of use, and should then be renewed as a matter of course.

Split pins must always be replaced with new ones of the correct size for the hole.

When thread-locking compound is found on the threads of a fastener which is to be re-used, it should be cleaned off with a wire brush and solvent, and fresh compound applied on reassembly.

Special tools

Some repair procedures in this manual entail the use of special tools such as a press, two or three-legged pullers, spring compressors, etc. Wherever possible, suitable readily-available alternatives to the manufacturer's special tools are described, and are shown in use. In some instances, where no alternative is possible, it has been necessary to resort to the use of a manufacturer's tool, and this has been done for reasons of safety as well as the efficient completion of the repair operation. Unless you are highly-skilled and have a thorough understanding of the procedures described, never attempt to bypass the use of any special tool when the procedure described specifies its use. Not only is there a very great risk of personal injury, but expensive damage could be caused to the components involved.

Environmental considerations

When disposing of used engine oil, brake fluid, antifreeze, etc, give due consideration to any detrimental environmental effects. Do not, for instance, pour any of the above liquids down drains into the general sewage system, or onto the ground to soak away. Many local council refuse tips provide a facility for waste oil disposal, as do some garages. If none of these facilities are available, consult your local Environmental Health Department, or the National Rivers Authority, for further advice.

With the universal tightening-up of legislation regarding the emission of environmentally-harmful substances from motor vehicles, most vehicles have tamperproof devices fitted to the main adjustment points of the fuel system. These devices are primarily designed to prevent unqualified persons from adjusting the fuel/air mixture, with the chance of a consequent increase in toxic emissions. If such devices are found during servicing or overhaul, they should, wherever possible, be renewed or refitted in accordance with the manufacturer's requirements or current legislation.

OIL CARE
FOLLOW THE CODE

OIL BANK LINE
0800 66 33 66

Note: It is antisocial and illegal to dump oil down the drain. To find the location of your local oil recycling bank, call this number free.

The jack supplied with the vehicle tool kit should only be used for changing roadwheels. When carrying out any other kind of work, raise the vehicle using a hydraulic jack, and always supplement the jack with axle stands positioned under the vehicle jacking points.

When jacking up the vehicle with a hydraulic jack, position the jack head under one of the relevant jacking points (note that the jacking points for use with a hydraulic jack are different to those for use with the vehicle jack). **Do not** jack the vehicle under the sump or any of the steering or suspension components. Supplement the jack using axle stands. The jacking points and axle stand positions are shown in the accompanying illustrations **(see illustrations)**.

⚠️ *Warning: Never work under, around, or near a raised vehicle, unless it is adequately supported in at least two places.*

Location of jacking points for vehicle jack

Front jacking point for hydraulic jack or axle stands

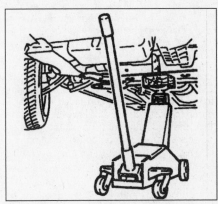

Rear jacking point for hydraulic jack or axle stands

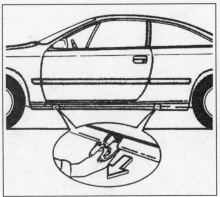

When raising the front of the vehicle, locate the jack underneath the centre of the subframe. Note the use of the block of wood placed on the jack head

Radio/cassette unit Anti-theft System

The radio/cassette unit fitted as standard equipment by Vauxhall is equipped with a built-in security code, to deter thieves. If the power source to the unit is cut, the anti-theft system will activate. Even if the power source is immediately reconnected, the radio/cassette unit will not function until the correct security code has been entered. Therefore, if you do not know the correct security code for the radio/cassette unit, do not disconnect the battery negative terminal of the battery, or remove the radio/cassette unit from the vehicle.

Refer to the Audio handbook supplied in the owner's handbook pack, for further details of how to use the code.

If you should lose or forget the code, seek the advice of your Vauxhall dealer. On presentation of proof of ownership, a Vauxhall dealer will be able to unlock the unit and provide you with a new security code.

Introduction

A selection of good tools is a fundamental requirement for anyone contemplating the maintenance and repair of a motor vehicle. For the owner who does not possess any, their purchase will prove a considerable expense, offsetting some of the savings made by doing-it-yourself. However, provided that the tools purchased meet the relevant national safety standards and are of good quality, they will last for many years and prove an extremely worthwhile investment.

To help the average owner to decide which tools are needed to carry out the various tasks detailed in this manual, we have compiled three lists of tools under the following headings: *Maintenance and minor repair*, *Repair and overhaul*, and *Special*. Newcomers to practical mechanics should start off with the *Maintenance and minor repair* tool kit, and confine themselves to the simpler jobs around the vehicle. Then, as confidence and experience grow, more difficult tasks can be undertaken, with extra tools being purchased as, and when, they are needed. In this way, a *Maintenance and minor repair* tool kit can be built up into a *Repair and overhaul* tool kit over a considerable period of time, without any major cash outlays. The experienced do-it-yourselfer will have a tool kit good enough for most repair and overhaul procedures, and will add tools from the *Special* category when it is felt that the expense is justified by the amount of use to which these tools will be put.

Maintenance and minor repair tool kit

The tools given in this list should be considered as a minimum requirement if routine maintenance, servicing and minor repair operations are to be undertaken. We recommend the purchase of combination spanners (ring one end, open-ended the other); although more expensive than open-ended ones, they do give the advantages of both types of spanner.

☐ *Combination spanners:*
  Metric - 8 to 19 mm inclusive
☐ *Adjustable spanner - 35 mm jaw (approx.)*
☐ *Spark plug spanner (with rubber insert) - petrol models*
☐ *Spark plug gap adjustment tool - petrol models*
☐ *Set of feeler gauges*
☐ *Brake bleed nipple spanner*
☐ *Screwdrivers:*
  Flat blade - 100 mm long x 6 mm dia
  Cross blade - 100 mm long x 6 mm dia
  Torx - various sizes (not all vehicles)
☐ *Combination pliers*
☐ *Hacksaw (junior)*
☐ *Tyre pump*
☐ *Tyre pressure gauge*
☐ *Oil can*
☐ *Oil filter removal tool*
☐ *Fine emery cloth*
☐ *Wire brush (small)*
☐ *Funnel (medium size)*
☐ *Sump drain plug key (not all vehicles)*

Repair and overhaul tool kit

These tools are virtually essential for anyone undertaking any major repairs to a motor vehicle, and are additional to those given in the *Maintenance and minor repair* list. Included in this list is a comprehensive set of sockets. Although these are expensive, they will be found invaluable as they are so versatile - particularly if various drives are included in the set. We recommend the half-inch square-drive type, as this can be used with most proprietary torque wrenches.

The tools in this list will sometimes need to be supplemented by tools from the *Special* list:

☐ *Sockets (or box spanners) to cover range in previous list (including Torx sockets)*
☐ *Reversible ratchet drive (for use with sockets)*
☐ *Extension piece, 250 mm (for use with sockets)*
☐ *Universal joint (for use with sockets)*
☐ *Flexible handle or sliding T "breaker bar" (for use with sockets)*
☐ *Torque wrench (for use with sockets)*
☐ *Self-locking grips*
☐ *Ball pein hammer*
☐ *Soft-faced mallet (plastic or rubber)*
☐ *Screwdrivers:*
  Flat blade - long & sturdy, short (chubby), and narrow (electrician's) types
  Cross blade – long & sturdy, and short (chubby) types
☐ *Pliers:*
  Long-nosed
  Side cutters (electrician's)
  Circlip (internal and external)
☐ *Cold chisel - 25 mm*
☐ *Scriber*
☐ *Scraper*
☐ *Centre-punch*
☐ *Pin punch*
☐ *Hacksaw*
☐ *Brake hose clamp*
☐ *Brake/clutch bleeding kit*
☐ *Selection of twist drills*
☐ *Steel rule/straight-edge*
☐ *Allen keys (inc. splined/Torx type)*
☐ *Selection of files*
☐ *Wire brush*
☐ *Axle stands*
☐ *Jack (strong trolley or hydraulic type)*
☐ *Light with extension lead*
☐ *Universal electrical multi-meter*

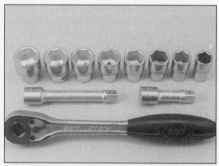

Sockets and reversible ratchet drive

Brake bleeding kit

Torx key, socket and bit

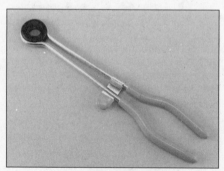

Hose clamp

Angular-tightening gauge

Special tools

The tools in this list are those which are not used regularly, are expensive to buy, or which need to be used in accordance with their manufacturers' instructions. Unless relatively difficult mechanical jobs are undertaken frequently, it will not be economic to buy many of these tools. Where this is the case, you could consider clubbing together with friends (or joining a motorists' club) to make a joint purchase, or borrowing the tools against a deposit from a local garage or tool hire specialist. It is worth noting that many of the larger DIY superstores now carry a large range of special tools for hire at modest rates.

The following list contains only those tools and instruments freely available to the public, and not those special tools produced by the vehicle manufacturer specifically for its dealer network. You will find occasional references to these manufacturers' special tools in the text of this manual. Generally, an alternative method of doing the job without the vehicle manufacturers' special tool is given. However, sometimes there is no alternative to using them. Where this is the case and the relevant tool cannot be bought or borrowed, you will have to entrust the work to a dealer.

- [ ] *Angular-tightening gauge*
- [ ] *Valve spring compressor*
- [ ] *Valve grinding tool*
- [ ] *Piston ring compressor*
- [ ] *Piston ring removal/installation tool*
- [ ] *Cylinder bore hone*
- [ ] *Balljoint separator*
- [ ] *Coil spring compressors (where applicable)*
- [ ] *Two/three-legged hub and bearing puller*
- [ ] *Impact screwdriver*
- [ ] *Micrometer and/or vernier calipers*
- [ ] *Dial gauge*
- [ ] *Stroboscopic timing light*
- [ ] *Dwell angle meter/tachometer*
- [ ] *Fault code reader*
- [ ] *Cylinder compression gauge*
- [ ] *Hand-operated vacuum pump and gauge*
- [ ] *Clutch plate alignment set*
- [ ] *Brake shoe steady spring cup removal tool*
- [ ] *Bush and bearing removal/installation set*
- [ ] *Stud extractors*
- [ ] *Tap and die set*
- [ ] *Lifting tackle*
- [ ] *Trolley jack*

Buying tools

Reputable motor accessory shops and superstores often offer excellent quality tools at discount prices, so it pays to shop around.

Remember, you don't have to buy the most expensive items on the shelf, but it is always advisable to steer clear of the very cheap tools. Beware of 'bargains' offered on market stalls or at car boot sales. There are plenty of good tools around at reasonable prices, but always aim to purchase items which meet the relevant national safety standards. If in doubt, ask the proprietor or manager of the shop for advice before making a purchase.

Care and maintenance of tools

Having purchased a reasonable tool kit, it is necessary to keep the tools in a clean and serviceable condition. After use, always wipe off any dirt, grease and metal particles using a clean, dry cloth, before putting the tools away. Never leave them lying around after they have been used. A simple tool rack on the garage or workshop wall for items such as screwdrivers and pliers is a good idea. Store all normal spanners and sockets in a metal box. Any measuring instruments, gauges, meters, etc, must be carefully stored where they cannot be damaged or become rusty.

Take a little care when tools are used. Hammer heads inevitably become marked, and screwdrivers lose the keen edge on their blades from time to time. A little timely attention with emery cloth or a file will soon restore items like this to a good finish.

Working facilities

Not to be forgotten when discussing tools is the workshop itself. If anything more than routine maintenance is to be carried out, a suitable working area becomes essential.

It is appreciated that many an owner-mechanic is forced by circumstances to remove an engine or similar item without the benefit of a garage or workshop. Having done this, any repairs should always be done under the cover of a roof.

Wherever possible, any dismantling should be done on a clean, flat workbench or table at a suitable working height.

Any workbench needs a vice; one with a jaw opening of 100 mm is suitable for most jobs. As mentioned previously, some clean dry storage space is also required for tools, as well as for any lubricants, cleaning fluids, touch-up paints etc, which become necessary.

Another item which may be required, and which has a much more general usage, is an electric drill with a chuck capacity of at least 8 mm. This, together with a good range of twist drills, is virtually essential for fitting accessories.

Last, but not least, always keep a supply of old newspapers and clean, lint-free rags available, and try to keep any working area as clean as possible.

Micrometers

Dial test indicator ("dial gauge")

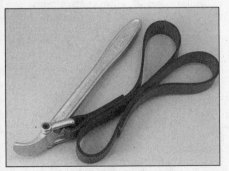

Strap wrench

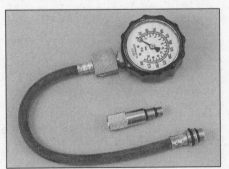

Compression tester

Fault code reader

This is a guide to getting your vehicle through the MOT test. Obviously it will not be possible to examine the vehicle to the same standard as the professional MOT tester. However, working through the following checks will enable you to identify any problem areas before submitting the vehicle for the test.

Where a testable component is in borderline condition, the tester has discretion in deciding whether to pass or fail it. The basis of such discretion is whether the tester would be happy for a close relative or friend to use the vehicle with the component in that condition. If the vehicle presented is clean and evidently well cared for, the tester may be more inclined to pass a borderline component than if the vehicle is scruffy and apparently neglected.

It has only been possible to summarise the test requirements here, based on the regulations in force at the time of printing. Test standards are becoming increasingly stringent, although there are some exemptions for older vehicles. For full details obtain a copy of the Haynes publication Pass the MOT! (available from stockists of Haynes manuals).

An assistant will be needed to help carry out some of these checks.

The checks have been sub-divided into four categories, as follows:

1 Checks carried out **FROM THE DRIVER'S SEAT**

2 Checks carried out **WITH THE VEHICLE ON THE GROUND**

3 Checks carried out **WITH THE VEHICLE RAISED AND THE WHEELS FREE TO TURN**

4 Checks carried out on **YOUR VEHICLE'S EXHAUST EMISSION SYSTEM**

1 Checks carried out **FROM THE DRIVER'S SEAT**

Handbrake

☐ Test the operation of the handbrake. Excessive travel (too many clicks) indicates incorrect brake or cable adjustment.

☐ Check that the handbrake cannot be released by tapping the lever sideways. Check the security of the lever mountings.

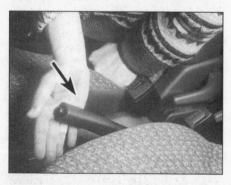

Footbrake

☐ Depress the brake pedal and check that it does not creep down to the floor, indicating a master cylinder fault. Release the pedal, wait a few seconds, then depress it again. If the pedal travels nearly to the floor before firm resistance is felt, brake adjustment or repair is necessary. If the pedal feels spongy, there is air in the hydraulic system which must be removed by bleeding.

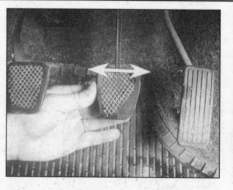

☐ Check that the brake pedal is secure and in good condition. Check also for signs of fluid leaks on the pedal, floor or carpets, which would indicate failed seals in the brake master cylinder.

☐ Check the servo unit (when applicable) by operating the brake pedal several times, then keeping the pedal depressed and starting the engine. As the engine starts, the pedal will move down slightly. If not, the vacuum hose or the servo itself may be faulty.

Steering wheel and column

☐ Examine the steering wheel for fractures or looseness of the hub, spokes or rim.

☐ Move the steering wheel from side to side and then up and down. Check that the steering wheel is not loose on the column, indicating wear or a loose retaining nut. Continue moving the steering wheel as before, but also turn it slightly from left to right.

☐ Check that the steering wheel is not loose on the column, and that there is no abnormal

movement of the steering wheel, indicating wear in the column support bearings or couplings.

Windscreen and mirrors

☐ The windscreen must be free of cracks or other significant damage within the driver's field of view. (Small stone chips are acceptable.) Rear view mirrors must be secure, intact, and capable of being adjusted.

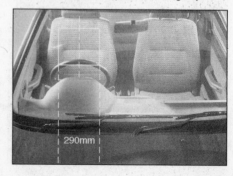

290mm

Seat belts and seats

Note: *The following checks are applicable to all seat belts, front and rear.*

☐ Examine the webbing of all the belts (including rear belts if fitted) for cuts, serious fraying or deterioration. Fasten and unfasten each belt to check the buckles. If applicable, check the retracting mechanism. Check the security of all seat belt mountings accessible from inside the vehicle.

☐ The front seats themselves must be securely attached and the backrests must lock in the upright position.

Doors

☐ Both front doors must be able to be opened and closed from outside and inside, and must latch securely when closed.

2 Checks carried out WITH THE VEHICLE ON THE GROUND

Vehicle identification

☐ Number plates must be in good condition, secure and legible, with letters and numbers correctly spaced – spacing at (A) should be twice that at (B).

☐ The VIN plate and/or homologation plate must be legible.

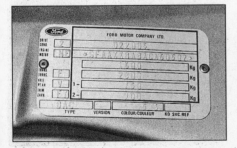

Electrical equipment

☐ Switch on the ignition and check the operation of the horn.

☐ Check the windscreen washers and wipers, examining the wiper blades; renew damaged or perished blades. Also check the operation of the stop-lights.

☐ Check the operation of the sidelights and number plate lights. The lenses and reflectors must be secure, clean and undamaged.

☐ Check the operation and alignment of the headlights. The headlight reflectors must not be tarnished and the lenses must be undamaged.

☐ Switch on the ignition and check the operation of the direction indicators (including the instrument panel tell-tale) and the hazard warning lights. Operation of the sidelights and stop-lights must not affect the indicators - if it does, the cause is usually a bad earth at the rear light cluster.

☐ Check the operation of the rear foglight(s), including the warning light on the instrument panel or in the switch.

Footbrake

☐ Examine the master cylinder, brake pipes and servo unit for leaks, loose mountings, corrosion or other damage.

☐ The fluid reservoir must be secure and the fluid level must be between the upper (**A**) and lower (**B**) markings.

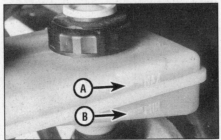

☐ Inspect both front brake flexible hoses for cracks or deterioration of the rubber. Turn the steering from lock to lock, and ensure that the hoses do not contact the wheel, tyre, or any part of the steering or suspension mechanism. With the brake pedal firmly depressed, check the hoses for bulges or leaks under pressure.

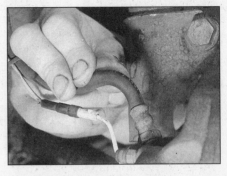

Steering and suspension

☐ Have your assistant turn the steering wheel from side to side slightly, up to the point where the steering gear just begins to transmit this movement to the roadwheels. Check for excessive free play between the steering wheel and the steering gear, indicating wear or insecurity of the steering column joints, the column-to-steering gear coupling, or the steering gear itself.

☐ Have your assistant turn the steering wheel more vigorously in each direction, so that the roadwheels just begin to turn. As this is done, examine all the steering joints, linkages, fittings and attachments. Renew any component that shows signs of wear or damage. On vehicles with power steering, check the security and condition of the steering pump, drivebelt and hoses.

☐ Check that the vehicle is standing level, and at approximately the correct ride height.

Shock absorbers

☐ Depress each corner of the vehicle in turn, then release it. The vehicle should rise and then settle in its normal position. If the vehicle continues to rise and fall, the shock absorber is defective. A shock absorber which has seized will also cause the vehicle to fail.

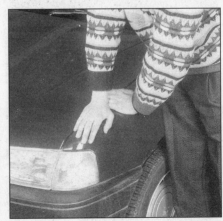

Exhaust system

☐ Start the engine. With your assistant holding a rag over the tailpipe, check the entire system for leaks. Repair or renew leaking sections.

3 Checks carried out **WITH THE VEHICLE RAISED AND THE WHEELS FREE TO TURN**

Jack up the front and rear of the vehicle, and securely support it on axle stands. Position the stands clear of the suspension assemblies. Ensure that the wheels are clear of the ground and that the steering can be turned from lock to lock.

Steering mechanism

☐ Have your assistant turn the steering from lock to lock. Check that the steering turns smoothly, and that no part of the steering mechanism, including a wheel or tyre, fouls any brake hose or pipe or any part of the body structure.
☐ Examine the steering rack rubber gaiters for damage or insecurity of the retaining clips. If power steering is fitted, check for signs of damage or leakage of the fluid hoses, pipes or connections. Also check for excessive stiffness or binding of the steering, a missing split pin or locking device, or severe corrosion of the body structure within 30 cm of any steering component attachment point.

Front and rear suspension and wheel bearings

☐ Starting at the front right-hand side, grasp the roadwheel at the 3 o'clock and 9 o'clock positions and shake it vigorously. Check for free play or insecurity at the wheel bearings, suspension balljoints, or suspension mountings, pivots and attachments.
☐ Now grasp the wheel at the 12 o'clock and 6 o'clock positions and repeat the previous inspection. Spin the wheel, and check for roughness or tightness of the front wheel bearing.

☐ If excess free play is suspected at a component pivot point, this can be confirmed by using a large screwdriver or similar tool and levering between the mounting and the component attachment. This will confirm whether the wear is in the pivot bush, its retaining bolt, or in the mounting itself (the bolt holes can often become elongated).

☐ Carry out all the above checks at the other front wheel, and then at both rear wheels.

Springs and shock absorbers

☐ Examine the suspension struts (when applicable) for serious fluid leakage, corrosion, or damage to the casing. Also check the security of the mounting points.
☐ If coil springs are fitted, check that the spring ends locate in their seats, and that the spring is not corroded, cracked or broken.
☐ If leaf springs are fitted, check that all leaves are intact, that the axle is securely attached to each spring, and that there is no deterioration of the spring eye mountings, bushes, and shackles.

☐ The same general checks apply to vehicles fitted with other suspension types, such as torsion bars, hydraulic displacer units, etc. Ensure that all mountings and attachments are secure, that there are no signs of excessive wear, corrosion or damage, and (on hydraulic types) that there are no fluid leaks or damaged pipes.
☐ Inspect the shock absorbers for signs of serious fluid leakage. Check for wear of the mounting bushes or attachments, or damage to the body of the unit.

Driveshafts (fwd vehicles only)

☐ Rotate each front wheel in turn and inspect the constant velocity joint gaiters for splits or damage. Also check that each driveshaft is straight and undamaged.

Braking system

☐ If possible without dismantling, check brake pad wear and disc condition. Ensure that the friction lining material has not worn excessively, (A) and that the discs are not fractured, pitted, scored or badly worn (B).

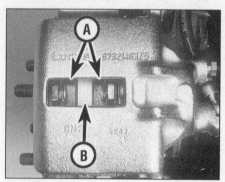

☐ Examine all the rigid brake pipes underneath the vehicle, and the flexible hose(s) at the rear. Look for corrosion, chafing or insecurity of the pipes, and for signs of bulging under pressure, chafing, splits or deterioration of the flexible hoses.
☐ Look for signs of fluid leaks at the brake calipers or on the brake backplates. Repair or renew leaking components.
☐ Slowly spin each wheel, while your assistant depresses and releases the footbrake. Ensure that each brake is operating and does not bind when the pedal is released.

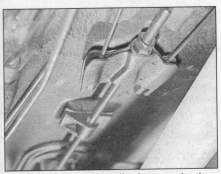

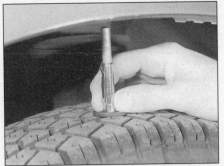

☐ Examine the handbrake mechanism, checking for frayed or broken cables, excessive corrosion, or wear or insecurity of the linkage. Check that the mechanism works on each relevant wheel, and releases fully, without binding.

☐ It is not possible to test brake efficiency without special equipment, but a road test can be carried out later to check that the vehicle pulls up in a straight line.

Fuel and exhaust systems

☐ Inspect the fuel tank (including the filler cap), fuel pipes, hoses and unions. All components must be secure and free from leaks.

☐ Examine the exhaust system over its entire length, checking for any damaged, broken or missing mountings, security of the retaining clamps and rust or corrosion.

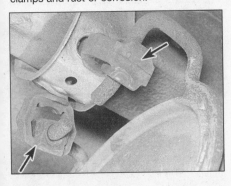

Wheels and tyres

☐ Examine the sidewalls and tread area of each tyre in turn. Check for cuts, tears, lumps, bulges, separation of the tread, and exposure of the ply or cord due to wear or damage. Check that the tyre bead is correctly seated on the wheel rim, that the valve is sound and

properly seated, and that the wheel is not distorted or damaged.

☐ Check that the tyres are of the correct size for the vehicle, that they are of the same size and type on each axle, and that the pressures are correct.

☐ Check the tyre tread depth. The legal minimum at the time of writing is 1.6 mm over at least three-quarters of the tread width. Abnormal tread wear may indicate incorrect front wheel alignment.

Body corrosion

☐ Check the condition of the entire vehicle structure for signs of corrosion in load-bearing areas. (These include chassis box sections, side sills, cross-members, pillars, and all suspension, steering, braking system and seat belt mountings and anchorages.) Any corrosion which has seriously reduced the thickness of a load-bearing area is likely to cause the vehicle to fail. In this case professional repairs are likely to be needed.

☐ Damage or corrosion which causes sharp or otherwise dangerous edges to be exposed will also cause the vehicle to fail.

4 Checks carried out on YOUR VEHICLE'S EXHAUST EMISSION SYSTEM

Petrol models

☐ Have the engine at normal operating temperature, and make sure that it is in good tune (ignition system in good order, air filter element clean, etc).

☐ Before any measurements are carried out, raise the engine speed to around 2500 rpm, and hold it at this speed for 20 seconds. Allow

the engine speed to return to idle, and watch for smoke emissions from the exhaust tailpipe. If the idle speed is obviously much too high, or if dense blue or clearly-visible black smoke comes from the tailpipe for more than 5 seconds, the vehicle will fail. As a rule of thumb, blue smoke signifies oil being burnt (engine wear) while black smoke signifies unburnt fuel (dirty air cleaner element, or other carburettor or fuel system fault).

☐ An exhaust gas analyser capable of measuring carbon monoxide (CO) and hydrocarbons (HC) is now needed. If such an instrument cannot be hired or borrowed, a local garage may agree to perform the check for a small fee.

CO emissions (mixture)

☐ At the time of writing, the maximum CO level at idle is 3.5% for vehicles first used after August 1986 and 4.5% for older vehicles. From January 1996 a much tighter limit (around 0.5%) applies to catalyst-equipped vehicles first used from August 1992. If the CO level cannot be reduced far enough to pass the test (and the fuel and ignition systems are otherwise in good condition) then the carburettor is badly worn, or there is some problem in the fuel injection system or catalytic converter (as applicable).

HC emissions

☐ With the CO emissions within limits, HC emissions must be no more than 1200 ppm (parts per million). If the vehicle fails this test at idle, it can be re-tested at around 2000 rpm; if the HC level is then 1200 ppm or less, this counts as a pass.

☐ Excessive HC emissions can be caused by oil being burnt, but they are more likely to be due to unburnt fuel.

Diesel models

☐ The only emission test applicable to Diesel engines is the measuring of exhaust smoke density. The test involves accelerating the engine several times to its maximum unloaded speed.

Note: It is of the utmost importance that the engine timing belt is in good condition before the test is carried out.

☐ Excessive smoke can be caused by a dirty air cleaner element. Otherwise, professional advice may be needed to find the cause.

Engine

- [ ] Engine fails to rotate when attempting to start
- [ ] Engine rotates, but will not start
- [ ] Engine difficult to start when cold
- [ ] Engine difficult to start when hot
- [ ] Starter motor noisy or excessively rough in engagement
- [ ] Engine starts, but stops immediately
- [ ] Engine idles erratically
- [ ] Engine misfires at idle speed
- [ ] Engine misfires throughout the driving speed range
- [ ] Engine hesitates on acceleration
- [ ] Engine stalls
- [ ] Engine lacks power
- [ ] Engine backfires
- [ ] Oil pressure warning light illuminated with engine running
- [ ] Engine runs-on after switching off
- [ ] Engine noises

Cooling system

- [ ] Overheating
- [ ] Overcooling
- [ ] External coolant leakage
- [ ] Internal coolant leakage
- [ ] Corrosion

Fuel and exhaust systems

- [ ] Excessive fuel consumption
- [ ] Fuel leakage and/or fuel odour
- [ ] Excessive noise or fumes from exhaust system

Clutch

- [ ] Pedal travels to floor - no pressure or very little resistance
- [ ] Clutch fails to disengage (unable to select gears)
- [ ] Clutch slips (engine speed increases, with no increase in vehicle speed)
- [ ] Judder as clutch is engaged
- [ ] Noise when depressing or releasing clutch pedal

Manual transmission

- [ ] Noisy in neutral with engine running
- [ ] Noisy in one particular gear
- [ ] Difficulty engaging gears
- [ ] Jumps out of gear
- [ ] Vibration
- [ ] Lubricant leaks

Automatic transmission

- [ ] Fluid leakage
- [ ] Transmission fluid brown, or has burned smell
- [ ] General gear selection problems
- [ ] Transmission will not downshift (kickdown) with accelerator fully depressed
- [ ] Engine will not start in any gear, or starts in gears other than Park or Neutral
- [ ] Transmission slips, shifts roughly, is noisy, or has no drive in forward or reverse gears

Driveshafts

- [ ] Clicking or knocking noise on turns (at slow speed on full-lock)
- [ ] Vibration when accelerating or decelerating

Braking system

- [ ] Vehicle pulls to one side under braking
- [ ] Noise (grinding or high-pitched squeal) when brakes applied
- [ ] Excessive brake pedal travel
- [ ] Brake pedal feels spongy when depressed
- [ ] Excessive brake pedal effort required to stop vehicle
- [ ] Judder felt through brake pedal or steering wheel when braking
- [ ] Brakes binding
- [ ] Rear wheels locking under normal braking

Suspension and steering systems

- [ ] Vehicle pulls to one side
- [ ] Wheel wobble and vibration
- [ ] Excessive pitching and/or rolling around corners, or during braking
- [ ] Wandering or general instability
- [ ] Excessively stiff steering
- [ ] Excessive play in steering
- [ ] Lack of power assistance
- [ ] Tyre wear excessive

Electrical system

- [ ] Battery will not hold a charge for more than a few days
- [ ] Ignition/no-charge warning light remains illuminated with engine running
- [ ] Ignition/no-charge warning light fails to come on
- [ ] Lights inoperative
- [ ] Instrument readings inaccurate or erratic
- [ ] Horn inoperative, or unsatisfactory in operation
- [ ] Windscreen/tailgate wipers inoperative, or unsatisfactory in operation
- [ ] Windscreen/tailgate washers inoperative, or unsatisfactory in operation
- [ ] Electric windows inoperative, or unsatisfactory in operation
- [ ] Central locking system inoperative, or unsatisfactory in operation

Introduction

The vehicle owner who does his or her own maintenance according to the recommended service schedules should not have to use this section of the manual very often. Modern component reliability is such that, provided those items subject to wear or deterioration are inspected or renewed at the specified intervals, sudden failure is comparatively rare. Faults do not usually just happen as a result of sudden failure, but develop over a period of time. Major mechanical failures in particular are usually preceded by characteristic symptoms over hundreds or even thousands of miles. Those components that do occasionally fail without warning are often small and easily carried in the vehicle.

With any fault-finding, the first step is to decide where to begin investigations. Sometimes this is obvious, but on other occasions, a little detective work will be necessary. The owner who makes half a dozen haphazard adjustments or replacements may be successful in curing a fault (or its symptoms). However, you will be none the wiser if the fault recurs, and ultimately you may have spent more time and money than was necessary. A calm and logical approach will be found to be more satisfactory in the long run. Always take into account any warning signs or abnormalities that may have been noticed in the period preceding the fault - power loss, high or low gauge readings, unusual smells, etc. - and remember that failure of components such as fuses or spark plugs may only be pointers to some underlying fault.

The pages that follow provide an easy-reference guide to the more common problems that may occur during the operation of the vehicle. These problems and their possible causes are grouped under headings denoting various components or systems, such as Engine, Cooling system, etc. The Chapter and/or Section that deals with the problem is also shown in brackets. Whatever the fault, certain basic principles apply. These are as follows:

Verify the fault. This is simply a matter of being sure that you know what the symptoms are before starting work. This is particularly important if you are investigating a fault for someone else, who may not have described it very accurately.

Do not overlook the obvious. For example, if the vehicle will not start, is there petrol in the tank? (Do not take anyone else's word on this particular point, and do not trust the fuel gauge either!) If an electrical fault is indicated, look for loose or broken wires before digging out the test gear.

Cure the disease, not the symptom. Substituting a flat battery with a fully charged one will get you off the hard shoulder, but if the underlying cause is not attended to, the new battery will go the same way. Similarly, changing oil-fouled spark plugs for a new set will get you moving again, but remember that the reason for the fouling (if it was not simply an incorrect grade of plug) will have to be established and corrected.

Do not take anything for granted. Particularly, do not forget that a "new" component may itself be defective (especially if it's been rattling around in the boot for months). Also do not leave components out of a fault diagnosis sequence just because they are new or recently fitted. When you do finally diagnose a difficult fault, you will probably realise that all the evidence was there from the start.

Test equipment

The electronic control units fitted to all Calibra models, for engine management, have diagnostic capabilities so that they can store a wide variety of system faults. You can read the faults using a simple hand-held device called TECH 1 **(see illustration)**. If you have one of these, you should use it whenever you think there is something wrong with your car, before resorting to other fault-finding techniques.

TECH 1 is supplied with a variety of program modules, and you will need to specify your vehicle model, engine type and year of manufacture to obtain the correct modules. To test for faults, switch off the ignition and connect TECH 1 to the diagnostic plug on the wiring harness in the engine compartment, then follow the TECH 1 Operating Instructions. When you have rectified a fault, connect TECH 1 again and cancel the fault so that it is removed from the system memory. Then you will need to test for faults again, in case there are more of them.

If you do not have TECH 1, you should try and get your vehicle to a dealer whenever a fault occurs. They will be able to find the fault within a few seconds, using TECH 1, saving you many hours of work. Some dealers have a

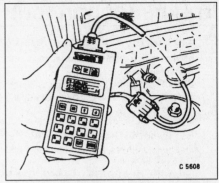

TECH 1 hand held diagnostic reader

more sophisticated piece of floor-standing equipment called TECH 15 which gives diagnostic information on a computer display, and uses a CD-ROM which contains data on a wide variety of vehicles.

The electronic control unit in your Calibra responds to certain faults by running the vehicle in "limp home" mode, so that it operates with reduced efficiency while you drive to the nearest garage. For example, on some vehicles with both crankshaft and camshaft phase sensors, the engine will run at a constant speed of 4,500 revs if one of the sensors fails.

On vehicles fitted with an anti-theft warning system, there is an additional diagnostic plug alongside the alarm siren, so that you can connect TECH 1 and obtain diagnostic information on the alarm system. If an alarm has been triggered, you can read the alarm code giving the sensor that triggered the alarm.

Engine

Engine fails to rotate when attempting to start

☐ Battery terminal connections loose or corroded (see *"Weekly checks"*).
☐ Battery discharged or faulty (Chapter 5).
☐ Broken, loose or disconnected wiring in the starting circuit (Chapter 5).
☐ Defective starter solenoid or switch (Chapter 5).
☐ Defective starter motor (Chapter 5).
☐ Starter pinion or flywheel ring gear teeth loose or broken (Chapters 2A and 5).
☐ Engine earth strap broken or disconnected (Chapter 5).

Engine rotates, but will not start

☐ Fuel tank empty.
☐ Battery discharged (engine rotates slowly), (Chapter 5).
☐ Battery terminal connections loose or corroded (see *"Weekly checks"*).
☐ Ignition components damp or damaged (Chapters 1 and 5).
☐ Broken, loose or disconnected wiring in the ignition circuit (Chapters 1 and 5).
☐ Worn, faulty or incorrectly gapped spark plugs (Chapter 1).
☐ Fuel injection system fault (Chapter 4A).
☐ Major mechanical failure (e.g. camshaft drive), (Chapter 2A or 2B).

Engine difficult to start when cold

☐ Battery discharged (Chapter 5).
☐ Battery terminal connections loose or corroded (see *"Weekly checks"*).
☐ Worn, faulty or incorrectly gapped spark plugs (Chapter 1).
☐ Fuel injection system fault (Chapter 4A).
☐ Other ignition system fault (Chapters 1 and 5).
☐ Low cylinder compressions (Chapter 2A).

Engine difficult to start when hot

☐ Air filter element dirty or clogged (Chapter 1).
☐ Fuel injection system fault (Chapter 4A).
☐ Low cylinder compressions (Chapter 2A).

Starter motor noisy or excessively rough in engagement

☐ Starter pinion or flywheel ring gear teeth loose or broken (Chapters 2A and 5).
☐ Starter motor mounting bolts loose or missing (Chapter 5).
☐ Starter motor internal components worn or damaged (Chapter 5).

Engine (continued)

Engine starts, but stops immediately

- ☐ Loose or faulty electrical connections in the ignition circuit (Chapters 1 and 5).
- ☐ Vacuum leak at the throttle body or inlet manifold (Chapter 4A).
- ☐ Blocked injector/fuel injection system fault (Chapter 4A).

Engine idles erratically

- ☐ Air filter element clogged (Chapter 1).
- ☐ Vacuum leak at the throttle body, inlet manifold or associated hoses (Chapter 4A).
- ☐ Worn, faulty or incorrectly gapped spark plugs (Chapter 1).
- ☐ Uneven or low cylinder compressions (Chapter 2A).
- ☐ Camshaft lobes worn (Chapter 2A or 2B).
- ☐ Timing belt incorrectly tensioned (Chapter 2A or 2B).
- ☐ Blocked injector/fuel injection system fault (Chapter 4A).

Engine misfires at idle speed

- ☐ Worn, faulty or incorrectly gapped spark plugs (Chapter 1).
- ☐ Faulty spark plug HT leads (Chapter 1).
- ☐ Vacuum leak at the throttle body, inlet manifold or associated hoses (Chapter 4A).
- ☐ Blocked injector/fuel injection system fault (Chapter 4A).
- ☐ Distributor cap cracked or tracking internally (where applicable), (Chapter 1).
- ☐ Uneven or low cylinder compressions (Chapter 2A).
- ☐ Disconnected, leaking, or perished crankcase ventilation hoses (Chapter 4B).

Engine misfires throughout the driving speed range

- ☐ Fuel filter choked (Chapter 1).
- ☐ Fuel pump faulty, or delivery pressure low (Chapter 4A).
- ☐ Fuel tank vent blocked, or fuel pipes restricted (Chapter 4A or 4B).
- ☐ Vacuum leak at the throttle body, inlet manifold or associated hoses (Chapter 4A).
- ☐ Worn, faulty or incorrectly gapped spark plugs (Chapter 1).
- ☐ Faulty spark plug HT leads (Chapter 1).
- ☐ Distributor cap cracked or tracking internally (where applicable), (Chapter 1).
- ☐ Faulty ignition coil (Chapter 5).
- ☐ Uneven or low cylinder compressions (Chapter 2A).
- ☐ Blocked injector/fuel injection system fault (Chapter 4A).

Engine hesitates on acceleration

- ☐ Worn, faulty or incorrectly gapped spark plugs (Chapter 1).
- ☐ Vacuum leak at the throttle body, inlet manifold or associated hoses (Chapter 4A).
- ☐ Blocked injector/fuel injection system fault (Chapter 4A).

Engine stalls

- ☐ Vacuum leak at the throttle body, inlet manifold or associated hoses (Chapter 4A).
- ☐ Fuel filter choked (Chapter 1).
- ☐ Fuel pump faulty, or delivery pressure low (Chapter 4A).
- ☐ Fuel tank vent blocked, or fuel pipes restricted (Chapter 4A or 4B).
- ☐ Blocked injector/fuel injection system fault (Chapter 4A).

Engine lacks power

- ☐ Timing belt incorrectly fitted or tensioned (Chapter 2A or 2B).
- ☐ Fuel filter choked (Chapter 1).

- ☐ Fuel pump faulty, or delivery pressure low (Chapter 4A).
- ☐ Uneven or low cylinder compressions (Chapter 2A).
- ☐ Worn, faulty or incorrectly gapped spark plugs (Chapter 1).
- ☐ Vacuum leak at the throttle body, inlet manifold or associated hoses (Chapter 4A).
- ☐ Blocked injector/fuel injection system fault (Chapter 4A).
- ☐ Brakes binding (Chapters 1 and 9).
- ☐ Clutch slipping (Chapter 6).

Engine backfires

- ☐ Timing belt incorrectly fitted or tensioned (Chapter 2A or 2B).
- ☐ Vacuum leak at the throttle body, inlet manifold or associated hoses (Chapter 4A).
- ☐ Blocked injector/fuel injection system fault (Chapter 4A).

Oil pressure warning light illuminated with engine running

- ☐ Low oil level, or incorrect oil grade (see "Weekly checks").
- ☐ Faulty oil pressure warning light switch (Chapter 12).
- ☐ Worn engine bearings and/or oil pump (Chapter 2A).
- ☐ High engine operating temperature (Chapter 3).
- ☐ Oil pressure relief valve defective (Chapter 2A).
- ☐ Oil pick-up strainer clogged (Chapter 2A).

Engine runs-on after switching off

- ☐ Excessive carbon build-up in engine (Chapter 2A).
- ☐ High engine operating temperature (Chapter 3).
- ☐ Fuel injection system fault (Chapter 4A).

Engine noises

Pre-ignition (pinking) or knocking during acceleration or under load

- ☐ Ignition timing incorrect/ignition system fault (Chapters 1 and 5).
- ☐ Incorrect grade of spark plug (Chapter 1).
- ☐ Incorrect grade of fuel (Chapter 1).
- ☐ Vacuum leak at the throttle body, inlet manifold or associated hoses (Chapter 4A).
- ☐ Excessive carbon build-up in engine (Chapter 2A).
- ☐ Blocked injector/fuel injection system fault (Chapter 4A).

Whistling or wheezing noises

- ☐ Leaking inlet manifold or throttle body gasket (Chapter 4A).
- ☐ Leaking exhaust manifold gasket or pipe-to-manifold joint (Chapter 4B).
- ☐ Leaking vacuum hose (Chapters 4A, 4B, 5, 9 and 12).
- ☐ Blowing cylinder head gasket (Chapter 2A or 2B).

Tapping or rattling noises

- ☐ Worn valve gear or camshaft (Chapter 2A or 2B).
- ☐ Ancillary component fault (coolant pump, alternator, etc.) (Chapters 3, 5, etc.).

Knocking or thumping noises

- ☐ Worn big-end bearings (regular heavy knocking, perhaps less under load), (Chapter 2A or 2B).
- ☐ Worn main bearings (rumbling and knocking, perhaps worsening under load), (Chapter 2A or 2B).
- ☐ Piston slap (most noticeable when cold), (Chapter 2A).
- ☐ Ancillary component fault (coolant pump, alternator, etc.) (Chapters 3, 5, etc.).

Cooling system

Overheating

- [ ] Insufficient coolant in system (see "*Weekly checks*").
- [ ] Thermostat faulty (Chapter 3).
- [ ] Radiator core blocked, or grille restricted (Chapter 3).
- [ ] Electric cooling fan or thermoswitch faulty (Chapter 3).
- [ ] Pressure cap faulty (Chapter 3).
- [ ] Ignition timing incorrect/ignition system fault (Chapters 1 and 5).
- [ ] Inaccurate temperature gauge sender unit (Chapter 3).
- [ ] Airlock in cooling system (Chapter 1).

Overcooling

- [ ] Thermostat faulty (Chapter 3).
- [ ] Inaccurate temperature gauge sender unit (Chapter 3).

External coolant leakage

- [ ] Deteriorated or damaged hoses or hose clips (Chapter 1).
- [ ] Radiator core or heater matrix leaking (Chapter 3).
- [ ] Pressure cap faulty (Chapter 3).
- [ ] Water pump seal leaking (Chapter 3).
- [ ] Boiling due to overheating (Chapter 3).
- [ ] Core plug leaking (Chapter 2A).

Internal coolant leakage

- [ ] Leaking cylinder head gasket (Chapter 2A or 2B).
- [ ] Cracked cylinder head or cylinder bore (Chapter 2A or 2B).

Corrosion

- [ ] Infrequent draining and flushing (Chapter 1).
- [ ] Incorrect coolant mixture or inappropriate coolant type (see "*Weekly checks*").

Fuel and exhaust systems

Excessive fuel consumption

- [ ] Air filter element dirty or clogged (Chapter 1).
- [ ] Fuel injection system fault (Chapter 4A).
- [ ] Ignition timing incorrect/ignition system fault (Chapters 1 and 5).
- [ ] Tyres under-inflated (see "*Weekly checks*").

Fuel leakage and/or fuel odour

- [ ] Damaged or corroded fuel tank, pipes or connections (Chapter 4A).

Excessive noise or fumes from exhaust system

- [ ] Leaking exhaust system or manifold joints (Chapters 1 and 4B).
- [ ] Leaking, corroded or damaged silencers or pipe (Chapters 1 and 4B).
- [ ] Broken mountings causing body or suspension contact (Chapter 1).

Clutch

Pedal travels to floor - no pressure or very little resistance

- [ ] Broken clutch cable (Chapter 6).
- [ ] Incorrect clutch cable adjustment (Chapter 6).
- [ ] Broken clutch release bearing or fork (Chapter 6).
- [ ] Broken diaphragm spring in clutch pressure plate (Chapter 6).

Clutch fails to disengage (unable to select gears).

- [ ] Incorrect clutch cable adjustment (Chapter 6).
- [ ] Clutch disc sticking on transmission input shaft splines (Chapter 6).
- [ ] Clutch disc sticking to flywheel or pressure plate (Chapter 6).
- [ ] Faulty pressure plate assembly (Chapter 6).
- [ ] Clutch release mechanism worn or incorrectly assembled (Chapter 6).

Clutch slips (engine speed increases, with no increase in vehicle speed).

- [ ] Incorrect clutch cable adjustment (Chapter 6).
- [ ] Clutch disc linings excessively worn (Chapter 6).
- [ ] Clutch disc linings contaminated with oil or grease (Chapter 6).
- [ ] Faulty pressure plate or weak diaphragm spring (Chapter 6).

Judder as clutch is engaged

- [ ] Clutch disc linings contaminated with oil or grease (Chapter 6).
- [ ] Clutch disc linings excessively worn (Chapter 6).
- [ ] Clutch cable sticking or frayed (Chapter 6).
- [ ] Faulty or distorted pressure plate or diaphragm spring (Chapter 6).
- [ ] Worn or loose engine or transmission mountings (Chapter 2A or 2B).
- [ ] Clutch disc hub or transmission input shaft splines worn (Chapter 6).

Noise when depressing or releasing clutch pedal

- [ ] Worn clutch release bearing (Chapter 6).
- [ ] Worn or dry clutch pedal bushes (Chapter 6).
- [ ] Faulty pressure plate assembly (Chapter 6).
- [ ] Pressure plate diaphragm spring broken (Chapter 6).
- [ ] Broken clutch disc cushioning springs (Chapter 6).

Manual transmission

Noisy in neutral with engine running

☐ Input shaft bearings worn (noise apparent with clutch pedal released, but not when depressed), (Chapter 7A).*

☐ Clutch release bearing worn (noise apparent with clutch pedal depressed, possibly less when released), (Chapter 6).

Noisy in one particular gear

☐ Worn, damaged or chipped gear teeth (Chapter 7A).*

Difficulty engaging gears

☐ Clutch faulty (Chapter 6).

☐ Worn or damaged gear linkage (Chapter 7A).

☐ Incorrectly adjusted gear linkage (Chapter 7A).

☐ Worn synchroniser units (Chapter 7A).*

Jumps out of gear

☐ Worn or damaged gear linkage (Chapter 7A).

☐ Incorrectly adjusted gear linkage (Chapter 7A).

☐ Worn synchroniser units (Chapter 7A).*

☐ Worn selector forks (Chapter 7A).*

Vibration

☐ Lack of oil (Chapter 1).

☐ Worn bearings (Chapter 7A).*

Lubricant leaks

☐ Leaking differential output oil seal (Chapter 7A).

☐ Leaking housing joint (Chapter 7A).*

☐ Leaking input shaft oil seal (Chapter 7A).*

Although the corrective action necessary to remedy the symptoms described is beyond the scope of the home mechanic, the above information should be helpful in isolating the cause of the condition. This should enable the owner can communicate clearly with a professional mechanic.

Automatic transmission

Note: *Due to the complexity of the automatic transmission, it is difficult for the home mechanic to properly diagnose and service this unit. For problems other than the following, the vehicle should be taken to a dealer service department or automatic transmission specialist. Do not be too hasty in removing the transmission if a fault is suspected, as most of the testing is carried out with the unit still fitted.*

Fluid leakage

☐ Automatic transmission fluid is usually dark in colour. Fluid leaks should not be confused with engine oil, which can easily be blown onto the transmission by airflow.

☐ To determine the source of a leak, first remove all built-up dirt and grime from the transmission housing and surrounding areas using a degreasing agent, or by steam-cleaning. Drive the vehicle at low speed, so airflow will not blow the leak far from its source. Raise and support the vehicle, and determine where the leak is coming from. The following are common areas of leakage:

a) Fluid pan or "sump" (Chapter 1 and 7B).

b) Dipstick tube (Chapter 1 and 7B).

c) Transmission-to-fluid cooler pipes/unions (Chapter 7B).

Transmission fluid brown, or has burned smell

☐ Transmission fluid level low, or fluid in need of renewal (Chapter 1)

☐ Internal clutches overheating (Chapter 7B)

General gear selection problems

☐ Chapter 7B deals with checking and adjusting the selector cable on automatic transmissions. The following are common problems that may be caused by a poorly adjusted cable:

a) Engine starting in gears other than Park or Neutral.

b) Indicator panel indicating a gear other than the one actually being used.

c) Vehicle moves when in Park or Neutral.

d) Poor gear shift quality or erratic gear changes.

Transmission will not downshift (kickdown) with accelerator pedal fully depressed

☐ Low transmission fluid level (Chapter 1).

☐ Incorrect selector cable adjustment (Chapter 7B).

Engine will not start in any gear, or starts in gears other than Park or Neutral

☐ Incorrect starter/inhibitor switch adjustment (Chapter 7B).

☐ Incorrect selector cable adjustment (Chapter 7B).

Transmission slips, shifts roughly, is noisy, or has no drive in forward or reverse gears

☐ There are many probable causes for the above problems, but the home mechanic should be concerned with only one possibility - fluid level. Before taking the vehicle to a dealer or transmission specialist, check the fluid level and condition of the fluid as described in Chapter 1. Correct the fluid level as necessary, or change the fluid and filter if needed. If the problem persists, professional help will be necessary.

Driveshafts

Clicking or knocking noise on turns (at slow speed on full-lock)

☐ Lack of constant velocity joint lubricant, possibly due to damaged gaiter (Chapter 8).

☐ Worn outer constant velocity joint (Chapter 8).

Vibration when accelerating or decelerating

☐ Worn inner constant velocity joint (Chapter 8).

☐ Bent or distorted driveshaft (Chapter 8).

Braking system

Note: *Before assuming that a brake problem exists, make sure that the tyres are in good condition and correctly inflated, that the front wheel alignment is correct, and that the vehicle is not loaded with weight in an unequal manner. Apart from checking the condition of all pipe and hose connections, any faults occurring on the anti-lock braking system should be referred to a Vauxhall dealer for diagnosis.*

Vehicle pulls to one side under braking

☐ Worn, defective, damaged or contaminated brake pads/shoes on one side (Chapters 1 and 9).
☐ Seized or partially seized front brake caliper/wheel cylinder piston (Chapters 1 and 9).
☐ A mixture of brake pad/shoe lining materials fitted between sides (Chapters 1 and 9).
☐ Brake caliper or backplate mounting bolts loose (Chapter 9).
☐ Worn or damaged steering or suspension components (Chapters 1 and 10).

Noise (grinding or high-pitched squeal) when brakes applied

☐ Brake pad or shoe friction lining material worn down to metal backing (Chapters 1 and 9).
☐ Excessive corrosion of brake disc or drum. This may be apparent after the vehicle has been standing for some time (Chapters 1 and 9).
☐ Foreign object (stone chipping, etc.) trapped between brake disc and shield (Chapters 1 and 9).

Excessive brake pedal travel

☐ Faulty master cylinder (Chapter 9).
☐ Air in hydraulic system (Chapters 1 and 9).
☐ Faulty vacuum servo unit (Chapter 9).

Brake pedal feels spongy when depressed

☐ Air in hydraulic system (Chapters 1 and 9).
☐ Deteriorated flexible rubber brake hoses (Chapters 1 and 9).
☐ Master cylinder mounting nuts loose (Chapter 9).
☐ Faulty master cylinder (Chapter 9).

Excessive brake pedal effort required to stop vehicle

☐ Faulty vacuum servo unit (Chapter 9).
☐ Disconnected, damaged or insecure brake servo vacuum hose (Chapter 9).
☐ Primary or secondary hydraulic circuit failure (Chapter 9).
☐ Seized brake caliper or wheel cylinder piston(s) (Chapter 9).
☐ Brake pads incorrectly fitted (Chapters 1 and 9).
☐ Incorrect grade of brake pads fitted (Chapters 1 and 9).
☐ Brake pads contaminated (Chapters 1 and 9).

Judder felt through brake pedal or steering wheel when braking

☐ Excessive run-out or distortion of discs (Chapters 1 and 9).
☐ Brake pads worn (Chapters 1 and 9).
☐ Brake caliper or brake backplate mounting bolts loose (Chapter 9).
☐ Wear in suspension or steering components or mountings (Chapters 1 and 10).

Brakes binding

☐ Seized brake caliper (Chapter 9).
☐ Incorrectly adjusted handbrake mechanism (Chapter 9).
☐ Faulty master cylinder (Chapter 9).

Rear wheels locking under normal braking

☐ Faulty brake pressure regulator (Chapter 9).

Suspension and steering

Note: *Before diagnosing suspension or steering faults, be sure that the trouble is not due to incorrect tyre pressures, mixtures of tyre types, or binding brakes.*

Vehicle pulls to one side

☐ Defective tyre (see "*Weekly checks*").
☐ Excessive wear in suspension or steering components (Chapters 1 and 10).
☐ Incorrect front wheel alignment (Chapter 10).
☐ Accident damage to steering or suspension components (Chapter 1).

Wheel wobble and vibration

☐ Front roadwheels out of balance (vibration felt mainly through the steering wheel), (Chapters 1 and 10).
☐ Rear roadwheels out of balance (vibration felt throughout the vehicle), (Chapters 1 and 10).
☐ Roadwheels damaged or distorted (Chapters 1 and 10).
☐ Faulty or damaged tyre (see "*Weekly checks*").
☐ Worn steering or suspension joints, bushes or components (Chapters 1 and 10).
☐ Wheel bolts loose.

Excessive pitching and/or rolling around corners, or during braking

☐ Defective shock absorbers (Chapters 1 and 10).
☐ Broken or weak spring and/or suspension component (Chapters 1 and 10).
☐ Worn or damaged anti-roll bar or mountings (Chapter 10).

Wandering or general instability

☐ Incorrect front wheel alignment (Chapter 10).
☐ Worn steering or suspension joints, bushes or components (Chapters 1 and 10).
☐ Roadwheels out of balance (Chapters 1 and 10).
☐ Faulty or damaged tyre (see "*Weekly checks*").
☐ Wheel bolts loose.
☐ Defective shock absorbers (Chapters 1 and 10).

Excessively stiff steering

☐ Lack of steering gear lubricant (Chapter 10).
☐ Seized track rod end balljoint or suspension balljoint (Chapters 1 and 10).
☐ Incorrect front wheel alignment (Chapter 10).
☐ Steering rack or column bent or damaged (Chapter 10).
☐ Failure of power steering - see "*Lack of power assistance*" below.

Suspension and steering (continued)

Excessive play in steering

☐ Worn steering column intermediate shaft universal joint (Chapter 10).
☐ Worn steering track rod end balljoints (Chapters 1 and 10).
☐ Worn rack-and-pinion steering gear (Chapter 10).
☐ Worn steering or suspension joints, bushes or components (Chapters 1 and 10).

Lack of power assistance

☐ Broken or incorrectly adjusted auxiliary drivebelt (Chapter 1).
☐ Incorrect power steering fluid level (see "Weekly checks").
☐ Restriction in power steering fluid hoses (Chapter 1).
☐ Faulty power steering pump (Chapter 10).
☐ Faulty rack-and-pinion steering gear (Chapter 10).

Tyre wear excessive

Tyres worn on inside or outside edges

☐ Tyres under-inflated (wear on both edges) (see "Weekly checks").
☐ Incorrect camber or castor angles (wear on one edge only), (Chapter 10).

☐ Worn steering or suspension joints, bushes or components (Chapters 1 and 10).
☐ Excessively hard cornering.
☐ Accident damage.

Tyre treads exhibit feathered edges

☐ Incorrect toe setting (Chapter 10).

Tyres worn in centre of tread

☐ Tyres over-inflated (see "Weekly checks").

Tyres worn on inside and outside edges

☐ Tyres under-inflated (see "Weekly checks").

Tyres worn unevenly

☐ Tyres/wheels out of balance (Chapter 10).
☐ Excessive wheel or tyre run-out (Chapter 10).
☐ Worn shock absorbers (Chapters 1 and 10).
☐ Faulty tyre (see "Weekly checks").

Electrical system

Note: *For problems associated with the starting system, refer to the faults listed under "Engine" earlier in this Section.*

Battery will not hold a charge for more than a few days

☐ Battery defective internally (Chapter 5).
☐ Battery terminal connections loose or corroded (see "Weekly checks").
☐ Auxiliary drivebelt worn or incorrectly adjusted (Chapter 1).
☐ Alternator not charging at correct output (Chapter 5).
☐ Alternator or voltage regulator faulty (Chapter 5).
☐ Short-circuit causing continual battery drain (Chapters 5 and 12).

Ignition/no-charge warning light remains illuminated with engine running

☐ Auxiliary drivebelt broken, worn, or incorrectly adjusted (Chapter 1).
☐ Alternator brushes worn, sticking, or dirty (Chapter 5).
☐ Alternator brush springs weak or broken (Chapter 5).
☐ Internal fault in alternator or voltage regulator (Chapter 5).
☐ Broken, disconnected, or loose wiring in charging circuit (Chapter 5).

Ignition/no-charge warning light fails to come on

☐ Warning light bulb blown (Chapter 12).
☐ Broken, disconnected, or loose wiring in warning light circuit (Chapter 12).
☐ Alternator faulty (Chapter 5).

Lights inoperative

☐ Bulb blown (Chapter 12).
☐ Corrosion of bulb or bulbholder contacts (Chapter 12).
☐ Blown fuse (Chapter 12).
☐ Faulty relay (Chapter 12).
☐ Broken, loose, or disconnected wiring (Chapter 12).
☐ Faulty switch (Chapter 12).

Instrument readings inaccurate or erratic

Instrument readings increase with engine speed

☐ Faulty voltage regulator (Chapter 12).

Fuel or temperature gauges give no reading

☐ Faulty gauge sender unit (Chapters 3 and 4A).
☐ Wiring open-circuit (Chapter 12).
☐ Faulty gauge (Chapter 12).

Fuel or temperature gauges give continuous maximum reading

☐ Faulty gauge sender unit (Chapters 3 and 4A).
☐ Wiring short-circuit (Chapter 12).
☐ Faulty gauge (Chapter 12).

Horn inoperative, or unsatisfactory in operation

Horn operates all the time

☐ Horn push either earthed or stuck down (Chapter 12).
☐ Horn cable-to-horn push earthed (Chapter 12).

Horn fails to operate

☐ Blown fuse (Chapter 12).
☐ Cable or cable connections loose, broken or disconnected (Chapter 12).
☐ Faulty horn (Chapter 12).

Horn emits intermittent or unsatisfactory sound

☐ Cable connections loose (Chapter 12).
☐ Horn mountings loose (Chapter 12).
☐ Faulty horn (Chapter 12).

Electrical system (continued)

Windscreen/tailgate wipers inoperative, or unsatisfactory in operation

Wipers fail to operate, or operate very slowly

- [ ] Wiper blades stuck to screen, or linkage seized or binding (Chapters 1 and 12).
- [ ] Blown fuse (Chapter 12).
- [ ] Cable or cable connections loose, broken or disconnected (Chapter 12).
- [ ] Faulty relay (Chapter 12).
- [ ] Faulty wiper motor (Chapter 12).

Wiper blades sweep over too large or too small an area of the glass

- [ ] Wiper arms incorrectly positioned on spindles (Chapter 1).
- [ ] Excessive wear of wiper linkage (Chapter 12).
- [ ] Wiper motor or linkage mountings loose or insecure (Chapter 12).

Wiper blades fail to clean the glass effectively

- [ ] Wiper blade rubbers worn or perished (see "*Weekly checks*").
- [ ] Wiper arm tension springs broken, or arm pivots seized (Chapter 12).
- [ ] Insufficient windscreen washer additive to adequately remove road film (see "*Weekly checks*").

Windscreen/tailgate washers inoperative, or unsatisfactory in operation

One or more washer jets inoperative

- [ ] Blocked washer jet (Chapter 1).
- [ ] Disconnected, kinked or restricted fluid hose (Chapter 12).
- [ ] Insufficient fluid in washer reservoir (see "*Weekly checks*").

Washer pump fails to operate

- [ ] Broken or disconnected wiring or connections (Chapter 12).
- [ ] Blown fuse (Chapter 12).
- [ ] Faulty washer switch (Chapter 12).
- [ ] Faulty washer pump (Chapter 12).

Washer pump runs for some time before fluid is emitted from jets

- [ ] Faulty one-way valve in fluid supply hose (Chapter 12).

Electric windows inoperative, or unsatisfactory in operation

Window glass will only move in one direction

- [ ] Faulty switch (Chapter 12).

Window glass slow to move

- [ ] Regulator seized or damaged, or in need of lubrication (Chapter 11).
- [ ] Door internal components or trim fouling regulator (Chapter 11).
- [ ] Faulty motor (Chapter 12).

Window glass fails to move

- [ ] Blown fuse (Chapter 12).
- [ ] Faulty relay (Chapter 12).
- [ ] Broken or disconnected wiring or connections (Chapter 12).
- [ ] Faulty motor (Chapter 12).

Central locking system inoperative, or unsatisfactory in operation

Complete system failure

- [ ] Blown fuse (Chapter 12).
- [ ] Faulty relay (Chapter 12).
- [ ] Broken or disconnected wiring or connections (Chapter 12).
- [ ] Faulty control module (Chapter 12).

Latch locks but will not unlock, or unlocks but will not lock

- [ ] Faulty master switch (Chapter 12).
- [ ] Broken or disconnected latch operating rods or levers (Chapter 11).
- [ ] Faulty relay (Chapter 12).
- [ ] Faulty control module (Chapter 12).

One solenoid/motor fails to operate

- [ ] Broken or disconnected wiring or connections (Chapter 12).
- [ ] Faulty solenoid/motor (Chapter 12).
- [ ] Broken, binding or disconnected latch operating rods or levers (Chapter 11).
- [ ] Fault in door latch (Chapter 11).

A

ABS (Anti-lock brake system) A system, usually electronically controlled, that senses incipient wheel lockup during braking and relieves hydraulic pressure at wheels that are about to skid.

Air bag An inflatable bag hidden in the steering wheel (driver's side) or the dash or glovebox (passenger side). In a head-on collision, the bags inflate, preventing the driver and front passenger from being thrown forward into the steering wheel or windscreen.

Air cleaner A metal or plastic housing, containing a filter element, which removes dust and dirt from the air being drawn into the engine.

Air filter element The actual filter in an air cleaner system, usually manufactured from pleated paper and requiring renewal at regular intervals.

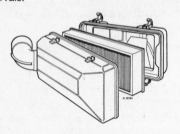

Air filter

Allen key A hexagonal wrench which fits into a recessed hexagonal hole.

Alligator clip A long-nosed spring-loaded metal clip with meshing teeth. Used to make temporary electrical connections.

Alternator A component in the electrical system which converts mechanical energy from a drivebelt into electrical energy to charge the battery and to operate the starting system, ignition system and electrical accessories.

Alternator (exploded view)

Ampere (amp) A unit of measurement for the flow of electric current. One amp is the amount of current produced by one volt acting through a resistance of one ohm.

Anaerobic sealer A substance used to prevent bolts and screws from loosening. Anaerobic means that it does not require oxygen for activation. The Loctite brand is widely used.

Antifreeze A substance (usually ethylene glycol) mixed with water, and added to a vehicle's cooling system, to prevent freezing of the coolant in winter. Antifreeze also contains chemicals to inhibit corrosion and the formation of rust and other deposits that would tend to clog the radiator and coolant passages and reduce cooling efficiency.

Anti-seize compound A coating that reduces the risk of seizing on fasteners that are subjected to high temperatures, such as exhaust manifold bolts and nuts.

Anti-seize compound

Asbestos A natural fibrous mineral with great heat resistance, commonly used in the composition of brake friction materials. Asbestos is a health hazard and the dust created by brake systems should never be inhaled or ingested.

Axle A shaft on which a wheel revolves, or which revolves with a wheel. Also, a solid beam that connects the two wheels at one end of the vehicle. An axle which also transmits power to the wheels is known as a live axle.

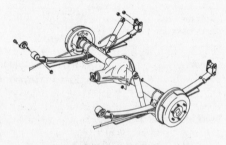

Axle assembly

Axleshaft A single rotating shaft, on either side of the differential, which delivers power from the final drive assembly to the drive wheels. Also called a driveshaft or a halfshaft.

B

Ball bearing An anti-friction bearing consisting of a hardened inner and outer race with hardened steel balls between two races.

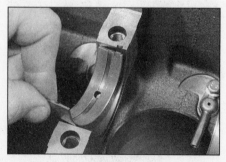

Bearing

Bearing The curved surface on a shaft or in a bore, or the part assembled into either, that permits relative motion between them with minimum wear and friction.

Big-end bearing The bearing in the end of the connecting rod that's attached to the crankshaft.

Bleed nipple A valve on a brake wheel cylinder, caliper or other hydraulic component that is opened to purge the hydraulic system of air. Also called a bleed screw.

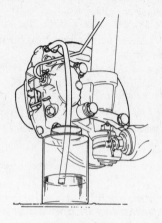

Brake bleeding

Brake bleeding Procedure for removing air from lines of a hydraulic brake system.

Brake disc The component of a disc brake that rotates with the wheels.

Brake drum The component of a drum brake that rotates with the wheels.

Brake linings The friction material which contacts the brake disc or drum to retard the vehicle's speed. The linings are bonded or riveted to the brake pads or shoes.

Brake pads The replaceable friction pads that pinch the brake disc when the brakes are applied. Brake pads consist of a friction material bonded or riveted to a rigid backing plate.

Brake shoe The crescent-shaped carrier to which the brake linings are mounted and which forces the lining against the rotating drum during braking.

Braking systems For more information on braking systems, consult the *Haynes Automotive Brake Manual*.

Breaker bar A long socket wrench handle providing greater leverage.

Bulkhead The insulated partition between the engine and the passenger compartment.

C

Caliper The non-rotating part of a disc-brake assembly that straddles the disc and carries the brake pads. The caliper also contains the hydraulic components that cause the pads to pinch the disc when the brakes are applied. A caliper is also a measuring tool that can be set to measure inside or outside dimensions of an object.

Camshaft A rotating shaft on which a series of cam lobes operate the valve mechanisms. The camshaft may be driven by gears, by sprockets and chain or by sprockets and a belt.

Canister A container in an evaporative emission control system; contains activated charcoal granules to trap vapours from the fuel system.

Canister

Carburettor A device which mixes fuel with air in the proper proportions to provide a desired power output from a spark ignition internal combustion engine.

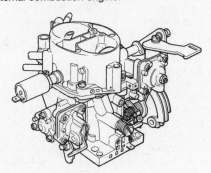

Carburettor

Castellated Resembling the parapets along the top of a castle wall. For example, a castellated balljoint stud nut.

Castellated nut

Castor In wheel alignment, the backward or forward tilt of the steering axis. Castor is positive when the steering axis is inclined rearward at the top.

Catalytic converter A silencer-like device in the exhaust system which converts certain pollutants in the exhaust gases into less harmful substances.

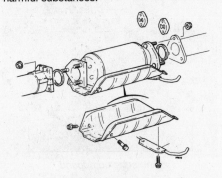

Catalytic converter

Circlip A ring-shaped clip used to prevent endwise movement of cylindrical parts and shafts. An internal circlip is installed in a groove in a housing; an external circlip fits into a groove on the outside of a cylindrical piece such as a shaft.

Clearance The amount of space between two parts. For example, between a piston and a cylinder, between a bearing and a journal, etc.

Coil spring A spiral of elastic steel found in various sizes throughout a vehicle, for example as a springing medium in the suspension and in the valve train.

Compression Reduction in volume, and increase in pressure and temperature, of a gas, caused by squeezing it into a smaller space.

Compression ratio The relationship between cylinder volume when the piston is at top dead centre and cylinder volume when the piston is at bottom dead centre.

Constant velocity (CV) joint A type of universal joint that cancels out vibrations caused by driving power being transmitted through an angle.

Core plug A disc or cup-shaped metal device inserted in a hole in a casting through which core was removed when the casting was formed. Also known as a freeze plug or expansion plug.

Crankcase The lower part of the engine block in which the crankshaft rotates.

Crankshaft The main rotating member, or shaft, running the length of the crankcase, with offset "throws" to which the connecting rods are attached.

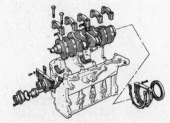

Crankshaft assembly

Crocodile clip See Alligator clip

D

Diagnostic code Code numbers obtained by accessing the diagnostic mode of an engine management computer. This code can be used to determine the area in the system where a malfunction may be located.

Disc brake A brake design incorporating a rotating disc onto which brake pads are squeezed. The resulting friction converts the energy of a moving vehicle into heat.

Double-overhead cam (DOHC) An engine that uses two overhead camshafts, usually one for the intake valves and one for the exhaust valves.

Drivebelt(s) The belt(s) used to drive accessories such as the alternator, water pump, power steering pump, air conditioning compressor, etc. off the crankshaft pulley.

Accessory drivebelts

Driveshaft Any shaft used to transmit motion. Commonly used when referring to the axleshafts on a front wheel drive vehicle.

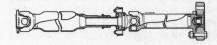

Driveshaft

Drum brake A type of brake using a drum-shaped metal cylinder attached to the inner surface of the wheel. When the brake pedal is pressed, curved brake shoes with friction linings press against the inside of the drum to slow or stop the vehicle.

Drum brake assembly

E

EGR valve A valve used to introduce exhaust gases into the intake air stream.

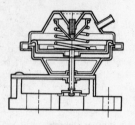

EGR valve

Electronic control unit (ECU) A computer which controls (for instance) ignition and fuel injection systems, or an anti-lock braking system. For more information refer to the *Haynes Automotive Electrical and Electronic Systems Manual.*

Electronic Fuel Injection (EFI) A computer controlled fuel system that distributes fuel through an injector located in each intake port of the engine.

Emergency brake A braking system, independent of the main hydraulic system, that can be used to slow or stop the vehicle if the primary brakes fail, or to hold the vehicle stationary even though the brake pedal isn't depressed. It usually consists of a hand lever that actuates either front or rear brakes mechanically through a series of cables and linkages. Also known as a handbrake or parking brake.

Endfloat The amount of lengthwise movement between two parts. As applied to a crankshaft, the distance that the crankshaft can move forward and back in the cylinder block.

Engine management system (EMS) A computer controlled system which manages the fuel injection and the ignition systems in an integrated fashion.

Exhaust manifold A part with several passages through which exhaust gases leave the engine combustion chambers and enter the exhaust pipe.

Exhaust manifold

F

Fan clutch A viscous (fluid) drive coupling device which permits variable engine fan speeds in relation to engine speeds.

Feeler blade A thin strip or blade of hardened steel, ground to an exact thickness, used to check or measure clearances between parts.

Feeler blade

Firing order The order in which the engine cylinders fire, or deliver their power strokes, beginning with the number one cylinder.

Flywheel A heavy spinning wheel in which energy is absorbed and stored by means of momentum. On cars, the flywheel is attached to the crankshaft to smooth out firing impulses.

Free play The amount of travel before any action takes place. The "looseness" in a linkage, or an assembly of parts, between the initial application of force and actual movement. For example, the distance the brake pedal moves before the pistons in the master cylinder are actuated.

Fuse An electrical device which protects a circuit against accidental overload. The typical fuse contains a soft piece of metal which is calibrated to melt at a predetermined current flow (expressed as amps) and break the circuit.

Fusible link A circuit protection device consisting of a conductor surrounded by heat-resistant insulation. The conductor is smaller than the wire it protects, so it acts as the weakest link in the circuit. Unlike a blown fuse, a failed fusible link must frequently be cut from the wire for replacement.

G

Gap The distance the spark must travel in jumping from the centre electrode to the side

Adjusting spark plug gap

electrode in a spark plug. Also refers to the spacing between the points in a contact breaker assembly in a conventional points-type ignition, or to the distance between the reluctor or rotor and the pickup coil in an electronic ignition.

Gasket Any thin, soft material - usually cork, cardboard, asbestos or soft metal - installed between two metal surfaces to ensure a good seal. For instance, the cylinder head gasket seals the joint between the block and the cylinder head.

Gasket

Gauge An instrument panel display used to monitor engine conditions. A gauge with a movable pointer on a dial or a fixed scale is an analogue gauge. A gauge with a numerical readout is called a digital gauge.

H

Halfshaft A rotating shaft that transmits power from the final drive unit to a drive wheel, usually when referring to a live rear axle.

Harmonic balancer A device designed to reduce torsion or twisting vibration in the crankshaft. May be incorporated in the crankshaft pulley. Also known as a vibration damper.

Hone An abrasive tool for correcting small irregularities or differences in diameter in an engine cylinder, brake cylinder, etc.

Hydraulic tappet A tappet that utilises hydraulic pressure from the engine's lubrication system to maintain zero clearance (constant contact with both camshaft and valve stem). Automatically adjusts to variation in valve stem length. Hydraulic tappets also reduce valve noise.

I

Ignition timing The moment at which the spark plug fires, usually expressed in the number of crankshaft degrees before the piston reaches the top of its stroke.

Inlet manifold A tube or housing with passages through which flows the air-fuel mixture (carburettor vehicles and vehicles with throttle body injection) or air only (port fuel-injected vehicles) to the port openings in the cylinder head.

J

Jump start Starting the engine of a vehicle with a discharged or weak battery by attaching jump leads from the weak battery to a charged or helper battery.

L

Load Sensing Proportioning Valve (LSPV) A brake hydraulic system control valve that works like a proportioning valve, but also takes into consideration the amount of weight carried by the rear axle.

Locknut A nut used to lock an adjustment nut, or other threaded component, in place. For example, a locknut is employed to keep the adjusting nut on the rocker arm in position.

Lockwasher A form of washer designed to prevent an attaching nut from working loose.

M

MacPherson strut A type of front suspension system devised by Earle MacPherson at Ford of England. In its original form, a simple lateral link with the anti-roll bar creates the lower control arm. A long strut - an integral coil spring and shock absorber - is mounted between the body and the steering knuckle. Many modern so-called MacPherson strut systems use a conventional lower A-arm and don't rely on the anti-roll bar for location.

Multimeter An electrical test instrument with the capability to measure voltage, current and resistance.

N

NOx Oxides of Nitrogen. A common toxic pollutant emitted by petrol and diesel engines at higher temperatures.

O

Ohm The unit of electrical resistance. One volt applied to a resistance of one ohm will produce a current of one amp.

Ohmmeter An instrument for measuring electrical resistance.

O-ring A type of sealing ring made of a special rubber-like material; in use, the O-ring is compressed into a groove to provide the sealing action.

O-ring

Overhead cam (ohc) engine An engine with the camshaft(s) located on top of the cylinder head(s).

Overhead valve (ohv) engine An engine with the valves located in the cylinder head, but with the camshaft located in the engine block.

Oxygen sensor A device installed in the engine exhaust manifold, which senses the oxygen content in the exhaust and converts this information into an electric current. Also called a Lambda sensor.

P

Phillips screw A type of screw head having a cross instead of a slot for a corresponding type of screwdriver.

Plastigage A thin strip of plastic thread, available in different sizes, used for measuring clearances. For example, a strip of Plastigage is laid across a bearing journal. The parts are assembled and dismantled; the width of the crushed strip indicates the clearance between journal and bearing.

Plastigage

Propeller shaft The long hollow tube with universal joints at both ends that carries power from the transmission to the differential on front-engined rear wheel drive vehicles.

Proportioning valve A hydraulic control valve which limits the amount of pressure to the rear brakes during panic stops to prevent wheel lock-up.

R

Rack-and-pinion steering A steering system with a pinion gear on the end of the steering shaft that mates with a rack (think of a geared wheel opened up and laid flat). When the steering wheel is turned, the pinion turns, moving the rack to the left or right. This movement is transmitted through the track rods to the steering arms at the wheels.

Radiator A liquid-to-air heat transfer device designed to reduce the temperature of the coolant in an internal combustion engine cooling system.

Refrigerant Any substance used as a heat transfer agent in an air-conditioning system. R-12 has been the principle refrigerant for many years; recently, however, manufacturers have begun using R-134a, a non-CFC substance that is considered less harmful to

the ozone in the upper atmosphere.

Rocker arm A lever arm that rocks on a shaft or pivots on a stud. In an overhead valve engine, the rocker arm converts the upward movement of the pushrod into a downward movement to open a valve.

Rotor In a distributor, the rotating device inside the cap that connects the centre electrode and the outer terminals as it turns, distributing the high voltage from the coil secondary winding to the proper spark plug. Also, that part of an alternator which rotates inside the stator. Also, the rotating assembly of a turbocharger, including the compressor wheel, shaft and turbine wheel.

Runout The amount of wobble (in-and-out movement) of a gear or wheel as it's rotated. The amount a shaft rotates "out-of-true." The out-of-round condition of a rotating part.

S

Sealant A liquid or paste used to prevent leakage at a joint. Sometimes used in conjunction with a gasket.

Sealed beam lamp An older headlight design which integrates the reflector, lens and filaments into a hermetically-sealed one-piece unit. When a filament burns out or the lens cracks, the entire unit is simply replaced.

Serpentine drivebelt A single, long, wide accessory drivebelt that's used on some newer vehicles to drive all the accessories, instead of a series of smaller, shorter belts. Serpentine drivebelts are usually tensioned by an automatic tensioner.

Serpentine drivebelt

Shim Thin spacer, commonly used to adjust the clearance or relative positions between two parts. For example, shims inserted into or under bucket tappets control valve clearances. Clearance is adjusted by changing the thickness of the shim.

Slide hammer A special puller that screws into or hooks onto a component such as a shaft or bearing; a heavy sliding handle on the shaft bottoms against the end of the shaft to knock the component free.

Sprocket A tooth or projection on the periphery of a wheel, shaped to engage with a chain or drivebelt. Commonly used to refer to the sprocket wheel itself.

Starter inhibitor switch On vehicles with an

automatic transmission, a switch that prevents starting if the vehicle is not in Neutral or Park.

Strut See MacPherson strut.

T

Tappet A cylindrical component which transmits motion from the cam to the valve stem, either directly or via a pushrod and rocker arm. Also called a cam follower.

Thermostat A heat-controlled valve that regulates the flow of coolant between the cylinder block and the radiator, so maintaining optimum engine operating temperature. A thermostat is also used in some air cleaners in which the temperature is regulated.

Thrust bearing The bearing in the clutch assembly that is moved in to the release levers by clutch pedal action to disengage the clutch. Also referred to as a release bearing.

Timing belt A toothed belt which drives the camshaft. Serious engine damage may result if it breaks in service.

Timing chain A chain which drives the camshaft.

Toe-in The amount the front wheels are closer together at the front than at the rear. On rear wheel drive vehicles, a slight amount of toe-in is usually specified to keep the front wheels running parallel on the road by offsetting other forces that tend to spread the wheels apart.

Toe-out The amount the front wheels are closer together at the rear than at the front. On front wheel drive vehicles, a slight amount of toe-out is usually specified.

Tools For full information on choosing and using tools, refer to the *Haynes Automotive Tools Manual*.

Tracer A stripe of a second colour applied to a wire insulator to distinguish that wire from another one with the same colour insulator.

Tune-up A process of accurate and careful adjustments and parts replacement to obtain the best possible engine performance.

Turbocharger A centrifugal device, driven by exhaust gases, that pressurises the intake air. Normally used to increase the power output from a given engine displacement, but can also be used primarily to reduce exhaust emissions (as on VW's "Umwelt" Diesel engine).

U

Universal joint or U-joint A double-pivoted connection for transmitting power from a driving to a driven shaft through an angle. A U-joint consists of two Y-shaped yokes and a cross-shaped member called the spider.

V

Valve A device through which the flow of liquid, gas, vacuum, or loose material in bulk may be started, stopped, or regulated by a movable part that opens, shuts, or partially obstructs one or more ports or passageways. A valve is also the movable part of such a device.

Valve clearance The clearance between the valve tip (the end of the valve stem) and the rocker arm or tappet. The valve clearance is measured when the valve is closed.

Vernier caliper A precision measuring instrument that measures inside and outside dimensions. Not quite as accurate as a micrometer, but more convenient.

Viscosity The thickness of a liquid or its resistance to flow.

Volt A unit for expressing electrical "pressure" in a circuit. One volt that will produce a current of one ampere through a resistance of one ohm.

W

Welding Various processes used to join metal items by heating the areas to be joined to a molten state and fusing them together. For more information refer to the *Haynes Automotive Welding Manual*.

Wiring diagram A drawing portraying the components and wires in a vehicle's electrical system, using standardised symbols. For more information refer to the *Haynes Automotive Electrical and Electronic Systems Manual*.

Note: *References throughout this index are in the form - "Chapter number" • "page number"*

Haynes Manuals – The Complete List

Title	Book No.
ALFA ROMEO	
Alfa Romeo Alfasud/Sprint (74 - 88) up to F	0292
Alfa Romeo Alfetta (73 - 87) up to E	0531
ALFA ROMEO	
Audi 80 (72 - Feb 79) up to T	0207
Audi 80, 90 (79 - Oct 86) up to D & Coupe (81 - Nov 88) up to F	0605
Audi 80, 90 (Oct 86 - 90) D to H & Coupe (Nov 88 - 90) F to H	1491
Audi 100 (Oct 82 - 90) up to H & 200 (Feb 84 - Oct 89) A to G	0907
Audi 100 & A6 Petrol & Diesel (May 91 - May 97) H to P	3504
Audi A4 (95 - Feb 00) M to V	3575
AUSTIN	
Austin/MG/Rover Maestro 1.3 & 1.6 (83 - 95) up to M	0922
Austin/MG Metro (80 - May 90) up to G	0718
Austin/Rover Montego 1.3 & 1.6 (84 - 94) A to L	1066
Austin/MG/Rover Montego 2.0 (84 - 95) A to M	1067
Mini (59 - 69) up to H	0527
Mini (69 - Oct 96) up to P	0646
Austin/Rover 2.0 litre Diesel Engine (86 - 93) C to L	1857
BEDFORD	
Bedford CF (69 - 87) up to E	0163
Bedford/Vauxhall Rascal & Suzuki Supercarry (86 - Oct 94) C to M	3015
BMW	
BMW 316, 320 & 320i (4-cyl) (75 - Feb 83) up to Y	0276
BMW 320, 320i, 323i & 325i (6-cyl) (Oct 77 - Sept 87) up to E	0815
BMW 3-Series (Apr 91 - 96) H to N	3210
BMW 3- & 5-Series (sohc) (81 - 91) up to J	1948
BMW 520i & 525e (Oct 81 - June 88) up to E	1560
BMW 525, 528 & 528i (73 - Sept 81) up to X	0632
CITROEN	
Citroën 2CV, Ami & Dyane (67 - 90) up to H	0196
Citroën AX Petrol & Diesel (87 - 97) D to P	3014
Citroën BX (83 - 94) A to L	0908
Citroën C15 Van Petrol & Diesel (89 - Oct 98) F to S	3509
Citroën CX (75 - 88) up to F	0528
Citroën Saxo Petrol & Diesel (96 - 98) N to S	3506
Citroën Visa (79 - 88) up to F	0620
Citroën Xantia Petrol & Diesel (93 - 98) K to S	3082
Citroën XM Petrol & Diesel (89 - 98) G to R	3451
Citroën ZX Diesel (91 - 93) J to L	1922
Citroën ZX Petrol (91 - 94) H to M	1881
Citroën 1.7 & 1.9 litre Diesel Engine (84 - 96) A to N	1379
COLT	
Colt/Mitsubishi 1200, 1250 & 1400 (79 - May 84) up to A	0600
FIAT	
Fiat 500 (57 - 73) up to M	0090
Fiat Cinquecento (93 - 98) K to R	3501
Fiat Panda (81 - 95) up to M	0793
Fiat Punto Petrol & Diesel (94 - Oct 99) L to V	3251
Fiat Regata (84 - 88) A to F	1167

Title	Book No.
Fiat Tipo (88 - 91) E to J	1625
Fiat Uno (83 - 95) up to M	0923
Fiat X1/9 (74 - 89) up to G	0273
FORD	
Ford Capri II (& III) 1.6 & 2.0 (74 - 87) up to E	0283
Ford Capri II (& III) 2.8 & 3.0 (74 - 87) up to E	1309
Ford Cortina Mk IV (& V) 1.6 & 2.0 (76 - 83) up to A	0343
Ford Escort (75 - Aug 80) up to V	0280
Ford Escort (Sept 80 - Sept 90) up to H	0686
Ford Escort & Orion (Sept 90 - 97) H to P	1737
Ford Escort Mk II Mexico, RS 1600 & RS 2000 (75 - 80) up to W	0735
Ford Fiesta (76 - Aug 83) up to Y	0334
Ford Fiesta (Aug 83 - Feb 89) A to F	1030
Ford Fiesta (Feb 89 - Oct 95) F to N	1595
Ford Fiesta Petrol & Diesel (Oct 95 - 97) N to R	3397
Ford Granada (Sept 77 - Feb 85) up to B	0481
Ford Granada & Scorpio (Mar 85 - 94) B to M	1245
Ford Ka (96 - 99) P to T	3570
Ford Mondeo Petrol (93 - 99) K to T	1923
Ford Mondeo Diesel (93 - 96) L to N	3465
Ford Orion (83 - Sept 90) up to H	1009
Ford Sierra 4 cyl. (82 - 93) up to K	0903
Ford Sierra V6 (82 - 91) up to J	0904
Ford Transit Petrol (Mk 2) (78 - Jan 86) up to C	0719
Ford Transit Petrol (Mk 3) (Feb 86 - 89) C to G	1468
Ford Transit Diesel (Feb 86 - 99) C to T	3019
Ford 1.6 & 1.8 litre Diesel Engine (84 - 96) A to N	1172
Ford 2.1, 2.3 & 2.5 litre Diesel Engine (77 - 90) up to H	1606
FREIGHT ROVER	
Freight Rover Sherpa (74 - 87) up to E	0463
HILLMAN	
Hillman Avenger (70 - 82) up to Y	0037
HONDA	
Honda Accord (76 - Feb 84) up to A	0351
Honda Civic (Feb 84 - Oct 87) A to E	1226
Honda Civic (Nov 91 - 96) J to N	3199
HYUNDAI	
Hyundai Pony (85 - 94) C to M	3398
JAGUAR	
Jaguar E Type (61 - 72) up to L	0140
Jaguar MkI & II, 240 & 340 (55 - 69) up to H	0098
Jaguar XJ6, XJ & Sovereign; Daimler Sovereign (68 - Oct 86) up to D	0242
Jaguar XJ6 & Sovereign (Oct 86 - Sept 94) D to M	3261
Jaguar XJ12, XJS & Sovereign; Daimler Double Six (72 - 88) up to F	0478
JEEP	
Jeep Cherokee Petrol (93 - 96) K to N	1943
LADA	
Lada 1200, 1300, 1500 & 1600 (74 - 91) up to J	0413
Lada Samara (87 - 91) D to J	1610
LAND ROVER	
Land Rover 90, 110 & Defender Diesel (83 - 95) up to N	3017
Land Rover Discovery Diesel (89 - 95) G to N	3016
Land Rover Series IIA & III Diesel (58 - 85) up to C	0529

Title	Book No.
Land Rover Series II, IIA & III Petrol (58 - 85) up to C	0314
MAZDA	
Mazda 323 (Mar 81 - Oct 89) up to G	1608
Mazda 323 (Oct 89 - 98) G to R	3455
Mazda 626 (May 83 - Sept 87) up to E	0929
Mazda B-1600, B-1800 & B-2000 Pick-up (72 - 88) up to F	0267
MERCEDES BENZ	
Mercedes-Benz 190, 190E & 190D Petrol & Diesel (83 - 93) A to L	3450
Mercedes-Benz 200, 240, 300 Diesel (Oct 76 - 85) up to C	1114
Mercedes-Benz 250 & 280 (68 - 72) up to L	0346
Mercedes-Benz 250 & 280 (123 Series) (Oct 76 - 84) up to B	0677
Mercedes-Benz 124 Series (85 - Aug 93) C to K	3253
MG	
MGB (62 - 80) up to W	0111
MG Midget & AH Sprite (58 - 80) up to W	0265
MITSUBISHI	
Mitsubishi Shogun & L200 Pick-Ups (83 - 94) up to M	1944
MORRIS	
Morris Ital 1.3 (80 - 84) up to B	0705
Morris Minor 1000 (56 - 71) up to K	0024
NISSAN	
Nissan Bluebird (May 84 - Mar 86) A to C	1223
Nissan Bluebird (Mar 86 - 90) C to H	1473
Nissan Cherry (Sept 82 - 86) up to D	1031
Nissan Micra (83 - Jan 93) up to K	0931
Nissan Micra (93 - 99) K to T	3254
Nissan Primera (90 - Aug 99) H to T	1851
Nissan Stanza (82 - 86) up to D	0824
Nissan Sunny (May 82 - Oct 86) up to D	0895
Nissan Sunny (Oct 86 - Mar 91) D to H	1378
Nissan Sunny (Apr 91 - 95) H to N	3219
OPEL	
Opel Ascona & Manta (B Series) (Sept 75 - 88) up to F	0316
Opel Ascona (81 - 88) (Not available in UK see Vauxhall Cavalier 0812)	3215
Opel Astra (Oct 91 - Feb 98) (Not available in UK see Vauxhall Astra 1832)	3156
Opel Calibra (90 - 98) (See Vauxhall/Opel Calibra Book No. 3502)	
Opel Corsa (83 - Mar 93) (Not available in UK see Vauxhall Nova 0909)	3160
Opel Corsa (Mar 93 - 97) (Not available in UK see Vauxhall Corsa 1985)	3159
Opel Frontera Petrol & Diesel (91 - 98) (See Vauxhall/Opel Frontera Book No. 3454)	
Opel Kadett (Nov 79 - Oct 84)	0634
Opel Kadett (Oct 84 - Oct 91) (Not available in UK see Vauxhall Astra & Belmont 1136)	3196
Opel Omega & Senator (86 - 94) (Not available in UK see Vauxhall Carlton & Senator 1469)	3157
Opel Omega (94 - 99) (See Vauxhall/Opel Omega Book No. 3510)	
Opel Rekord (Feb 78 - Oct 86) up to D	0543

Title	Book No
Opel Vectra (Oct 88 - Oct 95)	
(Not available in UK see Vauxhall Cavalier 1570)	3158
Opel Vectra Petrol & Diesel (95 - 98)	
(Not available in UK see Vauxhall Vectra 3396)	3523

PEUGEOT

Title	Book No
Peugeot 106 Petrol & Diesel (91 - 98) J to S	1882
Peugeot 205 (83 - 95) A to N	0932
Peugeot 305 (78 - 89) up to G	0538
Peugeot 306 Petrol & Diesel (93 - 99) K to T	3073
Peugeot 309 (86 - 93) C to K	1266
Peugeot 405 Petrol (88 - 96) E to N	1559
Peugeot 405 Diesel (88 - 96) E to N	3198
Peugeot 406 Petrol & Diesel (96 - 97) N to R	3394
Peugeot 505 (79 - 89) up to G	0762
Peugeot 1.7/1.8 & 1.9 litre Diesel Engine (82 - 96) up to N	0950
Peugeot 2.0, 2.1, 2.3 & 2.5 litre Diesel Engines (74 - 90) up to H	1607

PORSCHE

Title	Book No
Porsche 911 (65 - 85) up to C	0264
Porsche 924 & 924 Turbo (76 - 85) up to C	0397

PROTON

Title	Book No
Proton (89 - 97) F to P	3255

RANGE ROVER

Title	Book No
Range Rover V8 (70 - Oct 92) up to K	0606

RELIANT

Title	Book No
Reliant Robin & Kitten (73 - 83) up to A	0436

RENAULT

Title	Book No
Renault 5 (Feb 85 - 96) B to N	1219
Renault 9 & 11 (82 - 89) up to F	0822
Renault 18 (79 - 86) up to D	0598
Renault 19 Petrol (89 - 94) F to M	1646
Renault 19 Diesel (89 - 95) F to N	1946
Renault 21 (86 - 94) C to M	1397
Renault 25 (84 - 92) B to K	1228
Renault Clio Petrol (91 - May 98) H to R	1853
Renault Clio Diesel (91 - June 96) H to N	3031
Renault Espace Petrol & Diesel (85 - 96) C to N	3197
Renault Fuego (80 - 86) up to C	0764
Renault Laguna Petrol & Diesel (94 - 96) L to P	3252
Renault Mégane & Scénic Petrol & Diesel (96 - 98) N to R	3395

ROVER

Title	Book No
Rover 213 & 216 (84 - 89) A to G	1116
Rover 214 & 414 (89 - 96) G to N	1689
Rover 216 & 416 (89 - 96) G to N	1830
Rover 211, 214, 216, 218 & 220 Petrol & Diesel (Dec 95 - 98) N to R	3399
Rover 414, 416 & 420 Petrol & Diesel (May 95 - 98) M to R	3453
Rover 618, 620 & 623 (93 - 97) K to P	3257
Rover 820, 825 & 827 (86 - 95) D to N	1380
Rover 3500 (76 - 87) up to E	0365
Rover Metro, 111 & 114 (May 90 - 96) G to N	1711

SAAB

Title	Book No
Saab 90, 99 & 900 (79 - Oct 93) up to L	0765
Saab 900 (Oct 93 - 98) L to R	3512
Saab 9000 (4-cyl) (85 - 95) C to N	1686

SEAT

Title	Book No
Seat Ibiza & Cordoba Petrol & Diesel (Oct 93 - Oct 99) L to V	3571
Seat Ibiza & Malaga (85 - 92) B to K	1609

SKODA

Title	Book No
Skoda Estelle (77 - 89) up to G	0604
Skoda Favorit (89 - 96) F to N	1801
Skoda Felicia Petrol & Diesel (95 - 99) M to T	3505

SUBARU

Title	Book No
Subaru 1600 & 1800 (Nov 79 - 90) up to H	0995

SUZUKI

Title	Book No
Suzuki SJ Series, Samurai & Vitara (4-cyl) (82 - 97) up to P	1942
Suzuki Supercarry (86 - Oct 94) C to M	3015

TALBOT

Title	Book No
Talbot Alpine, Solara, Minx & Rapier (75 - 86) up to D	0337
Talbot Horizon (78 - 86) up to D	0473
Talbot Samba (82 - 86) up to D	0823

TOYOTA

Title	Book No
Toyota Carina E (May 92 - 97) J to P	3256
Toyota Corolla (Sept 83 - Sept 87) A to E	1024
Toyota Corolla (80 - 85) up to C	0683
Toyota Corolla (Sept 87 - Aug 92) E to K	1683
Toyota Corolla (Aug 92 - 97) K to P	3259
Toyota Hi-Ace & Hi-Lux (69 - Oct 83) up to A	0304

TRIUMPH

Title	Book No
Triumph Acclaim (81 - 84) up to B	0792
Triumph GT6 & Vitesse (62 - 74) up to N	0112
Triumph Spitfire (62 - 81) up to X	0113
Triumph Stag (70 - 78) up to T	0441
Triumph TR7 (75 - 82) up to Y	0322

VAUXHALL

Title	Book No
Vauxhall Astra (80 - Oct 84) up to B	0635
Vauxhall Astra & Belmont (Oct 84 - Oct 91) B to J	1136
Vauxhall Astra (Oct 91 - Feb 98) J to R	1832
Vauxhall/Opel Calibra (90 - 98) G to S	3502
Vauxhall Carlton (Oct 78 - Oct 86) up to D	0480
Vauxhall Carlton & Senator (Nov 86 - 94) D to L	1469
Vauxhall Cavalier 1600, 1900 & 2000 (75 - July 81) up to W	0315
Vauxhall Cavalier (81 - Oct 88) up to F	0812
Vauxhall Cavalier (Oct 88 - 95) F to N	1570
Vauxhall Chevette (75 - 84) up to B	0285
Vauxhall Corsa (Mar 93 - 97) K to R	1985
Vauxhall/Opel Frontera Petrol & Diesel (91 - Sept 98) J to S	3454
Vauxhall Nova (83 - 93) up to K	0909
Vauxhall/Opel Omega (94 - 99) L to T	3510
Vauxhall Vectra Petrol & Diesel (95 - 98) N to R	3396
Vauxhall/Opel 1.5, 1.6 & 1.7 litre Diesel Engine (82 - 96) up to N	1222

VOLKSWAGEN

Title	Book No
Volkswagen Beetle 1200 (54 - 77) up to S	0036
Volkswagen Beetle 1300 & 1500 (65 - 75) up to P	0039
Volkswagen Beetle 1302 & 1302S (70 - 72) up to L	0110
Volkswagen Beetle 1303, 1303S & GT (72 - 75) up to P	0159
Volkswagen Golf & Jetta Mk 1 1.1 & 1.3 (74 - 84) up to A	0716
Volkswagen Golf, Jetta & Scirocco Mk 1 1.5,1.6 & 1.8 (74 - 84) up to A	0726
Volkswagen Golf & Jetta Mk 1 Diesel (78 - 84) up to A	0451
Volkswagen Golf & Jetta Mk 2 (Mar 84 - Feb 92) A to J	1081
Volkswagen Golf & Vento Petrol & Diesel (Feb 92 - 96) J to N	3097
Volkswagen LT vans & light trucks (76 - 87) up to E	0637
Volkswagen Passat & Santana (Sept 81 - May 88) up to E	0814
Volkswagen Passat Petrol & Diesel (May 88 - 96) E to P	3498
Volkswagen Polo & Derby (76 - Jan 82) up to X	0335
Volkswagen Polo (82 - Oct 90) up to H	0813
Volkswagen Polo (Nov 90 - Aug 94) H to L	3245
Volkswagen Polo Hatchback Petrol & Diesel (94 - 99) M to S	3500
Volkswagen Scirocco (82 - 90) up to H	1224
Volkswagen Transporter 1600 (68 - 79) up to V	0082
Volkswagen Transporter 1700, 1800 & 2000 (72 - 79) up to V	0226
Volkswagen Transporter (air-cooled) (79 - 82) up to Y	0638
Volkswagen Transporter (water-cooled) (82 - 90) up to H	3452

VOLVO

Title	Book No.
Volvo 142, 144 & 145 (66 - 74) up to N	0129
Volvo 240 Series (74 - 93) up to K	0270
Volvo 262, 264 & 260/265 (75 - 85) up to C	0400
Volvo 340, 343, 345 & 360 (76 - 91) up to J	0715
Volvo 440, 460 & 480 (87 - 97) D to P	1691
Volvo 740 & 760 (82 - 91) up to J	1258
Volvo 850 (92 - 96) J to P	3260
Volvo 940 (90 - 96) H to N	3249
Volvo S40 & V40 (96 - 99) N to V	3569
Volvo S70, V70 & C70 (96 - 99) P to V	3573

YUGO/ZASTAVA

Title	Book No.
Yugo/Zastava (81 - 90) up to H	1453

AUTOMOTIVE TECHBOOKS

Title	Book No.
Automotive Brake Manual	3050
Automotive Carburettor Manual	3288
Automotive Diagnostic Fault Codes Manual	3472
Automotive Diesel Engine Service Guide	3286
Automotive Disc Brake Manual	3542
Automotive Electrical and Electronic Systems Manual	3049
Automotive Engine Management and Fuel Injection Systems Manual	3344
Automotive Gearbox Overhaul Manual	3473
Automotive Service Summaries Manual	3475
Automotive Timing Belts Manual – Austin/Rover	3549
Automotive Timing Belts Manual - Ford	3474
Automotive Timing Belts Manual – Peugeot/Citroën	3568
Automotive Timing Belts Manual – Vauxhall/Opel	3577
Automotive Welding Manual	3053
In-Car Entertainment Manual (3rd Edition)	3363

OTHER TITLES

Title	Book No.
Haynes Diesel Engine Systems & Data Book (91 -00)	3548
Haynes Petrol Models Data Book (94 - 00)	3718

CL09.04/00

Preserving Our Motoring Heritage

< The Model J Duesenberg Derham Tourster. Only eight of these magnificent cars were ever built – this is the only example to be found outside the United States of America

Almost every car you've ever loved, loathed or desired is gathered under one roof at the Haynes Motor Museum. Over 300 immaculately presented cars and motorbikes represent every aspect of our motoring heritage, from elegant reminders of bygone days, such as the superb Model J Duesenberg to curiosities like the bug-eyed BMW Isetta. There are also many old friends and flames. Perhaps you remember the 1959 Ford Popular that you did your courting in? The magnificent 'Red Collection' is a spectacle of classic sports cars including AC, Alfa Romeo, Austin Healey, Ferrari, Lamborghini, Maserati, MG, Riley, Porsche and Triumph.

A Perfect Day Out

Each and every vehicle at the Haynes Motor Museum has played its part in the history and culture of Motoring. Today, they make a wonderful spectacle and a great day out for all the family. Bring the kids, bring Mum and Dad, but above all bring your camera to capture those golden memories for ever. You will also find an impressive array of motoring memorabilia, a comfortable 70 seat video cinema and one of the most extensive transport book shops in Britain. The Pit Stop Cafe serves everything from a cup of tea to wholesome, home-made meals or, if you prefer, you can enjoy the large picnic area nestled in the beautiful rural surroundings of Somerset.

> John Haynes O.B.E., Founder and Chairman of the museum at the wheel of a Haynes Light 12.

< Graham Hill's Lola Cosworth Formula 1 car next to a 1934 Riley Sports.

The Museum is situated on the A359 Yeovil to Frome road at Sparkford, just off the A303 in Somerset. It is about 40 miles south of Bristol, and 25 minutes drive from the M5 intersection at Taunton.
Open 9.30am - 5.30pm (10.00am - 4.00pm Winter) 7 days a week, *except Christmas Day, Boxing Day and New Years Day*
Special rates available for schools, coach parties and outings Charitable Trust No. 292048